Beginning Mac OS® X Programming

Michael Trent and Drew McCormack

WILEY

Wiley Publishing, Inc.

Beginning Mac OS® X Programming

Published by
Wiley Publishing, Inc.
10475 Crosspoint Boulevard
Indianapolis, IN 46256
www.wiley.com

Copyright © 2005 by Wiley Publishing, Inc., Indianapolis, Indiana

Published simultaneously in Canada

ISBN-10: 0-7645-7399-3

ISBN-13: 978-0-7645-7399-6

Manufactured in the United States of America

10 9 8 7 6 5 4 3 2 1

1B/QX/QX/QV/IN

Library of Congress Cataloging-in-Publication Data
Trent, Michael, 1972-
    Beginning Mac OS X programming / Michael Trent and Drew McCormack.
        p. cm.
    Includes index.
    ISBN-13: 978-0-7645-7399-6 (paper/website)
    ISBN-10: 0-7645-7399-3 (paper/website)
    1. Mac OS. 2. Operating systems (Computers) 3. Macintosh
(Computers)—Programming. I. McCormack, Drew, 1971- II. Title.
    QA76.76.063T74565 2005
    005.4'46—dc22
                                              2005010351

About the Authors

Michael Trent has been programming in Objective-C since1997 and programming Macs since well before that. He is a regular contributor to Steven Frank's www.cocoadev.com website, technical reviewer for numerous books and magazine articles, and occasional dabbler in Mac OS X open source projects. Currently, he is using Objective-C and Apple Computer's Cocoa frameworks to build professional and consumer applications for Mac OS X. Michael holds a Bachelor of Science in Computer Science and a Bachelor of Arts in Music from Beloit College of Beloit, Wisconsin. He lives in Pittsburgh, Pennsylvania, with his family.

Drew McCormack has a Ph.D. in Chemical Physics and works as a computational scientist in the Theoretical Chemistry group at the Free University in Amsterdam. He is involved in developing the Quantum Chemistry software ADF (www.scm.com), which is run the world over on computers ranging from desktop Macs to massive supercomputers. He programs regularly in Python, C++, Objective-C, Fortran, and Bash, and in his spare time develops the Cocoa financial software Trade Strategist (www.trade-strategist.com). Drew maintains the Maniacal Extent website—a reference to the *chaotic dimension*, time—which details his various interests and activities (www.maniacalextent.com).

Credits

Acquisitions Editor
Katie Mohr

Senior Development Editor
Jodi Jensen

Technical Editor
Terrence Talbot

Production Editor
Felicia Robinson

Copy Editor
Kim Cofer

Editorial Manager
Mary Beth Wakefield

Vice President & Executive Group Publisher
Richard Swadley

Vice President and Publisher
Joseph B. Wikert

Project Coordinator
Erin Smith

Graphics and Production Specialists
April Farling
Carrie Foster
Lauren Goddard
Denny Hager
Joyce Haughey
Amanda Spagnuolo
Julie Trippetti

Quality Control Technicians
Leeann Harney
Jessica Kramer
Joseph Niesen
Carl Pierce
Dwight Ramsey

Media Development Specialists
Angela Denny
Kit Malone
Travis Silvers

Proofreading and Indexing
TECHBOOKS Production Services

For Angela and Katie —MT

For Jennifer and Gileesa —DM

Contents

Contents

Contents

Contents

Contents

Contents

Contents

Acknowledgments

I would like to thank Steve Kochan for his help with this project early on. Thanks also to Brett Halle and Pete Steinauer for their encouragement. Most of all, I would like to thank my wife, Angela, and my daughter, Katie, for putting up with all the late nights. —*Michael Trent*

I wish to thank my wife, Jennifer, and daughter, Gileesa, for suffering my wacky schemes; my brother Cody McCormack, for being my mentor; and Pier Philipsen for being my sounding board in all matters technical. —*Drew McCormack*

Introduction

Mac OS X represents the union of many different operating system technologies. At its core you will find Unix, an operating system once reserved for high-end servers and workstations, now found on common desktop systems. With Unix comes a whole history of tools, computer languages, and runtime environments. At a higher level, you will find Carbon, a library made from elements of the original Macintosh operating system. Although it is no longer responsible for managing the hardware itself, the Mac OS API remains, providing special services unique to the Macintosh. Mac OS X also includes Cocoa, derived from the application toolkits found on NeXTSTEP and OpenStep — a result of Apple's merger with NeXT in 1997. Other technologies have found their way into Mac OS X through the open source community, and Apple is hard at work developing new technologies unique to Mac OS X.

Although the operating system is composed of all these separate pieces, Mac OS X still looks and feels like a single piece of software. The Macintosh's legendary user interface still shines brightly today, providing a consistent look and feel for the applications on your system. When you sit down to use your computer, it just works for you. And aside from a few cosmetic differences, say using a command-line interface or a graphical interface, rarely are you aware of the differences between all these operating system technologies.

Under the covers there are fundamental differences between these operating system technologies. For example, Carbon still provides its own special memory data types, and Cocoa requires its own object-oriented runtime. But there are no firm boundaries between these technologies; Cocoa can call Carbon API and vice versa. And though these technologies have their own history, strengths, and weaknesses, they are all still part of the same Mac OS X operating system.

Who This Book Is For

This book is for anyone who wants to get started writing programs that run on Mac OS X. Every Mac OS X system comes with everything you need: a complete set of development tools and resources. But finding the place to start can be challenging. This book provides a great starting point for programming on Mac OS X and shows you how to find more information on your own.

This book will appeal most to the hobbyist programmer who already has some exposure to a programming language. Experience with C or Objective-C, although helpful, is not required. You can learn the basics of these languages, as well as concepts like *object-oriented programming*, as you go.

If you are an experienced programmer familiar with one aspect of Mac OS X programming (such as shell scripting or Carbon), you can use this book to explore other aspects of Mac OS X programming. In addition, you learn how to incorporate these new techniques into your existing programming style.

How This Book Is Structured

This book takes a hands-on approach to learning the material using the Wrox "Try It Out" format. After you learn about a particular element, you are presented with step-by-step instructions that walk you through using that element. You are encouraged to follow along on your own system by typing the examples, running them, and if necessary debugging when they don't work quite right. A detailed explanation of the example follows the step-by-step instructions under a "How It Works" heading.

Some examples take the form of small stand-alone projects, designed to illustrate one particular concept or technique. When appropriate, examples build on material presented in earlier chapters or examples, providing an opportunity to see the new material in a non-trivial context. Many of the examples focused on Mac OS X application development build on an application called Slide Master, a functional image/ slide show browser that you build piece by piece. Whenever possible, larger tasks have been broken down into smaller examples to make them easier to digest.

Each chapter includes a few exercises at the end, again illustrating the lessons presented earlier. You can work through these examples on your own, at your own pace. Complete answers to each exercise are provided in the appendix, so you can check your work or get a hint if you get stuck. Keep in mind that in programming there's usually more than one way to do something; our solution isn't necessarily the only correct solution.

Chapters are collected into three broad categories, or parts: Mac OS X Developer Resources, Application Programming, and Script Programming. This keeps related material together and helps with the flow of information from topic to topic. You are encouraged to cover the material in order so that you don't miss anything. But if you want to skip ahead to learn about a specific topic, make a point of coming back to the earlier material at a later time.

Here's a brief summary of what you'll find in each chapter:

In Chapter 1, "The Mac OS X Environment," you learn about Mac OS X's system architecture. You also get a little hands-on experience using Mac OS X's built-in command-line interface.

In Chapter 2, "Developer Tools," you find out about the resources that come with your copy of Mac OS X. You also learn how to find current versions of these resources on the Internet.

In Chapter 3, "Xcode," you explore the application used to build Mac OS X programs. A few simple examples introduce you to writing source code, building a finished product, and debugging programs one line of code at a time.

Chapter 4, "Interface Builder," walks you through the process of designing a graphic user interface on Mac OS X. Examples in this chapter illustrate useful techniques for building an interface that conforms to Apple's guidelines.

In Chapter 5, "The Application," you pick apart the individual elements that make up an application on Mac OS X. You learn how application resources are stored and how applications work in multiple languages.

Chapter 6, "The C Language," offers a brief introduction to the C programming language. If you are new to C, you will want to read this chapter before continuing on to Chapters 7, 8, or 9. In addition to learning how to write programs in C, you learn how non-trivial C programs are divided among several source files.

Chapter 7, "The Objective-C Language," builds on Chapter 6 to teach you about Objective-C, the object-oriented language used by the Cocoa application frameworks.

In Chapter 8, "Using the Cocoa Frameworks," you discover how to write your own Cocoa applications, from designing a user interface, to writing the final code. The Cocoa application frameworks do a lot of work for you, freeing you up to concentrate on the unique aspects of your own application.

Chapter 9, "Using the Carbon Frameworks," explores how to build user interfaces with Carbon and how to use Carbon interfaces, such as QuickTime, from within Cocoa programs.

In Chapter 10, "Overview of Scripting Languages," you examine scripting languages available on the Mac OS X system. Many of these languages extend Mac OS X's command-line interface in one way or another. You get a sense of what sets each language apart and what tasks each language is best suited to perform.

Chapter 11, "The Bash Shell," covers Mac OS X's default command-line interpreter in detail. You learn how to write shell scripts that interact with command-line tools installed on your system.

In Chapter 12, "AppleScript and AppleScript Studio," you learn about Apple's high-level application scripting language, AppleScript. AppleScript enables you to communicate with and automate tasks in Mac OS X applications. You can also use AppleScript to build graphic user interfaces using AppleScript Studio.

Chapter 13, "Using Scripts Wthin Applications," illustrates how your applications can interact with command-line tools and other scripts. Although graphic applications and command-line tools seem very different, you can easily integrate the two on Mac OS X.

The appendix provides solutions to the exercises that appear at the end of each chapter throughout the book.

Appendix A, "Exercise Answers, " provides the solutions to the exercises that appear at the end of each chapter throughout the book. Also be sure to check out Appendix B, "Developer Resources," and Appendix C, "Developer Tools Roadmap." These two appendixes offer valuable information that you may find helpful as you develop applications.

What You Need to Use This Book

As we mentioned earlier, your Mac OS X installation already has everything you need to get started. You will also need an Internet connection to access Apple Computer's developer website. We used the Safari web browser to access these pages, but other web browsers (Internet Explorer, Firefox, and so on) should work fine.

Examples and figures in this book were made using Mac OS X 10.4 "Tiger" and Xcode 2.0. You can follow along with an earlier version of Mac OS X and Xcode if you like. Although the screen shots will not match exactly, the code examples will still compile and run. Earlier versions of Xcode can be obtained at no charge from Apple's website. You can find more information on Apple's developer website, Apple Developer Connection, in Chapter 2.

Conventions

To help you get the most from the text and keep track of what's happening, we've used a number of conventions throughout the book.

> **Boxes like this one hold important, not-to-be forgotten information that is directly relevant to the surrounding text.**

Tips, hints, tricks, and asides to the current discussion are offset and placed in italics like this.

As for styles used in the text

- ❑   We *highlight* important words in italics when they are introduced.
- ❑   We show keyboard strokes like this: Ctrl-A.
- ❑   We show file and folder names, URLs, and code within the text in a special monofont typeface, like this: `persistence.properties`.
- ❑   We present code in two different ways:

```
In code examples we highlight new and important code with a gray background.
```

```
The gray highlighting is not used for code that is less important in the present
context or has been shown before.
```

On the Website

As you work through the examples in this book, you may choose either to type in all the code manually or use the source code files that accompany the book. All the source code used in this book is available for download at `www.wrox.com`. Once at the site, simply locate the book's title either by using the Search box or one of the topic lists and click the Download Code link. You can then choose what you want to download from a list of files zipped by chapter.

Because many books have similar titles, you may find it easiest to search by ISBN; for this book the ISBN is 0-7645-7399-3 (changing to 978-0-7645-7399-6 as the new industry-wide 13-digit ISBN numbering system is phased in by January 2007).

After you download the code, just decompress it with your favorite compression tool. Mac OS X 10.3 and later supports uncompressing zip files directly in the Finder. Alternatively, you can go to the main Wrox code download page at `http://www.wrox.com/dynamic/books/download.aspx` to see the code available for this book and all other Wrox books.

Errata

We make every effort to ensure that there are no errors in the text or in the code. However, no one is perfect, and mistakes do occur. If you find an error in one of our books, like a spelling mistake or faulty piece of code, we would be very grateful for your feedback. By sending in errata you may save another reader hours of frustration; at the same time, you are helping us provide higher quality information.

To find the errata page for this book, go to http://www.wrox.com and locate the title using the Search box or one of the topic lists. When the information page for the book appears, click the Errata link in the middle of the page. On this page, you can view all errata that has been submitted for this book and posted by Wrox editors. A complete book list, including links to each book's errata, is also available at www.wrox.com/misc-pages/booklist.shtml.

If you don't spot "your" error on the book's Errata page, click the Errata Form link in the paragraph just above the actual listing of errata or go to www.wrox.com/contact/techsupport.shtml. Complete the form to send us the error you have found. We'll check the information and, if appropriate, post a message to the book's errata page and fix the problem in subsequent editions of the book.

p2p.wrox.com

For author and peer discussion, join the P2P forums at p2p.wrox.com. The forums are a web-based system for you to post messages relating to Wrox books and related technologies and interact with other readers and technology users. The forums offer a subscription feature to email you topics of interest of your choosing when new posts are made to the forums. Wrox authors, editors, other industry experts, and your fellow readers are present on these forums.

At http://p2p.wrox.com you will find a number of different forums that will help you not only as you read this book, but also as you develop your own applications. To join the forums, just follow these steps:

1. Go to p2p.wrox.com and click the Register link.

2. Read the terms of use and click Agree.

3. Complete the required information to join as well as any optional information you want to provide and click Submit.

4. You will receive an email with information describing how to verify your account and complete the joining process.

You can read messages in the forums without joining P2P but in order to post your own messages, you must join.

After you join, you can post new messages and respond to messages other users post. You can read messages at any time on the Web. If you would like to have new messages from a particular forum emailed to you, click the Subscribe to this Forum icon by the forum name in the forum listing.

For more information about how to use the Wrox P2P, be sure to read the P2P FAQs for answers to questions about how the forum software works as well as many common questions specific to P2P and Wrox books. To read the FAQs, click the FAQ link on any P2P page.

Part I: Mac OS X Developer Resources

The Mac OS X Environment

Welcome to the wonderful world of Mac OS X, the next-generation operating system from Apple Computer!

The Mac OS X operating system powers modern Macintosh computers. After many long years and a few scrapped attempts to modernize the older Mac OS operating system, Apple released Mac OS X in April of 2001. Since then, Apple has released a steady stream of upgrades and system updates. This book was written around Mac OS X version 10.4, "Tiger," the latest version.

In order to write software for Mac OS X, you need to know your way around the system. By now you may already be familiar with Mac OS X's applications and user interface style. Those things all rest on top of a number of subsystems and services that make up the Mac OS X operating system.

In this chapter you learn

- ❑ How the Mac OS X operating system is structured, including what the major areas of the system are and how they work together
- ❑ How to use Mac OS X's command-line interface
- ❑ How applications take advantage of the operating system services on Mac OS X
- ❑ How Apple encourages a common look and feel for Mac OS X applications

Introducing the Mac OS X

What comes to mind when you think of Mac OS X? Is it the applications you use? Perhaps you recall Mac OS X's distinctive user interface? Or maybe you think of Mac OS X's stability? In truth, Mac OS X embodies all these things.

The Mac OS X operating system is often described as a collection of layers, as seen in Figure 1-1.

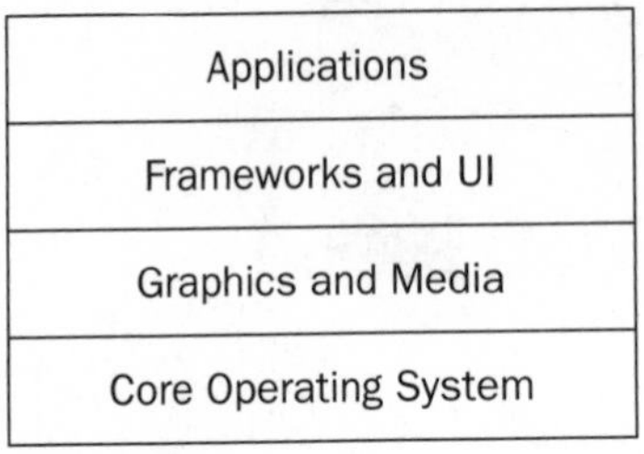

Applications
Frameworks and UI
Graphics and Media
Core Operating System

Figure 1-1

You are probably already familiar with the topmost layer: the applications that run on Mac OS X (like Mail, iTunes, Safari, and so on). These applications are all written against a collection of application *frameworks*. These frameworks are special libraries that provide the code and all the other resources (icons, translated strings, and so on) to perform common tasks. For example, the Cocoa framework contains a number of resources necessary to make a Cocoa application.

All Mac OS X applications use graphics to some extent, ranging from simply presenting its user interface to processing graphical data like QuickTime movies. The system provides several specialized libraries for working with graphics and graphics files.

These layers rest on the broad shoulders of the core operating system, which at the lowest level is responsible for making your Macintosh run. For example, the core OS handles reading from and writing to your hard drive and random access memory (RAM), it manages your network connections, it powers down the computer when it falls to "sleep," and so on. In fact, any program that talks to your hardware in any way ultimately goes through the core OS.

Throughout this book you examine Mac OS X in detail through Slide Master, an application that builds and displays photo slide shows. You will build Slide Master bit-by-bit as you learn more about how the elements of Mac OS X come together. The Slide Master application and its source code can be downloaded from Wiley's website; so you can check your work against our complete solution as you go.

This is a good time to take a quick tour of Slide Master. You can download Slide Master from Wiley's website, make a slide show, and view your handiwork. In doing so, you touch on all the major areas of the Mac OS X operating system.

Try It Out   Slide Master

1. Download the files for this chapter from www.wrox.com. Refer to the Introduction for instructions on finding the files you need from the Wrox website. You can search for the book by its ISBN number: 978-0-7645-7399-6. You are looking for a file named Chapter01.zip.

2. Uncompress the Chapter01.zip archive using your favorite decompression tool. (Mac OS X 10.3 and later supports uncompressing .zip files directly in the Finder.) Inside you will find the Slide Master application, a folder of pictures called Images, and a folder of source code.

3. Run the Slide Master application by double-clicking it in Finder. The application opens an untitled document window.

4. Add the pictures in the Images folder to Slide Master by choosing Slide Show ⇨ Add Slide. You can select all the files at once from the open panel. The images appear in a drawer to the side of the document window and the main window displays the selected image, as shown in Figure 1-2. You can use the arrow keys to change the selection.

Figure 1-2

5. Export a slide show as a QuickTime movie by choosing File ⇨ Export. Slide Master writes out a QuickTime movie and opens it with QuickTime Player.

6. Save your document by choosing File ⇨ Save.

How It Works

Slide Master is a document-based application, which means that it provides a user interface for individual documents. In this case, documents are collections of slides that you can sift through and export as QuickTime movies. Slide Master documents can be opened, saved, and closed using the File menu. Other document-based applications also support printing, although Slide Master does not.

Much of the functionality you see here comes from Slide Master's application framework: Cocoa. The Cocoa application frameworks provide the implementation for the things you see on the screen: windows, pictures, menus, buttons, and so on. Cocoa also provides support for managing the document: reading and writing document files, closing the document when its window is closed, and routing menu commands to the selected document. Finally, Cocoa provides tools for storing application data, including working with user preferences and storing lists of items in memory.

Of course Slide Master uses QuickTime to generate movie files. You are probably already familiar with QuickTime, both through QuickTime Player and through web browsers that support the display of

QuickTime movies. But QuickTime also makes most, if not all, of its functionality available to applications through its framework interface.

When you save a Slide Master document, the document file contains a list of image files that are part of your slide show, not the actual images themselves. As a result, these documents can be relatively small. Behind the scenes, Slide Master uses aliases to track these image files so that they can be found if the files are moved around on your disk. These aliases are the same aliases you can create in the Finder, although they are embedded in your document rather than saved separately to disk. Slide Master uses the Carbon application framework for working with aliases. Even though Slide Master is a Cocoa application, it can still access many of the services available in Carbon.

You learn more about Cocoa, Carbon, QuickTime, and other technologies later in this chapter, and as you proceed through this book.

The Core Operating System

The heart of Mac OS X is based on the Unix operating system. Unix was developed by AT&T in the early 1970s. In those days, computers were large and expensive, and Unix was intended as a way to share computing resources between multiple users at once. It was likely that an organization at that time could afford only one computer for all its members, and Unix provided a way for people to use that computer simultaneously without getting in each other's way.

Over the years, Unix development has split off into many distinct "flavors" of Unix, all headed up by different groups of people, all with somewhat different goals. BSD and Linux are two such examples. Each version of Unix shares some portion of the original vision and typically implements a common set of libraries and commands.

Unix is regarded as a robust operating system whose scalability and innate networking capability make it ideal for use as a server. In fact, most of the modern day Internet is powered by Unix servers of one version or another. It turns out that these features are also desirable in modern desktop operating systems. So it is no surprise when seeking to modernize the original Macintosh operating system, Apple turned to Unix.

Mac OS X's core operating system is a Unix flavor called *Darwin*. Like most Unix flavors, Darwin's source code is freely available, allowing interested parties to see exactly how the core operating system works. Apple maintains several resources for programmers interested in Darwin, including a way for people-at-large to contribute changes and bug fixes back to Apple.

Although Mac OS X tries to hide Darwin from the average user, there are some places where the Unix command-line pokes through. The most obvious example is the Terminal application, found in `/Application/Utilities`. You can use Terminal to work directly with Darwin's command-line tools. A more subtle example includes the way you describe file locations on Mac OS X: by using a *file path*. A file path is a string of text that describes a file's location.

The original Mac OS operating system abhorred file paths and tried its best to avoid them; but even so it devised a convention for describing a path to a file. Mac OS file paths are composed of a disk volume name followed by several folder names and possibly a file, all separated by colons, as in `Macintosh HD:Applications:Utilities:Terminal.app`.

> ### Program, Process, Application — What's the Difference?
>
> Much of the time you can use the terms *program* and *process* interchangeably to refer to something that's *executable*. But these terms do have distinct definitions. The word *program* refers to a file on disk containing a series of computer instructions. When this file is executed (or run, launched, and so on) the computer starts processing the instructions in the file. *Process* describes the act of executing the file. To borrow an example from the kitchen, it may help to think of a program as a recipe for baking a cake, and process as the act of baking that cake.
>
> Ultimately, an *application* is just a program. On Mac OS X, however, programs can take many forms: simple tools typed in a command-line interface, a program you can double-click in the Finder, a plug-in file loaded by other programs, and so on. To avoid some confusion, we use the term *application* in this book to refer specifically to those programs that appear in the Finder; we use the term *program* when no distinction is necessary.

Although there are places where this old convention still exists, Mac OS X mostly uses Unix's method of describing file paths: a series of directories from the *root* directory all separated by slashes, as in `/Applications/Utilities/Terminal.app`. The root directory contains all the files and directories on a Mac OS X system and is referred to simply as `/`. The path `/Applications` refers to a file or directory named `Applications` in the root directory. A path that begins with the root slash is called an *absolute* (or *full*) *path* because it describes a precise file location. If the root slash is not included, the path is called a *relative path* because it is relative to your current location.

> *If you look in* `/Applications/Utilities` *in the Finder, you might notice that there is no* `Terminal.app`; *instead there's just a program called Terminal. By default, Finder and other applications hide file extensions such as* `.app` *and* `.txt` *from you. So the application at* `/Applications/Utilities/Terminal.app` *appears simply as Terminal. The Core OS makes no attempt to hide extensions from you; if you browse the file system using Mac OS X's command-line interface, you can see all these extensions. You learn more about Mac OS X's command-line interface later in this chapter.*

Darwin is composed of several parts, including a *kernel*, a system library, and numerous commands, as illustrated in Figure 1-3.

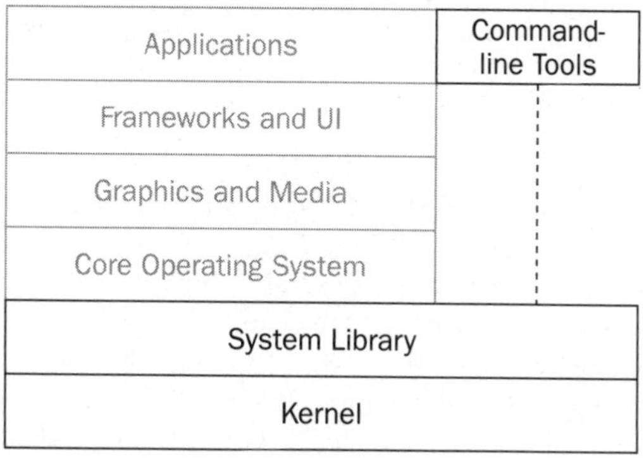

Figure 1-3

The Kernel

The heart of a Unix operating system is its *kernel*. The kernel is the program that loads when the computer is first turned on and is responsible for managing all the hardware resources available to the computer. The kernel is also responsible for running the other programs on the system, scheduling process execution so that they can share the central processing unit (CPU) and other resources, and preventing one process from seeing what another process is doing. These last two responsibilities are more commonly known as *pre-emptive multi-tasking* and *protected memory*, respectively.

Because Unix prevents programs from accessing the computer hardware or other programs directly, it protects against the most common forms of system crashes. If a process misbehaves in one way or another, the system simply terminates the process and continues on its way. In other words, the misbehaving process crashes. In some operating systems, a misbehaving process can stomp all over other applications, or even break the operating system itself, before the system is able to terminate the process. As a result, poorly written programs can cause the entire computer to freeze or crash. Not so on Unix; because a process cannot modify other processes, including the kernel, there is virtually no risk of a bad process bringing down the entire operating system.

Although the kernel is responsible for accessing hardware, much of the knowledge of specific hardware details is delegated to *device drivers*. Device drivers are small programs that are loaded directly into the kernel. Whereas the kernel might know how to talk to hard disks, for example, in general, a specific device driver knows how to talk to specific makes and models of hard disks. This provides a way for third parties to add support for new devices without having to build it into Apple's kernel. Mac OS X includes default drivers for talking to a wide variety of devices, so much of the time you won't need to install separate drivers when you install new third-party hardware.

The System Library

The kernel is responsible for critical functions such as memory management and device access, so programs must ask the kernel to perform work on its behalf. Programs communicate with the kernel through an application program interface (API) provided by a special library. This library defines some common data structures for describing system operations, provides functions to request these operations, and handles shuttling data back and forth between the kernel and other programs. This library is simply called the *system library*.

As you might imagine, every program on Mac OS X links against this library, either directly or indirectly. Without it, a program would be unable to allocate memory, access the file system, and perform other simple tasks.

What Is an API?

All libraries and frameworks provide a collection of functions and data structures that programs can use to perform a task. For example, the system library provides functions for reading from files; QuickTime provides functions for playing back QuickTime movies. These functions and data structures are collectively known as the library's *application program interface*, or API.

The system library takes the form of a dynamic library installed as /usr/lib/libSystem.B.dylib. Mac OS X also includes a framework called System.framework in /System/Library/Frameworks that refers to this library. The files that define the Darwin interface live in the /usr/include directory. By the way, neither of these directories is visible from Finder; Mac OS X actively hides much of the complexity of Darwin from the average Mac user.

Unix Commands

Unix users interact with their systems using command-line tools. These tools typically perform very specialized functions, such as listing files in a directory or displaying files on-screen. The advantage of supplying many specialized tools lies in the way commands can be combined to form more sophisticated commands. For example, a command that lists the contents of a directory can be combined with a program that lists text in "pages" for easy reading.

As you have learned, you use the Terminal application to gain access to Darwin's command-line tools.

The following Try It Out looks at Darwin's command-line interface. You start by browsing files using the command-line, looking up command information in Darwin's online help system, and running a command that displays its own arguments.

Try It Out   Experiencing Darwin's Command-Line Interface

1. Before you get started, you need to make sure the command-line tools have been installed on your system. Although Mac OS X comes with a full set of Unix commands, they are an optional part of the install process. Using the Finder, make sure a folder named BSD.pkg exists in the /Library/Receipts directory. If it does, you can move directly to step 3. Otherwise, continue to the next step.

2. Insert the first Mac OS X Installation CD and run the installer. From there you can customize your install and select only the BSD.pkg. When the installer finishes, you are ready to proceed.

3. In the Finder, go to Applications ➪ Utilities and launch the Terminal application. You will see a few status lines of text ending in a command-line prompt (your lines may look slightly different than what is shown here):

```
Last login: Sat May 15 23:28:46 on ttyp1
Welcome to Darwin!
Macintosh:~ sample $
```

4. When using Terminal there are commands that let you navigate the file system. The Terminal application always keeps track of where you are, maintaining the notion of your *current directory*. You can display the contents of the current directory using the ls (list) command that follows. As a matter of fact, the Terminal window is currently "in" your home directory. Your results may vary from what's printed here, but they will match what you see in the Finder when you browse your home directory. (Throughout this book, any text you are asked to type on the command line is indicated in **bold**.)

```
Macintosh:~ sample $ ls
Desktop        Library        Music          Public
Documents      Movies         Pictures       Sites
```

5. You can display more information about the files in your home directory by passing additional arguments, called *flags*, into `ls`. By using `ls -l`, you can build what is often called a *long list*. Again, your results may differ from what is printed here:

```
Macintosh:~ sample$ ls -l
total 0
drwx------   3 sample  sample  102 16 May 01:20 Desktop
drwx------   3 sample  sample  102 16 May 01:20 Documents
drwx------  17 sample  sample  578 16 May 01:20 Library
drwx------   3 sample  sample  102 16 May 01:20 Movies
drwx------   4 sample  sample  136 16 May 01:20 Music
drwx------   3 sample  sample  102 16 May 01:20 Pictures
drwxr-xr-x   4 sample  sample  136 16 May 01:20 Public
drwxr-xr-x   5 sample  sample  170 16 May 01:20 Sites
```

6. You can view the contents of a specific directory by specifying its name as the argument to `ls`. Note that this argument can co-exist with other flags you might want to use:

```
Macintosh:~ sample$ ls -l Library
total 0
drwx------   2 sample  sample   68 16 May 01:20 Application Support
drwx------   2 sample  sample   68 16 May 01:20 Assistants
drwx------   4 sample  sample  136 16 May 01:20 Audio
drwx------   3 sample  sample  102 16 May 01:20 Caches
drwx------   2 sample  sample   68 16 May 01:20 ColorPickers
drwx------   3 sample  sample  102 16 May 01:20 Favorites
drwx------  11 sample  sample  374 16 May 01:20 FontCollections
drwx------   2 sample  sample   68 16 May 01:20 Fonts
drwx------   2 sample  sample   68 16 May 01:20 Internet Plug-Ins
drwx------   2 sample  sample   68 16 May 01:20 Keyboard Layouts
drwx------   8 sample  sample  272 16 May 01:20 Preferences
drwx------   2 sample  sample   68 16 May 01:20 Printers
drwx------   2 sample  sample   68 16 May 01:20 Sounds
drwx------   4 sample  sample  136 16 May 01:20 iMovie
```

7. Two new questions immediately come to mind: exactly what is `ls -l` telling you, and what other flags can you pass into `ls`? The answer to both of these questions resides in Darwin's online help system, which is better known as the Unix Manual. You can consult the manual by using the `man` command and including the name of another command as the argument:

```
Macintosh:~ sample$ man ls
LS(1)                    BSD General Commands Manual                    LS(1)


NAME
     ls - list directory contents

SYNOPSIS
     ls [-ABCFGHLPRTWZabcdfghiklmnopqrstuwx1] [file ...]

DESCRIPTION
     For each operand that names a file of a type other than directory, ls
     displays its name as well as any requested, associated information.  For
     each operand that names a file of type directory, ls displays the names
     of files contained within that directory, as well as any requested, asso-
     ciated information.
```

```
        If no operands are given, the contents of the current directory are dis-
        played.  If more than one operand is given, non-directory operands are
        displayed first; directory and non-directory operands are sorted sepa-
        rately and in lexicographical order.

        The following options are available:

        -A      List all entries except for . and ... Always set for the super-
  :
```

8. The arguments you are allowed to pass to a Unix command depend entirely on the command. As you have seen, the `ls` command accepts file names, and the `man` command accepts the names of other Unix commands. The `echo` command accepts arbitrary arguments and simply repeats them on the screen. It turns out that this command is especially useful when writing shell scripts, as you see in Chapter 10.

```
Macintosh:~ sample$ echo hello, my name is sample
hello, my name is sample
```

How It Works

In spite of appearances, Terminal doesn't understand any of the commands you just entered. In fact, Terminal's only job is to read input from your keyboard and display text coming from a special program called a *shell*. Terminal starts your shell for you when its window appears. The shell is a special program that provides a command-line prompt, parses instructions into command names and lists of arguments, runs the requested commands, and passes back the resulting text.

Once the shell has decided which command to launch, the shell starts that command and passes the remaining flags and arguments into the command for further evaluation. That's why `ls`, `man`, and `echo` all interpret their arguments in different ways. Flags are also interpreted by individual commands, so it's not uncommon to use a particular flag in more than one Unix command, although the flag might have different meanings.

One thing to watch out for: Unix shells historically are *case-sensitive*, meaning that the command `LS` is not the same as `ls`, the directory `library` is not the same as the directory `Library`, and so on. Mac OS X's default file system, HFS+, is case-insensitive, and much of the time the shell can figure out what you mean. But if you had some trouble with the commands in the preceding Try It Out, make sure you entered the text exactly as it appears here.

You have only just scratched the surface of what the shell can do. You will continue to learn more about the shell as you continue through the book.

Graphics and Media Layers

Much of the user experience on Mac OS X is built around graphics. All the elements you see on the screen — windows, menus, buttons, text — are graphics. It comes as no surprise that Mac OS X has several subsystems dedicated to graphics, as shown in Figure 1-4.

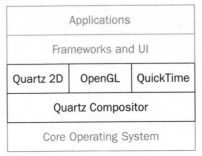

Figure 1-4

Mac OS X provides a rich graphics library for doing two-dimensional drawing, called Quartz 2D. The Quartz 2D library is specific to Mac OS X, although it uses industry-standard graphic formats, such as PDF. Mac OS X also includes OpenGL for those interested in three-dimensional drawing. Although popularized by cross-platform video games, Mac OS X itself uses OpenGL for certain operations. Finally, QuickTime is built into Mac OS X, providing support for what Apple occasionally calls four-dimensional drawing. QuickTime is also available for Microsoft Windows operating systems, and for older versions of Mac OS. All these programming libraries rely on the Quartz Compositor for actually drawing their content.

The following sections look at these subsystems in more detail.

The Quartz Compositor

The Quartz Compositor is a private system service that oversees all graphics operations on Mac OS X. Apple does not provide a means for developers to interact with the Quartz Compositor directly, so we won't look at it in detail here. The Quartz Compositor plays such an important role in Mac OS X's graphic strategy, however, it pays to understand what it does.

Among its many duties, the Quartz Compositor handles these tasks:

❑ **Manages all the windows on your screen:** While the actual look of the window may come from an application or an application framework like Cocoa or Carbon, the Quartz Compositor provides most of the window's guts: where the window sits on the screen, how the window casts its drop shadow, and so on.

❑ **Ensures that graphics are drawn appropriately, regardless of which library or libraries an application may be using:** In fact, an application may use commands from Quartz 2D, OpenGL, and QuickTime when drawing a given window. The Quartz Compositor ensures that the drawing reaches the screen correctly.

❑ **Collects user events from the Core Operating System and dispatches them to the Application Frameworks layer:** User events such as keystrokes and mouse movements are collected from drivers in the Core Operating System and sent on to the Quartz Compositor. Some of these events are passed along where they may be interpreted by the application. The Quartz Compositor will also send its own special events through to the application for responding to special conditions, such as when the user brings the application to the foreground or when a window needs to be updated.

The Quartz Compositor was designed with modern best practices for graphics in mind. For example, the drawing coordinate space uses floating-point values, allowing for sub-pixel precision and image smoothing. Compositing operations can take advantage of available hardware, such as the G4's Altivec vector unit. Transparency is supported natively and naturally in all drawing operations.

Apple has been able to capitalize on this architecture to provide a number of exciting features, such as Quartz Extreme and Exposé. Quartz Extreme allows graphic operations to take full advantage of the graphics processing unit (GPU) found on modern video cards to provide hardware-accelerated drawing. This has two benefits. The GPU is specially optimized for common drawing operations, so drawing is much faster than when using the computer's CPU. Second, by offloading drawing onto the GPU in the video card, Quartz Extreme frees up the CPU for other tasks. Although in the past developers needed to use OpenGL to do hardware-accelerated drawing, Quartz Extreme provides this support to Quartz 2D as well, and ultimately to QuickTime. Exposé allows the user to quickly view all windows at once. It is a very handy way to find a specific window that might be buried underneath a number of other windows, as shown in Figure 1-5.

The Quartz Compositor is one of the most innovative features on Mac OS X. Although you will not be working with it directly in this book, you will feel its influence in almost everything you do.

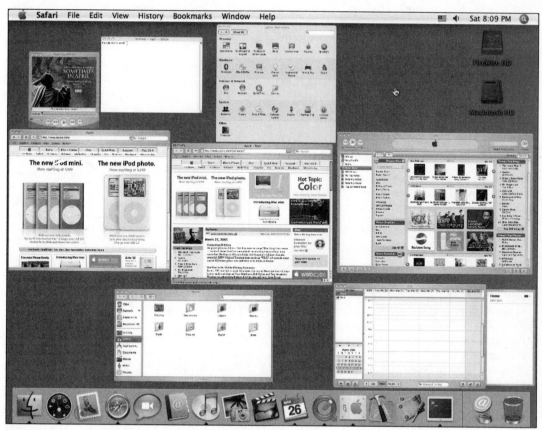

Figure 1-5

What Are PDF Files?

PDF stands for Portable Document Format. The PDF standard was invented by Adobe as a means for describing documents that can be displayed or printed virtually anywhere. The file specification itself is *open*, meaning the public-at-large can view the format and write their own tools for reading and generating PDF documents. Adobe continues to own and develop the standard.

Mac OS X reads and writes PDF documents as its preferred native image file format. You can save any document in PDF format simply by "printing" it and clicking Save as PDF in Mac OS X's print panel. PDF files can be displayed in Mac OS X's Preview application. Even screen shots are saved in PDF format.

Quartz 2D

The Quartz 2D graphic library is Mac OS X's native graphics library. It is responsible for all the two-dimensional drawing performed by Mac OS X. As you might imagine, Quartz 2D provides an interface for drawing two-dimensional shapes, such as lines and rectangles, and compositing images. It is also capable of drawing sophisticated curves, arbitrary shapes expressed as paths or vectors, and drawing color gradients. Quartz 2D also includes support for generating and displaying PDF files.

The Quartz 2D programming interface is provided by CoreGraphics, which is part of the ApplicationServices framework: `/System/Library/Frameworks/ApplicationServices.framework`. The Quartz 2D API is very powerful and is best approached by an experienced programmer. In this book, you focus more on the drawing API in the Application Frameworks layer, which is a little easier to use.

OpenGL

OpenGL is a powerful, cross-platform graphics library for doing 2D and 3D graphics. Although OpenGL is owned by SGI, the OpenGL specification is governed by an independent consortium called the OpenGL Architecture Review Board — ARB for short. As a voting member of the ARB, Apple contributes to the OpenGL community as a whole, in addition to improving the state of OpenGL on Mac OS X.

One of OpenGL's most compelling features is its tight integration with video card technology. Many OpenGL commands, such as image and shape drawing, blending and texture-mapping, can be performed directly by the video card's GPU. Recall that the GPU is optimized to perform these operations very quickly, and once graphic operations have been unloaded onto the video card, the CPU is free to perform other computational functions. The net result of this tight integration is very fast drawing.

Performance combined with its cross-platform nature makes OpenGL uniquely suited for certain kinds of situations, including scientific research, professional video editing, and games. If you have played a 3D video game on Mac OS X, you've seen OpenGL in action. For that matter, if you have used one of Mac OS X's built-in screen saver modules, you've seen OpenGL.

OpenGL's programming interface is spread across two frameworks: core OpenGL functionality lives in the OpenGL framework (`/System/Library/Frameworks/OpenGL.framework`), and a basic cross-platform Application Framework called GLUT resides at `/System/Library/Frameworks /GLUT.framework`. As with Quartz 2D, the OpenGL API is fairly advanced, and better suited for more experienced programmers.

QuickTime

Apple Computer invented QuickTime back in 1991 as a way to describe, author, and play back video on Macintosh computers running System 6 and System 7. Since then, QuickTime has exploded into a cross-platform library encompassing a variety of multimedia file formats and algorithms. QuickTime provides tools for working with digital video, panoramic images, digital sound, MIDI, and more. It has spawned entire genres of software, including CD-ROM adventure games, digital audio/video editing suites, and desktop video conferencing.

Mac OS X increased Apple's commitment to QuickTime by building it directly into the operating system. Though versions of QuickTime shipped with Mac OS releases since the earliest days of QuickTime, Mac OS X actually relies on QuickTime in ways earlier OS versions did not. For example, Finder uses QuickTime to allow you to preview video and audio files directly in the Finder when using column view. Mac OS X's Internet connectivity apps, including iChat and Safari, make substantial use of QuickTime.

It is interesting to note that because QuickTime predates Mac OS X by ten years, its programming interface does not leverage Quartz 2D directly. QuickTime instead uses an older two-dimensional graphics library that is part of Carbon, called QuickDraw. The QuickDraw graphics library dates back to the earliest Macintosh computers, and through the years it has been extended to support color displays, off-screen drawing, color correction, and other features. Although QuickDraw has been replaced by Quartz 2D within most of Mac OS X, programmers must still use QuickDraw data structures to work with QuickTime.

The QuickTime API is supplied by the QuickTime framework: `/System/Library/Frameworks/ QuickTime.framework`. The QuickTime programming interface has undergone nearly 15 years of evolution, and many of its concepts are quite advanced. We look at some of QuickTime's more humble roots in Chapter 8.

Application Frameworks and UI

All applications rely on common interface elements to communicate with the user. By packaging these elements in a library, an operating system can make sure all applications look and behave the same way. And the more functionality the operating system provides "for free," the less work application developers need to do themselves.

Toward that end, Mac OS X provides a number of application frameworks, as shown in Figure 1-6, upon which programmers can build their applications: Cocoa, Carbon, and the Java JDK. These frameworks, described in more detail in the following sections, all provide the basic concepts essential for application design: how events are processed by the application, how window contents are organized and drawn, how controls are presented to the user, and so on.

It is important that all applications present their UI in a consistent manner, regardless of which application framework the program uses. In other words, all windows, menus, buttons, text fields, and so on should look and behave the same way on Mac OS X. These UI elements together on Mac OS X form a distinctive user experience that Apple calls the Aqua user interface. Consistency among apps is so important that Apple has published guidelines enumerating the proper way to use Aqua user interface elements; these guidelines are called the Apple Human Interface Guidelines.

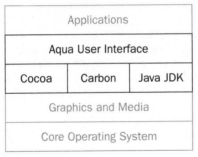

Figure 1-6

Each of these application frameworks is appropriate in different situations. In addition, these application frameworks are not mutually exclusive. An application may draw on features from all three frameworks.

Cocoa

The Cocoa application framework provides programmers with a means of building feature-rich Mac OS X applications quickly. The roots of Cocoa lie in NeXTSTEP, the operating system that powered NeXT computers in the early 1990s. When Apple announced Mac OS X in 1998, the API was re-christened Cocoa, and introduced alongside Carbon as Mac OS X's application development strategy.

Cocoa is an object-oriented API written in Objective-C, an object-oriented language descended from ANSI C and Smalltalk. Programmers work with Cocoa by creating objects and hooking them together in various ways. Objects provide a convenient way for programmers to extend basic application functionality without having to design the entire application from the ground up. Put another way, Cocoa allows you to focus on writing the code that makes your application unique, rather than forcing you to write the code that all applications must share.

The Cocoa API is divided between two frameworks:

❑ **The AppKit framework** (`/System/Library/Frameworks/AppKit.framework`): Provides high-level objects and services for writing applications, including Aqua user interface elements.

❑ **The Foundation framework** (`/System/Library/Frameworks/Foundation.framework`): Provides objects and services useful for all programs, such as collection data types, Unicode string support, and so on.

These features are separated into two separate frameworks so programs can use Foundation's utility classes without having to bring in a full graphic user interface; for example, a command-line tool written in Objective-C might simply use Foundation.

In addition, Java bindings for Cocoa are available, allowing Java programmers access to AppKit and Foundation objects. This book focuses on using Cocoa with Objective-C.

Carbon

What we know as Carbon today started out as the programmatic interface to the original Macintosh operating system. Although sufficient for writing Macintosh applications, the API had some problems that made transitioning to a new core operating system impossible. In 1998, Apple set out to revise the traditional Mac OS API and eliminate these problems, which would give existing Macintosh developers an easy path for migrating their code to Mac OS X. This revised API was called Carbon.

If you are interested in porting a traditional Mac OS application to Mac OS X, Carbon is a good place to start. However, with 20 years of refinement comes a fair amount of baggage; working in Carbon can be repetitive and time consuming. If you are starting a new project, or if you are trying to build an Aqua interface for a program originally developed on another platform, you may be better off using Cocoa. That said, a number of features in Mac OS X still use Carbon concepts and data structures in their APIs, such as QuickTime. A Mac OS X programmer should be familiar with how Carbon works in order to use these features.

The Carbon API is built around a collection of C interfaces, spread across several frameworks, including the Carbon framework (`/System/Library/Frameworks/Carbon.framework`), the Core Services framework (`/System/Library/Frameworks/CoreServices.framework`), and the ApplicationServices framework (`/System/Library/Frameworks/ApplicationServices.framework`). The Carbon framework includes a number of interfaces for working with high-level concepts, such as user interface elements, online help, and speech recognition. CoreServices provides interfaces for working with lower-level Carbon data structures and services. ApplicationServices fits somewhere between the other two, building on CoreServices to provide important infrastructure supporting the high-level interfaces in the Carbon framework, such as Apple events, font and type services, and speech synthesis.

Java JDK

Mac OS X comes with built-in support for Java applications. Java is an object-oriented programming language created by Sun Microsystems for developing solid applications that can deploy on a wide variety of machines. Java itself is best thought of as three separate technologies: an object-oriented programming language, a collection of application frameworks, and a runtime environment, as described in the following list:

- ❑ **Java the programming language:** Designed to make writing programs as safe as possible. Toward that end, Java shields the programmer from certain concepts that often are a source of trouble. For example, because programmers often make mistakes when accessing memory directly, Java doesn't allow programmers to access memory in those ways.

- ❑ **Java the application framework:** Provides a number of ways to develop applications using the Java programming language. Java and Cocoa are similar in many ways; for example, many of the objects and concepts in Cocoa also appear in Java.

- ❑ **Java the Virtual Machine:** Provides the runtime environment, called a virtual machine, in which all Java programs live. This virtual machine protects Java programs from subtle differences one encounters when trying to deploy programs on a variety of systems. For example, different systems may have widely divergent hardware characteristics, or supply different kinds of operating system services, and so on. The Java Virtual Machine levels the playing field for all Java apps, so that Java programmers do not need to worry about these issues themselves.

Java's greatest strength lies in that you can easily write applications that are deployable on a wide variety of computers and devices. In this respect Java has no equal. On the other hand, for the purposes of writing a Mac OS X–specific application, the Java application frameworks have some serious drawbacks. Because Java must deploy on several different computers, Java's approach to application design tends to focus on commonly available technologies and concepts. It is difficult to gain access to features unique to Mac OS X, such as the power of CoreGraphics, through Java's application frameworks, because those features are not available on all Java systems. Because this book focuses on technologies specific to Mac OS X, we will not examine Java in further detail.

Apple Human Interface Guidelines

All Mac OS X programs share a specific look and feel that makes them instantly recognizable as Mac OS X programs. This creates the illusion that all the applications on your system were designed to work together — even though your applications may have been designed by different people, all with different interests. Once you learn how to use one application, you have a pretty good idea of how to use all applications.

Apple provides a document, called the Apple Human Interface Guidelines, that spells out how Mac OS X applications should look and behave. Applications written against one of Mac OS X's application frameworks start with a bit of an advantage: all the user interface elements provided by these frameworks meet the specifications in the Apple Human Interface Guidelines. All the controls in Figure 1-7 are drawn using the Cocoa application framework; notice that they all look like Mac OS X controls.

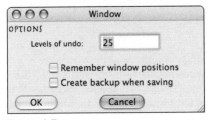

Figure 1-7

Unfortunately, simply using the right controls isn't enough to make an Aqua-compliant interface. A large part of user interface design is in collecting and organizing controls so they make sense. The Apple Human Interface Guidelines provide metrics for how far apart related controls and groups of controls should be and where certain kinds of controls should go. The Aqua guidelines specify specific fonts and font sizes for UI elements. It also specifies when certain features are appropriate, such as default buttons, hierarchical menu items, and so on. Figure 1-8 illustrates the same controls from Figure 1-7, laid out in compliance with the Apple Human Interface Guidelines; note it looks much cleaner.

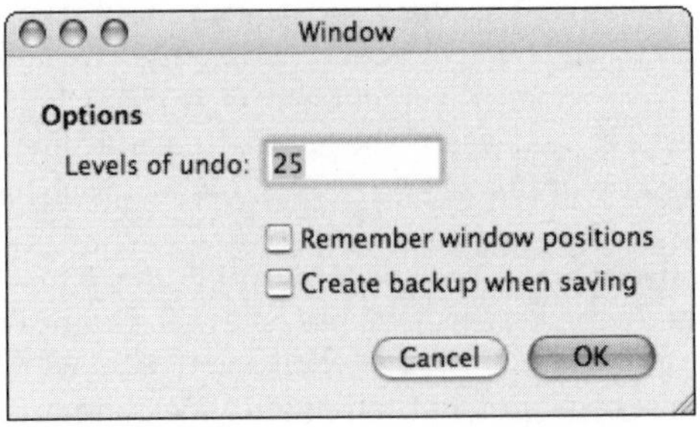

Figure 1-8

The information in the Apple Human Interface Guidelines is quite extensive. It covers all the user interface elements available within Mac OS X, such as windows, menus, controls, separators, text labels, and icons. All Mac OS X programmers should be familiar with the Apple Human Interface Guidelines in order to know what correct Aqua user interfaces are supposed to look like, and how they're supposed to behave.

Summary

You have seen how the major elements of Mac OS X come together on your computer. The applications you use every day are but one element. These applications are built on application frameworks, system services, and ultimately Mac OS X's core operating system; all these pieces contribute to your application experience. The high-level picture might look something like Figure 1-9.

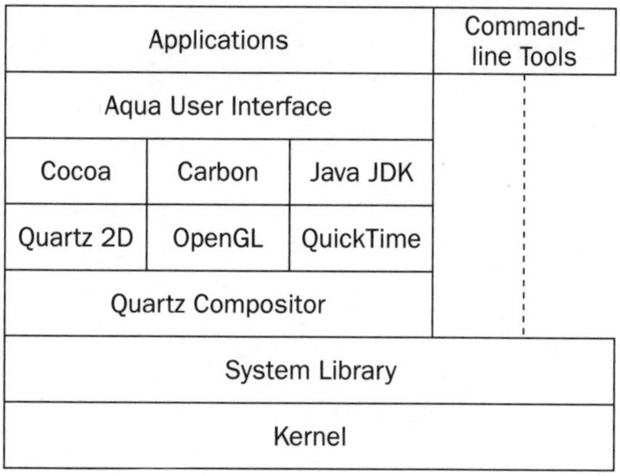

Applications			Command-line Tools
Aqua User Interface			
Cocoa	Carbon	Java JDK	
Quartz 2D	OpenGL	QuickTime	
Quartz Compositor			
System Library			
Kernel			

Figure 1-9

In this chapter you learned

- ❏ How the Core OS, Core Graphics, and application libraries form the heart of the Mac OS X operating system
- ❏ How to use the Terminal application to access Mac OS X's command-line interface
- ❏ How the Cocoa and Carbon application frameworks are organized
- ❏ How the Apple Human Interface Guidelines encourage a common look and feel across all Mac OS X applications

In the next chapter, you learn about the developer resources bundled with Mac OS X. This includes tools used during the development process, as well as online documentation and other resources. Before proceeding, you can use the exercises that follow to practice some of the things you learned in this chapter. You can find the solutions to these exercises in Appendix A.

Exercises

1. The `apropos` command returns a list of manual pages that match one or more keywords. Try entering the following commands into Terminal:

    a. apropos copy

    b. apropos copy file

    c. apropos "copy file"

    Which of these commands provides the best result?

2. You have seen how you can use `man` to read the online help for a specific command. Type `man man` into Terminal and read about what `man` is capable of. For example, what does `man -k "copy file"` do?

Developer Tools

Since the earliest releases of Mac OS X, a complete set of developer tools has come bundled with the operating system. These tools range from text editors and compilers to debuggers and performance analyzers. Mac OS X even comes with a large collection of developer documentation and examples to help explain how these developer tools and development libraries should be used. Those interested in programming on Mac OS X have everything they need to get started.

Apple Computer also has a large developer support website called Apple Developer Connection or ADC, found at http://developer.apple.com/. Here Apple posts the most updated versions of its developer tools, documentation, and examples. This site also provides resources for small businesses interested in developing and distributing a product to the Macintosh community. If you are an ADC member, you can even file bug reports on Apple's software to help resolve issues you may discover on your own.

In this chapter you learn

- ❑ How to install the developer tools that came with your copy of Mac OS X
- ❑ Where to find the tools and documentation you just installed
- ❑ How to use the Apple Developer Connection website

Installing the Developer Software

As we have said, Apple bundles development tools along with the Mac OS X operating system. However, these tools are often an optional part of the installation process, and all the necessary components might not yet be installed on your system. If your copy of Mac OS X came pre-installed on a new Macintosh, these tools may be installed already. Otherwise, you need to install the necessary pieces from your Mac OS X CDs.

In Mac OS X 10.4 "Tiger," developer tools are spread across two different installer packages. The first package, BSD, contains a collection of command-line tools that may be useful when writing programs on Mac OS X. If you followed along with Chapter 1, you already have this package installed. If you skipped this part of Chapter 1, find your Mac OS X installation CDs and install them now. Just run the main installer, click the Configure button in the lower-left corner, and select the BSD package.

Developer Applications

The Mac OS X developer package includes several applications for your use during the development process. You can find most of these applications in the /Developer/Applications folder. Some of these tools are essential, such as those used for editing source code and building programs. Other tools are more specialized, such as the performance analysis tools and graphics utilities. In the sections that follow, you learn about many of these tools and how you can put them to use.

Build Tools

Of the programs installed in /Developer/Applications, two stand out as being indispensable in the development process: Xcode and Interface Builder. Together they include all the functionality required to design, build, and debug programs on Mac OS X.

Xcode is the centerpiece of Mac OS X's development environment. It includes tools for writing, building, and debugging programs all in a single application. Xcode also provides easy access to much of the developer documentation on your system. Xcode scales easily from building command-line tools and applications, to building libraries and plug-ins. You learn much more about Xcode in Chapter 3.

Interface Builder builds Carbon and Cocoa user interfaces for use in Xcode projects. You build interfaces by arranging windows, controls, and other elements graphically with your mouse. You learn much more about Interface Builder in Chapter 4.

Both Xcode and Interface Builder are up to the challenge of building whatever program you might need. In fact, Apple uses these same tools to build most of the applications and frameworks that make up Mac OS X. And by making Xcode and Interface Builder available with Mac OS X, Apple is giving you a great head start on building your software.

Performance Tools

Once you have dealt with the petty matters of writing some software and working out the bugs, your thoughts may turn to the question of performance. When you run your program you may see the spinning wait cursor (or the *rainbow wheel* or *spinning pizza of death*, whatever you call it). This cursor means your program has stopped processing user events and has become temporarily unresponsive. This unresponsiveness can be caused by many factors that normally boil down to two root causes: excess computation and memory management problems. In other words, *time* vs. *space*.

Mac OS X includes several utilities for examining where you spend your time and how you allocate your memory. These tools all live in /Developer/Applications/Performance Tools. When used properly, they can help you track down your performance problems.

On Programs, Stacks, and Backtraces

Programs are made up of a series of machine instructions gathered into functions or routines. These functions normally call other functions to do work. Your program can't exit a given function until all that function's sub-functions have completed. You might think of these functions as a stack of plates at a cafeteria. When your program enters a function, push a plate on the stack; when the function completes, pop the plate off the stack. The topmost plate represents your program's current function.

This metaphor for describing how functions work is so natural we refer to a program's list of running functions as its *stack, frame stack,* or *call stack.* The individual function calls are sometimes called *frames.*

Debugging tools often show you where you are in your program by displaying the entire stack. Traditionally you start with the current frame and work all the way back to the very first function. This list is called a *backtrace* because you *trace back* from the current frame.

All these utilities work by analyzing your program's state as it runs. These kinds of tools are generally known as *profilers.* Profilers normally require you to build your program in a special way, so that the utility can carefully watch your program's execution. Mac OS X's utilities require no such preprocessing and can be run on any application, whether you wrote it or not. They work by periodically (several times a second) peeking at your program's stack and aggregating the results.

The following table lists some of the performance tools available on your system. These tools are covered in more depth in the next several sections.

Tool	Description
MallocDebug	Watches how your program allocates memory.
ObjectAlloc	Watches how your program manages reference-counted objects and debugs autorelease problems.
Quartz Debug	Debugs performance problems related to drawing.
Sampler	Shows how your program's call stack changes over time.
Shark	Samples the performance of the entire system.
Spin Control	Automatically samples programs when they display the wait cursor.
Thread Viewer	Watches how your program creates and uses threads.

MallocDebug

MallocDebug keeps track of when your application allocates and frees memory. It records the position in your program's call stack where each allocation occurs, allowing you to find places where you're using a lot of memory. MallocDebug even does leak analysis for you, showing places where your program lost its reference to memory without freeing it. If you aren't quite sure what memory allocation means or what a leak is, don't worry; you learn more about this in Chapter 6. Figure 2-1 shows MallocDebug in action.

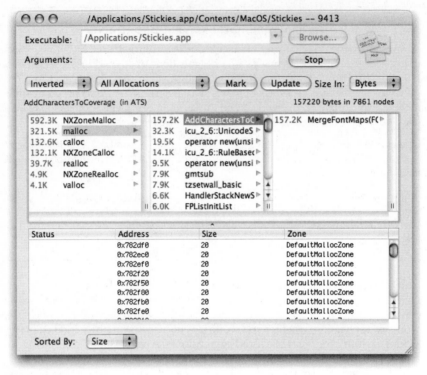

Figure 2-1

To learn more about MallocDebug, read through the documentation found under its Help menu. You'll find release notes, some instruction on how to use the program, and some hints on using MallocDebug effectively.

ObjectAlloc

ObjectAlloc is similar to MallocDebug in that it watches memory allocation, but ObjectAlloc is specifically useful for tracking reference-counted memory objects like Objective-C objects and CoreFoundation data structures. Figure 2-2 shows ObjectAlloc's main interface.

Reference counting is a memory management technique where you keep track of the number of things referring to a piece of memory. If someone is interested in the memory they *retain* it, or increase the memory's reference count by one. When they are done with the memory they *release* it, or decrease the reference count by one. When an object's reference count goes to 0, its memory is freed. Foundation introduces an interesting concept called *autoreleasing*. Autoreleasing is way of marking an Objective-C object to be released later on. It's useful for hanging onto an object temporarily without worrying about precisely when it is released.

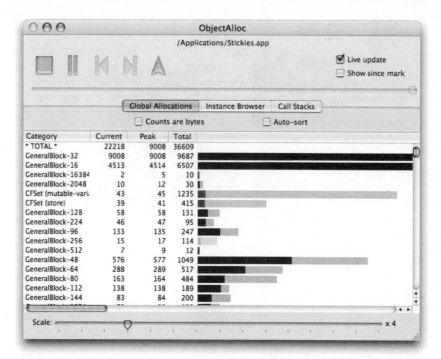

Figure 2-2

You may encounter a number of problems with reference counting. Like with normal memory, you can leak the object, which means that your program loses reference to an object without first releasing it. Objective-C's autorelease mechanism can also cause performance problems. If you autorelease a very large number of objects at the same time, you cause your program's total memory allocation to run up very high and then drop down all at once. This usage pattern can cause Mac OS X's memory management system to work harder to keep your program running. As with MallocDebug, don't panic if you're not quite sure what to make of reference counting or memory management in general. You learn more about this in Chapter 7.

Quartz Debug

Quartz Debug is a simple utility that allows you to examine the way in which your program draws to the screen. Mac OS X's graphics system is feature-rich, allowing for dynamic, transparent drawing common in the Aqua interface. But this also means drawing can be expensive, especially if you aren't careful about what you draw and when. Figure 2-3 shows the Quartz Debug application.

Mac OS X's application frameworks are explicit about what area of the screen needs to be redrawn at any time. For example, when you scroll through a long document, the system normally needs to redraw only the portion of the document that's now in view; the rest of the window can simply be moved to a new position. Programs that aren't careful might end up redundantly drawing the same thing several times, instead of only once. This needlessly wastes processing power.

You can use Quartz Debug to watch for these problems. Quartz Debug can instruct Mac OS X's window server to highlight the areas of your screen as they're refreshed. This allows you to check for unnecessary drawing. If you check the Autoflush Drawing option, you can watch your interfaces build piece by piece. You can even use Quartz Debug to temporarily disable Quartz Extreme, measure your screen's redraw performance, and get diagnostic information about the windows open on your computer.

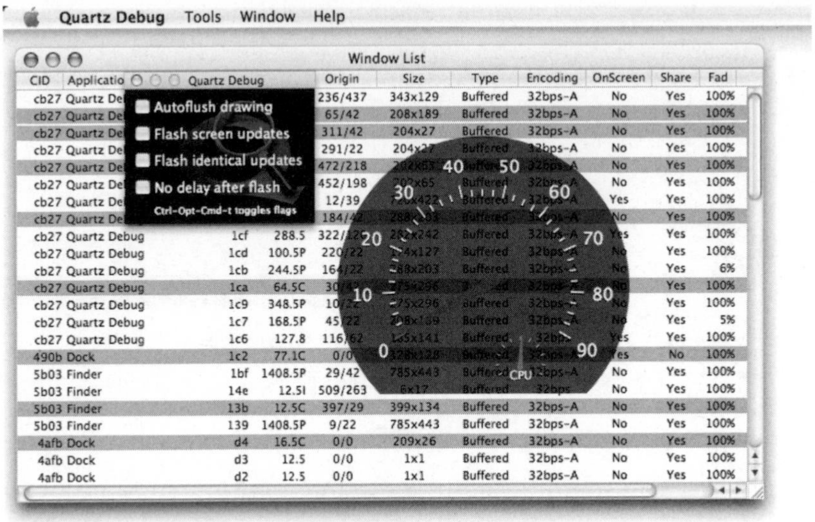

Figure 2-3

There is no online help available for Quartz Debug, but the application is easy to use. You can learn a fair amount of how drawing on Mac OS X works simply by playing with Quartz Debug's features.

Sampler

Sampler shows you how a program's call stack changes over time. You begin by launching a program (or connecting to a program already running) and recording its state as you use the program. When you finish recording you can analyze the results to find out where your program spent most of its time during the recording period.

Sampler works by pausing your program several times a second and recording your program's call stack at that point in time. It then trends the data in several ways, including measuring the frequency of each specific frame in the call stack, and tracking the size of the call stack changes. For example, if a specific function call appears in half your program's call stacks, Sampler calls that out.

Sampler provides three different views of your data, each in its own tab: Browser, Outline, and Trace. The Outline tab displays the functions in your program's call stack in an outline view sorted by frequency. You can use this tab to drill down and see where your program is spending its time. Figure 2-4 shows an example of the outline view. The Browser tab displays this same information as a browser, rather than an outline view. The Browser tab can be useful when you are looking at a specific section of the call stack. The Trace tab contains a graph representing the depth of each call stack in your sample data. You can use this view to get a sense of what your program is doing by watching the shape of the graph. Repeating jagged patterns suggests you're performing a lot of work in one or more loops. In all three views, you're normally looking for functions (or branches of functions) that are chewing up more time than you expected.

To learn more about Sampler, read through the documentation found under Sampler's Help menu. These notes include lots of background information and usage tips to help you get the most out of Sampler.

Figure 2-4

Shark

Apple provides a special set of tools called the Common Hardware Understanding Development Tools or CHUD Tools for short. These tools work very closely with your Mac's hardware to diagnose performance problems. The CHUD Tools are available separately from Apple, but they also come with the other Mac OS X developer tools. You'll find a folder at /Developer/Applications/Performance Tools/CHUD if these tools are installed; if you don't have these tools, you can install them from your Tiger install disks or download them from http://developer.apple.com/tools/performance/.

Of all the CHUD Tools from Apple, the most popular is Shark, as shown in Figure 2-5. Although part of the CHUD toolset, you will find Shark in /Developer/Applications/Performance Tools, not in the CHUD folder.

Shark is similar to Sampler in that it records programs' call stacks over a period of time and trends the results. Shark differs from Sampler in that it samples your entire system, not just a single application. Shark takes your call stack data one step further by showing your frame's assembly code, and even the source code, if available. So when Shark indicates you're spending a suspicious amount of time in a particular function, you can actually view the source code for that function right there. And if that isn't enough, Shark even suggests specific ways in which you can improve your function's performance. The only catch is that some of Shark's advice is appropriate only for advanced programmers.

You can find a complete user guide under Shark's Help menu. Shark also comes with a PowerPC assembly command reference guide to help you understand Shark's assembly code view.

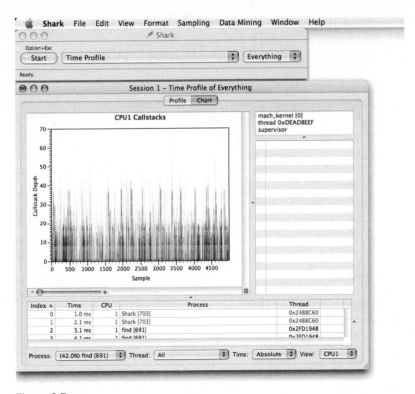

Figure 2-5

Spin Control

Imagine that your program has become unresponsive. It no longer responds to user events, and Mac OS X automatically shows the spinning wait cursor. You want to sample your program to find out what is chewing up its time, but by the time you launch Sampler and get ready to record your application, it has returned from its busy state and is working again.

Spin Control can help you deal with these situations by automatically sampling applications that go into the busy state (display the spinning wait cursor). The Spin Control interface shown in Figure 2-6 is fairly simple; you just start Spin Control and wait for your app to go off and start spinning. Once that happens, Spin Control generates a sample report like the one produced by Sampler. Because Spin Control works passively, you can just start it and leave it running as you go about your business.

Thread Viewer

Every process on Mac OS X uses one or more *threads* to process machine instructions. A thread basically represents the capability to do work on the system at any given time. In the same way in which Mac OS X's pre-emptive multi-tasking kernel can run two processes at the same time, a process with two threads can do two activities at the same time.

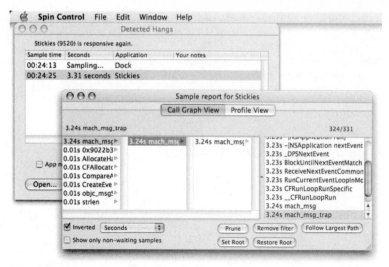

Figure 2-6

Programmers often turn to threads to improve program performance. For example, on Macintosh systems with more than one CPU, a programmer can use threads to perform work on both CPUs at once. Also, a program like the Finder might perform a long file copy operation in a background thread while responding to user events in the main thread.

But writing multi-threaded programs can be challenging because programmers must deal with the fact a program is performing two or more things at once. You can get into trouble if two threads start competing for the same resource. For example, if you have two programs trying to write to the same file at the same time, the file contents might get mixed up. Similarly, multiple threads trying to write to the same data structures might instead scramble their program's memory. Creating additional worker threads comes at some cost, so you can actually hinder performance if you get carried away with threads.

Thread Viewer allows you to easily see the state of your program's threads. Each thread is plotted in a bar graph, allowing you see when it's busy and when it's idle, as shown in Figure 2-7. Like with Shark and Sampler, you can access your threads' call stacks directly from the graph to get an exact idea of what each thread is doing.

Help is available from Thread Viewer's Help menu, although not as much as is available with Sampler or Shark.

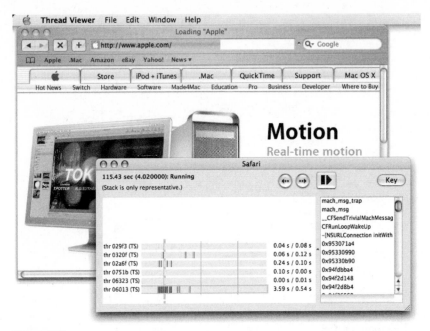

Figure 2-7

Other Utilities

Mac OS X's developer tools include other utilities that can make your life easier. Though not as indispensable as Xcode, Interface Builder, or the performance tools, it's worth spending some time getting to know them. A number of the more interesting utilities appear in the following table and are described in more depth in the next sections. All these tools live at /Developer/Applications/Utilities, except where otherwise noted.

Tool	Description
FileMerge	Compares two files or directory trees, and merges the differences.
Icon Composer	Builds icon files (.icns) used for your application.
PackageMaker	Builds Installer packages.
Pixie	Magnifies portions of your screen to look for minute drawing problems.
Property List Editor	Edits Property List files.
Script Editor	Writes and tests AppleScript programs.

FileMerge

FileMerge lets you compare two text files side by side and see how they differ. As you scroll through the files, FileMerge highlights places where text has been added, removed, or moved within the files. You can also use FileMerge to compare entire directories of files, as shown in Figure 2-8.

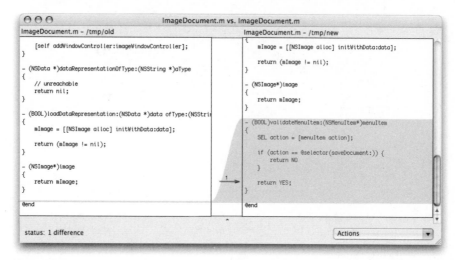

Figure 2-8

FileMerge gets its name from its ability to merge changes between two files into a third file. You simply scroll through both files and for each change pick which one you want to keep. You can then save a new version of the file that contains all the common text with the changes you specified. This is very useful when looking at two versions of the same Xcode project. You can use FileMerge to see where the two projects differ and select which changes you want to keep on a change-by-change basis.

Icon Composer

Icon Composer, shown in Figure 2-9, is a small utility for making Mac OS X icon files (.icns files). Unlike its name suggests, you cannot draw icons in Icon Composer; you need to draw your icons in some other program and save various sizes of the icons out as separate files. You can then drag your files into Icon Composer and save the result as a .icns file. You learn more about using .icns files in Chapter 5.

PackageMaker

PackageMaker builds packages for use in Installer, Mac OS X's built-in software installer. Once you've written your own programs, you might want to distribute them as packages to help simplify the installation process for your users. You simply point PackageMaker at a directory of files, fill out the form shown in Figure 2-10, and create your package.

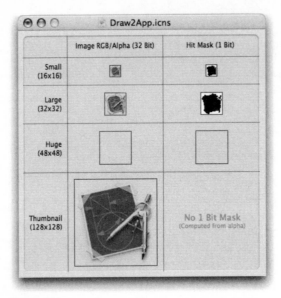

Figure 2-9

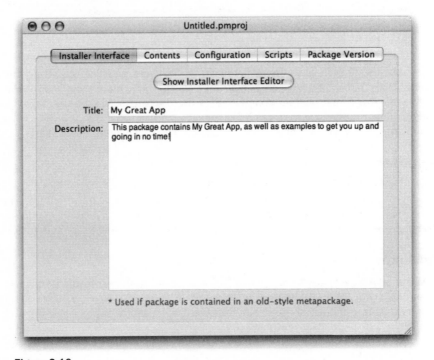

Figure 2-10

Packages can actually support a lot of custom functionality, more than can be configured using PackageMaker's interface. To enable packages' advanced features, you need to get into the details of the package format. PackageMaker's online help contains detailed notes on the package format, along with a few examples.

Pixie

Pixie magnifies the area of the screen under your mouse cursor, as shown in Figure 2-11. It can also display color values for the pixels on your screen. You can find Pixie in /Developer/Applications/ Graphics Tools.

These features are very useful when designing custom UI elements and other graphics for your programs. Unlike other developer tools, Pixie includes some usage notes in its About box in the Pixie menu, rather than in its Help menu. In fact, Pixie doesn't even have a Help menu. However, the program is easy to master.

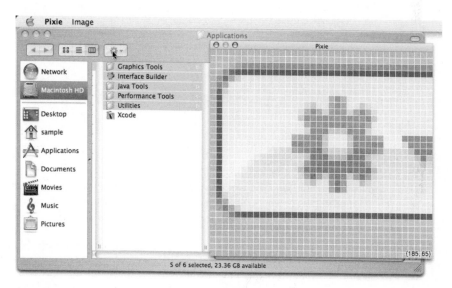

Figure 2-11

Property List Editor

Property List Editor is, as its name implies, a program that edits *property lists*. Property lists are text files that store structured data. Actually, property lists are a specific kind of XML file designed to store information that can be described as strings, numbers, arrays, or key/value pairs. Property List Editor displays property lists in an outline view so that you can easily navigate them, as shown in Figure 2-12.

Property lists are commonly used for such things as application preferences, configuration files, and even some document formats. You learn more about property lists and see some examples of how they are used in Chapter 5.

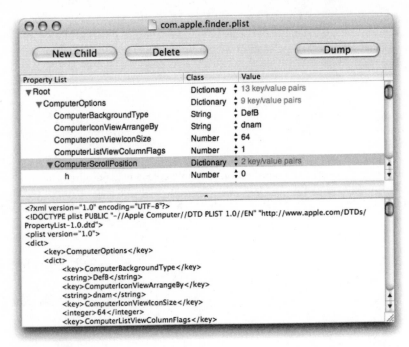

Figure 2-12

Script Editor

Script Editor is an application for writing and running AppleScripts. Strictly speaking, Script Editor isn't a developer tool; it's a standard part of Mac OS X. You can find Script Editor in /Applications/AppleScript.

Script Editor is a specialized tool for working with AppleScripts. It validates your AppleScript syntax as you write and uses colors and text styles to highlight various parts of your script. You can also run AppleScripts from Script Editor and display the results in the main editor window, as shown in Figure 2-13. Once you've written an AppleScript, you can save it as a self-contained application for future use; this lets you distribute AppleScripts without sharing your script's code with others. These applications are really just simple AppleScripts, not full-featured applications like TextEdit or Finder.

You can, however, use AppleScript to write full-featured applications. Apple calls this technology AppleScript Studio. You use Xcode and Interface Builder to build AppleScript Studio applications. As a result, you will probably edit your AppleScript Studio script files in Xcode as well. But Script Editor is still useful for writing small, self-contained scripts.

You learn more about AppleScript and AppleScript Studio in Chapter 12.

Command-Line Tools

As you learned in Chapter 1, Unix development is traditionally done through command-line tools. Although Mac OS X includes applications for designing, building, and debugging programs on Mac OS X, the developer packages include several powerful command-line tools as well. In fact, many of the applications you've read about in this chapter have command-line equivalents.

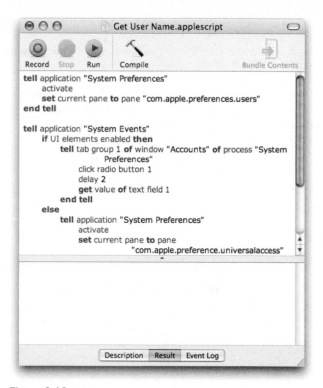

Figure 2-13

Some of the more interesting command-line utilities appear in the following table and are described in more detail in the next sections. You access these tools through the Terminal application.

Tool	Description
cc / gcc	Compiles C and other programming languages.
diff	Compares two files or directory trees.
gdb	Debugs programs written in C and other programming languages.
GetFileInfo / SetFile	Reads and writes Finder-specific file settings.
Rez / DeRez	Converts HFS+ resource forks into text files and vice versa.
sample	Shows how your program's call stack changes over time.
sh / bash / tcsh	Interprets Unix commands and runs shell scripts.
top	Tracks performance statistics for the entire system.

cc / gcc

Since the very beginning, Unix operating systems have come with a built-in C compiler: cc. In the old days, this compiler was necessary to install software: you would download a program's source code and compile it specifically for your system.

Sometime later, the Free Software Foundation created and distributed a free, multi-language compiler called gcc. The organization's goal was to ensure computer users would always have access to a royalty-free compiler they could use without cost. Today gcc has essentially replaced cc on most modern Unix systems, and Mac OS X is no exception. Even if you type cc instead of gcc, you get the gcc compiler.

Of course, Mac OS X's primary tool for building programs is Xcode, as you see in Chapter 3. In reality, Xcode uses the gcc compiler for building your C, C++, and Objective-C code. But you can still drive the gcc compiler yourself from the command-line. This is especially useful for compiling software intended for other Unix systems on Mac OS X.

diff

diff is a command-line tool for examining two text files and showing how they differ, much like FileMerge. The method for comparing two files is fairly straightforward. The following example shows a method has been added to a new version of the ImageDocument.m file. diff supports many options for customizing its output, and you can learn a lot more about this utility from its manual (man) page.

```
Macintosh:~ sample$ diff old/ImageDocument.m new/ImageDocument.m
60a61,71
> - (BOOL)validateMenuItem:(NSMenuItem*)menuItem
> {
>     SEL action = [menuItem action];
>
>     if (action == @selector(saveDocument:)) {
>         return NO
>     }
>
>     return YES;
> }
>
Macintosh:~ sample$
```

gdb

gdb is a source-level debugger distributed by the Free Software Foundation. You can use it to step through your program's call stack as it's running, examine your program's variables and the contents of its memory, and so on. If your program crashes while you're debugging it, gdb shows you precisely where it crashed. Like the Unix shell, you interact with gdb by issuing command-line instructions, as shown in the following example:

```
Macintosh:~ sample$ gdb Slide\ Master.app/Contents/MacOS/Slide\ Master
GNU gdb 5.3-20030128 (Apple version gdb-309) (Thu Dec  4 15:41:30 GMT 2003)
Copyright 2003 Free Software Foundation, Inc.
...
Reading symbols for shared libraries .... done
(gdb) break main
Breakpoint 1 at 0xedf68: file /Projects/Slide Master/main.m, line 13.
(gdb) run
Starting program: Slide Master.app/Contents/MacOS/Slide Master

Breakpoint 1, main (argc=1, argv=0xbffffe9c) at /Projects/Slide Master/main.m:13
13          return NSApplicationMain(argc, argv);
(gdb)
```

You've learned that the primary tool for debugging programs on Mac OS X is Xcode. But just as Xcode uses the gcc tool to compile your program's source code, Xcode actually uses gdb to help you debug your program. Xcode provides a nice graphical interface on top of gdb that is easy to learn and well suited for most debugging tasks. Once in a while programmers drop down to gdb's command line to access the debugger's more advanced features. You can learn more about Xcode in Chapter 3; if you're interested in learning more about gdb, you can bring up an extensive command reference by typing help at the (gdb) prompt.

GetFileInfo / SetFile

Most Macintosh computers use a file system called HFS+, invented by Apple in 1998 as the replacement to the older HFS file system. One of the features of the HFS file system is the capability to store special metadata for use by the Finder and other parts of the operating system. For example, every file on HFS can have a 4-character *type code* that identifies the file's contents (like a file extension) and a 4-character *creator code* that links that file back to the program that created it. Files and folders on HFS can also be marked invisible.

Historically, Apple doesn't include user-friendly ways of checking or modifying this information; it's meant to be used privately by the operating system itself. However, developers often need access to this information during the development or debugging process, or when preparing their files for installation. Mac OS X's developer tools include two utilities for reading and writing these settings: GetFileInfo and SetFile. You can learn more about these utilities from their man pages.

Rez / DeRez

Another feature of the HFS and HFS+ file systems is the capability to store multiple files at a given path. The files you see in the Finder and in Terminal are what HFS thinks of as a *data fork*; another common fork is the *resource fork*. Resource forks were designed to store Carbon Resource Manager data structures in arbitrary files without affecting that file's data fork content. For example, a text file could store a custom icon, a file version, and other information in its resource fork; the text file's contents (text) would remain in the data fork.

Today, Apple discourages the use of resource forks on Mac OS X because they don't play well with other file systems and platforms. For example, a Windows user who receives an HFS+ file as an email attachment might receive only half the file (its data fork) or receive a file in some strange hybrid format; in either of these cases, the file may be unusable. However, Apple still supplies tools for working with these forks because they're helpful for Carbon developers.

In the earliest days of Macintosh programming, programmers used a program called Rez to create resource forks from special text files, called *Rez files* (.r). Rez files use a special syntax for defining Carbon Resource Manager resources, as shown in the following code. The DeRez utility transforms the data in the opposite direction, converting a resource-fork into a Rez file. Today Rez and DeRez can convert data between Rez files and modern data-fork resources (.rsrc).

```
#include "AboutBox.h"
#include "Carbon.r"
#include "Localize.r"

resource 'WIND' (kAboutWindowID, purgeable) {
        {100, 100, 215, 400}, noGrowDocProc, invisible, goAway, 0, ABOUTBOXTITLE,
alertPositionMainScreen
```

```
};

resource 'STR#' (kAboutStrings, purgeable) {
        {
        ABOUTSTRING1;
        ABOUTSTRING2;
        ABOUTSTRING3;
        };
};
```

Modern Carbon programmers typically trust Xcode to handle their Rez files for them. Again Xcode simply talks to the `Rez` command-line tool to convert Rez files into data-fork resource files. You can learn more about `Rez` and `DeRez` from their man pages; you learn more about resources and Carbon programming in Chapter 8.

sample

`sample` is a command-line tool that generates Sampler reports. It's fairly simple to use; you just enter the name or *process identifier* of the program you want to sample and the number of seconds you want to record, as shown in the following code example: A process identifier is a unique number that identifies the process on your system. You can find a process's identifier using command-line tools like `ps` or `top`, or using the Activity Monitor application.

```
Macintosh:/tmp sample$ sample Finder 2
Sampling process 256 each 10 msecs 200 times
Sample analysis of process 256 written to file /tmp/Finder_256.sample.txt
Macintosh:~ sample$
```

Output is saved to a file in the `/tmp/` directory by default. Although not as user-friendly as the Sampler application, you may find yourself using `sample` quite a bit, especially if you spend a lot of time in Terminal. It's often faster to type `sample Finder 2` than to go and find Sampler, launch it, attach to the Finder, and so on. You can also open `sample` reports in Sampler by choosing File ➪ Open Trace. You can learn more about the options you can pass to `sample` from its man page.

sh / bash / tcsh

In Chapter 1 you learned how to run command-line functions from Terminal. Again, the Terminal itself knows nothing about how to interpret your commands. Instead it delegates all that responsibility to the Unix shell.

The original Unix shell is called `sh` (for *shell*) and supports a fairly simple command language. Every `sh` command begins with a program name. This program is responsible for parsing the other arguments in the `sh` command and doing the requested work. The `sh` command language also includes support for redirecting a program's input and output to files. For example, you can capture all the output from a command by redirecting its output to a file. Realizing the utility of `sh`'s command language, its authors devised a means of processing commands from a file rather than from user input. These files are called *shell scripts* because they are *scripts* of *shell* commands.

But `sh` is not without limitations, and many people have sought to build a better shell to replace `sh`. Individual shells come into, and subsequently out of, favor all the time. Two modern `sh` replacements include `bash` (the "Bourne Again Shell," a reference to one of the original `sh` authors) and `tcsh`, both of which come with Mac OS X. `bash` is a modern replacement derived (if only in spirit) from the original `sh` command syntax. It is quite common on Linux and other Unix systems and is the default shell for Mac OS X. `tcsh` is a modern replacement for an older shell, `csh`, which featured a number of improvements over the original `sh` command: a history and command aliases.

You can find shells installed with other fundamental command-line utilities in `/bin`. You can run a shell simply by typing its name in the command-line; the `exit` command quits out of the shell. You can change your default shell with the `chsh` command, as shown in the following code. The change takes effect when you open a new Terminal window:

```
Macintosh:~ sample$ chsh -s /bin/tcsh
chsh: netinfo domain "." updated
Macintosh:~ sample$
```

You learn more about the shell and shell scripting in Chapter 10. You can also learn a lot about how individual shells work, including their command syntax and other features, by reading their man pages.

Top

`top` displays system performance statistics such as CPU load, memory usage, and processor time consumed per process in your Terminal window. Unlike the other performance tools you've learned about so far, `top` updates itself automatically and displays its results live. It is the command-line equivalent of the Activity Monitor utility found in `/Applications/Utilities`.

Although it's really more of a system maintenance command than a developer tool, `top` is useful as a developer tool. Because `top` displays its results live, you can use it to watch how your program's CPU load and memory requirements change while you are using your program. For example, you should make sure your program is using 0% of the CPU when you aren't actively using the program; using CPU unnecessarily will affect the battery life on portable machines. Also make sure your program is using a minimum of other system resources: threads, memory, and so on. You can learn a lot more about how to use `top` from its man page.

Developer Documentation and Examples

Mac OS X includes a lot of documentation for people interested in writing Mac OS X programs. You have already seen some examples of this documentation, such as the online help that comes with most of the system's developer tools. Documentation also exists for frameworks like Carbon and Cocoa; this includes API reference, conceptual or high-level documentation, and even examples that illustrate how these frameworks should be used.

Much of Mac OS X's developer documentation resides in the `/Developer/ADC Reference Library` folder. Here you will find an API reference, high-level documentation, release notes, and other documentation resources. This folder is further subdivided by library or technology. For example, you will find a `Carbon` subdirectory containing Carbon-specific documentation in `/Developer/ADC Reference Library`. And these technology-specific subdirectories are often further subdivided by topic.

If you know what you're looking for, you might choose to just dive right into these directories. But if you're new to this material and want a bit more information, you can open the `index.html` file in your favorite web browser, as shown in Figure 2-14. This provides a little more context for each of the directories in `/Developer/ADC Reference Library` and may help you track down the information you need if you're not exactly sure where to find it.

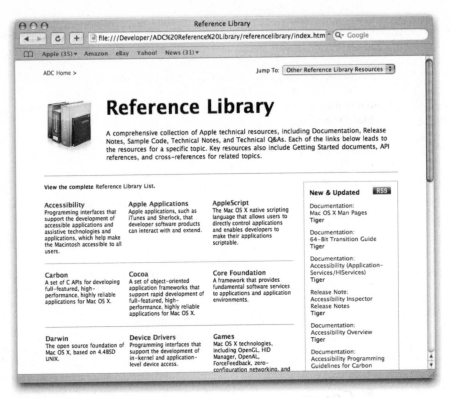

Figure 2-14

Mac OS X also includes examples of how to use many of the frameworks on your system. You can find some of these examples in /Developer/ADC Reference Library, and others in /Developer/ Examples. Like the ADC Reference Library, the Examples directory is subdivided by technology and topic; however the examples aren't collected into an index like the documentation. So you need to do a little bit of exploring to learn about what's available. For example, you can find many Cocoa examples in the /DeveloperExamples/AppKit directory.

Earlier you learned how to use Mac OS X's man page system to get help for command-line tools. Although man pages aren't strictly intended as developer documentation, they do contain a lot of information specifically for developers. For example, most of Mac OS X's Darwin API reference is published through man pages rather than HTML or PDF documents. The same is true of some third-party libraries and languages, such as OpenGL, Tcl, and Perl.

Conceptual Documentation

When you're learning how to use a particular library or framework on Mac OS X, one of the first places you should turn to is the framework's conceptual documentation. The conceptual documentation is designed to teach you the fundamentals of using that framework, such as describing basic data structures and concepts and how the different parts of the framework interact with each other and with other frameworks. The conceptual documentation also contains tutorials that illustrate how the pieces come together and give you a chance to practice what you've learned.

The best place to find this conceptual documentation is in the HTML index: `/Developer/ADC Reference Library/documentation/index.html`. When you select a technology from the main index, you are taken to a page listing the materials specific to that technology. You can find conceptual documentation listed in a Resources section in a column marked Fundamentals. Figure 2-15 shows the Cocoa Reference Library page, with the conceptual documentation listed in the Cocoa Resources section.

The documents shown in the following table and explained in more detail in the following sections describe important Mac OS X concepts that aren't specific to individual technologies. You have already learned about some of them in Chapter 1, but they bear repeating. You can find these documents in the Mac OS X section of the documentation index.

Document	Description
Apple Human Interface Guidelines	Describes the elements of the Aqua user interface.
Mac OS X Technology Overview	Describes Mac OS X's system architecture.
Xcode 2.0 User Guide	Describes the Xcode program in detail.

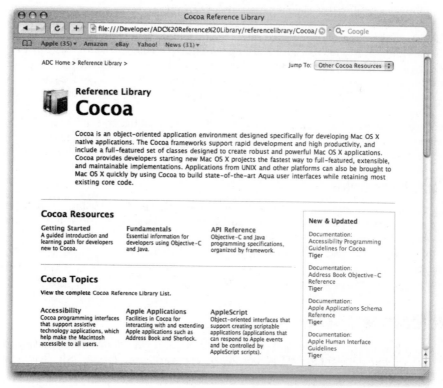

Figure 2-15

Apple Human Interface Guidelines

You already learned about the role of the Apple Human Interface Guidelines in Chapter 1. To recap, the Apple Human Interface Guidelines describes how Aqua user interface elements should look and behave, how they should interact with each other, when to develop your own custom controls, and how to make them "fit in" with the rest of Aqua. In other words it defines the rules all Mac OS X applications are supposed to follow. You can find this document in the Mac OS X section of the documentation index; or you can navigate to it in the Finder at `/Developer/ADC Reference Library/documentation/ UserExperience/Conceptual/OSXHIGuidelines/index.html`.

Mac OS X Technology Overview

The Mac OS X Technology Overview describes how the various pieces of Mac OS X come together into a complete system. It includes an overview of information you can't find easily in other places, including

- ❑ Mac OS X's directory layout
- ❑ File system issues specific to Mac OS X
- ❑ How bundles, applications, and frameworks are packaged
- ❑ Strategies for internationalizing Mac OS X software

Although the Technology Overview goes into a reasonable amount of detail on these topics, it stops short of providing an API reference for working with the technologies themselves. So, for example, you should turn to the System Overview to learn what a bundle is, what features they offer, and conceptually how bundles are used. After you understand all this, you can turn to Carbon- or Cocoa-specific documentation to learn about the particular API available for working with bundles directly.

The Technology Overview is available in the Mac OS X section of the documentation index; or you can navigate to it in the Finder at `/Developer/ADC Reference Library/documentation/MacOSX/ Conceptual/OSX_Technology_Overview/index.html`.

Xcode 2.0 User Guide

The Xcode application is a complex tool. Although it's easy to get started using Xcode to write Mac OS X programs, there are many advanced features lurking beneath its surface. You will find a fairly thorough explanation of Xcode's features in the Xcode 2.0 User Guide. You can find this document in the Tools section of the documentation index, or you can navigate to it in the Finder at `/Developer/ADC Reference Library/documentation/DeveloperTools/Conceptual/XcodeUserGuide20/ Contents/Resources/en.lproj/index.html`.

API Reference

After you understand the fundamental concepts behind a particular framework and work through a tutorial or two, you will want to roll up your sleeves and start writing some code. Before too long, you will have questions about how the framework's API handles a certain problem, or if it provides a particular feature. To find the answers, you can turn to the framework's API reference.

As with conceptual documentation, the best place to find API reference is in the HTML index: /Developer/ADC Reference Library/referencelibrary/index.html. You will find API reference listed in a technologies Resources section in a column marked API Reference.

The exact contents of an API reference file depend on the technology. Figure 2-16 shows the Application Kit Reference for Objective-C. The top-level page links to additional pages for individual Objective-C classes and other information. Class pages contain documentation for each of the class's methods.

Figure 2-17 shows one such method entry; the page defines the method signature and then describes the function's inputs and outputs, expected behavior, and anything else you need to know to use the function.

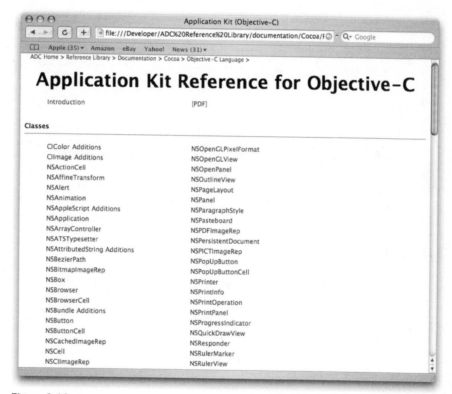

Figure 2-16

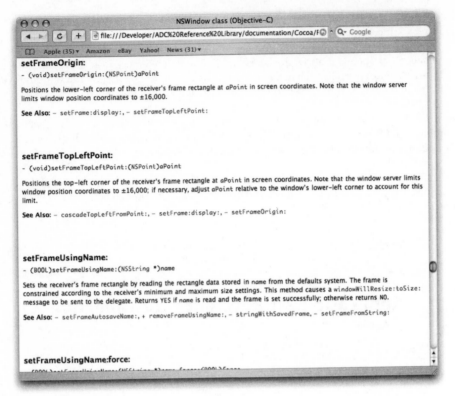

Figure 2-17

By comparison, the Carbon Function Index shown in Figure 2-18 lists all the functions available through the Carbon framework in alphabetical order.

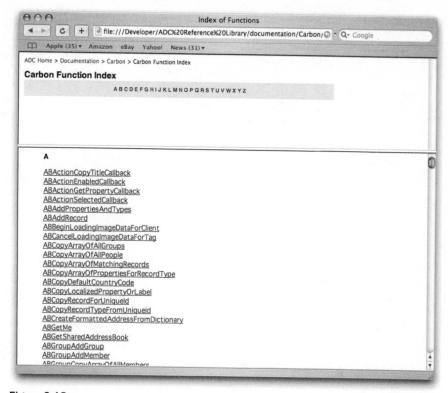

Figure 2-18

When you select a function, you get the function's C prototype as well as information about how that function is used, as shown in Figure 2-19.

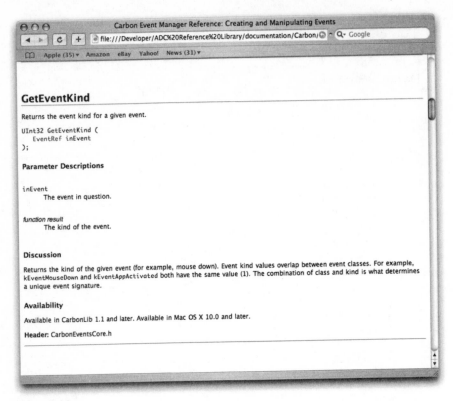

Figure 2-19

Again, you learn more about C and Objective-C in Chapters 6 and 7, so you don't need to worry about those details right now.

This API reference is arguably the most important piece of Mac OS X's developer documentation. You use it to discover what a framework is capable of and to learn how to write code that uses that framework's specific features. Without the API reference you could still learn a lot about a framework's API definition from its header files, but you'd have to guess at what the interface does and how it's used. Feel free to bookmark the reference pages you visit often so that you can return to them quickly.

Examples

You can find a bunch of examples in /Developer/ADC Reference Library/samplecode/ and also in /Developer/Examples. These examples are editable by any user with administrative privileges. If you created your user account when you installed Mac OS X, or when you turned on your new computer for the first time, you have an administrator account. That means you can open and build these projects right where they are. However it's still a good idea to always make copies of these examples before you build them; that way if you accidentally edit or change something, you can always go back to the original.

These examples range from small snippets of code that illustrate specific points to full-blown applications. For example, you will find the complete source code to TextEdit, SimpleText, and Sketch available here. You should already be familiar with TextEdit, the text editor that lives in /Applications. The TextEdit source code shows how to build a complete Cocoa application, including working with documents, basic scriptability, and printing. TextEdit is quite old for a Cocoa app, and doesn't use some of the newer additions to Cocoa, such as Cocoa's document abstraction. SimpleText follows in a similar spirit; you may be familiar with SimpleText as the editor that came with older versions of Mac OS. Although useful, SimpleText doesn't use some of the newer features of Carbon. Sketch is a drawing application written in Cocoa; it's a little more current than the TextEdit example. You can find pre-built versions of SimpleText and Sketch in /Developer/Applications/Utilities/Built Examples.

Man Pages

In Chapter 1 you learned about the Unix *manual* and how you can use the man command to view information about Mac OS X's command-line programs. Even the command-line tools installed by the developer packages have man pages. But the manual contains information beyond command-line reference.

Most of the Darwin programmer documentation lives in the manual system. This includes API reference for the C functions in the system libraries. It also contains API reference for other libraries and languages that are part of Darwin, including entries for Perl, Tcl, and OpenSSL. In addition, you can find notes on file formats, directory layouts, and other conceptual documentation in the manual.

Man pages are gathered into different sections, with each section indexed by numbers. Historically, these sections have special meaning, as shown in the following table.

Section	Description
1	Commands
2	System Calls
3	Library Functions
4	Devices and Device Drivers
5	File Formats
6	Games
7	Miscellaneous
8	System Maintenance

Although most of the man pages available on Mac OS X still follow this old format, there are some things to consider. Information about command-line utilities tend to live in sections 1 and 8. Similarly, C API reference for Darwin is spread between sections 2 and 3; the difference between these sections is somewhat obscure. Although section 4 includes a few manual pages related to devices and device drivers, you won't find information about IOKit, Mac OS X's driver layer, in the man system. Instead, you can find IOKit information in /Developer/ADC Reference Library, along with other Mac OS X–specific technologies.

Other projects have expanded the original section list to meet their own needs. For example, Perl documentation lives in section *3pm*, which is sort of a part of section 3. You really don't need to worry about these new sections (or sections in general) except when you have trouble pulling up certain man pages.

When you ask for a manual page, man searches its sections for a matching page and returns the first one it finds. So if pages in two or more sections share the same name, man displays only one of those files. In these cases, you have to ask for the proper section number in addition to the page name. For example, man 2 open asks the system for the open man page in the System Calls section, not the page in the Commands section. You can use the apropos or man -k commands you learned about in Chapter 1 to print page names and section numbers that match specific keywords, as shown here:

```
Macintosh:~ sample$ man -k "copy file"
CpMac(1)                - copy files preserving metadata and forks
File::Copy(3pm)         - Copy files or filehandles
cp(1)                   - copy files
cpio(1)                 - copy file archives in and out
ditto(8)                - copy files and directories to a destination directory
```

Also, if you know that a page appears in more than one section, but you're not sure which, you can use man -a to print all the pages that match a specific name. For example, man -a open displays all the open man pages, one after another.

Mac OS X's man pages live in the /usr/share/man directory. This directory is part of the underlying Darwin system and isn't visible from Finder by default. You can either use Terminal or choose Finder's Go ⇨ Go to Folder command to examine this directory. Here you'll find the individual sections broken out for you, each one containing the individual man files. Most of these files appear in an old Unix text markup language called troff that you won't be able to read in normal text editors, web browsers, or word processors. Oh, why /usr/share/man you ask? Find the answer in the hier man page.

Apple Developer Connection

Mac OS X is constantly evolving, and the same is true of its developer information. Apple is constantly revising its tools, documentation, and examples to reflect the changes in Mac OS X and the needs of its developers. You can tap into this information from the Apple Developer Connection (ADC) website: http://developer.apple.com/. Figure 2-20 shows the Apple Developer Connection home page at the time this book was written. Like all things on the Internet, it may change by the time you read this.

Some of the information is available to the public-at-large, and those pages can be viewed using any web browser. Other content is available with an Apple Developer Connection account. You can sign up for an Online Membership to the ADC program for free, which gives you access to most, if not all, of the material on the ADC website. You can learn more about the ADC membership levels at http://developer.apple.com/membership/.

Once you're online, you will find a treasure trove of information, ranging from programming content to Macintosh business details. For example, you can find information to help you promote your Mac OS X product. Or you might find information about debugging Mac OS X's kernel. Some highlights of the ADC website follow.

Figure 2-20

Documentation

The ADC website contains the most recent versions of Mac OS X's developer documentation, and many links into this documentation appear on the ADC home page. You can also find the ADC Reference Library at the following URL: `http://developer.apple.com/referencelibrary/`. This page, shown in Figure 2-21, should look familiar to you — it's an Internet version of the developer documentation index on your hard drive: `file:///Developer/ADC%20Reference%20Library/referencelibrary/index.html`.

In fact, the similarities between the ADC website and the documentation on your hard drive are not coincidental. The documentation installed with your developer tools is a snapshot of the ADC website, ensuring that you have complete and reasonably recent information even if you aren't connected to the Internet. And if you are connected, your local files contain links to resources in the ADC website, creating a seamless bridge between both sets of documentation.

From the ADC Reference Library, you can dive into the individual content areas and look around, or you can start browsing the most recently added and updated files. A New & Updated section appears in the upper-right corner of the web page, listing a few of the most recent additions by date. You can bring up a larger list, as shown in Figure 2-22, by clicking the View Reference Library Revision List link at the bottom of this section. The Reference Library Revision List page contains a complete list of changes going back several months.

Figure 2-21

Each technology-specific area, such as QuickTime or AppleScript, has its own New & Updated section and revision list. You can easily browse changes to a technology's documentation by clicking its link from the Reference Library home page and then selecting its reference list link.

All the documentation in the ADC Reference Library is available without an ADC membership. You should be able to access this information quickly and easily using your favorite web browser.

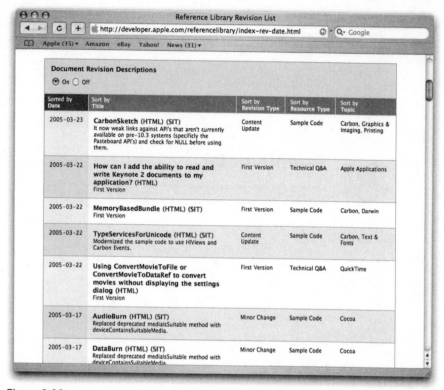

Figure 2-22

Examples

The ADC website also includes developer examples to help you learn more about how Mac OS X's technologies work. They are cross-referenced throughout the ADC website, so there are many ways to discover these examples. The most direct way is to follow the link from the Apple Developer Connection home page to the Sample Code area at `http://developer.apple.com/samplecode/`. Figure 2-23 shows the contents of the Sample Code page. Notice that the information is indexed by technology, just like the other areas of the ADC website.

You can also jump to the Sample Code content from other areas of the reference library. For example, if you are viewing the Cocoa Documentation section of the Reference Library, you can jump directly to the Cocoa Sample Code page using the Jump To popup menu in the upper-right corner of the page. After you are on the Cocoa Sample Code page, you can jump back to the Reference Library using the same popup.

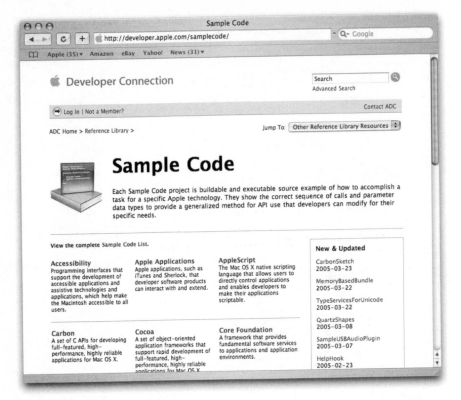

Figure 2-23

The similarities don't stop there. The Cocoa Sample Code section shown in Figure 2-24 mirrors the layout of the Cocoa Reference Library page. For example, a New & Updated section in the upper-right corner shows the recent changes to the Cocoa Sample Code area. Sample code is organized by Topic, just like the Reference Library. After you learn your way around the Reference Library, you'll have no trouble finding things in the Sample Code area.

But the similarities between the website and the files on your hard drive end there. The examples available on the ADC website are not the same examples installed in your /Developer/Examples directory. For example, you won't find the TextEdit or Sketch examples on the ADC website. Instead, you will find a large collection of additional examples there. This probably works to your advantage: you have more examples available to you than those installed on your hard drive.

All the examples in the ADC Source Code library are available free without an ADC membership.

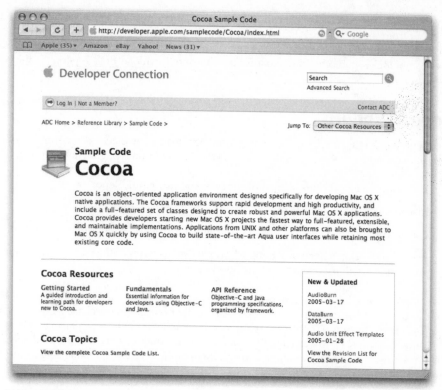

Figure 2-24

Mailing Lists

Apple maintains a number of mailing lists about specific developer topics. These mailing lists are available at `http://lists.apple.com/`. Here you can discuss various topics with other interested users and developers. Apple also provides archives of older messages, so you can easily check if a question has already appeared on a mailing list. All of Apple's mailing lists are publicly available. You only need an email address to subscribe to a mailing list. You can browse old mailing list archives using your favorite web browser.

Developer Tools

Apple also provides tool updates on the Apple Developer Connect website. Unlike the Reference Library and Sample Code areas, the tool downloads are available only to ADC members. However, these tools are available with the free Online Membership plan.

When you log into the ADC account with your membership, you'll see a special members-only section cordoned off from the rest of the ADC site. Here you have access to a Download Software menu where you'll find updates to developer tools like Xcode and Web Objects, Software Development Kits (SDKs) for other technologies, and other downloads. You can even download PDF versions of the entire ADC Reference Library.

Developer Support

Another benefit of having an Apple Developer Connection account is access to a number of developer support services. All these services are available from the ADC home page. These services include

❑   The ability to report bugs against Apple software using Bug Reporter

❑   Discounts on Apple hardware

❑   Use of Apple's compatibility labs in Cupertino and Tokyo, by appointment only

❑   Access to Developer Technical Support, which can help you with your programming problems/questions, one support incident at a time

The level of service available to you depends on your membership plan. For example, Bug Reporter and mailing lists are available to all ADC members. All member levels can purchase support incidents for access to Developer Technical Support; paying membership levels get a few starting support incidents with their memberships. Hardware discounts and access to compatibility labs are available for paying memberships only. You can find a complete breakdown of the services available at each membership level at http://developer.apple.com/membership/.

Business Resources

You will find a Business Resources menu on the right side of the Apple Developer Connection home page. Here Apple provides useful information for businesses interested in selling Macintosh software. Some of the information in this section links back to Developer Support content, such as information on Apple's compatibility labs and hardware discount services. But you will also find information about the Macintosh marketplace in general, including product guides and information about other Macintosh software and hardware vendors. Some third parties also offer their products and services to ADC members at a discount. Although this information isn't helpful if you're trying to learn how to write programs for Mac OS X, it is a great place to start if you're interested in selling your software to others.

Summary

Apple provides a number of developer tools and information to help you write programs on Mac OS X. Much of this information is stored locally in /Developer for quick access. Recent information is available at the Apple Developer Connection website at http://developer.apple.com/.

In this chapter you learned

- ❑ How to install the developer tools that came with your copy of Mac OS X
- ❑ Where to find the tools and documentation you just installed
- ❑ How to use the Apple Developer Connection website

In the next chapter, you learn about the Xcode application, which provides the tools you need to develop Mac OS X programs. Before proceeding, however, try the exercises that follow to test your understanding of the material covered in this chapter. You can find the solutions to these exercises in Appendix A.

Exercises

1. Use Sampler to watch the Stickies program launch. Let the program sit idle for a few seconds before stopping the sample process. Where did Sampler spend most of its time? If you need some help using the Sampler application, check the documentation under the Help menu.

2. Use the GetFileInfo and SetFile command-line tools to look-up and change Finder-specific information about files on your disk:

   a. How can you use GetFileInfo to check if a file or folder will be visible in the Finder? Here's a hint: you need to check the file's *invisible* attribute. Consult the GetFileInfo man page for help.

   b. What arguments would you pass to the SetFile command to make a file or folder invisible? Again, SetFile's man page may help you.

   c. Make a directory named Secrets invisible with the SetFile command. Since you have to use Terminal to run SetFile, you might as well create the Secrets directory in Terminal as well. Use the mkdir command to create Secrets in your home directory.

   Once you've set Secrets' invisible attribute the file should not appear in the Finder. However, you may need to re-launch the Finder to see your change; you can do that using the Force Quit menu item under the Apple menu. You can also use GetFileInfo to verify the invisible attribute is set properly.

   Also you will need to refer to SetFile and GetFileInfo by their full paths in order for your shell to find them. For example /Developer/Tools/SetFile. This is because your command shell doesn't automatically look in /Developer/Tools for command-line tools. You learn more about how the shell works in Chapter 10.

3. Which man sections contain a page named intro on your system? Use a single man command to read them all. Feel free to consult man's man page for help at any time.

Xcode

When programming for Mac OS X you spend most of your time in Xcode. Xcode is an Integrated Development Environment, or IDE, meaning that Xcode provides all the tools you need to write, build, and debug Mac OS X programs in a single application.

Xcode's text editing tools are specifically designed for writing computer programs. Source code is typically displayed in a small monospaced font so that programmers can tell at a glance if their code is formatted properly. In addition, source code can be color-coded so that specific parts of the program stand out. For example, comments that aren't compiled into your program may appear in a different color from the rest of the code.

Xcode also provides tools for building your source code in easy reach. You can easily change your build settings to adapt to different situations, such as testing or deploying your program. If for some reason your code will not compile, Xcode displays the list of errors encountered in the build process and allows you to fix your mistakes.

After your code has compiled into the final application, you can launch the program directly from Xcode. If the program doesn't work right, or if it crashes, you can diagnose the problem using Xcode's built-in debugger. The debugger allows you to walk through your program line by line and examine the state of your program's variables as it runs.

During the development process, you may find yourself checking and double-checking the developer documentation on your system. Xcode provides a full-featured documentation browser within easy reach, so you don't need to fumble with a web browser or PDF viewer to review the API. A number of shortcuts make looking up specific functions, methods, and data types very easy.

In the sections to follow, you learn

- ❑ How to create new projects in Xcode
- ❑ How to organize files in an Xcode project
- ❑ How Xcode can help you write and format your code
- ❑ How to build and run your application, and examine your project in Xcode's built-in debugger
- ❑ How to access online documentation through Xcode

Starting a New Project

Every application starts out as a blank page or lump of clay. You are responsible for shaping that figurative page or lump into the application you see in your mind's eye. This really is a creative process very much like writing, painting, or sculpting, except that your medium is source code.

Xcode gives you a head start with a new project by supplying you with templates that include some of the basic files, code, and other resources you need to get started. All these resources are bundled together into an Xcode *project*, which provides a way for you to organize all the files for your program in a single place.

Create a Default Project

1.   Launch `/Developer/Applications/Xcode.app`. If this is your first time launching Xcode, you need to answer a few questions before you can proceed. Don't worry about those settings for now, just go with the defaults. You can change them later if you like.

2.   Choose File ⇨ New Project. A New Project Assistant window appears, like the one shown in Figure 3-1.

Figure 3-1

3.   Scroll down to the Command Line Utility group, select Standard Tool, and click Next. The assistant gives you a chance to name your project and choose the directory it will live in, as shown in Figure 3-2.

Figure 3-2

4.   Name your project `Hello`, pick a directory in which to save your new project (use your `Documents` directory if you aren't sure), and click Finish. At this point, you see Xcode's project interface, as shown in Figure 3-3. The project window contains a toolbar, a Groups & Files list on the left side, and a larger file list on the right side. The file list on the right contains three entries, a `Hello` application, a `Hello.1` file, and a `main.c` file.

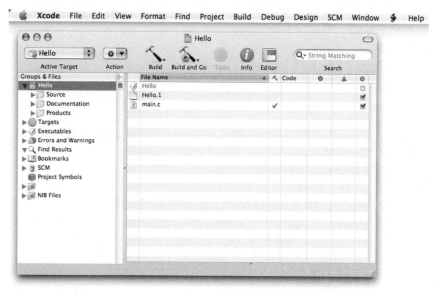

Figure 3-3

5. Double-click `main.c`, and the file appears in a new window. Notice that `main.c` already contains the following code. Keep this code for now:

```c
#include <stdio.h>

int main (int argc, const char * argv[]) {
    // insert code here...
    printf("Hello, World!\n");
    return 0;
}
```

6. Click the Build and Go button in `main.c`'s window. Xcode flashes some status information at the bottom of `main.c`'s window, and a new window appears and displays the following message. Your results may not match exactly.

```
[Session started at 2005-03-05 17:17:28 -0800.]
Hello, World!

Hello has exited with status 0.
```

How It Works

When you create a new project, Xcode also creates simple *source files* for you. The content of the source files depends on the kind of project you created; but generally the source files represent a general placeholder so that you can get the ball rolling. Because you are creating a simple command-line tool, Xcode created a very basic C program shell. Normally you replace the placeholder code with something more original.

> *When describing computer programs written in languages that require compilation, we refer to the text file containing human-readable instructions as source code. Source files typically use special file extensions that identify the language the source code is written in. For example, the .c extension designates code written in C, Objective-C programs end in .m, and C++ files generally use .cpp. Some source files are meant to share common data structures and interfaces among several other files. Those files are called header files, or simply headers. C, Objective-C, and C++ use the .h file extension to designate header files.*

After the program was built, you asked Xcode to run the program for you. This particular workflow, first build and then run, is so common that Xcode provides a single command to perform both functions: Build and Go. Xcode's Build menu calls this Build and Run, but it's the same thing.

Xcode ran the program and displayed the results in the Run Log window. When the program finished, Xcode printed the following:

```
Hello has exited with status 0
```

This means that the program ran to completion without errors. All Mac OS X programs return a numeric error code when they finish: By convention, 0 means the program ran correctly and any other value means something went wrong. Notice that your program explicitly returned its error code just before it ended:

```
    return 0;
```

Working with Files

Like the Finder, Xcode allows you to specify how your project files are organized. Unlike the Finder, your changes don't necessarily reflect how the files are stored on disk. Just as it does when creating a project, Xcode automates some of the busy work of creating new source files.

Try It Out   **Using Xcode's Groups & Files Viewer**

1. Create a new Standard Tool Command Line Utility project and name it Hello2.

2. Close the Hello2 project group; then Option-click the disclosure triangle to open it again. The project group and all its subgroups will expand, as shown in Figure 3-4. Notice that the Products file Hello2 is drawn in red; that's because the Hello2 program doesn't exist yet.

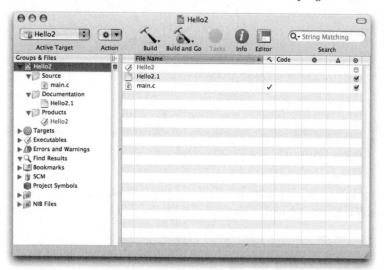

Figure 3-4

3. Click on each of the groups below the Hello2 project group. Notice the contents of the file list changes to match the contents of your selection. When the Hello2 project group is selected, all the files in Hello2 appear in the list; when Source is selected, only main.c appears in the list.

4. Option-click the Source group. Make sure you click to the right of the disclosure triangle. You can now rename the Source group to My Source Files.

5. Option-click main.c and rename your source file to Hello2.c.

6. Click Hello2.1 and drag it into your My SourceFiles group.

7. Select the Documentation group and press the Delete key. The group is removed from your project.

8. Select Hello2.1 again and choose File ⇨ Group. A new group appears containing the Hello2.1 file, and the group is ready to be renamed. Name this new group Man Pages.

9. Drag the new Man Pages group to the same level as the My Source Files and Products groups. If you have trouble, drag down and to the left toward the Products group's disclosure triangle; make sure the circle at the end of the drag indicator is to the left of the Products group folder icon. Figure 3-5 shows what your project should look like now.

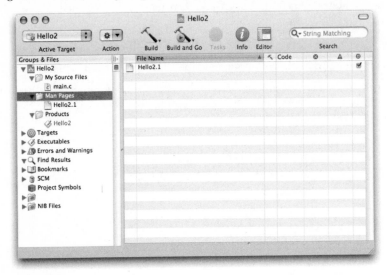

Figure 3-5

10. Select your My Source Files group and choose File ➪ New File. A New File assistant appears, resembling Figure 3-6, and allows you to select the kind of file you want to create.

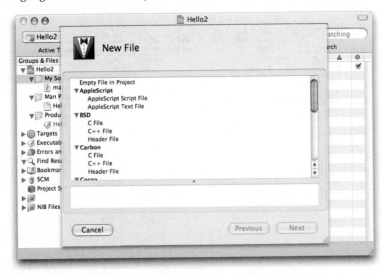

Figure 3-6

11. Select Carbon C File and click the Next button. The assistant changes, giving you a chance to name your file, as shown in Figure 3-7.

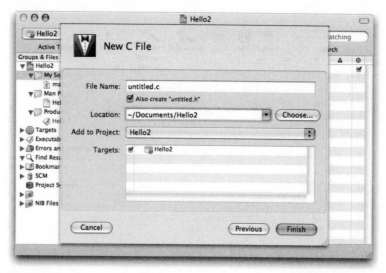

Figure 3-7

12. Name the file `Example.c`.

13. Make sure the checkbox named Also Create "Example.h" in Figure 3-7 is checked. Ignore the other settings for now.

14. Click Finish. A window appears containing your new header file. Close this window.

15. Select the Hello2 project group. Your project should now resemble Figure 3-8.

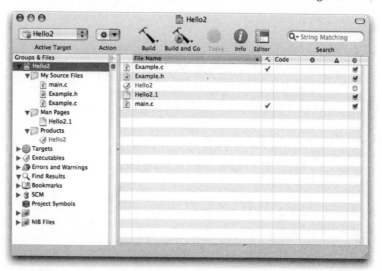

Figure 3-8

16. Select the group named Implementation Files. In Xcode 2.0, this group might not have a name. If that's the case, it will be the unnamed group just below the Project Symbols group. The list of files changes to include only your .c files.

17. Select the group named Project Symbols. The file list changes to a list of symbols, including the symbol name, the kind of symbol it is, and the file where the symbol can be found, as shown in Figure 3-9.

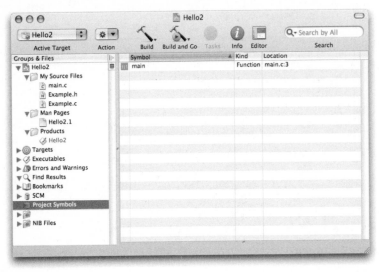

Figure 3-9

18. Double-click the entry for the main symbol. Hello2.c appears with the first line of the main function selected.

How It Works

The Groups & Files list uses the Option key to enable various quick shortcuts. You used the Option key to rename files and groups and to open all the subgroups within a parent group. There often are many ways to perform a given task in Xcode, including a command in the main menu bar or in a contextual menu, or clicking, command-clicking, or Option-clicking text. Your toolbar might also include an Action popup menu that provides quick access to some of the commands you'll find in the contextual menu.

When you rename files, Xcode actually changes the name of the file on disk. In this example, the file main.c changed to Hello2.c when the file was renamed. This is often very helpful, because Xcode tends to lose track of source files if you rename them in the Finder or in Terminal. Remember, if Xcode cannot find a file, it will draw its name in red.

Xcode uses *groups* to organize your code. Although groups resemble folders like what you might see in the Finder, they don't necessarily map to real folders. Groups are just containers in which you can organize your files. You can create them, rename them, remove them, and copy files in and out of them, however you like, without affecting how your source files are stored on disk.

Your project has some built-in groups for organizing information you might want within easy reach. For example, you can pull up a list of recent find results in the Find Results group, get a quick list of all your build problems in the Errors and Warnings group, or see all the *symbols* defined within your project from the Project Symbols group.

> *The term "symbol" refers to the names of elements within a source file or program, including function names, variable names, class names, data type names, structure definitions, and so on. For example, all C programs define a function symbol named "main" representing the start of the program.*

Xcode also provides something called *smart groups*. Smart groups filter your source file based on a set of rules. For example, the Implementation Files group is a smart group that displays all files that end with .c or .m file extensions. Smart group rules are specified using *regular expressions*, which is a small but sophisticated language for recognizing patterns within strings. You can Get Info on a smart group to see what patterns the group is filtering on.

When you created a new source file, Xcode helped out by automatically supplying a new header file with the same name. Xcode also added a little bit of code to get us started. These templates vary by the kind of file you are creating, so it's a good idea to start with a file template that most closely resembles what you need.

Writing Your Code

Most of your time in Xcode will be spent reading and writing the source files that make up your program. Xcode's source code editor has a number of features to make this time as productive as possible. Some of these features are passive, such as drawing different parts of your source code in different colors or styles. This helps you quickly recognize elements of your program at a glance. Other features are active, such as providing commands for quickly formatting large areas of code.

In the following example you write a small C program called Calculator that lets you add and subtract numbers. The program consists of two functions: the main function, which interacts with the user using Mac OS X's command-line interface, and a calculate function that does some arithmetic. The calculate function takes two numbers and an operator and returns the result of applying the operator to the numbers. If you aren't familiar with the C programming language, don't worry too much about what the code is doing; this is really just a chance to get used to Xcode's text editor. Alternatively, you can skip ahead to Chapter 6 where you learn about writing programs in C.

Try It Out   **Working in the Code Editor**

1. Choose Xcode ➪ Preferences. Xcode's Preferences window appears.

2. If necessary, select the General preference pane.

3. Check the Open Counterparts In Same Window button.

4. Select the Text Editing preference pane.

5. Check the Show Line Numbers button. The Show Gutter button should already be checked; if not, you will want to check Show Gutter as well.

6. Click OK. Xcode's Preferences window closes.

7. Create a new Standard Tool Command Line Utility project and name it `Calculator`.

8. Select the Source group and create a new Carbon C File named `Calculate.c` in your project. Make sure you create the accompanying header file `Calculate.h`. A source editor window resembling Figure 3-10 appears on-screen, displaying the contents of `Calculate.h`. The window is composed of a main toolbar at the top, an empty status area, a small button bar, and a large text editing area. In particular, this small button bar contains grayed-out left and right arrows, a popup menu with `Calculate.h` already selected, and a few other tools.

Figure 3-10

9. Remove the following line of code from your file:

```
#include <Carbon/Carbon.h>
```

10. Add the following line of code to the file:

```
int calculate(int a, int b, char operator);
```

11. Choose View ➪ Switch to Header/Source File. The source editor window switches to display the contents of `Calculate.c`. Notice that the left arrow is no longer grayed out and the popup menu now says `Calculate.c`.

12. Click the left arrow. This moves you back to the last file you were working with: `Calculate.h`. The back button disables itself while the right forward button is enabled.

13. Save your changes to `Calculate.h` now. Simply use the Save command as normal.

14. Click the popup menu to view its contents. You will see entries for `Calculate.h` and `Calculate.c` as well as an item that clears the file history.

15. Select `Calculate.c` from the file history popup menu. Once again, the contents of the source editor change to reflect `Calculate.c`.

16. Add the following code to the end of the file, typed exactly as shown here. As you enter the code, notice that Xcode draws different parts of your program in different colors. The added color is called *syntax coloring* and helps you spot keywords, strings, and so on in your code.

```c
#include <stdio.h>
#include <stdlib.h>

int calculate(int a, int b, char operator)
{
int result

switch (operator) {
case '+':
result = a + b;
break;
case '-'
result = a - b;
break;
default:
printf("unknown operator: %c\n", operator)
exit(1);
}

return result;
}
```

17. Select all the text within the `calculate` function. That corresponds to lines 17–31 in Figure 3-11.

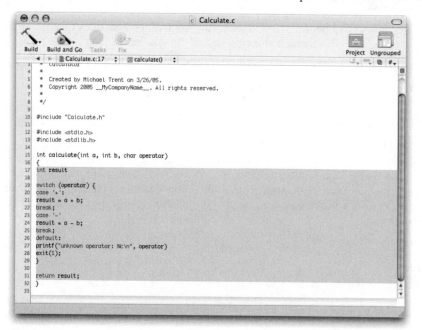

Figure 3-11

18. Choose Format ➪ Shift Right. The selection indents four spaces to the right.

19. Select the three lines of code that comprise the first `case` statement. That corresponds to lines 20–22 in Figure 3-11.

20. Press Command-] to invoke the Shift Right command. The selection indents four more spaces to the right.

21. Change the selection to the last two lines in that same `case` statement, lines 21 and 22 in Figure 3-11, and indent the text four more spaces to the right.

22. Repeat steps 19–21 until the `switch` statement is indented as shown here:

```
switch (operator) {
    case '+':
        result = a + b;
        break;
    case '-'
        result = a - b;
        break;
    default:
        printf("unknown operator: %c\n", operator)
        exit(1);
}
```

23. Make sure your text insertion point is in the `calculate` function; if not click line 19 to set the selection. By now you may have noticed there is a second popup menu in the small button bar, next to the file history popup menu. The menu currently says `calculate()`.

24. Move the text insertion point cursor to the very top of the file. Use the mouse if you like, or press Command-up arrow on your keyboard. The second popup menu changes to <No selected symbol>.

25. Click this second popup to reveal its menu. You will see a small menu with a single item: `calculate()`. This menu is showing you all the symbols in your file.

26. Select the `calculate()` item. The selection changes to highlight the `calculate` function's name.

27. Save your changes to `Calculate.c` and close the window.

28. Double-click `main.c` from your project's file list in the right side of the project window. If you have trouble finding `main.c`, look in your project's Source group in the Groups & Files list. The file appears in a new source editor.

29. Replace the contents of `main.c` with the code below. Use your Tab key to indent text as you type. Like the Shift Right command, the Tab key will insert four spaces into your file; unlike the Shift Right command, the spaces are added at the insertion point, not at the beginning of the line. If you get into trouble, you can fix your indenting with the Shift Left and Shift Right menu commands.

```
#include <stdio.h>
#include <stdlib.h>

#include "Calculate.h"

int main (int argc, const char * argv[])
{
```

```
int a, b, count, answer;
char op;

// print the prompt
printf("Enter an expression: ");

// get the expression
count = scanf("%d %c %d", &a, &op, &b);
if (count != 3) {
    printf("bad expression\n");
    return 1
}

// perform the computation
answer = calculate(a, b, op);

// print the answer
printf("%d %c %d = %d\n", a, op, b, answer);

return 0;
}
```

30. Save your changes to main.c.

31. Command–double-click the word calculate in your main function. The Calculate.c file appears in a window, with the calculate function name selected.

How It Works

You started by turning on line numbers in Xcode's *gutter*. The gutter is the region just to the left of the source editor's text area. The line numbers are a handy way to keep track of precisely where you are in a source file. You also configured Xcode to use the same source editor for viewing your source and header files. This is a handy feature for easily switching between a header and its implementation.

You might be wondering why you created new files using Xcode's Carbon C File template. The truth is that the Carbon templates are a convenient way to create new .c files even if you aren't going to write Carbon code. You weren't going to use Carbon in this project, so you removed the line of code that brings in all the Carbon headers:

```
#include <Carbon/Carbon.h>
```

Xcode retains a history of files you have viewed in a given source editor. You can easily flip through these files using the source editor's small button bar, called a *Navigation Bar*. The Navigation Bar includes forward and back buttons like you might find in a web browser. It also includes a history popup to select any of the files in your file history, regardless of how far forward or back they are. The history popup will use darkened file icons to remind you about unsaved files.

The Navigation Bar also includes a popup button of symbols defined in your source files. In this example, each of your files contained only one symbol, a function; but normally source files contain many symbols. The symbol popup menu is a helpful way to search for a specific symbol. You can jump directly to the place where a symbol is defined by Command–double-clicking the symbol name as it appears in your source file. This is helpful if you can't remember exactly where a symbol is defined, saving you the step of searching for it.

As you noticed earlier, Xcode drew different parts of your program in different colors. This helps you distinguish between various parts of your program at a glance. For example, comments might be drawn in green, reserved language keywords might be drawn in purple, strings might be drawn in red, and so on. You probably also noticed Xcode drew your text in a monospaced font. Since all characters have the same width — even spaces — it's easy to align your text vertically.

If for whatever reason you do not like the default colors or font settings, you can easily change them in Xcode's Syntax Coloring preferences panel. For each part of your program (strings, comments, and so on), you can specify the specific color, font, size, and style (such as bold or italic) to use. For example, you could display your source code in a nice fixed-width font, but display your comments in a hot pink symbol font if you thought that might help.

Although C, Objective-C, and C++ languages do not require you to indent your code, code written in these languages by convention is indented. Although specific styles of indenting exist, there can be a wide variation between individual programmers. You will probably end up using Shift Left and Shift Right a lot.

A Second Look at Indenting

In the previous example you learned two different ways of indenting your code: using the Tab key to insert four spaces at the text insertion point, and using the Shift Left and Shift Right menu commands to quickly remove or insert four spaces at the beginning of a line. Xcode provides a third way of indenting your code: indenting automatically.

Try It Out   **Indenting Automatically**

1. In Xcode, open your Calculator project from the previous Try It Out.

2. Open the `Calculate.c` file in a source editor.

3. Select all the text and press Command-[(Shift Left) repeatedly until all the code is mashed against the left side of the window.

4. Without changing the selection, choose Format ➪ Re-Indent. Xcode indents all your code for you.

5. Save your changes to `Calculate.c` and close the window.

6. Open Xcode's Preferences panel.

7. Select the Indentation toolbar item.

8. Turn on Syntax-Aware Indenting and leave the other settings alone. Your settings should match those in Figure 3-12.

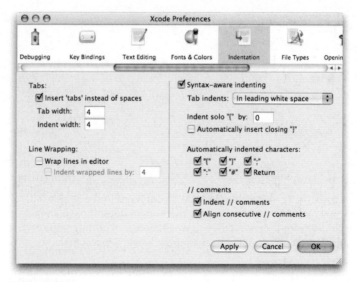

Figure 3-12

9. Click OK to save your preference changes.

10. Open `main.c` and delete all the text in the file.

11. Re-enter the code from the previous example. The code is reprinted here for your convenience. This time, do not do any formatting yourself; do not press the Tab key or add extra spaces, and do not use the Shift Left or Shift Right menu commands:

```c
#include <stdio.h>
#include <stdlib.h>

#include "Calculate.h"

int main (int argc, const char * argv[])
{
    int a, b, count, answer;
    char op;

    // print the prompt
    printf("Enter an expression: ");

    // get the expression
    count = scanf("%d %c %d", &a, &op, &b);
    if (count != 3) {
        printf("bad expression\n");
        exit(1)
    }

    // perform the computation
```

```
        answer = calculate(a, b, op);

        // print the answer
        printf("%d %c %d = %d\n", a, op, b, answer);

        return 0;
}
```

12. Save your changes to `main.c`.

How It Works

Xcode's Re-Indent command looks at the selection and neighboring code and tries its best to indent the selection appropriately. You can find the Re-Indent command in the source editor's contextual menu as well as on the Format menu. Unfortunately, the menu item doesn't have a macro assigned by default. If you find yourself using Re-Indent often, you might consider adding your own macro. You can use Xcode's Key Bindings preferences panel to customize Xcode's menu macros.

By turning auto-indenting on in Preferences, Xcode automatically formats your code as you type. You don't need to use the Tab key or the Shift Left or Shift Right menu commands to line up your code. Both auto-indenting and the Re-Indent command use the same formatting algorithms, so the features play well together. Because you won't need to stop and format your code manually, auto-indenting can save you a lot of time.

However, neither indenting method is perfect. Under some rare circumstances the Re-Indent command might misinterpret how you want your code to be formatted. Or maybe you don't agree with the style in which Xcode indents your text. Perhaps you just find auto-indenting distracting. If any of these are true, you can simply fall back to the Tab key and Shift Left and Shift Right menu items to manually format your code.

Building and Running

After you have written a reasonable amount of code, the urge to build your project may strike. Building your project is the first step toward validating that you have entered your code correctly. Of course, compiling does not guarantee your program actually works! Remember: computers only understand what you said, not what you meant. Once you build your project, however, you can run your program and make sure it does what you want.

In the next Try It Out example, you actually build the `Calculator` project you saw earlier. Along the way, you correct a few build errors introduced during the editing process. Finally, you verify that Calculator works correctly by running the program and testing its results.

Try It Out   Building Your Calculator Project

1. In Xcode, open your `Calculator` project you created and saved earlier.

2. Click the Build button. If you entered the code exactly as it was provided earlier, the project will fail to compile. The project window's status area notes that the build failed, and the Errors and Warnings group appears drawn in red.

3. Select the Errors and Warnings group. The file area changes to display a list of build errors, resembling Figure 3-13.

Calculator
Calculator
Active Target
Action
Build
Build and Go
Tasks
Info
Editor
String Matching
Search
Groups & Files
Calculator
Source
main.c
Calculate.h
Calculate.c
Documentation
Products
Targets
Executables
Errors and Warnings
Find Results
Bookmarks
SCM
Project Symbols
NIB Files
Message
In function `main':
error: parse error before '}' token
error: parse error at end of input
Location
main.c:0
main.c:19
main.c:29
Build failed for target "Calculator" using build style "Development" (2 errors)
Failed 2

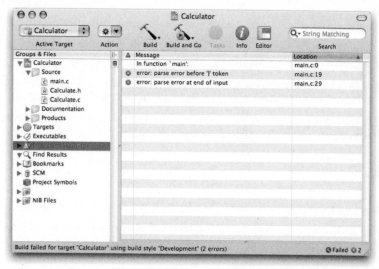

Figure 3-13

4. Double-click the first error in the list. A source editor appears with the contents of `main.c`. A line of code is selected near where the error occurred, as seen in Figure 3-14. Line 18 is missing a semicolon.

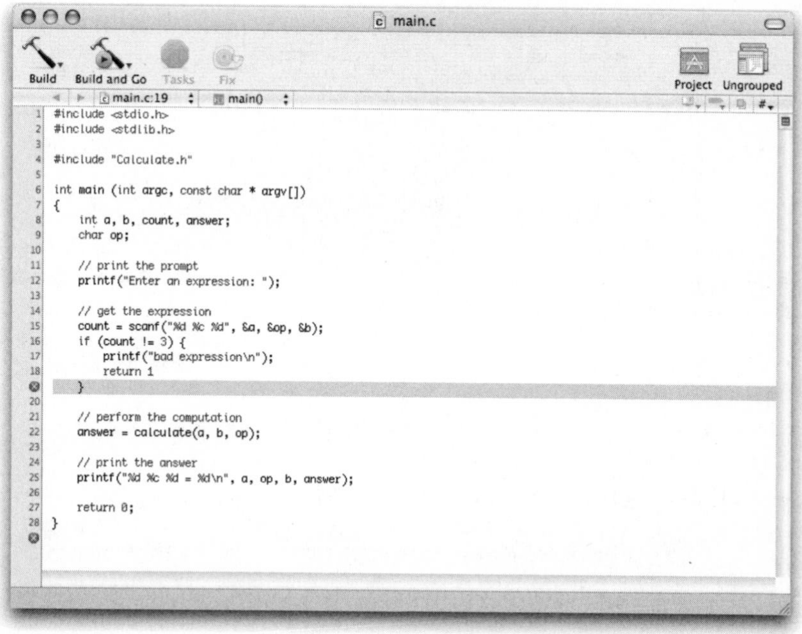

main.c
Build
Build and Go
Tasks
Fix
Project
Ungrouped
main.c:19
main()
1 #include <stdio.h>
2 #include <stdlib.h>
4 #include "Calculate.h"
6 int main (int argc, const char * argv[])
7 {
8 int a, b, count, answer;
9 char op;
11 // print the prompt
12 printf("Enter an expression: ");
14 // get the expression
15 count = scanf("%d %c %d", &a, &op, &b);
16 if (count != 3) {
17 printf("bad expression\n");
18 return 1
}
21 // perform the computation
22 answer = calculate(a, b, op);
24 // print the answer
25 printf("%d %c %d = %d\n", a, op, b, answer);
27 return 0;
28 }

Figure 3-14

5. Add a semicolon to line 18:

```
return 1;
```

6. Save `main.c` and close its editor window.

7. Try rebuilding `Calculator`. The build will fail again, and the Errors and Warnings group will change to show errors in `Calculate.c`.

8. Choose Build ⇨ Build Results. A window resembling Figure 3-15 appears and lists the build errors along with a few other controls. This window is called the Build Results window.

9. Double-click the first error for `Calculate.c`. Again, a source editor window appears showing you the contents of `Calculate.c`. The line right before the error is missing a semicolon.

10. Add a semicolon to line 17:

```
int result;
```

11. Choose Build ⇨ Build Results to go back to the Build Results window.

12. Double-click the second error in the list. Line 24 becomes selected, as shown in Figure 3-16. The `case` statement on line 23 should end with a colon.

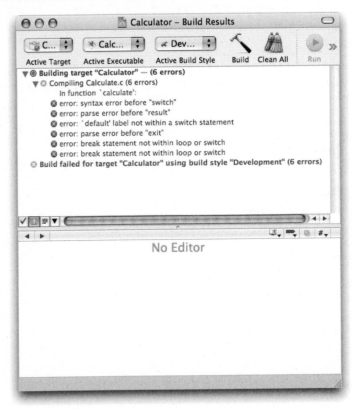

Figure 3-15

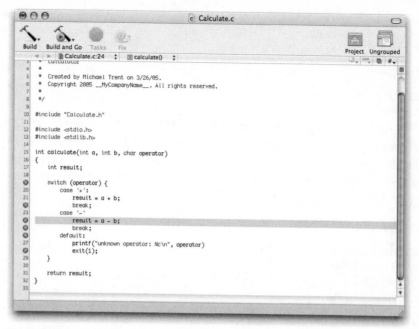

Figure 3-16

13. Add a colon at the end of line 23:

```
case '-':
```

14. Go back to the Build Results window and double-click each of the remaining errors looking for obvious problems. Notice that line 27 is also missing a semicolon.

15. Add a semicolon to line 27:

```
printf("unknown operator: %c\n", operator);
```

16. Save Calculate.c and close its source window.

17. Rebuild Calculator again using the Build button on the Build Results window. This time the compile should succeed.

18. In the project window, click and hold the Build and Go button. A menu appears showing you a number of options.

19. Select Run from the Build and Go popup menu. A new window appears, displaying the contents of your program. This window is called the Run Log window. Calculator asks you to enter an expression, as shown here. So far, so good.

```
Enter an expression:
```

20. Enter 44 + 7, and press Return. The Run Log displays the results of your program. It looks like it's working correctly:

```
Enter an expression: 44 + 7
44 + 7 = 51

Calculator has exited with status 0.
```

21. Run Calculator again by clicking the Run button on the Run Log window.

22. Enter 44 – 7 and press Return. The Run Log will display the following results. Again, so far so good.

```
Enter an expression: 44 - 7
44 - 7 = 37

Calculator has exited with status 0.
```

23. Run Calculator again, and enter 6 * 9. This time Calculator prints an error message and quits early. Although it's unfortunate that Calculator doesn't know how to multiply, that doesn't qualify as a bug in your program. You simply haven't taught it how to multiply yet.

```
Enter an expression: 6 * 9
unknown operator: *

Calculator has exited with status 1.
```

24. Run Calculator again, and enter two plus two. Calculator prints a new error message and quits. Again, this is the expected result.

```
Enter an expression: two plus two
bad expression

Calculator has exited with status 1.
```

25. Close the Run Log window.

26. Return to the Build Results window and click the Clean All button. A warning appears, as shown in Figure 3-17, advising that you are about to delete your compiled program.

27. Click the Clean All Targets button. Xcode does a little work, and your Build Results window notes that the command succeeded.

28. Change the Active Build Style button from Development to Deployment.

29. Click the Build button. The build should now succeed.

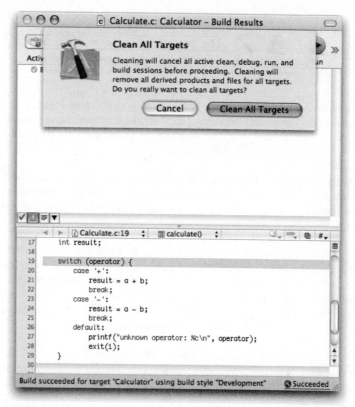

Figure 3-17

How It Works

You started by changing your project's toolbar to Icon & Text mode. This isn't so much an Xcode feature as it is a feature of all Mac OS X toolbars. The Icon & Text mode helps you learn the names of the toolbar buttons; once you are comfortable with what the icons mean, you can switch back to Icon mode if you like. You will encounter a number of toolbars in Xcode and Interface Builder. This book will always refer to toolbar items by name, not by icon.

When you asked Xcode to build your project, Xcode actually did a number of smaller tasks for you and presented the results all at once. The first thing Xcode did was convert all your source code to machine-friendly instructions using a tool called a *compiler*. The compiler's main job is to take your instructions written in a programming language like C or Objective-C and convert it to instructions understandable by your computer's CPU. These instructions are called *object code*. Object code is typically stored in special files, called *object files*; these files are transitional in nature and their existence was handled entirely by Xcode.

The second thing Xcode did while building your project was to combine all your object files together to form an executable binary file. This process is called *linking* and it is performed using a special tool called, you guessed it, a *linker*. A linked file is self-contained and can easily be copied and used on other computers, assuming those computers are running the same operating system and are in the same processor family.

Either of these processes may encounter problems such as syntax errors, missing files, and the like. Xcode reports these errors in the Errors and Warnings group and in the Build Results window. You must address these errors before you can link and run your program. The Calculator code contained a few minor syntax errors to help you practice fixing these problems.

Notice that Xcode actually reported more problems in your program than you fixed. A single error in a source file may actually result in several problems within the C compiler. So the fact that adding a semicolon to one line of code in `main.c` fixed all the compile errors there is not all that surprising. This is true of Objective-C and C++ as well.

When working on fairly small projects, it is easy to think Xcode will simply build all the files in your project. In reality, Xcode builds all of the files in the current *target*. A target collects all the files, resources, and settings required to build a specific program. An Xcode project can contain several targets. For example, a project that builds an application, a framework, and a plug-in would be composed of three different targets. Although the target abstraction is a powerful feature for people working on larger or more complicated projects, this book focuses on examples with only one target.

Xcode's Build Styles allows you to generate your object code differently depending on what you intend to do with your program. A specific build style contains options for the compiler, linker, and other build tools that control the way your project builds. For example, the Development build style tells the compiler to generate debugging symbols along with your code, and might tell the linker not to fully link your program. The Deployment build style doesn't generate debugging symbols, but it does enable optimizations and instructs the linker to fully link your program so you can distribute it to other people.

Xcode also has a command for cleaning your build results: Clean All. The Clean All command removes the build results associated with your entire project. Build results include temporary files like your project's object files and some other information cached by Xcode; it also includes your compiled program. You typically use this command to make sure your next project build starts from a clean state and won't get any left over state from a previous build. You might also clean your project before giving the source code to someone else because build results can add several megabytes to your source directory.

Using the Debugger

Sometimes your program won't work properly, and even after you spend hours staring at your source code it isn't obvious what has gone wrong. For times like these, Xcode has a built-in debugger. The debugger allows you to step through your code as the program is running and watch the state of your variables change.

Try It Out　　**Debugging Changes to Calculator**

1. In Xcode, open your `Calculator` project that you saved earlier.

2. Open the Build Results window.

3. Make sure the Active Build Style popup reads Development; change it if necessary.

4. Clean your build results by clicking the Clean All button.

5. Close the Build Results window.

6. Open `Calculate.c`.

7. Make a copy of the second `case` statement at lines 23–25, and paste them back at line 26. The calculate function should look like the following code:

```
int calculate(int a, int b, char operator)
{
    int result;

    switch (operator) {
        case '+':
            result = a + b;
            break;
        case '-':
            result = a - b;
            break;
        case '-':
            result = a - b;
            break;
        default:
            printf("unknown operator: %c\n", operator);
            exit(1);
    }

    return result;
}
```

8. Change `case '-':` at line 26 to `case '*':`.

9. Save `Calculate.c`.

10. Build and run your project.

11. Enter 4 * 5. `Calculator` prints the following result. Obviously, something is wrong.

```
Enter an expression: 4 * 5
4 * 5 = -1

Calculator has exited with status 0.
```

12. Open `main.c`.

13. Click in the gutter on the left side of the window at line 6, where the main function is defined. A marker appears there, as shown in Figure 3-18.

14. Choose Build ➪ Build and Debug. A new window appears called Debugger, and your program starts. A few moments later, the debugger stops at the first line of code in your main function, as shown in Figure 3-19. The current line of code is highlighted in red and marked with a red arrow.

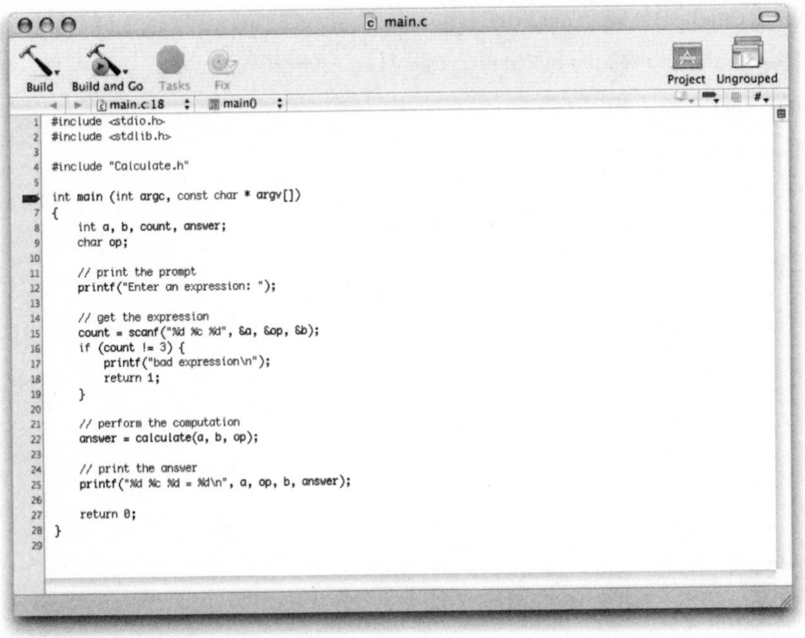

Chapter 3

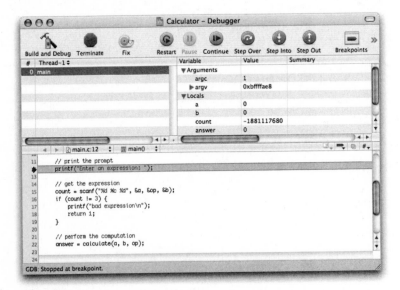

Figure 3-18

Figure 3-19

15. Click the Step Over button. The selection advances to line 15.

16. Click the Step Over button again. The selection disappears, and the debugger's toolbar changes so that only the Pause and Terminate buttons are enabled.

17. Choose Debug ➪ Standard I/O Log. A new window appears that resembles Figure 3-20. The contents of the window should look familiar: this is the output of your `Calculator` program.

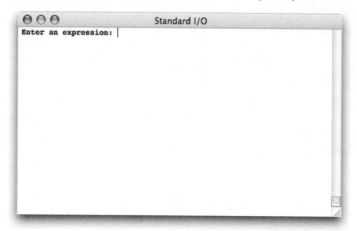

Figure 3-20

18. Enter 4 * 5. The Debug window enables itself, and line 16 is selected. In addition, the entries for a, b, count, and op in the Variable table all change to reflect your expression. Figure 3-21 shows what the debugger should look like.

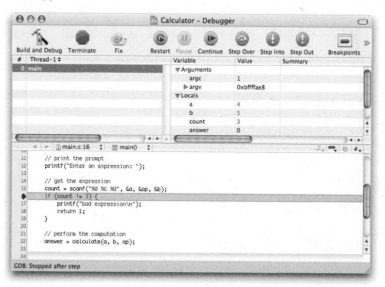

Figure 3-21

19. Click the Step Over button. The selection advances to line 22.

20. Click the Step Into button. The debugger changes to display the contents of the Calculate.c file, where line 19 is selected. The calculate symbol appears at the top of the listing the debugger's upper-left corner.

21. Click the Step Over button. The selection advances to line 27, as shown in Figure 3-22. And now the problem becomes clear. You changed the calculate function to include a new * operator, but you didn't change the logic that computes the answer to multiply your numbers together. It looks like b, which is currently 5, will be subtracted from a, currently 4, to yield –.

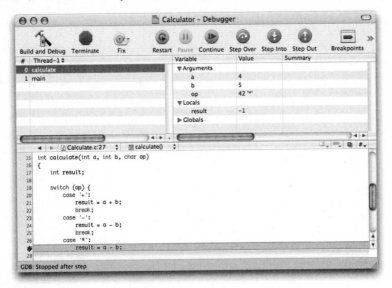

Figure 3-22

22. Click the Step Over button. Sure enough, the Variable table shows result changing to –1.

23. Click the Terminate button.

24. Without leaving the debugger, correct Calculate.c by changing the operator at line 27 from - to *.

25. Choose Build ⇨ Build and Run. Xcode realizes one of your files contains unsaved changes, and your project needs to be recompiled. Before compiling, a panel appears asking if you want to save your changes to Calculate.c.

26. Click Save All. Xcode saves Calculate.c and compiles your project. Assuming that you didn't make any mistakes, the Run Log window appears on screen showing that your program is in progress.

27. Enter 4 * 5. Calculator prints the following result. It looks like you've fixed the problem.

```
Enter an expression: 4 * 5
4 * 5 = 20

Calculator has exited with status 0.
```

How It Works

You started by changing your build style to Development and cleaning any previous build results. Before you try to debug a program make sure you are working with a Development build. Otherwise, the debugger will not be able to work properly. Another good habit to form now is always using the Build and Debug command to start the debugger. Sometimes when you are debugging you will make changes to your source code. Build and Debug will live up to its name and rebuild your project before starting the debugger; this will make sure your source code and your program are in sync with each other.

Xcode's debugger has the power to pause its target program, control when the program's instructions are fed to the processor, and examine or change the contents of the program's memory. A paused program is actually in a state of suspended animation: a process exists, but machine instructions are not being processed. The debugger can also execute your program a few instructions at a time. This allows you to watch how your program's state changes bit-by-bit as it's running. The following table lists a number of common debugging commands.

Command	Description
Restart	Terminates the current debug session and starts a new one from the beginning. This is useful if you find you've missed the point where a bug occurred.
Pause	Suspends your program, allowing you to see which lines of code are currently being executed as well as your program's variables.
Continue	Resumes execution of a suspended program.
Step Over	Advances the program to the next line of code. If the current line of code is a function call, Step Over simply allows it to run normally as if it were a single instruction. In other words, this command steps over the function.
Step Into	Advances the program to the next line of code. If the current line of code is a function call, Step Into descends into the function call. In other words, this command steps into the function.
Step Out	Advances the program until the current function ends.
Step Into Instruction	Like Step Into except that this command runs your program one machine instruction at a time. Note that a single line of source code may be expanded into several machine instructions.

The marker that appeared when you clicked on the source editor's gutter is called a *break point*. Break points instruct the debugger to pause (*break*) your program when you reach that spot (*point*) in the file. If you don't set a break point, the debugger simply runs your program until you click the Pause button, your program completes normally, or your program crashes.

You may have noticed that although you set a break point on line 6, the debugger actually stopped on line 12. Xcode allows you to set break points on arbitrary lines in your source file, even places where there isn't any code. In those cases, Xcode's debugger stops at the first opportunity after the break point.

The debugger displays the state of your program's variables in the Variable table. Each variable is displayed along with its value. If a variable changes as you step through your code, Xcode draws the variable in red. The Variable table isn't for display only; you can actually change a variable's value simply by double-clicking the Value cell and entering a new value.

The debugger also displays your current stack history in the list in the Debugger's upper-left corner. This list shows your program's Stack. Each entry in the Stack represents a function call, or *stack frame*. The topmost entry represents the function your program is currently "in"; that function was called by the second entry in the list, which was called by the third entry, and so on. You can click on a stack frame to see your program's state at that function. The Stack is extremely useful for figuring out how your program ended up in the current function.

There isn't enough room in the debugger to display your program's output, so Xcode provides a separate window, called the Standard I/O window, for that purpose. The window gets its name from *standard I/O*, which is the name of the mechanism command-line tools use to read and write data in the Terminal. This window is otherwise just like the Run Log window.

Xcode's Debug window includes a source editor, so you can easily keep track of where you are in your program. This source editor works the same as the other source editors you have seen: you can edit code, you can use source editor's history to switch between files, and so on. This is really useful when you find a simple bug in your program: just correct the code in the debugger, rebuild, and try again.

Online Documentation

Xcode provides a ton of documentation within easy reach. This includes API documentation for various system frameworks, conceptual documentation that illustrates how various services should be used, and Darwin's man page system. In the following Try It Out example, you learn how to use the documentation tools in Xcode to access the online Cocoa documentation. The techniques illustrated here apply to other online documentation, such as Carbon, QuickTime, and so on.

Try It Out   Searching the Online Documentation

1. Create a new Foundation Tool project named Greetings.

2. Open Greetings.m. A source editor window appears.

3. Replace the contents of main.m with the following code:

```
#import <Foundation/Foundation.h>

int main (int argc, const char *argv[])
{
    NSAutoreleasePool *pool = [[NSAutoreleasePool alloc] init];

    NSString *user = NSFullUserName;
    NSString *time = nil; // get the current time ...

    printf("Hello %s,\n", [user UTF8String]);
    printf("It is now %s.\n", [time UTF8String]);

    [pool release];
    return 0;
}
```

Notice you haven't actually initialized the `time` variable to something useful. You need to find some kind of function or method call that returns the current time.

4. Choose Help ⇨ Documentation. A new window appears titled Reference Library – Developer Documentation, as shown in Figure 3-23. The window is composed of a main toolbar at the top, a Search Groups list, Bookmarks list, Navigation Bar, and a large Reference Library area. The Navigation Bar behaves exactly like the one in the source editor, allowing you to quickly navigate your file history and current symbols.

5. Click the Cocoa group from the Search Groups list. The window displays documentation specific to the Cocoa framework. This is the same online documentation you saw earlier in Chapter 2.

6. Click the API Reference link in the Cocoa Resources section.

7. Click Foundation Reference for Objective-C (HTML) in the API Reference section of the documentation viewer. A list of Foundation topics appears, including classes, protocols, functions, and related documents.

8. Select `NSDate` from the list of Foundation classes. The Documentation window displays information about `NSDate`.

9. Click the symbol popup in the Navigation Bar. A list of documentation topics appears, beginning with high-level concepts and ending with method documentation for `NSDate`.

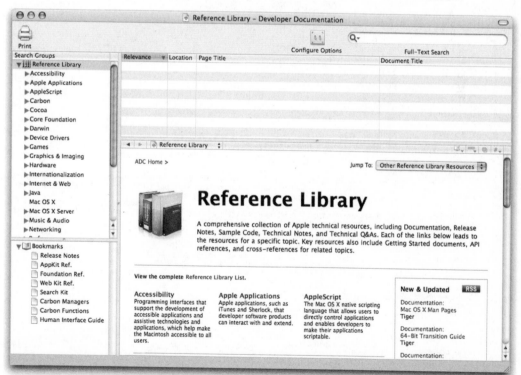

Figure 3-23

10. Select `descriptionWithCalendarFormat:timeZone:locale:` from the symbol popup. The Documentation window jumps to the entry describing `descriptionWithCalendarFormat:timeZone:locale:`, as shown in Figure 3-24.

This method returns the current time with a particular formatting. The example provided in the documentation looks like what you are looking for.

11. Switch back to your `Greetings.m` window.

12. Change line 8 to match the following code and save the file:

```
NSString *time = [[NSDate date] descriptionWithCalendarFormat:@"%H:%M:%S %Z"
                                                      timeZone:nil
                                                        locale:nil];
```

13. Build and run the project. The Run Log appears, displaying a message indicating the program crashed on launch:

```
Greetings has exited due to signal 11 (SIGSEGV).
```

14. Run the program in the debugger by selecting Debug from the project window's Build and Go button. The debugger appears, displaying the precise place where the program crashed, as noted in Figure 3-25.

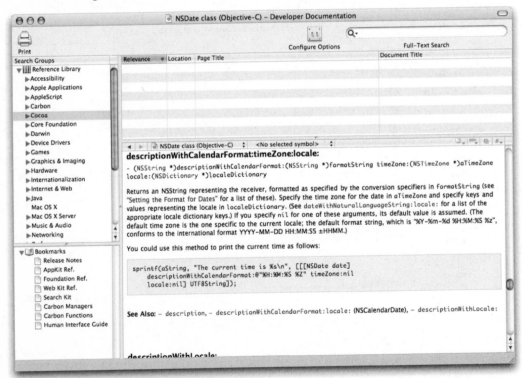

Figure 3-24

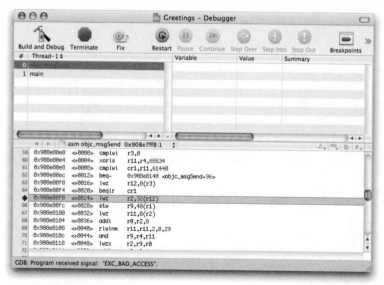

Figure 3-25

15. Click the entry for main in the Stack table. The debugger updates to match the contents of Figure 3-26. It looks like the program has crashed trying to print the full user name.

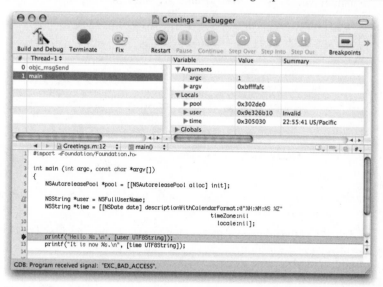

Figure 3-26

16. Stop debugging the program by clicking the Terminate button.

17. Option–double-click NSFullUserName. The Documentation window appears, displaying some information for NSFullUserName. It turns out that this symbol is a function call, not a constant.

18. Return to `main.m` and change line 7 to match this code:

```
NSString *user = NSFullUserName();
```

19. Build and run the project. The Run Log appears, displaying your full Mac OS X user name, the current time, and a short message indicating the program ran successfully. Your results should be similar to the following:

```
Hello Your Name,
It is now 01:31:39 US/Pacific.

Greetings has exited with status 0.
```

20. Return to the Documentation window.

21. Click in the search field at the top of the Documentation window.

22. Enter `NSString`. Notice the Symbol table automatically updates itself as you type. Eventually an entry for the `NSString` Objective-C class percolates to the top of the list.

23. Select `NSString` from the Symbol table. The Documentation window displays documentation for the `NSString` class.

24. Select `UTF8String` from the symbol popup menu (it's toward the very bottom). It looks like `UTF8String` returns a `const char *` type, which should be exactly what `printf` expects.

25. Return to `Greetings.m` and Option–double-click `printf`. Although `printf` appears in the Documentation window's search field, an exact match will not appear in the Symbol table.

26. Choose Help ⇨ Open Man Page. A small panel appears resembling Figure 3-27.

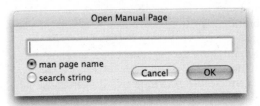

Figure 3-27

27. Enter `printf` and click OK. The Documentation window changes to display the man page for the `printf` command-line tool.

28. Choose Help ⇨ Open man page. Again, enter `3 printf` and click OK. The Documentation window now displays information for the `printf` function call.

How It Works

The code in this example looks a little different from the earlier examples because it is Objective-C. Don't worry about following along with the specifics of what this program is doing; you learn more about Objective-C in Chapter 6.

In this example, you ran the debugger without first setting a break point. Recall that the debugger executes your program until it hits a break point, terminates normally, you click the Pause button, or the program crashes. Because you knew the program was going to crash shortly after launch, you just let the debugger show you where the crash occurred. Of course, you could have set a break point early and stepped through your code until the program eventually crashed.

The Documentation window displays information about many of the high-level frameworks on the system. You can navigate the documentation in three different ways:

❑ Browse through the documentation as you might browse through a website, clicking through a series of hyperlinked entries. This is a great approach if you aren't quite sure what you are looking for.

❑ Search for documentation on specific symbols, such as classes, functions, and so on, by typing the symbol name into the search field. This is a great approach if you are looking for more information on a specific thing.

❑ Jump to entries by holding down the Option key while double-clicking on symbols in your source files. Recall earlier you Command–double-clicked a symbol to jump to that symbol's definition in your program. For example, Option–double-clicking NSDate displays documentation for Cocoa's NSDate class in the Documentation window, whereas Command–double-clicking NSDate displays NSDate's definition in the NSDate.h header file.

You searched through the Cocoa documentation looking for information on a specific topic: getting the string representing the current time. Sometimes it can be hard to find the information you are looking for, either because it doesn't turn up in your searches or because you're not sure what you're looking for. In those cases, it's often helpful to just browse through the documentation and look at some of the conceptual documentation and sample code available on the system. This technique is true of Carbon, QuickTime, and other libraries, not just Cocoa.

Although there is a Darwin group in the Documentation window, the Darwin man page system is not integrated into the search methods just listed. Man pages must be specifically requested by name using a separate Open Man Page command. Recall from Chapter 2 that manual pages are organized into separate sections. If necessary, you can specify the section name along with the page, such as in the case of 3 printf. While not as user friendly as other features in Xcode, this command might save you from having to launch Terminal just to read some documentation.

Summary

The Mac OS X development workflow is built around the Xcode IDE. You used Xcode to write and build a number of small projects. Xcode's source editor gave you a hand by providing several tools for arranging and navigating your source code. The integrated build system and run log turned your code into a useful program. And when things didn't go right, the debugger allowed you to see what was really going on in your program. Xcode even threw in a documentation browser for good measure.

The Documentation window also includes a Tools group where you can find documentation for most of the developer tools in Mac OS X, including Xcode. This chapter presents enough information to help you get started with Xcode. You can learn a lot more about Xcode by reading its online manual.

In this chapter you learned

❑ How to create new projects in Xcode by starting with a template that matches the kind of project you want to make.

❑ How to organize files in an Xcode project. You can structure the contents of your project's Groups & Files list however you like. When you select a group in the Groups and Files list, Xcode displays all the files in that group in the file list on the right side of the project window.

❑ How Xcode can help you write and format your code. You can manually format your code using the Tab key and Shift Left and Shift Right menu commands, or you can configure Xcode to automatically indent your code while you type.

❑ How to build and run your application and examine your project in Xcode's built-in debugger. Xcode shows your current position right in your source code window, so you can follow along as your program runs. You can also watch your program's variables as you step through your program.

❑ How to access online documentation through Xcode's built-in Documentation window. This allows you to access the ADC Reference Library documentation directly within Xcode.

In the next chapter, you learn how to use Interface Builder, a tool for building graphical user interfaces. Before proceeding, however, try the exercises that follow to test your understanding of the material covered in this chapter. You can find the solutions to these exercises in Appendix A.

Exercises

1. Look up the man page for the functions in the following table:

Function
printf
scanf
pow

2. The Calculator program can only perform integer math. Extend Calculator to do double-precision floating-point computations. These double-precision values will use the double data type, rather than the int data type. For example, you need to change the calculate function to accept and return doubles instead of ints. Feel free to skip ahead to Chapter 6 if you want to learn more about these data types. But this is mostly an opportunity to practice using Xcode to build and run a program.

   The "3 printf" and "3 scanf" man pages tell you how to read and write double-precision numbers to standard I/O. Make sure the decimal point is printed only when necessary:

```
Enter an expression: 1 + 2
1 + 2 = 3

Enter an expression: 1 + 2.1
1 + 2.1 = 3.1
```

3. Common mathematical functions and operators appear in the following table. Extend your `Calculator` changes in Exercise 2 to incorporate these new operators.

Name	Key	Function/Operator	Example
Divide	" / "	/	x = y / z;
Integer Divide	" \ "	/	x = (int)y / (int)z;
Modulo	" % "	%	x = (int)y % (int)z;
Power	" ^ "	pow()	x = pow(y, z);

You need to add the following line of code near the top of `Calculate.c`, along with the other `include` statements:

```
#include <math.h>
```

Interface Builder

Interface Builder, as its name implies, is a tool for building graphical user interfaces. You design interfaces by dragging windows, controls, and other elements into your interface and arranging them with your mouse. People often refer to this kind of tool as a *WYSIWYG* editor because What You See Is What You Get. Because you're already familiar with these techniques (moving files, sorting your email, and so on), it's easy to get started designing user interfaces in Interface Builder.

All your interface information is stored in a *nib* file. Nib files can describe the interface for an entire interface, or they can describe only a subset of an interface, such as a menu bar or window. As such, nib files are used by plug-ins (like System Preferences panes) as well as applications.

You can use Interface Builder design interfaces for both Carbon and Cocoa applications. Once your interface has been built, you can test the interface and make sure everything has been laid out correctly. Although the techniques involved are the same for either development library, Cocoa and Carbon interfaces differ in a number of key ways. In this chapter, you learn the fundamentals of using Interface Builder; you learn more about Cocoa- and Carbon-specific features in Chapters 8 and 9, respectively.

In this chapter you learn

- ❑ How to build menus and controls
- ❑ How to make windows resizable
- ❑ How to use Interface Builder's Inspector to configure individual interface elements
- ❑ How to test your interface directly in Interface Builder

Starting a New Interface

Like Xcode, Interface Builder has templates that help you get started with a new nib file. These templates are grouped by application framework, so you can quickly zero in on the kind of interface you need.

Try It Out   **Create a New Interface**

1. Launch /Developer/Applications/Interface Builder. If this is the first time you've run Interface Builder, you might see a Release Notes window. Close this window for now; you can always open it again by choosing Help ⇨ Release Notes. You should see a Starting Point window resembling Figure 4-1.

Figure 4-1

2. Choose Carbon Main Menu With Menu Bar from the Starting Point window. Four new windows appear, as shown in Figure 4-2. The Untitled window represents your nib file and contains a menu bar and a window. The contents of the menu bar and window are displayed in detail in their own windows. The fourth window, known as the Palettes window, contains user interface elements.

3. Before going any further, Control-click anywhere on the Palettes window's toolbar and select Icon & Text from the popup menu. This displays the name of each palette along with its icon. Some of the palettes have long names, so there won't be enough room to see all the palette items at once. You can either resize the window or click on the chevron to pick items that aren't visible.

4. Close the window representing your interface's main window. This window is simply named Window and has no content.

5. Double-click the MainWindow icon in your nib's Instances tab. The window representing the main window reappears.

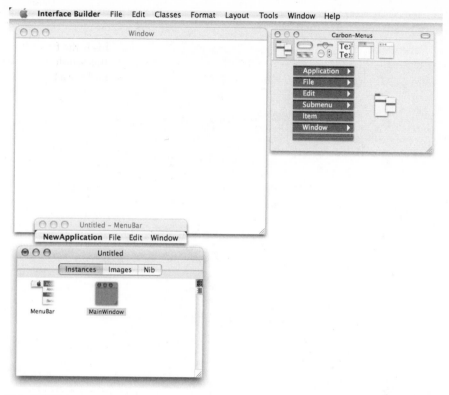

Figure 4-2

6. Double-click the MainWindow icon's label. The label changes to an editable text field, allowing you to rename the window icon in your nib file. Change its name to My Window. Notice that the title of the window you opened in the previous step doesn't change.

7. From the menu bar, choose Tools ➪ Show Inspector. An Inspector window like the one shown in Figure 4-3 appears. It displays the settings for your main window.

8. Click the Menu bar icon in your interface's Instances tab. The contents of the Inspector window change to reflect the settings of your main menu. This behavior is common among all inspector windows; Inspector contents change along with the current selection.

9. Choose File ➪ Test Interface. Interface Builder opens your interface in a program called Carbon Simulator. The Carbon Simulator displays your menu bar and window, as shown in Figure 4-4.

10. Quit Carbon Simulator, and you are returned to Interface Builder.

Figure 4-3

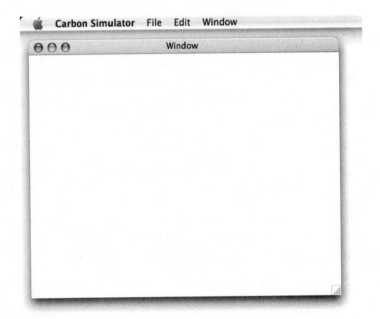

Figure 4-4

How It Works

When you create a new nib file in Interface Builder, it offers to initialize the file from one of a series of templates. Interface Builder needs to know if the interface is going to be used with Carbon or Cocoa. Even if you want to start from a blank slate, you need to specify the empty template appropriate for your application framework.

Your nib file appears in a small window, which provides a place to store menu bars, windows, and other user interface elements. Interface Builder refers to the elements in your interface as *instances*, and sets aside a special tab for storing them. An instance is essentially a specific item of a particular type. If your nib file contains two windows, you will find two window instances in your nib file's Instances tab. In this example, you created a nib file with menu bar and window instances. Icons in your nib's Instances tab can be renamed; the name is merely a label for your benefit, it has no bearing on the final user interface.

Instance contents are displayed graphically within Interface Builder using additional windows. For example, your application's main menu was represented within a window. And representing an application's main window as a window seems natural enough. In the examples that follow, you edit these interface elements by manipulating the instances.

Interface Builder provides two powerful tools in the form of utility panels: the Inspector and the Palettes window. The Inspector window displays information about the current selection. You use the Inspector to customize the instances in your nib file. The Palettes window contains different kinds of interface elements. The specific contents of the Palettes window depends on the kind of interface being edited (Carbon or Cocoa) and on what developer tools you have installed. Normally, you use the Palettes window by dragging interface elements into your nib file, or into your window or menu bar windows.

After your interface has been designed, you can quickly check your work with the Test Interface command. Test Interface runs your interface in a special simulation mode, giving you the opportunity to try out the controls, check that your window's keyboard focus moves properly when you press the Tab key, verify that windows look good when they are resized, and similar tasks. Cocoa interfaces are run directly within Interface Builder, and Carbon interfaces are loaded into a separate program called Carbon Simulator. In either case, you can quit the simulation by pressing Command-Q or by selecting Quit from your interface's menu bar.

It is interesting to note at this point that Interface Builder did not generate any source code in order to test your interface. The behavior of your interface is controlled entirely by the Cocoa and Carbon frameworks. All the information necessary to rebuild your interface is stored in your nib file and is interpreted by the Cocoa and Carbon frameworks at runtime. You learn more about how Cocoa and Carbon use nib files in Chapters 8 and 9.

Building Menus

Every Mac OS X program has a main menu bar — that familiar sight at the top of your computer's screen. Although every application adds its own menus and menu items, there is a fair amount of similarity between each program. Most programs have File, Edit, Window, and Help menus, for example. The guidelines for how menus should look and behave can be found in the Apple Human Interface Guidelines, which you learned about in Chapter 2.

In this Try It Out example, you create a menu bar for a Carbon application. Interface Builder provides some nice graphical tools for building menus, and it also sets up many of the common menus for you.

Try It Out   Building Carbon Menus

1. In Interface Builder, create a new Carbon Menu Bar project. Note that you can open the Starting Point window by choosing File ⇨ New, if necessary. Three windows appear: your untitled interface window, the Palettes window, and a window representing your nib's menu bar.

2. Click once on the File menu in your menu bar window. The File menu drops down, as shown in Figure 4-5. Notice that a bunch of items have already been filled in for you.

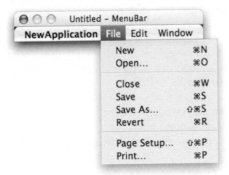

Figure 4-5

3. Click once on the New item your nib's File menu. The New menu item will be selected.

4. Choose Tools ⇨ Show Inspector to open the Inspector. The Inspector displays the settings for the new menu item.

5. Change the settings to match those in Figure 4-6. Notice that as you change the settings, the menu item updates itself accordingly.

6. Double-click the NewApplication menu on the left side of your interface's menu bar. You can rename the menu to something more appropriate.

7. Name the menu `Carbon Example` and press Return. The name is changed.

8. Click the Carbon Example menu name to reveal a menu with a single item: About NewApplication.

9. Click the About NewApplication item. Note the Inspector automatically changes to display the settings for this menu item.

10. Rename the item to `About Carbon Example` using the Inspector. Don't forget to press Return when you're finished changing the text.

Figure 4-6

11. Select the Menus palette in the Palettes toolbar. It should look like Figure 4-7. Notice that the Menus palette contains a number of menu items along the left side.

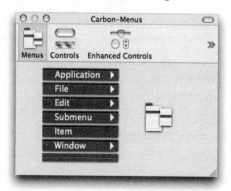

Figure 4-7

12. Be sure the Carbon Example menu is still open and drag the menu item named Item from the Menus palette to the end of the Carbon Example Menu. A new Item item is added to the end of the menu.

13. Rename this new item to Preferences by double-clicking the item and changing its name.

14. Now double-click near the right edge of the Preferences item. See Figure 4-8 for an exact placement of where to click. A box appears, indicating that you've selected that portion of the menu item.

Figure 4-8

15. Press the comma (,) key. The item's Menu Key changes to Command-,.

16. Drag the Submenu menu item from the Menus palette into your interface's menu bar. Drop the menu item between the Edit and Window menus. A new Submenu menu appears in the menu bar, as shown in Figure 4-9. If you need to, you can re-order the menu items by dragging them.

Figure 4-9

17. Rename the Submenu menu to Extras.

18. Select the Extras menu sole Item menu item.

19. Rename the item to Empty The Trash and change its settings to match those shown in Figure 4-10. Notice that the Menu Key has been set to Command-E and the Dynamic option is checked.

20. Click the Empty The Trash item once more to make sure it's selected; then duplicate the item by choosing Edit ⇨ Duplicate.

21. Rename the item to Shred The Trash and check the Option key check box, as shown in Figure 4-11.

22. Choose File ⇨ Test Interface. Your interface is loaded into the Carbon Simulator application.

23. Check the Carbon Simulator and File menu to be sure your changes took effect.

24. Click once on the Extras menu to reveal the menu. Notice that there is only a single menu item: Empty The Trash.

25. Hold down the Option key. The Extras menu item changes to Shred The Trash.

Figure 4-10

Figure 4-11

How It Works

Every application in Mac OS X has a main menu bar. This menu bar is composed of several menus, which are in turn composed of menu items. Interface Builder normally creates a main menu bar for you. You can add menus and menu items to your nib by dragging these items in from Interface Builder's Palette window.

Interface Builder's Menus palette contains several items of interest. Figure 4-12 illustrates the Menus palette for both Carbon and Cocoa.

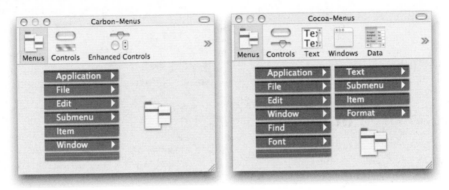

Figure 4-12

The Menus palette contains these things:

❑ **Empty menus and menu items, such as Submenu and Item:** You can drag the Submenu menu into the main menu bar to create new menus, or you can drag it into other menus to create submenus.

❑ **Pre-built menus such as Application, File, Text, and Format:** Some of these items are automatically included in the main menu bar, and some can be added manually for enabling certain kinds of operations. For example, if you're working on a text editing application, you might want to add Text and Font menus to your menu bar.

❑ **A blank menu separator:** Menu separators help group menu items into collections of related items. They aren't selectable; they simply separate other menu items. You add them to menus exactly like adding other kinds of items; just drag them into the menu from the Menus palette.

❑ **An icon representing a menu:** Like the Submenu item, this icon represents an individual menu. However, this menu can't be dragged into the menu bar or other menus; it can only be dragged into your nib's Instances tab. This is useful for defining menus that don't live in your main menu bar, such as contextual menus or Dock menus.

After you've arranged your menus the way you want them, you can edit the individual menu items. You can do simple tasks such as naming the item and setting its Menu Key from the menu itself by double-clicking the menu item. More complicated changes require Interface Builder's Inspector.

Note that the Carbon Simulator's application menu did not change to Carbon Example, even though you changed the nib file. Although there is an entry in the nib for your application menu, the system does not actually use its name at runtime. Instead, it uses the application's display name, which is stored in the application's bundle. You learn more about the application's bundle in Chapter 5.

One of the more interesting features of Mac OS X is the capability to create *alternate* or *dynamic* menu items. Alternate items allow applications to hide less commonly used menu items from view unless a specific modifier key (usually Option) is pressed. In this example, you created a menu item Empty The Trash that changes to Shred The Trash when the option key is pressed. An example of alternate menus in action is the Finder's File menu. If you tap the Option key while holding down the File menu you see a number of menu items change. For example, File ⇨ Close Window changes to File ⇨ Close All. Note that alternate menu items must share the same menu key character but use different modifier keys in order to work properly.

You haven't learned how to actually make these menu items do anything yet; that is, you haven't learned how to hook the menu items up to specific application commands. The method for wiring up controls to an application depends on the application framework. You learn more about this in Chapters 8 and 9.

A Second Look at Menus

Although menus are basically the same regardless of which application framework was used to build the application, there are some differences in the way you build menus for Carbon and Cocoa systems. In the preceding example, you built a simple menu bar.

In this Try It Out example, you build a similar interface; but this time it's for a Cocoa application.

Try It Out   **Building Cocoa Menus**

1.   In Interface Builder, create a new Cocoa Application project. Your nib window, the Palettes window, a window representing your interface's menu bar, and a blank window appear. Notice in Figure 4-13 that the nib window looks a little different than those shown in the previous examples.

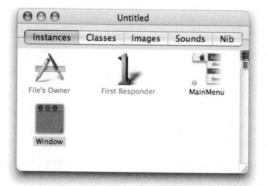

Figure 4-13

2.   Select the Window icon in the nib's Instances tab and press the Delete key. The icon and the blank window disappear.

3. Rename the NewApplication menu on the left side of your interface's menu bar by double-clicking its name. Name the menu `Cocoa Example` and press Return.

4. Click the Cocoa Example menu to reveal its menu. Note that this time the menu has a number of menu items, including a Preferences menu item. Figure 4-14 shows what the Cocoa Example menu should look like.

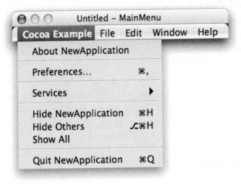

Figure 4-14

5. Rename the About NewApplication item to `About Cocoa Example`. While you're here, also rename the Hide NewApplication and Quit NewApplication items to `Hide Cocoa Example` and `Quit Cocoa Example`.

6. Drag the Submenu menu item from the Menus palette into your interface's menu bar and drop it between the Edit and Window menus. A new Submenu menu appears. Again, you can re-order the menu items by dragging them with the mouse, if necessary.

7. Rename the Submenu menu to `Extras`.

8. Select the Extras menu sole Item menu item.

9. Rename the item to `Empty The Trash` and set its Menu Key to Command-Shift-E.

10. Choose Edit ⇨ Duplicate to duplicate the Empty The Trash menu item.

11. Change the new item's name to `Shred The Trash` by double-clicking the item title in the menu.

12. Change the item's Menu Key to Command-Option-Shift-E by double-clicking the Menu Key (Command-Shift-E) and pressing Command-Option-Shift-E.

13. If necessary, open the Inspector window by choosing Tools ⇨ Show Inspector. The Inspector displays the settings for this menu item, as shown in Figure 4-15. Note the Inspector displays different options than in the previous example.

14. Check the Treat as an Alternate of the Previous Item* check box. If this check box isn't enabled, make sure the Empty The Trash and Shred The Trash menu items have the same Menu Key character (E) and use a different set of modifiers.

15. Choose File ⇨ Test Interface. Your menu bar appears on-screen.

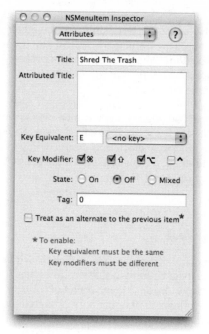

Figure 4-15

16. Check the Cocoa Example menu to make sure your changes took effect.

17. Check the Extras menu both with and without the option key to make sure your alternate menu item works correctly. Notice that both menu items are disabled.

How It Works

In contrast to the Carbon examples you've seen up until now, Cocoa nibs have two additional instances: File's Owner and First Responder. These special items are defined by Cocoa, and they're used to bind controls to the application code. They cannot be removed or renamed; as a result Interface Builder draws their labels in gray. You can simply ignore these items for now.

The menus in the default menu bar also contain more items. The Application menu already contains menu items for Preferences, Hide, Show All, and so on; the Edit menu contains submenus for Find, Spelling, and Speech. In some cases this is because Cocoa provides this support automatically (Find, Spelling, Speech) and in other cases this is simply to encourage programmers to follow the Apple Human Interface Guidelines (Preferences).

One major area in which defining menu items differs between Cocoa and Carbon applications is in the Inspector. The settings available to Carbon menu items are different from those available to Cocoa applications; in particular, Carbon menu items have a large number of check boxes associated with them. Again, this is a case where Cocoa offers to make things easier for you by handling the details automatically. Interface Builder provides controls for only the most common settings; to change other settings you need to write some code.

You might be wondering why Empty The Trash used Command-E in the Carbon example and Command-Shift-E in the Cocoa example. The default Cocoa menu bar already includes an item in the Edit ⇨ Find command that uses the Command-E menu key. If you set the Extras menu items to Command-E and Command-Option-E, they wouldn't work properly. One fix is to remove the Find submenu from your example since it isn't really important here; but in general, it's better to pick menu keys that aren't reserved by common system items.

When you tested your interface, you noticed the new menu items were disabled. Cocoa automatically handles enabled/disabled states for its menu items. In general, if a menu item is hooked up to something, Cocoa enables the item; otherwise the item is disabled. You haven't learned how to hook up menu items yet, so these items are disabled. Again, you learn more about hooking your interface up to your program's source code in Chapters 8 and 9.

Building Windows

Applications use windows in many different ways. Document windows, like those used by word processors or image viewers, tend to be large, resizable windows that contain only a few user interface elements. Utility windows and inspectors tend to have a lot of controls packed into a small area. Dialog and sheets are often the simplest windows, containing only enough items to ask a simple question and collect an answer from the user.

Interface Builder's drag-and-drop interface should be well suited for building windows. Theoretically, all you need to do is drag some controls into your window and you're good to go. In practice, you also need to make sure the controls are arranged properly in the window, accounting both for your application's needs and the spacing rules set forth in the Apple Human Interface Guidelines. Fortunately for you, Interface Builder includes some useful tricks that make this easy.

In the following Try It Out, you build a window to be used as a *modal* dialog box or a sheet. A modal window locks out portions of your application's interface until you close that window. Modal dialog boxes block the entire application, whereas sheets block access only to the window in which they're anchored. The window contains a number of controls arranged in a specific layout. The window also includes OK and Cancel buttons that allow the user to dismiss the window. As is often the case with small dialog boxes and sheets, this window will not be resizable.

Try It Out   Building a Dialog Window

1. In Interface Builder, create a new Cocoa Empty project. Your nib window appears. Unlike the earlier examples, no other windows are associated with your interface yet.

2. Select the Windows palette from the Palettes toolbar. The Palettes window should look like Figure 4-16.

3. Drag the Window item from the Windows palette into your nib's Instances tab. An instance named Window is added to your nib file and a blank window representing that instance appears.

4. Choose Tools ⇨ Show Inspector to open the Inspector. The Inspector displays the settings for the new window. The Inspector's main popup menu should read Attributes.

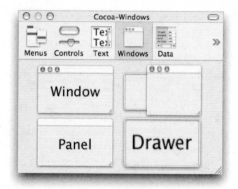

Figure 4-16

5. Uncheck the Close, Minimize, and Zoom (and resize) buttons. The Inspector should resemble Figure 4-17.

Figure 4-17

6. Switch to the Text palette from the Palettes toolbar, as shown in Figure 4-18. The Text palette contains controls for displaying static and editable text.

7. Hold the mouse over the first item in the palette: a simple text field. After a few seconds a help tag displays the name of the control; in this case, NSTextField.

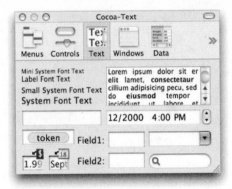

Figure 4-18

8. Drag the System Font Text label out of the palette into the center of your window. This creates a new text label in your window.

9. Double-click the label in your window to change its text. Replace System Font Text with `First Name:`. Click once outside the label to end the text entry process.

10. Select the label by clicking it. Control points appear around the text.

11. Resize the label to fit its text by dragging the right side of the box to the left. In this case, Interface Builder won't let you make the label smaller than its text, so just move the right edge as far as it will go.

12. Drag the label toward the upper-left corner of the window. As you approach the corner, blue guides appear about 20 pixels from the left and top of the window. Figure 4-19 shows these guides in action. These guides help suggest a place for your label that is consistent with the Apple Human Interface Guidelines.

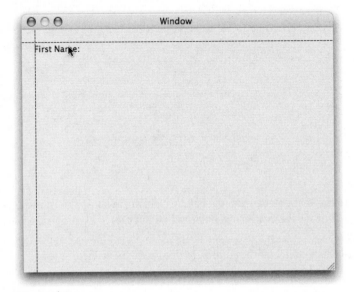

Figure 4-19

13. Be sure the label is selected. The Inspector displays information about this label.

14. Change the label's text to be right aligned by clicking the third control in the list of Alignment buttons. Figure 4-20 shows the Inspector with right alignment selected.

Figure 4-20

15. Drag an editable text field box out of the Text palette and into your window.

16. Move the text field so that it sits to the right of the First Name: label. Guides shown in Figure 4-21 appear to suggest the proper distance between the text field and its label. A guide also aligns the label and text field's base lines.

17. Be sure the text field is selected and choose Size from the Inspector's popup menu. The Inspector displays size and layout information for your text field, as shown in Figure 4-22.

18. Change the text field's layout width to 200 pixels. Don't forget to press Return to end editing. The text field immediately changes to reflect this new size.

19. Use the mouse to select both items and choose Edit ➪ Duplicate. New items appear on top of the originals, offset a few pixels down and to the right.

20. Drag the new items directly below the originals. The left edges should line up. As you move down, Interface Builder may suggest two positions right next to each other: one when the text fields are 6 pixels away and one when the text field is 8 pixels away. Choose the greater of these two gaps.

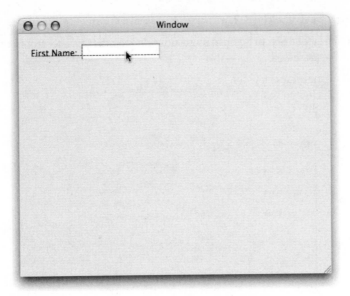

Figure 4-21

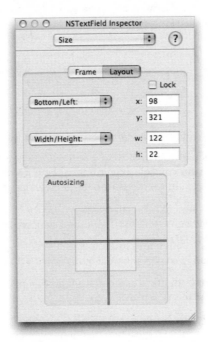

Figure 4-22

21. Rename the new label from First Name: to Last Name:.

22. Duplicate the first two items again, and position the new items directly below the First Name: and Last Name: fields.

23. Rename the new label to Email:. Figure 4-23 shows the window's layout so far. Notice that the controls are aligned to the top and left of the window, but there is a lot of unused space below and to the right.

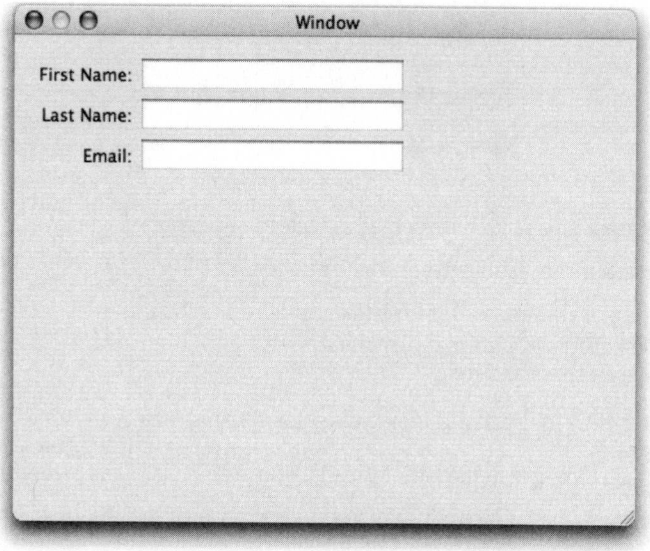

Figure 4-23

24. Make the window narrower by clicking in the window's resize control and dragging it to the left. As before, Interface Builder uses guides to suggest a reasonable distance between the window's right edge and your controls. Don't worry about keeping your window's height exactly the same; you can tighten up the window's lower edge once you've finished adding items to the window.

25. Switch to the Controls palette from the Palettes toolbar, as shown in Figure 4-24. The Controls palette contains a collection of buttons, sliders, and other interesting things.

26. Drag a normal push button out of the palette into your window.

27. Move the button to the right side of the window below the Email: text field. Guides appear suggesting a position about 20 pixels away from the window's right edge and 20 pixels away from the text field.

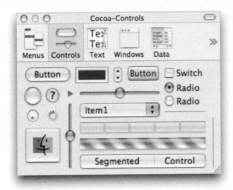

Figure 4-24

28. Select the Attributes section from the Inspector's main popup menu.

29. Use the Inspector to change the button's title to OK.

30. Set the button's key equivalent to Return by selecting Return from the Inspector's Key Equiv. popup menu. The OK button is displayed with a dark highlight, indicating the Return key can be used to choose this button.

31. Drag a new push button from the Controls palette into your window. Position this button to the left of your OK button. Again, Interface Builder's guides will suggest a reasonable place for this button: about 12 pixels to the left of the OK button and 20 pixels below the Email: text field.

32. Use the Inspector to name this button `Cancel` and set its key equivalent to Escape.

33. Now you can finish resizing the window so that it fits all its controls snugly. The guides suggest the proper 20-pixel buffer between the controls and the window's edges. Figure 4-25 illustrates your final window.

Figure 4-25

34. Choose File ➪ Test Interface. Your window appears onscreen, giving you a chance to test out your controls.

35. Press Command-Q to end the test.

How It Works

You build window interfaces much like you build menu interfaces: by dragging interface elements out of the Palettes window into your interface. When building windows, Interface Builder uses guides to automatically suggest layouts consistent with the Apple Human Interface Guidelines. These guides appear when you move and resize interface elements.

Even though you removed your window's close, resize, and minimize controls, you were still able to resize, close, and minimize that window when designing your interface. The window Interface Builder uses to represent the interface you're editing can always be resized, closed, and minimized. Think of this representation as Interface Builder's window editor, not actually your window. Once you test the interface you will find your window really isn't resizable.

The Palettes window contains dozens of controls spread across several individual palettes. Displaying both the icons and text for the Palettes toolbar can help you learn what each palette represents, although at the expense of screen space. Similarly, individual palette items can sometimes be difficult to identify by their icons alone. If you hold the mouse over a palette item, the name of that item appears in a help tag. For Cocoa controls, this name also doubles as its Cocoa class name. You learn more about this in Chapter 8.

When laying out the first text field, you used the Inspector to set its size to a specific value. You also used the Inspector to edit button and label attributes. These values lived in different views of the Inspector, and each view was accessible through the Inspector's popup menu. Interface Builder buries a lot of interesting, framework-specific functionality in these Inspector views. You learn more about some of these views in Chapters 8 and 9, but you might take some time to explore other panels on your own.

You resized your text label to exactly fit its text contents by making the label smaller. Interface Builder wouldn't let you make the label smaller than its text. This is only true when the text label starts out larger than its text. If the label is currently too small to display all the text, or if the label currently fits the text exactly, Interface Builder lets you make the text field as large or as small as you want.

Making Windows Resizable

When designing windows, you need to consider what will happen when the user tries to resize them. For some windows, such as simple sheets and dialog boxes, you may choose to prohibit resizing. But most user-friendly interfaces allow the user to resize windows as they see fit.

An interface element normally responds in two possible ways when a window is resized. The element may remain stationary, fixed in an area of the screen, or the element may change size along with the window. Some elements may do both: remain fixed vertically and resize themselves horizontally. Interface Builder provides tools for defining what happens to its contents when a window is resized.

In the following Try It Out, you build a simple resizable Cocoa window. Figure 4-26 shows the window in two sizes. Don't worry too much about what this interface is supposed to represent; it's really just an opportunity to practice item layout.

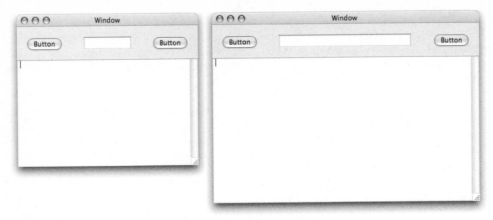

Figure 4-26

Try It Out   Building a Resizable Cocoa Window

1. In Interface Builder, create a new Cocoa Empty project. Your nib window appears.

2. Drag a Window item from the Windows palette into your nib's Instances tab. An instance named Window is added to your nib file and a blank window representing that instance appears.

3. Choose Tools ➪ Show Inspector to open the Inspector. The Inspector displays the settings for the new window.

4. Verify that the Miniaturize, Close, and Resize buttons are all checked.

5. Drag a button from the Controls palette and place it in the upper-left corner of your window. Use the guides to place the button a comfortable distance of 20 pixels from the window edges.

6. Drag a second button from the Controls palette and place it in the upper-right corner of your window.

7. Drag a text field from the Text palette and place it between the two buttons. Use the guides to make sure that the text field lines up vertically with the buttons. Don't worry about centering the text field right now.

8. Make sure the text field is selected. If not, select it using the mouse.

9. Hold down the Option key and move the mouse over the window. Special red guides appear to measure out the distance from the text field's boundaries to those of the window. Figure 4-27 shows these guides in action. The specific horizontal distances may differ from those shown here.

10. While still holding down the Option key, tap the left or right arrow key on the keyboard. This nudges the text field by a single pixel. Continue nudging the text field until it is centered in the window.

11. Drag a multi-line text view object from the upper-right corner of the Text palette and into your window. Position it such that it fills the window's remaining space, as shown in Figure 4-28. If you have trouble finding the text view object, use the help tags to find an item named *NSTextView*.

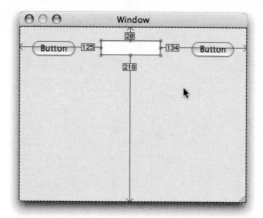

Figure 4-27

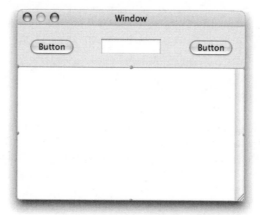

Figure 4-28

12. Choose File ➪ Test Interface to check your work. Your window is displayed in test mode.

13. Grab the window by its resize control and resize the window in a bunch of different directions Start using small circular motions and move toward progressively larger movements. You'll find the controls seem pinned to the lower-left corner of the window. If you make the window very small, the buttons and text field will be pushed off the top of the window. If you make the window very large, the items sit still as the window grows underneath them.

14. Press Command-Q to quit test mode. Interface Builder's user interface returns to normal.

15. Select the button in your window's upper-left corner.

16. Press Command-3 to open the Inspector's Size view. Figure 4-29 shows the layout values, along with an unusual Autosizing control. The Autosizing control is composed of two dark lines intersecting a light gray rectangle.

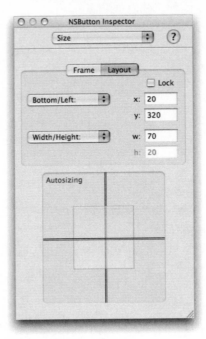

Figure 4-29

17. Click the Autosizing control's dark line segments below and to the right of the gray box. The clicked line segments change to springs, as shown in Figure 4-30. If you click the wrong line segment, just click it again and the spring changes back to a straight line.

Figure 4-30

18. Click the button in the upper-right corner of your window.

19. Click the Autosizing control's dark line segments below and to the left of the gray box. The Autosizing control should look like Figure 4-31.

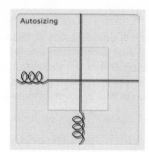

Figure 4-31

20. Select the text field at the top of the window.

21. Click the Autosizing control's dark line segment below the gray box.

22. Click the horizontal line running through the gray box. It also changes to a spring, as shown in Figure 4-32.

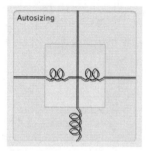

Figure 4-32

23. Select the text view at the bottom of the window.

24. Click the Autosizing control's line segments within the gray box. The control should look like the one in Figure 4-33.

Figure 4-33

25. Choose File ⇨ Test Interface to check your work. Your window appears in test mode.

26. Resize the window in a bunch of different directions. At first it looks like the interface is resizing correctly. The buttons stay in their corners, the text field expands and contracts horizontally, and the text view fills the remaining available space. But if you make the window too small, the text field goes away; once that's happened, making the window large again leaves the text field in an unusual state. The solution to this problem is to set a minimum size for the window.

27. Quit out of test mode using Command-Q. Interface Builder's user interface returns to normal.

28. Click between one of your buttons and the text field to select the underlying window. Alternatively, you can select the window icon in your interface document's Instances tab. Figure 4-34 shows the Inspector's Size controls for your window.

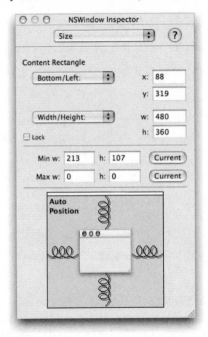

Figure 4-34

29. Click the Current button on the same line as the Min label, as shown in Figure 4-35. This sets the window's minimum size to match the window's current size.

30. Choose File ⇨ Test Interface to check your work.

31. Resize the window in a bunch of different directions. The window elements will resize correctly. The window won't shrink beyond the dimensions specified in step 29.

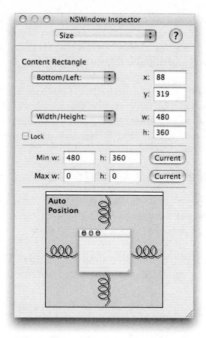

Figure 4-35

How It Works

Initially your window's controls seemed pinned to the lower-left corner of the window. In Cocoa programming, graphics coordinates are normally relative to a window's lower-left corner. So without any additional resizing information, a control is pinned to the lower-left corner by default.

You used a special control, an Autosizing control, for configuring how Cocoa interface elements resize. This Autosizing control consists of two dark lines that intersect a light gray rectangle. The light gray rectangle represents the interface element, or control, you are editing, and the dark lines describe how your interface element responds when its parent window changes. You can turn the dark lines into springs by clicking them with the mouse; what effect this has depends on which part of the line you clicked.

The four line segments outside the light gray rectangle represent the distance between your control and the window's border. A straight line means that the control's position doesn't change along that edge. This has the effect of anchoring the control in a specific location. A spring means the distance between the interface element's edge and the window's edge may change when the window is resized. Here you changed the upper-left button's bottom and right sides to springs, and left the other two sides straight; this basically locked the button against the upper-left corner of the window.

The two line segments within the light gray rectangle represent the size of your interface element. Straight lines mean the size remains constant, and springs mean the size can change. You changed the text field's horizontal line segment to a spring, and left the vertical line straight. This allowed the text field's width to change with the window while keeping the height constant.

Sometimes you can get into trouble when a window gets too small. This often happens when you have one or more controls that change size along with the window. The solution to this problem is to set your window's minimum size. Normally your layout in Interface Builder already is the minimum size; it's easier to design a small interface and allow it to grow bigger than the other way around.

The resizing rules for controls and windows often aren't obvious at a glance, and manually checking each control's Autosizing values can be tedious. The Test Interface command again proves its value by providing a quick and easy way to test your resize logic within Interface Builder. It also encourages experimentation; if you're not sure what a specific set of Autosizing values will do, just test it out.

A Second Look at Resizing Windows

The Autosizing tool you learned about in the preceding example is specific to Cocoa interfaces. Carbon uses a different set of controls for setting resize logic. Although the controls are different, the essential concept of locking an edge to its parent's edge remains the same.

In the following Try It Out example, you build a simple resizable Carbon window. Figure 4-36 shows the window in two sizes. Again, this interface is meant just as an opportunity to practice item layout.

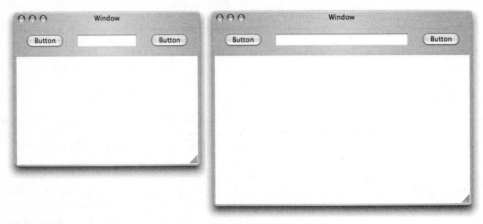

Figure 4-36

Try It Out Building a Resizable Carbon Window

1. In Interface Builder, create a new Carbon Empty project. Your nib window is displayed.

2. Select the Windows palette from the Palettes toolbar, as shown in Figure 4-37. The Windows palette contains two kinds of windows: a normal document window with Close, Minimize, and Zoom buttons, and a movable modal dialog box.

3. Drag a Document Window item from the Windows palette into your nib's Instances tab. An instance named Window is added to your nib file and a blank window representing that instance appears.

4. Choose Tools ⇨ Show Inspector to open the Inspector. The Inspector displays the settings for the new window.

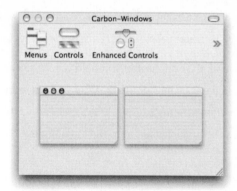

Figure 4-37

5. Verify that the Close, Minimize, Resize, and Zoom buttons are all checked.

6. Check the Metal button. This makes the text controls stand out against the Carbon window's background.

7. Drag a button from the Controls palette and place it in the upper-left corner of your window. Use the guides to place the button a comfortable distance from the window edges.

8. Drag second button from the Controls palette and place it in the upper-right corner of your window.

9. Drag a text field from the Text Based Controls palette and place it between the two buttons. Use the guides to make sure the text field lines up vertically with the buttons. Use the arrow keys to make sure the text field is centered in the window.

10. Drag a text view object from the upper-right corner of the Text Based Controls palette and into your window. Position it such that it fills the window's remaining space, as shown in Figure 4-38. If you have trouble finding the text view object, use the help tags to find an item named *Text View*.

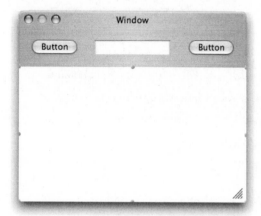

Figure 4-38

11. Choose File ⇨ Test Interface to check your work. Your window appears in the Carbon Simulator.

12. Grab the window by its resize control and resize the window in a bunch of different directions. You'll find that the interface seems pinned to the upper-left corner of the window. If you make the window very small, the buttons and text field will be pushed off the bottom of the window.

13. Quit the Carbon Simulator using Command-Q and return to Interface Builder.

14. Select the button in your window's upper-left corner.

15. Press Command-4 to open the Inspector to the Layout view. Figure 4-39 shows the four popup menus available in the Layout view.

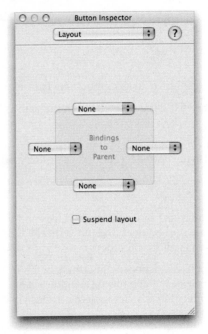

Figure 4-39

16. Change the Layout view's left popup menu to Left and top popup menu to Top.

17. Select the button in your window's upper-right corner.

18. Change the Layout view's right popup menu to Right and top popup menu to Top.

19. Select the text field at the top of the window.

20. Change the Layout view's left popup menu to Left, top popup menu to Top, and right popup menu to Right.

21. Select the text view at the bottom of the window.

22. Change the Layout view's left popup menu to Left, top popup menu to Top, right popup menu to Right, and bottom popup menu to Bottom.

23. Choose File ⇨ Test Interface to check your work. Your window appears in the Carbon Simulator.

24. Resize the window in a bunch of different directions. Start using small circular motions and move toward progressively larger movements. All the controls in the window do what you expect: the buttons stay in their corners, the text field expands and contracts horizontally, and the text view fills the remaining available space. If you make the window too small, the text field will go away. But this problem is easily correctable by simply making the window larger.

25. Press Command-Q to quit test mode and return to Interface Builder.

How It Works

Carbon elements separate layout controls into their own Inspector view. This view contains four popup menus, one for each edge of the control you are editing. These popup menus let you bind your control's edges to those of its parent window. This one set of menus accommodates both locking a control's position and allowing it to resize.

If you bind a control to a single edge or adjacent edges, the control is locked to that position. Here you bound the upper-left button against the window's left and top edges by setting the left popup menu to Left and the top popup menu to Top.

If you bind a set of opposite edges, such as the left and right edge, the control resizes with the window. Here you made the text field horizontally resizable by setting the left popup menu to Left and the right popup menu to Right. You also made the text view completely resizable by setting all four popup menus.

In this example, you basically always set the left popup menu to Left, the top popup menu to Top, and so on. This is generally the case for windows that resize out from the center. Note that you can get into trouble if you reverse the binding directions. For example, if you make an item resizable by setting the left popup to Right and the right popup to Left, the control will not resize correctly.

Note that initially the controls were pinned to the upper-left corner of your window. In Carbon programming, graphics coordinates are relative to a window's upper-left corner. This is different from what you saw in the Cocoa example, where the windows were pinned to the lower-left corner by default. Carbon and Cocoa treat drawing coordinates differently for historical reasons. You should avoid this issue entirely by making sure you specify resize information for all your interface elements.

This example did not include instructions for setting your window's minimum size. Interface Builder does not include controls for setting a window's minimum size directly. Carbon applications generally need to handle this case through custom source code.

Summary

Interface Builder is a powerful tool that's essential for designing user interfaces on Mac OS X. It allows you to design, build, and test user interfaces using simple editing concepts, such as drag and drop. Interface Builder also lets you fine-tune your interfaces using its Inspector.

In this chapter, you learned how to

❑   Build menus and controls by dragging them from Interface Builder's Palettes window into your interface

❑   Make windows and their contents resizable

❑   Use Interface Builder's Inspector to configure individual interface elements

❑   Test your interface directly in Interface Builder

In the next chapter, you learn about the structure of a Mac OS X application. Before proceeding, however, try the exercises that follow to test your understanding of the material covered in this chapter. You can find the solutions to these exercises in Appendix A.

Exercises

1.   Modify the example dialog you built in the Try It Out "Building a Dialog Window" to make it resizable. All the controls should be pinned to the upper-left corner of the window. Allow the text fields to expand when the window is resized.

2.   Carbon and Cocoa both support a tab control that lets you display several sets of controls in the same area. Unlike the examples you've seen so far, you can actually put controls inside a tab control: simply switch to the tab you want and drag buttons, text fields, and the like into that tab.

Build the interface shown in Figure 4-40 using a Cocoa nib file. This window need not be resizable.

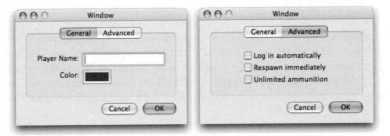

Figure 4-40

Part II: Application Programming

The Application

Mac OS X applications seem simple enough. They appear with friendly icons that bounce in the Dock when you launch them, display a window or two, and then you're on your way. If you want, you can move the application out of the system-wide /Applications directory and into a folder of your choosing. You can even drag some applications into Mail or iChat to send a copy to your friends!

But in reality, Mac OS X applications are sophisticated things. They are composed of executable code, a user interface, and other resources. An application can even include files that translate the user interface into other languages. When packaged correctly, an application looks and feels as if it really were a single file. This packaging scheme is called a *bundle*, or sometimes *wrapper* or *package*.

Bundles organize executable code and other resources at the file level by storing files in a special directory tree. The bundle format can store resources for specific languages and countries (called *localizations*) as well as resources that are language-independent. Bundles can also store executable code for various platforms, allowing the system to pick a specific version of a program based on the system on which it's running. The Finder, Dock, and other Mac OS X programs treat bundles as if they were single files, giving you the flexibility of a directory tree with the convenience of a file.

Although applications themselves are self-contained, they do store some data in other places on your computer. These data normally represent things like your application preferences, the directory that opens by default when you bring up an Open panel, the contents of an Open Recent menu, and the like. All these settings are stored in one of a few common locations using a common file format.

In this chapter you learn

❑ How applications and other bundles are structured

❑ What kind of files you find in a bundle

❑ How application preferences are stored

Basic Bundle Structure

Mac OS X uses bundles for a number of file formats, including applications, frameworks, plug-ins, and certain kinds of documents. You are already familiar with applications and frameworks. Plug-ins are bundles that can be loaded into applications or frameworks at runtime. For example, graphics programs commonly use plug-ins to import functionality into the application. Also, the QuickTime framework can load new codecs, importers, and other things with plug-ins. Some applications use bundles to store document data. For example, Interface Builder .nib files and Xcode project files are both bundles. Not all documents are bundles, however.

Bundles offer a number of different features depending on the specific kind of bundle format in use. No one format takes advantage of all bundle features. The following table outlines the features supported for each bundle format.

	Applications	Frameworks	Plug-ins	Documents
Opaque Directory	✓		✓	✓
Versioned Bundles		✓		
The Info.plist File	✓	✓	✓	
Executable Code	✓	✓	✓	
Global Resources	✓	✓	✓	✓
Localized Resources	✓	✓	✓	

Opaque Directory

Various parts of the operating system, including the Finder, Dock, and Open / Save panels can treat a bundle directory as if it really were a single file. This prevents people from casually viewing a bundle's contents and making changes to its files and directories. Because users can't see inside these bundles, we refer to them as *opaque directories*.

Opaque directories are common for applications, plug-ins, and document bundle types. When users open one of these bundles in the Finder, they expect an application to launch (either the selected application or an application that works with the selected plug-in or document). As a result, these bundles are opaque. Framework bundles are not opaque because you need to look inside a framework to see its header files, documentation, and other browsable resources.

The system keeps track of opaque bundle directories in a number of ways. The first way is simply by checking the file extension. All application bundles (directories that end in .app) are made opaque automatically. The second way is by setting a piece of file meta-data called a *bundle bit*. If a directory's bundle bit is set, the system knows it should treat the bundle as a file, and not as a directory. Thirdly, an application can register a file extension for bundled document types with the system; when the system encounters a directory with that extension, it knows it needs to be treated as a file. This is normally also how document icons are associated with files on Mac OS X.

Versioned Bundles

Frameworks on Mac OS X actually use an older bundle format than other bundle types. This type supports a built-in bundle versioning scheme where all the bundle's files are separated into special subdirectories within the bundle. This allows several versions of a framework to safely live within a single framework bundle.

At the top level of the bundle you will find a `Versions` directory that stores all the version-specific subdirectories. Normally frameworks are versioned by a single English letter, starting with *A*. However, frameworks can also use more meaningful version numbers.

Along with the `Versions` directory you will find *symbolic links* pointing to specific files and directories in the current version. This helps people find and work with the current bundle version without having to know which version they are actually using. When a program is first built, it normally uses the current version of the bundle. However, the program keeps track of the version it used at build time. If a new version of the framework is added in the future, the application continues to look for the version it built against. The application runs only if that older framework version is still installed.

A symbolic link, or symlink, is a special Unix file that refers to another file or directory. When you open a symbolic link, Mac OS X opens the symbolic link's target file or directory instead. You normally create symbolic links using the `ln` *command in Terminal.*

Because symbolic links are part of the Unix system, they use paths to refer to these target files. There is no guarantee a symbolic link points to a valid target file. For example, the target may have been deleted, or someone might have moved or renamed it.

Symbolic links resemble alias files created by Mac OS X's Finder. The major difference between symbolic links and aliases is that aliases use a method other than a file path to refer to its targeted files. As a result, aliases continue to point to their target file even if the target is moved or renamed. On the other hand, alias files do not work with traditional Unix commands, which expect full paths.

Here is an example of a versioned bundle:

```
FunFramework.framework
FunFramework.framework/FunFramework
FunFramework.framework/Resources
FunFramework.framework/Versions
FunFramework.framework/Versions/A
FunFramework.framework/Versions/A/FunFramework
FunFramework.framework/Versions/A/Resources
FunFramework.framework/Versions/A/Resources/English.lproj
FunFramework.framework/Versions/A/Resources/English.lproj/InfoPlist.strings
FunFramework.framework/Versions/A/Resources/Info.plist
FunFramework.framework/Versions/Current
```

More modern bundles do not support versioning. Instead of gathering their files up into a versions directory, they push their bundle contents into a `Contents` directory at the top level, as shown in the following code:

```
FunBundle.bundle
FunBundle.bundle/Contents
FunBundle.bundle/Contents/Info.plist
FunBundle.bundle/Contents/MacOS
FunBundle.bundle/Contents/MacOS/FunBundle
FunBundle.bundle/Contents/Resources
FunBundle.bundle/Contents/Resources/English.lproj
FunBundle.bundle/Contents/Resources/English.lproj/InfoPlist.strings
```

The Info.plist File

Most bundles contain a special file called an `Info.plist`, which contains special information about the bundle: its name, a human readable copyright string, an identifier meant to uniquely represent the bundle, and other settings. The `Info.plist` file is commonly used by application, framework, and plug-in bundles to provide specific information about their features to the system. You will find the `Info.plist` at the top level of the bundle's content directory.

The `Info.plist` is a *property list*. Property lists are special files that can hold an arbitrary hierarchy of data on Mac OS X. Data can be referenced either by name (known as a *key*) or with a numeric index, depending on how the data is organized. Data in the `Info.plist` file is most often looked up by key. The following table provides keys commonly found in the `Info.plist` file, along with an explanation of their use.

Info.plist Key	Usage
CFBundleDocumentTypes	A list of document types supported by an application. Each entry in this list includes the document's type, file extension, HFS file type, and a reference to its icon, and other settings.
CFBundleExecutable	The file name of the executable found within the bundle. Common to application and plug-in bundles.
CFBundleGetInfoString	Text displayed by the Finder when the user brings up the Info window for this bundle.
CFBundleIconFile	The file name of this bundle's icon. This key is used only for application bundles.
CFBundleIdentifier	A string representing a unique identifier for this bundle. These strings are normally expressed in a format beginning with a company's reversed domain name followed by the program name. For example, `com.apple.mail` or `com.wrox.Slide Master`.
CFBundleName	The name of the bundle. This key can be localized, so it takes precedence over the bundle's file name when determining what name to display to the user.
CFBundlePackageType	A four-character code representing the bundle's "Type" code. It is normally "APPL" for applications and "FMWK" for frameworks. Plug-in bundles might use a variety of type codes.
CFBundleSignature	A four character code representing this bundle's "Creator" code used to identify this bundle. It is typically used by Mac OS X when deciding which application should open a document by default.
CFBundleVersion	The version string for this version; for example, "1.0.3" or "4.1b3fc2."
NSMainNibFile	For Cocoa applications, the name of the nib file containing the main menu.
NSPrincipalClass	The name of an Objective-C class designated as the principal class for a Cocoa application or plug-in bundle. In the case of Cocoa applications, this must either be `NSApplication` or an `NSApplication` subclass.

The keys shown in the preceding table represent only the most common `Info.plist` keys used by the system. Other keys do exist but are appropriate only for certain situations, such as for applications that run without appearing in the Dock. You can also define your own data keys if you want.

Bundles with an `Info.plist` file often also contain one or more `InfoPlist.strings` files. These strings files contain localized copies of human-readable values in the `Info.plist`. For example, the `CFBundleGetInfoString` key represents text displayed when the user examines the bundle in the Finder, and normally is translated along with other strings in the bundle. However, other values, such as `CFBundleIdentifier`, are not meant to be localized. You learn more about localization in the section "Localized Resources" later in this chapter.

You can find more information about `Info.plist` keys in Mac OS X's conceptual documentation for Runtime Configuration: `/Developer/ADC Reference Library/documentation/MacOSX/Conceptual/BPRuntimeConfig/Concepts/ConfigFiles.html`.

Executable Code

Bundles can contain executable code, as is the case for application, framework, and plug-in bundles. Executable files live in a special directory named after the system for which the code is intended. Mac OS X defines two such directories: `MacOS` for native Mac OS X programs and `MacOSClassic` for programs that must run natively on Mac OS 9 or earlier. This mechanism allows one bundle to contain code that runs natively on Mac OS X and earlier systems.

Global Resources

All bundles support *global resources*, which are files required by the bundle regardless of what platform or localization the bundle is running under. For example, global resources might include file icons, images, sounds, and other resources that don't need to be translated. Global resources live in a `Resources` directory inside the bundle's content directory.

The system provides functions for searching a bundle's contents for its resources. These functions will always find global resources before returning other kinds of resources, so don't think of global resources as a "default" resource available when all else fails. Global resources are meant to be truly localization independent.

Localized Resources

In contrast to global resources, *localized resources* are meant to contain resources that are appropriate only for a specific language or locale. For example, localized resources might include user interface (`.nib`) files, Unicode strings (`.strings`) files, and other resources that may need to be translated into other languages.

Localized resources live in *Language Project* directories, commonly known as *lprojs* (named for their `.lproj` file extension), which live in the bundle's `Resources` directory. Language project directories gather up resources for a specific language or locale into a single directory named after that language or locale. For example, files appropriate for English speakers will be grouped together into an `English.lproj` directory.

Again, the system provides functions for searching bundles for localized resources, assuming a global version of the resource does not exist. The system searches for localizations according to the user's settings in the International System Preferences pane. By separating code and global resources from resources that need to be localized, it's easy to see how Mac OS X makes it easy to support single applications that can seamlessly run in many languages.

Although technically any bundle can hold localized resources, document bundles normally are not localized.

Examining Application Bundles

Although the Finder goes out of its way to display bundles as files, it does provide some tools for peeking into package contents. You can use the Finder to view and install localizations for individual applications. You can also open the bundle directly and examine the entire application bundle.

Unix commands make no attempt to disguise the true nature of application bundles — the very concept of bundles is alien to a Unix system. Terminal is another good way to reveal the contents of an application.

In the Try It Out example that follows, you use both Finder and Terminal to examine the contents of the Mail Application's bundle.

Try It Out   Examining the Mail Application

1. In the Finder, select /Applications/Mail.

2. Control-click the Mail application's icon. A contextual menu appears.

3. Select Get Info from the contextual menu. A panel appears that resembles Figure 5-1.

Figure 5-1

4. Open the Languages section by clicking its disclosure triangle. The panel resizes to reveal a list of languages, as seen in Figure 5-2.

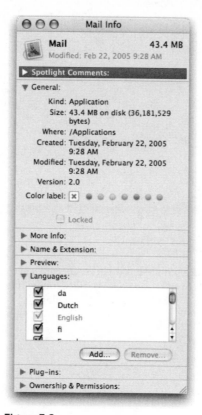

Figure 5-2

5. Uncheck one of the languages in the list; it's a good idea to pick a language that you aren't currently using. We chose to turn off Spanish.

6. Close the Get Info panel.

7. Control-click the Mail icon again and select the Show Package Contents menu item. A new Finder window appears and contains a folder named Contents.

8. Select the Contents folder without opening it.

9. Change the window to Column mode by choosing View ⇨ as Columns. The Finder window displays a number of files and folders, as shown in Figure 5-3.

10. Select the MacOS directory. Inside you will see a single file named Mail.

11. Select that Mail file. Finder claims Mail is a Unix Executable File.

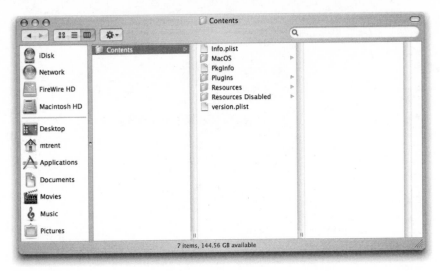

Figure 5-3

12. Scroll the Finder window to the left if necessary and select Contents/Resources. This directory is full of all kinds of files: AppleScript files, image files saved in TIFF format, lproj directories, and so on. Figure 5-4 shows a few of those files.

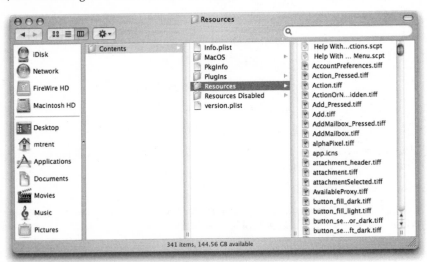

Figure 5-4

13. Scroll down until you see an lproj directory and select it. Figure 5-5 shows the Finder window with da.lproj selected. The lproj directory contains a number of other files, primarily Interface Builder and Strings files.

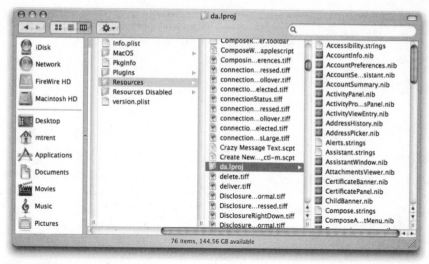

Figure 5-5

14. Select the `Contents/Resources Disabled` directory. You will see a directory representing the language you disabled in step 5; for example, `Spanish.lproj`.

15. Close this window.

16. In another Finder window Get Info on `/Applications/Mail` again.

17. Go to the Languages section and re-enable the language you turned off before.

18. Close the Info panel.

19. Launch `/Applications/Utilities/Terminal`.

20. Change the current directory to `/Applications` using the `cd` command:

```
Macintosh:~ sample$ cd /Applications
Macintosh:/Applications sample$
```

21. Type `find Mail.app`. Pages of information will scroll by. You can use Terminal's scroll bar to go back and see the whole list. Here is a portion of the results:

```
Macintosh:/Applications sample$ find Mail.app
Mail.app
Mail.app/Contents
Mail.app/Contents/Info.plist
Mail.app/Contents/MacOS
Mail.app/Contents/MacOS/Mail
Mail.app/Contents/PkgInfo
Mail.app/Contents/PlugIns
Mail.app/Contents/PlugIns/MailWebPlugIn.bundle
Mail.app/Contents/PlugIns/MailWebPlugIn.bundle/Contents
Mail.app/Contents/PlugIns/MailWebPlugIn.bundle/Contents/Info.plist
Mail.app/Contents/PlugIns/MailWebPlugIn.bundle/Contents/MacOS
Mail.app/Contents/PlugIns/MailWebPlugIn.bundle/Contents/MacOS/MailWebPlugIn
Mail.app/Contents/PlugIns/MailWebPlugIn.bundle/Contents/version.plist
```

```
Mail.app/Contents/Resources
Mail.app/Contents/Resources/ Help With Rule Actions.scpt
Mail.app/Contents/Resources/ Help With Scripts Menu.scpt
Mail.app/Contents/Resources/AccountPreferences.tiff
Mail.app/Contents/Resources/Action.tiff
Mail.app/Contents/Resources/Action_Pressed.tiff
[ ... ]
```

22. Quit Terminal.

How It Works

When you run an application, the Finder looks inside the application's bundle and selects the appropriate executable for your system. In the preceding case of Mail, there was only one executable file: `Mail.app/Contents/MacOS/Mail`. That executable file is the "real" Mail program.

Also when you run an application, the system decides which language to use. This choice is driven by your settings in the International System Preferences pane and by the `lprojs` available in your application. The system goes through each language in the International preference pane's list in order until it finds an `lproj` for that language. The application then uses the files in that `lproj` directory for its user interface. This selection process is all automatic; the application programmer only needs to make sure localized resources are available for a given language. In the case of Mail, the system looks for localized resources in `Mail.app/Contents/Resources/English.lproj` when running in English. The system only pulls resources from one localization; it does not mix and match resources from multiple localizations.

The other files that make up the Mail application live in the global resources directory, `Mail.app/Contents/Resources`. The files stored in this directory do not contain language-specific information. In this example, the global resource directory contains a lot of TIFF images (`.tiff`), icon files (`.icns`), and so on. Normally, image files display the same image regardless of language, so they are commonly treated as global resources.

Finder provides a contextual menu command for opening up a bundle and seeing its contents. This is useful for all kinds of bundles that masquerade as files, not just applications. The Finder also includes UI for examining the languages available to an application and for adding or removing them. When you disabled a localization, its `lproj` directory was moved out of `Resources` and into a `Resources Disabled` directory. The system ignores `Resources Disabled` directories when searching for localizations.

The Unix `find` command walks down a directory tree and performs a variety of operations on the files and directories it finds. In this example, you told `find` to walk through the entire `Mail.app` directory tree and print the path to each file or directory therein. People new to Unix commands are often confused by `find` because its name suggests it scrounges through directories looking for specific files ("find me this file!"). Although `find` can do that, it is capable of a whole lot more; you may discover that even the basic way you used `find` in this example is extremely useful. When you have some time, read through `find`'s manual page entry to learn what it is capable of.

Building an Application Bundle

Bundles are basically directories, and building a bundle could be as simple as just creating a folder in the Finder. However, much of the bundle's power is wrapped up in its specific directory tree and `Info.plist` file. Xcode manages most of the complexity of building bundles for you as part of your project build process.

In the following Try It Out, you explore this capability in Xcode by building the project and application bundle for the Slide Master application. If you haven't already done so, you will want to download the Slide Master source from www.wrox.com. You can use our copy of Slide Master to copy from if you get into trouble. You can also pull icons and other resources out from our copy.

Try It Out   **Building the Slide Master Bundle**

1.   In Xcode, create a new Cocoa Document-based Application named Slide Master.

2.   Build and run the new project. After a few moments of building, your new Slide Master application appears. Right now the application just displays a window saying Your document contents here. Slide Master appears in the Dock using a generic app icon, as shown in Figure 5-6.

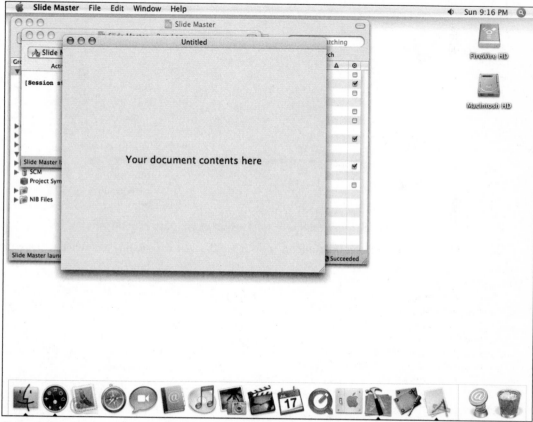

Figure 5-6

3.   Choose Slide Master ⇨ About NewApplication. An About panel appears with some default credits and the generic app icon.

4.   Quit Slide Master.

5.   In Terminal, type cd but don't press return. Make sure you leave a space after the cd command.

6. In Finder, locate your new Slide Master program.

7. Drag the Slide Master icon from Finder into your Terminal window. The path to the application appears on your Terminal command line, resembling Figure 5-7. Your results will differ depending on where your Slide Master project lives. Normally you will find your built programs in a new directory called build inside your project directory.

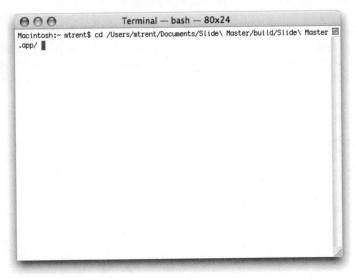

Figure 5-7

8. Press Return to change the current directory to that of your application bundle.

9. Enter find . to list the entire contents of your bundle. The list should resemble the following:

```
.
./Contents
./Contents/Info.plist
./Contents/MacOS
./Contents/MacOS/Slide Master
./Contents/PkgInfo
./Contents/Resources
./Contents/Resources/English.lproj
./Contents/Resources/English.lproj/Credits.rtf
./Contents/Resources/English.lproj/InfoPlist.strings
./Contents/Resources/English.lproj/MainMenu.nib
./Contents/Resources/English.lproj/MainMenu.nib/classes.nib
./Contents/Resources/English.lproj/MainMenu.nib/info.nib
./Contents/Resources/English.lproj/MainMenu.nib/objects.nib
./Contents/Resources/English.lproj/MyDocument.nib
./Contents/Resources/English.lproj/MyDocument.nib/classes.nib
./Contents/Resources/English.lproj/MyDocument.nib/info.nib
./Contents/Resources/English.lproj/MyDocument.nib/objects.nib
```

10. Switch back to Xcode and select Slide Master in the Groups & Files list. The file list changes to display the source files and other resources that make up your project.

11. Open `Credits.rtf`. This is where the credits you saw in step 3 came from. Go ahead and make the credits more meaningful to you. Then save and close the file.

12. Choose Project ⇨ Add To Project. A sheet appears where you can choose files to add.

13. Navigate to the Slide Master project you downloaded from `www.wrox.com` and select `appl.icns`. If you haven't downloaded the project yet, you can borrow TextEdit's icon from here: `/Developer/ Examples/AppKit/TextEdit/Edit.icns`. When you select the file, the sheet shown in Figure 5-8 appears.

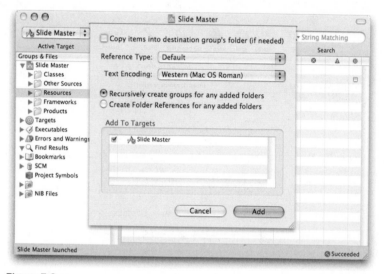

Figure 5-8

14. Check the Copy Items Into Destination Group's Folder check box and click the Add button to dismiss the sheet. The file will appear in your Groups & Files list.

15. Rename the icon file to `appl.icns`.

16. Choose Project ⇨ Add To Project again and then add `slim.icns` to your project. Again, borrow from TextEdit if you don't have the Slide Master example project handy. Make sure you copy the file into your project.

17. Drag your icon files into the Resources group. Your project should resemble the one shown in Figure 5-9.

18. Open the Targets group in the Groups & Files list.

19. Select the item representing your Slide Master application.

20. Get Info for this target by choosing File ⇨ Get Info. A Target Info window appears, displaying settings for your target.

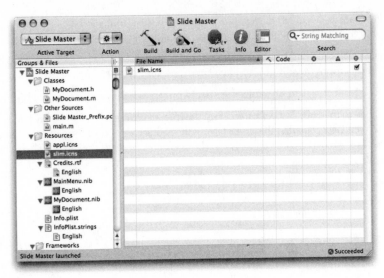

Figure 5-9

21. Select the Build tab in the Target Info window. The window displays lists of build options, as shown in Figure 5-10. Note `Product Name` is set to `Slide Master` and `Wrapper Extension` is set to `app`.

Figure 5-10

22. Select the Properties tab in the Target Info window. You will now see an area where you can enter information about your application, as shown in Figure 5-11.

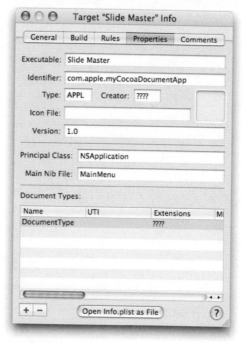

Figure 5-11

23. Change Identifier to `com.wrox.Slide Master`.

24. Change Icon File to `appl.icns`.

25. Change Creator to `Slid`.

26. Verify that Version is `1.0`. Your Target Info window should now resemble the one shown in Figure 5-12.

27. Close the Target Info window.

28. Build and run the new project. After building, Slide Master should launch and your icon should appear in the Dock.

29. Choose Slide Master ⇨ About NewApplication. The About panel now uses your application icon and your updated credits text.

30. Choose File ⇨ Open. An Open panel appears, allowing you to browse for files. However, all the files will be grayed out and unselectable.

31. Cancel out of the Open panel and quit Slide Master.

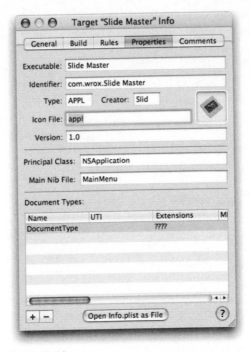

Figure 5-12

32. Re-open the Target Info window by double-clicking the Slide Master target; if necessary, select the Properties button. Notice a table named Document Types at the bottom of the window. The table has one entry, for a document named `DocumentType`.

33. Change the entry for `DocumentType` to match the information in Figure 5-13.

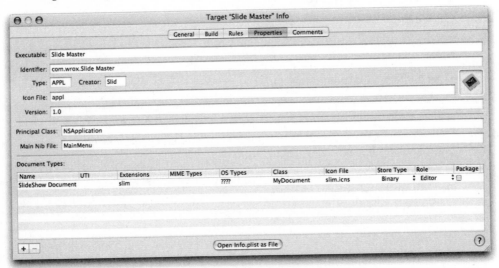

Figure 5-13

34. Build and run the new project. After building, Slide Master should launch.

35. Choose File ⇨ Open. An Open panel should now allow you to select files ending with a `.slim` extension. If you don't happen to have any `.slim` files, save some slide shows from the version of Slide Master you downloaded off the Web. If you haven't downloaded Slide Master yet, just use TextEdit to create a text file with a `.slim` extension.

36. Open a slide show file. Again, your placeholder window appears.

37. Quit Slide Master.

38. Find and open the `Info.plist` file in Xcode's Groups & Files list. If you have trouble, select the Slide Master project group and enter `Info` in the toolbar's Search field. When you open the file, a source editor appears, displaying the contents of your `Info.plist` file; it should resemble the one shown in Figure 5-14. You will see that the results in this file match the values you entered into your target's Info panel shown in Figure 5-13.

Figure 5-14

How It Works

Slide Master works with slide show documents (`.slim` files), so the Cocoa Document-based Application template is the logical choice for your project. This project template is set up to emit a complete Cocoa application at build time. When you built the project, Xcode laid out Slide Master's bundle directory structure and copied default resources into it. The result is a normal application, although one that doesn't do much yet.

Much of your program's bundle is derived from its project files. For example, your application's credits file and icon are stored in files embedded in the application bundle. In fact, your entire user interface is copied into the application bundle. The bundle also includes information about what document types your program will recognize, and what icon to use for those types. This document binding information is stored in the bundle's `Info.plist` file.

If necessary, you can change key details of your bundle from the Build tab in Xcode's Target Info window. For example, you can customize your bundle's extension or rename your `Info.plist` file to something else. Normally, you don't need this kind of control for applications and frameworks, but plug-in bundles often use custom file extensions.

Xcode provides several ways to modify your `Info.plist` file. One way is to use the Properties tab in Xcode's Target Info window, which is convenient for projects that do not require anything special of their `Info.plist` file. Alternatively, you can simply open your project's `Info.plist` file in a source editor and view the raw property list XML. This is useful for those projects that require custom settings in their `Info.plist` file. Recall the `Info.plist` file can contain any number of data keys, not just those shown here.

Navigating through deep directory trees can be a tedious task in Terminal, for novice and expert users alike. Terminal and the Unix shell include a number of shortcuts that make this chore easier. One such shortcut is the capability to drag files and folders into Terminal instead of typing their entire path. This allows those comfortable with the Finder to save a bit of typing.

The Slide Master icons have unusual names: `appl.icns`, `slim.icns`, and so on. These files have been named after the HFS file type those icons represent. For example, `appl` represents the application and `slim` represents slide show documents. This is not a requirement by Xcode or the system, it is merely a way to remember what each icon is for. You can name icons whatever you like, provided you enter the proper filename in your program's `Info.plist`.

Application Preferences

Most programs provide a preferences panel that allows users to customize the application to fit their needs. By convention, applications are supposed to store their preferences in a specific place with a specific file format. The system also provides tools that encourage developers to enforce these conventions.

Try It Out   **Examining Preference Files**

1. Launch `/Applications/TextEdit`. TextEdit displays a new, untitled text document.

2. Choose TextEdit ➪ Preferences. A Preferences window appears, as shown in Figure 5-15.

3. Click the Restore All Defaults button. This returns TextEdit's preferences to what they were when Mac OS X was first installed. If you have already customized TextEdit's preferences, you might write down your settings so that you can restore them later.

4. Close the Preferences window.

5. Enter some text in the text document. Anything will do; you just need enough text for TextEdit to note that the document needs to be saved.

6. Save the document to the Desktop. Name it `Document`.

7. Quit TextEdit.

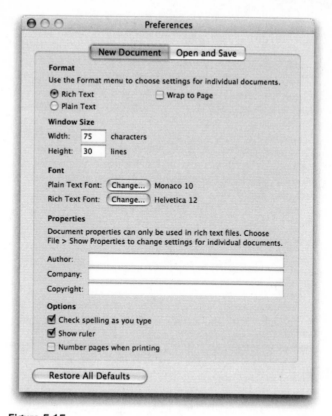

Figure 5-15

8. In Finder go to the `Library/Preferences` directory in your home directory. You will see a number of files and folders. The majority of files are property lists, or `.plist` files.

9. Open the `com.apple.TextEdit.plist` file. The file should open in a program called Property List Editor, as seen in Figure 5-16.

10. Option-click the disclosure triangle next to the Root entry. The outline expands to show the entire contents of the property list file.

11. Click the Dump button. The text view at the bottom of the window displays the contents of the file in XML form.

12. Quit Property List Editor.

13. Launch `/Applications/Utilities/Terminal`.

Figure 5-16

14. Enter defaults read com.apple.TextEdit. The Terminal displays a large amount of data in an ordered fashion, as illustrated in the following code. Your results may not match this exactly:

```
[Macintosh:~] sample% defaults read com.apple.TextEdit
{
    NSNavLastRootDirectory = "~/Desktop";
    NSRecentDocumentRecords = (
        {
            "_NSLocator" = {
                "_NSAlias" = <00000000 016e0002 00000c4d 6163696e 746f7368 20484400
00000000 00000000 00000000 0000bc93 a1cc482b 00000003 4dab0c44 6f63756d 656e742e
72746600 00000000 00000000 00000000 00000000 00000000 00000000 00000000 00000000
00000000 00000000 00000000 00000000 0000000c 13e9bd0f ae290000 00000000 0000ffff
ffff0000 09200000 00000000 00000000 00000000 00074465 736b746f 70000010 00080000
bc94124c 00000011 00080000 bd101099 00000001 000c0003 4dab0003 4d9e0000 5f8f0002
002e4d61 63696e74 6f736820 48443a55 73657273 3a6d7472 656e743a 4465736b 746f703a
446f6375 6d656e74 2e727466 000e001a 000c0044 006f0063 0075006d 0065006e 0074002e
00720074 0066000f 001a000c 004d0061 00630069 006e0074 006f0073 00680020 00480044
00120021 55736572 732f6d74 72656e74 2f446573 6b746f70 2f446f63 756d656e 742e7274
66000013 00012f00 00150002 000dffff 0000>;
            };
        }
    );
    "NSTableView Columns NSNavOutlineColumnSettings.v1" = (
        <040b7479 70656473 74726561 6d8103e8 84014084 8484084e 53537472 696e6701
8484084e 534f626a 65637400 8584012b 1c4e534e 61764469 73706c61 794e616d 6546696c
6550726f 70657274 7986>,
```

```
        225,
        <040b7479 70656473 74726561 6d8103e8 84014084 8484084e 53537472 696e6701
8484084e 534f626a 65637400 8584012b 184e534e 61764d6f 64446174 6546696c 6550726f
70657274 7986>,
        117
    );
    "NSTableView Sort Ordering NSNavOutlineColumnSettings.v1" = (
        <040b7479 70656473 74726561 6d8103e8 84014084 8484084e 53537472 696e6701
8484084e 534f626a 65637400 8584012b 1c4e534e 61764469 73706c61 794e616d 6546696c
6550726f 70657274 7986>,
        1
    );
}
```

15.   Launch TextEdit again and open the Preferences window.

16.   Uncheck the Delete Backup File check box found on the Open And Save tab and close the Preferences window.

17.   Choose File ➪ Open Recent ➪ Clear Menu. TextEdit forgets the contents of the Open Recent menu.

18.   Quit TextEdit.

19.   In Terminal, enter `defaults read com.apple.TextEdit` again. The output of the `defaults` command will change to resemble the following:

```
[Macintosh:~] sample% defaults read com.apple.TextEdit
{
    DeleteBackup = 0;
    NSNavLastRootDirectory = "~/Desktop";
    NSRecentDocumentRecords = ();
    "NSTableView Columns NSNavOutlineColumnSettings.v1" = (
        <040b7479 70656473 74726561 6d8103e8 84014084 8484084e 53537472 696e6701
8484084e 534f626a 65637400 8584012b 1c4e534e 61764469 73706c61 794e616d 6546696c
6550726f 70657274 7986>,
        225,
        <040b7479 70656473 74726561 6d8103e8 84014084 8484084e 53537472 696e6701
8484084e 534f626a 65637400 8584012b 184e534e 61764d6f 64446174 6546696c 6550726f
70657274 7986>,
        117
    );
    "NSTableView Sort Ordering NSNavOutlineColumnSettings.v1" = (
        <040b7479 70656473 74726561 6d8103e8 84014084 8484084e 53537472 696e6701
8484084e 534f626a 65637400 8584012b 1c4e534e 61764469 73706c61 794e616d 6546696c
6550726f 70657274 7986>,
        1
    );
}
```

20.   Enter `defaults write com.apple.TextEdit DeleteBackup 1`. Terminal command should accept the command without comment.

21.   Again enter `defaults read com.apple.TextEdit`. The results should resemble the following:

```
[Macintosh:~] sample% defaults write com.apple.TextEdit DeleteBackup 1
[Macintosh:~] sample% defaults read com.apple.TextEdit
{
```

```
        DeleteBackup = 1;
        NSNavLastRootDirectory = "~/Desktop";
[ ... ]
```

22. Launch TextEdit and open the Preferences window. The Delete Backup File check box is selected again.

23. Quit TextEdit.

24. In Terminal, enter `defaults read com.apple.screensaver`. An error message appears, claiming that the `com.apple.screensaver` domain doesn't exist.

25. Enter `defaults -currentHost read com.apple.screensaver`. Some Screen Saver settings should appear. If they don't, change your Screen Saver settings in System Preferences and try again.

26. Enter `ls ~/Library/Preferences/ByHost`. You will see a number of files, including one beginning with `com.apple.screensaver`:

```
Macintosh:~ sample$ defaults read com.apple.screensaver
Domain com.apple.screensaver does not exist
Macintosh:~ sample$ defaults -currentHost read com.apple.screensaver
{
    idleTime = 300;
    moduleName = "Computer Name";
    modulePath =
"/System/Library/Frameworks/ScreenSaver.framework/Versions/A/Resources/Computer
Name.saver";
}
Macintosh:~ sample$ ls ~/Library/Preferences/ByHost
com.apple.screensaver.000d93c27c30.plist
[ ... ]
```

How It Works

Most applications store preferences of some kind. Normally preferences are edited in an application's Preferences pane. Other settings might be set more transparently, such as an application that remembers its window positions. Mac OS X will even save some settings on an application's behalf, such as the contents of the File ⇨ Open Recent menu.

Normally your application preferences are stored in your `Library/Preferences` directory. By designating a place for preferences to be stored, the system makes it easy for you to manage your own preference files (for example, by removing old preferences if necessary) and discourages applications from writing preferences in other, less appropriate, places.

Actually, Mac OS X defines a number of places in which programs can store preference files. Consider that a Mac OS X system might have multiple user accounts. Since preferences are generally user-specific, each user has his or her own collection of preferences. However, some preferences may be appropriate for all users on the system. Also consider that in larger networked environments, home directories might live on a file server, and the user might share the same home directory among several computers. Some preferences may be appropriate only for a specific system, whereas other preferences might be shared among all systems. The following table outlines the various preferences directories on a Mac OS X system.

Directory	Purpose
~/Library/Preferences	Normally user preferences are saved into their Library/Preferences directory. In large networked environments, these settings are appropriate for all machines the user might log into. This is the most common location for preferences on a Mac OS X system.
~/Library/Preferences/ByHost	User preferences specific to a particular machine are stored in a ByHost subdirectory of the user's Preferences directory. For example, screen savers tend to make assumptions based on a computer's display hardware, and thus save machine-specific preferences. Normally these machine-specific preference files are tagged with the computer's primary Ethernet address as a simple means of uniquely identifying individual computers.
/Library/Preferences	Preferences specific to all users on a given system are saved in the system-wide /Library/Preferences directory. For example, preferences related to starting up your computer or for running Software Update are stored here. But in general such settings are rare.
/Network/Library/Preferences	In large networked environments, preferences intended for all users on all machines can be written to a special file server directory found at /Network/Library/Preferences. These settings, too, are rare.

In addition to providing common places for saving preference files, Mac OS X provides a common file format for saving preference data: the property list. As you saw in the Info.plist, property lists can hold a wide variety of structured data. This makes property lists ideal for storing application preferences as well.

Preferences are meant to be created lazily. Application installers shouldn't install preference files along with other file data; instead application preferences should be created by the application when the user actually sets a preference. In addition, the application doesn't need to write out every preference value when it saves a file; it can write out only values that differ from the default settings. You saw this when looking at TextEdit's preferences: the NSRecentDocumentRecords and DeleteBackup keys were absent when they had nothing meaningful to store. Of course, you were able to manually set DeleteBackup to its default value, but you could also have simply removed the DeleteBackup key entirely.

Applications that use Mac OS X's built-in preferences system benefit from a number of features. One of these benefits is a convenient API for working with preferences files. In the case of Cocoa applications, the system takes care of reading and writing your preferences automatically; the application only needs to work with the preference values themselves. Carbon programs need to do a little extra work to find the right preference file and save out changes but otherwise work only with individual preference values. You learn more about these APIs in Chapters 8 and 9.

Another benefit of using Mac OS X's built-in preferences system is that a number of tools exist for working with preference files. These tools include the Property List Editor application and the defaults command-line tool you saw in this example. Property List Editor is a normal document-based application that works with property list files in general. The defaults tool is specifically designed to work with preference files. When using defaults you reference settings by their *preference domain* rather than by filename. An application's preference domain is normally the same as its CFBundleIdentifier. You can use the -currentHost flag to easily distinguish between normal and machine-specific preferences. You can learn more about the defaults command by reading its man page.

You may have noticed that the defaults command displays preference information in a format completely different from the property list format you've seen in Xcode. Normally, property list files are written in XML, a language well suited for describing nested groups of arbitrary data. You saw this when looking at Slide Master's Info.plist file in Xcode's source editor. The defaults command appears to display the same data but in a format using square and curly brackets to designate groups of values. It turns out this is actually an obsolete version of the property list file, used in systems prior to Mac OS X. Although the newer XML format has officially replaced the older format, the older format is a little easier to read; it is sometimes used when displaying property list data to a developer, as in the case of the defaults command.

Both Property List Editor and defaults allow you to change the contents of your preference files. This comes with a quick word of caution. Although the property list format is common to most preference files, the semantic meaning of the contents of the property list is specific to the application that wrote the file. Editing an application's preference file by hand may result in causing that application to misbehave or crash if you make an inappropriate change. If you get into trouble with a corrupt or damaged preference file, just delete it; the application creates a new one.

Not all applications follow these conventions. Some applications write their own preference file format to the Library/Preferences directory; some store their files in other places entirely. This can actually cause problems for certain kinds of Macintosh environments. For example, many administration tools make use of the standard preference locations and file formats to allow system administrators to easily configure entire rooms of Macintosh computers at once. Applications that do not save in standard locations using the standard format will not play well with these tools.

Summary

In this chapter, you learned that

❑   Mac OS X uses bundles to wrap a collection of files into self-contained directories that appear as files in Finder and other programs.

❑   Bundles store external resources, including those intended for specific localizations.

❑   The system provides standard locations and file formats for storing preference files, and tools for viewing and editing them.

In the next chapter, you learn about the C programming language. C is commonly used in writing Carbon programs, and it also forms the base of the Objective-C programming language used by Cocoa. Before proceeding, however, try the exercises that follow to test your understanding of the material covered in this chapter. You can find the solutions to these exercises in Appendix A.

Exercises

1. You have seen how an application's bundle structure defines various properties for an application. Use the techniques for examining bundles you learned in this chapter to answer the following questions.

   a. How many document types does the TextEdit application support?

   b. What is the Preview application's bundle signature?

   c. What is Terminal's bundle identifier?

   d. Some document types actually are bundles rather than solitary files. Examine a number of nib files. What kind of files might you find in an Interface Builder file?

   e. What is the current bundle version of the AppKit framework?

   f. What is the current bundle version of the JavaVM framework?

2. The defaults command provides a convenient way for working with application preferences from Terminal. You can read and write preference values without having to manually find and edit the preference file. Use the defaults command to perform the following tasks; if necessary check the defaults man page for help.

   a. List all your machine-independent preference domains.

   b. List all your machine-specific preference domains.

   c. Display your Terminal preferences.

   d. Display HIToolbox's preferences.

   e. Create a new preference file called MyExamplePref with a single key Autosave set to 1.

   f. Add a key colors to your MyExamplePref preference with an array of values: red, orange, yellow.

   g. Delete the Autosave key from your MyExamplePref preference.

6

The C Language

C is probably the most successful programming language that there has ever been. Whether you realize it or not, most of the software you use daily has something to thank C for. Operating systems, such as Mac OS X, are invariably written in C, and most of the applications still with us from the days of Mac OS 9 and earlier rely on the Carbon framework, which is written in C (see Chapter 9). Popular languages, such as Java, also take much of their syntax from C. Let's face it, apart from the fact that it is still very much in use today, C is the Latin of computer languages.

C also forms the basis of Objective-C , which is a more modern variant used for most new application development on Mac OS X. Objective-C is the core language for the Cocoa frameworks, which you learn about in Chapter 8.

Half the battle of learning to program new applications on Mac OS X is learning to program in Objective-C, which you learn about in Chapter 7. And more than half of that battle is learning C. Objective-C is a superset of C, meaning it has everything that C has and a bit more. If you already know C, you are well on the way to mastering Objective-C and Cocoa development (Chapter 8).

In this chapter, you learn the basics of C, which will serve you well whether or not you continue to develop for Mac OS X. By the end, you should be able to read existing C code without too much trouble, and you will have the prerequisites for learning to write programs in Objective-C.

In this chapter you learn

❑ How to write programs in the C programming language

❑ How to write C programs using the structured programming style used in the Mac OS X C frameworks, including CoreFoundation, Carbon, and QuickTime

A Little History

C is the mother of many popular languages, including Objective-C, Java, and C++. Even scripting languages such as Perl owe much to this venerable old workhorse. C began its journey to greatness at Bell Labs in 1969, where Ken Thompson and Dennis Ritchie created it. It was used to write the first Unix operating system, from which Mac OS X ultimately descends. Other operating systems, like Windows and Mac OS, also owe a lot to C.

In 1989, the American National Standards Institute (ANSI) published the first official standard for C. C was already very popular by this time, but standardization is always an important point in the history of a programming language. Before this, a watershed book by Brian Kernighan and Dennis Ritchie, *C Programming Language* (Prentice Hall), had become the de facto standard for C. In 1999, the International Standards Organization (ISO) published an update to the 1989 standard, known to developers as C99.

These days, C is used as a modern *assembler*. C was one of the first *high-level* languages, but relative to more modern programming languages such as Objective-C and Java, it is actually quite low level. For programmers, it has transplanted much of the functionality of assembler and is often only used when performance is critical.

Assembler is a very low-level language that is normally used only by computers as an intermediate step to producing object code, which can be run by the computer's CPU. In the early days of computers — sometimes still today — a programmer often had to write assembler code to get high performance because hand-tuned assembler could sometimes yield more efficient code than a compiler produces.

Getting Started

Every C program begins execution in the main function. It is the first piece of code that is run, and it's responsible for ensuring that other parts of your code are executed appropriately. Sometimes a main function can be a few lines, as is often the case in software written with the Cocoa frameworks (see Chapter 8), and at other times it may constitute the whole program. Here is a simple example to get started:

```
#include <stdio.h>

int main (int argc, const char * argv[]) {
    printf("Why me? Why C?");
    return 0;
}
```

The first line in this snippet is called a *preprocessor directive:*

```
#include <stdio.h>
```

The preprocessor, which is explained in more detail later in the chapter, is a program that passes over the source code, modifying it, before the compiler is called to turn the program into binary *machine code* that the computer can run. This particular line tells the preprocessor to replace the directive with all the text from the file stdio.h. The file stdio.h is part of the standard C library, and the preprocessor automatically knows where to find it. This type of file is known as a *header file*, and it contains definitions that can be used in C programs. Header files are an important part of C, and you generally need to write many of them to define the functions and data structures in your programs.

The main function itself begins on the next line:

```
int main (int argc, const char * argv[]) {
```

The word int at the beginning of the line is known as the *return type*. It is the type of number that the main function returns to the environment in which it was started. For a main function, the return type is a whole number or *integer*, which is written as int in C. Returning a value of zero from the main function indicates that the run was successful, and any non-zero value indicates an error occurred.

Returning 0 to indicate success may seem odd if you have worked with other programming languages. This oddity also carries over into Unix, which is based on C; Unix commands also return 0 to indicate success, with a non-zero value returned if an error arises.

The main function is listed next to int, followed by a block of code in parentheses. This block of code is known as the *parameter list*. The main function can be passed a number of character strings by the environment that runs it. For example, if a program is started on the command line, a number of file names or some options that control the program's behavior could be passed to the main function. The parameter list contains *parameters*, in this case argc and argv. Parameters in turn are *variables*, which are entities in which you can store values. In this case, argc has the type int, which means it is an integer. Its value is the number of strings being passed to the main function. argv holds the character strings themselves. The type of argv is quite involved, so we leave that discussion for later in the section "Characters and Strings."

The *body* of the main function is included between braces (that is, {...}), and looks like this:

```
printf("Why me? Why C?");
return 0;
```

The first of these two lines is a *function call*. A *function* is a separate unit of code that you can jump to in order to carry out some task, before returning to the original point in the code. A function is not unlike the main function itself: it has a number of parameters, executes a block of source code, and returns a value. The function in this case is called printf, and its definition is in the header file stdio.h included earlier. This is a popular C function that prints a character string to the program's output. In this case, the text Why me? Why C? should appear in the output of the program when it is run.

The final line of the main function just returns the integer number 0. As explained earlier, this indicates to the environment running the program that it succeeded. The return statement is used to return values and exit the main function immediately.

Note that each of the lines of code in the example main function end in a semicolon. C does not assume a line has ended until it sees a semicolon, whether a return has been inserted or not. So this code is equivalent to the return statement used above:

```
return
   0;
```

C makes no distinction between the two. Note that unlike some other languages, you do not need any character to indicate that a line continues. C takes the opposite approach — you need a character to indicate a line has ended.

In the next Try It Out, you compile your first C program with Xcode and run it. The program in question is an old favorite: Hello World. Xcode inserts a Hello World program whenever it creates a new C project.

Try It Out   Compiling and Running a C Program with Xcode

1.   Create a new Standard Tool project with Xcode. You can find Standard Tool in the New Project panel under Command Line Utility. Call the project MyFirstMain.

2.   In the Groups & Files view on the left, open the Source group, and click main.c so you can view its source in the editor. You will need to drag the split in the view on the right to see the editor under the details table.

3. You should already see the following code, which is inserted by Xcode:

```
#include <stdio.h>

int main (int argc, const char * argv[]) {
    // insert code here...
    printf("Hello, World!\n");
    return 0;
}
```

4. Compile and run this program by clicking the Build and Go toolbar item. The Run Log window (shown in Figure 6-1) should appear.

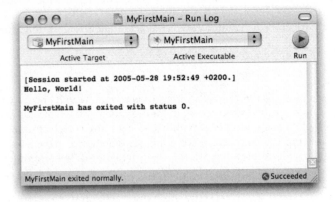

Figure 6-1

How It Works

This is an example of the infamous Hello World program that is the bane of every beginning programmer, whatever the language they are learning. It simply prints out "Hello, World!" when it is run, as you will have seen, we hope, in the Run Log, and you can also see it in Figure 6-1. The greeting can be found between the session start time and exit status.

> *Apple, with its uncanny knack for the fine details, has apparently spent more effort on punctuation than most in its Hello World program.*

The details of this example are very similar to the main function discussed earlier. This main function also uses the definitions provided in the header file stdio.h, and in particular, the function printf. The main function generated by Xcode includes a *comment line*, not present in the earlier example. The comment line looks like this:

```
// insert code here...
```

A *comment* is a message to the programmer, which is ignored by the compiler. The double forward slashes tell the compiler to ignore any text that appears up to the end of the line (that is, next return character). The comment is telling you that the code given is disposable, and can be replaced by your own, which hopefully does something more useful than printing out "Hello, World!".

Apart from the text destined for display, the `printf` statement includes two extra characters that you may have found perplexing: `\n`. These two characters together in a C string indicate that a new line character should be inserted. C does not insert new line characters automatically after printing a string; you have control over where and when new lines appear in the output.

Variables and Data Types

The `main` functions in the previous sections demonstrate that even the simplest of C programs include operations on data, even if it is just writing it to the program output. Any non-trivial program needs to be able to represent different types of data, and reference it in a way that a programmer can understand. C has many built in data types, including integer, decimal, and character types. To store and reference data, C has *variables*, which are labels applied to pieces of data.

You should already recognize the fundamental integer type of C: `int`. It appeared in the previous sections as the type of the variable `argc`. An `int` is a whole number that can be positive, negative, or zero. There are also other variations on the integer, including integers that cannot take negative values (`unsigned int`), integers that take up less space but have a more restricted range of values (`short int`), and integers that take up more space but can take a wider range of values (`long int`). The following table provides the most important integer types in C.

Integer Type	Minimum Value	Maximum Value	Size in Bytes
int	-2147483648	2147483647	4
short int	-32768	32767	2
long int	-2147483648	2147483647	4
unsigned int	0	4294967295	4

There are other variations on these types, but these are by far the most important and the ones you will encounter the most.

Now that you know what integer types are available, it would be nice to know how you use them. You can create integer *literals* in your code, which are values inserted directly, but you can also create integer variables, which can be used to store integers, and can change value while the program is running. Here is a piece of code to demonstrate some of the things you can do with integers:

```c
#include <stdio.h>

int main( int argc, const char * argv[] ) {
    int var1;
    int var2, var3 = 5;
    var1 = 10;

    var2 = var1 * var3;
    printf("var2 is %d\n", var2);  // Should be 50

    unsigned int var4 = 4294967295;
```

```
        printf("var4 is %u\n", var4);  // Should be 4294967295

        var4 = var4 + 1;
        printf("var4 is %u\n", var4);  // Should be 0

        return 0;
}
```

There is quite a lot happening in this code, so we will take it one step at a time, beginning with the variables at the start of the `main` function:

```
int var1;
int var2, var3 = 5;
var1 = 10;
```

The first two lines are *declarations*: they declare the type of a variable. In this case, the variables `var1`, `var2`, and `var3` are all of the `int` type. `var3` is not only declared, it is also initialized to the value 5, and so 5 will be put in the memory associated with `var3` when it is created. You can also see from the declaration of `var2` and `var3` that multiple variables of the same type can be declared on the same line if commas separate them.

> You may be wondering if the variable names chosen have any significance. The answer is no. They can be just about anything you like, with a few limitations: Variable names can contain only the alphanumeric characters and the underscore character, and variable names cannot begin with a number. Other than that, you are free to choose any variable names you like, but try to make them understandable so that others reading your code can follow it more easily.

The next two lines perform an arithmetic operation on the variables, and print the value of `var2`:

```
var2 = var1 * var3;
printf("var2 is %d\n", var2);  // Should be 50
```

`var2` is first set to the value of `var1` multiplied by `var3`, and then the `printf` function, which you were introduced to previously, prints the value of `var2` to the program's output. The expected value is 50, or 10 by 5, as indicated in the comment.

Don't concern yourself with the form of the string passed to the `printf` function — the details are discussed later in the chapter, in the section on Input/Output (I/O).

The next lines introduce an unsigned integer variable, and demonstrate what can happen if you are not wary of the range limitations in the preceding table:

```
unsigned int var4 = 4294967295;
printf("var4 is %u\n", var4);  // Should be 4294967295

var4 = var4 + 1;
printf("var4 is %u\n", var4);  // Should be 0
```

The variable `var4` is declared and set to a very particular number. If you look to the preceding table, you will see that this is the maximum value in the range of unsigned integers. The next line prints `var4`, and the value should be as expected. However, the `var4` is then incremented by one, which takes it outside the range of allowed values for `unsigned int`. What happens? The program continues without error, but `var4` will *wrap* around to the lower limit of its range, namely zero. This behavior can be expected with all of C's numerical types, and you should be on your guard not to introduce hard-to-find bugs in this way.

The variable `var4` was declared in the middle of the `main` function, not at the beginning. Some programming languages, including C originally, require that all declarations appear at the beginning of the function in which they appear. This has recently changed in the case of C so that you are allowed to declare variables anywhere in the code.

You can't get far with integers alone, so C has a variety of decimal number types. These are referred to as *floating-point* numbers in C, because the decimal point is able to "float" to any position in the number. The following table shows the most important floating-point numbers you will encounter in C programs.

Floating-Point Type	Smallest Value	Largest Value	Size in Bytes
float	1.175494e-38	3.402823e+38	4
double	2.225074e-308	1.797693e+308	8

In this case, the largest negative number has not been presented, because it has the same magnitude as the largest value, but the smallest representable non-zero number has been given instead. Infinitely many decimal numbers exist, even between two values like 0.0 and 1.175494e-38 that are very close together. A computer can't represent any decimal number, so it uses the closest number it can find whenever a floating-point number arises that it can't represent exactly.

If you already have experience with other programming languages, you may be wondering when we are going to discuss Boolean types. A Boolean value is one that can be true or false. Actually, C didn't originally have a Boolean type. Instead, zero was treated as false, and any other number as true. This is still the common approach in C programs, though C99 did introduce a Boolean type to the language: `bool`.

Operators

In the previous examples, you could see some simple operators in use, adding and multiplying numbers and variables. C has a variety of different operators, some that you will need to use nearly every time you sit down to program, and others that you rarely see. The following table shows some of the most important arithmetic and logical operators in C.

Operator	Symbol	Description	Example
Addition	+	Adds two numbers together.	5.46 + 7.2
Subtraction	–	Subtracts second number from first.	8 – 6
Multiplication	*	Multiplies two numbers together.	7 * 19.5

Table continued on following page

Operator	Symbol	Description	Example
Division	/	Divides the first number by the second.	10 / 2
Modulus	%	Finds remainder after integer division.	11 % 2
Logical OR	||	True if one or both expressions are true.	1 || 0
Logical AND	&&	Only true if both expressions are true.	1 && 1
Not	!	True if expression is false, and vice versa.	!0
Increment	++	Increase integer variable by one.	++i
Decrement	--	Decrease integer variable by one.	--i
Addition Assignment	+=	Add LHS to RHS and assign value to LHS.	i += j
Subtraction Assignment	-=	Subtract LHS from RHS and assign LHS.	i -= j
Assignment	=	Assign variable on LHS to RHS.	i = 5
Equality	==	Test if two values are equal.	1 == 1
Inequality	!=	Test if two values are not equal.	1 != 1
Greater Than	>	Test if first value is greater than the second value.	10 > 5
Less Than	<	Test if first value is less than the second value.	10 < 5
Greater or Equal	>=	Test if first value is greater than or equal to the second value.	10 >= 5
Less or Equal	<=	Test if first value is less than or equal to the second value.	15 <= 19

LHS = Left Hand Side

RHS = Right Hand Side

The table begins with the usual suspects of arithmetic operators. These behave pretty much as you would expect. The only one to be wary of is the division operator. If you divide an integer number by another integer number, the result is always an integer, whether the numbers divide exactly or not. For example, in the following expression the variable var ends up taking the value 2, not 2.2:

```
int var = 11 / 5;
```

Even in this case the variable will be 2.0, rather than 2.2:

```
float var = 11 / 5;
```

Integer division can lead to some very interesting bugs if you are not careful. A general rule of thumb for avoiding integer division is to make sure that when you want the correct floating-point number to come out of a division of two numbers, one of them has to be a floating-point number. Here are some ways you can ensure that:

```
float var1 = 11 / 5;      // No good! We want var1 to be 2.2, not 2.0
float var2 = 11.0 / 5;    // Fine. Now var2 is 2.2

float var3 = 11;
float var4 = var3 / 5;    // Again fine. var3 is a float, so float division is used.
```

If you are now cursing C for having ever being invented, note that sometimes you may actually want the result of an integer division. And furthermore, you may want the remainder left after the division. You can use the modulus operator in such instances:

```
int anInt = 5;
int divInt = anInt / 2;   // divInt will become 2
int modInt = anInt % 2;   // modInt will become 1
```

In this example, integer division is used to get the whole number of times that 2 goes into anInt, and the modulus gets the leftover. You could use the modInt value to test whether anInt is odd or even, for example.

Logical operators appear next in the table. These are most commonly used in tests. For example, in the following code, a number is tested to see if it is outside a given range:

```
if ( x < 0 || x > 5 ) printf("x is outside the range 0 to 5 inclusive.");
if ( x < 0 && x > 5 ) printf("Wrong! x can't be in two places at once.");
if ( x < 0 && !(x < -5) ) printf("x is -5, -4, -3, -2, or -1");
if ( x < 0 && x >= -5 ) printf("x is -5, -4, -3, -2, or -1 (again)";
```

The if statement, which tests an expression and carries out the corresponding action in the case of a true (non-zero) result, has been introduced here. The if statement is discussed in detail later in this chapter, but here it shows typical uses of logical operators. Each test compares the integer variable x with integer constants, like 0 and 5, to see if the variable is in a given range. The first test, for example, checks if x is less than 0, or greater than 5. If it is, a message is printed to indicate that x falls outside the range 0 to 5 inclusive.

The third if statement demonstrates the NOT operator. The test is whether x is less than 0 and not less than –5. In other words, this tests if x is greater than or equal to –5, and less than 0, as indicated by the very next test. Note the brackets used with the NOT operator: these ensure that the expression x < -5 is evaluated before the NOT operator is applied. If you don't do this, you could get some very unexpected results. For example, if x is equal to 6, then x < -5 should be false, so ! (x < -5) will be true. But !x < -5 will be false! That's because the NOT operator has *precedence* over the less-than operator, so the expression will be evaluated like this: !x is evaluated first, and has the value 0 (false), because x is 6, which corresponds to true. So now the comparison is 0 < -5, which is false.

> *You need to be careful to consider operator precedence in your expressions, and use parentheses to enforce your will whenever in doubt. Precedence of operators is discussed later in this section.*

C has various operators for changing the value of a variable. The increment operator, ++, is used to increase an integer by 1. The decrement operator, --, reduces an integer by 1. Any of the basic arithmetic operators can also be combined with an equals sign to produce an operator that first evaluates the right-hand side (RHS) of the expression, performs an operation between the left and right sides, and lastly, assigns the result to the variable on the left. Here are some examples of these types of operators:

```
int i = 5;
i++;        // i is now 6
i--;        // i is 5 again
i += 1;     // i is now 6
i *= 2;     // i is now 12, i.e., 6 * 2

int j = 2;
i -= j + 1;  // i is 9
```

The last two statements demonstrate clearly how these operators work. In the last expression, i is set to be the value of itself minus the RHS. The following would be exactly equivalent:

```
i = i - (j + 1);
```

This is actually a good way to remember how these operators work. Simply imagine an expression using the assignment operator, =, in which the LHS also appears at the beginning of the RHS.

The remaining operators are fairly self-explanatory. There are the usual comparison operators, such as greater than, less than, greater than or equal, and less than or equal. The equality operator is ==, which you should be careful not to confuse with the assignment operator =. The following is a common bug made by beginning C programmers:

```
int a = 1, b = 2;
if ( a = b ) printf("a was equal to b");
```

If you think this code will not print anything, think again. The expression a = b assigns a to b. In other words, it sets a to the value of b, which is 2. The if statement tests the value of a after the assignment, which is non-zero, so the result of the test is considered to be true, and the printf statement is performed, printing the text.

One thing you may be wondering is the order in which operators are evaluated in C, or the *operator precedence*. Following is a table that gives the operators in order of precedence. Operators appearing in a given row have the same precedence, with the level of precedence decreasing down the table. Expressions are evaluated in order from the operator of highest precedence to that of lowest precedence. To override operator precedence, you can always turn to parentheses, the contents of which are evaluated before any operators.

Operator Precedence

! ++ --
* / %
+ -
< <= >= >
== !=
&&
||
= += -=

Now that you know about simple data types and operators, it's time to move on to more advanced data types. In the next section, you learn about arrays and closely related types known as pointers, which enable you to store multiple data values in a single variable.

Arrays and Pointers

Integers and floating-point variables are useful to be sure, but what do you do if you need to represent lots of numbers of the same type? Coming up with unique variable names for each one could be quite tiresome. Take the following code, for example:

```
int var0 = 1;
int var1 = 5;
int var2 = 3;
int var3 = 2;
...
int var9 = 7;
```

If you had to make up variable names to represent a thousand values like this, you would soon lose any interest you might have had in writing C programs.

Luckily, C provides *array variables*, which are variables containing many values of the same data type. If you consider the preceding code, you will notice that each variable name starts with var and has a number appended to make it unique. Arrays work the same way, except the number, or *index*, is not part of the variable's name. Here is an example similar to the preceding code, but using an array instead of multiple simple variables:

```
int var[10];
var[0] = 1;
var[1] = 5;
var[2] = 3;
var[3] = 2;
...
var[9] = 7;
```

The array variable var contains 10 integers. You can see that from the way it has been declared: the number 10 in square brackets is the size of the array. The indexes are used to access the *elements* of the array range between 0 and 9, and appear in the square brackets directly after the variable name. Array indexes in C always begin at 0; this differs from some other programming languages that begin counting at 1.

> *If the preceding examples have you wondering what the advantage of using arrays is over lots of different variables, you will have to wait until we get to the section on loops to find out. The advantage may not be evident looking at the examples so far, where each array element has been assigned on a separate line of code, but it will become clearer when you have a means of moving through the elements of an array without explicitly referring to each one individually.*

If you don't explicitly set the value of an array element, its value is undefined. It could have any value, and you shouldn't try to access its value until you have *initialized* it. There is a shorthand way of initializing an array that can save you typing in the same variable name over and over. When you declare the array, you can set its contents, like so:

```
int var[10] = {1,5,3,2,2,3,4,5,6,7};
```

The numbers in the braces on the right are used to initialize the contents of the array var. Actually, the size of the array is even optional in this case, because the compiler can see how long the array should be from the number of entries used to initialize the array, so the following is also legal:

```
int var[] = {1,5,3,2,2,3,4,5,6,7};
```

You still need to include the square brackets to indicate that the variable is an array, but you do not need to enter the size of the array explicitly.

An array is stored as a block of *contiguous* memory, meaning here are no gaps in the data. The computer stores the numbers together, with var[1] just before var[2], which is just before var[3], and so forth. The C compiler calculates where a particular array element is by calculating how far it is *offset* from the beginning of the array. So the array is stored as the memory address of var[0], and whenever another element of the array is accessed, the compiler simply calculates how far it is from var[0], giving its address in memory. For example, var[2] is two steps from var[0], so it must be stored two memory addresses after the address of var[0].

In C, a variable that holds a memory address is known as a *pointer*. You can create pointers explicitly in your programs, and retrieve the pointer of any variable. You can also perform *pointer arithmetic*, calculating new pointers from existing ones. Here is some code to demonstrate basic properties of pointers:

```
int *p;
int a = 5;
p = &a;
printf("%d\n", *p);  // This should print 5

*p = 2;
printf("%d\n", a);  // This should print 2
```

A pointer is declared whenever an asterisk appears before the variable's name. In the preceding code, int *p; declares a pointer variable called p. This pointer points to the address in memory of an int. The value of p was not initialized, so you don't know what it is pointing to in the beginning, and you shouldn't use it until it has been assigned.

After declaring and initializing an int variable called a, on the next line the pointer is assigned to the address of a, like this

```
p = &a;
```

The operator & is called the *address-of operator*. It gives the memory address of the variable it precedes, in this case a. This address has been assigned to the pointer p, so p points to a.

The value pointed to by p is printed next:

```
printf("%d\n", *p);
```

It is important to recognize the distinction between the pointer's value, which is an address in memory, and the value it points to, which is an int in this case. To access the pointer's value, you simply use the pointer variable, like when the pointer was assigned to the address of a. When you want to access the value pointed to by the pointer, you need to *dereference* it by inserting an asterisk immediately in front of the pointer variable. This asterisk tells the compiler to use the value that the pointer points to, rather than the memory address stored in the pointer. Because p points to a's address, the value of a is printed, namely 5.

> When you are first learning C, it is easy to confuse dereferencing a pointer with declaring a pointer because both use the asterisk character in the same way. You should try to make this distinction in your head early on: inserting an asterisk when declaring a variable indicates that the variable is a pointer to the type, and inserting an asterisk in other parts of the code indicates that the value pointed to by the pointer will be used, not the memory address stored in the pointer.

Pointer dereferencing is demonstrated further on the next line of code:

```
*p = 2;
```

In this case, the value pointed to by p is set to 2. Since p points to the same memory as a, this will also change the value of a. When a is printed on the last line, the output should show 2 instead of the initial value of 5.

How big is a pointer variable? The answer depends on the type of computer and operating system you are using. In Mac OS X Panther and earlier operating systems, the size of a pointer was 32 bits or 4 bytes. You may have heard that Mac OS X Panther was a 32-bit Operating System; this refers to the size of the pointers used to store memory addresses. Mac OS X "Tiger" has support for both 32-bit and 64-bit pointers, which makes it possible for an application to address much more memory. This is the reason Tiger is referred to as a 64-bit Operating System.

Pointers and arrays are closely related in C, as you may have gathered from the preceding discussion. An array is represented internally as a pointer to some memory, and in C programming, it is quite common to use the two interchangeably, as this example shows:

```
int a[3];
*a = 2;       // Sets a[0]
*(a+1) = 5;   // Sets a[1]
*(a+2) = 10;  // Sets a[2]

int *p;
p = &a[1];
printf("%d\n", *p);      // Should print a[1], which is 5
printf("%d\n", *(p-1));  // Should print a[1-1], which is a[0], which is 2
```

An array a has been declared, but its contents have been set as if a were a pointer. That's because in C an array and a pointer are equivalent. Take the first assignment:

```
*a = 2;
```

This sets the value pointed to by an int pointer to 2. The variable a points to the first element of the array — the element at index 0 — so setting *a sets the first element of a.

The next two lines are a little more involved:

```
*(a+1) = 5;   // Sets a[1]
*(a+2) = 10;  // Sets a[2]
```

You can do arithmetic with pointers, just like you can with integers. When you add an integer to a pointer, the result is a new pointer offset from the original by the amount added. Adding 1 to an int pointer results in the memory address of the next int in memory. Adding 2 results in a memory address that is 2 integers further in memory. In the example, *(a+1) is equivalent to a[0+1], which is a[1], so the value of a[1] is set to 5. The same logic can be applied to the line for *(a+2).

The last block of code in the example introduces a new pointer, p, which is set to the address of array element a[1], like this:

```
p = &a[1];
```

The right-hand side of this expression uses the address-of operator, &. It takes the address of the array element a[1], which means p is assigned the address of a[1]. You could also write the equivalent expression:

```
p = a+1;
```

Hopefully the examples of pointer arithmetic have taught you enough to realize that these two expressions achieve the same end result.

The last two lines of the example print the value pointed to by p, and the int in the memory address preceding p. The latter is given by the expression *(p-1). This pointer arithmetic demonstrates that you aren't restricted to merely adding offsets to pointers, but can also subtract them. You can even use operators such as ++ and -- with pointers, as well as += and -=.

In the following Try It Out, you write a program to test your knowledge of pointer arithmetic. The program asks you questions about pointers used to access data stored in an array, and you enter the answers in the console. When you are finished, a score is printed to tell you how many you got right.

Try It Out   Working with Pointers

1. Create a new Standard Tool project with Xcode and name it Pointy.

2. Open the main function in the editor by opening the Source group in the Groups & Files view and clicking the main.c file. You may need to drag the split view on the right in order to see the editor.

3. Replace the default code provided by Xcode with the following in main.c:

```
#include <stdio.h>

/* Pointy is a program to test your pointer arithmetic.
   The user is asked to answer questions about the value pointed
   to by an integer pointer. */
int main (int argc, const char * argv[]) {

    printf("Pointy: A program to test your pointer arithmetic\n");

    int intArray[] = {10,20,30,40,50};
    printf("The variable intArray holds these values: %d %d %d %d %d\n",
        intArray[0], intArray[1], intArray[2], intArray[3], intArray[4] );

    int answer;
```

```
    int score = 0;

    // Question 1
    int *p;
    p = intArray + 3;
    printf("p is set to 'intArray + 3'. What is the value of *p? ");
    scanf("%d", &answer);
    if ( answer == *p ) {
        ++score;
        printf("Very good!\n");
    }
    else {
        printf("No, the answer is %d\n", *p);
    }

    // Question 2
    ++p;
    printf("After applying ++p, what is the value of *p? ");
    scanf("%d", &answer);
    if ( answer == *p ) {
        ++score;
        printf("Very good!\n");
    }
    else {
        printf("No, the answer is %d\n", *p);
    }

    // Question 3
    p = &intArray[4] - 1;
    printf("p is set to &a[4] - 1. What is the value of *p? ");
    scanf("%d", &answer);
    if ( answer == *p ) {
        ++score;
        printf("Very good!\n");
    }
    else {
        printf("No, the answer is %d\n", *p);
    }

    printf("You got %d out of 3.\n", score);

    return 0;
}
```

4. Build and run the program by clicking the Build and Go toolbar item.

5. You should see the Run Log appear, with some introductory text and a question. Type the answer to the question, and the questions that follow, into the Run Log console. Be sure only to enter integer values in response to the questions, or the program may behave unexpectedly.

6. You should be told after each question whether you have the answer correct, and at the end you will be told your score. Keep rerunning the program by pressing the Run button in the Run Log window until you get all questions right.

How It Works

The code for this example may seem complex at first, but it is very repetitive. It begins by initializing some data, and then asks three questions. The source code for each question is virtually identical, so only the code used to ask the first question is discussed.

Duplication of code that is the same or almost the same throughout your program is a bad idea, because when you need to change something, you need to track down all of the different pieces of copied code and change those as well. This is a big waste of time and effort, and can introduce bugs. A better way is to write the code once in a function, and call the function at each point that you need to execute the code. Functions are introduced and discussed later in the chapter.

Before the main function even starts, there is some introductory text in the form of a comment for the programmer. You have already seen single line comments, which begin with a // and continue to the end of the line, but in this case the multiple line variety is used. Multiple line comments can be one or more lines long, begin with the symbols /*, and end with */. Anything in between is completely ignored by the compiler.

After printing an introductory message, the main function begins like this:

```
int intArray[] = {10,20,30,40,50};
printf("The variable intArray holds these values: %d %d %d %d %d\n",
    intArray[0], intArray[1], intArray[2], intArray[3], intArray[4] );

int answer;
int score = 0;
```

This initializes the variable intArray to be an array of integers, with five entries. The printf statement writes the values in the array to output, so that the user can see what is in the array, and is able to answer the questions. Two other variables are also declared, answer and score. score, which will be used to count how many questions are answered correctly, is initialized to 0. The answer variable is used to store the answers typed in by the user.

The code for the first question looks like this:

```
// Question 1
int *p;
p = intArray + 3;
printf("p is set to 'intArray + 3'. What is the value of *p? ");
scanf("%d", &answer);
if ( answer == *p ) {
    ++score;
    printf("Very good!\n");
}
else {
    printf("No, the answer is %d\n", *p);
}
```

A new pointer variable p is declared, and set to be intArray+3. A printf statement then prompts the user to enter the answer to a question about *p, the value pointed to by p.

A second function, scanf is used to read what the user types. scanf is also from the header file stdio.h, and reads anything entered on *standard input*, which in this case is what the user types on the keyboard. Do not concern yourself too much with the call to scanf; it simply expects to read an integer from input, and puts the value of the integer read into the int variable answer. You will learn more about scanf in the section on Input/Output later in this chapter.

Another new construction is introduced on the next lines: the if/else statement. You have already seen if statements, and this is simply a variation on the theme. If the value in round parentheses evaluates to a non-zero number, it is considered to be true, and the code in the braces following the if is evaluated. If the expression in the parentheses is zero, it is considered false, and the code in the braces after the else statement is evaluated instead. The if/else construction is described in detail later in the chapter.

In the preceding example, the value entered by the user, which is stored in the variable answer, is compared for equality with the value pointed to by p. If it is the same, the user was right, so the score variable is incremented and a congratulatory message is printed. If the user was wrong, the correct answer is printed, and the score variable is left unchanged.

After all questions have been answered, the program writes the user's score and stops.

Conditional Branching

In the previous section, you became acquainted with *conditional branching*, whether you realized it or not. *Branching* occurs in a program when execution can jump to different parts of the code depending on the situation. The term branching refers to the way that program execution can follow different paths, like a monkey climbing a tree, or someone rowing up a river. In the case of the if/else construction, the program chooses between jumping to the block of code just after the if statement, or to the block of code after the else statement. The path followed depends on whether the condition in parentheses is true or false. This explains the "conditional" in "conditional branching": the branch followed depends on whether a condition is true or false.

Consider the following if/else construct:

```
if ( everestIsHigh ) {
    printf("Everest is apparently a high mountain");
}
else {
    printf("Which world do you originate from?");
}
```

This is the same form of if/else used in the previous example. If the value in parentheses, everestIsHigh, evaluates to a non-zero value, the code in the if block will be evaluated; otherwise, the code in the else block is evaluated. Each code block is enclosed in braces, and may consist of zero or more statements. The placement of the braces is entirely at your discretion, because C ignores extra white space, including new lines. The following rewriting of the example is also perfectly legal, but not advisable:

```
if ( everestIsHigh ) { printf("Everest is apparently a high mountain"); } else
{
    printf("Which world do you originate from?"); }
```

Common conventions for brace placement include putting the opening brace at the end of a line, and the end brace alone on a line, like the first example in the preceding text, and putting each brace on a separate line, like this:

```
if ( everestIsHigh )
{
    printf("Everest is apparently a high mountain");
}
else
{
    printf("Which world do you originate from?");
}
```

You may also see this variation:

```
if ( everestIsHigh )
    {
    printf("Everest is apparently a high mountain");
    }
else
    {
    printf("Which world do you originate from?");
    }
```

The point is that all of these variations are legal in C. It is up to you to choose a style that makes your code legible for yourself and other programmers that may need to read your code.

If you have only a single statement in a code block, it is even possible to leave out the braces altogether:

```
if ( everestIsHigh )
    printf("Everest is apparently a high mountain");
else
    printf("Which world do you originate from?");
```

In practice this can be a risky exercise, because if you ever need to add an extra statement to one or other of the code blocks, chances are you will forget to add the braces. Take a look at this code, for example:

```
if ( everestIsHigh )
    printf("Everest is apparently a high mountain");
else
    printf("Which world do you originate from?");
    ++i;
```

This code is equivalent to the following:

```
if ( everestIsHigh ) {
    printf("Everest is apparently a high mountain");
}
else {
    printf("Which world do you originate from?");
}
++i;
```

However, it is not equivalent to this code, as you may have thought:

```
int everestIsHigh = 1;
if ( everestIsHigh ) {
    printf("Everest is apparently a high mountain");
```

```
    }
    else {
        printf("Which world do you originate from?");
        ++i;
    }
```

It is reasonable, however, to leave out the braces when you use a solitary `if`, without an `else` branch, as shown in the following:

```
    if ( everestIsHigh ) ++highMountainCount;
```

You have already seen this form of `if` in many of the examples. It is fairly safe to use, because you are unlikely to accidentally forget to add braces when you add a new statement to the `if` block.

Often you don't have only two different branches to choose from, but rather you have a whole range of choices. You can use `if/else if/else` constructions in such cases:

```
    float mountainHeight = 6000.0; // Height in feet
    if ( mountainHeight > 15000.0 ) {
        printf("A monster!");
    }
    else if ( mountainHeight > 10000.0 ) {
        printf("I've seen bigger.");
    }
    else if ( mountainHeight > 5000.0 ) {
        printf("You call that a mountain!");
    }
    else {
        printf("Mountain? Or molehill?");
    }
```

The `if/else if/else` construct is basically a number of `if` statements chained together, with an optional `else` at the end. The code following the first condition that evaluates to true is used, and all other code is skipped. In the example, the `mountainHeight` variable is tested to see if it is greater than `15000.0` feet. If so, `A monster!` is printed, and execution continues after the last `else` branch—all other branches are ignored. If the first test fails, the condition of the first `else if` is tested. If that is true, `I've seen bigger.` is printed and execution jumps to after the `else`, and so on. If none of the `else if` conditions evaluate to true, the code in the `else` block is performed.

C includes another conditional branching construction for choosing between discrete integer values: `switch/case`. The `if/else if/else` construction is general, and can be used whenever you have multiple branches. The `switch/case` construction is less general, but a bit more compact, and can help improve the legibility of your programs. Here is an example of `switch/case`:

```
    int age = 3;
    switch (age) {
        case 0:
            printf("Newborn\n");
            break;
        case 1:
            printf("Baby\n");
            break;
        case 2:
```

```
    case 3:
        printf("Toddler\n");
        break;
    case 4:
        printf("Pre-schooler\n");
        break;
    case 5:
        printf("School Kid\n");
        break;
    default:
        printf("That ain't no kid!\n");
}
```

`switch` is used to branch based on the value of an integer variable. In the preceding example, the age of a child is represented as an integer. The `switch` statement tests the value of `age` against each `case` in order. The `case` statement includes a single integer value, followed by a colon. If the integer in the `case` equals the value of the variable in the `switch`, the code under the `case` is executed.

Despite what you might expect, once a `case` has been matched, all of the code below that `case` is executed up until a `break` statement is encountered, even if some or all of that code appears under a different `case`. `switch/case` is different from `if/else if/else` in this sense, because after an `if` or `else if` block has been evaluated, execution automatically jumps to the end. With `switch/case`, you are responsible for making sure that the program jumps to the end when it should. You do this with the `break` keyword.

In the preceding example, `case 2:` appears immediately in front of `case 3:`, and includes no code of its own. If the child is two years old, execution continues from the `case 2:` branch to the `case 3:` branch, where `Toddler\n` gets printed. Only after the `break` statement does execution jump to the end of the `switch`. The other `cases` each have a single call to `printf`, followed by a `break`. The optional `default` block is equivalent to `else`: it gets executed if no other case matches.

The last conditional branching construction discussed here is actually an operator: a *ternary* operator. It is ternary because it has three parts. You can use the ternary operator as a shorthand way of choosing one value or another based on the value of a condition. Here it is in action:

```
// Ice cream id's
const int CHOCOLATE = 0;
const int STRAWBERRY = 1;

// People id's
const int MOM = 0;
const int DAD = 1;

// Set person
int person = DAD;

// Dad's favorite is Chocy
int favorite;
favorite = ( person == DAD ? CHOCOLATE : STRAWBERRY );
```

The ternary operator appears at the end of this example:

```
person == DAD ? CHOCOLATE : STRAWBERRY
```

The ternary operator consists of a condition — in this case the comparison between the variable `person` and the constant `DAD` — followed by a question mark, and then two expressions separated by a colon. The ternary operator is used here to set the value of the variable `favorite`, according to the value of `person`. If `person` is equal to `DAD`, `favorite` is set to the value of `CHOCOLATE`, and otherwise it is set to `STRAWBERRY`.

It is a good idea to enclose the ternary operator in parentheses when it is used in expressions like the one above, because they help avoid surprises that can arise due to operator precedence.

The ternary operator's condition appears before the question mark. If the condition evaluates to a non-zero value, it is considered true, and the value of the expression before the colon is evaluated and returned. If the condition evaluates to zero (that is, false), the value of the expression after the colon is used.

To clarify matters, the statement containing the ternary operator in the preceding code is equivalent to the following more verbose `if/else` construct:

```
if ( person == DAD ) {
    favorite = CHOCOLATE;
}
else {
    favorite = STRAWBERRY;
}
```

The ternary operator can be useful for writing more compact code, when there are only two branches and branching is being used to set a variable or to evaluate part of a larger expression, as in the following:

```
const int FEET = 0;
const int INCHES = 1;
float height = 6.0;
int units = FEET;
float heightInInches = ( units == FEET ? 12 : 1 ) * height;
```

In this example, the ternary operator has been embedded in a larger expression, rather than being used to set a variable directly. The value of the variable `units` is compared with the value of the variable `FEET`. If the value of `units` is in feet, the ternary operator evaluates to 12; otherwise, it is 1. The operator thus chooses the conversion factor for multiplying by the height. If the `units` are already inches, the conversion factor is 1, but if the `height` variable is in feet, it is multiplied by 12 to convert the value into inches.

You may have noticed the keyword `const` used in the preceding examples. It is not strictly necessary, but it can help prevent bugs. `const` tells the compiler that the value of a variable may not change after it has been initialized. If you try to change the value of a `const`, you will get an error from the compiler.

Constant variables are often given names that are all capitalized. This is a convention to make code more readable, but is not a requirement of the C language itself.

Loops

If there is one thing that computers are good at, it is repetitive tasks. C has various constructs for repeating a block of code, which is known as *looping*. Looping is also a form of branching because at the end of a loop, execution can either continue or return to the beginning of the loop.

The simplest form of loop in C is the `while` loop. `while` keeps looping until a condition is no longer true. The condition is tested whenever execution returns to the beginning of the loop after each *iteration*. A `while` loop takes this form:

```
while ( condition ) {
    ...
}
```

The order of events in a `while` loop goes as follows: When the `while` is encountered, the condition in parentheses is tested. If it is true, the block of code between the braces after the `while` is executed, and execution jumps from the closing brace back to the `while` statement, where the condition is tested again. This continues until the condition evaluates to zero (false), at which point execution jumps to immediately after the last brace and continues.

Here is a concrete example of a `while` loop:

```
int i = 0;
while ( i < 2 ) {
    printf("%d\n", i);
    ++i;
}
```

The execution of this example code proceeds as follows:

1. When the `while` is first encountered, i is equal to 0, which is less than 2, so execution jumps to the code in the braces.

2. The `printf` statement is executed, printing 0 to standard output.

3. i is then incremented to 1.

4. At the closing brace, execution jumps back to the `while`, and again performs the test. Since i is 1, and this is still less than 2, the code in the braces is executed again.

5. After execution has jumped back to the `while` again, i is equal to 2. Since 2 is not less than 2, the condition is not met, so the program jumps to the last brace, and continues with the rest of the program. The code between the braces is not performed in this case.

A disadvantage of `while` loops is that if you are not careful, you can end up in an *infinite loop*. This arises when the condition in the `while` statement never evaluates to false, and no other provision for escaping the loop is made. Here is about the simplest infinite loop you can think of:

```
while (1) {
}
```

If you run this code, and wait for it to end, you could be waiting a while (pardon the pun). Since 1 never equates to 0, the loop will never finish — it will be infinite.

> *This concept is so important to computing, that Apple named its campus driveway after it. The street address of the Apple campus is 1 Infinite Loop.*

Nevertheless, you will occasionally see a `while` loop with condition equal to 1. Does that mean such loops will never end? Not necessarily, because you can *break out* of a loop in other ways. The C command break, which you encountered in the context of switch/case statements, can also be used to escape a while loop, like this:

```
int i = 0;
while (1) {
    if ( i >= 5 ) break;
    printf("%d\n", i);
    ++i;
}
```

This code is actually equivalent to the first while loop example given previously. It will loop until i is greater than or equal to 5, at which point the if condition will evaluate to true, and the break will be performed. Execution then jumps immediately to the closing brace, and continues.

> break **is not only useful for** switch **and** while **statements; it can actually be used anytime you want to escape a block of code enclosed in braces. Execution is immediately transferred to the closing brace, and continues from there.**

Another common loop in C programming is the for loop. In theory, you can do everything a for loop can do with a while loop, but the for loop is often easier to read and understand. The structure of a for loop is a little more complex, but after you get used to it, it is straightforward enough. It takes the following form:

```
for ( initialization; condition; update ) {
    ...
}
```

As you can see, the for loop has parentheses just like the while loop, but it expects more than just a single condition. Three entries are required, separated by semicolons. The first is an initialization statement, which is performed only once at the beginning. The second is a condition for whether the loop should continue, just like the while loop has. The last are statements that are executed at the beginning of each new iteration, which are usually used to update indexing variables.

A for loop typically looks something like this:

```
int i;
for ( i = 0; i < 2; ++i ) {
    printf("%d\n", i);
}
```

This code performs the same operations as the first example of while shown previously. The program flow goes like this:

1. When the for loop is first encountered, the initialization block is executed, setting i to 0.

2. The condition is then checked, and since i is less than 2, the code in the braces is executed.

3. The printf statement prints the value of i, which is 0, to standard output.

4. Control jumps from the closing brace back to the for statement. The update statement is executed first, incrementing i to 1.

5. Next the condition is tested. Because i is still less than 2, the code in braces is executed again, and 1 is printed.

6. When the for statement is encountered for the third time, the update operation increments i to 2. Then the condition is checked, but this time it is false, so control jumps immediately to the closing brace without performing the printf, and continues with the rest of the program.

for loops are most commonly used to perform operations on arrays. Here is an example of adding the elements of two arrays, and storing the result in a third:

```
int array1[] = {1,2,3,4,5};
int array2[] = {2,3,4,5,6};
int array3[5];

int i;
for ( i = 0; i < 5; ++i ) {
    array3[i] = array1[i] + array2[i];
}

for ( i = 0; i < 5; ++i ) printf("%d ", array3[i]);
printf("\n");
```

Arrays array1 and array2 are initialized to each hold five elements. The array array3 is given a size, but its elements are not initialized. The for loop loops over i values from 0 to 4 inclusive, executing the summation in braces, which sets the elements of array3 to the sum of the corresponding elements of array1 and array2. The last for loop prints the values of array3 one after the other, separated by a space. The last printf adds a new line character to the end.

> *The for loop responsible for printing array3 did not include any braces. In this case it was not necessary, because there was only one statement to be performed. This is a general aspect of C.*

You should take careful notice of the form of the for loops used in the preceding code, because it is very common. Whenever you need to iterate over the elements of an array, you generally use a for statement with these three characteristics:

❑ An index variable is initialized to 0.

❑ The condition expression requires the index variable to be less than the array length.

❑ The index is incremented after each iteration.

This structure is summarized by the following form:

```
int i;
for ( i = 0; i < array_length; ++i ) {
    ...
}
```

If you stick to this formula for iterating array elements, you should rarely go astray.

> `for` loops often lead to what are called off-by-one or fence-post bugs, particularly for beginner programmers. An off-by-one bug arises when the loop iterates one too many or too few times, either not treating all of the array elements, or treating too many and going outside the bounds of the array. (The latter can lead to program crashes known as segmentation faults, because the segment of memory assigned to the array was exceeded.)
>
> The best way to avoid these types of bugs is to develop a convention that works, and always use that convention. The `for` loop convention shown is a good example. If you always use `i < array_length`, for example, instead of sometimes using `i <= array_length - 1`, you are much less likely to make a mistake.

In the following Try It Out, a program is developed that uses loops to perform a simple statistical analysis of some data stored in an array.

Try It Out   Statistical Analysis of Array Data

1. Create a new Standard Tool project with Xcode and call it Statistics.

2. Open the file main.c in the editor by clicking it in the Groups & Files view. You can find it in the group Source.

3. Replace the default code inserted by Xcode with the following:

```c
#include <stdio.h>
#include <stdlib.h>

int main (int argc, const char * argv[]) {
    const int DATA_SIZE = 1000;
    float heightData[DATA_SIZE];

    // Initialize data randomly.
    int i;
    for ( i = 0; i < DATA_SIZE; ++i ) {
        float randNum = (float)rand() / RAND_MAX;  // From 0.0 to 1.0
        heightData[i] = 150.0 + ( randNum * 70.0 ); // 150.0 to 220.0 centimeters
    }

    // Calculate statistics
    float maxHeight = 0.0, minHeight = 1000.0;
    float sum = 0.0, average;
    for ( i = 0; i < DATA_SIZE; ++i ) {
        sum += heightData[i];
        if ( heightData[i] > maxHeight ) maxHeight = heightData[i];
        if ( heightData[i] < minHeight ) minHeight = heightData[i];
    }
    average = sum / DATA_SIZE;

    // Print results
    printf("Average Height (cm): %f\nMaximum Height (cm): %f\nMinimum Height (cm): %f\n",
        average, maxHeight, minHeight);

    return 0;
}
```

4. Click the Build and Go toolbar item to compile and run the program.

5. Verify that the Run Log that appears contains results similar, although not exactly the same, as in Figure 6-2.

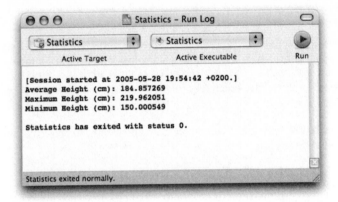

Figure 6-2

How It Works

This program calculates a number of statistics for a data array of the heights of 1,000 people, given in centimeters. Rather than use real data, the data is generated randomly within a realistic range of values. The statistics calculated are the average or mean, the maximum height, and the minimum height. You will need to use the techniques in this example many times in your C programming. For example, calculating the maximum or minimum value in an array is a very common programming task.

The declaration of the array holding the data makes use of a constant integer called DATA_SIZE:

```
const int DATA_SIZE = 1000;
float heightData[DATA_SIZE];
```

Using a constant like this is good practice. If instead of using a constant, you just typed 1000 anywhere in your program that the array size was needed, you would soon discover that changing the amount of data can be very inconvenient. You have to find every point in the code where you typed 1000, and change it to the new size. If you use a constant variable, as in the example, you have to change only the value of the constant whenever you want to change the size of your array. The rest of the program is automatically updated, because there is no reference to 1000, only to the constant variable.

The code to randomly initialize the height data looks like this:

```
// Initialize data randomly.
int i;
for ( i = 0; i < DATA_SIZE; ++i ) {
    float randNum = (float)rand() / RAND_MAX;   // From 0.0 to 1.0
    heightData[i] = 150.0 + ( randNum * 70.0 ); // 150.0 to 220.0 centimeters
}
```

This loops over the elements in the array. For each element, a random number between 0.0 and 1.0 is generated, and put in the variable randNum. randNum is used to generate a value for the height between 150.0 and 220.0 centimeters, which is inserted in the heightData array.

> *The function* rand *returns an* int *between 0 and the constant* RAND_MAX. *The declarations of both* rand *and* RAND_MAX *come from the* stdlib.h *file that has been included at the beginning of the program.*

To generate a random float between 0.0 and 1.0, the int returned by rand is first converted to a float, like this:

```
(float)rand()
```

This is called a *cast*. You force the compiler to convert the int from rand into a float. Putting a data type in parentheses like this tells the compiler you want to cast the number or variable that follows to a different type.

The random float is divided by the int RAND_MAX, so the result is a float between 0.0 and 1.0. The floating-point number randNum is then used to generate a height between 150.0 and 220.0. You can verify for yourself that the code given achieves this result, if randNum is between 0.0 and 1.0.

The statistics are calculated in the second loop:

```
// Calculate statistics
float maxHeight = 0.0, minHeight = 1000.0;
float sum = 0.0, average;
for ( i = 0; i < DATA_SIZE; ++i ) {
    sum += heightData[i];
    if ( heightData[i] > maxHeight ) maxHeight = heightData[i];
    if ( heightData[i] < minHeight ) minHeight = heightData[i];
}
average = sum / DATA_SIZE;
```

In order to calculate the average, the sum of all heights is first calculated, and then divided by the total number of people. The variable sum is used to accumulate the sum of heights. It is first initialized to 0.0, and has heightData[i] added to it each iteration of the loop. The variable average is set to sum divided by DATA_SIZE after the loop.

To calculate the maximum height, the variable maxHeight is used. It is first initialized to a very small height value, namely 0.0. In each iteration of the loop, heightData[i] is compared with the current value of maxHeight. If it is larger, maxHeight is set to heightData[i], which is the new maximum height. If not, no action is taken. When the loop completes, maxHeight will hold the largest value in the array.

Evaluating the minimum height is similar, except the variable used to accumulate it, minHeight, is initialized to a very large value. Whenever heightData[i] is smaller than minHeight, minHeight is updated.

The last lines of the main function simply print out the values of average, minHeight, and maxHeight.

Functions

Many of the examples you have seen thus far have included the printf statement, but what is printf exactly? printf is a *function* in the C standard library that prints a string to standard output. A function is a block of code that can be executed from any other point in your program. When you execute a function, you are said to be *calling* it. When you call a function, your program performs the code in the *function body*, before returning to the point of the call.

> The standard library is a collection of functions and constants provided with every C compiler. It includes functions for reading and writing files, and manipulating strings, among other things. C programmers need to use the standard library in virtually every piece of code they write.

Here is a simple example of a function, with calling code:

```
#include <stdio.h>

int AddFunc(int a, int b) {
    return a + b;
}

int main( const int argc, const char *argv[] ) {
    printf("%d\n", AddFunc(1,2) );
    return 0;
}
```

This defines a function called AddFunc, which adds two ints together. The function has two *parameters*, which are called a and b. Parameters are variables that are initialized with values passed to the function when it is called. The values passed are called *arguments*, and in the preceding example, the arguments to AddFunc are 1 and 2, the numbers appearing in parentheses after AddFunc in the printf statement.

When the function AddFunc is called from inside the printf statement, it initializes the variables a and b to the values of the arguments passed, which in this case are 1 and 2. It then returns the value of a + b, which is 3, to the calling code. The *return value* is then used at the point in the code that the call was instigated, so in this case, the value 3 would be printed by printf.

Functions are not required to take any arguments, nor are they required to return anything. You can use the keyword void when there is nothing to return, and/or to be passed in via the parameter list, like this:

```
void DoNothingFunc( void ) {
    }
```

You must use void when there is no return value, but the void in the parameter list is optional, so you could rewrite DoNothingFunc like this:

```
void DoNothingFunc() {
    }
```

When a function is called, it must already have been declared. You could try to keep all of your functions in order, so that each has been declared before any other function needs to call it, but this is a hassle, and, in certain cases, impossible. Instead, C allows you to declare a function without writing its body (or *implementation*). These function declarations are known as *signatures*.

It is possible in C for two functions to call one another, and even that a function call itself. (The latter is known as *recursion*.) In the case of two functions calling one another, it is not possible to declare each function before each call without using function signatures.

Here is an example in which two functions call one another, with both functions' signatures declared in the beginning:

```c
#include <stdio.h>

// Function signatures
unsigned int calcSum(unsigned int n, unsigned int sum);
unsigned int addToSum(unsigned int n, unsigned int sum);

/* Adds the numbers from n to 10 to sum,
   and returns the result. */
unsigned int calcSum(unsigned int n, unsigned int sum) {
    if ( n > 10 )
        return sum;
    else
        return addToSum(n, sum);
}

// Used by calcSum
unsigned int addToSum(unsigned int n, unsigned int sum) {
    return calcSum(n+1, n+sum);
}

// Main function
int main() {
    printf( "%d\n", calcSum(1, 0) );
    return 0;
}
```

This mechanics of this example are quite involved, but the important thing for you to realize is that calcSum calls addToSum, even though calcSum's implementation appears first. This is possible, because addToSum has already been declared before the definition of calcSum, by means of a function signature at the beginning. The signature is nothing more or less than the interface that appears at the beginning of a function, which defines the function's name, parameter list, and return value.

Without going into too much detail, the example demonstrates a rather obscure way of adding up the numbers from 1 to 10. calcSum is called first from main with the value 1 for the parameter n, and 0 for sum. Since n is not greater than 10, calcSum calls addToSum, passing 1 and 0 as arguments. addToSum calls back to calcSum, but passes the value of n+1 and n+sum as arguments. Back in calcSum, the new value of n is 2, and sum is 1. Since n is still not greater than 10, addToSum is again called, this time with 2 and 1 as arguments. This merry-go-round continues until n is greater than 10, at which point calcSum returns sum, which is the sum of numbers to that point.

This is a rather complex piece of recursion, and you should not worry yourself too much with it. It is only important that you understand that a function can call another function before it is defined, as long as its signature has been declared.

There is one more aspect of C functions that you should grasp before moving on, and it has to do with the arguments passed. C follows a convention known as *pass-by-value*. What this means in practice is that any argument passed to a function is copied before it is used in the function, and any changes you make to the corresponding parameter have no effect on the argument. Here is an example to demonstrate this important point:

```c
void func(int param) {
    param = 5;
}

int main() {
    int a = 2;
    func(a);
    printf("%d\n", a);
    return 0;
}
```

The million-dollar question is: What will be printed? You may say 5, because when you call `func`, it sets `param` to 5, but alas you would be wrong. Because C uses pass-by-value, the argument a passed in `main` to `func` is copied, so that when the parameter `param` is modified in `func`, the original argument does not change. After returning to the `main` function, the variable a is still 2, and this is what gets printed.

But what if you do want to change a variable passed to a function? How can you do it? The simple answer is that you must pass a pointer to the variable, rather than the variable itself. Here is the preceding example rewritten so that a really does get modified by `func` before returning to `main`:

```c
void func(int *param) {
    *param = 5;
}

int main() {
    int a = 2;
    func(&a);
    printf("%d\n", a);
    return 0;
}
```

If you run this version of the program, 5 will be printed for the value of a. Notice that `func` now expects a pointer to an `int`. It sets the value pointed to by the pointer `param` to 5 by using the dereferencing operator `*`. The call to `func` uses the address-of operator `&` to pass a pointer to a, rather than a itself. When `func` sets the value pointed to by `param` to 5, it is actually setting a to 5, because `param` is a copy of the memory address of a.

When you pass a pointer to a function, the function receives a copy of the pointer, just as with any other type, but the data pointed to by the pointer is not copied. This means that you can allow a function to change a variable passed to it by passing the pointer to the variable, rather than the variable itself. The pointer will be copied, but the function will still be able to access the data pointed to by dereferencing the pointer copy.

The only exception to the pass-by-value rule is arrays. The contents of an array that gets passed to a function are not copied; instead, the array is passed as a pointer to its first element. This pointer itself is copied, but the array data is not. If the function makes changes to the data in the array, the array data will reflect these changes after the function returns.

Characters and Strings

Since beginning your sojourn into C, you have made use of many strings. Each `main` function gets passed an array of strings, for example, and every `printf` call has at least one string. Discussion of strings was put off until now because they are a bit more difficult to use than other basic data types like `int` and `float`.

As you will undoubtedly have guessed, you can create a literal string by simply putting it between double quotation marks. But how do you declare a string variable? This is trickier, because a string variable is actually an array of characters, which have the type `char` in C.

`char` variables have a size of 1 byte. They can represent ASCII characters, which include letters and numbers, as well as punctuation. A literal `char` is a single character between single quotation marks. Here is an example of creating a `char` variable, and setting it to the letter *A*:

```
char cVar = 'A';
```

A `char` can also change its value, just like an `int` or `float`. You could change the value of `cVar` later in the program to *b*, like this:

```
cVar = 'b';
```

As with any variable, if you don't want the value of a character variable to change, you can make it constant:

```
const char constCharVar = 'c';
```

Because an array is equivalent to a pointer to the first element of the array, and strings are just arrays of `chars`, strings are usually given the type `char*`. Here is an example of initializing a string:

```
char *myString = "Hello, World!";
```

This string can be printed like this:

```
printf("%s", myString);
```

To declare a string without initializing it to a literal value, you simply follow the same steps that you would take to declare an array:

```
char anotherString[100]; // This string has room for 100 chars
```

But how do you set the characters in this array once the array has been declared? The first approach is to use the usual means of setting the elements in an array, like this:

```
anotherString[0] = "H";
anotherString[1] = "e";
anotherString[2] = "l";
anotherString[3] = "l";
anotherString[4] = "o";
anotherString[5] = "\0";
```

Printing `anotherString` will result in `Hello` appearing in the output. Take careful note of the last character entered into the string, "\0". This is known as the *terminating null character*. Because C stores arrays as a simple pointer to the first element, it doesn't actually know how long they are after they are declared. Strings inherit this problem from arrays, so in order to tell the compiler where the string ends, you have to insert the terminating null character. The terminating null character has the special form of a backslash followed by a zero.

> *You may have noticed that there was no terminating null character used in the literal strings above. Literal strings have a terminating null character added automatically. The only thing you have to remember is to make enough space in your strings to accommodate this extra character. For example, if your literal string has 10 characters, and you want to copy its contents into a string variable, your variable will need to be at least 11 characters long in order to contain the 10 characters of the literal string and the terminating null character.*

Setting the characters in a string one-by-one, as in the preceding example, may only be convenient for certain applications. It wasn't very convenient in this particular case, for example. It would be better if you could just copy the contents of a literal string directly into the string variable. C doesn't provide direct language support for such an operation. The following, for example, will *not* copy the contents of a literal into a string variable, despite what you might expect:

```
char stringVar[10];
stringVar = "Hello";
```

What this code does is take the pointer corresponding to stringVar, and assign it to the address of the first char in the literal "Hello". This is probably not what you want.

Even though there is no built-in language support for copying string contents, C provides functions to do so in its standard library. You need to include the file string.h in order to use these functions. Here is an example of copying a string with a function from string.h:

```
#include <string.h>
...
char stringVar[10];
strcpy(stringVar, "Hello");
```

strcpy copies the contents of the second string into the first, including the terminating null character. If there is no terminating null character in the second string, your program will likely crash when it is run. In this example, there is a terminating null, because a literal string always has a hidden terminating null character.

> *C is reasonably compact when compared to some other languages. A lot of functionality is provided in the standard library, rather than via the language itself. Where other languages provide built-in string manipulation operations, C provides most of this through functions in the standard library. Even* printf, *which is used to print to output, is simply a function in the standard library.*

Another function from string.h is strncpy, which can be used to copy one string into another, up to a maximum number of characters. It can be a bit safer to use than strcpy, because it will not go on forever looking for a terminating null character. Here is the preceding example, using strncpy instead of strcpy:

```
#include <string.h>
...
char stringVar[10];
strncpy(stringVar, "Hello", 10);
```

In this instance, a maximum length of 10 has been used because you know that stringVar cannot accommodate more than 10 characters.

There are many other functions in the standard library for working with strings. The following table gives some of the more useful functions declared in the file string.h.

Function	Signature	Description
strcat	char *strcat(char *first, const char *second)	Appends/concatenates the second string to the end of the first. Returns the modified first string.
strncat	char *strncat(char *first, const char *second, int n)	Appends/concatenates the second string to the end of the first, taking at most *n* characters. Returns the modified first string.
strcmp	int strcmp(const char *first, const char *second)	Compares the two strings. A return value less than 0 means that the first string precedes the second alphabetically; a value of 0 means the two strings are equal; and a positive value means the first string comes after the second.
strncmp	int strncmp(const char *first, const char *second, int n)	Compares the two strings as in strcmp, but only up to a maximum of *n* characters.
strstr	char *strstr(const char *first, const char *second)	Searches for the second string in the first string. If it is found, a pointer to the first character of the second string in the first is returned. If it is not found, NULL is returned.
strlen	int strlen(const char *first)	Returns the length of the string passed.

The table of functions for manipulating strings is fairly straightforward, but the keyword NULL may have you worried. If so, worry not. NULL is actually just another way of saying 0, and is used to indicate that a pointer is not pointing to any useful address. In the table, it can be returned from strstr whenever the second string is not found in the first string. You can compare the pointer returned with NULL to see if the string was found.

Returning NULL for a pointer in C is a very common way of saying that something didn't go to plan. Perhaps an error occurred, or something was not found, as is the case for strstr. Passing NULL as the value of a pointer to a function is a common way of telling the function that the corresponding argument is not needed for this call.

You've probably noticed that in many examples, though not all, the main function has two parameters, with a signature like this:

```
int main( const int argc, const char* argv[] );
```

None of the examples to this point have actually made use of these parameters, so what are they? These parameters allow arguments to be passed to a program when it is run. The number of arguments passed is argc, or the *argument count*. The values of the arguments passed in are stored in argv, the *argument values*. argc is a simple integer, but the declaration of argv is more involved. argv is an array of pointers to char. A pointer to char is a string, so argv is actually an array of strings. Each entry in the array is a different argument for the main function.

You can access these arguments like this:

```
int main( const int argc, const char* argv[] ) {
    printf("arg0 is %s", argv[0]);
    printf("arg1 is %s", argv[1]);
    return 0;
}
```

The first entry in the array, argv[0], is reserved for the name of the program. The other entries, up to index argc-1, are the arguments for the program. How these arguments are passed to the program depends on the manner in which the program is run.

> The %s given in printf is a formatting directive, which is used to print string variables. This, and other aspects of formatting, are covered in the next section.

Sometimes you will see a main function declared like this:

```
int main( const int argc, const char** argv );
```

In this case, the second parameter is given as a *pointer to a pointer*. Because an array is equivalent to a pointer in C, this declaration is equivalent to the preceding one.

Input/Output

Programs aren't very useful unless you can get data into and out of them. This aspect of computing is known as *Input/Output* or *I/O*. You have already seen many examples of I/O earlier in the chapter. Every time a program contains printf or scanf, it is performing I/O, either printing data to output, or reading it from input. It is also common to read or write from files. This section covers basic aspects of I/O in C programming.

As you are now well aware, printf can be used to print strings to standard output. Variables and other values can be embedded in the string via format characters, which are preceded by a %. The following table provides the most important format characters.

Format Characters	Types
%d, %i	int, short, long
%u	unsigned int
%f, %e, %g	float, double
%c	char
%s	char* (string)
%p	pointer

The format characters appear in the string passed to `printf`. Expressions for the values corresponding to the format characters appear after the string, separated by commas. Here is an example of printing a complex string containing several values:

```
int i = 5;
float f = 100.6;
char *str = "This is the winter of our discontent";

printf("Shakespeare said: \"%s\". \n\tThis, while he ate %d eggs, "
       "each weighing %f grams.\n", str, i+10, f);
```

If you can't fit a string on one line, you can either leave it as a single line and let it wrap around in your editor, or you can break it in two, as in this example. Two neighboring string literals are concatenated to form a single string, which is passed to `printf`.

The use of quotations inside a string is made possible by *escaping* the special meaning of the quotation marks. You do this by adding a backslash character before each quotation mark. This principle applies to all characters with special meaning. Another example is the `%` symbol, which generally implies a format character. If you want to print the backslash character itself, you need to use two backslashes together.

Non-formatting characters with a special meaning are preceded by a backslash. For example, `\n` represents a new line character, and `\t` is the tab character. If you want to print `\n` or `\t` rather than a new line or tab, you can again use the double backslash trick, entering `\\n` or `\\t` in your string.

You are not restricted to simple variables and literals in calls to `printf`. As you can see from the example, any expression is allowed. In this case, `i+10` has been passed. Of course, this applies to functions in general, not just `printf`.

> *If you take the time to type in the preceding example and run it, don't be too surprised if the weight of each egg in the example is not printed as 100.6 grams, but something like 100.599998 grams. This has to do with the way the computer stores floating-point numbers. It cannot internally represent all floating-point numbers, so it represents only some, and chooses the closest internal representation it can find for any given value. In this case, 100.599998 is the closest float to 100.6 that the computer can represent.*

When you want to read something in from standard input, you use `scanf`, which reads a string with a particular format, in the same way that `printf` writes one. The same format characters that apply to `printf` also apply to `scanf`. Here is an example of using `scanf` to read two floating-point numbers, and one integer, from standard input (the user's keyboard):

```
#include <stdio.h>

int main() {
    float f1, f2;
    int i;
    printf("Enter two floats and an int: ");
    scanf("%f%f%d", &f1, &f2, &i);
    printf("You typed: %f, %f, and %d.\n", f1, f2, i);
    return 0;
}
```

The program is simple enough: it requests the user to type in two floats, followed by an int, using the printf function. scanf is then used to read the numbers in. The format characters in the string passed as first argument to scanf indicate what value types can be expected. After the format string, a list of pointers to variables is passed. (You can tell that pointers are being passed because each variable is preceded by an &, the dereferencing operator.)These variables will contain the values read after the call. Finally, another printf statement writes the data read back out again.

Note that scanf takes pointers to variables as arguments, and not the variables themselves, as is the case for printf. This is because scanf must change the variables' values inside the function. As you learned earlier in this chapter, because C uses pass-by-value, the only way to change the value of a variable passed to a function is to pass the address of the variable to be modified, rather than its value.

If you try this out, you will find that scanf is fairly tolerant of your input, although results may be meaningless if you don't type in what is requested. For example, if you enter an int instead of a float, it works fine, because an integer number can be easily converted to a floating-point number. But try entering a float in place of the requested int, and you may get surprising results, depending on the form of the float that you enter. 4.5 will give 4, which is not so surprising, but .3 gives 6, which is a little more difficult to fathom!

White space in the format string is ignored by scanf, unlike printf, so the following statement is equivalent to the original:

```
scanf("%f %f %d", &f1, &f2, &i);
```

Two functions that are not directly related to I/O, but which are closely related to scanf and printf, are sscanf and sprintf. These functions behave very similarly to scanf and printf, except that they read and write to and from strings, respectively, rather than input and output. Here is a simple example of using sscanf and sprintf:

```
char str[34];
sprintf( str, "Have a nice birthday on the %dth.", 20 );
printf("%s\n", str);

int i;
float f;
char s[20];
char *readStr = "20 1.4 hey there";
sscanf( readStr, "%d%f%s", &i, &f, s );
printf("%d:%f:%s\n", i, f, s);
```

If you compile and run this in a `main` function, you will see output something like this:

```
Have a nice birthday on the 20th.
20:1.400000:hey
```

`sprintf` includes the same parameters as `printf`, except it takes an extra one at the beginning of the parameter list, which is the string it is to write into. In this case, the variable `str` is passed, which is 34 characters long. If you count how many letters there are in the output string, you should come to 33. So an extra `char` has been included in the variable `str`. This is by design: if you recall, a string should include a terminating null character, and that occupies the extra place. In general, you should make your strings at least one larger than the maximum expected number of meaningful characters that they need to contain.

`sscanf` has the same parameters as `scanf`, but it too has an extra string at the beginning of the parameter list. It reads out of this string, according to the format passed as the second argument. In this case, it reads the int 20, the `float` 1.4, and the string `hey`. You will notice that it stopped reading the string at the first white space rather than continuing on to read in `there`. `sscanf` and `scanf` assume white space delineates the end of an entry.

Variations of `scanf` and `printf` also exist for reading and writing to files: `fscanf` and `fprintf`. Not surprisingly, these functions take the same arguments as `scanf` and `printf`, with the addition of an extra `FILE` pointer passed first. The following example opens two files, reading from one, and writing to the other, using `fscanf` and `fprintf`, respectively:

```c
#include <stdio.h>

int main() {
    FILE *inpFile, *outFile;

    // Open files
    inpFile = fopen("/var/tmp/temp.inp", "r");
    outFile = fopen("/var/tmp/temp.out", "w");

    // Read from inpFile
    float f1, f2, f3;
    fscanf( inpFile, "%f%f%f", &f1, &f2, &f3 );

    // Write to outFile
    fprintf( outFile, "The three floats were: %f, %f, and %f.", f1, f2, f3 );

    // Close files
    fclose(inpFile);
    fclose(outFile);

    return 0;
}
```

This program begins by declaring two pointers to variables of the type `FILE`. The `FILE` type is not as simple as a `float` or `int`. It is a `struct`, which you will learn about later in the chapter. In the meantime, you can use `FILE` pointers without actually understanding what they contain or how they work.

In this case, the function `fopen` is used to open two files, and the `FILE` pointers are assigned to the return values. `fopen` takes two parameters: a string with the path to the file and a string indicating the operations permitted on the file.

The second parameter tells `fopen` whether the file is for reading, writing, or some combination. The following table shows strings that can be passed as the second argument to `fopen`.

String	File Operation
r	Read only.
w	Write only.
a	Append to the end of an existing file.
r+	Read and write an existing file.
w+	Read and write a new file.
a+	Read and write an existing file, beginning at the end.

In the example, for the input file `"r"` is passed, indicating it will be read, and `"w"` is passed for the output file, indicating it will only be written to.

> *The paths chosen for the files were both in the directory* /var/tmp. *This is a good directory to practice with reading and writing files because everything there is treated as temporary and disposable, and it is less likely that you will accidentally overwrite or change an important file.*

`fscanf` and `fprintf` work as expected, taking the respective file pointers as first argument. After reading data from `inpFile`, and writing the same data to `outFile`, both files are closed using the function `fclose`. After `fclose`, the `FILE` pointers are no longer valid, and should not be used.

Many other functions are defined in the standard library for reading and writing standard input and output, and files. The following table gives some of the more important functions, for use in your programs.

Function	Signature	Description
gets	`char *gets(char *line);`	Reads a string from standard input up to a new line character, and copies the string into the `line` variable. It also returns the pointer to the `line` string. If the end of file is encountered before a line is read, the `line` variable is not set, and NULL is returned.
fgets	`char *fgets(char *line, int n, FILE *file);`	Same as `gets`, except that it reads from the file associated with the file pointer file. A maximum of n-1 characters can be read. If a new line is encountered, or the maximum number of characters reached, the line is returned, including the new line, and a terminating null character.
getchar	`char getchar();`	Reads a single character from standard input.
fgetc	`char fgetc(FILE *file);`	Reads a single character from the file passed. If the end of the file is encountered, the special value EOF is returned.

In the following Try It Out you write a program called *Grepper*, which is a simplified version of the Unix command *grep*. Grepper goes through a file one line at a time, searching for a string passed to it when run. If it finds the string in a line, the whole line is printed. In this way you can see whether a file contains a particular word, for example, and the lines on which the word appears.

Try It Out   Searching a File

1. Create a new Standard Tool project in Xcode and call it Grepper.

2. Open the source file main.c and replace the contents with the following code:

```
#include <stdio.h>
#include <string.h>

// Global constants
const int MAX_STRING_LENGTH = 256;

// Main function
int main (int argc, const char * argv[]) {

    // Make sure there are two arguments given, the filename
    // and the search string
    if ( argc != 3 ) return 1; // Indicate error

    // Get input file paths from standard input
    const char *inpPath = argv[1];

    // Get string to search for
    const char *searchString = argv[2];

    // Open files
    FILE *inpFile;
    inpFile = fopen(inpPath, "r");

    // Loop over lines in the input file, until there
    // are none left
    char line[MAX_STRING_LENGTH];
    while ( fgets(line, MAX_STRING_LENGTH-1, inpFile) ) {
        if ( strstr(line, searchString) ) {
            printf("In file %s:\t%s", inpPath, line);
        }
    }

    // Close files
    fclose(inpFile);

    return 0;
}
```

3. Build the program by clicking the Build toolbar item.

4. Select the Grepper executable in the Executables group of the Groups & Files view.

5. Choose File ➪ Get Info or use the key combination Command-I.

6. Open the Arguments tab in the Grepper Info window, and click the + button to add a new argument. Enter a path to any text file that you would like to search for a string. (This could even be the main.c program in the Grepper project itself.)

191

7. Add a second argument, and enter the string you would like to search for in the file. The Grepper Info window should now look similar to Figure 6-3.

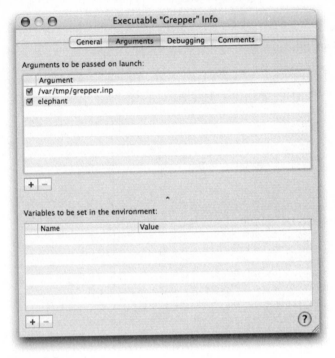

Figure 6-3

8. Now run the program and monitor the Run Log for results. You should see each of the lines from the input file that contains the search string.

How It Works

Grepper utilizes many of the skills that you have learned to this point in the chapter, from string handling to I/O, and conditional branching to loops. After the `#include` statements, a variable is declared outside the `main` function. This variable has *global scope*, which means it can be accessed from anywhere in the program, not just inside a particular function, for example. In this case it could also have been placed inside the `main` function, but there will be other cases where the variable needs to be accessed outside of `main` as well, and making it global is one way to facilitate this.

In general, global variables should be avoided, because they can make a program more difficult to understand. You can't see the variable being passed through to a function via the parameter list, so it can make it difficult to follow the flow of data in a program. One case where global data is acceptable is for constant variables that need to be accessed at many points throughout a program. The previous example, MAX_STRING_LENGTH, is just such a case, because it stipulates the size of string variables used throughout Grepper.

> The *scope* in *global scope* refers to where a particular variable can be accessed, and how long it remains in existence. Variables with global scope are visible everywhere in a program, and exist for the run time of the program, but for most variables, this isn't the case. Variables declared inside functions are created when the function begins, and destroyed when it ends. These variables are called *local variables* because they exist only locally to the function. In fact, variables declared in any code block — a section of code enclosed in braces — exist only while that block is executing.

The main function first checks that argc is 3, because it expects to be passed exactly three values in argv. The first, as always, is the name of the executable itself. The next is the path to the file that should be scanned, and the last is the string that is sought in the file. You entered these input parameters in the inspector window of the Grepper executable just before you ran it. Xcode passes these parameters to Grepper when it starts.

If there are three arguments, the next action taken is to assign the last two arguments to variables, one for the input file path (inpPath), and one for the string (searchString). The inpPath variable is then used with fopen to open the input file for reading.

The program then begins to loop over lines, checking each one for the string:

```
char line[MAX_STRING_LENGTH];
while ( fgets(line, MAX_STRING_LENGTH-1, inpFile) ) {
    if ( strstr(line, searchString) ) {
        printf("In file %s:\t%s", inpPath, line);
    }
}
```

Just before the loop, a string variable is created to store each line of the file. It is given the length defined earlier at global scope. This should be adequate as long as your file does not have any very long lines. *Very long* in this case is greater than 255 characters because MAX_STRING_LENGTH is 256 and you should always leave one character over for the terminating null character.

The condition for the while loop needs some explaining. It is a call to a function that you haven't seen before: fgets. fgets is declared in the file string.h, which has been included at the beginning of the program. The fgets function reads a line of text from the file passed as third argument, up to a maximum length given by the second argument. So it keeps reading until it either encounters a new line character (\n), or reaches the maximum line length. In either case, it sets the value of the string passed as first argument to the line read, and returns the same string variable via its return parameter. If the end of the file is reached before anything is read, it returns NULL.

You may be puzzling as to why both the first parameter value and the return value are set to the line string. One reason is that you can easily test if anything was read, and thus whether you should keep reading. That is precisely how it has been used here: the while loop will continue until a zero value is returned by fgets. NULL is a zero value, so it will keep reading lines until the end of the file is encountered.

The if construct in the loop uses the function strstr, which was introduced in the section called "Characters and Strings." This function searches the string passed as first argument for the string passed second. If it finds the second string in the first, a pointer to the location of the second string in the first is returned. If it is not found, NULL is returned. The if tests whether the return is non-zero, so any line for which NULL is returned by strstr is ignored, while any line containing the search string will be printed.

The last lines of `main` simply close the input file, and return 0, indicating success.

> *Grepper assumes that no line will exceed 255 characters, plus one terminating null character. If a line is longer than this, Grepper will not operate correctly. This type of situation is referred to as buffer overflow, and is a common source of security breaches. For example, an unscrupulous hacker could use buffer overflow to cause a program like FTP to crash, and run more malicious programs in its place. If your programs are potentially security risks, you should take extra care to put checks into your code that ensure buffer overflow can't happen.*

Data Structures

To this point in the chapter, you have dealt with only simple data types such as `int`, `float`, and `char`. C was one of the first languages to facilitate *structured programming*, part of which entails creating more complex data relationships than you have seen so far. C provides a number of constructions to group data together, and this section introduces you to them.

Sometimes it is necessary to represent variables that can take only a few discrete values. For example, a variable representing the type of a pet could be represented by an integer restricted to a small range of values. Such a variable is referred to as an *enumerated type*. C provides the `enum` data type to represent enumerated types. Consider this example:

```c
typedef enum { DOG, CAT, BIRD } Pet;

Pet myPet = CAT;

switch (myPet) {
    case DOG:
        printf("I have a dog!\n");
        break;
    case CAT:
        printf("I have a cat!\n");
        break;
    case BIRD:
        printf("I have a bird!\n");
        break;
    default:
        printf("I have an undefined beast\n");
}
```

The keyword `typedef` is used in conjunction with the keyword `enum` to define a new type called `Pet`. This type can take three meaningful values: `DOG`, `CAT`, and `BIRD`. A variable called `myPet` is then declared to be of the type `Pet`, and is initialized to `CAT`. A `switch` statement checks the type of `myPet`, printing a message depending on its value.

C simply represents enumerated types as integers, so they can be used anywhere an `int` can be used. For example, you can subscript an array with an `enum`:

```c
int averagePetLifetime[3];

averagePetLifetime[DOG] = 20;
averagePetLifetime[CAT] = 15;
averagePetLifetime[BIRD] = 5;
```

Unless indicated otherwise, the first entry in an enum gets the value 0; the second, 1; the third, 2; and so forth. You can override this behavior by explicitly indicating the integers corresponding to the entries, like this:

```
typedef enum { DOG = 1, CAT = 2, BIRD = 3} Pet;
```

Whenever no integer is explicitly assigned to one of the values, it is given the value of the previous value incremented by 1. So this example could also be written as follows:

```
typedef enum { DOG = 1, CAT, BIRD} Pet;
```

In theory, you can do without enums in your programming, but your code becomes considerably easier to read if you use them because the values assigned have a clear meaning. Assigning a variable to DOG is much easier to understand than assigning it to 1, where 1 only implies a dog.

Another data structure available in C is the struct. A struct allows you to group variables together. Here is a struct you might use to represent a person:

```
typedef enum { BLUE, GREEN, BROWN } EyeColor;

struct Person {
    char *firstName, *secondName;
    char *address;
    float height;
    float weight;
    EyeColor eyeColor;
};
```

The struct can include variables of any type, including other structs. To use a struct, you need to make a variable, or *instance*, like this:

```
struct Person me;
```

You can then access the variables inside the struct using the . operator. To set them, you can do this:

```
me.firstName = "Bob";
me.secondName = "Bobbs";
me.address = "1 Holy Smoke Crescent, Who Knows Where, USA";
me.height = 180.0;
me.weight = 90.0;
me.eyeColor = BLUE;
```

To use the variables, you can do this:

```
float weightInPounds = me.weight * KILOS_TO_POUNDS;
```

In other words, the members of a struct are just like ordinary variables in every way, except that you have to reference them by giving the name of the struct variable, followed by a point, and then the name of the member.

Most programmers find typing in struct Person me; annoying after a while, so they use the same trick you saw for enums; namely, they define the struct as a new type. The following code shows you how:

```
typedef struct Person_ {
    char *firstName, *secondName;
    char *address;
    float height;
    float weight;
    EyeColor eyeColor;
} Person;

Person me;
me.height = 180.0;
```

As you can see, this saves you typing `struct` in front of every variable you declare. If you look carefully, you will see two names ascribed to the `struct`: `Person_` and `Person`. `Person` is actually not the name of a `struct`, but a type, which in this case happens to be a `struct` called `Person_`. The name of the `struct`, `Person_`, may be omitted, in which case you have an *anonymous struct*. However, it is good practice to name a `struct`, even if you don't have any immediate reason to. That's because you sometimes need to make reference to the `struct` inside its own definition:

```
typedef struct ListNode_ {
    float value;
    struct ListNode_ *nextNode;
} ListNode;
```

It is perfectly legal in C to include pointer variables to the `struct` you are declaring inside the declaration itself. If you used an anonymous `struct`, this would not be possible, because you can't refer to the `struct`'s type, and the type name `ListNode` is yet to be declared.

This example also demonstrates that, just as with any other type of variable, you can declare a variable that is a pointer to a `struct`. When you want to access a member of such a variable, it looks like this:

```
(*me).address = "55 Melancholy Road, Loserville";
```

You first have to dereference the pointer to the `struct`, and then apply the `.` operator to get the address. This is not very pretty, so C provides the following equivalent notation:

```
me->address = "55 Melancholy Road, Loserville";
```

The hyphen followed by a greater-than symbol is a shorthand way of accessing the members of a pointer to a `struct`.

Memory Management

Up to this point, all the variables you have created have been stored in a part of memory known as the *stack*. The stack is a *contiguous* block of memory, meaning that it forms one continuous segment unbroken by gaps. Whenever a function is entered, the local variables declared there are *pushed* onto the end of the stack. When the function returns, the variables are *popped* off the stack again, effectively destroying them.

Stack variables can't be used for every situation, so C also gives you access to another part of memory for storing variables called the *heap* or *free store*. When you put a variable *on the heap*, you are responsible for managing its memory yourself. In other words, you have to request that the memory be assigned to the variable, and you are also responsible for freeing the memory when you are finished with it. If you don't do this, you can end up with a *memory leak*, where the amount of memory used by your program rises over time, perhaps even causing your computer to slow or crash.

Variables that have their values stored on the heap are always pointers. They point to the location in memory where the data is stored. Here is an example of creating and freeing a heap variable:

```c
#include <stdlib.h>
#include <stdio.h>

int main() {
    float *heapVar;
    heapVar = malloc( sizeof(float) );

    *heapVar = 4.0;
    printf( "%f\n", *heapVar );

    free(heapVar);

    return 0;
}
```

The variable `heapVar` is declared as a pointer, and then assigned to the return value of the function `malloc`, which is declared in `stdlib.h`. `malloc` stands for *memory allocation*; it takes a single argument, which is an integer indicating how many bytes of memory are required to hold the variable. You could enter 4 here, because you know that a `float` has 4 bytes, but this would be a mistake: If `float` were to be redefined on the Mac to have more than 4 bytes, or, if you port your program to a platform where `float` has 8 bytes, your code will no longer run.

Instead of *hard coding* the size of `float`, you can use the function `sizeof` to find out how many bytes are in a `float`. `sizeof` will work with any data type, including pointers, though you should be careful not to confuse the size of the pointer itself with the size of what it is pointing to. In this example the return value of `sizeof(float)` is passed to `malloc`, which allocates the requested 4 bytes, and returns a pointer to the memory.

> `malloc` **returns a special kind of pointer called a** *void pointer*. **A void pointer is a general pointer to memory, with no associated data type. You can declare a void pointer variable with the type** `void*`.
>
> **Rather than having to provide a different version of** `malloc` **for each pointer type, the designers of C elected to have a single function that returns a void pointer. A void pointer can be cast to any other type of pointer implicitly by the compiler, so they effectively killed all birds with one stone.**

After assigning what `heapVar` points to, the memory is destroyed or *freed*. `free` is a bit easier to use than `malloc` because you don't have to pass a size. You simply pass the pointer, and the memory it points to on the heap will be freed for use at a later point in time.

`malloc` and `free` will work with any C data type, as long as you remember that you need to use it with pointer variables. Here is an example of creating a *linked list* of floating-point values:

```c
#include <stdlib.h>
#include <stdio.h>

int main() {

    typedef struct ListNode_ {
        float data;
        struct ListNode_ *nextNode;
    } ListNode;

    typedef struct List_ {
        ListNode *firstNode;
        ListNode *currentNode;
    } List;

    // Create a list on the stack, and add a node to it
    List list;
    list.firstNode = malloc(sizeof(ListNode));
    list.firstNode->data = 2.0;
    list.firstNode->nextNode = NULL; // NULL indicates there are no more nodes
    list.currentNode = list.firstNode;

    // Add a new node in front of the other one
    ListNode *newNode = malloc(sizeof(ListNode));
    newNode->data = 3.0;
    newNode->nextNode = list.firstNode;
    list.firstNode = newNode;

    // Print out the values in the list
    list.currentNode = list.firstNode;
    while ( list.currentNode ) {
        printf("Node value: %f\n", list.currentNode->data);
        list.currentNode = list.currentNode->nextNode;
    }

    // Free the memory of all nodes
    list.currentNode = list.firstNode;
    while ( list.currentNode ) {
        ListNode *next = list.currentNode->nextNode;
        free(list.currentNode);
        list.currentNode = next;
    }

    return 0;
}
```

A linked list is a data container, which has similarities to C's arrays. The primary difference is that they can grow and shrink to fit the amount of data they need to store. C does not have any built-in linked list type, but you can certainly create linked lists in C using structs, *as shown in the example. A more advanced implementation would provide functions for adding data to the list, and removing it again.*

A linked list is made up of zero or more nodes. Each node holds a piece of data, in this case a float. The nodes are linked together in the sense that the first node in the list has a pointer to the second, which has a pointer to the third, and so forth. The last node points to NULL, indicating that the list is finished.

Nodes are represented by the type ListNode, which is a struct that contains a single float, and a pointer to the next node in the list:

```
typedef struct ListNode_ {
    float data;
    struct ListNode_ *nextNode;
} ListNode;
```

Note that the struct, ListNode_, is referenced inside the struct itself in order to define a pointer to the next node.

The List type is a struct that has two pointers, one to the first node in the list, and one to the current node, which may be used while *traversing* or moving through the list:

```
typedef struct List_ {
    ListNode *firstNode;
    ListNode *currentNode;
} List;
```

The List is declared and initialized as follows:

```
// Create a list on the stack, and add a node to it
List list;
list.firstNode = malloc(sizeof(ListNode));
list.firstNode->data = 2.0;
list.firstNode->nextNode = NULL; // NULL indicates there are no more nodes
list.currentNode = list.firstNode;
```

The firstNode member of the struct variable list is assigned to the pointer returned from malloc. Once the memory for the node has been allocated, the data can be set, in this case to 2.0. The nextNode pointer in the ListNode struct is assigned to NULL, to reflect the fact that this is the last node in the list at this point. Finally, the currentNode pointer in list is assigned to the newly created node.

The next portion of code inserts a second node at the beginning of the list. This is slightly more complex, because the newly inserted node must point to the first node created:

```
// Add a new node in front of the other one
ListNode *newNode = malloc(sizeof(ListNode));
newNode->data = 3.0;
newNode->nextNode = list.firstNode;
list.firstNode = newNode;
```

The primary difference is that the nextNode pointer in newNode is set to the firstNode pointer of list. The firstNode variable is then updated to point to newNode, making it the first node in the list. It is important that these operations are carried out in this order. If instead list.firstNode was assigned to newNode, there would be no way of assigning newNode->nextNode to the original node in the list.

> You could use list.currentNode *to set* newNode->nextNode, *but this is not a general solution to the problem. If for some reason* list.currentNode *was pointing to a different node in the list, there would be no pointers to the first node, and no way to determine its address in memory.*

The next section of code prints the values of the list. This demonstrates how you can traverse a list with a loop:

```
// Print out the values in the list
list.currentNode = list.firstNode;
while ( list.currentNode ) {
    printf("Node value: %f\n", list.currentNode->data);
    list.currentNode = list.currentNode->nextNode;
}
```

`list.currentNode` is first initialized to the first node. A `while` loop is used to move through the list, until the `currentNode` is NULL, which indicates the end of the list has been reached. The data stored in the current node is printed each time around the loop, and `list.currentNode` is updated to point to the following node.

The final `while` loop is similar, although not exactly the same. Its purpose is freeing the memory that was allocated for the nodes earlier in the program:

```
// Free the memory of all nodes
list.currentNode = list.firstNode;
while ( list.currentNode ) {
    ListNode *next = list.currentNode->nextNode;
    free(list.currentNode);
    list.currentNode = next;
}
```

The current node of `list` is again set to the first node, and the `while` loop continues until `list.current Node` is NULL. The difference lies in an extra pointer declared inside the body of the loop: `next`. This is used to temporarily store the address of the next node in the list. The reason this is necessary is that the current node is being freed, and the `nextNode` pointer will be freed with it. Without the temporary pointer, you would not know the memory address of the next node in the list, and could not free the nodes in the rest of the list.

The Preprocessor

Now you are going to cover a topic that isn't really part of the C language at all: the *C preprocessor*. A preprocessor is a program that goes through a piece of code before it is passed to the compiler, and modifies it. The C preprocessor is heavily used by C programmers, and derived variants like C++ and Objective-C.

On Mac OS X, the standard C compiler is gcc, which is part of the GNU Compiler Collection (GCC). To confuse matters, the preprocessor is part of gcc, so you may not even realize that you are using it. Usually it runs before the compiler automatically. If you want to use the gcc preprocessor without compiling afterward, you can pass the −E −P options.

The C preprocessor is used for a range of tasks, most of which ensure that compilation can proceed without a hitch. Here are some ways in which the C preprocessor is used:

❑ To incorporate the source code of one file in another file.

❑ To include different code based on some condition, such as whether you are debugging.

❑ To replace a macro label wherever it is found with a piece of code. For example, replacing PI with a number like 3.1415972.

In this section, you learn how you can achieve these goals with the C preprocessor.

When you communicate with the preprocessor in your source code, you give it *directives*. These are commands to do something, and they are all preceded by a # symbol. The first directive, and probably most widely used, is #include. Its purpose is to tell the preprocessor to include the text of another file in the current file, at the position of the #include. Here is an example:

```
My birthday is on
#include "Birthday"
at
#include "Venue"
```

When the preprocessor sees the #include lines in a source file, it will look for the files Birthday and Venue. If the preprocessor finds the values, it will insert the text contained in these files into the source file, replacing the #include directives. The preprocessed file might end up looking something like this:

```
My birthday is on
March the 21st
at
Under the C
```

All of this happens before the compiler itself is called, so the compiler will never see the #include, only the text from Birthday and Venue.

You will undoubtedly have noticed that the preceding example is not C. What this demonstrates is that the C preprocessor is not part of the C language, and doesn't care what contents are in the file that it is processing. In fact, the C preprocessor is often used with other languages, like Fortran, which doesn't have a preprocessor of its own.

The #include directive is very important in C programming. Nearly every source file will have one or more includes, like the example. These includes are used to import declarations of functions and data structures needed to compile the source code. Without the #include directive, the programmer would have to duplicate these declarations in each source file that required them.

The #include directive can also be used to include declarations from a library or framework. In this case, rather than quotes, triangular parentheses are used:

```
#include <math.h>
```

This directive includes the file math.h from the C standard library, which defines a number of mathematical functions and constants.

The C preprocessor also allows you to define *macros*. A macro is effectively a label for a piece of text that will be inserted whenever the macro label is found in the file. Here is a simple example:

```
#define MY_AGE 21
```

This defines the macro MY_AGE to be 21. Note that MY_AGE is not the number 21, but a string with the value 21. Macros are just strings of characters to the preprocessor. You could equally write the following, and the preprocessor would not complain:

```
#define MY_AGE twenty something
```

This directive would replace any instances of MY_AGE in the file with the text twenty something. Whether that makes sense will depend on what you are using the macro for. In any case, the preprocessor itself will not complain, but the compiler may not like what it finds in the preprocessed file.

Although the preprocessor will generally treat macro definitions with numbers as strings of characters, it is capable of simple arithmetic operations, and in such cases a number string can be handled as an integer. This is explained further a little later.

Using a macro is very easy — you simply insert the macro's label in your file wherever you like. Here is a simple example:

```
Since turning MY_AGE a few months ago, I have had an overwhelming desire to learn
C. Perhaps mid-life is finally upon me!
```

The preprocessor replaces MY_AGE with the string 21, giving the following preprocessed source:

```
Since turning 21 a few months ago, I have had an overwhelming desire to learn C.
Perhaps mid-life is finally upon me!
```

The only restriction on where you can place a macro is that it should not appear in a string, between quotations. If it does, the preprocessor will treat the macro label as a literal string, and not replace it. For example, the following will remain unchanged by the preprocessor, because MY_AGE appears in quotations:

```
Since turning "MY_AGE" a few months ago, I have had an overwhelming desire to learn
C. Perhaps mid-life is finally upon me!
```

Interestingly, you can also define macros that define nothing at all. This is useful for using the preprocessor for conditional branching. Yes, even the preprocessor is capable of checking for conditions, and taking different actions accordingly. The following defines a condition for the preprocessor:

```
#define USE_SMALL_BUFFER
```

After the preprocessor sees this line, it will consider USE_SMALL_BUFFER to be defined, even though it has not been assigned a value.

By now you will probably have realized that macros are usually named in uppercase letters, with underscores separating words. This is a convention only to help distinguish them from standard variables. The preprocessor does not require you to use the convention, but it is good to do so. Otherwise, other programmers may have trouble understanding your code.

The preprocessor can check conditions with the #ifdef and #ifndef directives:

```
#ifdef USE_SMALL_BUFFER
const int bufferSize = 1024;
#else
const int bufferSize = 2048;
#endif
```

An equivalent way of writing this code is as follows:

```
#ifndef USE_SMALL_BUFFER
const int bufferSize = 2048;
#else
const int bufferSize = 1024;
#endif
```

In both these cases, the `#else` block is optional. The `#ifdef` directive checks if a macro has been defined earlier. If it has been, the text up until the next directive is included. If the macro has not been defined, the text following is not included, but any text after the `#else` directive — if it exists — will be included. The `#ifndef` directive is exactly the opposite of `#ifdef` — its text is included if a macro is *not* defined.

`#ifdef` is actually a shorthand way of writing `#if defined`. There is also an `#elif` directive, which stands for else if. This allows you to include many different branches, each one with a different block of text. The first matching block is included. For example:

```
#if defined USE_SMALL_BUFFER
const int bufferSize = 1024;
#elif defined USE_MEDIUM_BUFFER
const int bufferSize = 2048;
#else
const int bufferSize = 4096;
#endif
```

The preprocessor first checks if `USE_SMALL_BUFFER` is defined. If it is, the line setting `bufferSize` to `1024` is included. If `USE_SMALL_BUFFER` is not defined, the `#elif` condition is tested; if `USE_MEDIUM_BUFFER` is defined, the line setting `bufferSize` to `2048` is included. Finally, if neither of the conditions is met, the line in the `#else` block is included, setting the `bufferSize` variable to `4096`.

Simple arithmetic is also allowed in macro definitions. Take this reworking of the preceding example:

```
#define BUFFER_BLOCK_SIZE 1024

#if defined USE_SMALL_BUFFER
    #define BUFFER_SIZE BUFFER_BLOCK_SIZE
#elif defined USE_MEDIUM_BUFFER
    #define BUFFER_SIZE BUFFER_BLOCK_SIZE * 2
#else
    #define BUFFER_SIZE BUFFER_BLOCK_SIZE * 4
#endif

const int bufferSize = BUFFER_SIZE;
```

Here you can see that it is possible to use a previously defined macro in the definition of a new one. The macro `BUFFER_BLOCK_SIZE` is used to define the macro `BUFFER_SIZE`, and simple arithmetic used in the last two definitions.

The arithmetic allowed in conditionals like these is not very advanced, but is adequate for most purposes. You can use simple integer arithmetic, such as adding or subtracting, but arithmetic with decimal numbers is not possible. You can compare integers and strings, testing for equality, or for one value being greater or less than another. Here is an example demonstrating some of the arithmetic operators available:

```
#define MY_AGE 21
#define MIDDLE_AGE 40
#define OLD_AGE 60

#if MY_AGE >= OLD_AGE * MIDDLE_AGE
printf("Humans do not live that long.\n");
#elif MY_AGE > \
      OLD_AGE + MIDDLE_AGE
printf("Should you be using a computer at your age?\n");
#elif MY_AGE >= OLD_AGE
printf("Better sit down.\n";
#elif MY_AGE == MIDDLE_AGE
printf("Life is just beginning.\n");
#elif MY_AGE > MIDDLE_AGE
printf("Better slow down.\n");
#else
printf("A spring chicken, eh?\n");
#endif
```

This example is intended to demonstrate the use of arithmetic operators with the preprocessor and is not intended to reflect the authors' personal definitions of middle and/or old age, or the activities appropriate for a person of a given age.

Jokes aside, the preceding code includes the operators *, +, >, >=, and ==. You should also have noticed this strange looking construction:

```
#elif MY_AGE > \
      OLD_AGE + MIDDLE_AGE
```

Apart from the strange logic used, the backslash is new. A backslash at the end of a preprocessor line is a *line continuation* symbol. It indicates to the preprocessor that the next line belongs with the current one, and should be treated as a single logical expression. The preceding is equivalent to the following:

```
#elif MY_AGE > OLD_AGE + MIDDLE_AGE
```

The preprocessor requires that a line be explicitly continued, rather than explicitly terminated, as does the C language.

Macros are not just restricted to simple string substitution. They can actually take arguments, assuming a role more like that of functions. Here is an example of a macro that calculates the maximum of two different numbers:

```
#define MAX(a, b) ( a > b ? a : b )
```

Consider this code:

```
float f = MAX(1.0, 10.0);
```

It will look like this after the preprocessor is finished with it:

```
float f = (1.0 > 10.0 ? 1.0 : 10.0 );
```

Note that the preprocessor doesn't actually evaluate the macro; it simply performs a textual substitution of the arguments passed to it, and then inserts the result directly in the code.

Macros with arguments can be particularly useful when you have some code that can be applied for many different types. Instead of writing a different function for each of the possible types, each with a slightly different parameter list, you could write one macro. MAX is actually a good example of this principle because it works regardless of the type of number you feed to it:

```
float f = MAX(1.0, 10.0);
int i = MAX(5, 2);
```

As you can see, the same macro, MAX, is used with both floating-point numbers and integers in this example. You could not do this with a function: you would need to have one function to find the maximum of two floats (MaxFloats), and one to find the maximum of two ints (MaxInts).

The examples you have seen to this point in the chapter have all been concentrated in a single file, with the code executed directly in the main function. Of course, this is practical only for the simplest of programs. Usually, many different files are used, and then code organization becomes an issue. The next section deals with how you should organize your C programs.

Organizing Programs

As explained in Chapter 3, C programs typically comprise many source files with the extension .c. These files contain the *definitions* of the functions and variables that make up the program. Each source file is usually accompanied by a *header* file, which has the extension .h. A header file declares the parts of the source file that should be visible to the rest of the program, which may include macros, global variables, data types, and function signatures. Any .c file can utilize the declarations in a header file by including it with the #include preprocessor directive.

Take the following example: You have a function called DoSomething, and a struct called Monkey, and you want to put them into a separate file from the main function. You could write a header file, Monkey.h, which contains declarations and definitions, like this:

```
#ifndef MONKEY_H
#define MONKEY_H

typedef struct {
    char *name;
} Monkey;

void DoSomething(Monkey *monkey);

#endif
```

The first thing you will notice is that there are some preprocessor directives that don't have anything to do with the code itself. These directives are called *guards*. Definitions such as the struct Monkey can only be defined once, or the compiler will report an error. To avoid this, the guard is introduced, to ensure that the definitions in the header file only get imported once, no matter how many times #include "Monkey.h" appears.

The first line of the guard checks if the macro MONKEY_H is defined. If not, the preprocessor includes the definitions and declarations, and also defines MONKEY_H. The next time the header is included, MONKEY_H is defined, and the code is excluded. In this way, the declarations and definitions in Monkey.h are included only once per compilation.

The main.c file can use the definitions and declarations in Monkey.h by including it, like this:

```
#include <stdio.h>
#include "Monkey.h"

int main() {
    return 0;
}
```

The struct Monkey and the function DoSomething are now accessible inside the main function, as shown in the following:

```
#include <stdio.h>
#include "Monkey.h"

int main() {
    Monkey monkey;
    monkey.name = "Bonzo";
    DoSomething(&monkey);
    return 0;
}
```

The last piece of the puzzle is the Monkey.c file, which must provide a definition of DoSomething. Here is one possibility:

```
#include "Monkey.h"

void DoSomething(Monkey *monkey) {
    printf("%s stands on his head.\n", monkey->name);
}
```

Because the Monkey.c file also needs the definitions and declarations in Monkey.c, it also includes the header file Monkey.h. The Monkey.c file includes a definition of the function DoSomething, which simply prints a sentence using the name of the Monkey passed to it.

The struct Monkey does not get defined in Monkey.c because it was already defined in Monkey.h. Monkey must be defined in Monkey.h; otherwise, the compiler doesn't know what member variables it includes and cannot compile files such as main.c that access the variables of Monkey. This is not the case for the function DoSomething because the compiler needs to know only the signature of a function in order to compile the call in main.c. The implementation of DoSomething is not needed, so it is defined in DoSomething.c.

In general, you need to give the compiler enough details in a header file that it can compile any file using the header, but no more than that. Every time you make a change to a header file, any file that includes that header must be recompiled when you click Build. If your program becomes large, you will want to put the bare minimum in header files, so that you don't spend your time waiting for unnecessarily long builds for every small change you make.

In the following sections, to finish up your exploration of C, you are going to write a program that spans multiple files and uses many of the aspects of C you have read about in this chapter. The program itself is a simple address book, which allows you to add addresses, retrieve them, and save them to disk.

Try It Out Getting Started with MyAddressBook

1. Create a new Standard Tool project in Xcode and call it MyAddressBook.

2. Create a new C file called `Person.c` in the Source group. To do this, select the Source group in the Groups & Files view on the left, and then choose File ⇨ New File. Under the file group Carbon, choose C File, and click the Next button. Enter the name, and make sure that the Also Create "Person.h" check box is selected, as shown in Figure 6-4. When you are ready, click the Finish button, and Xcode creates two files: `Person.c` and `Person.h`.

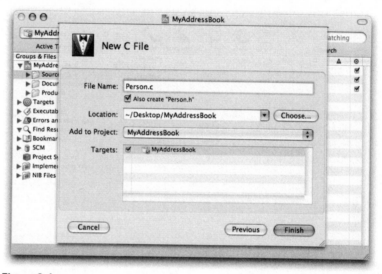

Figure 6-4

3. Replace the contents of the `Person.h` and `Person.c` files, as well as `main.c`, with the code given in the following listing:

Person.h

```c
#ifndef PERSON_H
#define PERSON_H

typedef struct {
    char *name;
    char *address;
} Person;

Person* AllocPerson();
void InitPerson( Person *person, char *name, char *address );
void DeallocPerson( Person *person );

#endif
```

Person.c

```c
#include "Person.h"
#include <stdio.h>
#include <stdlib.h>


Person* AllocPerson() {
    return malloc( sizeof(Person) );
}


void InitPerson( Person *person, char *name, char *address ) {
    int nameLength = strlen(name) + 1;
    person->name = malloc( sizeof(char) * nameLength );
    strcpy( person->name, name );

    int addressLength = strlen(address) + 1;
    person->address = malloc( sizeof(char) * addressLength );
    strcpy( person->address, address );
}


void DeallocPerson( Person *person ) {
    free( person->name );
    free( person->address );
    free( person );
}
```

main.c

```c
#include <stdio.h>
#include "Person.h"

int main () {
    Person *person = AllocPerson();
    InitPerson(person, "Joe Citizen", "1 Hopalong Avenue, MediumRare, USA");
    printf("Name: %s\nAddress: %s\n", person->name, person->address);
    DeallocPerson(person);
    return 0;
}
```

4. Compile and run the program by clicking the Build and Go toolbar item.

How It Works

The MyAddressBook program is considerably more complex than anything you have seen to this point. It makes use of all the aspects of C that you have already encountered, and uses them in a particular style of *structured programming* that is very common in C programming.

> *The style of programming demonstrated in this example is used, for example, in the Mac OS X frameworks CoreFoundation and QuickTime. Even if you don't end up programming in C, at some point you will inevitably need to use one of these frameworks, or one of the other C frameworks in Mac OS X. When that time comes, the information you have garnered from this example will serve you very well.*

In structured programming, data is arranged into structs, and functions are written to operate on the data in each struct. Together, the struct and functions that operate on it are referred to as an *Abstract*

Data Type (ADT), because they represent an abstraction of something, like a person or an automobile. This style of programming lays the foundations for object-oriented programming, and you learn about it in Chapter 7, which covers Objective-C.

You should generally begin to study a program that you are not familiar with by considering the *interfaces* it declares. These are the entities in a program that are visible to other parts of the program, and are given in the header files. From the header files, you can learn how a program is structured, and get a general idea of how it works, without knowing the finer details of how things are implemented.

You can find the interface of the `Person` ADT in `Person.h`. The `Person` ADT stores two strings: one to contain the name of the person, and another to contain the address. The only functions declared are for *constructing* and *destructing* the `Person` instance. Functions that allocate memory, initialize the ADT, and deallocate memory are common to all ADTs.

Every ADT provides methods for construction and destruction. Construction is the process of allocating memory for an ADT and initializing its data. Usually `malloc` is used to allocate memory. Destruction is freeing the memory associated with an ADT, usually with the `free` function, as well as any other resources it might be using, such as files.

The `Alloc...` functions allocate memory to store the ADT in. Mostly, the implementation of an `Alloc...` function simply calls `malloc` and returns the pointer to the new memory. This is the case for `AllocPerson`.

The `Init...` functions allocate and initialize any variables in the ADT. The `Dealloc...` method frees the data structures, as well as the ADT variable itself. As you can see in the preceding code, `DeallocPerson` frees the memory associated with the `name` and `address` variables, and then frees the `Person` struct itself.

The `main` function is some simple test code to create a new `Person`, print its data, and deallocate it again. Writing test code in this manner as you go can be very useful, rather than leaving your testing until the end when the whole program is written. Testing late in the game can make finding bugs much more difficult than if you test small chunks of the program at a time.

The `main` function demonstrates the pattern used for constructing and destructing ADT variables when using structured programming. Memory for the variable is first allocated by calling an `Alloc...` function, rather than using `malloc` directly:

```
Person *person = AllocPerson();
```

The pointer returned is assigned to the pointer variable used to represent the instance. Note that this variable is always a pointer. After the allocation of memory, an `Init...` function is called:

```
InitPerson(person, "Joe Citizen", "1 Hopalong Avenue, MediumRare, USA");
```

This allocates memory for any variables in the type and initializes them. When it is no longer needed, the variable is deallocated:

```
DeallocPerson(person);
```

This pattern of allocation, initialization, and deallocation is an important aspect of structured programming and object-oriented programming, which are introduced in Chapter 7.

Having written the `Person` ADT, in the following Try It Out you write the `AddressBook` ADT, which stores multiple `Person` instances and can be used to save them to file.

Try It Out   **Writing the AddressBook ADT**

1. Open the MyAddressBook project in Xcode, and using the approach described in the preceding Try It Out for creating files for the `Person` ADT, add files called `AddressBook.c` and `AddressBook.h`.

2. Insert the following code in the new files, and replace the existing `main` function as well:

AddressBook.h

```
#ifndef ADDRESSBOOK_H
#define ADDRESSBOOK_H

#include "Person.h"
#include <stdio.h>

typedef struct {
    Person **persons; // An array of pointers to Person
    int numPersons;
    int maxNumPersons;
} AddressBook;

AddressBook* CreateAddressBook( const char *pathToAddressBookFile );

AddressBook* AllocAddressBook();
void InitAddressBook( AddressBook *addressBook, const int maxNumPersons );
void InitAddressBookWithFile( AddressBook *addressBook, FILE *file);
void DeallocAddressBook( AddressBook *addressBook );

AddressBook* AddPerson( AddressBook *addressBook, Person *person );

Person* FindPerson( AddressBook *addressBook, char *name );

void SaveToFile( AddressBook *addressBook, FILE *file);

#endif
```

AddressBook.c

```
#include "AddressBook.h"
#include <stdio.h>
#include <stdlib.h>


void ReadLine( FILE *file, char *line, const int maxLength ) {
    fgets(line, maxLength-1, file);
        // This reads up to new line, and includes new line
    int l = strlen(line);
    line[l-1] = '\0';
        // Replace the new line character with a null terminating char
}


// Create an address book. If the address book file exists, create the book
// from the file. Otherwise, create an empty address book.
```

```c
AddressBook* CreateAddressBook( const char *pathToAddressBookFile ) {
    AddressBook *addressBook = AllocAddressBook();
    FILE *file;
    file = fopen( pathToAddressBookFile, "r" );
    if ( NULL == file ) {
        // Create new address book
        InitAddressBook( addressBook, 1000 );
    }
    else {
        // Read address book from file
        InitAddressBookWithFile( addressBook, file );
        fclose(file);
    }
    return addressBook;
}


AddressBook* AllocAddressBook() {
    return malloc( sizeof(AddressBook) );
}


void InitAddressBook( AddressBook *addressBook, const int maxNumPersons ) {
    addressBook->persons = malloc( sizeof(Person*) * maxNumPersons );
    addressBook->maxNumPersons = maxNumPersons;
    addressBook->numPersons = 0;
}


void InitAddressBookWithFile( AddressBook *addressBook, FILE *file ) {
    int numPersons, maxNumPersons;
    fscanf(file, "%d", &numPersons);
    fscanf(file, "%d", &maxNumPersons);
    fgetc(file); // Remove the new line character

    // Call the other initializer first.
    InitAddressBook( addressBook, maxNumPersons );

    int i;
    for ( i = 0; i < numPersons; ++i ) {
        int nameLength, addressLength;

        // Read person's name
        char name[256];
        ReadLine( file, name, 255 );

        // Read person's address
        char address[256];
        ReadLine( file, address, 255 );

        // Create new person
        Person *p = AllocPerson();
        InitPerson( p, name, address );

        // Add person to address book
        AddPerson( addressBook, p );
```

```
        }
    }


    void DeallocAddressBook( AddressBook *addressBook ) {
        // Dealloc all Persons first
        int i;
        for ( i = 0; i < addressBook->numPersons; ++i )
            DeallocPerson(addressBook->persons[i]);

        // Now free persons array
        free(addressBook->persons);

        // Free address book
        free(addressBook);
    }


    // Adding a person passes ownership of the person to the AddressBook.
    // The return value is the address book if the person was added successfully,
    // NULL otherwise.
    AddressBook* AddPerson( AddressBook *addressBook, Person *person ) {
        int n = addressBook->numPersons;

        // Check that the persons array is big enough. Otherwise indicate error.
        if ( ++n > addressBook->maxNumPersons ) return NULL;

        // Array is big enough, so add the new person.
        addressBook->numPersons = n;
        addressBook->persons[n-1] = person;

        return addressBook;
    }


    // Find a person in the address book according to their name. If the person
    // with the name is not found, NULL is returned.
    Person* FindPerson( AddressBook *addressBook, char *name ) {
        int i;
        for ( i = 0; i < addressBook->numPersons; ++i ) {
            Person *person = addressBook->persons[i];
            if ( strcmp( person->name, name ) == 0 ) return person;
        }
        return NULL;
    }


    void SaveToFile( AddressBook *addressBook, FILE *file) {
        fprintf(file, "%d\n", addressBook->numPersons);
        fprintf(file, "%d\n", addressBook->maxNumPersons);

        int i;
        for ( i = 0; i < addressBook->numPersons; ++i ) {
            Person *p = addressBook->persons[i];
```

```
            fprintf(file, "%s\n", p->name);
            fprintf(file, "%s\n", p->address);
        }
    }
```

main.c
```
#include <stdio.h>
#include "Person.h"
#include "AddressBook.h"

int main () {
    AddressBook *addressBook = AllocAddressBook();
    InitAddressBook(addressBook, 1000);

    // Add a person to the address book
    Person *person = AllocPerson();
    InitPerson(person, "Joe Citizen", "1 Hopalong Avenue, MediumRare, USA");
    AddPerson(addressBook, person);

    // Add another
    person = AllocPerson();
    InitPerson(person, "Jill Citizen", "2 Hopalong Avenue, MediumRare, USA");
    AddPerson(addressBook, person);

    // Search for person in the address book
    person = FindPerson(addressBook, "Joe Citizen");
    printf("Found person\nName: %s\nAddress: %s\n", person->name, person->address);

    DeallocAddressBook(addressBook);
    return 0;
}
```

3.   Compile and run the program by clicking the Build and Go toolbar item.

How It Works

The AddressBook ADT is declared in the header file AddressBook.h. The data of AddressBook is declared in the following struct:

```
typedef struct {
    Person **persons; // An array of pointers to Person
    int numPersons;
    int maxNumPersons;
} AddressBook;
```

The numPersons variable is used to store the number of entries currently in the address book, and maxNumPersons stores the upper limit on the number allowed. The entries themselves are stored in the variable persons. The double asterisk next to the label persons indicates that it is a pointer to a pointer to a Person. In this case, it will be used as an array of Person pointers; this is the same thing, because an array is simply represented as a pointer to its first element.

Although a double asterisk can represent an array of pointers, it is not always so. It is often used simply as a pointer to a pointer to a single data value. You cannot tell by looking at the variable declaration which is the case, so it's important to make your code clear by choosing appropriate variable names and using comments.

213

The functions declared for AddressBook are the following:

```
AddressBook* CreateAddressBook( const char *pathToAddressBookFile );

AddressBook* AllocAddressBook();
void InitAddressBook( AddressBook *addressBook, const int maxNumPersons );
void InitAddressBookWithFile( AddressBook *addressBook, FILE *file);
void DeallocAddressBook( AddressBook *addressBook );

AddressBook* AddPerson( AddressBook *addressBook, Person *person );

Person* FindPerson( AddressBook *addressBook, char *name );

void SaveToFile( AddressBook *addressBook, FILE *file);
```

The AllocAddressBook function is provided for allocating memory for an AddressBook. Two different functions are provided for initializing an AddressBook after it has been allocated: InitAddressBook and InitAddressBookWithFile. The function CreateAddressBook allocates and initializes an AddressBook in one call, and DeallocAddressBook is responsible for deallocating the memory associated with an AddressBook, and all of its member variables.

The other functions declared in the AddressBook.h file are AddPerson, for adding a new Person; FindPerson, for finding an existing Person; and SaveToFile, for saving the whole AddressBook to a file. This file can be read later to initialize a new AddressBook with the same information as the one saved, using the function InitAddressBookWithFile.

The InitAddressBook function in AddressBook.c looks like this:

```
void InitAddressBook( AddressBook *addressBook, const int maxNumPersons ) {
    addressBook->persons = malloc( sizeof(Person*) * maxNumPersons );
    addressBook->maxNumPersons = maxNumPersons;
    addressBook->numPersons = 0;
}
```

This function allocates an array of pointers to Persons and sets addressBook->persons with it. The other initializer function, InitAddressBookWithFile, calls InitAddressBook to do the initial memory allocation before adding addresses from file:

```
void InitAddressBookWithFile( AddressBook *addressBook, FILE *file ) {
    int numPersons, maxNumPersons;
    fscanf(file, "%d", &numPersons);
    fscanf(file, "%d", &maxNumPersons);
    fgetc(file); // Remove the new line character

    // Call the other initializer first.
    InitAddressBook( addressBook, maxNumPersons );

    int i;
    for ( i = 0; i < numPersons; ++i ) {
        int nameLength, addressLength;

        // Read person's name
        char name[256];
```

```
        ReadLine( file, name, 255 );

        // Read person's address
        char address[256];
        ReadLine( file, address, 255 );

        // Create new person
        Person *p = AllocPerson();
        InitPerson( p, name, address );

        // Add person to address book
        AddPerson( addressBook, p );
    }
}
```

The loop reads from file one person at a time. The number of Persons in the file is read first, along with the maximum number of Persons allowed in the address book. After the call to InitAddressBook, the loop reads one name and address at a time, allocates and initializes a new Person with the information, and adds it to the AddressBook with the AddPerson function.

The order in which the data is read from file in InitAddressBookWithFile has to be exactly the same as the order in which it was written. The function SaveToFile is used for writing the AddressBook to file:

```
void SaveToFile( AddressBook *addressBook, FILE *file) {
    fprintf(file, "%d\n", addressBook->numPersons);
    fprintf(file, "%d\n", addressBook->maxNumPersons);

    int i;
    for ( i = 0; i < addressBook->numPersons; ++i ) {
        Person *p = addressBook->persons[i];
        fprintf(file, "%s\n", p->name);
        fprintf(file, "%s\n", p->address);
    }
}
```

As you can see, it first prints the number of Persons, and the maximum number allowed. This is exactly the same order that InitAddressBookWithFile read them in. The loop prints the name and address of each person in turn, in the same order in which they are read.

> The capability to store information even after a program stops running is known as *persistence*. This can entail storing data on file, but could also involve more advanced means such as using a database. Being able to save your ADTs to some form of storage, and retrieve them again, is very useful, and many ADTs will define functions for performing these actions.

The function CreateAddressBook can be used to allocate and initialize a new AddressBook in a single function call. The function first checks to see if there is already an AddressBook stored on file. If so, it initializes the new AddressBook with the information stored using the function InitAddressBookWithFile:

```
AddressBook* CreateAddressBook( const char *pathToAddressBookFile ) {
    AddressBook *addressBook = AllocAddressBook();
```

```
    FILE *file;
    file = fopen( pathToAddressBookFile, "r" );
    if ( NULL == file ) {
        // Create new address book
        InitAddressBook( addressBook, 1000 );
    }
    else {
        // Read address book from file
        InitAddressBookWithFile( addressBook, file );
        fclose(file);
    }
    return addressBook;
}
```

To check if the file exists, an attempt is made to open it with fopen. If a NULL pointer is returned, the file does not exist. If there is no file, an empty AddressBook is initialized with the function InitAddressBook.

The AddPerson function in AddressBook.c adds a Person pointer to the end of the persons array:

```
AddressBook* AddPerson( AddressBook *addressBook, Person *person ) {
    int n = addressBook->numPersons;

    // Check that the persons array is big enough. Otherwise indicate error.
    if ( ++n > addressBook->maxNumPersons ) return NULL;

    // Array is big enough, so add the new person.
    addressBook->numPersons = n;
    addressBook->persons[n-1] = person;

    return addressBook;
}
```

Care is taken to check that there is room for adding the new Person, by comparing the new value of addressBook->numPersons with the maximum allowed value addressBook->maxNumPersons. The latter is used to allocate the persons array in InitAddressBook; ignoring the maximum would cause data to be written outside the array, and either corrupt other data or crash the program.

To find a person in the AddressBook, the FindPerson function simply loops over all of the Persons in the persons array, and checks if a match is found for the name passed:

```
Person* FindPerson( AddressBook *addressBook, char *name ) {
    int i;
    for ( i = 0; i < addressBook->numPersons; ++i ) {
        Person *person = addressBook->persons[i];
        if ( strcmp( person->name, name ) == 0 ) return person;
    }
    return NULL;
}
```

The strcmp function compares the name passed with the name of a Person in the persons array. If they match — if 0 is returned — the Person is returned from FindPerson. If no Person matches, NULL is returned.

The last function you should consider is the `DeallocAddressBook` function because it demonstrates the sort of actions you must take to clean up when you destruct an ADT variable:

```c
void DeallocAddressBook( AddressBook *addressBook ) {
    // Dealloc all Persons first
    int i;
    for ( i = 0; i < addressBook->numPersons; ++i )
        DeallocPerson(addressBook->persons[i]);

    // Now free persons array
    free(addressBook->persons);

    // Free address book
    free(addressBook);
}
```

You can see that a call is made to every `Person` in the `persons` array. This brings up the issue of *ownership*, because by deleting a `Person`, the `AddressBook` is assuming that no other part of the program needs to use it anymore. The `AddressBook` is considered to own any `Person` passed to the `AddPerson` function and is thus responsible for deleting it when the time comes.

An important part of memory management when programming with this structured form of C is to decide who owns each variable, and is thus responsible for deleting it. Not making a clear decision about this could lead to memory leaks, or variables being deallocated when they are still needed.

The `DeallocAddressBook` function continues by freeing the `persons` array. Note that this happens after all of the `Persons` contained in the array have been deallocated. If you freed the array first, you would not have any way to access its contents. The final act of `DeallocAddressBook` is to deallocate the `AddressBook` itself.

The `main` function is again used for testing purposes:

```c
int main () {
    AddressBook *addressBook = AllocAddressBook();
    InitAddressBook(addressBook, 1000);

    // Add a person to the address book
    Person *person = AllocPerson();
    InitPerson(person, "Joe Citizen", "1 Hopalong Avenue, MediumRare, USA");
    AddPerson(addressBook, person);

    // Add another
    person = AllocPerson();
    InitPerson(person, "Jill Citizen", "2 Hopalong Avenue, MediumRare, USA");
    AddPerson(addressBook, person);

    // Search for person in the address book
    person = FindPerson(addressBook, "Joe Citizen");
    printf("Found person\nName: %s\nAddress: %s\n", person->name, person->address);

    DeallocAddressBook(addressBook);
    return 0;
}
```

It creates an AddressBook instance, adds two Person instances to it with the AddPerson function, searches for one of the Persons with the FindPerson function, and prints details of the Person found.

With the basic data storage ADTs now defined for MyAddressBook, the next Try It Out moves on to deal with an ADT called Controller, which interacts with the user of the program and modifies the AddressBook instance according to requests from the user.

Try It Out   **Finishing Off MyAddressBook**

1. Using the approach described earlier for creating files for the Person and AddressBook ADTs, add files called Controller.c and Controller.h to the MyAddressBook project.

2. Insert the following code into the new files and replace the existing main function:

Controller.h

```c
#ifndef CONTROLLER_H
#define CONTROLLER_H

#include <stdio.h>
#include "Person.h"
#include "AddressBook.h"

typedef struct {
    AddressBook *addressBook;
    char *pathToAddressBookFile;
} Controller;

Controller* AllocController();
void InitController(Controller *controller);
void DeallocController(Controller *controller);

void PrintIntroductoryMessage(Controller *controller);
void PrintUserOptions(Controller *controller);

int ProcessUserChoice(Controller *controller, char c);
void ProcessNewPersonRequest(Controller *controller);
void ProcessFindPersonRequest(Controller *controller);
void ProcessSaveRequest(Controller *controller);

#endif
```

Controller.c

```c
#include "Controller.h"
#include <stdio.h>
#include <stdlib.h>
#include "Person.h"
#include "AddressBook.h"


Controller* AllocController() {
    return malloc( sizeof(Controller) );
}


void InitController(Controller *controller) {
```

```
        controller->pathToAddressBookFile = "/var/tmp/addressbook.txt";
        controller->addressBook = CreateAddressBook(controller->pathToAddressBookFile);
}


void DeallocController(Controller *controller) {
    DeallocAddressBook( controller->addressBook );
    free(controller);
}


void PrintIntroductoryMessage(Controller *controller) {
    printf("Welcome to MyAddressBook\n");
    printf("With this program, you can add addresses, retrieve them,\n"
           "and store them on file.\n");
}


void PrintUserOptions(Controller *controller) {
    printf("\nYou can either\n"
           "a) Add an address\n"
           "f) Find an address, or\n"
           "s) Save your addresses\n"
           "q) Save and Quit\n");
    printf("Please enter your choice (a, f, s, or q): ");
}


// Return value is 1 if the program should stop running, and 0
// if it should continue.
int ProcessUserChoice(Controller *controller, char choice) {
    int shouldStop = 0;
    switch (choice) {
        case 'a':
            ProcessNewPersonRequest(controller);
            break;
        case 'f':
            ProcessFindPersonRequest(controller);
            break;
        case 's':
            ProcessSaveRequest(controller);
            break;
        case 'q':
            ProcessSaveRequest(controller);
            shouldStop = 1;
            break;
        default:
            printf("You entered an invalid choice. Try again.\n");
    }
    return shouldStop;
}


void ProcessNewPersonRequest(Controller *controller) {
    char name[256];
    printf("You chose to add an address.\n");
```

```
        printf("Please enter the name of the person to add: ");
        gets(name);

        char address[256];
        printf("Please enter the address of the person on one line: ");
        gets(address);

        Person *p = AllocPerson();
        InitPerson( p, name, address );

        if ( ! AddPerson( controller->addressBook, p ) )
            printf("An error occurred while trying to add the new address.\n");
}


void ProcessFindPersonRequest(Controller *controller) {
    char name[256];
    printf("You chose to find an address.\n");
    printf("Please enter the name of the person to find: ");
    gets(name);

    // Print details of person if found. Otherwise tell the user that
    // the person could not be found.
    Person *p = FindPerson( controller->addressBook, name );
    if ( p )
        printf("The address of %s is\n%s\n", p->name, p->address );
    else
        printf("The address of %s could not be found.\n", name );
}


void ProcessSaveRequest(Controller *controller) {
    FILE *file = fopen(controller->pathToAddressBookFile, "w");
    SaveToFile(controller->addressBook, file);
    fclose(file);
}
```

main.c

```
#include <stdio.h>
#include "Person.h"
#include "AddressBook.h"
#include "Controller.h"

int main () {
    Controller *controller = AllocController();
    InitController(controller);

    PrintIntroductoryMessage(controller);

    // Main run loop
    int exitMainLoop = 0;
    while ( !exitMainLoop ) {
        PrintUserOptions(controller);
        char line[256];
        gets( line );
```

```
        if ( strlen(line) > 1 ) {
            printf("You entered too many characters. Try again.\n");
        }
        else {
            exitMainLoop = ProcessUserChoice( controller, line[0] );
        }
    }

    DeallocController(controller);

    return 0;
}
```

3. Compile and run the program by clicking the Build and Go toolbar item.

4. Follow the instructions printed by the program in the Run Log window. Add a few names and addresses. Search for one of the names you have entered, and also search for a name that you haven't added, just to see what happens. Try entering an invalid option to see how the program reacts.

5. When you have finished playing with MyAddressBook, choose the Save and Quit option. Now rerun the program, and search for one of the names you entered before you quit. The program should find and print the address, even though it was added in a different session.

How It Works

As you now know, the MyAddressBook program has three ADTs: `Person`, `AddressBook`, and `Controller`. A `Person` is a type that stores information about an entry in the address book, in particular, name and address. The `AddressBook` type contains many instances of the type `Person`, which represent all of the entries in the address book. The last ADT, `Controller`, is a type that interacts with the user, and updates the data objects as required.

> This design is known as *Model-View-Controller (MVC)*, and is very important in Cocoa programming, which you learn about in Chapter 8. Put simply, the data objects, like Person and `AddressBook`, make up the Model. The View is the interface with the user, in this case a console with keyboard input. (In Cocoa programming, the View is usually the Aqua Graphical User Interface.) The Controller is the intermediary between the View and the Model, and is in charge of keeping the two synchronized with one another.

The `Controller` has the usual functions for constructing and destructing the ADT, but it also includes functions that print information for the user and process user input:

```
typedef struct {
    AddressBook *addressBook;
    char *pathToAddressBookFile;
} Controller;

Controller* AllocController();
void InitController(Controller *controller);
void DeallocController(Controller *controller);

void PrintIntroductoryMessage(Controller *controller);
```

```
void PrintUserOptions(Controller *controller);

int ProcessUserChoice(Controller *controller, char c);
void ProcessNewPersonRequest(Controller *controller);
void ProcessFindPersonRequest(Controller *controller);
void ProcessSaveRequest(Controller *controller);
```

The `Controller` struct holds the `AddressBook` used in the program, in the variable `addressBook`. It also contains a path to the file where the address book can be saved.

The `Process...` functions handle different user requests. `ProcessNewPersonRequest` is for adding a new entry to the address book, and `ProcessFindPersonRequest` is for finding a person in the address book. Saving the address book to file is handled by `ProcessSaveRequest`. The `ProcessUserChoice` function takes a `char` entered by the user, and chooses the appropriate `Process...` method to call for that choice. If the user presses a, for example, the `ProcessUserChoice` function ends up calling `ProcessNewPersonRequest`.

The `Controller.c` file contains most of the code for interacting with the user. When the user makes a choice, the `main` function calls the function `ProcessUserChoice`:

```
int ProcessUserChoice(Controller *controller, char choice) {
    int shouldStop = 0;
    switch (choice) {
        case 'a':
            ProcessNewPersonRequest(controller);
            break;
        case 'f':
            ProcessFindPersonRequest(controller);
            break;
        case 's':
            ProcessSaveRequest(controller);
            break;
        case 'q':
            ProcessSaveRequest(controller);
            shouldStop = 1;
            break;
        default:
            printf("You entered an invalid choice. Try again.\n");
    }
    return shouldStop;
}
```

As you can see, this is really just a big `switch`. A processing method is chosen based on the letter entered by the user. When the user chooses q, the address book is saved by `ProcessSaveRequest`, and the flag `shouldStop` is set to 1. This causes the `main` function to exit.

When the user chooses to add a new address, the `ProcessNewPersonRequest` is called. It asks the user for the name and address of the new entry, creates a new `Person`, and adds it to the `AddressBook`:

```
void ProcessNewPersonRequest(Controller *controller) {
    char name[256];
    printf("You chose to add an address.\n");
    printf("Please enter the name of the person to add: ");
```

```
    gets(name);

    char address[256];
    printf("Please enter the address of the person on one line: ");
    gets(address);

    Person *p = AllocPerson();
    InitPerson( p, name, address );

    if ( ! AddPerson( controller->addressBook, p ) )
        printf("An error occurred while trying to add the new address.\n");
}
```

The address book is stored in the variable `controller->addressBook`, and gets created in the `Init Controller` function. Note that the return value of `AddPerson` is checked to see if it is `NULL`, because a `NULL` return value is used to indicate an error has occurred, such as when the array of `Persons` is too small to hold the new entry.

The `ProcessFindPersonRequest` is very straightforward: it simply calls the `AddressBook`'s `FindPerson` function, and returns the result.

The `ProcessSaveRequest` first opens a file for writing, and then asks the `AddressBook` to save its contents on the file using the `SaveToFile` function, and finally closes the file again:

```
void ProcessSaveRequest(Controller *controller) {
    FILE *file = fopen(controller->pathToAddressBookFile, "w");
    SaveToFile(controller->addressBook, file);
    fclose(file);
}
```

The path to where the `AddressBook` will be stored is fixed in this example, and initialized in `InitController` to `/var/tmp/addressbook.txt`. In a more advanced program, the user would be able to set this path.

The `Controller` creates a new `AddressBook` by calling the function `CreateAddressBook` from `AddressBook.c`. As you saw earlier, this function first checks to see if there is already an `AddressBook` stored on file. If so, it initializes the new `AddressBook` with the information stored using the function `InitAddressBookWithFile`. If not, it creates a new empty `AddressBook`.

The `main` function is relatively simple. It simply creates a `Controller`, asks it to print an introductory message for the user, and then loops until the `Controller` indicates it should stop:

```
int main () {
    Controller *controller = AllocController();
    InitController(controller);

    PrintIntroductoryMessage(controller);

    // Main run loop
    int exitMainLoop = 0;
    while ( !exitMainLoop ) {
        PrintUserOptions(controller);
        char line[256];
        gets( line );
```

```
        if ( strlen(line) > 1 ) {
            printf("You entered too many characters. Try again.\n");
        }
        else {
            exitMainLoop = ProcessUserChoice( controller, line[0] );
        }
    }

    DeallocController(controller);

    return 0;
}
```

Each iteration of the loop prints a request for the user to choose an operation. The function `PrintUser Options` is used for this purpose. The `main` function then reads the whole line of input typed by the user with the `gets` function. If this line is longer than one character, an error message is printed. If exactly one character was entered (excluding the new line character), the character is passed to the `Controller` function `ProcessUserChoice`, which takes the appropriate action. The `ProcessUserChoice` returns a non-zero value when the program should stop. After the loop exits, the `DeallocController` method frees the memory of the `Controller` and the `AddressBook` that it contains.

This concludes your exploration of the C programming language. C is useful in itself, but it becomes really useful as the basis for other languages, such as Objective-C, which you learn about in the next chapter. Ninety percent of Objective-C is just plain C, so having completed this chapter, you are well on your way to understanding Objective-C and learning to program with the Cocoa frameworks (see Chapter 8).

Summary

This chapter has been a crash course in the one of the most important languages on Mac OS X. Along the way you have learned

❑   That C is the Latin of programming languages, underpinning operating systems such as Mac OS X and fathering more modern languages such as Objective-C, Java, and C++.

❑   About various aspects of C, such as variables, pointers, functions, conditional branching, memory management, and looping.

❑   About structured programming in C, where data structures are coupled with functions to form abstract data types (ADTs). This style of programming is used in fundamental Mac OS X frameworks such as CoreFoundation, QuickTime, and Carbon. It is also the basis of object-oriented programming (OOP).

In the next chapter, you learn about Objective-C, which together with the Cocoa frameworks (Chapter 8) forms the basis of most new application development on Mac OS X. Before proceeding, however, try the exercises that follow to test your understanding of the material covered in this chapter. You can find the solutions to these exercises in Appendix A.

Exercises

1. Modify the Grepper C program so that it can search in multiple files for a string. Assume that the filenames are given as the first arguments to the main function, and that the search string is given last. Test it by adding more than one file to the arguments of the Grepper executable in Xcode. Also modify the program so that line numbers are printed after the filename in the program output.

2. Change MyAddressBook so that the user can request that an entry be removed from the address book.

The Objective-C Language

Objective-C is an *object-oriented* programming (OOP) language that forms the basis of most new software development on Mac OS X. It is a superset of the C programming language, which means that you can use C code directly in an Objective-C program. In fact, much of an Objective-C program is simply C. What's left is a small number of extensions to facilitate object-oriented programming, which can potentially make your life a lot easier as a programmer.

The philosophy of Objective-C is a minimalist one. The object-oriented (OO) features of Objective-C were designed to be a compact and easy-to-understand extension to C. This is in contrast to C++, for example, which is also a superset of C, but which includes many different extensions to standard C, and is relatively difficult to learn. Anyone that understands C++, or any other object-oriented language for that matter, can learn Objective-C in a few hours. For those with no understanding of object-oriented programming, Objective-C is one of the better languages with which to learn it, because of its simplicity.

Just because Objective-C is easy to learn, and simple to use, does not mean it gives away anything to other languages when it comes to expressiveness. In many ways, Objective-C is more powerful than other languages, by way of its dynamism, as you will learn as you proceed through this chapter. Cocoa developers, extolling the virtues of the Objective-C/Cocoa combination, often claim that they are much more productive than they ever were with any other combination of language and framework. After you have completed this chapter, and Chapter 8, which covers the Cocoa frameworks, you can be the judge.

In this chapter you learn

❑ What object-oriented programming (OOP) is, and its most important characteristics

❑ The extensions to C defined by the Objective-C language, including object-oriented programming

❑ How to write object-oriented programs in Objective-C, using the Foundation framework from Cocoa

Object-Oriented Programming

Before you begin to learn Objective-C, you need to know a little bit about what it was designed to achieve. *Object-oriented programming* (OOP) has really caught on only over the last 15 years or so, but is now the de facto standard for all programming languages. Nearly all development these days takes place in the object-oriented style — even in non-OO languages like C!

So what is OOP? The main distinction between programming in an object-oriented language like Objective-C, and programming in a procedural language like C, is that data and functions that operate on that data are grouped together into entities called *objects*. An *object* has both data and behavior: the data are the variables belonging to the object, and the behavior is defined by the object's functions.

An object is actually a variable or *instance* of a particular *class*. A class defines what data and functions a particular type of object has. For example, a class called Person could declare that Person objects have a name and address, and that they have functions to create a new Person, delete an existing Person, and perform operations like changing a Person's address.

> *If you worked through the chapter on C programming, you realize by now that OOP has many similarities with the structured programming example you encountered in the simple address book program MyAddressBook. Indeed, structured programming with Abstract Data Types (ADTs) was a forerunner of OOP, and is still used today to achieve some of the benefits of OOP in programming languages that do not support object orientation, such as C.*

The variables in an object are called *instance variables* or *attributes*. They are very similar to the variables in a C `struct`. The functions associated with an object are called *methods*, and are similar, though not the same, as functions in C.

An important aspect of OOP is being able to hide the data in an object from other parts of the program. This is known as *encapsulation*, because the object encapsulates its own data, and can choose how and what to make accessible to the rest of the program. Encapsulation is important, because it reduces the dependencies between different parts of a program. If you know that a certain variable can only be accessed from within a certain class, you have much less to think about when searching and changing code that uses that variable.

A second aspect of OOP is the capability to directly reuse the instance variables and member functions of one class in another class. This is known as *inheritance*, and classes related in this way often mimic the relationships found in the real world. For example, a dentist is a type of person. You could say that a dentist *inherits* the characteristics of a person, as well as possessing some unique attributes that a general person does not exhibit. If you were modeling this in an object-oriented (OO) program, you may create a class `Dentist`, which inherits all of the data (that is, attributes) and behavior (that is, member functions) of a class `Person`. `Dentist` is said to be a *subclass* of `Person`.

The last major aspect of OO programming languages not possessed by procedural languages is *polymorphism*. The word may be terrifying, but the meaning is less so: Polymorphism is the capability of something to behave differently depending on the circumstances. In the context of OOP, it refers to the ability of a single *method invocation* — the OO equivalent of a function call — to execute different code depending on an object's class.

To make the discussion more concrete, take a real-world example: A Man is a type of Person, and a Woman is a type of Person. Each could be considered subclasses of Person. Assume that a Person has a life expectancy, which depends on its specific type — its subclass. A Man, for example, may have a life expectancy of only 70 years, while a Woman may expect to live for 77 years. If you have an object of the class Person, you will get a different answer to the question "What is your life expectancy?" depending on the specific subclass of Person you are talking to. In programming terms, the same method invocation — lifeExpectancy, for example — either executes some code in the class Man or some code in the class Woman, depending on the type of Person used to invoke the method.

If this all seems a bit abstract, don't worry; it will become clearer when you see how these concepts are put in practice. At this point, it is only necessary that you get a vague feeling for what OOP is, and some of its more important attributes.

Classes and Objects

Objective-C takes the concepts presented in the previous section, and makes minimal extensions to C in order to implement them. Classes in Objective-C are comprised of two basic code structures: the *interface block* and the *implementation block*.

The interface block defines the interface of a class, which includes its instance variables and methods. The interface is usually found in a header file, because it should be accessible to the rest of the program. Here is an interface block for a class similar to the Person type defined in the MyAddressBook program from Chapter 6:

```
@interface Person : NSObject
{
    NSString *name;
    NSString *address;
}
-(id)initWithName:(NSString *)name andAddress:(NSString *)address;
-(void)dealloc;
-(NSString *)name;
-(NSString *)address;
@end
```

The interface block begins with the keyword @interface, and ends with @end. After the @interface keyword, the name of the class is given, followed by a colon, and the name of the *superclass*. The superclass of Person is NSObject, just as Person is a subclass of NSObject. Person inherits all of the data and methods of the class NSObject. NSObject is an important Cocoa class from which nearly all classes ultimately *descend*. You learn more about this class as you go.

After the superclass, a block in braces declares the data belonging to the class. This part of the class interface is similar in many ways to a C struct, and the preceding code bears a close resemblance to the struct Person used in the MyAddressBook program in Chapter 6. The main difference is that whereas C strings are represented by the simple type char*, in Objective-C/Cocoa programming, variables of the class NSString* are usually used instead.

> *The NS that appears at the beginning of every Cocoa class name is a prefix used to avoid naming conflicts. An application or framework will often use a unique prefix for class names, so that the chance of two different classes having the same name is minimized.*
>
> *The choice of NS may seem obscure, until you realize that Cocoa descends from a technology called NeXTSTEP, which was originally created by NeXT Computers, and later bought by Apple in 1996.*

After the instance variables, the method declarations appear. An Objective-C method signature looks considerably different to a C function, though there are many similarities, too. Like a C function, a method has a name, but this name is partitioned into sections, one for each parameter that the method declares. You learn more about how Objective-C methods are declared in the next section. For now, you simply need to recognize that the preceding example declares four different methods, one on each line.

The implementation block of the Person class could take the following form:

```
@implementation Person

-(id)initWithName:(NSString *)name andAddress:(NSString *)address {
...
}

-(void)dealloc {
...
}

-(NSString *)name {
...
}

-(NSString *)address {
...
}

@end
```

The implementation usually appears in a file with the extension .m, and the same base name as the header file in which the interface block appeared. In this case, the Person interface would probably be in the file Person.h, and the implementation in Person.m.

The implementation block is similar to the interface block, but has no data section. It contains the definitions of the methods declared in the interface block, between @implementation and @end keywords. The name of the class is given directly after the @implementation keyword, just as it was for the interface block.

In Objective-C, it is perfectly legal, and indeed common, to have multiple interface blocks, and multiple implementations per class. They don't even have to be in the same files. The extra blocks define *categories*, and the code in them has all of the same privileges as the main interface and implementation blocks. The only difference is that a category cannot define any new data: the interface block cannot declare instance variables, only methods.

Here is the interface block of a category for the Person class:

```
@interface Person ( MeasurementsCategory )
-(float)heightInMeters;
-(float)weightInKilos;
@end
```

The implementation would look like this:

```
@implementation Person ( MeasurementsCategory )

-(float)heightInMeters {
...
}

-(float)weightInKilos {
```

```
...
}

@end
```

As you can see, a category has an additional label, given in brackets after the class name in both the interface and implementation blocks. This label must be unique on a per-class basis, but can otherwise be any legal identifier. Note that the category implementation doesn't have to be in a separate implementation block, but can also be placed in an existing one.

In the `Person` example, a category called `MeasurementsCategory` has been defined. The interface block declares two methods: `heightInMeters` and `weightInKilos`. Note that there is no data block, because that is not allowed. In this case, the new methods could not simply return the value of an instance variable, unless that instance variable were to be included in the main interface block.

The methods declared in `MeasurementsCategory` are treated exactly the same as methods declared in the main interface block. Everything you learn in the following sections about methods and how they work applies equally well to category methods as methods declared in the main interface block.

Objective-C places no special restrictions on the kind of methods defined in a category. For example, you can replace an existing method in a category. This allows you to change the behavior of a class without writing a subclass. You should be wary, however, that you cannot easily call the original method from inside your category method when you do this.

Methods

Now you are going to take a closer look at how methods are defined, and called, or *invoked*, to be more consistent with the OO terminology.

Consider the first method of the `Person` class above:

```
-(id)initWithName:(NSString *)name andAddress:(NSString *)address;
```

The method's name is broken into two segments, `initWithName:` and `andAddress:`. The full name of this method is `initWithName:andAddress:`, which is quite a mouthful, but has the advantage that it reads like a sentence. After each section of the name, there is a colon, which is actually considered part of the name itself, and then a parameter. The type of the parameter is given in parentheses, followed by the parameter name.

It is also legal to have parameters with only a colon, and no preceding label, like this:

```
-(void)methodWith3Parameters:(NSString *)param1 :(float)param2 :(int)param3;
```

The method name in this case is `methodWith3Parameters:::` — the colons are significant.

The parameter types in a method declaration are also optional, but if you exclude them, the parameter is assumed to be an object. A generic object has the type `id` in Objective-C, as shown in the following method declaration:

```
-(void)doSomethingWithObject:(id)object1 andObject:(id)object2;
```

This is an equivalent declaration:

```
-(void)doSomethingWithObject:object1 andObject:object2;
```

By now you will have realized that Objective-C methods also have return values, just like C functions. In the first example in this section, the return value was of the type id, a generic object. In the subsequent examples, there was no return value, so the return type was given as void, just as in C.

The hyphen that you see preceding every method signature is not just for decoration; it indicates an *instance method*. An instance method is one that belongs to an object or instance of the class. Instance methods have an extra hidden argument passed to them when they are invoked: the object that the method belongs to. This object can be accessed inside an instance method using the variable self. For example, it is not uncommon to see methods something like the following in Objective-C classes:

```
-(void)run {
    [self takeYourMark];
    [self go];
}
```

Here the method run invokes two other methods, takeYouMark and go, both of which belong to the same class. It uses the self variable to refer to the object for which the other methods are invoked.

Another type of method is also found in Objective-C: the *class method*. Class methods are preceded by a + symbol rather than a hyphen. Class methods are shared by all objects of a particular class, and do not get passed an object hidden in the self variable; instead, the class itself is passed in via the self variable. Here is how you might declare a class method for the Person class:

```
+(int)totalNumberOfPersons;
```

This method describes a property of the class Person, and not of an individual Person object, so it is appropriate to make it a class method.

The only aspect of methods not yet considered is how you can actually invoke them. The syntax for invoking an Objective-C method is quite different to calling a C function. Here is an example of invoking one of the instance methods introduced earlier:

```
[obj doSomethingWithObject:arg1 andObject:arg2];
```

The whole invocation appears between square brackets. The object to which the method belongs — in this case the object obj — comes first, followed by the segmented method name. After each colon in the name, an argument is given. In this case, the argument variables are called arg1 and arg2.

Method invocations can be embedded in one another. Consider the following variation on the preceding example:

```
[[otherObj getObject] doSomethingWithObject:arg1 andObject:[anotherObj getArg]];
```

The original method invocation now has two additional invocations embedded within it. Each invocation is enclosed in square brackets. The first invokes the getObject method of the object otherObject. The return value of getObject becomes the object for which doSomethingWithObject:andObject: is invoked. The other embedded method is getArg, which is invoked for the object anotherObj, with the return value becoming the second argument to doSomethingWithObject:andObject:.

You may find the syntax used to invoke methods in Objective-C unusual at first, particularly if you are used to other calling conventions, but you soon get used to it, and when you do, you may even find it preferable to other styles. To better grasp how the Objective-C syntax works, here is the previous method as it might be written in Java or another C-like OO language:

```
otherObj.getObject().doSomething(arg1, anotherObj.getArg());
```

The Java way is a little shorter, but not as explicit about what arguments are being passed to doSomething. The Objective-C approach has the advantage of being more *self-documenting*, at the expense of being more verbose. Both approaches work well in practice, and which of the two is best is really just a question of personal preference.

Class methods are invoked the same way as instance methods, but they must be invoked on a class. You can give the class explicitly, like this:

```
[Person totalNumberOfPersons];
```

Alternatively, you can give the class via the class method of an object, like this:

```
[[person class] totalNumberOfPersons];
```

The variable person is assumed here to be an instance of the class Person. The method class returns the class of any object.

> *Class methods in Objective-C are a bit different to the analogous methods found in Java or C++. In Objective-C, class methods behave just like instance methods. They can be inherited and overridden, for example, concepts that you learn more about later in the chapter. In other languages, class methods — which are often called static methods — are more like C functions, and do not exhibit the OO characteristics of instance methods.*

In the following Try It Out, you rewrite in Objective-C the Grepper program that you saw in Chapter 6. This will give you an idea of what Objective-C looks like, and the way objects and classes are used.

Try It Out   Rewriting Grepper in Objective-C

1. Create a new project in Xcode. In the New Project panel, choose the project type Foundation Tool in the group Command Line Utility. Call the project Grepper in Objective-C.

2. Find the file Grepper in Objective C.m in the Source group of the Groups & Files list on the left. Select it so that its source code appears in the editor. To display the editor, you may need to drag open the split view on the right.

3. Replace the code in the open file, which was generated by Xcode, with the following:

```
#import <Foundation/Foundation.h>

int main (int argc, const char * argv[]) {
    NSAutoreleasePool * pool = [[NSAutoreleasePool alloc] init];

    @try {
        // Make sure there are two arguments given, the filename
        // and the search string
        if ( argc != 3 ) {
```

```
            NSException *exception =
                [NSException exceptionWithName:@"GrepperException"
                    reason:@"Wrong number of arguments passed to main."
                    userInfo:nil];
            @throw exception;
        }

        // Get input file path from standard input
        NSString *inpPathString = [NSString stringWithCString:argv[1]];

        // Get string to search for
        NSString *searchString = [NSString stringWithCString:argv[2]];

        // Read file into string
        NSString *fileString = [NSString stringWithContentsOfFile:inpPathString];

        // Split file string into lines
        NSArray *lines = [fileString componentsSeparatedByString:@"\n"];

        // Loop over lines, printing any that contain the search string
        NSFileHandle *so = [NSFileHandle fileHandleWithStandardOutput];
        NSEnumerator *lineEnum = [lines objectEnumerator];
        NSString *line;
        while ( line = [lineEnum nextObject] ) {
            // Find range of search string
            NSRange searchStringRange = [line rangeOfString:searchString];

            // If string was found, write it to standard output
            // Also add a new line character
            if ( searchStringRange.location != NSNotFound ) {
                NSString *s =
                    [NSString stringWithFormat:@"In file %@:\t%@\n",
                        inpPathString, line];
                [so writeData:[s dataUsingEncoding:NSUTF8StringEncoding]];
            }
        }

    }
    @catch (NSException *e) {
        NSLog(@"The following error occurred: %@", [e reason]);
    }

    [pool release];
    return 0;
}
```

4. Open the Targets group in the Groups & Files list, and select the Grepper in Objective C target. Choose File ⇨ GetInfo and click the Build tab. Scroll down until you see Enable Objective-C Exceptions, and select the check box next to it. Close the Info panel.

5. Click the Build toolbar item to compile the program.

6. Open the Executables group in Groups & Files, click the Grepper in Objective C executable, and again choose Get Info from the File menu. Select the Arguments tab, and add two arguments to the first table, by twice clicking the + button under the table. The first argument should be a path

to a text file that you would like to search in. (It could even be the source code for this example.) The second argument should be the string that will be sought in the file. Close the Get Info panel.

7. Click the Build and Go toolbar item to run the program. You should see the lines in the file you entered that contain the search string appear in the Run Log window.

How It Works

This example, though short, is dense with Cocoa classes, so you are not expected to grasp it all at once. However, you should try to get a feel for Objective-C code, and how closely intertwined Objective-C is with Cocoa. Cocoa is to Objective-C what the Standard Library is to C.

At the top of the file, there is a preprocessor directive that is not recognized by the standard C preprocessor: `#import`. `#import` is similar to `#include`, but it imports a file content only once. Any further imports are ignored. In other words, it fulfills the same role as the guards discussed in Chapter 6, but in a much easier and concise manner.

The `#import` statement imports the framework Foundation, which is part of Cocoa. It provides the functionality of Cocoa that is not related to the graphical user interface; that's why you can use it in a command-line tool like Grepper, which has no graphical interface.

The `main` function begins by creating an object of the type `NSAutoreleasePool`. This has to do with memory management, and you should ignore it for the time being; it is discussed in depth later.

The main body of the code appears in a block between the Objective-C keywords `@try` and `@catch`. These are used for exception handling. Exception handling is about treating exceptional occurrences and errors. Objective-C provides facilities for exception handling, like most other OO languages, that allow you to jump from anywhere in the `@try` block to the `@catch` block whenever an exception arises. An example of this appears at the top of the `@try` block:

```
if ( argc != 3 ) {
    NSException *exception =
        [NSException exceptionWithName:@"GrepperException"
            reason:@"Wrong number of arguments passed to main."
            userInfo:nil];
    @throw exception;
}
```

This is the same test performed in the original Grepper program, to make sure there were exactly two arguments passed when the program was started. In the original program, if the condition was not met, the program simply returned a non-zero value. In this case, an exception is thrown: an object of the class `NSException` is created, and the keyword `@throw` used to jump to the `@catch` block.

In the `@catch` block, the exception is caught, and the reason for the exception, which was included in the `NSException` when it was created, is output to the program log, using the function `NSLog`:

```
@catch (NSException *e) {
    NSLog(@"The following error occurred: %@", [e reason]);
}
```

`NSLog` is virtually the same in its workings as `printf`, but it expects to be passed an `NSString` as the first argument, not a `char*`. A literal `NSString` is created using double quotes, preceded by an `@` symbol. Note also the formatting character %@, which is used when an object is to be printed, in this case the reason for the exception, which is an NSString. When this formatting character is encountered, the description method of the object is called to get an NSString representing its value.

After the argument count test, several NSStrings are created:

```
// Get input file path from standard input
NSString *inpPathString = [NSString stringWithCString:argv[1]];

// Get string to search for
NSString *searchString = [NSString stringWithCString:argv[2]];

// Read file into string
NSString *fileString = [NSString stringWithContentsOfFile:inpPathString];

// Split file string into lines
NSArray *lines = [fileString componentsSeparatedByString:@"\n"];
```

Various methods are used to create the strings, including stringWithCString: to create strings from the char* string parameters of the main function, and stringWithContentsOfFile:, which reads the file at the path passed, and places its contents in an NSString object.

To make processing the file string easier, it is split into an array of lines. A Cocoa array class is used to contain the lines: NSArray. Other than NSString, NSArray is probably the most widely used Cocoa class there is. It is similar to an array in C, in that you can store and retrieve objects by index, but it is also more powerful. You learn more about it in Chapter 8, which covers the Cocoa frameworks.

The last part of the @try block loops through the lines in the NSArray, and searches each one for the search string passed to the main function:

```
NSFileHandle *so = [NSFileHandle fileHandleWithStandardOutput];
NSEnumerator *lineEnum = [lines objectEnumerator];
NSString *line;
while ( line = [lineEnum nextObject] ) {
    // Find range of search string
    NSRange searchStringRange = [line rangeOfString:searchString];

    // If string was found, write it to standard output
    // Also add a new line character
    if ( searchStringRange.location != NSNotFound ) {
        NSString *s =
            [NSString stringWithFormat:@"In file %@:\t%@\n",
                inpPathString, line];
        [so writeData:[s dataUsingEncoding:NSUTF8StringEncoding]];
    }
}
```

A class called NSEnumerator is used to move through the array. Its job is simply to enumerate the array, or move from one element to the next, and nothing more. The method nextObject returns the next object in the NSArray until there are none left, at which point nil is returned. The combination of NSArray, NSEnumerator, and the while loop as used here is very common in Cocoa programming.

The NSString method rangeOfString: is used to search each line for the string stored in the variable searchString. This method returns an NSRange, which is a standard C struct, *not* an Objective-C class. As a result, you can treat searchStringRange as a stack variable, rather than a pointer to a heap object. Objective-C requires all objects be allocated from the application heap, and must always be represented as pointers. You learn more about how to create an Objective-C object later in this chapter.

rangeOfString: returns an NSRange with its location variable set to the constant NSNotFound if the string is not found. The if statement checks searchStringRange to see for the string, and writes the line to standard output when it is found. Standard output is represented by the variable so, which is a variable of the class NSFileHandle. NSFileHandle is the Objective-C class equivalent of C's FILE type.

Data Hiding

An important aspect of OOP is encapsulation of data. Encapsulation requires that a language include facilities for *data hiding* so that the programmer can control access to data from outside a class. Objective-C provides three keywords for this purpose: @public, @protected, and @private. These keywords can be inserted into the data section of a class's interface block and applies to any data that follows, up to the end of the block or the next keyword.

For example, imagine that you want to restrict access to the name attribute of the Person class, but wish to make the address attribute directly accessible to the rest of the program. You could declare the class like this:

```
@interface Person : NSObject
{
    @public
    NSString *address;

    @private
    NSString *name;
}
...
@end
```

The @public keyword makes an instance variable globally accessible. Any part of your program can directly retrieve the value of a public variable or modify its value. The @private keyword indicates that data may be accessed only from within the specific class in which it appears, in this case Person. @protected gives access to the data from within the class in which it appears, but also from *descendents* of that class—subclasses of the class, subclasses of subclasses of the class, and so forth. If no keyword is given, instance variables are assumed to have protected accessibility.

In general, you should make as much data in your classes protected or private as possible. Public data is frowned upon in OOP, because any change in the way the data is represented in the class can potentially require global changes to your program. For example, imagine that instead of using an NSString to store the address in Person, you decide you want to use another class. Because your program has direct access to the address variable, you will have to track down every point in the program where the address is accessed and update the code. This is not only a time-consuming operation, but it can also be an error prone one, leading to bugs in your program.

So how should you access instance variables from outside the class itself? You should define methods explicitly for the purpose of getting and setting each instance variable that needs to be accessed from outside the class. Such methods are called *accessor methods* or *accessors*. Here is how you could declare the Person class with accessor methods, thus giving the rest of your program controlled access to the data it contains:

```
@interface Person : NSObject
{
    @private
    NSString *address;
    NSString *name;
}
-(NSString *)name;                            // Getter method for name
-(void)setName:(NSString *)newName;           // Setter method for name
-(NSString *)address;                         // Getter method for address
-(void)setAddress:(NSString *)newAddress;     // Setter method for address


...

@end
```

Accessors generally come in pairs, with a setter and a getter for each instance variable, but occasionally you may want to allow only data to be read, in which case you would only supply a getter. The getter simply returns the value of the instance variable, and the setter takes the new value of the variable as an argument, and sets the variable to that value.

Apart from restricting access to data, accessors also play a crucial role in memory management in Objective-C. They are thus even more important in Objective-C than in other languages, such as Java. A bit later, you learn how to write accessor methods, but for now it is enough to understand their purpose and importance.

Subclassing

Each class in Objective-C can have a *superclass* from which it inherits data and methods. Only *single inheritance* is allowed, meaning that each class may only have a maximum of one superclass.

Languages like C++ allow multiple inheritance, where each class may have many superclasses. Other languages, such as Java, do not. Multiple inheritance is a hotly debated issue among OO programmers: it seems like a powerful feature, but you also have to be careful how you use it, or it can lead to serious design issues and make a program difficult to understand.

Naming Conventions

The naming convention used in the example is that the getter shares the name of the instance variable, and the setter name begins with set, and ends with the variable name, in mixed-case format.

Naming of accessors in Objective-C/Cocoa programming is not simply a question of whatever takes your fancy. You should stick to the convention used here, because the Cocoa frameworks include various technologies, such as Bindings, that work only if your code adheres to the convention. Adopting a different naming scheme will effectively prevent you from using important features of Cocoa in your programs. You learn more about Bindings in Chapter 8.

Languages like Objective-C and Java have instead opted for single inheritance, but add a second mechanism to mimic one of the better aspects of multiple inheritance, namely, the ability to have two classes not in the same inheritance tree share some interface. Objective-C provides Protocols for this purpose, which are covered later in the chapter.

When you are programming with Cocoa in Objective-C, all of your objects will have a superclass. Most classes in a Cocoa program descend from the class NSObject, which contains much of the basic functionality in Cocoa, including memory management.

Recall from the discussion earlier in the chapter that a subclass inherits all of the data and methods of its superclass. So the following class inherits all the methods in SuperClass:

```
@interface SubClass : SuperClass
{
    @private
    int subClassInt;
}
-(id)init;
-(void)dealloc;
-(void)subClassMethod;
@end
```

If the SuperClass interface looks like this:

```
@interface SuperClass : SuperDuperClass
{
    @private
    int superClassInt;
}
-(id)init;
-(void)dealloc;
-(void)superClassMethod;
@end
```

SubClass will include the integer instance variable superClassInt, and the method superClassMethod, as if SubClass had declared them itself. (Note that the SubClass has no direct access to superClassInt, because it is private to SuperClass, but the data for superClassInt is included in SubClass.)

The SuperClass also inherits from SuperDuperClass, so all of the instance variables and methods in SuperDuperClass are also included in SubClass, as though it had declared them itself. SubClass is said to be a *descendent* of SuperDuperClass, and includes its methods and data via inheritance from SuperClass. SuperDuperClass is an *ancestor* of SubClass.

The following code makes use of the preceding SubClass, demonstrating that methods inherited from the superclass are first class methods of the subclass:

```
SubClass *subClassObj = [[SubClass alloc] init];
[subClassObj superClassMethod];
[subClassObj release];
```

The method alloc is inherited from NSObject, and allocates memory for the SubClass object. init initializes it, and returns a pointer, which is stored in the variable subClassObj. The method `superClassMethod`, which is defined in `SuperClass`, is then invoked on the `SubClass` object, as though it were defined in that class. Finally, the method `release` from `NSObject` is invoked in order to indicate that the object is no longer needed.

> `alloc` and `release` *form an integral part of memory management in Cocoa, and are covered in detail later in the chapter.*

You may have noticed that `SubClass` has declared a few methods that are also declared by `SuperClass`, namely `init` and `dealloc`. A subclass is allowed to redefine any of the methods it inherits from its superclass, and, implicitly, from any of its ancestors. This is called *overriding*. The subclass can even invoke the superclass method from inside the overriding method. This is a way of extending the functionality of a method in a subclass.

> *A subclass can override superclass methods, but it cannot override superclass instance variables. Two different instance variables cannot have the same name, even if one is in the superclass, and the other in a subclass.*

Take this typical implementation of `dealloc`, which is a method inherited from `NSObject`, and is used to deallocate an object when it is no longer needed:

```
-(void)dealloc {
    [instanceVar release];
    [super dealloc];
}
```

This method first invokes the `release` method of the instance variable `instanceVar`, and then invokes the `dealloc` method of the superclass. Methods in the superclass can be called using the variable `super`. Effectively, the `dealloc` method in the superclass has been extended to include the line invoking `release`.

The keyword `super` is used to access the contents of the superclass. In this case, the `dealloc` method of the superclass is invoked at the end of `dealloc` method of the subclass. This *chaining* of method invocations is very common in OOP.

> *Languages such as Java and C++ allow not only for method overriding, but also method overloading. Overloading is giving the same name to two different methods in a class. The methods are distinguished by their parameters, so it must be clear from the arguments passed in the calling code which of the overloaded methods is intended.*
>
> *Objective-C does not have method overloading, but it is not really needed, because the sectioned naming scheme adopted means that you will rarely want two methods to have the same name. For example, imagine that you have a method called `execute` in Java or C++, which is overloaded to either take an argument of type `ClassA`, or an argument of type `ClassB`. In Objective-C, the argument types are usually incorporated into the method name, so you would probably call the two methods something like `executeWithClassA:` and `executeWithClassB:`. This approach has the added advantage of making your code more readable.*

An object of a given class can always be used where an object of an ancestor class is expected. This is an example of polymorphism, and an extremely important concept in OOP. Because a descendent class contains all of the methods and data of its ancestors, objects of the descendent class can do everything defined by the ancestor classes (and more), and may thus be used wherever an object of the ancestor class is expected.

The easiest way to understand this is to consider an example. In the Foundation framework of Cocoa, the NSString class is used to represent string objects that are immutable, meaning they cannot change after they have been created. There is also a subclass of NSString called NSMutableString. NSMutableString inherits all of the data and methods of NSString, of course, and introduces a number of new methods that allow its contents to be modified. Because NSMutableString is a subclass of NSString, it can be used wherever an NSString is expected. Take this function, for example:

```
NSString* PrintAndReturnString(NSString *string) {
    NSLog(string);
    return string;
}
```

Looking at this function, you may be led to think that PrintAndReturnString can be used only with objects of the class NSString. This is not true. It can be used with objects of any class descending from NSString, including NSMutableString. So the following calling code is perfectly legal:

```
NSString *str = PrintAndReturnString(@"Some NSString");

NSMutableString *mstr = [NSMutableString stringWithString:@"Some NSMutableString"];
mstr = (NSMutableString *)PrintAndReturnString(mstr);
```

On the first line, a literal NSString is passed to the PrintAndReturnString function, and the return value assigned to the variable str. On the last two lines, an NSMutableString instance is created with the stringWithString: method, and this too is passed to PrintAndReturnString. In both calls to PrintAndReturnString, the object passed will be printed by the NSLog function, which is similar to C's printf function.

You may have noticed that assigning the return value to mstr on the last line required a cast to NSMutableString*. Wasn't it stated that you could use an NSMutableString wherever an NSString is expected? That's right, but it didn't say you could use an NSString wherever an NSMutableString is expected. The assignment of the return value of PrintAndReturnString to mstr attempts to assign an NSString* to an NSMutableString* variable. Although you know that the string returned from PrintAndReturnString is actually an NSMutableString, not just an NSString, the compiler does not know that, and must assume an NSString is being returned. To compile this code, you need to cast the NSString returned to an NSMutableString. This is called *downcasting*, because you are casting down the inheritance hierarchy, from an ancestor class to one of its descendents.

Being able to substitute objects of a descendent class wherever an object of an ancestor class is expected is the primary source of polymorphism in OO programs. Because you can use different descendent classes in the same code, like in PrintAndReturnString just shown, that code can be made to behave differently depending on the class of object used — it can behave polymorphically. Polymorphism is difficult to grasp at first, but an essential aspect of OOP.

Messaging

Now that you know about inheritance in Objective-C, you are ready to consider method invocation, or *messaging*. It is called messaging because it is like sending a message to an object, asking it to do something. Messaging has similarities to function calling, but it is important to realize that it is a higher-level operation: a single message will often entail several behind-the-scenes function calls.

When you send a message, like the following, a chain of events is set in progress:

```
[obj doSomething];
```

The function `objc_msgSend` is called, with the object and an identifier for the message `doSomething` passed as arguments. `objc_msgSend` is a function in the *Objective-C runtime*, which is a library of functions and data structures in every Objective-C program.

`objc_msgSend` performs a search for a function matching the arguments passed to it. It first looks in the class of `obj`, to see if a `doSomething` method has been defined there. If not, it moves to the superclass, to see if `doSomething` appears there. It then moves to the superclass of the superclass, and so forth, until a `doSomething` method is found. When `doSomething` is located, the corresponding function is called. If it is not found in any of the ancestors of the class of `obj`, an error occurs.

As you can see from this example, messaging is a high-level operation, often leading to several function calls. It is also very powerful, because a programmer can influence the messaging procedure in various ways. For example, it is possible to intercept any message that does not correspond to any method in the inheritance tree, and *forward* it to another object. This can be used, for example, to mimic multiple inheritance, or easily implement a so-called *proxy* class, which passes most of its messages on to another class or program, perhaps via a network.

Each method has a unique identifier in the Objective-C runtime, called a *selector*. A selector has the C type `SEL`. You can get the selector of a method by using the `@selector` keyword, as in this example:

```
[obj performSelector:@selector(doSomething) withObject:nil];
```

This method can be found in `NSObject`. It takes a selector and an object as arguments, and invokes the method passing the object as argument. If the object has the value `nil`, which is the Objective-C equivalent of `NULL` for object values, no argument is passed. The preceding line of code is thus equivalent to this:

```
[obj doSomething];
```

Selectors can be very powerful because they allow you to store method names in variables, and pass them around as arguments to functions or methods of other objects. It is possible, for example, to read a string from file, convert it to a selector using the Cocoa function `NSSelectorFromString`, and invoke the corresponding method of an object. This sort of flexibility is considerably more difficult to achieve in most other programming languages.

Protocols and Informal Protocols

Objective-C is a language with single inheritance, meaning that each class can have at most one super-class. But there is a mechanism for defining shared behavior between classes that are not related by inheritance: *protocols*. Protocols can be used to define a set of methods that a class must implement. It is a bit like a class without any data, consisting of an interface declaring the methods that are implemented, and nothing more. There is no limit to the number of protocols a class can conform to, and there is also no limit on the number of classes that can conform to a single protocol. With protocols, you can get some of the advantages of multiple inheritance, without the drawbacks.

Dynamic versus Static Typing

Programming languages generally fall into two basic categories: *statically typed* and *dynamically typed*. Statically typed languages such as C++ and Java require that the type of an object be explicitly known when the program is compiled, so that the compiler can check if it has been used in a valid way. This means that a programmer is often forced to explicitly cast object types in order to compile, making code more verbose and difficult to read. It also makes sending an arbitrary message to an object more involved, or, worse still, impossible. In C++, for example, it is not possible to send arbitrary messages to objects without manually building the capability into your program yourself.

Objective-C is a dynamically typed language, meaning that it does not require that an object type be given explicitly for the compiler to check. Instead, the type is effectively checked at *run time*, because whenever an object is used inappropriately—by sending it an invalid message, for example—an error will occur. By postponing *type checking* until run time, Objective-C can avoid the casting required in statically typed languages, making the code easier to read. It also makes it more flexible, because you can easily invoke arbitrary methods on objects, without having to indicate what object classes are involved in the transaction.

Static typing does have the advantage that it can catch certain programmer errors a bit faster than dynamic typing, because you don't have to run the program first. For this reason, Objective-C offers static typing extensions. In theory, you could give all object variables in your programs the type id, but it is generally better to include an explicit type where that is known. Objective-C allows you to do this, and you will be warned by the compiler if it detects that you are using an object in an invalid way. No error will arise though—only a warning—and your program will still compile. In contrast to statically typed languages, object types in Objective-C are used only to alert the programmer to potential problems, and are not needed to compile the code.

Here is an example of a protocol declaration:

```
@protocol Execute
-(void)execute;
-(void)stopExecution;
@end
```

This looks like an interface block without the data section, and with the `@interface` keyword replaced by `@protocol`. A protocol has no implementation block—it only defines interface. It is up to a class conforming to the protocol to provide the implementation. Here is the interface of a class called `Task` that conforms to the `Execute` protocol:

```
@interface Task : NSObject <Execute>
{
}

@end
```

Protocols that a class conforms to are added after the superclass in triangular brackets. If there are multiple protocols, they are separated by commas. It is not necessary to redeclare the protocol methods in the conforming class's interface block, though you can if you want to.

The implementation of `Task` must implement the methods in the `Execute` protocol, and could look like this:

```
@implementation Task

- (void) execute {
...
}

- (void) stopExecution {
...
}

@end
```

The implementation block makes no reference to the protocol, but must provide implementations for the methods declared in the protocol.

The advantage of protocols is that completely unrelated classes can conform to the same protocol, and thus be used in similar contexts. Imagine that in addition to `Task`, you have a second class that conforms to `Execute` called `Television`. There would seem to be no relation between `Task` and `Television`, but they both conform to `Execute`, so you could write a function similar to the following that would work with an object of either type:

```
void StartAndStop( id <Execute> executableObj ) {
    [executableObj execute];
    [executableObj stopExecution];
}
```

The parameter of this function has the type `id <Execute>`. The class is given first, which in this case is the generic `id` type. Any protocols that the object must conform to, such as `Execute`, are given next in triangular brackets. Because both `Task` and `Television` conform to `Execute` — they are both *executable* — an object of either type can be passed to the `StartAndStop` function. `StartAndStop` only uses the methods from the `Execute` protocol, and both `Task` and `Television` are required to define these methods.

You could call the `StartAndStop` function with any object conforming to the `Execute` protocol, like this:

```
Task *task = [[Task alloc] init];
StartAndStop(task);

Television *tele = [[Television alloc] init];
StartAndStop(tele);
```

Protocols are a powerful means of having two or more classes share interface, but they have one disadvantage: you have to implement all of the methods in the protocol in each class. Sometimes this is what you want, as in the `Execute` protocol, and sometimes it isn't. When you have a situation where you want to give classes the option of leaving some methods out, you can use an *informal protocol*.

An informal protocol is not an official language construction like a protocol — it is a convention. To create an informal protocol, you write an interface category declaring the methods of the informal protocol, and attach it to a class that is an ancestor of all of the classes that you want to be able to implement the informal protocol.

A common use for informal protocols is *delegation*. A *delegate* is an object that is sent messages by another object when certain events occur. Here is how you could declare an informal protocol for `Task` that contains delegate methods:

```
@interface NSObject (TaskDelegateMethods)
-(BOOL)executionShouldBegin:(Task *)task;
-(void)executionDidBegin:(Task *)task;
-(BOOL)executionShouldStop:(Task *)task;
-(void)executionDidStop:(Task *)task;
@end
```

The name of the informal protocol is arbitrary, but must be unique for the class. It is not used anywhere else in the program. You should choose a name that documents what the category is for, in this case defining delegate methods of the `Task` class.

Note that the category does not belong to `Task`, but to `NSObject`. That's because it doesn't declare methods that `Task` implements, but methods that can be implemented by a delegate of `Task`. The delegate can be of any class, and by using `NSObject`, most possibilities are covered, because most classes are descendents of `NSObject`. Adding a category to `NSObject` is the most common way of introducing an informal protocol for delegation purposes.

Here is how you could write a class that can act as delegate for `Task`:

```
@interface TaskObserver
{
}
@end


@implementation TaskObserver

-(BOOL)executionShouldBegin {
    ...
    return YES;
}

-(void)executionDidStop {
    ...
}

@end
```

The class `TaskObserver` contains no reference whatsoever to the `TaskDelegateMethods` informal protocol, though it does implement two of its methods. The method `executionShouldBegin:` is sent by a `Task` object to its delegate whenever the `execute` method is called, and execution is about to begin. The `Task` object passes itself as the only argument so that the delegate knows which `Task` object is sending the message. The use of the word *should* in the title is a convention that indicates that the delegate may determine whether or not the action may proceed. By returning a true value, the execution continues; a false value would prevent execution from proceeding.

In the Cocoa frameworks, BOOL *is defined to represent the type of Boolean values, since originally C had no such built-in type. (C99 does include a built-in* boolean *type.) In practice,* BOOL *is simply a C type.* BOOL *can take the value* YES, *which is simply defined to be a non-zero value, or* NO, *which is zero.*

The other method defined in `TaskObserver`, `executionDidStop:` is sent when the `stopExecution` method of `Task` is invoked, after execution has ended. Note that `TaskObserver` did not provide implementations for `executionDidBegin:` or `executionShouldStop:`. This is the primary advantage of an informal protocol over a formal one—a class can choose which of the methods it will implement.

One question remains: How does `Task` call its delegate? First, a class with a delegate usually supplies the accessor methods `setDelegate:` and `delegate`. A `TaskObserver` object could become a `Task` delegate with code similar to the following:

```
Task *task = [[Task alloc] init];
TaskObserver *observer = [[TaskObserver alloc] init];
[task setDelegate:observer];
```

`Task` then includes code similar to the following at any point that it needs to message its delegate:

```
id del = [self delegate];
if ( del && [del respondsToSelector:@selector(executionShouldBegin:)] )
    [del executionShouldBegin:self];
```

This code first gets the delegate and stores it in the local variable `del`, which is of the generic class type `id`. The `if` condition can be broken into two halves, joined by a logical `&&` operator. The first half of the condition checks if `del` is set, by seeing if it is `nil`, which is equivalent to zero or false. If `del` is set, it sends a message to it asking whether it implements the method `executionShouldBegin:`. The `NSObject` method `respondsToSelector:` is used for this purpose. If the delegate does implement the method, then the message `executionShouldBegin:` is sent, with `self`—the `Task` instance—as the argument. If `del` is not set, or it doesn't implement the `executionShouldBegin:` method, no action is taken.

The preceding example dealt with informal protocols as they are used to implement a delegation relationship, which is a common application, but by no means the only one. Whether you choose to use a protocol or an informal protocol in any given situation will depend on whether it makes sense for a class to only implement some of the methods declared. If so, an informal protocol is probably what you want. If an object must implement all methods, a formal protocol is the better choice.

Naming Conventions

At several points in this chapter you have encountered Objective-C conventions. Informal protocols are a good example of a concept that is not built into the language proper, but pervades Objective-C/Cocoa programming. Understanding conventions like this can be just as important as grasping the formal aspects of the language, such as its syntax.

Objective-C has many conventions, and some of them apply to naming. You may think that you can name functions, variables, and classes in any way you like, within the rules laid down by the Objective-C grammar. That is true, but if you do not stick to the naming conventions of Objective-C/Cocoa, your programs will be at a disadvantage, and not have access to certain functionality.

You have probably already worked out most of the naming conventions, simply by reading the example code. Classes and variables should be in mixed-case format, with all words beginning with a capital letter, and all other letters lowercase. The exception to this rule is that variable names should begin with a lowercase letter; classes begin with an uppercase letter. So you might have a class called `ClassWithALongName`, and a variable called `variableWithALongName`.

Accessor methods, which were introduced earlier, should also follow a convention: Setters should begin with `set`, and be followed by the corresponding variable in mixed-case form, such as `setVariableWithALong Name:`. Getters should have the same name as the variable they are accessing, such as `variableWithALong Name`.

Why is all of this so important? Cocoa assumes that you will follow these conventions, and builds that assumption into certain key technologies. One of these is *Task (KVC)*, which is used to implement *Bindings* that you learn about in Chapter 8. Key-Value Coding (KVC) allows you to get and set instance variables using strings, or *keys*, rather than calling an accessor directly. For example, to get the value of an instance variable called `date`, you could do the following:

```
NSDate *d = [obj valueForKey:@"date"];
```

Note that there is no call to the accessor `date`. Instead, the method `valueForKey:` searches the methods defined in the class of `obj`, looking for an accessor called `date`. If it finds one, it calls it, and returns the result. If not, it looks to see if there is an instance variable called `date`. If there is, it returns that directly.

You can also set `date` using KVC:

```
NSDate *d = [NSDate date];
[obj setValue:d forKey:@"date"];
```

In this case, the `setValue:forKey:` method looks for an accessor called `setDate:`. If it finds such an accessor, it is called with `d` as an argument. If `setDate:` does not exist in the class, `setValue:forKey:` checks for an instance variable called `date`. If such a variable is found, it is set to `d` directly.

> *The example is a bit artificial, because you should always call `setDate:` in your code, rather than `setValue:forKey:`. KVC should be reserved for cases where you want to program to a generic interface, rather than explicitly including methods like `setDate:` in your code. In other words, when you don't know what setters and getters you will need to call beforehand, use KVC; if you do know, use the standard accessors.*

KVC is an important part of Cocoa programming, which facilitates many of its cooler features. Interface Builder, for example, would not be nearly as powerful without KVC, and Bindings would probably not have materialized at all without KVC. These technologies rely on the ability to get and set object properties with keys, and in order for this to work, you need to follow the conventions laid down, or they will not work with your classes.

Creating and Destroying Objects

An important part of any OO programming language is being able to create and destroy objects. In Objective-C, creation or *instantiation* of objects occurs in two stages: allocation and initialization. The `NSObject` method `alloc` takes care of allocating the memory needed to store the instance variables of an object. You should practically never need to override `alloc` to implement your own memory allocation scheme.

Initialization occurs in a method called an *initializer*. An initializer is a just a method like any other, and could be given any name; however, Cocoa convention says that it should begin with `init`. Initializers are responsible for allocating and initializing any instance variables, as well as ensuring that an initializer in the superclass is called. Here is an example of an initializer:

```
-(id)init {
    if ( self = [super init] ) {
        [self setCount:0];
        [self setGreeting:@"Hello"];
    }
    return self;
}
```

The `if` statement may seem a bit strange. It first assigns the `self` variable to the return value of the `init` method in the superclass. In Objective-C it is acceptable for an initializer to replace an object with a different instance and return that, so assigning `self` to the return value of super's `init` is good practice, even though `self` generally will not change.

> In many OO languages, initializers, which are often called constructors, are special methods that are not inherited. In Objective-C, initializers are ordinary methods, which get inherited like any other. If you write a class that inherits an initializer, you may need to override the initializer if you want it to work as expected with your new class.

The return value of an assignment is simply the value of the left-hand side (LHS) after the assignment, in this case, the value of `self`. Another Cocoa convention says that if there is an error in an initializer, that initializer should return `nil`. So the value of `self` is first checked to make sure it is not `nil` by the `if` statement. If it is a non-`nil` value, the instance variables are initialized, which, in the preceding example, involves invoking two setter methods.

An initializer must return the object it has initialized. In the example, `self` is returned, which is the case for most of the initializers you will encounter. Returning the initialized object makes it easier to embed initializer invocations in longer expressions, like this:

```
Cat *cat = [[[Cat alloc] initWithName:@"Bob"] autorelease];
```

You learn about the `autorelease` method in the next section, but what this example demonstrates is the way in which initializers are often used in Objective-C code.

A class can have many initializers, but it only ever has one *designated initializer*. The designated initializer is yet another Objective-C convention. Usually, the designated initializer is the most general initializer in a class, the one that gives you the most control over the contents of an object. For example, take this class representing cats:

```
@interface Cat : NSObject
{
    NSString *name;
    unsigned age;
}
-(id)init;
-(id)initWithName:(NSString *)newName;
-(id)initWithName:(NSString *)newName andAge:(unsigned)newAge; // Designated

-(void)setName:(NSString *)newName;
-(NSString *)newName;
-(void)setAge:(unsigned)newAge;
-(unsigned)newAge;
@end
```

The three initializers belonging to the class `Cat` would probably be chained together in the implementation block, like this:

```
@implementation Cat

-(id)init {
    return [self initWithName:@"No Name"];
}

-(id)initWithName:(NSString *)newName {
    return [self initWithName:newName andAge:0];
}

-(id)initWithName:(NSString *)newName andAge:(unsigned)newAge {
    if ( self = [super init] ) {
        [self setName:newName];
        [self setAge:newAge];
    }
    return self;
}

...

@end
```

The designated initializer is the most general one, namely, `initWithName:andAge:`. It allows you the most control over the contents of a `Cat` object. Other initializers do no initializing of their own, but instead invoke other initializers to do the work for them. These invocations all end up back at the designated initializer, which actually takes the steps of invoking the superclass initializer, setting the instance variables, and returning the initialized object.

Because designated initializers are a convention, they have no language support. It is thus important that you document in your code which of the initializers in a class is designated. The reason this is important is that subclasses should nearly always call the designated initializer of their superclass. This prevents strange things from happening during the initialization process.

> `NSObject` *is the root of the whole Cocoa class hierarchy, and many of your classes will inherit directly from this class. The only initializer that* `NSObject` *has is* init, *which is the designated initializer by default. Whenever you subclass* `NSObject` *directly, you need to invoke the* init *method of the* super *variable.*

When you no longer need an object, you have to be able to delete it. In Cocoa, object deletion takes place in the `dealloc` method. You should never call the `dealloc` method directly though. Instead, you call either the `release` or `autorelease` methods when you don't need an object anymore. These methods, which are defined in `NSObject`, are covered in detail in the next section. They simply indicate that an object is no longer needed by a particular part of the program. When the object is not needed by any part of the program anymore, the `dealloc` method is called behind-the-scenes to delete it.

Here is the `dealloc` method for the `Cat` class:

```
-(void)dealloc {
    [name release];
    [super dealloc];
}
```

A `release` message is sent to the `name` string, to indicate that it is not needed anymore by the `Cat` object. If it is still being used by other parts of the program, it will not be deleted. When it is not needed anywhere in the program, the string's `dealloc` method will also be invoked.

Although you should never invoke the `dealloc` method of an object directly from outside a class, it is acceptable — indeed necessary — to invoke it from within the `dealloc` method of a subclass, as in the preceding example. The `dealloc` method, like an initializer, should always invoke the `dealloc` method of its superclass, usually after it has released the class's instance variables. If you don't do this, a memory leak will arise.

In addition to object initialization, Objective-C also provides a means of initializing data used class-wide. The `initialize` class method is called by the Objective-C once before a class is used for the first time. You can set up any data structures needed by the class in this method. Here is an example of setting user preference defaults in an `initialize` method, which is a common use of the method:

```
+(void)initialize {
    NSUserDefaults *defs = [NSUserDefaults standardUserDefaults];
    [defs registerDefaults:
        [NSDictionary dictionaryWithObject:@"/var/tmp" forKey:@"TempDir"]];
}
```

The class `NSUserDefaults` is used to store preferences for a program. The `standardUserDefaults` method returns a shared object that is used throughout the program. The `registerDefaults:` method sets default values, which are used when a particular preference has not been set explicitly somewhere else in the program, or found in the user's preferences file.

An `NSDictionary` is passed to the `registerDefaults:` method. An `NSDictionary` is a container class like an `NSArray`; but rather than using indexes to access stored data, `NSDictionary` uses *keys*. The data in an `NSDictionary` is unordered, so using an index to reference it makes no sense; instead, you supply a key, which is a label that uniquely identifies a particular data value. Usually `NSStrings` are used as keys, although this is not a requirement. The data value can be any object that you want to store in the dictionary. The `NSDictionary` used in the preceding code is created with only a single entry, which has the `NSString` key `@"TempDir"`, and the `NSString` value `@"/var/tmp"`.

Memory Management

Memory is managed in Objective-C/Cocoa using a scheme known as *reference counting*. Basically, the `NSObject` class contains an integer instance variable that keeps track of how many entities in the program are using a given object. When the integer, which is known as the *retain count*, drops to zero, the object is not needed anymore, and the `dealloc` method is called to delete it.

When you initialize an object, it is given a retain count of 1. If you take no further action, the object will remain in existence for the lifetime of the program. You indicate that an object is not needed by sending it a `release` message, which reduces the retain count by 1. If the retain count drops to 0, the object is deallocated.

You can also explicitly indicate that an object should remain in existence by sending it a `retain` message, which increases the retain count by 1. `retain` is used when a part of your code needs to ensure that an object instantiated elsewhere remains in existence.

In the same way that objects have a retain count of 1 when they are first initialized, they also have a retain count of 1 when they are copied using the NSObject *method* copy, *or a similar method like* copyWithZone: *or* mutableCopy. *Any copy method produces an object with a retain count of 1.*

In some cases you can't release an object, even if you do not need it anymore. One such case is when the object must be returned from a method or function. If you invoke release, the object may get deallocated, and then the return value would be undefined. For these cases, Cocoa provides the autorelease method. autorelease has the same effect as release, in that it decreases the retain count by 1, but this action is delayed to a later time. After you invoke autorelease, you can keep using the object without fear that it will be deallocated. At some later time, the retain count of the object will be automatically decreased by 1, and if the retain count drops to 0, the object will be deleted.

The workings of autorelease may seem mysterious, but there is really nothing sinister about it. When you invoke the autorelease method of an object, the object is passed to another object of the class NSAutoreleasePool. The autorelease pool stores a list of objects that need to be released at some later time. When the autorelease pool itself is released, and subsequently deallocated, it sends a release message to each of the objects on its list.

Usually NSAutoreleasePool operates behind the scenes in a Cocoa application, and you don't need to worry about the details of how it works, and when it is released. In some situations, such as when you write a program without a graphical interface, you will need to instantiate and release your own NSAutoreleasePool.

At this point you may think that memory management in Cocoa is a complex exercise, but nothing could be further from the truth. With the following simple guidelines it becomes a breeze:

❑ Any program unit (for example, a class or a function) that initializes, retains, or copies an object, is also responsible for releasing that object.

❑ Any invocation of an initializer, retain, or copy method should be balanced by a release or autorelease invocation.

❑ When an object is no longer needed by a program unit, but must be passed or returned to another program unit, autorelease should be used, rather than release.

❑ autorelease should be preferred to release, unless it would result in excessive memory consumption, due to an accumulation of many temporary objects, for example. Autoreleasing an object when it is first created reduces the risk of memory leaks, which can arise if you forget to release it later in the code, or an exception is thrown and not caught. Preferring autorelease to release also leads to a cleaner programming style, similar to languages like Java that have automatic garbage collection.

The next Try It Out contains an example that creates and releases many objects using the techniques described in this section.

Try It Out   Memory Management with Cats

1. Create a new Foundation Tool project in Xcode and name it Memories of Cats.

2. Select the Memories of Cats.m file in the Groups & Files view in the group Source. In the editor, replace the default code with the following:

```
#import <Foundation/Foundation.h>

@interface Cat : NSObject <NSCopying>
{
}
-(id)copyWithZone:(NSZone *)zone;
+(id)createCat;
@end


@implementation Cat

-(id)copyWithZone:(NSZone *)zone {
    return [[Cat alloc] init];
}

+(id)createCat {
    Cat *cat = [[Cat alloc] init];
    return [cat autorelease];
}

@end


int main() {
    NSAutoreleasePool *pool = [[NSAutoreleasePool alloc] init];
    Cat *cat1 = [[[Cat alloc] init] autorelease];
    Cat *cat2 = [Cat createCat];

    Cat *cat3 = [[Cat alloc] init];
    NSLog(@"Retain count of cat3 is: %i", [cat3 retainCount]); // Prints 1

    Cat *cat4 = [cat3 copy];
    NSLog(@"Retain count of cat3 is: %i", [cat3 retainCount]); // Prints 1
    NSLog(@"Retain count of cat4 is: %i", [cat4 retainCount]); // Prints 1

    [cat3 release];    // Deallocates cat3

    [cat4 retain];
    NSLog(@"Retain count of cat4 is: %i", [cat4 retainCount]); // Prints 2

    [cat4 release];
    NSLog(@"Retain count of cat4 is: %i", [cat4 retainCount]); // Prints 1

    [cat4 release];    // Deallocates cat4

    [pool release];    // Deallocates cat1 and cat2

    return 0;
}
```

3. Click the Build and Go toolbar item to compile and run the program.

4. Read the output in the Run Log, and try to understand what each of the memory management method invocations in the example are doing to the retain count of each of the Cat objects.

How It Works

This code is not intended to represent typical Cocoa code, and you should not write your programs to look like this. The point of the exercise is simply to get acquainted with the various memory management methods and monitor their effect on the retain count of objects.

A very sparse Cat class is declared and defined first. It contains no instance variables, and only two methods. The copyWithZone: method is required in order to allow Cat objects to be copied. It is declared in the NSCopying protocol, and used by the NSObject method copy. An NSZone is an object that describes a section of memory, but can be ignored here. The copyWithZone: method returns an exact copy of the messaged object. Since Cat has no instance variables, it is only necessary to initialize and return a new Cat.

The content of the main function is sandwiched between the instantiation and destruction of an NSAutoreleasePool. This keeps track of the autoreleased objects, and sends them a release message when the autorelease pool is deallocated.

The variable cat1 is initialized first, to a Cat object that is autoreleased. This Cat is automatically deallocated by the NSAutoreleasePool at the end of the function.

cat2 is initialized with a Cat returned by the class method createCat. createCat initializes a Cat, and autoreleases it before it is returned, so the net effect is the same as for cat1: the Cat returned is deallocated when the NSAutoreleasePool is deallocated.

> *The class method* createCat *falls into the category of convenience initializer. Many classes provide methods that initialize and return an autoreleased object, because it is easier for the user of the class than calling* alloc, init..., *and* autorelease. *By way of example,* NSString *has many such methods:* stringWithFormat:, stringWithString:, stringWithContentsOfFile: ... *the list is almost endless! All of these methods return an autoreleased object, so you don't need to release the objects in your code.*

cat3 is set to a Cat that is initialized by init, but not autoreleased. An NSLog call prints out the retain count on the next line, which should be 1, because a newly initialized object should have a retain count of 1. The retainCount method of NSObject returns the retain count of an object. A bit further on, cat3 gets copied, which does not affect its retain count, and then it gets released. At this point, the retain count drops to 0, so the Cat is deallocated immediately, with its dealloc method called.

cat4 is initialized to be a copy of cat3. As you can see by the code for the copyWithZone: method of the Cat class, the object returned has a retain count of 1, just as if it were newly initialized. This is a Cocoa convention—copied objects are returned with a retain count of 1. Two NSLog calls follow, which should verify that cat4 has a retain count of 1, and that cat3 is unaffected by the copy operation.

cat4 is then subject to a retain invocation, which increments its retain count to 2. This is again verified in a call to NSLog. A release follows, which decrements the retain count to 1, before cat4 finally meets its end at the hands of yet another release. Don't worry, cat4's passing is quick and humane, with immediate deallocation, rather than the prolonged agony of the NSAutoreleasePool.

Accessor Methods

You have already met accessor method interfaces earlier in the chapter, but you are about to find out how you can implement them. Accessor methods are even more important in Objective-C than they are in other languages, like Java, because they are used for systematic memory management. If you follow this system, you will rarely have any problem with memory leaks or disappearing objects in your code. If you don't, you may end up in an Objective-C grade horror movie.

> *Actually, the reference to a horror movie is appropriate, because Cocoa provides a class called* NSZombie *for tracking down memory management problems in which objects are released too many times, or sent messages after they have been deallocated.* NSZombie *is a class that comes into play when you set the environment variable* NSZombieEnabled *to* YES *before running your program.*

> *With the environment variable set, whenever an object is deallocated, its class is effectively changed to* NSZombie. *If a message is sent to the object after it has been deallocated, it will go to* NSZombie, *which will throw an exception telling you details of the mismanaged object.*

There are actually several ways to write accessor methods. Each approach works, and it is up to you to choose the one that you are most comfortable with. To demonstrate some of the ways of writing accessors, consider the following class interface:

```
@interface WeatherConditions
{
    float temperature;
    NSDate *date;
    WeatherStation *weatherStation;
}
-(float)temperature;
-(void)setTemperature:(float)newTemp;
-(NSDate *)date;
-(void)setDate:(NSDate *)newDate;
-(WeatherStation *)weatherStation;
-(void)setWeatherStation:(WeatherStation *)newStation;
@end
```

The question is, how do you implement the accessor methods in the WeatherConditions class?

The float variable temperature is an easy case, because it is a simple type, not an object. It does not need to be allocated or deallocated, so it can simply be returned from the getter, and set directly in the setter:

```
-(float)temperature {
    return temperature;
}

-(void)setTemperature:(float)newTemp {
    temperature = newTemp;
}
```

The NSDate variable date is a bit more difficult. It is a Cocoa class representing a time or date. A getter accessor is easy enough to write, because it can simply return the date instance variable, but the setter is more involved. Here is one approach:

```
-(NSDate *)date {
    return date;
}

-(void)setDate:(NSDate *)newDate {
    id old = date;
```

```
        date = [newDate retain];
        [old release];
    }
```

The setDate: method starts by storing the date instance variable in a temporary variable called old. It then updates the date instance variable to point to newDate, and retains it at the same time. The retain indicates that the newDate object is needed by the WeatherConditions object, and ensures it will not be deallocated. The last line of the setter releases the temporary variable old, which is the object that date used to be. This is to indicate that the old NSDate object is no longer needed by WeatherConditions, and may be deallocated if it is not needed elsewhere.

Why so much trouble just to set date? Why not simply release the old date and assign the new one while retaining it, as shown in the following:

```
-(void)setDate:(NSDate *)newDate {
    [date release];
    date = [newDate retain];
}
```

The problem with this is that it doesn't account for the case that newDate and date are the same object. If they are, the object will be released by the first line of the setter, and may be deallocated before the second line is executed. This is why it is necessary to first retain the new date, and only then release the old one.

Two other common ways exist of getting around the pathological case where the new object is the same as the old one. Here is one of them:

```
-(void)setDate:(NSDate *)newDate {
    [date autorelease];
    date = [newDate retain];
}
```

This does not suffer the fate of the previous version, because the autoreleased object is guaranteed to exist at least for the life of the method. The only disadvantage of this approach is that if there happen to be a lot of calls to setDate:, an unnecessarily high number of NSDate objects may end up hanging around waiting to be released by the NSAutoreleasePool. In most cases, this is not the case, but you should keep it in mind.

The second approach to the problem is to explicitly test if the two objects are the same:

```
-(void)setDate:(NSDate *)newDate {
    if ( newDate == date ) return;
    [date release];
    date = [newDate retain];
}
```

This method returns if the date instance variable happens to be the same object as the newDate parameter.

The setters all assume that it is desirable to retain the new NSDate. This implies that the NSDate object may be shared with other parts of the program, and will not be exclusive to the WeatherConditions object. It is often better to copy small objects, rather than retain them, like this:

```
-(void)setDate:(NSDate *)newDate {
    id old = date;
    date = [newDate copy];
    [old release];
}
```

Here, the WeatherConditions object creates its own copy of the NSDate, so it doesn't need to worry about another section of the code modifying the NSDate later on. For small objects, like NSDate and NSString, it is a good idea to use copy rather than retain, just to be sure that your class's encapsulation is not violated.

There is yet another way of writing accessor methods that turns the preceding approaches upside down. The setter can take any of the preceding forms, but the getter looks completely different. Here is an example of this last approach, as demonstrated on the weatherStation instance variable in the WeatherConditions class:

```
-(WeatherStation *)weatherStation {
    [[weatherStation retain] autorelease];
}

-(void)setWeatherStation:(WeatherStation *)newStation {
    id old = weatherStation;
    weatherStation = [newStation retain];
    [old release];
}
```

The getter in this example first retains the instance variable, and then autoreleases it. The net effect of this is that the WeatherStation's retain count is incremented by 1, and it has been added to the autorelease pool. At some later time, the pool will send a release message to the object, and its retain count will return to what it was before the invocation of the weatherStation method.

Some advocate this form of getter because it can avoid a very subtle problem in which one part of a program retrieves a pointer to an object, and another part of the program releases it before it can be used, like this:

```
void Func(WeatherConditions *conds) {
    WeatherStation *ws = [conds weatherStation];
    [conds release];
    NSLog([ws description]);
}
```

Here the WeatherStation variable ws is inadvertently deallocated by releasing the WeatherConditions instance conds, before it can be used in the call to NSLog. In this case, the problem is easily recognized, but other examples can arise that are more difficult to spot.

Cases like this are quite rare, and it is probably better to simply retain any object that you think may be in danger of being deallocated before it can be used, rather than litter your getters with retain and autorelease invocations.

There is one last link in the memory management chain: the dealloc method. dealloc must release any instance variables that a class has retained, copied, or initialized. This is what dealloc would look like for the WeatherConditions class:

```
-(void)dealloc {
    [weatherStation release];
    [date release];
    [super dealloc];
}
```

It is safe to use `release` here, rather than `autorelease`, because none of the instance variables are being returned.

In the following Try It Out, you rewrite the MyAddressBook program in Objective-C. This brings together all the aspects of Objective-C that you have learned here, and contrasts the style of Objective-C programming directly with programming in the C language.

Try It Out   Beginning MyAddressBook in Objective-C

1. Create a new project in Xcode. In the New Project panel, choose Foundation Tool in the Command Line Utility group. Name the project MyAddressBook in Objective C.

2. Create the files `Person.h` and `Person.m` in the Source group of the Groups & Files view. To do this, select the Source group and then choose File ⇨ New File. In the New File sheet, choose Objective-C Class in the Cocoa group. Name the file `Person.m` and ensure that the Also Create "Person.h" check box is checked.

3. Create files called `IOUtility.h` and `IOUtility.m` in the same way you created `Person.h` and `Person.m` in step 2.

4. Replace the default code in each of these files, as well as the default code in the file `MyAddressBook` in `Objective C.m`, with the following source code:

Person.h

```objectivec
#import <Foundation/Foundation.h>


@interface Person : NSObject {
    @private
    NSString *name;
    NSString *address;
}

-(id)initWithName:(NSString *)aName andAddress:(NSString *)anAddress; // Designated
-(id)initWithName:(NSString *)aName;

-(NSString *)name;

-(NSString *)address;
-(void)setAddress:(NSString *)newAddress;

-(NSString *)description;

@end
```

Person.m

```
#import "Person.h"

@implementation Person

-(id)initWithName:(NSString *)aName andAddress:(NSString *)anAddress {
    if ( self = [super init] ) {
        name = [aName copy];
        [self setAddress:anAddress];
    }
    return self;
}

-(id)initWithName:(NSString *)aName {
    return [self initWithName:aName andAddress:@"Address Unknown"];
}

-(void)dealloc {
    [name release];
    [address release];
    [super dealloc];
}

-(NSString *)name {
    return name;
}

-(NSString *)address {
    return address;
}

-(void)setAddress:(NSString *)newAddress {
    id old = address;
    address = [newAddress copy];
    [old release];
}

-(NSString *)description {
    return [NSString stringWithFormat:@"Name: %@\nAddress: %@", name, address];
}

@end
```

IOUtility.h

```
#import <Foundation/Foundation.h>

void WriteToStandardOutput(NSString *string);
NSString* ReadFromStandardInput();
```

IOUtility.m

```
#import "IOUtility.h"

void WriteToStandardOutput(NSString *string) {
    NSFileHandle *so = [NSFileHandle fileHandleWithStandardOutput];
```

```
        [so writeData:[string dataUsingEncoding:NSUTF8StringEncoding]];
    }

    // Reads input line, and removes new line character
    NSString* ReadFromStandardInput() {
        NSFileHandle *si = [NSFileHandle fileHandleWithStandardInput];
        NSData *data = [si availableData];
        NSString *string = [[[NSString alloc] initWithData:data
            encoding:NSUTF8StringEncoding] autorelease];
        NSCharacterSet *set =
            [NSCharacterSet characterSetWithCharactersInString:@"\n"];
        return [string stringByTrimmingCharactersInSet:set];
    }
```

MyAddressBook in Objective C.m

```
#import <Foundation/Foundation.h>
#import "Person.h"
#import "IOUtility.h"

int main (int argc, const char * argv[]) {
    NSAutoreleasePool *pool = [[NSAutoreleasePool alloc] init];

    Person *person = [[[Person alloc] initWithName:@"Joe Citizen"
        andAddress:@"1 Hopalong Avenue, MediumRare, USA"] autorelease];
    WriteToStandardOutput([person description]);

    [pool release];
    return 0;
}
```

5. Build and run the program by clicking the Build and Go toolbar item.

How It Works

The Person class is a *model* class, which is a class that is used to store data. It is quite similar to the abstract data type (ADT) of the same name used in the C version of the program. It contains two instance variables, both of which are NSStrings, which are used to store the name and address of an entry in the address book. (The C version contained two char* strings.)

The Person class demonstrates the use of initializer chaining, with a designated initializer. It also has accessor methods for the name and address instance variables. Note that there is no setter for the name attribute. This is a design decision: for the purposes of this address book program, it was decided that a person could not change name, although changing address should be allowed. Not providing a setName: method prevents a Person object from having its name changed. The name variable of Person is said to be *immutable*.

The Person class also contains the method description. This method is actually inherited from the NSObject class, and has been overridden. It can be used to provide a user-readable description of an object, in the form of an NSString. Anytime you use the stringWithFormat: method to create a new NSString and include the formatting character %@, which is the character for an object, the description method of the object is called and returns an NSString describing the object. The description method of Person is used in other parts of the program to write out the details of the Person for the user.

The `WriteToStandardOutput` function uses the class `NSFileHandle` to write to the standard output stream:

```
void WriteToStandardOutput(NSString *string) {
    NSFileHandle *so = [NSFileHandle fileHandleWithStandardOutput];
    [so writeData:[string dataUsingEncoding:NSUTF8StringEncoding]];
}
```

The class method `fileHandleWithStandardOutput` returns an `NSFileHandle` that corresponds to standard output. Writing to this file handle with the method `writeData:` causes the data to appear in standard output. The string passed to the `WriteToStandardOutput` method is converted into data in the UTF8 format, which is the format used by the console. The `NSString` method `dataUsingEncoding:` returns an autoreleased `NSData` object, which is a Cocoa class that wraps around raw bytes of data. The constant `NSUTF8StringEncoding` is used to indicate that the data format should be UTF8.

The `ReadFromStandardInput` function reads a line from the console, and returns it as an autoreleased `NSString`:

```
NSString* ReadFromStandardInput() {
    NSFileHandle *si = [NSFileHandle fileHandleWithStandardInput];
    NSData *data = [si availableData];
    NSString *string = [[[NSString alloc] initWithData:data
        encoding:NSUTF8StringEncoding] autorelease];
    NSCharacterSet *set =
        [NSCharacterSet characterSetWithCharactersInString:@"\n"];
    return [string stringByTrimmingCharactersInSet:set];
}
```

An `NSFileHandle` for standard input is retrieved with the method `fileHandleWithStandardInput`, and the line of data read in with `availableData`. The `NSData` object returned is converted to an `NSString` using the initializer `initWithData:encoding:`. The string created is autoreleased. A new string is created with the new line character removed from the end using the `NSString` method `stringByTrimmingCharactersInSet:`. An `NSCharacterSet` is simply a set of characters; the one used here contains only the new line character, so the `stringByTrimmingCharactersInSet:` method trims any new line characters from either end of the string, before returning the result.

The `main` function in this example is used for testing purposes. An `NSAutoreleasePool` is initialized at the beginning, and released at the end. In between, a `Person` object is created, and the function `WriteToStandardOutput` is used to write the `NSString` returned by the `Person`'s `description` method to standard output.

In the next Try It Out you write the `AddressBook` class, which stores the `Person` objects containing the addresses in the address book.

Try It Out   Writing the AddressBook Class

1. Open the MyAddressBook in Objective C project, and create the files `AddressBook.h` and `AddressBook.m` in the Source group of the Groups & Files view. Choose the file type Objective-C Class in the Cocoa group of the New File sheet.

2. Replace the default code in each of these files, as well as the contents of `MyAddressBook` in `Objective C.m`, with the following source code:

AddressBook.h

```
#import <Foundation/Foundation.h>

@class Person;

extern NSString *AddressBookFilePath;

@interface AddressBook : NSObject {
    @private
    NSMutableDictionary *personForNameDict;
}

+(id)sharedAddressBook;

-(id)init;
-(id)initWithFile:(NSString *)path;

-(void)writeToFile:(NSString *)path;
+(void)writeSharedAddressBookToFile;

-(void)addPerson:(Person *)newPerson;
-(Person *)personForName:(NSString *)name;

@end
```

AddressBook.m

```
#import "AddressBook.h"
#import "Person.h"

// Path to address book file
NSString *AddressBookFilePath = @"/var/tmp/addressbookobjc";

@implementation AddressBook

+(id)sharedAddressBook {
    static AddressBook *sharedAddressBook = nil;
    if ( ! sharedAddressBook ) {
        // Load from file if the file exists
        NSFileManager *fm = [NSFileManager defaultManager];
        if ( [fm fileExistsAtPath:AddressBookFilePath] ) {
            sharedAddressBook =
                [[AddressBook alloc] initWithFile:AddressBookFilePath];
        }
        else { // Create a new AddressBook
            sharedAddressBook = [[AddressBook alloc] init];
        }
    }
    return sharedAddressBook;
}

-(id)init {
    if ( self = [super init] ) {
        personForNameDict = [[NSMutableDictionary alloc] init];
    }
```

```
        return self;
    }

    -(void)dealloc {
        [personForNameDict release];
        [super dealloc];
    }

    -(id)initWithFile:(NSString *)path {
        if ( self = [super init] ) {
            personForNameDict = [[NSMutableDictionary alloc] init];
            NSString *string = [NSString stringWithContentsOfFile:path];
            NSScanner *scanner = [NSScanner scannerWithString:string];
            NSString *name, *address;
            while ( ![scanner isAtEnd] ) {
                [scanner scanUpToString:@"\n" intoString:&name];
                [scanner scanString:@"\n" intoString:NULL]; // Remove end of line
                [scanner scanUpToString:@"\n" intoString:&address];
                [scanner scanString:@"\n" intoString:NULL]; // Remove end of line
                Person *person = [[Person alloc] initWithName:name andAddress:address];
                [self addPerson:person];
                [person release];
            }
        }
        return self;
    }

    -(void)writeToFile:(NSString *)path {
        NSMutableString *string = [NSMutableString string];
        NSEnumerator *en = [personForNameDict objectEnumerator];
        Person *person;
        while ( person = [en nextObject] ) {
            [string appendString:[person name]];
            [string appendString:@"\n"];
            [string appendString:[person address]];
            [string appendString:@"\n"];
        }
        [string writeToFile:path atomically:YES];
    }

    +(void)writeSharedAddressBookToFile {
        [[AddressBook sharedAddressBook] writeToFile:AddressBookFilePath];
    }

    -(void)addPerson:(Person *)newPerson {
        [personForNameDict setObject:newPerson forKey:[newPerson name]];
    }

    -(Person *)personForName:(NSString *)name {
        return [personForNameDict objectForKey:name];
    }

@end
```

MyAddressBook in Objective C.m

```objc
#import <Foundation/Foundation.h>
#import "IOUtility.h"
#import "Person.h"
#import "AddressBook.h"

int main (int argc, const char * argv[]) {
    NSAutoreleasePool *pool = [[NSAutoreleasePool alloc] init];

    AddressBook *addressBook = [[[AddressBook alloc] init] autorelease];

    // Add a person to the address book
    Person *person = [[[Person alloc] initWithName:@"Joe Citizen"
        andAddress:@"1 Hopalong Avenue, MediumRare, USA"] autorelease];
    [addressBook addPerson:person];

    // Add another
    person = [[[Person alloc] initWithName:@"Jill Citizen"
        andAddress:@"2 Hopalong Avenue, MediumRare, USA"] autorelease];
    [addressBook addPerson:person];

    // Search for person in the address book
    person = [addressBook personForName:@"Joe Citizen"];
    WriteToStandardOutput(@"Found person");
    WriteToStandardOutput([person description]);

    [pool release];
    return 0;
}
```

3. Build and run the program by clicking the Build and Go toolbar item.

How It Works

The `AddressBook` class stores `Person` objects in a Foundation container class called `NSMutableDictionary`. An `NSMutableDictionary` stores key-value pairs, like an `NSDictionary`; in fact, it is a subclass of `NSDictionary`. The difference is that an `NSMutableDictionary` is mutable, and so can be modified after creation. You can add or remove key-value pairs to an existing `NSMutableDictionary`.

`AddressBook` has two methods for adding and finding `Person` objects:

```objc
-(void)addPerson:(Person *)newPerson {
    [personForNameDict setObject:newPerson forKey:[newPerson name]];
}

-(Person *)personForName:(NSString *)name {
    return [personForNameDict objectForKey:name];
}
```

The `addPerson:` method sets an object in the `personForNameDict` instance variable, with the `Person`'s name as the key. The `setObject:forKey:` method of `NSMutableDictionary` serves this purpose. Note that no attempt is made to check whether a `Person` with that name is already in the `NSMutableDictionary`, so the `newPerson` instance will replace any instance with the same name that already exists. A dictionary can only have one value per key.

The `personForName:` method can be used to retrieve a `Person` from the `AddressBook`. The `objectForKey:` method of `NSDictionary` is used, which returns the object corresponding to the key passed, or `nil`, if no object with that key exists in the dictionary.

The `init` and `dealloc` methods of `AddressBook` are responsible for initializing `personForNameDict`, and releasing it:

```
-(id)init {
    if ( self = [super init] ) {
        personForNameDict = [[NSMutableDictionary alloc] init];
    }
    return self;
}

-(void)dealloc {
    [personForNameDict release];
    [super dealloc];
}
```

However, you don't generally need to call `init` directly, because `AddressBook` is a *singleton* class, which means usually there is only one instance of `AddressBook` used in the whole program. The method `sharedAddressBook` is used to access this instance. Rather than creating a new `AddressBook`, `sharedAddressBook` is called, and takes care of initializing the `AddressBook` object:

```
+(id)sharedAddressBook {
    static AddressBook *sharedAddressBook = nil;
    if ( ! sharedAddressBook ) {
        // Load from file if the file exists
        NSFileManager *fm = [NSFileManager defaultManager];
        if ( [fm fileExistsAtPath:AddressBookFilePath] ) {
            sharedAddressBook =
                [[AddressBook alloc] initWithFile:AddressBookFilePath];
        }
        else { // Create a new AddressBook
            sharedAddressBook = [[AddressBook alloc] init];
        }
    }
    return sharedAddressBook;
}
```

A `static` variable called `sharedAddressBook` is declared, and initialized to `nil`. Being declared `static` means that it will not disappear when the method returns, but will remain for the life of the program. The `if` statement checks if the variable is `nil`; if not, it simply returns the `AddressBook` to the calling code. If the variable is `nil`, a new `AddressBook` must be created.

The new `AddressBook` can either be retrieved from file, which involves invoking the initializer `initWithFile:`, or created empty with the `init` initializer. The Foundation class `NSFileManager`, which is used to perform operations that are typically handled by Finder (for example, moving and removing files, creating directories), is used to check for the existence of the `AddressBook` file. The `fileExistsAtPath:` method returns `YES` if the file exists at the path passed, and `NO` otherwise. According to the return value of this method, the `sharedAddressBook` method chooses between the `initWithFile:` and `init:` methods to initialize the new `AddressBook` instance.

Reading and writing to and from file is achieved using the two methods initWithFile: and writeToFile:. (The convenience class method writeSharedAddressBookToFile: is also provided to write the shared address book to file; this simply invokes writeToFile:.) The writeToFile: method writes the name and address of each entry in the personForNameDict dictionary to file:

```
-(void)writeToFile:(NSString *)path {
    NSMutableString *string = [NSMutableString string];
    NSEnumerator *en = [personForNameDict objectEnumerator];
    Person *person;
    while ( person = [en nextObject] ) {
        [string appendString:[person name]];
        [string appendString:@"\n"];
        [string appendString:[person address]];
        [string appendString:@"\n"];
    }
    [string writeToFile:path atomically:YES];
}
```

An NSEnumerator object is used to move through the entries of the NSMutableDictionary. Each Person's name is appended to an NSMutableString, followed by the address. (NSMutableString is a subclass of NSString. The value of an NSMutableString can change after it is created, unlike instances of NSString.) After each string is appended, a new line character is appended, so that when the data is read back in, the end of each string can be located.

You may be starting to see a pattern emerge in the naming of certain Cocoa classes. NSString, which is immutable, has a subclass called NSMutableString, which is mutable. NSDictionary, which is immutable, has a subclass called NSMutableDictionary, which is mutable. In fact, many of the most important Cocoa Foundation classes have mutable and immutable variants.

The mutable classes have all the methods of the corresponding immutable classes, as well as extra methods for changing the object's attributes. For this reason, the mutable class is always a subclass of the immutable one.

The initWithFile: method reads the data back in, and adds it to the personForNameDict:

```
-(id)initWithFile:(NSString *)path {
    if ( self = [super init] ) {
        personForNameDict = [[NSMutableDictionary alloc] init];
        NSString *string = [NSString stringWithContentsOfFile:path];
        NSScanner *scanner = [NSScanner scannerWithString:string];
        NSString *name, *address;
        while ( ![scanner isAtEnd] ) {
            [scanner scanUpToString:@"\n" intoString:&name];
            [scanner scanString:@"\n" intoString:NULL]; // Remove end of line
            [scanner scanUpToString:@"\n" intoString:&address];
            [scanner scanString:@"\n" intoString:NULL]; // Remove end of line
            Person *person = [[Person alloc] initWithName:name andAddress:address];
            [self addPerson:person];
            [person release];
        }
    }
    return self;
}
```

The method begins by initializing the `personForNameDict`. After reading the contents of the file with the `NSString` method `stringWithContentsOfFile:`, an `NSScanner` is used to extract the names and addresses. `NSScanner` is a class that can scan through strings, looking for strings and numbers.

The `while` loop keeps iterating until the end of file is reached, which is signaled by the `NSScanner` method `isAtEnd` returning `YES`. Each iteration of the loop scans in the `name` and `address` strings with the method `scanUpToString:intoString:`, and discards the end of line character with the `scanString:intoString:` method. Passing `NULL` as the second argument to this method causes the string to be scanned, but ignored.

At the completion of each loop iteration, a new `Person` is created with the name and address read, and added to the `AddressBook` with the `addPerson` method.

The `main` function is again used for testing purposes. It creates an AddressBook object; adds two `Person` objects to it; searches for a `Person` with `personForName:`; and writes the details to standard output.

In the next Try It Out you write the `Controller` class, which is used to interact with the user. You also introduce a class that represents the different operations the user can perform. This section provides a good demonstration of inheritance and polymorphism in OOP.

Try It Out   Writing the Controller and Command Classes

1. Open the MyAddressBook in Objective C project, and create the files `Controller.h` and `Controller.m` in the Source group of the Groups & Files view. Choose the file type Objective-C Class in the Cocoa group of the New File sheet.

2. Similarly, create files called `Commands.h` and `Commands.m` in the Source group.

3. Replace the contents of each of these files, as well as the contents of `MyAddressBook in Objective C.m`, with the following source code:

Controller.h
```
#import <Foundation/Foundation.h>

@class AddressBook;

@interface Controller : NSObject {
}

-(void)printIntroductoryMessage;
-(BOOL)processUserRequest;
-(void)printUserOptions;
-(BOOL)processUserChoice:(NSString *)choice;

@end
```

Controller.m
```
#import "Controller.h"
#import "Commands.h"
#import "IOUtility.h"

static NSDictionary *commandClassForChoiceDict;

@interface Controller (PrivateMethods)
```

```objc
-(NSDictionary *)requestCommandInfoFromUser:(Class)commandClass;
@end

@implementation Controller

+(void)initialize {
    NSMutableDictionary *dict = [NSMutableDictionary dictionary];
    NSEnumerator *commEnum = [[Command commandClasses] objectEnumerator];
    Class c;
    while ( c = [commEnum nextObject] ) {
        [dict setObject:c forKey:[c commandIdentifier]];
    }
    commandClassForChoiceDict = [dict retain];
}

-(void)printIntroductoryMessage {
    NSString *message =
        @"Welcome to MyAddressBook\n"
        @"With this program, you can add addresses, retrieve them,\n"
        @"and store them on file.\n";
    WriteToStandardOutput(message);
}

-(BOOL)processUserRequest {
    // Offer user options
    [self printUserOptions];
    WriteToStandardOutput(@"Please enter a choice: ");

    // Read choice, and get first character
    NSString *choice = ReadFromStandardInput();
    choice = [choice substringToIndex:1];

    // Process choice
    return [self processUserChoice:choice];
}

-(void)printUserOptions {
    NSArray *commandClasses = [Command commandClasses];
    NSEnumerator *classEnum = [commandClasses objectEnumerator];
    NSMutableString *str = [NSMutableString stringWithString:@"The options are\n"];
    Class c;
    while ( c = [classEnum nextObject] ) {
        [str appendString:[c commandIdentifier]];
        [str appendString:@":\t"];
        [str appendString:[c commandDescription]];
        [str appendString:@"\n"];
    }
    WriteToStandardOutput(str);
}

-(BOOL)processUserChoice:(NSString *)choice {
    BOOL shouldStop = NO;
    NSString *outputString;
    Class commClass = [commandClassForChoiceDict objectForKey:choice];
    if ( Nil == commClass ) {
        outputString = @"Invalid choice.\n";
```

```
        }
        else {
            NSDictionary *infoDict = [self requestCommandInfoFromUser:commClass];
            AddressBook *ab = [AddressBook sharedAddressBook];
            Command *comm = [[[commClass alloc] initWithAddressBook:ab] autorelease];
            outputString = [comm executeWithInfoDictionary:infoDict];
            if ( nil == outputString ) {
                shouldStop = YES;
            }
            else { // Append new line
                outputString = [outputString stringByAppendingString:@"\n"];
            }
        }
        if ( nil != outputString ) WriteToStandardOutput(outputString);
        return shouldStop;
}

-(NSDictionary *)requestCommandInfoFromUser:(Class)commandClass {
    NSMutableDictionary *infoDict = [NSMutableDictionary dictionary];
    NSArray *reqInfo = [commandClass requiredInfoIdentifiers];
    if ( [reqInfo count] > 0 ) {
        WriteToStandardOutput(@"Please enter the following information:\n");

        // Request each piece of info, and enter in a dictionary.
        NSEnumerator *reqEnum = [reqInfo objectEnumerator];
        id req;
        while ( req = [reqEnum nextObject] ) {
            WriteToStandardOutput([NSString stringWithFormat:@"%@: ", req]);
            NSString *info = ReadFromStandardInput();
            [infoDict setObject:info forKey:req];
        }

    }
    return infoDict;
}

@end
```

Commands.h

```
#import <Foundation/Foundation.h>
#import "AddressBook.h"
#import "Person.h"

@interface Command : NSObject
{
    @private
    AddressBook *addressBook;
}
+(NSArray *)commandClasses;
-(id)initWithAddressBook:(AddressBook *)ab;
-(AddressBook *)addressBook;
@end

@interface Command (AbstractMethods)
```

```
+(NSString *)commandIdentifier;
+(NSString *)commandDescription;
+(NSArray *)requiredInfoIdentifiers;  // Info needed from the user
-(NSString *)executeWithInfoDictionary:(NSDictionary *)infoDict;
@end

@interface QuitCommand : Command
{
}
@end
```

Commands.m

```
#import "Commands.h"

static NSArray *commandClasses;

@implementation Command

+(void)initialize {
    commandClasses =
        [[NSArray arrayWithObjects:
            [QuitCommand class],
            nil] retain];
}

+(NSArray *)commandClasses {
    return commandClasses;
}

-(id)initWithAddressBook:(AddressBook *)ab {
    if ( self = [super init] ) {
        addressBook = [ab retain];
    }
    return self;
}

-(void)dealloc {
    [addressBook release];
    [super dealloc];
}

-(AddressBook *)addressBook {
    return addressBook;
}

@end


@implementation QuitCommand

+(NSString *)commandIdentifier {
    return @"q";
}

+(NSString *)commandDescription {
```

```
        return @"Save and quit";
    }

+(NSArray *)requiredInfoIdentifiers {
        return [NSArray array];
    }

-(NSString *)executeWithInfoDictionary:(NSDictionary *)infoDict {
        [AddressBook writeSharedAddressBookToFile];
        return nil;
    }

@end
```

MyAddressBook in Objective C.m

```
#import <Foundation/Foundation.h>
#import "IOUtility.h"
#import "Controller.h"

int main (int argc, const char * argv[]) {
    NSAutoreleasePool *outerPool = [[NSAutoreleasePool alloc] init];

    // Print introduction
    Controller *controller = [[[Controller alloc] init] autorelease];
    [controller printIntroductoryMessage];

    // Run loop
    BOOL exitRunLoop = NO;
    while ( !exitRunLoop ) {
        NSAutoreleasePool * pool = [[NSAutoreleasePool alloc] init];
        exitRunLoop = [controller processUserRequest];
        [pool release];
    }

    [outerPool release];
    return 0;
}
```

4. Compile and run the program by clicking the Build and Go toolbar item.

5. Follow the instructions in the Run Log window. Quit the program by entering a "q" at the prompt.

6. Rerun the program by selecting Run Executable in the Build and Go toolbar item popup menu. Try entering some invalid responses to see how the program reacts.

How It Works

This version of MyAddressBook is perhaps overkill for the simple problem it solves, but the intention is to expose you to as many of the principal Foundation classes of Cocoa as possible, and the OO features of Objective-C. You could easily produce a program that mimics the source code of the C version of MyAddressBook more closely, but it would not demonstrate the OO features of Objective-C very well. Instead, the design of MyAddressBook has been changed somewhat to make full use of OO features like inheritance and polymorphism.

The `Controller` class performs a similar role to the `Controller` ADT in the C version of MyAddressBook. It acts as the interface between the model classes, which store the data, and the user interface, which in this case is simply a console. It has methods for printing introductory messages, printing the options available to the user, and processing the user's choices. Most of these methods use the functions `WriteToStandardOutput` and `ReadFromStandardInput`, which were defined in the files `IOUtility.h` and `IOUtility.m`.

The `printUserOptions` method of the `Controller` class is responsible for printing the various commands a user can choose from:

```
-(void)printUserOptions {
    NSArray *commandClasses = [Command commandClasses];
    NSEnumerator *classEnum = [commandClasses objectEnumerator];
    NSMutableString *str = [NSMutableString stringWithString:@"The options are\n"];
    Class c;
    while ( c = [classEnum nextObject] ) {
        [str appendString:[c commandIdentifier]];
        [str appendString:@":\t"];
        [str appendString:[c commandDescription]];
        [str appendString:@"\n"];
    }
    WriteToStandardOutput(str);
}
```

What you will notice about this code is that there is no explicit mention of any of the options. There is no reference to adding a new person, saving the address book, or any other operation that the user can request. The C version of the program included a large `switch` statement that would call different processing functions based on the character entered by the user. Here the OO features of Objective-C have been used to create a more flexible design.

The way it works is this: Each option is represented by a subclass of the class `Command`. The `Command` class is called an *abstract class*, because you never actually create an instance of `Command`, only its subclasses. However, you do use the interface of `Command`, as you can see from the `printUserOptions` method.

`printUserOptions` begins by calling the `Command` class method `commandClasses`. This returns an `NSArray` containing all of the subclasses of `Command`, which represent the different options available to the user. The built-in Objective-C keyword `Class` is used to represent the generic type of classes, in the same way that `id` is the generic type of objects.

The `printUserOptions` method then initializes an `NSMutableString`. A `while` loop iterates over the `Command` subclasses, and calls the class methods `commandIdentifier` and `commandDescription`. The return values of these methods are `NSStrings`, which are appended to the `NSMutableString`. The strings returned represent the character option that the user can enter to select the command, and a description of what the command does, respectively. When all subclasses of `Command` have been queried, the `NSMutableString str` is written to standard output.

The `printUserOptions` method is a good example of OOP, and polymorphism, in particular. The methods `commandIdentifier` and `commandDescription` are declared in the interface of `Command`, but the `Command` class does not provide the implementation. Instead, the subclasses of `Command` implement the methods. When an invocation of `commandIdentifier` is made in the `while` loop, it ends up invoking the `commandIdentifier` method of a subclass of `Command`, not the `Command` class implementation.

To understand the design of the Command class hierarchy somewhat better, consider the Command class itself. Its interface can be found in Commands.h, and looks like this:

```
@interface Command : NSObject
{
    @private
    AddressBook *addressBook;
}
+(NSArray *)commandClasses;
-(id)initWithAddressBook:(AddressBook *)ab;
-(AddressBook *)addressBook;
@end

@interface Command (AbstractMethods)
+(NSString *)commandIdentifier;
+(NSString *)commandDescription;
+(NSArray *)requiredInfoIdentifiers;   // Info needed from the user
-(NSString *)executeWithInfoDictionary:(NSDictionary *)infoDict;
@end
```

The initializer takes an AddressBook object, which is needed by many of the Command subclasses. The AddressBook itself is stored in the Command class, and accessed from the subclasses using the addressBook accessor method. It also includes the commandClasses method that you have already seen, and the commandIdentifier and commandDescription class methods.

The *abstract methods* in the Command class—those without an implementation—are declared in a category. If you declare them in the main interface block of the class, the compiler issues a warning that it cannot find the methods' implementations. Using a category avoids the warning, as well as making it clear to other programmers that the methods are abstract.

The commandClasses method returns an NSArray that is also called commandClasses, which gets initialized in the initialize class method:

```
+(void)initialize {
    commandClasses =
        [[NSArray arrayWithObjects:
            [QuitCommand class],
            nil] retain];
}

+(NSArray *)commandClasses {
    return commandClasses;
}
```

At this point, only one command exists, QuitCommand, which saves the address book and quits the program. The commandClasses variable is declared at the top of the file:

```
static NSArray *commandClasses;
```

You have already seen the keyword static several times; it ensures that the variable remains in existence for the lifetime of the program.

The `initialize` method uses the `NSObject` method `class` to retrieve the `Class` type of each subclass of `Command`, and inserts them into a new `NSArray` with the method `arrayWithObjects:`. You will probably use this convenience constructor of `NSArray` often; it takes a comma-separated series of objects, and must be terminated by a `nil` argument.

Two other methods are included in the `Command` class interface. The first is `requiredInfoIdentifiers`, which returns an `NSArray` of `NSStrings`. Many of the `Command` subclasses need extra information in order to process a user request. For example, in order to add a new address to the address book, a person's name and address are needed. This method returns the strings used to identify the information that must be entered by the user.

The `Controller` class uses the returned array in the `requestCommandInfoFromUser:` method, in order to get the information from the user, and puts the results in a dictionary:

```
- (NSDictionary *) requestCommandInfoFromUser: (Class) commandClass {
    NSMutableDictionary *infoDict = [NSMutableDictionary dictionary];
    NSArray *reqInfo = [commandClass requiredInfoIdentifiers];
    if ( [reqInfo count] > 0 ) {
        WriteToStandardOutput(@"Please enter the following information:\n");

        // Request each piece of info, and enter in a dictionary.
        NSEnumerator *reqEnum = [reqInfo objectEnumerator];
        id req;
        while ( req = [reqEnum nextObject] ) {
            WriteToStandardOutput([NSString stringWithFormat:@"%@: ", req]);
            NSString *info = ReadFromStandardInput();
            [infoDict setObject:info forKey:req];
        }

    }
    return infoDict;
}
```

This method basically consists of a `while` loop that prints out a request for each piece of information required by the `Command`, and stores the user response in an `NSMutableDictionary` with the request string as key.

The last method of the `Command` class is `executeWithInfoDictionary:`. This method gets passed the dictionary of user responses created in `requestCommandInfoFromUser:` and executes the `Command`. The parameter `infoDict` holds the information requested from the user. If the `Command` has output, it can be returned as an `NSString`.

The only part of the puzzle not yet addressed is how the `Controller` actually creates a `Command` and executes it. That takes place in the `processUserChoice:` method:

```
- (BOOL) processUserChoice: (NSString *) choice {
    BOOL shouldStop = NO;
    NSString *outputString;
    Class commClass = [commandClassForChoiceDict objectForKey:choice];
    if ( Nil == commClass ) {
        outputString = @"Invalid choice.\n";
    }
    else {
        NSDictionary *infoDict = [self requestCommandInfoFromUser:commClass];
```

```
        AddressBook *ab = [AddressBook sharedAddressBook];
        Command *comm = [[[commClass alloc] initWithAddressBook:ab] autorelease];
        outputString = [comm executeWithInfoDictionary:infoDict];
        if ( nil == outputString ) {
            shouldStop = YES;
        }
        else { // Append new line
            outputString = [outputString stringByAppendingString:@"\n"];
        }
    }
    if ( nil != outputString ) WriteToStandardOutput(outputString);
    return shouldStop;
}
```

This method starts by attempting to retrieve a Class from the NSDictionary commandClassFor
ChoiceDict, which is the static variable created in the initialize method. This dictionary maps the
option characters that a user enters to the classes that represent the command in the program. The return
value of objectForKey: is assigned to the variable commClass, which is then compared to Nil. Nil is an
Objective-C keyword that is the zero-value of a Class variable, in the same way that nil is the zero-value
of the id type.

If a Command class is found that corresponds to the choice string, it is used with the methods described
earlier. First the Controller method requestCommandInfoFromUser: is invoked to create the
NSDictionary infoDict, which contains information for the Command. Then an object of the class
commClass is created, and assigned to the Command variable comm. comm is executed, with infoDict
passed as argument, and the returned string is stored in outputString. If outputString is not nil, it
is printed, and the method returns.

The advantage of the OO design used here is that the Controller class is quite generic. It makes no
reference to the various commands available to the user — this functionality has been split off into the
Command class hierarchy. To add a new command, which adds a person to the address book, for example,
you only have to write a new subclass of Command, and add the new class to the array returned by
commandClasses method of the Command class. The Controller class remains unaltered.

The main function creates the Controller object, and includes a run loop that repeatedly calls the
Controller to process the next user request:

```
    NSAutoreleasePool *outerPool = [[NSAutoreleasePool alloc] init];

    // Print introduction
    Controller *controller = [[[Controller alloc] init] autorelease];
    [controller printIntroductoryMessage];

    // Run loop
    BOOL exitRunLoop = NO;
    while ( !exitRunLoop ) {
        NSAutoreleasePool * pool = [[NSAutoreleasePool alloc] init];
        exitRunLoop = [controller processUserRequest];
        [pool release];
    }

    [outerPool release];
```

This code includes two NSAutoreleasePool instances. One is created to encompass the whole body of the main function. This one should exist in any Foundation Tool that you write, because otherwise you might end up with a memory leak. The controller instance, for example, is autoreleased, and the outerPool is responsible for releasing it at the end of the main function.

The second autorelease pool is inside the run loop. This one is not strictly necessary, but has been added to prevent memory usage increasing too much. If this pool did not exist, every autoreleased object created inside the loop would remain in existence until the whole program finished. This is wasteful of memory, so a second autorelease pool is created that releases autoreleased objects once per iteration of the run loop. This code also demonstrates that it is perfectly acceptable to use multiple NSAutoreleasePool objects. When an object's autorelease method is invoked, the object is added to the last pool created.

> The main function used in this example contains a while loop referred to as a run loop. You usually don't need to create a loop like this in Cocoa programming, because it is created for you. An object of the class NSRunLoop is used for this purpose.

In the following Try It Out, you add the Command subclasses that enable you to create and store addresses.

Try It Out   Adding Command Subclasses

1. Open the MyAddressBook in Objective C project and add the following source code to the bottom of the Commands.h and Commands.m files:

Commands.h
```
@interface NewPersonCommand : Command
{
}
@end

@interface FindPersonCommand : Command
{
}
@end

@interface SaveAddressBookCommand : Command
{
}
@end
```

Commands.m
```
@implementation NewPersonCommand

+(NSString *)commandIdentifier {
    return @"n";
}

+(NSString *)commandDescription {
    return @"Add a new address";
}

+(NSArray *)requiredInfoIdentifiers {
```

```objc
        return [NSArray arrayWithObjects:@"Name of person", @"Address", nil];
}

-(NSString *)executeWithInfoDictionary:(NSDictionary *)infoDict {
    NSString *name = [infoDict objectForKey:@"Name of person"];
    NSString *address = [infoDict objectForKey:@"Address"];
    Person *p = [[[Person alloc] initWithName:name andAddress:address]
        autorelease];
    [[self addressBook] addPerson:p];
    return [NSString stringWithFormat:
        @"Address for %@ was added to the address book.", name];
}

@end

@implementation FindPersonCommand

+(NSString *)commandIdentifier {
    return @"f";
}

+(NSString *)commandDescription {
    return @"Find an address";
}

+(NSArray *)requiredInfoIdentifiers {
    return [NSArray arrayWithObject:@"Name of person"];
}

-(NSString *)executeWithInfoDictionary:(NSDictionary *)infoDict {
    NSString *name = [infoDict objectForKey:@"Name of person"];
    Person *p = [[self addressBook] personForName:name];
    return ( p == nil ? @"Address not found" : [p description] );
}

@end

@implementation SaveAddressBookCommand

+(NSString *)commandIdentifier {
    return @"s";
}

+(NSString *)commandDescription {
    return @"Save address book";
}

+(NSArray *)requiredInfoIdentifiers {
    return [NSArray array];
}

-(NSString *)executeWithInfoDictionary:(NSDictionary *)infoDict {
    [AddressBook writeSharedAddressBookToFile];
    return @"Address book saved";
```

```
    }

@end
```

2. Modify the `initialize` method of the `Command` class in `Commands.m` as follows:

```objc
+(void)initialize {
    commandClasses =
        [[NSArray arrayWithObjects:
            [NewPersonCommand class],
            [FindPersonCommand class],
            [SaveAddressBookCommand class],
            [QuitCommand class],
            nil] retain];
}
```

3. Compile and run the program by clicking the Build and Go toolbar item.

4. Follow the instructions in the Run Log window. Enter a few names and addresses and then try to retrieve them again with a find request. Try saving the address book and then quit.

5. Rerun the program by selecting Run Executable in the Build and Go toolbar item popup menu. Try to find one of the addresses you entered before quitting in step 4.

How It Works

To improve your understanding of how the `Command` subclasses work, consider the `NewPersonCommand` class, which is used to add a new entry to the address book. For this, a person's name and address are needed. The `NewPersonCommand` class returns strings from the `requiredInfoIdentifiers` method that are used to request the user to enter a name and address:

```objc
+(NSArray *)requiredInfoIdentifiers {
    return [NSArray arrayWithObjects:@"Name of person", @"Address", nil];
}
```

The `executeWithInfoDictionary:` method of `NewPersonCommand` creates the new `Person` and adds it to the `AddressBook`:

```objc
-(NSString *)executeWithInfoDictionary:(NSDictionary *)infoDict {
    NSString *name = [infoDict objectForKey:@"Name of person"];
    NSString *address = [infoDict objectForKey:@"Address"];
    Person *p = [[[Person alloc] initWithName:name
        andAddress:address] autorelease];
    [[self addressBook] addPerson:p];
    return [NSString stringWithFormat:
        @"Address for %@ was added to the address book.", name];
}
```

The user-supplied information is passed to the method by the `Controller` via the `infoDict` `NSDictionary`. The identifiers returned from `requiredInfoIdentifier` are used as the keys to extract the information. A string is returned from the method that indicates that a new entry has successfully been added to the address book.

The other subclasses of `Command` that were introduced have a similar structure to `NewPersonCommand`; it is left to you to investigate them further on your own.

Summary

This chapter has introduced you to one of the most important languages on Mac OS X for applications development. You learned

❑   What object-oriented programming (OOP) entails, including the important concepts of encapsulation, inheritance, and polymorphism

❑   That Objective-C is a superset of C that introduces powerful OO programming capabilities with minimal extensions

❑   Aspects of Objective-C such as classes, protocols, categories, methods, data hiding, messaging, and memory management

❑   How to write a Foundation Tool in Objective-C that makes use of fundamental Cocoa classes from the Foundation framework, while leveraging the OO capabilities of Objective-C

In the next chapter, you learn about the Cocoa Frameworks, which form the basis of most new application development on Mac OS X and which are tightly coupled with Objective-C. Before proceeding, however, try the exercises that follow to test your understanding of the material covered in this chapter. You can find the solutions to these exercises in Appendix A.

Exercises

1.   In this exercise, you practice working with some of the most important Cocoa Foundation classes. You need to use these classes every time you write a Cocoa program, so it is essential that you get used to them.

Create a new Foundation Tool project called Discus, and in the Discus.m file, add code to store information about a few CDs and DVDs in your collection. Store details of each CD/DVD in an NSDictionary and use an NSArray to hold all the dictionaries. The details you might consider storing could include the type of media (CD or DVD); the title; where in your house it is located; and the artist or director. After the data has been stored in the array, retrieve a few pieces of information and print them to the console using the NSLog function.

Finally, look up NSArray in the Xcode documentation and read about the methods writeToFile: atomically: and initWithContentsOfFile:. Use these methods to save the data for your CD/DVD collection to a file on your desktop; then read it back in again. Write the whole NSArray to the console using NSLog to verify that it was read correctly. Also examine the contents of the file on your desktop in a text editor such as TextEdit.

2.   Update the Objective-C version of MyAddressBook so that it allows the user to remove an entry from the address book. Compare the changes you make in the Objective-C version to those you made in Exercise 2 of Chapter 6.

Using the Cocoa Frameworks

People use the word "Cocoa" in different ways to describe different things. For example, Cocoa can refer to the Objective-C programming language and dynamic runtime. In Chapter 7, you learned how to write simple programs in Objective-C. Some of that material, such as memory management, is specific to Cocoa.

Cocoa also applies to the Objective-C frameworks and libraries commonly used by Cocoa applications. Two principal frameworks among these include AppKit and Foundation. A few other smaller frameworks seem to be a part of the Cocoa family in one way or another, including the PreferencePanes and WebKit frameworks.

The Foundation framework contains Objective-C objects, protocols, and functions that are useful to Mac OS X programs in general, regardless of whether they are meant to be user-friendly applications or low-level system utilities. For example, things like collection classes, file I/O, and memory utilities are defined in Foundation. Also, some functionality commonly thought of as high-level application functionality lives in Foundation because it doesn't involve any user interface. Management of undo and user preferences are all part of Foundation.

The AppKit framework builds upon Foundation to implement classes essential for high-level applications, often limiting itself to graphic elements displayed on the screen. For example, windows, buttons, and menus are all AppKit features. Also, some specialized objects live in AppKit, even though they don't themselves define UI directly. One example of such algorithms are objects responsible for doing font and text layout.

As a topic, Cocoa is huge. The API reference alone would make a hefty book if it were all printed out. Fortunately Cocoa's API reference is installed on your hard drive, where you can search through it at your leisure. Rather than spending your time covering one or two Cocoa classes in great detail, this chapter illustrates some of the techniques used to build Cocoa applications, along with concrete examples. As you discover new Cocoa objects, you are encouraged to learn more about them in Cocoa API reference documentation built into Xcode.

Most of the examples in this chapter appear in the context of the Slide Master application. Each example builds on the information presented in the previous example. As a result you may find it easier to work through these examples in order. However, the information is gathered into specific topics, so you can jump right in and learn about specific areas if you prefer.

In this chapter you learn

- ❏ To use outlets, actions, and Cocoa Bindings to connect Cocoa application interfaces up to your custom source code.

- ❏ To present data in a document; including managing the document's windows and data, undoing changes, and storing the information in files.

- ❏ To extend existing Cocoa objects to meet your specific needs. For example, you will customize the way images are drawn, and handle specific keyboard events.

- ❏ To define a main menu bar and send commands to the current window.

- ❏ To tell your objects when some external resource changes, using notifications and Cocoa Bindings again.

- ❏ To use common interface elements such as open panels, table views, and drawers.

- ❏ To work with application preferences, including opening a modal preference panel, and reading and writing the standard preference file format.

Connecting Cocoa Interfaces

In earlier chapters you learned how to use Xcode to create a Cocoa application shell and use Interface Builder to design its user interface. Those examples stopped short of actually connecting the interface to code, because the details vary between Carbon and Cocoa. In fact Cocoa provides two different complimentary ways of hooking up user interfaces.

Older Cocoa applications and programs with fairly specialized needs may choose to work with the user interface directly. In these cases you are responsible for keeping the controls synchronized with the state if their application. In other words, you must initialize your controls with your application data and you must grab a new value from the controls when they change. This technique is direct and easy to grasp, but it can be hard to work with to create large user interfaces.

In Mac OS X 10.3 Panther, Apple introduced Cocoa Bindings, a new way of connecting Cocoa controls to custom Objective-C objects. Cocoa Bindings let you bind your application's controls to specific pieces of data. When your data changes, Cocoa Bindings will update the control; similarly, when the control changes, Cocoa Bindings will update your data. Cocoa Bindings helps to alleviate some of the tedium of connecting larger interfaces by hand; however, some specialized interfaces may be difficult to convert entirely to Cocoa Bindings.

Modern Cocoa applications use both techniques in their user interface. Fields that naturally reflect application data, such as text fields and sliders, may be connected using Cocoa Bindings. Other controls, such as push buttons and controls with customized drag and drop behavior, may continue to bind manually.

Connecting Interfaces Manually with Outlets and Actions

Before getting started with connecting Cocoa interfaces you need to understand a few simple concepts: *instances*, *actions*, and *outlets*. Everything you worked with in Interface Builder so far was an *instance*: menus and menu items, controls, windows, and so on. All of these items appear in your nib file's

Instances tab. Not only are these conceptually instances of each control, but they are also literally instances of Objective-C classes. That is to say, each element in your interface is one or more Objective-C objects. Recall from Chapter 6 that Objective-C objects are composed of instance variables and methods that operate on those variables.

An Interface Builder *action* is a specific kind of Objective-C method that is sent whenever a control is triggered. All actions have the same basic method signature: a void method that accepts a single argument.

```
- (IBAction) textFieldChanged: (id) sender;
```

Here IBAction is really the same as void; it's just a marker to remind you that this method is known to Interface Builder as an action. The sender parameter is normally a pointer to the control that triggered the action. For example, when you click the button, it will send its action message to a target object. You set both the target object and the action in Interface Builder.

Similarly, an *outlet* is an instance variable that points to another object known to Interface Builder. Objects often contain references to other objects to facilitate communication between these objects. In the case of the button mentioned earlier, the button needs to know about its target. Often these references are handled automatically but sometimes you need to explicitly tell one object about another object in Interface Builder. Outlets serve that purpose.

Most of the controls in Interface Builder's Palettes window have specific outlets and actions predefined. This gives you a good base to start from when hooking your controls up to something. Normally you will define your own classes within Interface Builder, define outlets and actions, and instantiate those classes. Then you can connect the interface up to your own classes and customize its behavior with code.

In the following examples you build a simple program, Email Formatter, that takes some text data and reformats it in a particular way. The user interface, as seen in Figure 8-1, should look familiar to you; it's similar to the "Building a Dialog Window" example in Chapter 4.

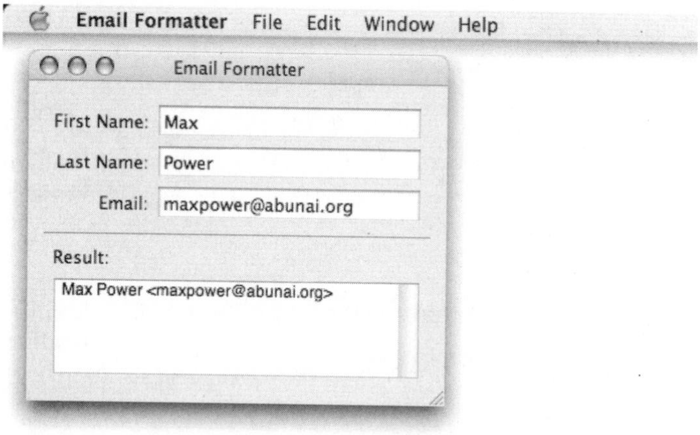

Figure 8-1

Interface Builder is easy to use, if not exactly intuitive, to create simple interfaces. But the process of binding objects to controls can be repetitive and difficult in larger examples. Interface Builder includes several time-saving shortcuts to help streamline this process, and you learn many of these shortcuts along the way.

After you've built the interface, you perform four basic steps to get the application working:

❑ First you set the key view loop so that the interface focus changes correctly when the user taps the Tab key. You didn't see this in Chapter 4 because this requires working with outlets; it's good practice before jumping in and creating your own objects.

❑ You declare a new Objective-C class inside Interface Builder that will manage your interface. This includes defining the class's outlets and actions.

❑ Then you instantiate the class within your nib file and connect it to your controls.

❑ Finally you complete your object's definition by writing some code in Xcode.

The following Try It Out walks you through building a simple interface.

Try It Out   **Building the Email Formatter Interface**

1.   In Xcode create a new Cocoa Application project named `Email Formatter`.

2.   Double-click the `MainMenu` nib file. It opens in Interface Builder.

3.   In Interface Builder, lay out the interface shown in Figure 8-2. If you need a refresher on arranging controls in Interface Builder, feel free to flip back to Chapter 4 and read the "Building Windows" section again. Don't forget to make these items resizable.

Figure 8-2

4.   Change the text view's settings to match those shown in Figure 8-3. Note the text view is not editable, and doesn't support multiple fonts.

Figure 8-3

5. Make sure the window is visible at launch time, as shown in Figure 8-4. Normally this setting is on by default.

Figure 8-4

How It Works

There isn't much new here, since you got a lot of practice building user interfaces in Chapter 4. However, there are some important things to note. One is the horizontal separator shown in Figure 8-2. This control lives in the Controls palette and is actually an instance of the NSBox object. As you might expect, NSBox is used to collect items into a box, but Interface Builder includes special one-dimensional NSBox instances for drawing horizontal and vertical lines in nib files.

Simple Cocoa Applications projects normally have only one window that contains most, if not all, of the application's user interface. These windows normally are visible on launch time, and Interface Builder provides a helpful check box for displaying the window automatically. This setting isn't appropriate when you have more than one window, such as in a document-based application; in those cases you tend to make windows visible programmatically. You learn more about documents later in this chapter.

NSTextView instances are very customizable, allowing you to adjust each one to your specific needs. In this case you just need a read-only view to display some string results; the text view should be selectable so you can copy text out of it and paste it into other applications. You can enable a bunch of other features in Interface Builder, including support for multiple fonts, undo/redo support, and automatic spell checking.

In the next Try It Out example, you define your window's key view loop so that you can use the Tab key to switch between controls in the window.

Try It Out   **Setting the Key View Loop**

1. In Interface Builder, arrange your MainMenu nib file, your window editor, and the Inspector window so that you can easily see all three windows at the same time. Make sure the window editor is the front-most window.

2. Hold down the Control key, click the editable First Name text field, and drag out without letting go of the mouse button. A line appears joining the text field to the mouse cursor, as shown in Figure 8-5.

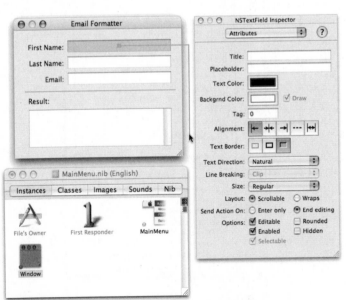

Figure 8-5

3.   Move the mouse over the editable Last Name text field and let go of the mouse button. The line will now join the two text fields, like in Figure 8-6. The Inspector window updates itself to display a Connections view, featuring a tab view containing Outlets and Target/Action tabs. The Target/Action tab is selected, and a number of methods appear in the action list.

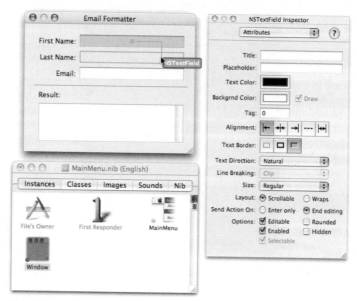

Figure 8-6

4.   Select the Outlets tab. A list of outlets appears in the Outlets list, including one named nextKeyView drawn in bold.

5.   Select the nextKeyView outlet and click the Connect button. Figure 8-7 shows the updated outlet list indicating that the nextKeyView outlet has been bound to a text field.

6.   Follow steps 2 through 5 again to connect the remaining objects to each other. Start by Control-dragging from the editable Last Name text field to the Email text field, and end by connecting the Result text view back to the First Name field. Note you'll need to switch to the Outlets tab every time; Interface Builder assumes you want to set the controls' actions first.

7.   Now Control-drag from the window instance in the MainMenu nib file to the First Name field. This time Interface Builder understands that you intend to set one of your window's outlets and the Outlet tab will be selected by default. Two outlets will be bold, shown in Figure 8-8: a delegate outlet and an initialFirstResponder outlet.

8.   Double-click the initialFirstResponder outlet. This connects the outlet as if you clicked the Connect button.

9.   Test the interface and verify the key view loop is correct by tabbing through the items. The key focus, normally indicated by a blue focus ring, should visit each control in turn. Note the text view doesn't get a focus ring. If the text view just swallows the Tab key (inserts a tab as text), that means you haven't marked the control non-editable yet; select the text view and uncheck the Editable box in the Inspector window's attributes view.

Figure 8-7

Figure 8-8

How It Works

You set outlets by Control-dragging from one instance to another. You must remember to start the drag from the object whose outlet you want to set. That is, if you want to set a window's `initialFirstResponder` outlet to a text field, you must start the drag from the window and end at the text field. You cannot set the window's outlets when starting the drag from another object.

When connecting the text controls to each other you had to manually select the Outlets tab each time. This is because Interface Builder assumes you want to set actions before you worry about outlets. In the future you can save some time by setting controls' outlets after you hook up their actions. Note that only controls have actions (by definition); when starting a drag from windows and other objects, Interface Builder will select the Outlet tab for you.

> *Mac OS X interfaces are meant to be navigable from the keyboard. At a minimum this means you can switch between text controls using the Tab key. However, you can turn on full keyboard access from the Keyboard & Mouse system preference pane; this allows you to tab between all kinds of controls.*

In Cocoa, controls are responsible for handling their own events. The selected control gets the first opportunity to handle incoming events. This control is called the *first responder*. Normally the control just handles the event itself. For example, a text field updates itself when you type text. If the control doesn't know how to interpret an event, it can pass the event to someone else. You learn more about the first responder and event handling later in this chapter.

When you press the Tab key, the first responder will attempt to change the focus to the next control in the window. Since a control needs to know what the next control should be, you supply that information by setting the control's `nextKeyView` outlet. Remember outlets are really special instance variables. When the first responder receives the tab event it will look at its `nextKeyView` instance variable and make the object it finds there the new first responder.

By default the Cocoa system will attempt to figure out what the next control should be based on the location of other controls in the window, but it's good practice to set the key view loop directly. The AppKit decides if it should use the default behavior or trust the settings in the controls by checking the window's `initialFirstResponder` outlet. `initialFirstResponder` points to the control that should be active when the window first appears on screen. If you want to define your own key view loop in Interface Builder, you must remember to set the window's `initialFirstResponder`.

In the next Try It Out example, you make a new Objective-C class that manages your interface. This includes defining the class's outlets and actions.

Try It Out Declaring a Custom Controller

1. Switch to your nib file's Classes tab. A collection of Cocoa classes appears in a browser view, resembling Figure 8-9. This browser displays a simplified version of the Cocoa class hierarchy, allowing you to see the superclass and subclasses for a given object. The class of the currently selected instance is selected in the browser.

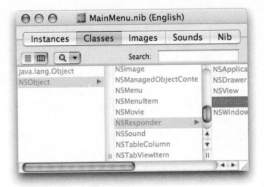

Figure 8-9

2. Scroll all the way left and select the NSObject base class. NSObject will be highlighted in the browser.

3. Select Classes ⇨ Subclass NSObject. A new class named MyObject appears in the second browser column, already selected and ready to be renamed.

4. Rename this class EmailController.

5. Open the Inspector window's Attributes view. The Inspector window displays the EmailController class's settings, as shown in Figure 8-10. Currently there are no outlets or actions defined for this class.

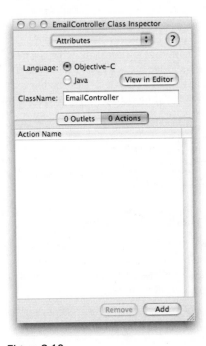

Figure 8-10

6. Click the Outlets tab and click the Add button. A new outlet named myOutlet appears in the Outlet table.

7. Rename the outlet firstNameField and set its Type to NSTextField.

8. While firstNameField is still selected, press the Return key. A new outlet named myOutlet appears, as if you clicked the Add button.

9. Name this outlet lastNameField and set its Type to NSTextField.

10. Create a new NSTextField outlet named emailField and an NSTextView outlet named resultTextView. The outlets table should now resemble Figure 8-11.

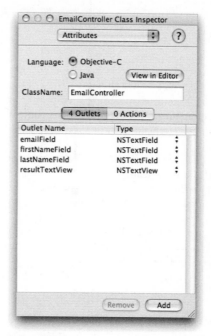

Figure 8-11

11. Switch to the Actions tab and click the Add button. A new action named myAction: appears in the Actions table.

12. Rename the action textFieldChanged:.

13. Choose Classes ⇨ Instantiate EmailController. Your nib file switches to the Instances tab where you will find a new object instance named EmailController, as shown in Figure 8-12.

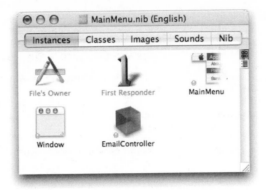

Figure 8-12

How It Works

Information about common Cocoa controls, including their outlets and actions, are built directly into Interface Builder. This information allows you to hook Cocoa controls to each other. You took advantage of these built-in settings to set your application's key view loop earlier in this example.

You can use the Classes tab to declare your own custom classes in Interface Builder. First you create a subclass from an existing class and then declare the instance variables (outlets) and methods (actions) you need to access from Interface Builder. Note you can often use the Return key to create new classes, outlets, and actions instead of menu items or other controls. This shortcut will save you a little time.

When creating an outlet you can tell Interface Builder what kind of class that outlet should be bound to. For example, you set the firstNameField's type to NSTextField, meaning this outlet is appropriate for text fields. This information is optional. If you supply it, Interface Builder helps check your nib for you. Otherwise, the field defaults to type id, which as you recall from Chapter 7 is appropriate for any type of object.

After you've declared your class, you can instantiate it in your nib file. This allows you to connect your object to other user interface elements in your nib file, as you see shortly. Note that you really are creating an instance of your object in your nib file; when your application starts up a new instance of your object will be created and initialized with the settings in the nib file. Your nib assumes ownership of this object, so you don't need to worry about retaining or releasing the object yourself.

In the next Try It Out, you create an instance of your Objective-C controller class and connect it to your user interface.

Try It Out   Connecting Controls to Your Controller

1. Before starting, note the contents of the MainMenu nib. Note the Window and EmailController instances have little yellow exclamation point badges next to them. If you hold the mouse over one of these objects, a warning appears in a help tag, as shown in Figure 8-13.

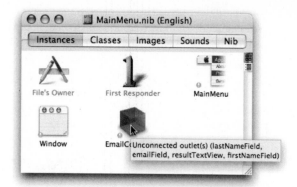

Figure 8-13

2. Control-drag from the `EmailController` instance to the Email text field. Note the Inspector window automatically displays its Connections view and selects the Outlets list, as in Figure 8-14. The text field outlets are all drawn in bold, and the first field, emailField, is selected for you. All you need to do is click the Connect button to set the emailField outlet.

Figure 8-14

3. Repeat step 2 to set the First Name and Last Name fields to the firstNameField and lastNameField outlets respectively, in that order. Remember to start dragging from the `EmailController` instance. Note that Interface Builder automatically selects the next available outlet in the Outlets list.

4. Set the `EmailController`'s `resultTextView` outlet to the Result text view. This time only the `resultTextView` outlet will be bold. Since it's the last available outlet, `resultTextView` will be selected automatically. Also, once you make the connection `EmailController`'s exclamation badge goes away.

5. Now Control-drag from the First Name text field to the `EmailController` instance as shown in Figure 8-15. That's right: start the drag from the text field, not the `EmailController`. The Connections inspector displays `EmailController`'s Actions list. As you may recall, `EmailController` has only one action: `textFieldChanged:`.

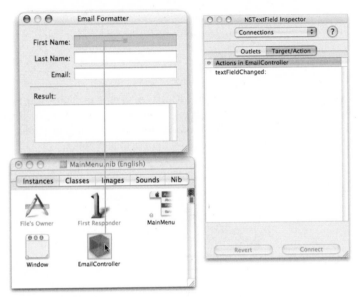

Figure 8-15

6. Double-click `textFieldChanged:` to set the action.

7. Repeat steps 5 and 6 to set the action for the Last Name and Email text fields. When you make the last connection the Window instance's exclamation badge will also disappear.

How It Works

You saw how to connect outlets in the previous example, and for the most part there were no surprises. However, you did learn about some helpful Interface Builder features that make this process a little easier.

Interface Builder drew some of the Outlets list entries in bold. Bold outlets are appropriate for the kind of object being connected. For example when connecting `EmailController` to a text field, the `firstNameField`, `lastNameField`, and `emailField` outlets appear in bold. This worked because you specified the outlet types in the previous example. If you left the types set to `id` all the outlets would appear bold all the time.

But Interface Builder's consistency checking didn't stop there. It drew yellow exclamation point badges next to instances that weren't completely configured. In the case of EmailController, Interface Builder warned you some of its outlets hadn't been set yet. A specific list of problems was available in the instance's help tag. Once you connected the outlets the badge went away.

When connecting EmailController's outlets, Interface Builder automatically selected the first appropriate outlet in the Outlets list. You can take advantage of this when wiring up larger interfaces. Because the Outlets list is always sorted alphabetically, you can save time by connecting fields as they appear in the list.

You also learned how to set actions. For the most part setting actions works just like setting outlets except you start the Control-drag operation from the control. This whole issue of Control-dragging can be a bit confusing for people new to Cocoa, since it's not always obvious where you should start dragging from. There is a simple rule to keep this straight: always start the Control-drag from the element you are modifying. The following table lists a few examples illustrating this point.

What You Want	What You Do
Set a window's initialFirstResponder to a text field.	The window is being modified, so Control-drag from the window to the text field.
Set a text field's nextKeyView to a button.	The text field is being modified, so Control-drag from the text field to the button.
Connect a button to an object's clickedOK: action.	The button is being modified, so Control-drag from the button to the object.

In the next Try It Out example, you write the code for your EmailController class. Then you will be able to build and run the Email Formatter program.

Try It Out   Writing Your Controller

1. Switch back to the Classes tab in the MainMenu nib file and select your EmailController class.

2. Choose Classes ⇨ Create Files for EmailController. A save panel appears, allowing you to pick a place to save some new source files, as shown in Figure 8-16.

3. Click OK to save the files in the default location.

4. Save the MainMenu file.

5. Switch to Xcode. Note EmailController.m and EmailController.h files have been added to your project. You may want to drag these files into your project's Classes group.

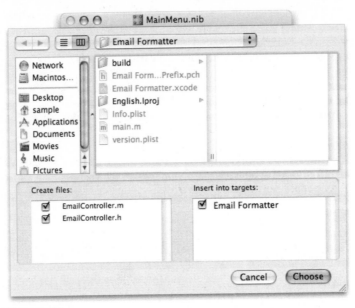

Figure 8-16

6. Open `EmailController.h`. The following code was generated from Interface Builder:

```
/* EmailController */

#import <Cocoa/Cocoa.h>

@interface EmailController : NSObject
{
    IBOutlet NSTextField *emailField;
    IBOutlet NSTextField *firstNameField;
    IBOutlet NSTextField *lastNameField;
    IBOutlet NSTextView  *resultTextView;
}
- (IBAction)textFieldChanged:(id)sender;
@end
```

7. Switch to `EmailController.m`. Again, the following generated code appears. Notice the `textFieldChanged:` method has been defined but is currently empty.

```
#import "EmailController.h"

@implementation EmailController

- (IBAction)textFieldChanged:(id)sender
{
}

@end
```

8. Add the following code to the `textFieldChanged:` method:

```
- (IBAction)textFieldChanged:(id)sender
{
    NSString *string = [NSString stringWithFormat:@"%@ %@ <%@>",
        [firstNameField stringValue],
        [lastNameField stringValue],
        [emailField stringValue]];

    [resultTextView setString:string];
}
```

9. Save your changes to `EmailController.m`.

10. Build and run your project. Xcode will compile your code, build your application wrapper, and run your program.

11. Insert values in the text fields. As you do so, the Result view displays the information formatted as a verbose email address. You can select the text in the Result field and copy and paste or drag and drop the full address into an email program like Mail.

How It Works

Interface Builder knows a lot about your `EmailController` object, including the names and types of `EmailController`'s outlets and the name of its action. This information was required for hooking your interface's controls up to a custom object. As an added bonus, Interface Builder can use this information to build starter files for `EmailController`. Interface Builder will even insert these files into your Xcode project for you.

Note that Interface Builder's understanding of your object isn't complete. Your object may include other instance variables that aren't relevant within the nib file; similarly you can define other methods that aren't meant to be invoked directly from controls. In this example, all you needed to do was supply some code for the `textFieldChanged:` method. For that matter, Interface Builder didn't generate any code at all for the other objects in your nib file.

This is a pretty big deal, especially if you've used WYSIWYG development environments that automatically generate the entire code for all of your interface elements. Those systems actually write large pieces of your source code for you as you change your interface layout. Although those tools spare you the time and trouble to write that code, it can be difficult to find where you should insert your own changes. If you make a mistake, you run the risk of losing your custom code the next time you make a trivial change to your interface. When using Cocoa, you only write the code that's unique to your application; all of the default control behaviors are provided directly by the Cocoa frameworks.

The `textFieldChanged:` method does three things. First, it gets the contents of the text fields using their `-stringValue` methods. The `NSTextField` objects inherit `-stringValue` from their superclass, `NSControl`. The `NSControl` class is the common ancestor for all controls that trigger actions when they change.

Second, the `textFieldChanged:` method builds a new `NSString` object that joins the other strings together using `+stringWithFormat:`. You may remember `NSString`'s `stringWithFormat:` and `NSLog` from Chapter 7. This string holds the newly formatted email address.

Third, it assigns the resulting string to the resultTextView using its -setString: method. Again, resultTextView is an instance of NSTextView, which in spite of appearances isn't really an NSControl subclass like NSTextField. As a result, it doesn't use the same methods for getting and setting data.

In Chapter 7 you also learned a little about how NSAutoreleasePool objects work; every example you saw created and released its own autorelease pool instance. You may be wondering why this example has no autorelease pool. It turns out it does, but AppKit is managing it for you. Every event is processed in its own autorelease pool, meaning all the temporary objects created during event handling are released before processing the next event. That also means you can't hang onto these autoreleased objects in an instance variable (or a global variable) without retaining them first. Note that's exactly what the NSTextView will do when you call setString:. As a general rule in Cocoa programs you don't need to worry about autoreleased objects as long as you never hang onto them between events.

After you've completed the textFieldChanged: method you can build and run your application. When your application's nib file loads, Cocoa creates and initializes your EmailController object. And when you change the text fields, textFieldChanged: is called to rebuild the result text view. If you want you can set a breakpoint in textFieldChanged:, run your application in Xcode's debugger, and watch as the result text view is rebuilt. Note that copy and paste, select all, drag and drop, and other features work without you doing anything special on your end; you are beginning to reap the benefits of Cocoa.

Working with Cocoa Bindings

You now have a pretty good idea of the work involved in connecting a Cocoa user interface. Most of the hard work is done in Interface Builder: you design your user interface, then you declare your classes, then you do a lot of Control-dragging to connect the interface to your custom classes. Once that's all done, all you have to do is fill in the remaining source code and you're good to go.

While this isn't a big deal for the Email Formatter example, there's a lot of busy work involved in building a large user interface. Consider an inspector window with dozens or hundreds of controls. Each control needs its own outlet, you have to remember to initialize the controls to useful values, and you have to remember to update the controls if somehow your data changes behind the scenes. You also need to track when each control changes using either separate actions or by funneling groups of controls into a single action. Even the Email Formatter application, which had only three editable controls, captured edits in a single action method. AppKit provides a number of little tricks, like control tags, to help facilitate this kind of control management. But there's another way hook up Cocoa user interfaces that avoids much of this busywork.

Apple introduced *Cocoa Bindings*, a new way of connecting Cocoa controls to your custom Objective-C objects, to deal with some of these scalability issues. Instead of connecting a control to outlet instance variables and action methods, Cocoa Bindings let you connect a control directly to an object's value. When the control changes Cocoa Bindings will update the value for you. What's more, when the value changes Cocoa Bindings will automatically update the control for you as well. There's a lot going on behind the scenes to make this work; but you really don't need to worry about how it works to get started with Cocoa Bindings.

In the following Try It Out, you build a version of Email Formatter that uses Cocoa Bindings to manage its user interface. After you build your user interface, three steps remain to complete the application:

❑ First, you create an NSObjectController instance and connect it to a custom data object. This is the Cocoa Bindings equivalent of the EmailController class from the first Email Formatter example.

❑ Second, you connect your controls up to the NSObjectController.

❑ Finally, you finish the implementation of your custom class in Xcode.

Try It Out   Building the Email Formatter 2 Interface

1. In Xcode create a new Cocoa Application project named Email Formatter 2.

2. Double-click the MainMenu nib file. It opens in Interface Builder.

3. In Interface Builder select the Window instance and press the Delete key to remove it from your nib file.

4. Now open the MainMenu nib file from your first Email Formatter program. You should be able to find it in Interface Builder's File ➪ Open Recent menu. If not, you can find it in your Email Formatter Xcode project.

5. Copy the Window instance from the first Email Formatter nib file by clicking the Window icon and choosing Edit ➪ Copy.

6. Close the original Email Formatter nib file.

7. Paste the Window into your new nib file by choosing Edit ➪ Paste.

8. Make sure the window is visible at launch time. When you pasted the window into your new nib file, Interface Builder may have turned this option off.

How It Works

Copying the Window instance from your first Email Formatter project to your second saved you a bit of time. For the most part, the entire Window instance structure was preserved, including the controls and their key view loop. However, all of your controls' actions were cleared. This is just as well, as you won't be setting actions in this example. The one unexplained mystery was Interface Builder cleared your window's "Visible at launch time" setting, and that was easily fixed.

In the next Try It Out, you declare an EmailAddress class to store the data displayed by your interface and create an NSObjectController instance to manage the relationship between your controls and the EmailAddress class.

Try It Out   Creating an NSObjectController

1. In your nib file's Classes tab create an NSObject subclass called EmailAddress. You don't need to worry about creating outlets or actions for this class.

2. Instantiate the EmailAddress class. A blue cube appears in your nib file's Instances tab representing your EmailAddress instance.

3. Select the Controllers palette in Interface Builder's Palettes window. Green cubes representing controller objects appear, like those in Figure 8-17. The middle object is the NSObjectController. You can confirm that by holding the mouse over its icon; a help tag with the object's class name will appear.

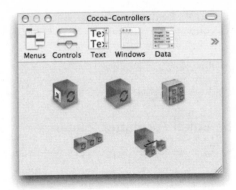

Figure 8-17

4.   Drag an NSObjectController instance out of the Bindings palette into your nib file's Instances tab.

5.   Set the NSObjectController's content outlet to your EmailAddress instance by Control-dragging from NSObjectController to the EmailAddress icon.

How It Works

Cocoa Bindings use NSController subclasses to marshal data between your custom objects and your controls. Currently there are three such NSController subclasses: NSObjectController, NSUserDefaultsController, and NSArrayController. NSArrayController is useful for working with arrays of custom objects, such as when working with lists of information. NSUserDefaultsController is a special kind of NSObjectController that reads and writes values to your preference file automatically. You added an NSObjectController object to your interface because your data object is a simple NSObject subclass.

You still created a custom class in Interface Builder, EmailAddress, even though you're working with Cocoa Bindings. This custom class won't talk to your controls directly; and as a result you didn't need to create any outlets or actions. Your NSObjectController instance will handle that for you. Instead EmailAddress will basically store the values that appear in your controls. Because NSObjectController will need this information, you connected your EmailAddress instance to NSObjectController's outlet.

In the next example, you connect the controls to your new NSObjectController instance.

Try It Out   **Connecting Controls to NSObjectController**

1.   Select the editable First Name text field in your Window editor.

2.   Select Bindings from your Inspector window's popup menu. A new view appears, as shown in Figure 8-18.

3.   Click the "value" disclosure triangle under the Value section to reveal the group of controls shown in Figure 8-19. Note that NSObjectController already appears in the Bind To popup menu.

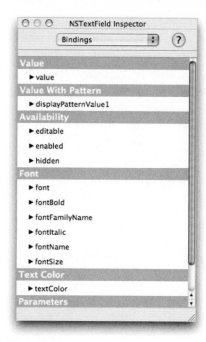

Figure 8-18

Figure 8-19

4. Enter `firstName` in the Model Key Path text field and press Return. Note the Bind check box will automatically enable itself, and the group of disabled controls under the Model Key Path value will become enabled.

5. Follow the preceding steps to set the Last Name text field's Model Key Path to `lastName` and the Email text field's Model Key Path to `email`.

6. Click once on the Result text view. Note the Bindings view will change to include only Availability and Parameters sections. Also note the Inspector window's title reads "NSScrollView Inspector."

7. Double-click the Result text view. The Inspector window's title is now "NSTextView Inspector," and the Bindings view includes a Value section.

8. Click the "value" disclosure triangle under the Value section to reveal the group of controls. These controls resemble the ones you saw in Figure 8-19.

9. Enter `formattedEmail` in the Model Key Path text field and press Return. Again note the disabled group of controls under Model Key Path will be enabled.

10. Turn off the Conditionally Sets Editable check box. The Bindings settings should match those shown in Figure 8-20.

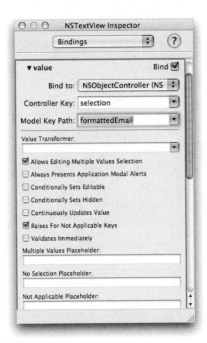

Figure 8-20

How It Works

You use the Bindings inspector to associate a user interface element with a particular piece of data. First you specify the NSController subclass you want to bind to using the Bind To popup menu. In this example, Interface Builder automatically selected your NSObjectController because it was the only one available in your nib file.

Then you specify a *controller key,* which helps provide some context when talking to your controller. In this example, and for all NSObjectController bindings, this value will always be selection. Other kinds of controllers, such as NSArrayController, can use the Controller Key value to access other kinds of information.

Finally you specify a *model key path* that identifies the data you are looking for. In this example, the model key path values are simply names of values in your EmailAddress object, although you haven't defined those values yet. In more sophisticated examples, the model key path might include a list of objects to traverse in order to find the data.

There are two subtle gotchas regarding your NSTextView. When you built your interface the first time (in the Email Formatter example) you turned off the ability to use multiple fonts. This allows you to treat the contents of the text view as a simple string, just like the preceding text fields. You see why this is important in the next section. If that option was enabled, Cocoa Bindings would expect you to work with NSData objects containing *rich text* data, like those found in RTF files. In that case, the Bindings view will show the "data" section in Figure 8-21 instead of the "value" section seen earlier in Figure 8-20. If you find yourself in this situation, just turn off the data binding shown in Figure 8-21, turn off the text view's Use Multiple Fonts check box, and then enable the value binding.

Figure 8-21

The second NSTextView gotcha involves editability. Again when you created the interface you turned off the NSTextView's Editable flag. If you use Cocoa Bindings, the Editable flag is ignored on default; instead editability can be controlled through the bindings themselves. That is, you can configure controls to be editable only when another condition is true; for example, you can enable one check box automatically when the check box above it is enabled. Because this text view must always be read-only, you have to turn off the Bindings view's Conditionally Sets Editable setting.

In the next example, you write the code for your `EmailAddress` model object. Then you will be able to build and run Email Formatter 2.

Try It Out   Writing Your EmailAddress Class

1. In Xcode, choose File ⇨ New File and create a new Cocoa Objective-C Class. Name the class file `EmailAddress.m` and opt to create the corresponding `EmailAddress.h` file.

2. Open `EmailController.h`. Xcode supplied the initial following code:

```
//
//  EmailAddress.h
//  Email Formatter 2
//
//  Created by sample on Fri Sep 10 2004.
//  Copyright (c) 2004 __MyCompanyName__. All rights reserved.
//


#import <Foundation/Foundation.h>


@interface EmailAddress : NSObject {

}

@end
```

3. Change the declaration of `EmailAddress` to include the following instance variables:

```
@interface EmailAddress : NSObject {
    NSString *firstName;
    NSString *lastName;
    NSString *email;
}

@end
```

4. Save your changes to `EmailAddress.h`.

5. Switch to `EmailAddress.m`. Here is the initial code:

```
//
//  EmailAddress.m
//  Email Formatter 2
//
//  Created by sample on Fri Sep 10 2004.
//  Copyright (c) 2004 __MyCompanyName__. All rights reserved.
//


#import "EmailAddress.h"


@implementation EmailAddress

@end
```

6. Add the following methods to the `EmailAddress` object:

```
@implementation EmailAddress

+ (void)initialize
{
    NSArray *keys = [NSArray arrayWithObjects:@"firstName",
        @"lastName",
        @"email",
        nil];

    [EmailAddress setKeys:keys
        triggerChangeNotificationsForDependentKey:@"formattedEmail"];
}

- (NSString*)formattedEmail
{
    if (firstName && lastName && email) {
        return [NSString stringWithFormat:@"%@ %@ <%@>", firstName, lastName,
email];
    }

    return nil;
}

@end
```

7. Save your changes to `EmailAddress.m`.

8. Build and run your project. Xcode compiles your code, builds your application wrapper, and runs your program.

How It Works

In this example you created the files for your custom Objective-C object in Xcode, instead of Interface Builder. Because you didn't define any outlets or targets for the `EmailAddress` class, Interface Builder wouldn't create any instance variables or methods for you. Xcode also provides more information in comments at the top of each file.

Your `EmailAddress` class used an `+initialize` class method to set some initial state when your program launched. The `+initialize` class method is special; rather than a method called by other code in your program, `+initialize` methods are called automatically by the Objective-C runtime before your class is accessed the first time. While this method is a good place to set global state required by your class before it is used, it does come with some risk. Because the `+initialize` method runs before your class is used it has the potential to slow down application launch, making your program seem sluggish. You should avoid costly operations such as reading from files or a network in these methods. In the case of `EmailAddress`, its +initialize method is fairly simple. But it's a good idea to use Sample, Shark, or the other performance tools you read about in Chapter 2 to measure your program's launch performance.

Cocoa Bindings will look for model key paths either in instance variables or accessor methods. You are already familiar with instance variables of course. Three of your key paths, `firstName`, `lastName`, and `email`, were defined as instance variables in your `EmailAddress` object. Because all three of these values need to be available to `EmailAddress` at any given time (in order to build the resulting formatted email address), instance variables were a convenient choice of implementation. All you had to do was make sure the instance variables' names matched the key paths in the nib file, and Cocoa Bindings managed the rest for you.

You may also remember accessor methods, methods used to get and set instance variable values, from Chapter 7. Your fourth key path, `formattedEmail`, was implemented as an accessor method. Doing so gave your `EmailAddress` object the opportunity to construct the `formattedEmail` value upon demand. If it were instead implemented as an instance variable you would need to find some other way of rebuilding the value when one of the text fields changed.

Note in both cases the specific data types for `EmailAddress`'s values were specified by the instance variable and accessor definitions themselves. You did not need to specify the exact type in your nib file. The Cocoa Bindings system recognizes many different data types. In this example you worked entirely with `NSString` instances; you could just have easily worked with simple scalar types like `int`, `float`, or `BOOL`. Other kinds of controls are better suited for working with other kinds of data types. For example, an `NSImageView` might work with `NSImage` instances directly; `NSTextViews` that display rich text work with `NSData` objects.

The mechanism for accessing your objects' values by a key path is called *Key Value Coding*, and is one of the technologies Cocoa Bindings is based on. You have already seen Key Value Coding in action accessing the values in your `EmailAddress` object. Key Value Coding also defines how the values for each key is found, how to handle requests for keys that aren't available, navigating through multiple objects to find specific data, and other advanced topics.

However, Key Value Coding doesn't explain why your application knew to request the `formattedEmail` value when your text fields changed. Early on, in your `+initialize` method, you used a class method called `+setKeys:triggerChangeNotificationsForDependentKey:` to tell Cocoa Bindings that `formattedEmail` depends on the values of your other keys. This method is built into `NSObject` and is part of a mechanism called *Key Value Observing*.

Key Value Observing is another core technology behind Cocoa Bindings. It refers to the ability for Cocoa Bindings to watch your objects, note when they change, and communicate that change to others. This is normally used to keep controls synchronized with their bound values. For example, when an object's value is changed through an accessor method, Key Value Observing will make sure the controls that refer to this value are updated automatically. This automatic update works only for changes made through accessor methods, not for direct assignment to instance variables. You can consider Key Value Coding equivalent to accessor methods for the purposes of observing. In this example, when your `NSObjectController` changed the value of `EmailAddress`'s `firstName`, `lastName`, and `email` values through Key Value Coding, Key Value Observing told the `NSObjectController` that the `formattedEmail` value also needed to be updated. Then the `NSObjectController` used Key Value Coding again to read the new value of `formattedEmail`.

This example has only just scratched the surface of Cocoa Bindings, Key Value Coding, and Key Value Observing. You see a few more examples of bindings throughout this chapter. If you want to learn more about bindings, including how bindings work and what they can do, you should check the Xcode's Documentation window. You can start by reading the conceptual documentation for Cocoa Bindings, available either through the Cocoa conceptual documentation list or through the `NSController` reference documentation.

The Model/View/Controller Design Pattern

You may have noticed the term "controller" appearing in both of the previous examples. In the first Email Formatter application, the word appears in the name of your custom Objective-C object, `EmailController`. In the second application, you learned Cocoa Bindings is built around a series of classes derived from `NSController`. And there are some similarities about how these controllers were used; in both cases your user interface was bound directly to your controller objects. This was not a coincidence.

Most Cocoa objects follow a programming convention known as the *Model/View/Controller* design pattern. Model/View/Controller, which is abbreviated MVC, refers to a particular way of organizing objects to encourage code reuse. Objects are separated into one of three categories, from which the MVC design pattern derives its name: *model* objects, *views*, and *controllers*.

A *model* encapsulates a particular set of data or an algorithm. They are normally limited in scope, and do not imply how the data is meant to be displayed. One example of a model object you've seen so far is `NSString`. `NSString` objects represent a Unicode character string; it supplies storage for the string data and methods for accessing and manipulating that data. At the same time, `NSString` doesn't provide any support for drawing strings in user interfaces. By keeping model objects focused on the data they represent, they are easily usable in any situation that calls for that kind of data.

Objects responsible for presenting information to the user are called *views*. Concrete examples of views abound in Cocoa; for example, windows, buttons, menus, and text fields are all views. Many AppKit classes even use the term in their class names, such as `NSTextView` and `NSImageView`. View objects aren't directly concerned with the details of how data is stored, or what the data might represent. This allows views to be easily reused whenever you need that kind of user interface element.

Controllers fill the gap between the general-purpose model and view objects. Mechanically, this means a controller pulls data out of the model and hands it to the view for display, and when the view changes (the user changed the value of a control) the controller pulls the new data out of the view and records it in the model. This also means the controller provides the context in which the model and view objects are used. For example, while an `NSString` is just a collection of Unicode characters, and an `NSTextField` knows how to draw an `NSString` in an editable control, the `EmailController` object knows that a particular string containing an email address should go into the Email `NSTextField` control. Because controllers are specific to a particular user interface, they normally aren't reusable in the same way model and view objects are. Cocoa Bindings try to solve this reusability problem by providing a standard mechanism for shuttling values between your model objects and your views.

The MVC design pattern is an abstract notion, and you can implement its concepts in different ways. For example, a controller object might also double as a model in a simple example where you aren't interested in re-using the model elsewhere. This was the case in your first Email Formatter application: the `EmailController` object was responsible for reacting to user interface changes as well as performing your model-specific behavior (converting the inputs into a formatted email address). On the other hand, Email Formatter 2's `EmailAddress` object was strictly a model object.

Also objects your application thinks of as views might actually be implemented as a small collection of objects that can be further described by the MVC design pattern. One great example of this is `NSTextView`, which you used to display formatted results in your Email Formatter applications. `NSTextView` works with `NSTextStorage` and `NSLayoutManager` behind the scenes to draw the requested text. `NSTextView` really is the view, as its name implies. NSTextStorage is a model object providing private storage for the string drawn in the view. You can think of the NSLayoutManager as the controller coordinating how the string data in NSTextStorage is drawn in the NSTextView view. And again, you treat this entire mechanism as a view for getting your text to appear on screen.

Working with Documents

The AppKit framework includes classes to help manage documents of information in a Cocoa program. When you use these classes, AppKit will handle your documents' files and windows for you. You need to focus on your documents' data and how you connect it to your user interface.

AppKit's document support can be used in two different ways, depending on how sophisticated your interface is or what kind of hurry you are in. In both cases you begin by creating your own custom subclass of NSDocument. The NSDocument class provides basic behavior for a document, including reading from and writing to files, tracking open windows, managing document changes and undo, printing, and so on.

Your NSDocument subclass can manage its own windows directly. In this case your NSDocument subclass will contain model code for storing document data in memory and working with files, as well as controller information such as populating the user interface, and updating the model when the interface changes (and vice versa).

Using NSDocument in this way has a few advantages for people new to Cocoa programming. Primarily it simplifies your application code by keeping all of your document knowledge in one class. It's easy to get started working with document-based applications using this method. Also, for very small projects with only a few objects, it may not make sense to burden the application with a more sophisticated design. On the other hand, more complicated classes may suffer by mingling interface controller code with the document model code.

AppKit provides an NSWindowController class that you can use to separate document model logic from its interface control. NSWindowController manages the life cycle of a window, including loading the window from a nib file, managing how the window appears on screen, and tearing everything down when the window is closed. In addition to providing general window behavior, a custom NSWindowController subclass can also manage a window's contents: the window controller can initialize its controls from your document's state, and update that state when the controls change.

Because NSDocument can handle window management itself, use of custom NSWindowControllers in a document-based application is largely optional. There are benefits to separating out document model logic from interface controller code. For example, you may want to create instances of your documents where you don't load a user interface, such in a background-only daemon or when handling AppleScript commands. Also, you will need to use NSWindowController subclasses if your application needs to display more than one window per document, such as in a CAD program. NSDocument can only handle one window per document by default.

Creating a New Document

In the following Try It Out, you build a simple image viewer application that uses a custom NSWindowController class along with a custom NSDocument class. Rather than building a small stand-alone example, you build this functionality directly into the Slide Master project you started in Chapter 5. This gives Slide Master the capability to view slides in individual windows, outside the context of a slide show, as shown in Figure 8-22. Images appear in their own window; if the window isn't large enough to display the entire image, scroll bars appear.

You add this functionality to Slide Master in four steps:

1. First you build Slide Master's image window. This window contains an `NSImageView` object that can display image data; the image view resides within an `NSScrollView` object that knows how to scroll views too large to fit in a specific area.

2. Next you define your custom `NSWindowController` and set it as the nib file's owner. This allows you to connect the interface to your custom controller class.

3. You create your custom `NSDocument` subclass in Xcode. This class is responsible for reading image data from disk.

4. Finally, you build an `NSWindowController` subclass responsible for loading the image window and initializing its contents.

Figure 8-22

Try It Out   Configuring a Scrollable Image View

1. In Xcode open the Slide Master project you created in Chapter 5. If you haven't built this project yet for some reason, flip back to Chapter 5 and follow the example in the "Building an Application Bundle" section.

2. Control-click the MyDocument nib file and choose the Reveal In Finder option from the contextual menu. The Finder will activate and display the MyDocument nib file.

3. Make a copy of the MyDocument nib file named ImageWindow.

4. In Xcode add ImageWindow to the Slide Master project. If you like, drag ImageWindow to the Resources group in your project's Groups & Files list.

5. Double-click the ImageWindow nib file. It will open in Interface Builder.

6. Replace the "Your document contents here" placeholder with an image view. You will find NSImageView control on the Containers palette; it looks like a picture of a mountain range set into the window, shown in Figure 8-23. Don't bother resizing the control; you manage the size of this image view programmatically in a custom NSWindowController class, which you do a little later.

Figure 8-23

7. Turn off the image view's border and scaling function. The Attributes inspector should resemble Figure 8-24. Note that when you turn the border off, the image view is no longer obviously visible in the window editor. Only its bounding box selection handles indicate the image view's location.

8. Select Layout ⇨ Make subviews of ⇨ Scroll View. The image view is replaced by a scroll view containing that image view.

9. Resize the scroll view so that it fills the entire screen. Also make sure the scroll view will grow and shrink as the window is resized.

10. Disable the scroll view's border and turn on Automatically Hide Scrollers. Also set the scroll view's background color to white. The Attributes inspector will resemble the one in Figure 8-25.

11. Double-click within the scroll view area; this selects the image view again.

12. Verify the image view will not grow or shrink when the window is resized, using the Size inspector.

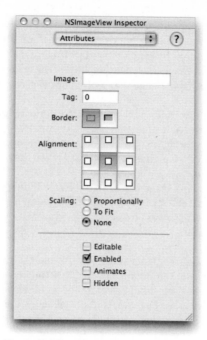

Figure 8-24

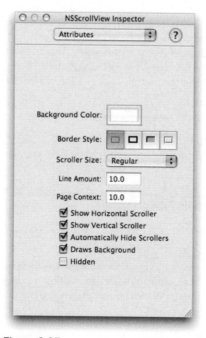

Figure 8-25

How It Works

The NSImageView class is a simple control that draws image data. It's useful in cases like this where you need to draw an image in a window. NSImageView objects can also be editable, meaning you can change the image by dragging in a new image file from the Finder. These kinds of image views are often called *image wells*, so called because editable image views often appear inset in the window.

Rather than exposing scroll bars as individual controls in Interface Builder, Cocoa provides a new view class that manages the entire scrollable area: NSScrollView. An NSScrollView instance does all of the work required for checking its size against the size of its contents and configuring the scroll bars accordingly. You can even tell NSScrollView to hide scroll bars when they aren't necessary.

You normally create NSScrollView instances using Interface Builder's "Make subviews of" menu item. This menu item takes the current selection and wraps it in a container view, such as NSScrollView or NSBox. Because NSScrollView instances are meaningless on their own, you cannot drag them into your interface from the Palettes window.

You can access an NSScrollView's contents simply by double-clicking in its content area. You will notice the selection rectangle change slightly to reflect the scroll view's contents. Also, the Inspector window will change to reflect the new selection. Selecting the scroll view again can be difficult, especially if the scroll view fills the entire window; one way is to double-click the window instance in the Instances tab. This will select the window's contents, which happens to be the scroll view.

When you built your interface, you didn't resize the NSImageView control, and you made sure that the control doesn't change size along with the window. This may seem odd when compared with the other examples you've seen so far. You didn't change the control's size because Slide Master controls its area programmatically. When you open a large image, Slide Master resizes the NSImageView to fit the image. If you did change the size of the control, that's okay; it will have no bearing on the finished product. You made sure the NSImageView doesn't resize with the window because its viewable area is being managed by an NSScrollView. When the window changes size, your NSScrollView changes with it, allowing you to see more of the picture. But the picture itself, including its size, remains constant — even when the window is resized.

In the following Try It Out, you declare a custom NSWindowController subclass and designate it the owner of your nib file. This is a prerequisite step for hooking your document's user interface up to your code.

Try It Out   Setting the Nib File's Owner

1. In your nib file's Classes tab, find the class named NSWindowController. It is a subclass of the NSResponder class, which itself is a subclass of NSObject.

2. Create an NSWindowController subclass called ImageWindowController. ImageWindowController should define one outlet, mImageView. Note that NSWindowController also defines an outlet called window.

3. Create the files for your ImageWindowController class and save them to the default location within the Slide Master project.

4. In your ImageWindow nib file's Instances tab, select the File's Owner instance.

5. Select the Inspector window's Custom Class inspector. A list of class names will appear with a class called `MyDocument` currently selected.

6. Change the File's Owner's current class to `ImageWindowController`.

7. Connect the `File's Owner's mImageView` and `window` outlets to the image view and document window.

8. Save the `ImageWindow` nib file.

How It Works

In Cocoa applications, nib files are opened on behalf of a particular object, which is known as the nib file's *owner*. You can think of the nib file's owner as the object that actually loaded the nib file. A nib file can reference its owner using the built-in File's Owner instance. Unlike other controller instances you've seen in Interface Builder so far, the File's Owner exists before the nib is loaded. For example, the `MainMenu` nib file is owned by the `NSApplication` class, because `NSApplication` is responsible for finding and loading the nib with the menu bar.

Your document interface is owned by its window controller, `ImageWindowController`. You defined your `ImageWindowController` class as a subclass of `NSWindowController`, which provides much of your custom class's functionality. Note that the `window` outlet is actually part of the `NSWindowController` superclass; you cannot delete or rename this outlet.

You use the Custom Class inspector to change the class of the selected instance. The Custom Class list displays only class names that are appropriate for the instance in question. In this case the File's Owner can be any kind of `NSObject` subclass, so the Custom Class list displayed a lot of choices. Once you defined your `ImageWindowController` class, you were able to make it the File's Owner's class. You can also use this technique to create and use a custom class for other instances. For example, you can create a custom subclass of `NSButton` and configure a button instance to use your class; in that case, the Custom Class list would only display `NSButton` and your custom subclass.

In the next Try It Out, you create `ImageDocument`, an `NSDocument` subclass, to manage Slide Master's image windows. You also modify your project so Slide Master recognizes image files as valid documents.

Try It Out   Writing a Custom NSDocument Subclass

1. Create new source files of Cocoa Objective-C `NSDocument`-subclass type, named `ImageDocument.h` and `ImageDocument.m`.

2. Open `ImageDocument.h` and define the `ImageDocument` class as follows:

```
@interface ImageDocument : NSDocument
{
    NSImage *mImage;
}

- (NSImage*)image;

@end
```

3. Open `ImageDocument.m`. Xcode added a lot of starter code to this file for you, including some usage notes. This provides a good place to start when hooking up your document functionality.

4. Replace the `ImageDocument.m` contents with the following code:

```objc
#import "ImageDocument.h"

#import "ImageWindowController.h"

@implementation ImageDocument

#pragma mark Document Initialization

- (id)init
{
    self = [super init];
    if (self) {

        // Add your subclass-specific initialization here.
        // If an error occurs here, send a [self release] message and return nil.

    }
    return self;
}

- (void)dealloc
{
    [mImage release];

    [super dealloc];
}

- (void)makeWindowControllers
{
    ImageWindowController *imageWindowController = nil;

    imageWindowController = [[[ImageWindowController alloc]
initWithWindowNibName:@"ImageWindow"] autorelease];

    [self addWindowController:imageWindowController];
}

- (NSData *)dataRepresentationOfType:(NSString *)aType
{
    // unreachable
    return nil;
}

- (BOOL)loadDataRepresentation:(NSData *)data ofType:(NSString *)aType
{
    mImage = [[NSImage alloc] initWithData:data];

    return (mImage != nil);
}

#pragma mark Slide Accessors

- (NSImage*)image
```

```
{
    return mImage;
}

#pragma mark Menu Management

- (BOOL)validateMenuItem:(NSMenuItem*)menuItem
{
    SEL action = [menuItem action];

    if (action == @selector(saveDocument:) ||
        action == @selector(saveDocumentAs:) ||
        action == @selector(saveDocumentTo:))
    {
        return NO;
    }

    return [super validateMenuItem:menuItem];
}

@end
```

5. Save the `ImageDocument` files.

6. In Xcode's project window, select the Slide Master target and choose Project ➪ Get Info. The Target Info window appears.

7. Select the Properties tab and add a new document type called Image Document. The Image Document type resembles the SlideShow Document type you added back in Chapter 5, with a few differences. Set the document Class to `ImageDocument`, set Extensions to `tif jpg gif pdf` (do not include a dot; separate the extensions with a space), and set the Role to Editor, as shown in Figure 8-26. You don't need an icon for this document type. Also, make sure the new Image Document type appears after the SlideShow Document type in the list; this way Slide Master continues to create untitled SlideShow Documents when you select File ➪ New.

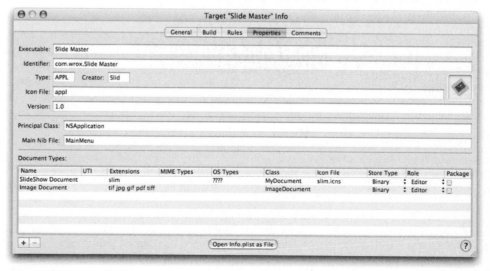

Figure 8-26

How It Works

Your NSDocument subclass needs to provide two pieces of information to Cocoa: how its windows should be loaded, and how its data should be read from and written to disk. Simple applications that use an NSDocument subclass as an interface controller as well as a document model can implement the windowNibName method:

```
- (NSString *)windowNibName;
```

The windowNibName method associates a nib file directly with that class. In other words, the document class is the File's Owner for the specified nib file.

Document classes that delegate window management to NSWindowController objects should use the makeWindowControllers method instead of windowNibName. Your document will use makeWindowControllers to initialize its window controllers. Window controllers normally manage windows found in a nib file, and in these cases you simply need to pass the nib file's name to initWithWindowNibName:. Once created, you can add the window controller to your document by calling addWindowController:. Note that this is the last time Slide Master's ImageDocument class deals with the image window interface; the rest is handled by ImageWindowController.

NSDocument defines several methods for reading and writing file data, the most common of which are dataRepresentationOfType: and loadDataRepresentation:ofType: as shown here:

```
- (NSData *)dataRepresentationOfType:(NSString *)aType;
- (BOOL)loadDataRepresentation:(NSData *)data ofType:(NSString *)aType
```

The NSData objects refer to the data being written to or read from file. NSData is a class that stores an arbitrary chunk of binary or text data. The aType variable stores the name of the document type describing the data. Document-based applications can use the same document class to work with different kinds of documents; if so, the document class can differentiate between the document types using this value. Recall from Chapter 5 this information lives in the application's Info.plist file, and you set it in Xcode's Target editor. Slide Master currently handles two kinds of documents: Image Documents and Slide Show Documents. Since each document type uses its own custom NSDocument subclass, you don't need to worry about the type value here.

AppKit uses an object called NSImage to store and work with image data. For example, NSImageView uses NSImage objects in much the same way NSTextView uses NSString objects. NSImage objects can be created from a variety of different sources, such as a path to a file or raw image data encoded in an NSData object. The ImageDocument class simply creates an NSImage object by passing the file data from loadDataRepresentation:ofType: to NSImage's initWithData: method. Note the resulting NSImage object is retained for the life of the document object.

Slide Master's ImageDocument class cannot save image data back out again. It is meant to be used as an image viewer only. As a result its dataRepresentationOfType: method returns nil instead of actually doing anything. It turns out this code path is unreachable, meaning it will never be called, because ImageDocument disables the Save and Save As menu items in its validateMenuItem: method.

The -validateMenuItem method is a special method that allows objects that respond to menu items to adjust the state of those items. Its primary use is to enable or disable menu items. Before a menu is activated the AppKit framework will look at that menu's items; for each item, AppKit will call its target's -validateMenuItem: method. If -validateMenuItem: returns YES, the item will be enabled; otherwise the menu will be grayed out.

Your `validateMenuItem:` method distinguishes between menu items by checking their actions directly. Each action is an Objective-C method selector, or `SEL` data type. You can refer to selectors as `SEL` variables by wrapping them with the `@selector()` directive. For example

```
@selector(saveAs:)
```

refers to your `ImageDocument`'s `saveAs:` method. `ImageDocument` simply checks for the save methods defined by the `NSDocument` superclass and returns `NO` when found. Otherwise `ImageDocument` will pass the message back to its superclasses.

Note `ImageDocument`'s instance variable has a special prefix: `m`. When working with larger classes it's often helpful to prefix your instance variables in some way so you can easily distinguish them from other kinds of variables. The practice of using `m` as a prefix comes from existing C++ conventions, but it works well for Objective-C objects, too. Apple reserves the underscore prefix (as in `_window`) to prefix Cocoa instance variables, so you should avoid that prefix in your own classes.

You added a few `#pragma mark` directives to your `ImageDocument` class. These directives have nothing to with how your class is compiled; they merely insert comments into Xcode's function popup menu in the navigation bar. You can even insert separator items into the function popup menu with the following code:

```
#pragma mark -
```

As you start adding more and more functions to a source file, the function popup can become hard to navigate. You can use the `#pragma mark` directives to identify groups of related symbols, and add some structure to the function popup.

In the next Try It Out example, you write `ImageWindowController`, a custom subclass of `NSWindowController`, responsible for coordinating your image window with the `ImageDocument` class. You will then be able to build and run Slide Master.

Try It Out   Writing a Custom NSWindowController Subclass

1. Open `ImageWindowController.h` and add a method called `resizeWindowToFitImage`. The entire `ImageWindowController` interface should look like the following code:

```
@interface ImageWindowController : NSWindowController
{
    IBOutlet id mImageView;
}

- (void)resizeWindowToFitImage;
@end
```

2. Open `ImageWindowController.m` and replace its contents with the following code:

```
#import "ImageWindowController.h"

#import "ImageDocument.h"

@implementation ImageWindowController

- (void)windowDidLoad
{
```

```
        NSImage *image = [[self document] image];

        [super windowDidLoad];

        // set the image
        [mImageView setImage:image];
        [mImageView setFrameSize:[image size]];

        // resize the window to fit the new image
        [self resizeWindowToFitImage];
    }

    - (void)resizeWindowToFitImage
    {
        NSWindow *window = [self window];
        NSRect rect = [window frame];
        NSPoint topLeftPoint;

        // get the window's top left point
        topLeftPoint.x = rect.origin.x;
        topLeftPoint.y = NSMaxY(rect);

        // size the window to fit our image size exactly
        rect = [window contentRectForFrameRect:rect];
        rect.size = [[[self document] image] size];
        rect = [window frameRectForContentRect:rect];

        // re-adjust the frame origin
        rect.origin.x = topLeftPoint.x;
        rect.origin.y = topLeftPoint.y - rect.size.width;

        // set the new window frame
        [window setFrame:rect display:[window isVisible]];
    }

@end
```

3. Save the `ImageWindowController` files.

4. Build and run Slide Master. The Slide Master application will now open various image files and display them in a simple window, much like the Preview application. As you resize the window, scroll bars appear. However, when the window is larger than the image data, the image will always draw in the lower-left corner rather than in the center of the window. If you are unable to open image files, check your Slide Master target Properties settings from the previous example; make sure that the document Class (`ImageDocument`) and Extensions (`tif jpg gif pdf`) settings are correct. If necessary, refer back to Figure 8-26.

5. Select the File menu and look at its menu items. Slide Master only views images, it doesn't edit them; the various save operations are disabled.

How It Works

`NSWindowController` calls its `windowDidLoad` method after its window has been loaded and before it appears on-screen. You can use this method to configure your window interface the first time. Since Slide Master's image window isn't editable, this is the only time the interface needs to be initialized.

Editable interfaces should factor code that initializes controls from its document values into a separate function that can be called whenever the underlying document has changed.

Slide Master automatically resizes its image windows to match the dimensions of the image data. All of the logic for doing this is contained in ImageWindowController's resizeWindowToFitImage method. ImageWindowController calls this method itself when initializing its controls from the document information.

In Cocoa, screen area is measured in rectangles. Cocoa rectangles are themselves described as having an origin point, and a size from that origin. The Foundation framework provides data types for all three of these values: NSRect, NSPoint, and NSSize. These types are C-style structures, not real Objective-C objects, defined like so:

```
typedef struct _NSPoint {
    float x;
    float y;
} NSPoint;

typedef struct _NSSize {
    float width;
    float height;
} NSSize;

typedef struct _NSRect {
    NSPoint origin;
    NSSize size;
} NSRect;
```

You can work these data types either by setting their values directly, or by using constructor functions like NSMakeRect or NSMakePoint.

Normally when changing the size of a window, you work with *frame rects,* or rectangles describing the area of the entire window including its title bar. Because you want your window to enclose an existing image, you need to specify the window's *content rect,* or the rectangle describing only the window's contents. NSWindow provides methods for converting between frame and content rect coordinates:

```
- (NSRect)contentRectForFrameRect:(NSRect)frameRect;
- (NSRect)frameRectForContentRect:(NSRect)contentRect;
```

When drawing in Cocoa, the coordinate plane's origin is the lower-left corner of the drawable area. For example, when drawing in a custom view, the origin is the lower-left corner of that view, and when positioning windows on screen, the origin is the lower-left corner of the screen. This complicates window positioning because conceptually we think of a window's upper-left corner as being the window's origin. ImageWindowController adjusts for that difference when programmatically resizing its image windows.

There is one problem with Slide Master's image document window: if you make the window larger than the image, the picture won't be centered in the window. The NSScrollView class draws its content in its origin, which you've just learned is the scroll view's lower-left corner. While reasonable behavior for something like a text view, image viewers look better when they center their content.

One fix for this problem is to change the nib file to resize the NSImageView instance along with the scroll view and window. You will also need to resize the image view in the nib file to match the size of its scroll view. Then the image will always draw in the center of the window when the window is larger than the image. NSImageView provides this behavior by default. But now you'll have another problem: if the window is smaller than the image, scroll bars will not appear. NSScrollView compares the size of its content view to its own size to configure the scroll bars; if both views are the same size, no scroll bars will appear. If you don't make the image view exactly match the scroll view size in the nib file, you will see even more unpredictable behavior within Slide Master.

In order to solve this problem cleanly you need to change the way your NSImageView resizes. When the window is larger than the image, the NSImageView should grow along with the window. This will allow you to take advantage of NSImageView's ability to center images in a large area. When the window is smaller than the image, the NSImageView should remain the same size as the image. Then NSScrollView will display scrollbars allowing you to reveal the portions of the image not currently on screen. Since NSImageView doesn't have this functionality already, you will need to create your own image view class that resizes the way you want. The easiest way to do that is by subclassing NSImageView. You learn how to do later in this chapter.

Replacing the Existing MyDocument Class

When you start a new Cocoa document-based application project in Xcode, Xcode creates some files to help you get started. These files are all named MyDocument. Although that name is good for very quick projects where you might not be interested in reusing or maintaining your code, you normally want to use more descriptive names for your Objective-C classes.

In this Try It Out, you replace Slide Master's MyDocument files with others that have more appropriate names. Along the way, you start building out the slide show user interface, although you hook it up in later examples.

Try It Out   Replacing the MyDocument Class

1. In Xcode, remove the MyDocument.h and MyDocument.m files.

2. Create new source files of type Cocoa Objective-C NSDocument-subclass, named SlideShowDocument.h and SlideShowDocument.m.

3. Create new source files of type Cocoa Objective-C NSWindowController-subclass, named SlideShowWindowController.h and SlideShowWindowController.m.

4. Rename the MyDocument nib file to SlideShowWindow.nib. (Recall from Chapter 3 that you can rename files by Option-clicking their names in the Groups & Files list.)

5. Open the SlideShowWindow nib file in Interface Builder.

6. In the nib file's Classes tab create a new NSWindowController subclass called SlideShowWindowController.

7. Set the File's Owner class to the new SlideShowWindowController class.

8. Make sure that the File's Owner's window outlet is connected to the document window instance. If not, make the connection.

9. Replace the "Your document contents here" placeholder with an image view. Resize the control to fill the window's available space, and make sure the image view shrinks and grows properly when its window is resized. Do not wrap the image view in a scroll view.

10. Use the Attributes inspector to disable the border for the image view. Make sure the image data will scale proportionally. The image view's attributes will resemble those in Figure 8-27.

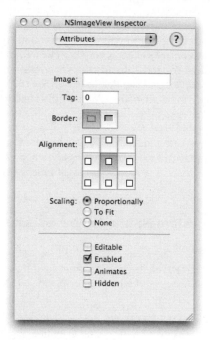

Figure 8-27

11. Save the SlideShowWindow nib file.

12. In Xcode's project window, select the Slide Master target and choose Project ⇨ Get Info. The Target Info window appears.

13. Select the Properties tab and change the class for the Slide Show Document from MyDocument to SlideShowDocument.

How It Works

Xcode always uses a MyDocument class for new document-based projects. The class name appears in source files, in the MyDocument nib file, and in the Info.plist. If you want your class names to be more relevant to your project, you will need to change all of these different areas. It's often easier to simply replace the source files with new ones than to rename them and change all the references to MyDocument within the source code. That leaves you with the task of updating the nib file and Info.plist by hand.

Subclassing Controls in Interface Builder

Occasionally you need to create your own custom controls to provide the right user experience within your application. Although you can create new controls from scratch by creating a custom NSControl subclass, you can often start from an existing control and just add your custom behavior. After all, if you need a special control that acts like a slider, you could save a lot of time and trouble by re-using the implementation in the NSSlider class.

Once you have defined a custom control, you will want to use that control in Interface Builder. This is simply a matter of declaring the control's class in your nib file's Classes tab, and changing a control instance to use your custom class. You have already seen examples of both these techniques: you have already created custom NSObject, NSDocument, and NSWindowController objects, and you have changed the class of a nib's File's Owner instance. You simply need to apply these techniques to other controls in your interface.

In the following Try It Out, you create a custom image view class that provides some custom resize logic for that view. This image view is meant to resize itself freely when its window changes size, as long as the image view is never smaller than its contents. This custom class simply inherits the rest of its behavior from the existing NSImageView class.

Try It Out   Creating a Custom NSImageView Subclass

1. Open the ImageWindow nib file in Interface Builder.

2. Double-click the NSScrollView in your document window to select its NSImageView. You'll know the NSImageView is selected when the Inspector window's title bar says NSImageView Inspector.

3. Manually resize the image view to match the area of your scroll view. The image view should be 507 pixels wide and 413 pixels high. If you have trouble resizing the view, try setting its origin to 0,0 using the Size inspector. Also make sure the image view grows and shrinks when its parent scroll view and window are resized.

4. Switch to your nib file's Classes tab. In Tiger, Interface Builder selects your window instance and highlights NSWindow in the class browser. You can click your image view instance to quickly select NSImageView in the class browser.

5. Create an NSImageView subclass called SlideImageView. The new subclass has no new outlets or actions.

6. Return to your nib file's Instances tab and select the NSImageView instance again.

7. Change the image view's custom class to SlideImageView using the Custom Class inspector.

8. Save the ImageWindow nib file.

9. Open the SlideShowWindow nib file in Interface Builder and repeat steps 4 through 7 to convert its NSImageView instance to a SlideImageView instance. If NSImageView doesn't appear in the Classes tab automatically, you'll find it in the following path: NSObject ➪ NSResponder ➪ NSView ➪ NSControl ➪ NSImageView.

10. Save the SlideShowWindow nib file.

11. In Xcode, create new source files of type Cocoa Objective-C object, named SlideImageView.h and SlideImageView.m.

12. Open `SlideImageView.h` and define the `SlideImageView` class as a subclass of `NSImageView`:

```
@interface SlideImageView : NSImageView
{
}
@end
```

13. Switch to `SlideImageView.m` and add a custom `setFrameSize:` method to the `SlideImageView` class:

```
@implementation SlideImageView

- (void)setFrameSize:(NSSize)viewSize
{
    NSScrollView *scrollView = [self enclosingScrollView];

    // if the image view is installed in a scroll view, make sure we preserve
    // the original file dimensions, so scroling works correctly.
    if (scrollView) {
        NSSize imageSize = [[self image] size];
        NSSize scrollSize = [scrollView documentVisibleRect].size;

        // first, disregard the area used by scroll bars (if any)
        viewSize.width = MIN(viewSize.width, scrollSize.width);
        viewSize.height = MIN(viewSize.height, scrollSize.height);

        // second, make sure the view is at least as big as the image itself
        viewSize.width = MAX(viewSize.width, imageSize.width);
        viewSize.height = MAX(viewSize.height, imageSize.height);
    }

    // set the adjusted frame size
    [super setFrameSize:viewSize];
}

@end
```

14. Replace `ImageWindowController`'s `windowDidLoad` method with the following code:

```
- (void)windowDidLoad
{
    [super windowDidLoad];

    // set the image
    [mImageView setImage:[[self document] image]];

    // resize the window to fit the new image
    [self resizeWindowToFitImage];
}
```

15. Save your changes to the `SlideImageView` and `ImageWindowController` files.

16. Build and run Slide Master. Now when you resize image documents, the image will remain centered when the window is large, and scroll bars will appear when the window is small.

How It Works

When you use a custom class for an object instantiated in the nib file, Cocoa will create an object of that class at run time, when your nib file is opened. This works much the same way as NSObject subclasses that reside in a nib's Instances tab. In both cases the objects are created and owned by the nib file.

Interface Builder will keep track of an object's original class even after you change the object's class. It uses this information to know what kind of control to draw in the nib file and what information should be displayed in the Inspector. Though you changed your NSImageView instance to a SlideImageView, Interface Builder still treated it like an NSImageView instance; you could set its attributes or reset its custom class if you like. On the other hand, if you created your SlideImageView subclass from a simple NSView instance, Interface Builder would not recognize the SlideImageView as an NSImageView subclass. Note the NSView instance in the Containers palette is labeled "Custom View" because normally you assign these objects a custom class.

Your SlideImageView extends the NSImageView class by providing a new setFrameSize: method. The setFrameSize: method is actually defined by the NSView superclass, and is used to change a view's size. This method will be called whenever the image document's window is resized, since the SlideImageView instance is still set to resize itself in the nib file. Before passing the resize request back to the default implementation, SlideImageView will make sure the new frame size is at least as large as its image data. That's simply a matter of checking the image size against the image's visible area, and using the larger of the two.

Because the image document uses an NSScrollView to manage the image's scroll bars, SlideImageView can ask the NSScrollView for its visible area. The NSScrollView class has a documentVisibleRect method that returns the visible area as an NSRect; this rectangle doesn't include the scroll view's scroll bars. You are familiar with using outlets to create relationships between two objects, and in this case you could have created an outlet in SlideImageView for storing a reference to the NSScrollView instance. However, the NSView class provides a convenience method called enclosingScrollView that returns the NSScrollView for any given view; if a view isn't in a scroll view, enclosingScrollView will return nil. This provides an easy alternative to using an outlet for this purpose.

Connecting Menus

In Cocoa menu items behave a lot like controls. For example, menu items can send an action to a target object. Unlike controls, which normally talk to specific controller objects, menu commands are usually handled by an application's current selection. For example, the Copy command will copy the information from the selected control, regardless of which control is selected. In either case you connect menus using the same kinds of techniques you've seen earlier in this chapter.

In the following Try It Out, you build Slide Master's menu bar. Most of Slide Master's custom interface is meant to be handled by the slide show document. You configure the menus in three steps:

❑ First, you design the menus in Interface Builder, and connect them to custom actions in the nib file's First Responder instance.

❑ Then, you declare an application delegate in your MainMenu nib file and write code in Xcode to handle one of the menu items.

❑ Finally, you implement the menu actions in a Slide Show document.

Try It Out   **Connecting Menus to the First Responder**

1. In Xcode, double-click the `MainMenu` nib file. The nib file opens in Interface Builder.

2. Rename the NewApplication menu to Slide Master. Also change the other occurrences of NewApplication in the Slide Master and Help menus to Slide Master.

3. Add an Import menu item to the File menu, as shown in Figure 8-28.

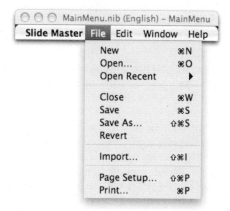

Figure 8-28

4. Drag the Submenu item from the Menus palette and insert it into the main menu bar between the Edit and Windows menus. Name the menu `Slide Show` and add the items in Figure 8-29.

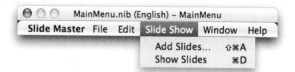

Figure 8-29

5. In your nib file's Classes tab find the entry named `FirstResponder`. It appears as a subclass of `NSObject`. The `FirstResponder` class is drawn in bold, indicating it is editable.

6. Add the following actions to the `FirstResponder` class:

Action
`addSlidesWithOpenPanel:`
`newSlideShowWithOpenPanel:`
`toggleSlideDrawer:`

7. Switch to the Instances tab and connect the following menu items to actions in the First Responder. Simply Control-drag from each menu item to the First Responder instance, and connect the item to the appropriate action.

Menu	Command	First Responder Action
File	Import . . .	`newSlideShowWithOpenPanel:`
Slide Show	Add Slide . . .	`addSlidesWithOpenPanel:`
Slide Show	Show Slides	`toggleSlideDrawer:`

8. Save the `MainMenu` nib file.

How It Works

Connecting menu items works just like connecting controls. Control-drag from the menu item to the target object, and select one of the target's actions. Although you didn't do so in this example, you can also assign menus and menu items to other objects' outlets.

The Slide Show menu items are meant to be sent to the currently active slide show document. Since you don't know which instance that might be at run time, or if there even is an active Slide Show document, you need a placeholder to reflect that information in your nib file. Your nib file's First Responder instance is exactly that placeholder. Recall from the Email Formatter examples that you manually set your window's `initialFirstResponder` to a specific item, and that the first responder changed as you tabbed from item to item.

Messages sent to the nib file's First Responder instance may not necessarily be handled by the first responder. It may instead be handled by one of a number of objects involved in handling events in your application. These objects collectively make up your *responder chain*, or the specific list of objects that might respond to a given event. If a particular instance doesn't respond to an event, it passes the event to the next element in the responder chain; this process continues until either the event is handled, or until the entire chain is searched. The following table shows basically how the responder chain interprets events.

Responder	Description
The key window's first responder	The key window is the window receiving keyboard events. This is often the same as the main window. However, windows derived from the `NSPanel` object may become key without being the main window. Inspector windows like Interface Builder's Inspector are often derived from `NSPanel`. The first responder by definition gets the first chance to respond to an event.
The key window	If its contents will not handle this event, the key window has an opportunity to do so.
The main window's first responder	The main window is the currently active `NSWindow` class. Again, its first responder gets the first chance to respond to an event.
The main window	Like the key window, the main window has the opportunity to handle events ignored by its contents.
The application	If the key and main windows or their contents don't handle an event, the `NSApplication` instance itself gets one last chance to handle the event.

Other instances might be involved in the responder chain as well. The window and application instances might have *delegate* objects associated with them. Delegate objects are other objects, often simply just NSObject subclasses, that can respond to messages in lieu of a particular object. If a window or application doesn't handle an event, the delegate will get a chance to handle it before the event is passed up the chain.

In the following Try It Out, you create an object to serve as Slide Master's application delegate. This delegate will be a part of Slide Master's responder chain and will be able to respond to menu events.

Try It Out   **Implementing an Application Delegate**

1. Open Slide Master's MainMenu nib file in Interface Builder if it isn't still open from the previous example.

2. In your nib file's Classes tab create an NSObject subclass called ApplicationDelegate. This object has no outlets or actions. Don't bother creating the files for this class yet.

3. Instantiate the ApplicationDelegate class in your nib file. An ApplicationDelegate object will appear in your nib file's Instances tab.

4. Connect the File's Owner's delegate outlet to the new ApplicationDelegate instance. Start by Control-dragging from the File's Owner instance.

5. Save the MainMenu nib file.

6. In Xcode create new source files of type Cocoa Objective-C class, named ApplicationDelegate.m and ApplicationDelegate.h.

7. Open ApplicationDelegate.h and declare the following action.

```
- (IBAction)newSlideShowWithOpenPanel:(id)sender;
```

8. Switch to ApplicationDelegate.m and define the newSlideShowWithOpenPanel: action in the ApplicationController instance as shown here.

```
- (IBAction)newSlideShowWithOpenPanel:(id)sender
{
    NSLog(@"ApplicationDelegate received newSlideShowWithOpenPanel:");
}
```

9. Save the ApplicationDelegate files.

10. Build and run Slide Master. The File ⇨ Import menu item should be enabled; when you select the menu item, a note appears in Xcode's run log:

```
2004-09-21 20:26:27.547 Slide Master[5645] ApplicationDelegate received
newSlideShowWithOpenPanel:
```

How It Works

The File's Owner instance in the MainMenu nib represents Slide Master's single instance of the NSApplication class. Recall the MainMenu nib file's owner is the NSApplication class, in part because this class is responsible for loading the main menu bar. You also learned the application object can forward events and other messages to a delegate object. Interface Builder provides an outlet for this delegate object, so you can easily assign your application's delegate in your nib file.

At this point in time the ApplicationDelegate object exists simply to receive the File ⇨ Import . . . menu item's action, newSlideShowWithOptions:. Slide Master takes advantage of the fact that events are forwarded to the application's delegate as part of the normal responder chain processing to receive this action without any special setup. You could also have connected the menu item directly to an ApplicationDelegate action if you had defined one such action in Interface Builder.

In the following Try It Out, you use the same principles to connect menu commands to your SlideShowDocument instances.

Try It Out   **Receiving Menu Commands in a Document**

1.   In Xcode, open the SlideShowDocument.h file and add the following method to the SlideShowDocument class.

```
- (void)addSlidesWithOpenPanel:(id)sender;
```

2.   Switch to SlideShowDocument.m and replace its contents with the following code. Note that the default windowNibName method was replaced by a makeWindowControllers method.

```
#import "SlideShowDocument.h"

#import "SlideShowWindowController.h"

@implementation SlideShowDocument

#pragma mark Document Initialization

- (void)makeWindowControllers
{
    SlideShowWindowController *slideShowWindowController = nil;

    slideShowWindowController = [[[SlideShowWindowController alloc]
initWithWindowNibName:@"SlideShowWindow"] autorelease];

    [self addWindowController:slideShowWindowController];
}

- (NSData *)dataRepresentationOfType:(NSString *)type {
    // Implement to provide a persistent data representation of your document OR
remove this and implement the file-wrapper or file path based save methods.
    return nil;
}

- (BOOL)loadDataRepresentation:(NSData *)data ofType:(NSString *)type {
    // Implement to load a persistent data representation of your document OR
remove this and implement the file-wrapper or file path based load methods.
    return YES;
}

#pragma mark Open Panel UI

- (void)addSlidesWithOpenPanel:(id)sender
```

```
{
    NSLog(@"SlideShowDocument received addSlidesWithOpenPanel:");
}

#pragma mark Undo Support

@end
```

3. Open the `SlideShowWindowController.h` file and add the following method to the `SlideShowWindowController` class:

```
- (void)toggleSlideDrawer:(id)sender;
```

4. Add the following code to the `SlideShowWindowController` implementation in `SlideShowWindowController.m`:

```
#import "SlideShowWindowController.h"

@implementation SlideShowWindowController

#pragma mark Window Initialization

#pragma mark Document Management

#pragma mark Event Handling

- (void)toggleSlideDrawer:(id)sender
{
    NSLog(@"SlideShowWindowController received toggleSlideDrawer:");
}

#pragma mark Table View Support

@end
```

5. Save your changes to the `SlideShowDocument` and `SlideShowWindowController` files.

6. Build and run the Slide Master project. The application will open with your preliminary slide show document interface. When a slide show document is active, the items in the Slide Show menu are active.

7. Open an image file by choosing File ⇨ Open. When the image document is active, the Slide Show menu items are no longer active.

8. Try selecting the Slide Show menu items. Xcode will display notes in the run log telling you the actions have fired.

How It Works

`NSWindowController` objects make themselves the delegate of the windows they maintain. As a result, they become part of the responder chain. You have already learned that NSDocuments insert themselves into the responder chain between the window's delegate and the `NSApplication` instance. This means between `SlideShowWindowController`, `SlideShowDocument`, and `ApplicationDelegate` instances, the `SlideShowWindowController` instance has the first opportunity to respond to events sent to the first responder, followed by the `SlideShowDocument`, and finally `ApplicationDelegate`.

Selecting Files with Open Panels

As you know, AppKit's NSDocument class handles your application's File ⇨ Open menu command for you. It reads the list of supported file extensions and file types out of your application's Info.plist file, and displays files of that type in an open panel. When you select one of those files, AppKit instantiates the document class appropriate for the selected file, and passes the file contents to the document.

Sometimes you need to drive the open panel yourself. You might be working on an application that doesn't have documents, or your document may itself refer to one or more files. In either case, working with the open panel is fairly easy.

The NSOpenPanel class defined by AppKit provides all of the functionality necessary to run an open panel modally, either as a sheet or as a separate dialog window. NSOpenPanel is itself based on the NSSavePanel class, used for driving a corresponding save file window. While NSSavePanel provides some of the basic implementation, NSOpenPanel extends this to include filtering for specific files and file types, returning multiple files, selecting directories as well as files, and other features.

In the following Try It Out, you use an open panel to add image files to a slide show document. You can add slides to an existing document by choosing the Slide Show ⇨ Add Slides command or by creating a new slide show document from a directory of slides using the File ⇨ Import command. The user interface for displaying the slide show won't exist yet, but you can verify Slide Master is working by stepping through the source code in the debugger.

You complete this example in four steps:

❑ First, you write a model object that represents a slide. This model object basically stores a slide's path and image data.

❑ Next, you add a list of slides to the SlideShowDocument class, including accessor methods for working with this list. The list will be backed by an NSMutableArray object.

❑ Then, you add code to SlideShowDocument to get a list of files from an NSOpenPanel sheet and add them to the document. You hook this code up to the Slide Show ⇨ Add Slides menu item.

❑ Finally, you add support to SlideShowDocument and ApplicationDelegate to create a new slide show document from an existing folder of images. This code is called from the File ⇨ Import menu item.

Try It Out   **Building a Simple Model Object**

1. In Xcode, create new source files of type Cocoa Objective-C class named Slide.h and Slide.m.

2. Open Slide.h and replace its contents with the following code:

```
#import <Cocoa/Cocoa.h>


@interface Slide : NSObject
{
    NSString    *mFilePath;
    NSImage     *mImage;
}
```

```objc
- (id)initWithPath:(NSString*)filePath;

- (NSString*)filePath;
- (NSImage*)image;

@end
```

3. Switch to `Slide.m` and replace its contents with the following code:

```objc
#import "Slide.h"

@implementation Slide

- (id)initWithPath:(NSString*)filePath
{
    self = [super init];
    if (self) {
        mFilePath = [filePath retain];
    }
    return self;
}

- (void)dealloc
{
    [mFilePath release];
    [mImage release];

    [super dealloc];
}

- (NSString*)filePath
{
    return mFilePath;
}

- (NSImage*)image
{
    if (!mImage) {
        mImage = [[NSImage alloc] initWithContentsOfFile:mFilePath];
    }

    return mImage;
}

@end
```

4. Save your changes to the `Slide` files.

How It Works

`Slide` is a simple Objective-C class that represents an image file within Slide Master's slide show document. It provides a convenient wrapper collecting an `NSImage` object together with the path where the image was found. The `initWithPath:`, `filePath`, and `image` methods define the core of this functionality.

Slide objects are created from an NSString containing a path to the image. If someone wants to get a Slide's path, the object can just return the path supplied to initWithPath:. But if someone wants the Slide's image data, that data must be read in from disk. You could read this data in Slide's initWithPath: method, which seems like the natural place to initialize an object's instance variables. But if you create and then destroy a Slide object without ever reading its image data, you will have wasted the time and memory required to read that image into memory. To prevent that kind of waste, Slide reads the image data on demand, the first time you call its image accessor. Programmers often call this kind of behavior *lazy initialization*, meaning data is loaded or initialized only when it's needed.

Note the Slide object is careful about retaining its path and image data. The file path is explicitly retained in the initWithPath: method, and the image data is simply alloc/init'ed in the image accessor. In both cases the object's reference count is > 0, and we can say the Slide object has taken ownership of these values. Of course, Slide must release these objects in its dealloc method.

In the next Try It Out, you define accessors for manipulating a SlideShowDocument's slides. These slides are stored in an NSMutableArray.

Try It Out   Using Mutable Arrays

1.   Open SlideShowDocument.h and replace its contents with the following code:

```
#import <AppKit/AppKit.h>

@class Slide;

@interface SlideShowDocument : NSDocument
{
    NSMutableArray *mSlides;
}

- (int)numberOfSlides;
- (Slide*)slideAtIndex:(int)index;
- (BOOL)addSlidesAtPaths:(NSArray*)paths;
- (void)removeSlidesAtIndexes:(NSIndexSet*)indexes;

- (void)addSlidesWithOpenPanel:(id)sender;

@end
```

2.   Switch to SlideShowDocument.m and add the following define near the top of the file:

```
#import "Slide.h"
```

3.   Switch to SlideShowDocument.m and add init and dealloc methods as shown in the following code:

```
#pragma mark Document Initialization

- (id)init
{
    self = [super init];
    if (self) {
        mSlides = [[NSMutableArray alloc] init];
```

```
    }
    return self;
}

- (void)dealloc
{
    [mSlides release];

    [super dealloc];
}
```

4. Add the following methods to `SlideShowDocument`, between the `Document Initialization` and `Open Panel UI` sections, as shown here:

```
#pragma mark Slide Accessors

- (int)numberOfSlides
{
    return [mSlides count];
}

- (Slide*)slideAtIndex:(int)index
{
    return [mSlides objectAtIndex:index];;
}

- (BOOL)addSlidesAtPaths:(NSArray*)paths
{
    NSEnumerator *enumerator = [paths objectEnumerator];
    NSString *path;
    BOOL result = YES;
    NSMutableArray *newSlides = [NSMutableArray array];

    while (path = [enumerator nextObject]) {
        Slide *slide = [[[Slide alloc] initWithPath:path] autorelease];

        if (slide) {
            NSLog(@"adding %@", path);

            [newSlides addObject:slide];
        } else {
            result = NO;
        }
    }

    if ([newSlides count]) {
        [mSlides addObjectsFromArray:newSlides];
    }

    return result;
}

- (void)removeSlidesAtIndexes:(NSIndexSet*)indexes;
{
    NSMutableArray *slideList = [NSMutableArray array];
```

```
    unsigned int index = [indexes firstIndex];

    while (index != NSNotFound) {
        Slide *slide = [mSlides objectAtIndex:index];

        NSLog(@"removing %@", [slide filePath]);

        [slideList addObject:slide];

        index = [indexes indexGreaterThanIndex:index];
    }

    if ([slideList count]) {
        // remove the slides from the master list
        [mSlides removeObjectsInArray:slideList];
    }
}

#pragma mark Open Panel UI
```

5.   Save your changes to the `SlideShowDocument` files.

How It Works

You begin by declaring the `Slide` class within the `SlideShowDocument` header file; this allows you to use the `Slide` class in instance variables and in method arguments and return values. One common way of doing this is simply importing the header that declares the `Slide` document class:

```
#import "Slide.h"
```

Note that when you edit a header file, Xcode will need to rebuild all of the files that import that header file. If you get in the habit of importing header files in other headers you may end up in a situation where the smallest change to one of your headers will cause your entire application to rebuild. For example, changing `Slide.h` might cause `SlideShowDocument.m` and `SlideShowWindowController.m` to rebuild in addition to `Slide.m`. If you're just importing a header file to bring in Objective-C classes, you can use Objective-C's `@class` directive to pre-declare the class name:

```
@class Slide;
```

This tells the compiler that the named symbol is going to be used to refer to Objective-C classes, allowing you to use pointers to the class as instance variables and method inputs and outputs without importing the class's header file. Note that you must still import the class's header file in your implementation file, so you can actually use objects of that class.

The `SlideShowDocument` class uses an `NSMutableArray` named `mSlides` to store a list of `Slide` objects. The `NSMutableArray` class is a variant of the `NSArray` class, both of which are collection classes provided by Foundation. You learned about `NSArray` and `NSMutableArray` in Chapter 7.

The `SlideShowDocument` class wants to vend its slide information to other clients, such as its window controller. However, directly exposing a pointer to its mutable slide list would allow clients to change that list behind `SlideShowDocument`'s back, which might not be a very good thing at all. Instead `SlideShowDocument` exposes its own methods for working with this list that, while similar in nature to `NSArray` or `NSMutableArray` API, is specific to working with `SlideShowDocument` and its slide list. On the other hand, exposing the list of slides as an `NSArray` would make it easier to use Key Value Coding and Cocoa Bindings with `SlideShowDocuments`.

The `addSlidesAtPaths:` method does a lot of work, and it's worth understanding what it's doing in detail. In broad terms, `addSlidesAtPaths:` takes a list of file paths, inserts them into the slide list at the specified index, and returns `YES` if all the files were added correctly. The following three activities define this procedure: walking the list of paths, creating a slide, and adding the slide to the list.

You used `NSEnumerator` to access every path in the `paths` array. You may remember `NSEnumerator` from Chapter 7. It provides a convenient way to access every object in an array and is usually found in a `while` loop. You can also use `NSArray`'s `objectAtIndex:` method to get specific objects from an array.

After you have a path from the path list, you can easily create a `Slide` object from the supplied file path. If the `Slide` object could not be created, the `slide` variable will be set to `nil`, and `addSlidesAtPaths:` will note the operation failed. On success, however, the new slide is added to a temporary item list.

The `addSlidesAtPaths:` method uses the `newSlides` temporary item list to store the list of new slides that will be added to `SlideShowDocument`'s slide list. Once built, the `newSlides` array is passed to `NSMutableArray`'s `addObjectsFromArray:` method. This allows `addSlidesAtPaths:` to update the list a single time once all the slides have been created. Recall you cannot safely change an `NSMutableArray` while traversing it with an `NSEnumerator` object. The `newSlides` list helps avoid this problem, at the expense of a little extra memory.

The corresponding `removeSlidesAtIndexes:` method removes one or more slides from `SlideShowDocument`'s slide list. The algorithm is very similar to `addSlidesAtPaths:` in that it builds a temporary array of slides, which it passes to `NSMutableArray`'s `removeObjectsInArray:` method. In this case slides are referred to by numeric index, instead of referring to slides by path. Foundation provides a class called `NSIndexSet` that stores groups of numeric indexes in an efficient manner. `NSIndexSet` is a new addition to the Cocoa frameworks, and some Foundation or AppKit classes have been updated to use them to refer to selection objects. But not all classes support them; for example, you cannot remove objects from a mutable array based on an `NSIndexSet`. In these cases, you can enumerate the index set manually and fall back to an existing selection mechanism. `removeObjectsInArray:` uses the `NSIndexSet` to build a temporary array, which it will then pass to `NSMutableArray`'s `removeObjectsInArray:` method to do the deletion. After getting the first index in the `indexes` index set with `firstIndex`, `removeSlidesAtIndex:` calls `indexGreaterThanIndex:` in a `while` loop until it receives `NSNotFound`.

Both `addSlidesAtPaths:` and `removeSlidesAtIndexes:` include `NSLog` statements so you can watch what the program is doing in Xcode's Run Log. These `NSLog` calls work around the problem that the slide show window's user interface hasn't been built yet. You remove these `NSLog` statements later on.

In the next Try It Out, you use an open panel to select one or more files to be added to the `SlideShowDocument`. The open panel will run as a sheet, rather than a dialog.

Try It Out **Running an Open Panel**

1. Open SlideShowDocument.m and add the following PrivateMethods category definition at the top of the file, between the existing #import directives and SlideShowDocument's implementation section. The first several lines of SlideShowDocument.m appear in the following:

```
#import "SlideShowDocument.h"

#import "SlideShowWindowController.h"
#import "Slide.h"

@interface SlideShowDocument (PrivateMethods)
- (void)openPanelDidEnd:(NSOpenPanel *)openPanel returnCode:(int)returnCode
contextInfo:(void *)contextInfo;
@end

@implementation SlideShowDocument
```

2. Replace the existing Open Panel UI section with the following code:

```
#pragma mark Open Panel UI

- (void)openPanelDidEnd:(NSOpenPanel *)openPanel returnCode:(int)returnCode
contextInfo:(void *)contextInfo
{
    if (returnCode == NSOKButton) {
        [self addSlidesAtPaths:[openPanel filenames]];
    }
}

- (void)addSlidesWithOpenPanel:(id)sender
{
    NSArray *windowControllers = [self windowControllers];
    NSWindow *window = nil;

    // make sure our document has a window. without a window we cannot run
    // the sheet.
    if ([windowControllers count]) {
        window = [[windowControllers objectAtIndex:0] window];
    }

    if (window) {
        NSOpenPanel *openPanel = [NSOpenPanel openPanel];
        SEL selector = @selector(openPanelDidEnd:returnCode:contextInfo:);
        NSArray *types = nil;

        // get the list of image types
        types = [NSImage imageFileTypes];

        // configure the open panel
        [openPanel setAllowsMultipleSelection:YES];
        [openPanel setCanChooseDirectories:NO];
        [openPanel setCanChooseFiles:YES];
        [openPanel setResolvesAliases:YES];
```

```
                // run the open panel as a sheet
                [openPanel beginSheetForDirectory:nil
                                            file:nil
                                           types:types
                                   modalForWindow:window
                                    modalDelegate:self
                                    didEndSelector:selector
                                       contextInfo:nil];
        }
    }
```

3. Save your changes to the `SlideShowDocument` files.

4. Build and run the Slide Master project. Now, when you choose Slide Show ⇨ Add Slides, the open panel appears as a sheet on the slide show window. You can select one or more image files from this panel. When you press OK, the Run Log displays the paths of the items you selected.

How It Works

In this example, you laid the foundation for the next task: importing an entire directory of files. You began by declaring a method called `openPanelDidEnd:returnCode:contextInfo:`. This method is a private utility, intended to be used only from within the `SlideShowDocument` class. Objective-C doesn't have a concept of private methods; that is, methods that can be called only from within their own class. You can discourage other objects from using a method by omitting it from your class's header file. You can then define the methods in your implementation file using an Objective-C category. You learned about categories in Chapter 7.

You work with `NSOpenPanel` by getting a pointer to the shared open panel instance:

```
    NSOpenPanel *openPanel = [NSOpenPanel openPanel];
```

Once you have the shared instance you can configure the open panel to match your specific situation. For example, when adding slides with the Slide Show ⇨ Add Slides command, Slide Master configures the open panel to allow selection of multiple files. In contrast, the File ⇨ Import command allows only for choosing a single directory in the open panel. Either way, Slide Master resolves alias files, like those created by the Finder.

The open panel can be run either as a sheet or a dialog Dialog are processed *synchronously*. In other words, code that opens a dialog waits until the dialog is closed before continuing on its way. As a result, programming for dialog is easy; you simply call a method that invokes one (such as `NSOpenPanel`'s `runModalForTypes:` or `runModalForDirectory:file:types:`) to show and run the open panel, and check the return code to find out if the user confirmed or canceled the operation. Sheets are handled *asynchronously*, meaning code that starts a sheet operation will return right away, before the sheet has closed. This allows a sheet to lock out user events for the parent window, but allow other windows in your application to keep working. This also complicates the task of finding out how and when the sheet was dismissed.

`SlideShowDocument` runs the `NSOpenPanel` as a sheet by invoking its `beginSheetForDirectory:file:types:modalForWindow:modalDelegate:didEndSelector:contextInfo:` method. This method is easy to understand if you pick it apart section by section.

The first two parts of the method signature, beginSheetForDirectory: and file:, allow you to specify the directory or file that is selected by default in the open panel. SlideShowDocument passes nil in order to get the default behavior. The third part, represented by the type: segment, allows you to specify an array of file extensions and HFS types appropriate for this file. SlideShowDocument passes in the list of extensions and types that NSImage knows about, provided by the call to NSImage's imageFileTypes method. modalForWindow: takes the instance of the NSWindow the open panel will be anchored to. SlideShowDocument asks its window controller for the window instance. The last three arguments refer to a callback method that will be called when the NSOpenPanel is dismissed.

The first of these arguments, the modalDelegate: segment, refers to the object that will be notified when the sheet closes. This is normally the same object that requested the sheet in the first place, which in this example is the SlideShowDocument object. The didEndSelector: argument specifies the modal delegate's callback method that will fire when the sheet is dismissed. The method is specified by a SEL data type, which you can get using the @selector() function. According to the documentation from NSOpenPanel, these callbacks must match the following method signature (which matches method you declared earlier):

```
- (void)openPanelDidEnd:(NSOpenPanel *)sheet returnCode:(int)returnCode
contextInfo:(void *)contextInfo
```

That means the names in the method may be different as long as the number and types of arguments do not change. Finally, the contextInfo: segment designates a pointer that will be passed into the "did end selector" once the sheet ends. This provides an alternate way to pass information between the code that starts the sheet and the code that closes the sheet, which is especially helpful if this code is in different objects. If you aren't interested in this information, you can set it to nil.

Finally, your openPanelDidEnd:returnCode:contextInfo: method will take the result from the open panel and pass it to SlideShowDocument's addSlidesAtPaths: method. All it needs from the open panel is the list of file paths, which it gets using NSOpenPanel's filenames method.

In the next Try It Out, you write code for an Import menu command that asks the user for one or more files and then stores them in a new untitled document.

Try It Out   Creating a New Document

1. Open SlideShowDocument.h and add the following method to the SlideShowDocument interface:

```
+ (SlideShowDocument *)newFromFolderWithOpenPanel;
```

2. Switch to SlideShowDocument.m and add the following method declaration to your PrivateMethods category:

```
- (BOOL)importFolderAtPath:(NSString*)dirPath;
```

3. Add the newFromFolderWithOpenPanel class method at the top of the Document Initialization section:

```
#pragma mark Document Initialization

+ (SlideShowDocument *)newFromFolderWithOpenPanel
{
```

```
        SlideShowDocument *document = [[[SlideShowDocument alloc] init] autorelease];

        if (document) {
            NSOpenPanel *openPanel = [NSOpenPanel openPanel];
            int returnCode;

            // configure the open panel
            [openPanel setAllowsMultipleSelection:NO];
            [openPanel setCanChooseDirectories:YES];
            [openPanel setCanChooseFiles:NO];
            [openPanel setResolvesAliases:YES];

            // run the panel
            returnCode = [openPanel runModalForDirectory:nil
                                                    file:nil
                                                   types:nil];

            // if the user selected a directory, import the images found there.
            // if the user canceled, return nil and trust the autorelease pool
            // to release the document.
            if (returnCode == NSOKButton) {
                [document importFolderAtPath:[openPanel filename]];
            } else {
                document = nil;
            }
        }

        return document;
}
```

4. Add the following method at the end of the Slide Accessors section (right before the Open Panel UI section):

```
- (BOOL)importFolderAtPath:(NSString*)dirPath
{
    NSFileManager *fileManager = [NSFileManager defaultManager];
    NSMutableArray *paths = [NSMutableArray array];
    NSDirectoryEnumerator *enumerator = [fileManager enumeratorAtPath:dirPath];
    NSString *fileName;

    while (fileName = [enumerator nextObject]) {
        NSString *fullPath = [dirPath stringByAppendingPathComponent:fileName];
        [paths addObject:fullPath];
    }

    return [self addSlidesAtPaths:paths];
}
```

5. Open ApplicationDelegate.m and add the following #import directive near the top of the file:

```
#import "SlideShowDocument.h"
```

6. Replace the `newSlideShowWithOpenPanel:` method with the following code:

```
- (void)newSlideShowWithOpenPanel:(id)sender
{
    SlideShowDocument *slideDoc = [SlideShowDocument newFromFolderWithOpenPanel];

    if (slideDoc) {
        NSDocumentController *documentController = [NSDocumentController
sharedDocumentController];

        [slideDoc makeWindowControllers];
        [slideDoc showWindows];

        [documentController addDocument:slideDoc];
    }
}
```

7. Save your changes to the `SlideShowDocument` and `ApplicationDelegate` files.

8. Build and run your application. When you choose the File ⇨ Import command, you can choose a directory instead of individual images. When you select a directory, a new slide show document window appears. Xcode's Run Log displays the paths of the images found in the directory.

How It Works

You began by adding a new `newFromFolderWithOpenPanel` class method to `SlideShowDocument`. This class method provides a way for Slide Master to create a new slide show document pre-initialized with the contents of a directory chosen by the user. Because this is a class method, the method can be called without first instantiating `SlideShowDocument`. This is useful because this method is itself responsible for creating a `SlideShowDocument` instance.

Although the `newFromFolderWithOpenPanel` class method also drives the `NSOpenPanel`, its needs are very different from the `addSlidesWithOpenPanel:` method. Because the slide show document has just been created and its window isn't yet on-screen, you can't run the open panel as a sheet. Instead, `newFromFolderWithOpenPanel` runs the open panel as a modal dialog using the `runModalForDirectory:file:types:` method. Since `newFromFolderWithOpenPanel` doesn't need to customize the dialog, it passes `nil` in as all the arguments to `runModalForDirectory:file:types:`. When you click the OK button, the `newFromFolderWithOpenPanel` will make a call to `importFolderAtPath:`.

The `importFolderAtPath:` method enumerates the contents of the specified directory and passes its files to the existing `addSlidesAtPaths:` method. `SlideShowDocument` uses Foundation's `NSFileManager` object to get information about the file system. One of the features `NSFileManager` supplies is the ability to create an `NSDirectoryEnumerator` object for finding the contents of a directory. `NSDirectoryEnumerator` works just like the more general `NSEnumerator` class, except `NSDirectoryEnumerator` is designed to specifically return filenames. These filenames are relative to the directory you're enumerating, so you'll need to append it to the directory path to create an absolute file path. `NSString` provides some convenience methods for working with file paths that make this easy. For example, the method

```
NSString *fullPath = [dirPath stringByAppendingPathComponent:fileName];
```

creates a new autoreleased NSString object containing a path built by adding the fileName string to the dirPath string. You can find a complete list of NSString methods that aid in path arithmetic in the online reference for NSString.

Your ApplicatonDelegate's newSlideShowWithOpenPanel: method completes the menu action. First it acquires a new, pre-initialized SlideShowDocument instance using the newSlideShowWithOpenPanel class method. It then displays the document interface and adds it to the application's document list. The document list is maintained by a class called NSDocumentController. You rarely need to access this class directly in a document-based application; normally it works behind the scenes managing your documents for you. Since Slide Master has a customized way of creating new documents, it must talk to the document controller directly.

Remember the newSlideShowWithOpenPanel: is implemented in the ApplicationDelegate class so that the File ➪ Import menu command is always enabled. If you implemented newSlideShowWithOpenPanel: in SlideShowDocument or SlideShowWindowController you would only be able to use File ➪ Import if a document was already open.

Tracking Changes with Notifications

One of the common problems you may find yourself addressing over and over again in Cocoa programs, and in graphic user interface programs in general, is knowing when to redraw your application's interface. In the Model/View/Controller design pattern, the controller object is responsible for updating the model and then redrawing the appropriate views. You have seen how Cocoa Bindings uses Key Value Observing to implement this approach. When manually connecting your interface's outlets and actions, you'll need to look for other solutions to this problem.

The notion of just forcing this responsibility onto the controller makes sense, but it breaks down when you have several controllers: when one controller modifies the model data, the second controller needs to know the model has changed, so it can update itself accordingly. Consider the case of Slide Master's slide show document. The SlideShowWindowController defines the logic (or will define the logic) governing the slide show's user interface, including an image view and a table of slides. The SlideShowDocument provides storage for your model (a list of slides) as well as some common controller functionality, such as tracking open windows and handling events. If you change the slide show's data using a menu command, something needs to tell the SlideShowWindowController the slide data has changed.

Several traditional solutions to this problem exist, not including using Cocoa Bindings and Key Value Observing. Understanding these techniques will also help you understand how the Cocoa frameworks communicate with themselves. Some of these techniques include

- ❑ **Directly messaging other controller objects when a controller changes the model data:** For example, SlideShowDocument could directly message SlideShowWindowController when the document contents change. This is a brute-force solution to the problem; while it can get the job done, it requires teaching your controller objects about all the other objects. This can limit your ability to reuse these controllers in the future, and can complicate your code.

- ❑ **Messaging a specific object through a specific delegate protocol:** This works well when you expect only one other object to be interested in these changes. If you need multiple objects to respond to model changes, you're still left with this broader problem. You've seen a few trivial uses of delegate objects already; you learn more about delegate protocols later in this chapter.

❑ **Using a system to allow one object to broadcast messages to objects interested in those messages:** These messages are called *notifications*. This technique allows model objects to send, or *post*, notifications that their contents have changed without knowing what other objects (if any) are listening. Foundation provides a system for sending notifications based on the `NSNotification` and `NSNotificationCenter` classes.

In the following Try It Out, you use Cocoa's notification system to notify Slide Master's `SlideShowWindowController` when the `SlideShowDocument` state has changed. The `SlideShowDocument` object posts a notification when its slide list changes. Your `SlideShowWindowController` registers itself to receive these notifications from its document. When the notification is received, `SlideShowWindowController` reloads its user interface.

Try It Out   Sending and Receiving Notifications

1. In Xcode, open `SlideShowDocument.h` and add the following declaration above the `SlideShowDocument` interface block:

```
extern NSString *kSlideShowDocumentSlidesChangedNotification;
```

2. Switch to `SlideShowDocument.m` and add the corresponding definition at the top of the file, above `SlideShowDocument`'s `PrivateMethods` category:

```
NSString *kSlideShowDocumentSlidesChangedNotification =
@"SlideShowDocumentSlidesChangedNotification";
```

3. Add the following method to `SlideShowDocument`'s `PrivateMethods` category:

```
- (void)notifySlidesChanged;
```

4. Add the following method to the `Slide Accessors` group, after the `importFolderAtPath:` method:

```
- (void)notifySlidesChanged
{
    NSNotificationCenter *nc = [NSNotificationCenter defaultCenter];

    [nc postNotificationName:kSlideShowDocumentSlidesChangedNotification
                      object:self];
}
```

5. Change `addSlidesAtPaths:` and `removeSlidesAtIndexes:` to call the new `notifySlidesChanged` method after they change their `mSlides` instance variable. Also remove the `NSLog` statements you added in the previous example. Here are the complete definitions of `addSlidesAtPaths:` and `removeSlidesAtIndexes:`:

```
- (BOOL)addSlidesAtPaths:(NSArray*)paths
{
    NSEnumerator *enumerator = [paths objectEnumerator];
    NSString *path;
    BOOL result = YES;
    NSMutableArray *newSlides = [NSMutableArray array];
```

```
    while (path = [enumerator nextObject]) {
        Slide *slide = [[[Slide alloc] initWithPath:path] autorelease];

        if (slide) {
            [newSlides addObject:slide];
        } else {
            result = NO;
        }
    }

    if ([newSlides count]) {
        [mSlides addObjectsFromArray:newSlides];

        [self notifySlidesChanged];
    }

    return result;
}

- (void)removeSlidesAtIndexes:(NSIndexSet*)indexes;
{
    NSMutableArray *slideList = [NSMutableArray array];
    unsigned int index = [indexes firstIndex];

    while (index != NSNotFound) {
        Slide *slide = [mSlides objectAtIndex:index];

        [slideList addObject:slide];

        index = [indexes indexGreaterThanIndex:index];
    }

    if ([slideList count]) {
        // remove the slides from the master list
        [mSlides removeObjectsInArray:slideList];

        [self notifySlidesChanged];
    }
}
```

6. Open `SlideShowWindowController.m` and add the following `#import` directives near the top of the file:

```
#import "SlideShowDocument.h"
#import "Slide.h"
```

7. Add the following methods to the `Document Management` section:

```
- (void)setDocument:(NSDocument*)document
{
    NSNotificationCenter *nc = [NSNotificationCenter defaultCenter];

    // remove the exisitng notification, if any
    [nc removeObserver:self
```

```
                        name:kSlideShowDocumentSlidesChangedNotification
                object:[self document]];

    [super setDocument:document];

    // register a new notification, if any
    if (document) {
        [nc addObserver:self
                selector:@selector(slidesChanged:)
                    name:kSlideShowDocumentSlidesChangedNotification
                object:document];
    }
}

- (void)slidesChanged:(NSNotification*)notification
{
    SlideShowDocument *document = [self document];
    int i, count = [document numberOfSlides];

    NSLog(@"slides changed:");

    for (i = 0; i < count; i++) {
        NSLog(@"%@", [[document slideAtIndex:i] filePath]);
    }
}
```

8. Save your changes to the `SlideShowDocument` and `SlideShowWindowController` files.

9. Build and run the Slide Master project. Now when you add slides using the Slide Show ➪ Add Slides menu item, Xcode's Run Log continues displaying the paths of the items you selected.

How It Works

The `SlideShowDocument` will post a notification whenever it changes its `mSlides` array. The notification is a bit vague; it doesn't describe the nature of the change at all. However, it is a reasonable first pass at a slide changed notification.

Notifications are sent via the `NSNotificationCenter` object supplied by the Foundation framework. Every Cocoa application has a single default `NSNotificationCenter` instance for routing general-purpose notifications. You can get the default `NSNotificationCenter` instance from the `defaultCenter` method. Note that both `SlideShowDocument` and `SlideShowWindowController` use the default notification center.

`SlideShowDocument` posts notifications using `NSNotificationCenter`'s `postNotificationName: object:` method. All notifications are identified by a name. `SlideShowDocument.h` provides a constant symbol for its notification name, so `SlideShowDocument` and `SlideShowWindowController` can easily refer to the same notification name. `SlideShowDocument` passes itself in as `postNotificationName: object:`'s object value, indicating the specific object instance that triggered the notification. And that's all there is to it.

SlideShowWindowController registers for this notification in its setDocument: method. The NSWindowController base class defines the setDocument: method so that documents can tell their window controllers about themselves. When your window controller is added to your document instance, NSDocument will pass itself to the window controller's setDocument: method. Also, when the document is closed (or if the window controller is removed for some other reason), NSDocument will clear this value by passing nil into setDocument:.

Objects register for notifications by calling NSNotificationCenter's addObserver:selector:name:object: method. The first segment of the signature, addObserver:, represents the object interested in receiving the notification. The second segment, selector:, indicates the observer instance's method that will be called when the notification is posted. All notifications must match the following signature:

```
- (void)notificationMethod:(NSNotification*)notification;
```

The third segment, name:, refers to the specific notification being registered for. And finally the object: argument specifies an optional instance your object wants to listen to. If you supply an object, you will only receive notifications posted by that object. If you pass nil into the object: argument, you will receive notifications posted by all objects.

Similarly, NSNotificationCenter supplies a removeObserver:name:object: method for unregistering a notification observer. The observer, name, and object arguments all match those in the addObserver:selector:name:object: method. It is important you remove an object from the notification center before you deallocate it; if you fail to do so, the notification center might try to send a notification to a freed object, causing your program to crash. SlideShowWindowController is careful to unregister for notifications before it is closed by doing so in its setDocument: method, and in practice this works well. However, to be extra careful, SlideShowWindowController might also unregister in its dealloc method.

Currently SlideShowWindowController's slidesChanged: method just prints more diagnostics to Xcode's Run Log. Once the slide show window's user interface has been defined, the slidesChanged: method will actually update that interface instead of calling NSLog.

Using Drawers

Drawers provide a way to add ancillary controls to a window whose interface is otherwise busy displaying something else. Visually, drawers appear to be a special kind of window attached to a parent window, perhaps like a distant cousin of the sheet.

Slide Master uses a table view in its slide show documents for displaying lists of slides, as shown in Figure 8-30. The table view lives in a drawer where it can be tucked out of sight when it's not needed. The table view also controls which slide is visible in the slide show document window.

Figure 8-30

In the following Try It Out, you add a drawer to the slide show document interface. This example focuses on configuring the slide show drawer. You also flesh out the slide show window a little in preparation for later examples. You learn more about table views, for example, in the next section.

Try It Out   Adding a Drawer

1. Open the `SlideShowWindow` nib file in Interface Builder.

2. Drag a custom `NSView` instance from the Containers palette into your nib file. The `NSView` icon is labeled CustomView in the palette. When you drag the instance into your nib file, a view editor window appears. This view editor window works a lot like a window editor; you can change its size and drag controls and views into it.

3. Resize the custom view to 260 pixels wide and 350 pixels high. The exact dimensions aren't too important here, you just need enough room to work with.

4. Drag an `NSDrawer` instance from the Windows palette into your nib file's Instances tab. A drawer instance appears in your nib file, as shown in Figure 8-31.

Figure 8-31

5. Connect the NSDrawer instance's contentView, delegate, and parentWindow outlets to the custom view instance, File's Owner (SlideShowWindowController), and document window, respectively.

6. In your nib file's Classes tab, add three new outlets to the SlideShowWindowController class: mDrawer, mImageView, and mTableView.

7. Connect the File's Owner's mDrawer and mImageView outlet to the NSDrawer instance and NSImageView instance. For now, leave the mTableView outlet unassigned.

8. Grab a push button from the Controls tab and drag it into the document window; just drop it on top of the image view for now. Don't worry about naming it or positioning it anywhere specific.

9. Connect the button's action to the NSDrawer instance's toggle: action.

10. Test your interface by choosing Interface Builder's File ⇨ Test Interface command. You can show and hide the drawer by pushing the button you added in step 8. After the drawer is open, you can resize it by grabbing its edge. When you are satisfied the drawer is working, quit the test.

11. Select the push button and press the Delete key. The button goes away.

How It Works

The NSDrawer class is really a special kind of controller object that manages the drawer's state. It doesn't automatically provide a view object window editor for defining a view's content. Instead, you create a drawer by dropping an NSDrawer object into your nib file's Instances tab, and you configure it using Interface Builder's Inspector window. For example, you designate the drawer's parent window and content view through the parentWindow and contentView outlets. You can also hook controls up to built-in actions to open and close the drawer, such as the toggle: action.

The NSView class fundamentally provides two services within AppKit: managing drawing and handling user events. The task of managing drawing involves several things: defining an area in a window that can be drawn to, providing a coordinate space in which drawing operations can be described, and actually doing the drawing. Also, NSViews derive from the NSResponder class, meaning they can directly respond to user events; in other words, they can be part of the responder chain.

This union of drawing and event handling makes NSView objects well suited for controls and other interface elements. And it comes as no surprise that NSControl descends directly from NSView. The same is true of NSTextView, NSImageView, and other interface elements with the word "view" in their name. Also of the interesting properties of views is that they can contain other views. You've seen this in action many times. For example, NSScrollView instances commonly contain an NSImageView or NSTextView. A better example is NSWindow instances in Interface Builder: every window has a content view that describes the window's contents; when you add controls to a window in Interface Builder you are actually adding those controls to the window's content view.

Interface Builder will let you drag a generic NSView into a nib file's Instances tab rather than (or in addition to) just dragging it into a window editor. Because views can contain other views, Interface Builder will create an editor window, similar to the one created for NSWindow instances. This feature is especially helpful for defining a drawer's content view.

Working with Table Views

Tables are widely used in Mac OS X applications for displaying lists of information. You can see examples of it everywhere, from a list of messages displayed in Mail, to lists of files and build errors in Xcode. Table views often present information in multiple columns, with each column name appearing in the column's header. Columns and rows sometimes can be reordered within the table. AppKit supplies a single class that can be used in all of these situations: NSTableView.

The NSTableView class works with data in a different manner than other Cocoa controls. The controls you've seen so far, including text fields, text views, and image views, all use simple accessor methods to get and set the control's value. NSTableView does not store your list data itself; instead, it asks for your data on demand from another object, which NSTableView calls its data source. An NSTableView data source is an Objective-C object, perhaps simply an NSObject subclass that implements a special collection of methods, called a *protocol*. The NSTableView data source protocol specifies the methods used by the table view to get your object data. These are especially important when working with NSTableView objects directly, through Interface Builder outlets and actions.

You can also supply NSTableView data through Cocoa Bindings, using an NSArrayController to manage the list of your modal data. In this case, the table view will use the Key Value Coding mechanism to find your list data, not consult the data source directly. The data source object is still useful for providing other kinds of data, including responding to drag and drop operations.

In the following Try It Out, you complete the SlideShowDocument interface in two steps:

❏   First you add an NSTableView to the slide show's drawer. This includes configuring the table view's NSTableColumns.

❏   Then you define the data source methods that provide data to the table view, and display the selected slide in the image view. This example uses the traditional data source methods, rather than Cocoa Bindings, to better illustrate how NSTableView works.

Try It Out   Configuring Table Views in Interface Builder

1.   Open your SlideShowWindow nib file in Interface Builder and drag an NSTableView instance from the Data palette into your drawer's content view editor window. Resize the table to fill the available space, right up against the view's edges. Make sure this object will expand and contract when the window is resized.

2.   Change the table view's attributes to match those in Figure 8-32. Note that the row size is 34 pixels high, and the table view allows multiple, but not empty selections. Columns can be resized but not reordered, and rows are drawn with alternating background colors.

3.   Double-click the table view to actually select the table view, not its NSScrollView container.

4.   Connect the table view's dataSource and delegate outlets to the File's Owner instance.

5.   Click the first column's header in the table view to select it.

6.   Change the column's attributes to match those shown in Figure 8-33. Note the Header Title and Identifier fields have been set to Image, and the column is not resizable.

7.   Select the second column by clicking its header.

Figure 8-32

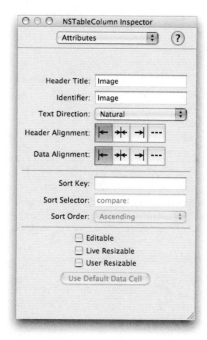

Figure 8-33

8. Change the column's Header Title and Identifier to Name, and make it non-editable.

9. Drag an NSImageCell instance from the Data palette to your NSTableView's Image column. You will find the NSImageCell instance near the palette's upper-left corner — it looks like a mountain in a narrow box. Make sure the Image column is selected before letting go of the mouse, as shown in Figure 8-34.

Figure 8-34

10. Connect File's Owner's mTableView outlet to the NSTableView instance.

11. Save your changes to the SlideShowWindow nib file.

How It Works

A single NSTableView instance in Interface Builder is actually composed of several instances. In this example you learned the table view itself resides in an NSScrollView, like the one you saw when you built Slide Master's image document window. The table view itself is composed of one or more NSTableColumn instances, which define the individual columns in the table. The NSTableColumn declares an NSCell object responsible for describing how the column's contents should be displayed. NSTableView's reference documentation mentions several other classes involved in defining the table view.

In this example you connected the table view's delegate and dataSource outlet to your SlideShowWindowController class through the File's Owner. This step is critical for loading data into your table view. You learn more about how the table view uses its delegate and dataSource in the next section.

A table view displays a list of data, where each row indicates a specific item in the list, and each column represents a particular attribute of that item. For example, in the Mail application's main viewer window, each row in the table represents an email message, and each column describes an attribute of that message: its title, its size, its sender, and so on. Table columns use an identifier to designate the specific property displayed by that column; each identifier is an NSString. This is similar to how Key Value Coding identifies values by a specific string key. In this table, each row represents a slide, and the slide's image and name will appear in the Image and Name columns.

Each NSTableColumn instance keeps track of an NSCell that the table view uses when drawing its data. In the past you had to set this information programmatically. Apple added common NSCells to Interface Builder's Data palette in Mac OS X 10.3 Panther specifically to make table views easier to configure. The slide show document uses an NSImageCell to display a slide's image in its table view.

Even though NSControl classes descend from NSView, and views manage drawing in Cocoa applications, NSControl classes don't actually do the drawing or event tracking themselves. Instead, controls delegate this responsibility to a corresponding NSCell class. These NSCell classes are responsible for actually drawing the control, tracking the mouse, and firing action methods when necessary. Nearly every NSControl class has a corresponding NSCell subclass that completes the control's implementation. For example NSButton has NSButtonCell, NSSlider has NSSliderCell, and so on.

> There is one case in which an NSControl class does all its own work: the NSScroller class used to implement scroll bars. NSScroller doesn't have a corresponding NSCell because scroll bars aren't meant to be used as general controls. Instead AppKit provides a special slider control (NSSlider, NSSliderCell) for that purpose.

By the same token, even though NSCells draw they don't come with the rest of drawing management functionality provided by NSView. It turns out that coordinating drawing with Mac OS X's window server and managing unique coordinate spaces can be time-consuming. Interfaces composed of thousands or tens of thousands of views spend a lot of time in view management, rather than doing more interesting work. Although you're not likely to drag one thousand controls from Interface Builder's Palettes window, a table view with many rows and columns can easily represent thousands of individual values. Rather than displaying each value in its own view, NSTableView uses an NSCell to draw the particular data within itself. After all, NSTableView is an instance of NSView; it's already set up its own drawing environment.

In the next Try It Out example, you extend your SlideShowWindowController object to be the data source for your table view. In other words, SlideShowWindowController controls what appears in the table.

Try It Out   Defining a Table Data Source

1. In Xcode, open SlideShowWindowController.h and change the SlideShowWindowController's interface block to match the following:

```
@class SlideImageView;

@interface SlideShowWindowController : NSWindowController
{
    IBOutlet NSDrawer       *mDrawer;
    IBOutlet SlideImageView *mImageView;
    IBOutlet NSTableView    *mTableView;
}

- (void)toggleSlideDrawer:(id)sender;

@end
```

2. Switch to `SlideShowWindowController.m` and add the following `#import` directive to the top of the file:

```
#import "SlideImageView.h"
```

3. Next add the following method to the `Window Initialization` section:

```
#pragma mark Window Initialization

- (void)windowDidLoad
{
    [super windowDidLoad];

    [mDrawer open];

    // set the initial selection
    if ([[self document] numberOfSlides]) {
        [mTableView selectRowIndexes:[NSIndexSet indexSetWithIndex:0]
                byExtendingSelection:NO];

        [mImageView setImage:[[[self document] slideAtIndex:0] image]];
    }
}
```

4. Replace the `slidesChanged:` method with the one listed here:

```
- (void)slidesChanged:(NSNotification*)notification
{
    // rebuild the table contents
    [mTableView reloadData];

    // readjust the selection
    [self tableViewSelectionDidChange:nil];
}
```

5. Replace the `Event Handling` section with the following code:

```
#pragma mark Event Handling

- (void)toggleSlideDrawer:(id)sender
{
    [mDrawer toggle:sender];
}

- (void)delete:(id)sender
{
    NSIndexSet *indexes = [mTableView selectedRowIndexes];
    [[self document] removeSlidesAtIndexes:indexes];
}

- (BOOL)validateMenuItem:(NSMenuItem*)menuItem
{
    BOOL result = YES;
    SEL action = [menuItem action];
```

```
        if (action == @selector(toggleSlideDrawer:)) {
            // allow the action, but customize the menu command
            int state = [mDrawer state];
            BOOL isOpen = (state == NSDrawerOpenState || state ==
NSDrawerOpeningState);
            NSString *title = isOpen ? @"Hide Slides" : @"Show Slides";

            [menuItem setTitle:title];
        }

        return result;
}
```

6. Add the following code to SlideShowWindowController's Table View Support section:

```
#pragma mark Table View Support

- (int)numberOfRowsInTableView:(NSTableView*)tableView
{
    return [[self document] numberOfSlides];
}

- (id)tableView:(NSTableView*)tableView
objectValueForTableColumn:(NSTableColumn*)tableColumn row:(int)rowIndex
{
    id result = nil;
    Slide *slide = [[self document] slideAtIndex:rowIndex];

    if ([[tableColumn identifier] isEqualToString:@"Image"]) {
        result = [slide image];
    } else if ([[tableColumn identifier] isEqualToString:@"Name"]) {
        NSString *path = [slide filePath];
        result = [NSString stringWithFormat:@"%@\n%@", [path lastPathComponent],
path];
    }

    return result;
}

- (void)tableViewSelectionDidChange:(NSNotification *)aNotification
{
    int selection = [mTableView selectedRow];
    NSImage *image = nil;

    if (selection != -1) {
        Slide *slide = [[self document] slideAtIndex:selection];

        image = [slide image];
    }

    [mImageView setImage:image];
}
```

7. Save your changes to SlideShowWindowController.m.

8. Build and run Slide Master. The Slide Master application appears with a blank slide show document window.

9. Choose Slide Show ➪ Add Slides and add some images to your slide show document. The new slides appear in the drawer, with the selected slide drawn in the main window.

10. Select some slides and choose Edit ➪ Delete. The slides are removed from the table.

How It Works

You have already learned that NSTableView will ask its data source object for information about the items to be displayed in the table view. You commonly designate this item by hooking up the table view's dataSource outlet. The table view will also give a delegate object the opportunity to further customize the table view's behavior. Often you will set the table view's delegate object to the same data source object; it's often easiest to encapsulate all of your table information into a single class.

An NSTableView instance communicates with its dataSource object using a specific *protocol*. Loosely defined, a protocol is a series of methods that define a particular way two objects communicate with each other. An object can talk with a second object simply by implementing the methods defined in the protocol. This usage of the word is similar to how the word is used when talking about networking.

The Objective-C language provides support for protocols in a couple of ways. You can use the Objective-C @protocol directive to create a named protocol. These protocols collect a group of methods under a specific protocol name. An Objective-C class can claim to be a member of the protocol by adding the protocol name as part of its @interface declaration. Once added, the class must implement all the methods defined in that protocol, or the compiler (and/or the Objective-C runtime) will generate an error. This kind of protocol is also known as a *formal protocol*, because objects formally declare their participation in the protocol, and must always support the protocol completely. The following pseudocode shows an example of a protocol and an object that adopts the protocol:

```
@protocol Copyable

- (id)copy;

@end

@interface String <Copyable>
{
    // ... etc ...
}
@end
```

Formal protocols are used rarely in the Cocoa frameworks because they're difficult to version in library code. Say a library publishes a protocol, and an application later adopts that protocol, and all is well. If the library adds a method to the protocol in its next version, existing protocol clients will suddenly no longer comply with the new protocol and fail to work. There are some examples of formal protocols within the Cocoa frameworks, although they are usually small examples. And the formal protocol is a good tool for the application programmer, where the code that defines and implements the protocol is contained in the same binary.

Because of this versioning issue, the Cocoa frameworks usually implement protocols using Objective-C categories. Recall from earlier that categories allow you to add methods to an existing object. The Objective-C language doesn't strictly require you to provide the implementation for a category along with the interface; you can simply use a category to declare a group of Objective-C methods you might be interested in calling if an object happens to implement them. Such protocols are called *informal protocols* because they don't require a class to formally declare participation in the protocol, and nor must the entire protocol be defined.

The NSTableView's data source protocol is an example of an informal protocol. All table view data sources must implement the following methods:

```
- (int)numberOfRowsInTableView:(NSTableView *)tableView;
- (id)tableView:(NSTableView *)tableView objectValueForTableColumn:(NSTableColumn
*)tableColumn row:(int)row;
```

These methods define the minimum amount of information required to present data in a table view. The data source's numberOfRows: method returns the number of rows that should appear in the table view. The tableView:objectValueFOrTableColumn:row: method returns the value to display in the cell identified by column and row. The NSTableView instance will call these methods as often as necessary to display your information.

NSTableView defines some additional methods for working with data, but those methods are optional; your data source needs to declare the methods only if you're interested in the functionality they provide. For example, editable tables must provide a tableView:setObjectValue:forTableColumn:row: method that allows the NSTableView to change the contents of a data value. AppKit's online reference contains a lot of information about NSTableView and the NSTableDataSource protocol.

The table view's delegate object is similar to the data source in that the table view communicates with its delegate through an informal protocol. However, the delegate methods do not directly pertain to the table data itself. For example, you added a tableViewSelectionDidChange: method to SlideShowWindowController; as a result, the table view will notify the window controller when its selection changes. Again, you can find a complete list of the delegate methods NSTableView might send your delegate in NSTableView's API reference.

Your SlideShowWindowController is interested in the selection so it can display an image in the main image view. When the document is first opened, the window controller will pick an appropriate initial selection. After that, the window controller will update the image whenever the table's selection changes.

SlideShowWindowController uses its validateMenuItem: method to change the title of one of its menu items. In a previous example you learned how to use validateMenuItem: to dynamically disable menu items. But you can use this method as an opportunity to change other menu item states as well. For example, in addition to changing an item's title, you can add a check mark to an item by calling its setState: method.

You may have noticed the slides do not draw with a white background like they do in the image document. In the ImageDocument nib file you set the background color in the NSScrollView instance. Because there is no scroll view in the SlideShowDocument nib, there is no background color. You fix this visual bug later when you learn about application defaults.

Handling Undo

The capability to easily undo or redo any change is a requirement for any application that considers itself user-friendly. Undo encourages users to experiment with your application's features. If they get into trouble they simply press Command-Z and their last change is undone.

Cocoa's document architecture provides support for undo and redo in your documents. But like other aspects of the document architecture, you must manage the finer details yourself. And that's only natural as every application handles their data differently.

In the following Try It Out, you add simple undo and redo support to Slide Master. The SlideShowDocument records the state of its mSlides list before every operation that changes that list. An undo operation is simply a matter of replacing the document's slide list with the one recorded earlier. This approach isn't particularly elegant or efficient, but it is simple.

Try It Out   **Handling Undo and Redo**

1.   In Xcode, open SlideShowDocument.m and add the following methods to SlideShowDocument's PrivateMethods category:

```
- (void)recordSlideChange;
- (void)handleUndo:(id)object;
```

2.   Call the recordSlideChange method before you change the mSlides list in addSlidesAtPaths: and removeSlidesAtIndexes:. The relevant part of addSlidesAtPaths: is shown in the following code:

```
if ([newSlides count]) {
        [self recordSlideChange];

        [mSlides addObjectsFromArray:newSlides];

        [self notifySlidesChanged];
    }
```

3.   Add the following code to the end of SlideShowDocument's implementation block:

```
#pragma mark Undo Support

- (void)recordSlideChange
{
    NSArray *slideCopy = [NSArray arrayWithArray:mSlides];

    [[self undoManager] registerUndoWithTarget:self
                                  selector:@selector(handleUndo:)
                                    object:slideCopy];

}

- (void)handleUndo:(id)argument
{
    NSArray *slides = (NSArray*)argument;

    [self recordSlideChange];
```

```
        [mSlides release];
        mSlides = [[NSMutableArray alloc] initWithArray:slides];

        [self notifySlidesChanged];
    }
```

4. Save your changes to SlideShowDocument.m.

5. Build and run Slide Master. Add some slides to your document and test undoing and redoing your changes. Note also that when you add slides to your document, a dot appears in the window's close button indicating the document contains unsaved data.

How It Works

The NSDocument class handles much of the undo infrastructure for you. Your NSDocument instance (rather, SlideShowDocument) creates a Foundation object called NSUndoManager to manage the list of undo commands. This list is often called the *undo stack* because when you undo a series of commands, you start with the most recent command and work your way backward. Menu commands such as Edit ➪ Undo and Edit ➪ Redo are captured by the document and forwarded to the undo manager. The undo manager then looks at the undo stack and passes the information it finds there to an object that can interpret that data. You are responsible for pushing data describing the current operation onto the undo stack and later interpreting that data when the user undoes the operation.

SlideShowDocument updates the undo stack by calling its recordSlideChange method whenever it changes the contents of the mSlides list. The recordSlideChanged registers the information required to undo the current information with SlideShowDocument's undo manager using registerUndoWithTarget:selector:object:. The first two arguments, target and selector, refer to the object that will handle the undo requests. In this case, SlideShowDocument will do the actual heavy lifting behind the undo operation. The selector must match the following method signature:

```
    - (void)handleUndo:(id)argument;
```

The object value refers to an Objective-C object that contains all the state required to undo the current operation. Since SlideShowDocument's entire document state is already stored in a single Objective-C object, the NSMutableArray mSlides, the recordSlideChange method passes the entire slide list. Note that since the slide list is mutable, recordSlideChange must make a non-mutable copy of the array before passing it to the NSUndoManager. If you simply passed the mSlides variable directly, the contents of NSUndoManager's slide array would change along with the contents of the document's slide array; this means undo and redo wouldn't actually do anything.

Of course, it's not always practical to record the entire document state for each undo operation. In these cases applications often record the minimum amount required to undo the requested change. For example, when you add a slide to your SlideShowDocument instance, the document could simply remember it needs to remove that slide. You could create a special Objective-C object for recording your individual undo commands, or you could store this state in an existing container object such as an NSDictionary.

When you select Edit ➪ Undo, the undo manager will call your document's handleUndo: method. This method receives the object passed into registerUndoWithTarget:selector:object: as its only argument. SlideShowDocument replaces its mSlides list with this argument, after being careful to convert the list back into a mutable array. And since handleUndo: changes the slide list, SlideShowDocument must remember to call its recordSlideChange method before making the switch; otherwise, the user won't be able to redo the command in the future.

Archiving Objective-C Objects

The Foundation framework provides several ways of retrieving data from files on disk. The right approach for you depends on the nature of your application and your data. Some of these methods are listed here:

❑ **Programs that need low-level access to files can use the NSFileHandle class to open files and read data.** NSFileHandle provides basic support for opening a file and reading a number of bytes from the file; you can pass the resulting data to NSString or NSNumber initialization methods to interpret the data as usable values. The NSStream subclasses, NSInputStream and NSOutputStream, provide low-level support for data that might reside in a number of different places: in the file system, in memory, on the network, and so on.

❑ **Common Foundation objects know how to write themselves to disk automatically.** For example, you can read and write an NSString using the initWithContentsOfFile: and writeToFile:atomically: methods. Other objects that can read and write themselves to disk include NSData, NSArray, and NSDictionary. Note you can use only the NSArray and NSDictionary classes to write out objects that can be found in property lists: NSData, NSDate, NSNumber, NSString, and other NSArray and NSDictionary objects. In fact, the NSDictionary and NSArray classes' writeToFile:atomically: method is normally how you write property lists.

❑ **You can encode one or more Objective-C objects into a single NSData item, and then write that NSData item to disk using its writeToFile:atomically: method.** This works well for programs that keep their state in Objective-C model objects. Foundation provides classes that manage this encoding process: NSArchiver and NSKeyedArchiver. Foundation also provides a protocol, NSCoding, that other objects can conform to; this allows you to pass your own objects to Foundation's archiving classes. Many Cocoa objects can be encoded by default, including all the property list classes mentioned above. Serialized data is stored in a binary format, unlike property lists, which are text.

You can use any of these techniques in your NSDocument subclass's file handling code. Xcode's template for new NSDocument subclasses is slightly biased toward the approach of encoding objects into an NSData object. This technique is fairly practical for Cocoa applications, where document state is normally stored in one or more model objects.

In the next Try It Out, you add support for reading and writing slide show files (.slim) to SlideShowDocument. These files are small binary files that contain lists of paths to individual image slides.

Try It Out   Archiving Objects

1. In Xcode, open Slide.h and add the NSCoding protocol to the Slide class's definition, as shown here:

```
@interface Slide : NSObject <NSCoding>
{
    NSString    *mFilePath;
    NSImage     *mImage;
}
```

2. Switch to `Slide.m` and add the following methods to the `Slide` implementation:

```
#pragma mark NSCoding Protocol

- (id)initWithCoder:(NSCoder *)decoder
{
    self = [super init];
    if (self) {
        if ([decoder allowsKeyedCoding]) {
            mFilePath = [decoder decodeObjectForKey:@"Slides"];
        } else {
            mFilePath = [decoder decodeObject];
        }
        [mFilePath retain];
    }
    return self;
}


- (void)encodeWithCoder:(NSCoder *)encoder
{
    if ([encoder allowsKeyedCoding]) {
        [encoder encodeObject:mFilePath forKey:@"Slides"];
    } else {
        [encoder encodeObject:mFilePath];
    }
}
```

3. Open `SlideShowDocument.m` and replace its file handling methods with the following code:

```
- (NSData *)dataRepresentationOfType:(NSString *)type
{
    NSMutableDictionary *fileDict = [NSMutableDictionary dictionary];
    NSData *result;

    // store the slides
    [fileDict setObject:mSlides forKey:@"Slides"];

    // store other settings

    // serialize the dictionary into a lump of data
    result = [NSKeyedArchiver archivedDataWithRootObject:fileDict];

    return result;
}

- (BOOL)loadDataRepresentation:(NSData *)data ofType:(NSString *)type
{
    NSDictionary *fileDict = nil;
    NSMutableArray *slides = nil;
    BOOL result = NO;

    fileDict = [NSKeyedUnarchiver unarchiveObjectWithData:data];

    slides = [NSMutableArray arrayWithArray:[fileDict objectForKey:@"Slides"]];
```

```
        if (slides) {
            [mSlides release];
            mSlides = [slides retain];
            result = YES;
        }

        return result;
    }
```

4. Save your changes to the `Slide` and `SlideShowDocument` files.

5. Build and run Slide Master. You can open and save your slide show documents as `.slim` files.

How It Works

Foundation defines a process for reading and writing Objective-C objects in a flat data buffer. This process is built around the `NSCoder` class. The `NSCoder` class is an *abstract* class, meaning that it is meant only to provide a common interface and implementation to its subclasses. You do not instantiate abstract classes directly; instead you access their functionality through its subclasses, which are called *concrete* subclasses. In this case, `NSCoder` defines an interface for reading and writing values to this flat data buffer; including other objects.

`NSCoder` and its subclasses can work only with objects that implement specific methods that define how the object should be read from and written to this binary buffer. Foundation provides the `NSCoding` protocol for this purpose:

```
@protocol NSCoding

- (void)encodeWithCoder:(NSCoder *)aCoder;
- (id)initWithCoder:(NSCoder *)aDecoder;

@end
```

An object receives an `encodeWithCoder:` method when someone passes that object to an `NSCoder` method, such as `encodeObject:` or `encodeObject:forKey:`. The object then encodes its own instance variables using additional `NSCoder` methods. Similarly, an object is initialized from the `initWithCoder:` method when someone decodes the binary stream. Note that `initWithCoder:` is meant to be a real initialization method—you need to properly initialize your object's superclass and set its instance variables.

Foundation provides two kinds of concrete subclasses of `NSCoder`: *archivers* and *keyed archivers*. Archivers write objects to the binary stream in a serial fashion; objects will be decoded in the same order they are encoded. This means your objects need to pay careful attention to the order in which your objects are archived so you can reverse that process. Serial archiving is performed with the `NSArchiver` and `NSUnarchiver` classes.

There are some maintenance issues with serial archivers, the most common being how to deal with adding new functionality to an object in the future. If you define a new version of your object that writes more data than the old object, older objects read in from file may not have all the necessary information to initialize your new object, and files saved with the new object will not work properly with older versions of your program. You can solve some of these problems by versioning your classes. This will allow you to upgrade older files to work with your new class, although it won't address compatibility with older systems.

Apple introduced *keyed archiving* to the NSCoder abstract class to help solve this problem. Keyed archiving records a name along with each individual value in the archive, much like how NSDictionary stores key/value pairs. As a result, you no longer need to worry about archiving and unarchiving data in the same order, and you won't have as much trouble with forward or backward compatibility. There is one major rule regarding compatibility: once you've defined a key, you cannot remove the key or change its meaning. You use keyed archiving through the NSKeyedArchiver and NSKeyedUnarchiver classes.

In general, you should use the keyed archivers instead of the older serial archivers, but be aware some code exists that still uses the serial archivers. You can figure out if your object is being coded in a keyed archive using the NSCoder class's allowsKeyedCoding method. If this method returns YES, you should use methods that encode or decode values by key; otherwise you can fall back to using the serial methods.

Note that object references decoded from an NSCoder subclass will have a limited life span. Depending on whether you are using a keyed archiver or a serial one, the object will be autoreleased or will be freed when the NSCoder subclass is destroyed. You need to retain these values if you want to use them outside the scope of your initWithCoder: method.

The Slide objects are simple model objects that store a path to an image file, and some cached image data. Because the image data can be very large, the Slide object only encodes its file path. Currently Slide Master trusts the file path will continue to point to an image file when a Slide is unarchived; that is, it assumes you haven't moved or deleted the image file. Clearly that might not be true. You deal with this bug in Chapter 9.

The SlideShowDocument encodes its data by asking the NSKeyedArchiver class to create an NSData instance from a root object. The root object represents SlideShowDocument's file data. Right now the root object is a dictionary with a single key, Slides, which points to your slide data.

Of course, you could simply have archived SlideShowDocument's mSlides instance variable directly instead of wrapping it in a dictionary. But since there is only one root object, and that object would be an array, you would be locked into a fairly rigid file format; you wouldn't be able to add new features to your file without affecting forward or backward compatibility. By instead using an NSDictionary, you get the same kind of benefits as keyed archiving in general. When working with file formats, remember careful planning now will save you a lot of worry in the future.

Application Preferences

Cocoa doesn't provide any special support for application preference windows, other than reserving a menu item for Preferences in new application nib files. You can simply apply the techniques and shortcuts you learned in earlier examples to build a window with controls, record the values when they change, and tell other parts of the application that they need to respond to that change. Cocoa Bindings do a very good job of managing this kind of problem.

In this example, you add a simple preference window to Slide Master, shown here in Figure 8-35. This window runs as a modal dialog just to keep things simple. You will use Cocoa Bindings to manage the values of the controls in your window, and observe the changes as they happen.

Figure 8-35

You complete the following Try It Out in two steps:

❑ First, you build the new user interface, including binding these controls with Cocoa Bindings.

❑ Then, you complete the custom code required to run the window modally and interpret the values.

Try It Out   **Creating a Preference Window Interface**

1. Open Slide Master's `MainMenu` nib file in Interface Builder.

2. Add an `orderFrontPreferencePanel:` action to the First Responder. Remember you can edit the First Responder instance from the Classes tab.

3. Connect your menu bar's Slide Master ➪ Preferences menu item to the First Responder's `orderFrontPreferencePanel:` action.

4. Save the `MainMenu` nib file.

5. Create a new empty Cocoa nib file. A new nib window appears, containing only the File's Owner and First Responder instances.

6. Build the window interface shown in Figure 8-36. The rectangular control is called a *color well*. You can find it on the Controls palette under the name `NSColorWell`.

Figure 8-36

7. Select the OK push button and set its tag to 1 using the Inspector.

8. In the color well's Bindings settings, select Shared User Defaults from the Bind To popup menu and change the Model Key Path to `backgroundColor`. Also select `NSUnarchiveWithData` from the Value Transformer combo box. The Bindings settings should now look like Figure 8-37. Also note that a Shared Defaults controller instance has appeared in the nib's Instances tab.

Figure 8-37

9. Create an `NSWindowController` subclass called `PreferencesWindowController` in the nib file's Classes tab. This class has one action: `handleOKCancel:`.

10. Switch to the Instances tab and change your File's Owner's custom class to `PreferencesWindowController` in the Inspector.

11. Connect the OK and Cancel buttons to the File's Owner's `handleOKCancel:` action.

12. Connect the File's Owner's `window` instance variable to your preference window.

13. Save your nib file with the name `PreferencesWindow`, and save it to your Slide Master project's `English.lproj` directory. Interface Builder asks if you want to add the nib file to your Slide Master project. Click the Add button to add the `PreferencesWindow` nib file to Slide Master.

How It Works

Cocoa Bindings provides an `NSController` subclass, called `NSUserDefaultsController`, for working with preferences. You can bind controls to this controller simply by choosing the Shared User Defaults option from the Bind To popup menu. Interface Builder will create the defaults controller instance for you.

Normally controls can work only with values that can be expressed as property list values: `NSString`, `NSDate`, `NSData`, `NSNumber`, and so on. Color values are defined by `NSColor` objects, which cannot be written to property lists or used directly with Cocoa Bindings. To deal with this problem, Cocoa Bindings can use a *value transformer* to convert an object into one suitable for use with property lists. Currently Cocoa Bindings provides one default value transformer for color wells and other controls, `NSUnarchiveFromData`. This value transformer will use the `NSArchiver` and `NSUnarchiver` classes to convert objects into `NSData` objects and back again. You need to use this value transformer when passing color values into Cocoa Bindings.

Your `PreferencesWindowController` subclass is primarily concerned with opening and closing the window, and running the window in a modal event loop. Because your preference controls are bound through Cocoa Bindings, you don't need to create outlets or actions to track them. `PreferencesWindowController` does provide a `handleOKCancel:` method for responding to the OK and Cancel buttons. This method distinguishes between the OK and Cancel buttons by checking the sender's tag value. The OK button's tag was set to 1, which is the same value defined by the `NSOKButton` constant you saw earlier.

In the next Try It Out example, you write the code that loads and drives the preferences window.

Try It Out   **Running the Modal Preferences Window**

1. In Xcode, create new files of type Cocoa Objective-C `NSWindowController` subclass, named `PreferencesWindowController.m` and `PreferencesWindowController.h`.

2. Open `PreferencesWindowController.h` and replace its contents with the following code:

```
#import <Cocoa/Cocoa.h>

@interface PreferencesWindowController : NSWindowController
{
}

+ (PreferencesWindowController*)sharedInstance;

- (IBAction)handleOKCancel:(id)sender;

- (void)runModal;

@end
```

3. Switch to `PreferencesWindowController.m` and define the `PreferencesWindowController` implementation as follows:

```
+ (PreferencesWindowController*)sharedInstance
{
    static PreferencesWindowController *sharedInstance = nil;

    if (sharedInstance == nil) {
        sharedInstance = [[PreferencesWindowController alloc]
initWithWindowNibName:@"PreferenceWindow"];
    }

    return sharedInstance;
}

- (void)runModal
{
    NSUserDefaultsController *defaultsController = [NSUserDefaultsController
sharedUserDefaultsController];

    // do not apply changes immediately; instead wait for the OK button.
    [defaultsController setAppliesImmediately:NO];
```

```
        // run the modal window
        int code = [NSApp runModalForWindow:[self window]];

        if (code == NSOKButton) {
            // save the defaults changes
            [defaultsController save:nil];
        } else {
            // discard the defaults changes
            [defaultsController revert:nil];
        }

        [self close];
}

- (IBAction)handleOKCancel:(id)sender
{
        // stop the modal loop and return the button's tag as the stop code
        [NSApp stopModalWithCode:[sender tag]];
}
```

4. Open `ApplicationDelegate.m` and add the following `#import` directive near the top of the file:

```
#import "PreferencesWindowController.h"
```

5. Add the following methods to the `ApplicationDelegate` implementation block:

```
- (void)applicationWillFinishLaunching:(NSNotification *)notification
{
        NSColor *color = [NSColor whiteColor];
        NSData *colorData = [NSArchiver archivedDataWithRootObject:color];
        NSDictionary *defaults = [NSDictionary dictionaryWithObjectsAndKeys:
            colorData, @"backgroundColor",
            nil];

        [[NSUserDefaults standardUserDefaults] registerDefaults:defaults];
}

- (void)orderFrontPreferencePanel:(id)sender
{
        [[PreferencesWindowController sharedInstance] runModal];
}
```

6. Open `SlideImageView.h` and add an `mBackgroundColor` instance variable and a `setBackgroundColor:` method. The following code shows the entire `SlideImageView` interface:

```
@interface SlideImageView : NSImageView
{
        NSColor *mBackgroundColor;
}

- (void)setBackgroundColor:(NSColor*)color;

@end
```

7. Switch to `SlideImageView.m` and add the following methods:

```
- (void)dealloc
{
    [mBackgroundColor release];

    [super dealloc];
}

- (void)setBackgroundColor:(NSColor*)color
{
    if (color != mBackgroundColor) {
        [mBackgroundColor release];
        mBackgroundColor = [color retain];
    }

    [self setNeedsDisplay:YES];
}

- (void)drawRect:(NSRect)rect
{
    if (mBackgroundColor) {
        [mBackgroundColor set];
        NSRectFill(rect);
    }

    [super drawRect:rect];
}
```

8. Open `SlideShowWindowController.m`, add the following `initWithWindowNibName:` and `dealloc` methods, and redefine the `windowDidLoad` method:

```
- (id)initWithWindowNibName:(NSString *)windowNibName
{
    self = [super initWithWindowNibName:windowNibName];

    if (self) {
        NSUserDefaults *userDefaults = [NSUserDefaults standardUserDefaults];

        // watch for backgroundColor changes
        [userDefaults addObserver:self
                       forKeyPath:@"backgroundColor"
                          options:NSKeyValueObservingOptionNew
                          context:NULL];
    }

    return self;
}

- (void)dealloc
{
    NSUserDefaults *userDefaults = [NSUserDefaults standardUserDefaults];

    // remove backgroundColor observer
    [userDefaults removeObserver:self forKeyPath:@"backgroundColor"];
```

```
        [super dealloc];
}

- (void)windowDidLoad
{
    NSUserDefaults *userDefaults = [NSUserDefaults standardUserDefaults];

    [super windowDidLoad];

    [mDrawer open];

    // set the initial selection
    if ([[self document] numberOfSlides]) {
        [mTableView selectRowIndexes:[NSIndexSet indexSetWithIndex:0]
                byExtendingSelection:NO];

        [mImageView setImage:[[[self document] slideAtIndex:0] image]];
    }

    // set the initial background color
    if (userDefaults) {
        NSData *data = [userDefaults objectForKey:@"backgroundColor"];
        NSColor *color = [NSUnarchiver unarchiveObjectWithData:data];

        [mImageView setBackgroundColor:color];

    }
}
```

9.   Add the following method to the Document Management section of
     SlideShowWindowController.m:

```
- (void)observeValueForKeyPath:(NSString *)keyPath ofObject:(id)object
change:(NSDictionary *)change context:(void *)context
{
    NSData *data = [change objectForKey:NSKeyValueChangeNewKey];
    NSColor *color = [NSUnarchiver unarchiveObjectWithData:data];

    [mImageView setBackgroundColor:color];
}
```

10. Save your changes to Slide Manager's source files.

11. Build and run Slide Master. You can bring up the preference panel by choosing Slide Master ⇨
     Preferences. When you change the color and click the OK button, all the open slide show docu-
     ments update themselves.

How It Works

PreferencesWindowController manages Slide Manager's preference panel. This class is a
singleton class, meaning there is always one instance of this class available at any time. The
PreferencesWindowController class guarantees this through its sharedInstance factory method.
The first time sharedInstance is called it will allocate and initialize the window controller; subsequent

calls to `PreferencesWindowController` will simply return this first instance. `ApplicationDelegate` should not release the instance returned by `sharedInstance` because it didn't explicitly allocate or copy the object itself.

The shared `PreferencesWindowController` instance runs its window as a modal dialog box by sending a `runModalForWindow:` message to an object named `NSApp`. `NSApp` is the shared instance of the `NSApplication` singleton class; `NSApp` is initialized by AppKit automatically when your program starts. You use the `NSApp` object to access certain kinds of AppKit features that are provided through the `NSApplication` interface. Running modal dialog and sheets are examples of `NSApplication` features. You can read the documentation for `NSApplication` to get a complete list of features available through the `NSApp` object.

`NSApplication`'s `runModalForWindow:` method will make the supplied window visible, and run that window in its own modal session. This means only that window will receive user events; other actions, such as clicking on other windows, are not permitted. The `runModalForWindow:` method will not return until something causes the modal session to stop. In this example, your OK and Cancel button handler, `handleOKCancel:`, ends the modal session by calling `NSApp`'s `stopModalWithCode:` method. You can also end a modal session by calling `NSApp`'s `stopModal` method.

The value passed into `stopModalWithCode:` will be returned by `runModalForWindow:`, providing a simple way to pass state from your OK and Cancel button handlers back to the code that started the modal session. `PreferencesWindowController` uses the predefined `NSOKButton` and `NSCancelButton` constants for this purpose, but you can use whatever values you want. You have the choice of completing the requested task either in your OK button action method, or later once `runModalForWindow:` concludes. Pick whichever technique works best for you.

Your `ApplicationDelegate` object does two more things now: it registers a set of initial user defaults when Slide Master launches, and it runs the `PreferencesWindowController` dialog box when the Preferences menu item is selected. The `NSApplication` class defines two dozen or so messages it might send to its delegate object, one of which is `applicationWillFinishLaunching:`. The `ApplicationDelegate` object will receive this message early in the application's launch cycle, making it a reasonably good place to initialize your application state.

The Cocoa class for working with user preferences is `NSUserDefaults`. You acquire the instance of this singleton class using its `standardUserDefaults` class method. You can access individual default values using methods similar to `NSMutableDictionary:` `objectForKey:`, `setObject:forKey:` and so on; you have already learned how to access these values using Cocoa Bindings. You can register a set of initial default values that `NSUserDefaults` will use when a value can't be found in the preferences file. For example, if Slide Master's preference file is missing or damaged, it will simply use [`NSColor whiteColor`] for the `backgroundColor` value.

You extended the `SlideImageView` to draw a solid background color if one was supplied to its `setBackgroundColor:` method. Although the `SlideImageView` class could talk to `NSUserDefaults` directly to get the background color, it's better to make this class as reusable as possible. A view object like `SlideImageView` shouldn't know anything about controller-level functionality such as user defaults.

`SlideImageView` overrides `NSImageView`'s `drawRect:` method to change the way the object is drawn. If a background color has been supplied, it will fill its area with the requested color; if not,

`SlideImageView` will default to `NSImageView`'s original behavior and not draw a background at all. This allows you to add the feature to `SlideImageView` for your slide show document without worrying about breaking your image document interface. Also, when someone calls `SlideImageView`'s `setBackgroundColor` method, the image view will redraw itself using the `setNeedsDisplay:` method.

The `SlideShowWindowController` enables the new `backgroundColor` feature in `SlideImageView`. When a window is first opened, it sets the image view's background color to the current default value. It reapplies the background color value when it notices the value has changed.

> *Remember that color values can't be stored in* `NSUserDefaults` *directly as* `NSColor` *objects; instead Cocoa Bindings is embedding the* `NSColor` *object in an* `NSData` *object using* `NSArchiver`.

`SlideShowWindowController` uses Cocoa Bindings' Key Value Observing protocol to note when the preferences have been updated. Of course, you could have used `NSNotification` for this purpose instead: the `PrefernecesWindowController` would post a notification when you clicked OK, and the `SlideShowWindowController` could catch that notification. This is convenient because Cocoa Bindings is already responsible for managing the preference window's UI, and it saves you the trouble of defining new notification names.

You listen for changes using `NSObject`'s `addObserver:forKeyPath:options:context:` method, which is part of the `NSKeyValueObserving` protocol. You send this message to the object you want to watch, in this case the shared `NSUserDefaults` object. The first argument represents the object listening for changes; in this case, the `SlideShowWindowController` object. The second object defines the key the observer is listening for. Recall you defined the `backgroundColor` key in your nib file earlier; that's the value you're interested in. The third argument is an options field; it currently can be set to `NSKeyValueObservingOptionNew`, `NSKeyValueObservingOptionOld`, or a combination of the two: `(NSKeyValueObservingOptionNew|NSKeyValueObservingOptionOld)`. These values indicate if the observing object is interested in learning about the new value, the old value, or both values. Finally the context is passed along to the observer when the value changes.

All observer objects must implement a `observeValueForPathKey:ofObject:change:context:` method, which is also part of the `NSKeyValueObserving` protocol. This method returns information about the observed value, including its parent object and its key path, and information about the change itself. `SlideShowWindowController` asks the change dictionary for the new value using `NSKeyValueChangeNewKey`. This value is available to `SlideShowWindowController` because it passed `NSKeyValueObservingOptionNew` in as the option to `addObserver:forKeyPath:options:context:`. Once `SlideShowWindowController` has the new color value, it resets the image view's background color.

As when using notifications, you must unregister an observer object before it is destroyed; otherwise you run the risk of sending a message to a freed object, which will result in your application crashing. `SlideShowWindowController` registers the observer in its `initWithWindowNibName:` function and unregisters itself in its `dealloc` function. This is another good place, in addition to `setDocument:`, to tear down notification code; in fact, since the image's background color state doesn't rely on document state at all, `initWithWindowNibName:` is probably the best choice for registering your observer.

Responding to Keyboard Events

Most Cocoa controls handle keyboard events automatically. For example, NSTextField controls automatically update their contents when you type, NSTableView objects will change their selection when you press the arrow keys, and so on. The responder chain routes events directly to these objects so you don't have to worry about event processing yourself. Sometimes you need to extend an object to handle a certain kind of event. For example, you might need to change a button's behavior when you Option-click it.

This is another case where subclassing an existing Cocoa control is a good solution to this problem. You just want to write the code specific to your situation, and inherit the rest of the control's behavior from its super class. Most of the time, your objects can simply pass the event farther down the responder chain, and handle the event in your NSWindowController subclass (or your window delegate, if you aren't using NSWindowController).

In the following Try It Out, you extend Slide Master's slide show document's image view to respond to keyboard events. For example, you delete the currently selected slides by pressing the Delete key. Pressing the arrow keys will also advance the selection, just like when the table view is selected. Because you are already using a custom NSImageView subclass, SlideImageView, you won't need to edit your nib files at all.

Try It Out   Responding to Keyboard Events

1. In Xcode, open SlideImageView.m and add the following methods to the class. These methods are already defined by NSResponder, one of SlideImageView's superclasses, so you really don't need to add these methods to your header file.

```
- (void)keyDown:(NSEvent*)event
{
    // explicitly forward this to the next responder
    [[self nextResponder] keyDown:event];
}

- (void)mouseDown:(NSEvent*)event
{
    // force this view to become the first responder so it routes events
    // through the responder chain.
    [[self window] makeFirstResponder:self];
}
```

2. Open SlideShowWindowController.m and add a category of private methods, as shown here:

```
@interface SlideShowWindowController (PrivateMethods)
- (void)selectNewRow:(BOOL)forward byExtendingSelection:(BOOL)extend;
- (void)delete:(id)sender;
@end
```

3. Add the following methods to SlideShowWindowController.m's Event Handling section:

```
- (void)selectNewRow:(BOOL)forward byExtendingSelection:(BOOL)extend
{
    int selection = [mTableView selectedRow];
```

```
        int count = [[self document] numberOfSlides];

        // if there are no slides, do nothing
        if (count == 0) {
            return;
        }

        // pick a new selection based on the current selection
        if (selection == -1) {
            selection = forward ? 0 : count-1;
        } else {
            selection += forward ? 1 : -1;
        }

        // if the selection as advanced off the end, wrap around
        if (!extend) {
            if (selection < 0) {
                selection = count-1;
            } else if (selection >= count) {
                selection = 0;
            }
        }

        // update the selection
        [mTableView selectRow:selection byExtendingSelection:extend];
    }

- (void)keyDown:(NSEvent*)event
{
        unichar ch = [[event characters] characterAtIndex:0];
        BOOL isShiftDown = ([event modifierFlags] & NSShiftKeyMask) != 0;

        switch (ch) {
            case 0x7f: // delete
            case NSDeleteFunctionKey:
                [self delete:nil];
                break;
            case NSUpArrowFunctionKey:
            case NSLeftArrowFunctionKey:
                [self selectNewRow:false byExtendingSelection:isShiftDown];
                break;
            case NSDownArrowFunctionKey:
            case NSRightArrowFunctionKey:
                [self selectNewRow:true byExtendingSelection:isShiftDown];
                break;
            default:
                [super keyDown:event];
        }
    }
```

4. Save your changes to SlideImageView.m and SlideShowWindowController.m.

5. Build and run Slide Master. Now when the image view is selected, such as when the document first opens or if you click on the image view, you can cycle through the slides by pressing the arrow keys. You can also remove the selected slides by pressing the Delete key.

How It Works

The default implementation of `NSImageView` forwards keyboard events to the next object in the responder chain. So while defining `SlideImageView`'s `keyDown:` method isn't strictly necessary, it's useful to see how event forwarding works. On the other hand, the default `NSImageView` implementation won't become the first responder when you click on it, so you need to manually make the `SlideImageView` instance the first responder in `mouseDown:`.

When you press a key with the image view selected, the event will be forwarded to your `SlideShowWindowController` instance. Recall that the responder chain begins with a window's contents, includes the window and its delegate, and ends with the `NSApplication` singleton; also recall `NSWindowController` establishes itself as its window's delegate. As a result you can receive these keyboard events simply by implementing the `keyDown:` method.

You can look at a keyboard event by asking the `NSEvent` instance for the characters the event represents. Normally these characters represent basic keystrokes: A, B, C, and so on; but many keys produce keystrokes of non-printable characters, such as your keyboard's function keys or arrow keys. AppKit's `NSEvent.h` file provides constant values for working with these keys. Some common keystrokes, however, don't have constant values, including the Delete key. You need to provide the numeric code for these keys yourself. If you aren't sure which code a key will generate, you can set a breakpoint in your `keyDown:` method, type a key, and then check the resulting `NSEvent` object.

`SlideShowWindowController` uses a switch statement to process keystrokes, since a number of buttons are bound to the same action. For example, the Delete and Forward Delete keys delete the current selection. Because you already defined the `delete:` action called by Edit ⇨ Delete to do the same thing, `SlideShowWindowController` can simply call `delete:` to get the same effect. Unhandled keys are forwarded to the `SlideShowWindowController`'s superclass; this gives `NSWindowController` a chance to handle the event before passing it to the next object in the responder chain.

The code for adjusting the table selection is collected into a single private method, `selectNewRow: byExtendingSelection:`. This method can select the next row or the previous row, depending on the value of its `forward` variable. First it gets the current selection from the table view; if there is a selection, it advances to the next (or previous) row. Normally the selection will wrap around when you get to one end of the list. You can also extend the selection by holding down the Shift key while pressing one of the arrow keys, in which case the selection will not wrap around when you reach the end.

Summary

You learned a lot in this chapter, including the following:

❑   How to bind your application's user interface to your custom code. Interface Builder's outlets and actions allow you to manage this relationship directly, although it can be tedious in larger programs. Cocoa Bindings provide an easier way of coordinating your data with your user interface, although it may not be appropriate in all cases. Fortunately, you can use both of these techniques within the same program to get the best of both worlds.

❑   How to manage documents using Cocoa's document-based application architecture. The Cocoa frameworks provided a lot of the basic behavior for free; such as managing common menu items, naming untitled documents, positioning new windows, and so on. You needed to fill in some key details to pull the whole thing together, including how to interpret your document files, managing undo, and the actual business of binding your document data to its user interface.

❑ How to extend existing Cocoa objects through subclassing. Interface Builder even works with your custom subclasses, providing a convenient way to extend existing controls like NSImageView and NSButton.

❑ How to use the responder chain and the first responder to route menu commands to the active document. You also learned how to receive and forward events along the responder chain.

❑ How to send and receive notifications using NSNotification and NSNotificationCenter. You can use these tools to track changes that aren't directly tied to a user event, such as when a data structure changes. You can also use Cocoa's Key Value Observing in some of these situations.

❑ How to work with application preferences. These tasks include displaying a preference user interface, storing the preferences on disk, and responding to preference changes within your application.

In the next chapter, you learn about using the Carbon frameworks. You also practice using Carbon and Cocoa in the same application. Before proceeding, however, try the exercises that follow to test your understanding of the material covered in this chapter. You can find the solutions to these exercises in Appendix A.

Exercises

1. Slide Master can display images as individual documents, as well as in a collection of slides in a slide show. Extend Slide Master to open an image in its own document when you double-click an entry in the slide show document's table view. Try to use NSDocumentController to open the requested file.

2. Change the slide show document to print the name of the current slide in the main slide show window. Implement the feature by printing the name directly in the SlideImageView. No nib file changes should be necessary. AppKit provides some additions to Foundation's NSString class for drawing strings directly in a view; you may find these methods helpful.

3. If the slide show document's image view is selected, you can delete the current slide simply by pressing the Delete key. However, if the table view is selected, the delete key simply beeps at you. Fix this bug by extending the table view to respond to the Delete key.

   Note that unlike with SlideImageView you can't actually forward the keyDown: event to your SlideShowWindowController using the responder chain. That's because the table view actually resides in a drawer window, which is separate from your slide show window and the SlideShowWindowController. Instead, try sending the keyDown: event to the table view's delegate object.

Using the Carbon Frameworks

Much of the technology behind the Carbon frameworks has been around a long time, well before Mac OS X was conceived. The first Macintosh computers shipped with an operating system that provided windows, menus, and controls to application programmers. The API in that first system evolved over time to include new functionality such as color, sound, power management, and later Internet networking and multimedia support. The System 6 and System 7 software lines gave way to Mac OS 8 and Mac OS 9 before ultimately the original Mac OS was officially retired in 2002. Even so, most of the APIs from traditional Mac OS live on in Mac OS X, repackaged into the Carbon frameworks.

The API at the center of the traditional Mac OS was referred to as the *Macintosh Toolbox*. Originally Macintosh software was written directly against the Toolbox API using a programming language called Pascal. Later Apple provided a C interface to the Toolbox that could be used by C and C++ programmers, but even to this day you can find evidence of its Pascal heritage.

The Macintosh Toolbox provides a fairly low-level interface to its functionality. You are responsible for handling most aspects of your program's operation. For example, when your program receives an event, you must figure out what the event means and then respond to that event appropriately. As a result, you are responsible for providing a lot of infrastructure code that may not be entirely relevant to the problem you are trying to solve.

In the past, Macintosh Toolbox programmers developed their own object-oriented application frameworks to simplify the problem of application development. Two popular Macintosh application frameworks were Apple's MacApp and Metrowerks PowerPlant. These frameworks encouraged consistency and code re-use by wrapping the Toolbox API in C++ objects; and once you got up to speed, you could write Macintosh programs more quickly. However, these frameworks had a steep learning curve, as you needed to know Toolbox programming as well as programming against the specific application framework. This limited adoption of these technologies, especially among programming hobbyists.

A few years prior to Mac OS X, Apple started providing more high-level APIs for working with common interface concepts, known as the *Human Interface Toolbox*. On Mac OS X systems, this functionality is encapsulated in the HIToolbox framework. The Human Interface Toolbox continues to provide a C API to its features, although it benefits from object-oriented design concepts. In fact, some recent additions to the Human Interface Toolbox were influenced by AppKit concepts, such as `HIView` and `HITextView`.

Although you can write user interface code using both traditional Toolbox and modern Human Interface Toolbox APIs on Mac OS X, Apple has focused much of its development efforts on the Human Interface Toolbox. Traditional Toolbox programming relies on Carbon Resource Manager data structures for defining application interfaces, and Apple no longer provides user-friendly tools for editing these files. On the other hand, the Human Interface Toolbox uses Carbon nib files created in Interface Builder.

After digging in to Carbon Events, you may find that using Carbon for doing high-level UI is a bit more complicated than using Cocoa. You are responsible for providing much of the basic infrastructure required by your program, infrastructure you might get "for free" from Cocoa. People interested in writing applications for Mac OS X might prefer to use Cocoa for their user interfaces. However, the Carbon interface API appeals to programmers who want this fine-grain control, programmers writing plug-ins that need to display UI in other Carbon applications, and programmers who need to deploy their application on other operating systems such as Mac OS 9 or Windows. Although the Carbon API is not available for Windows, both the Carbon and Windows API use C, which can simplify the process of reusing UI code; that is, you don't have to struggle with a language barrier.

One way Apple has tried to level the playing field between Carbon and Cocoa is through the CoreFoundation framework. CoreFoundation provides a C interface to many of the same data structures and algorithms found in Foundation: Unicode string support, mutable arrays and dictionaries, and so on. Although CoreFoundation is written in C, it has an object-oriented design in which data is encapsulated into private structures and accessed through functions. In this sense, CoreFoundation data structures are objects, like those in Foundation. Some CoreFoundation objects are so similar to Foundation that they can actually be used in place of real Foundation Objective-C objects, a practice referred to as *Toll-Free Bridging*. For example, you can pass Foundation's `NSString` object into a function that expects CoreFoundation's `CFStringRef` objects. You learn more about Toll-Free Bridging later in this chapter.

The Carbon frameworks include a lot of useful features other than UI. These low-level APIs behave the same regardless of how you implement your user interface code. For example, you can use Carbon file handling code from a Cocoa application.

In this chapter you learn

- ❑ How to manage memory using functions supplied by Carbon, CoreFoundation, and Darwin
- ❑ How to use Carbon Events to connect Carbon application interfaces up to your custom source code
- ❑ How to call the Carbon APIs from Cocoa applications
- ❑ How to track local files even if they are moved or renamed using the Carbon File Manager
- ❑ How to use the Carbon APIs to write out a simple QuickTime movie

Memory Management in Carbon

Carbon programs generally use C functions to create and destroy memory. You learned about the `malloc` and `free` memory functions in Chapter 6, and Carbon programs can certainly make use of these functions. Carbon provides its own memory-management functions, mostly for historical reasons. CoreFoundation also defines its own memory-management conventions, in part because its objects are reference counted. The following sections describe Carbon and CoreFoundation memory-management functions in more detail.

Carbon Memory Functions

Carbon provides its own functions for allocating memory. Although these functions used to be the native memory functions for the traditional Mac OS 9 operating system, they now eventually call down into the `malloc` memory functions. The Carbon functions exist now largely for source compatibility with existing code. In addition, the terminology for working with memory has made its way into other parts of the Carbon API. Understanding Carbon memory conventions can help you understand how other older libraries, such as QuickTime, are meant to be used.

Carbon Pointers

Carbon manages contiguous chunks of memory using the `NewPtr` and `DisposePtr` functions. These functions behave basically the same way as `malloc` and `free`. The `NewPtr` function returns a pointer to memory of a specific size, and `DisposePtr` allows the system to reclaim that memory. You will see the verbs *New* and *Dispose* used frequently within Carbon for creating and destroying specific data structures, such as `NewWindow` and `DisposeWindow`.

Although conceptually the same as `malloc` and `free`, you should resist the urge to pass memory created by `NewPtr` into `free`, or memory created by `malloc` into `DisposePtr`. These functions are equivalent, but not identical. Also, if you call a specific function that creates a data structure, you should use a corresponding function to destroy that structure if available. For example, windows created with `NewWindow` should be destroyed by `DisposeWindow`, not by `DisposePtr`. Note that some type-specific allocators do not have corresponding deallocators, so in those cases you will need to call `DisposePtr`.

Carbon Handles

The original Macintosh computers were severely memory constrained, limited to 128KB or 512KB of RAM. To make matters worse, the early systems didn't support virtual memory. Mac OS introduced a number of techniques, such as the handle, that allowed programmers to conserve as much memory as possible. A *handle* is a pointer that points into a block of *master pointers*, which in turn point to real memory. This pointer-to-pointer approach allowed the operating system to rearrange the contents of memory to improve runtime performance. The operating system could move the contents of memory from one area of RAM to another, and update a handle's master pointer, without changing or invalidating the handle itself.

You can use `NewHandle` and `DisposeHandle` to create and destroy handles, as shown in the following pseudocode:

```
typedef struct {
    Point origin;
    float radius;
} Circle;
```

```
Point center; // set elsewhere

Circle **sun = NewHandle(sizeof(Circle));

if (sun) {
    (*sun)->origin = center;
    (*sun)->radius = 3.0;

    // do something interesting ...

    DisposeHandle((Handle)sun);
}
```

The only real difference between pointers and handles in this example is the need to dereference the sun variable twice: first to get the handle's master pointer, and a second time to get to the data. All this double-dereferencing can become a bit tedious, and can have a negative impact on your program's performance. If you need to do a lot of handle accesses in a large loop, you might find your program spends a lot of its time simply getting to the master pointer. In those cases Mac OS programmers would get and cache their master pointer as in the pseudocode here:

```
if (sun) {
    Circle *sunPtr;

    HLock((Handle)sun);

    sunPtr = *sun;
    sunPtr->origin = center;
    sunPtr->radius = 3.0;

    // do something interesting ...

    HUnlock((Handle)sun);
    DisposeHandle((Handle)sun);
}
```

Remember Mac OS could rearrange the contents of memory by resetting a handle's master pointer. If the operating system decided to rearrange your program's memory while you were looking at a handle's master pointer, your program might dereference an invalid master pointer and crash. Mac OS programmers could avoid this problem by asking the operating system to leave a handle alone, using the HLock and HUnlock functions. Mac OS would not rearrange a locked handle's master pointer.

Of course, Mac OS X features modern memory management, including a first-class virtual memory system. There isn't any need for many of the handles features on Mac OS X, and Apple discourages using them for general memory needs. Handle functions still exist for compatibility with older source code (although you no longer need to worry about memory being rearranged) and some Carbon data structures and API still use the Handle pointer types. So it's still useful to know how to use handles even on Mac OS X.

Carbon provides additional memory functions in the NewPtr and NewHandle families. For example, the NewPtrClear function allocates a buffer that has been filled with zeros. Carbon's Memory Manager reference documentation has a complete list of memory functions available through Carbon.

CoreFoundation Memory Conventions

The CoreFoundation framework, which is often considered one of the Carbon frameworks, provides C-level API for low-level system utilities, such as collection classes, file I/O, and XML parsing. Many data types defined by CoreFoundation resemble Objective-C objects vended by the Foundation framework. For this reason you might think of CoreFoundation as "Foundation for C programs."

Most CoreFoundation data types are *opaque*, meaning structure contents are not exposed through CoreFoundation's header files. All CoreFoundation's opaque data type names end with a `Ref` suffix. Carbon often uses this convention as well, such as in the case of `WindowRef` and `ControlRef`. Because you can't access the contents of an opaque data type directly, you must use function calls to query or change the data's state. When used properly, opaque data types can provide some of the benefits of object-oriented code, such as data encapsulation.

These opaque data types force CoreFoundation objects to be allocated on the heap, just like Foundation objects. You create new CoreFoundation objects using a `CFCreate...` function. For example, the `CFCreateArray` function creates a `CFArrayRef` object. Also, all CoreFoundation functions with *copy* in their names create a new instance of an object; you must explicitly dispose of these objects yourself once you are done with them. For example, `CFBundleCopyBundleURL` returns a newly allocated `CFURLRef` object from an existing `CFBundleRef` object, and you must dispose of this `CFURLRef` object yourself. You can dispose of any CoreFoundation object using `CFRelease`.

CoreFoundation objects are reference counted, just like Foundation objects. You can use `CFRetain` to take ownership of a CoreFoundation object by incrementing its reference count. You can yield ownership, or decrement its reference count, using the `CFRelease` function. Note that CoreFoundation does not support the concept of an autorelease pool.

Connecting Carbon Interfaces

Every control in a Carbon nib file can have a unique key that identifies the control within your application. This key is called a `ControlID` and is composed of the following bits of information:

```
struct ControlID {
    OSType signature;
    SInt32 id;
};
```

The `signature` field is an `OSType` that identifies the owner of the control; in an application, this is normally the application's creator code. The `id` field is simply a signed number. Each of your controls will have a unique `id` number. Traditionally these numbers start at 128 and increase in value.

Action controls, such as buttons or text fields, have an associated command that takes place when the control is changed or used. Control commands are identified by 32-bit identifiers, which resemble `OSType` codes. Carbon handles some actions automatically, such as `quit` for quitting an application.

Together these `ControlID` and command values function like Cocoa outlets and actions, except you must manage the controls manually. Cocoa will automatically set your outlet instance variables when your nib is loaded, and will simply call your Objective-C method actions at the appropriate times. In Carbon programming, you must find the control yourself using its `ControlID` if you want to work with the control (such as ask it for its value). Also, you must manually register callback functions to receive events from the operating system, and interpret the events yourself.

In this example you build a Carbon version of the Email Formatter application you saw in Chapter 8. Not only is this program a fairly simple introduction to working with Carbon interfaces, but it also provides a basis for comparison between designing interfaces in Carbon and Cocoa. You build this program in three steps:

❑ First you build the user interface in Interface Builder. This includes setting the `ControlID` and command values for each control.

❑ Then you write custom code to initialize and respond to your user interface.

❑ Finally, you extract the data from your controls, modify the data, and then update your interface with the result.

The following Try It Out walks you though building an interface for a Carbon email formatter.

Try It Out   Building the Carbon Email Formatter Interface

1. In Xcode, create a new Carbon Application project named `Carbon Email Formatter`.

2. Double-click the `main` nib file to open it in Interface Builder.

3. In Interface Builder's Inspector window, change your `MainWindow` instance's Theme Brush to Dialog, the Position to Center, and make sure the Compositing check box is on. Also rename your window as `Carbon Email Formatter`. The Inspector should resemble the one shown in Figure 9-1.

Figure 9-1

4. Add the text fields, labels, and horizontal line shown in Figure 9-2. The editable text fields are 200 pixels wide. You will find the horizontal line on the Controls palette.

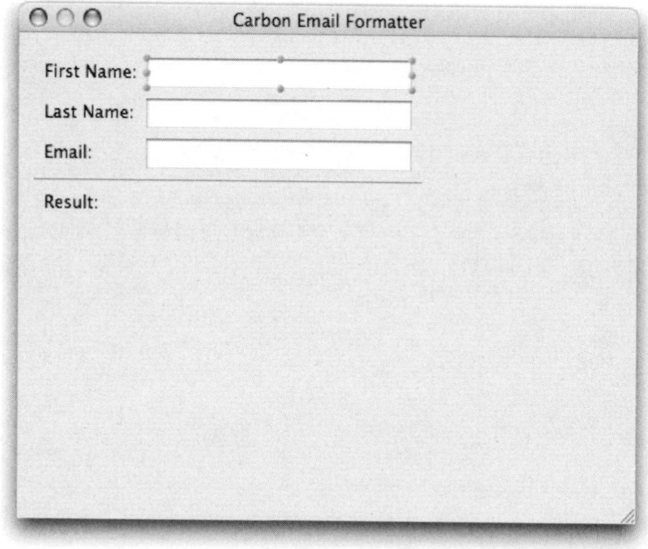

Figure 9-2

5. Drag a Text View control from the Text Based Controls palette to your window. The text control will simply look like a white box.

6. In the Inspector, check the Text View's Read Only, Output Text in Unicode, Always Wraps at View Edge, and Mono Styled Text check boxes. The Inspector should resemble Figure 9-3.

7. Select Layout ⇨ Embed in ⇨ Scroll View to wrap the Text View control in a Scroll View. Scroll bars will appear in your window. Note the Inspector window's title has changed to ScrollView Inspector, and displays settings for the Scroll View.

8. In the Inspector window, uncheck the Scroll View's Scroll Horizontally check box.

9. Position the new Scroll View and resize the window as shown in Figure 9-4.

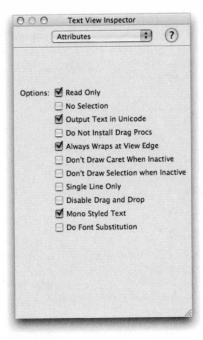

Figure 9-3

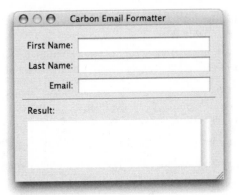

Figure 9-4

10. Select the first text field and select the Control inspector in the Inspector window. The Control view shown in Figure 9-5 includes a Signature and an ID field for setting the control's `ControlID`, and a Command field for setting the control's command ID.

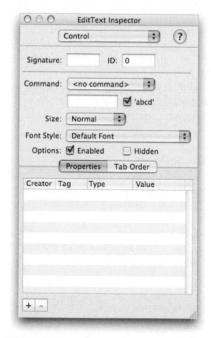

Figure 9-5

11. Set the Signature, ID, and Command codes for all three text fields using the values in the following table.

Text Field	Signature	ID	Command
First Name	EFmt	128	rslt
Last Name	EFmt	129	rslt
Email	EFmt	130	rslt

12. Double-click the Scroll View to select the Text View contained within. The Inspector's title bar changes to read Text View Inspector.

13. Set the Text View's Signature, ID, and Command codes using the values in the following table.

Text View	Signature	ID	Command
Result	EFmt	131	<no command>

14. Save your changes to the `main` nib file.

How It Works

You use Interface Builder's Control inspector to set a Carbon control's `ControlID` and command codes. Your controls' `ControlID` values should all use the same Signature value: your application's creator code. Here the `EFmt` code refers to "Email Formatter." Each control should use a unique value for its ID. Controls that trigger a command when they change should supply a four-character command code. Interface Builder supplies a list of commands automatically handled by Carbon for quick access; but ordinarily you will make up your own command code. Here the `rslt` code indicates the program should calculate its "result."

Carbon controls like the Text View can be embedded in scroll views, very much like Cocoa views can. Interface Builder will automatically select a Carbon Scroll View for Carbon interfaces, and an `NSScrollView` instance for Cocoa interfaces. Clicking once on the control simply selects the scroll view; you need to double-click the view to select its content.

The Carbon text fields are actually Carbon `ControlRef` instances. `ControlRefs` are a Human Interface Toolbox data structure that represents a control. The `ControlRef` API defines a common way to access a control, including setting and retrieving the control's data, modifying how the control is displayed, and so on.

The Human Interface Toolbox also includes a view mechanism called `HIView`. The `HIViewRef` data structure performs some of the same functions as Cocoa's `NSView` object: managing drawing in an area of a window. `HIViewRef` types are a special kind of `ControlRef`, and in some cases you can interact with these data structures as if they were controls. Your text view is actually an instance of an `HITextView`, which is a special text control based on the `HIView` mechanism.

In the following Try It Out you add code that responds to the user's changes. You also run your program and verify that your code is working.

Try It Out   Responding to Carbon Events

1. Open `main.c` in Xcode. The file already contains the following source code, created by Xcode:

```
#include <Carbon/Carbon.h>

int main(int argc, char* argv[])
{
    IBNibRef            nibRef;
    WindowRef           window;

    OSStatus            err;

    // Create a Nib reference passing the name of the nib file (without the
    // .nib extension) CreateNibReference only searches into the application
    // bundle.
    err = CreateNibReference(CFSTR("main"), &nibRef);
    require_noerr( err, CantGetNibRef );

    // Once the nib reference is created, set the menu bar. "MainMenu" is the
    // name of the menu bar object. This name is set in InterfaceBuilder when
    // the nib is created.
```

```
                err = SetMenuBarFromNib(nibRef, CFSTR("MenuBar"));
                require_noerr( err, CantSetMenuBar );

                // Then create a window. "MainWindow" is the name of the window object.
                // This name is set in InterfaceBuilder when the nib is created.
                err = CreateWindowFromNib(nibRef, CFSTR("MainWindow"), &window);
                require_noerr( err, CantCreateWindow );

                // We don't need the nib reference anymore.
                DisposeNibReference(nibRef);

                // The window was created hidden so show it.
                ShowWindow( window );

                // Call the event loop
                RunApplicationEventLoop();

    CantCreateWindow:
    CantSetMenuBar:
    CantGetNibRef:
     return err;
    }
```

2. Add the following #define directives to the top of the main.c file. Note that these values match those you used in your nib file:

```
#define kApplicationSignature     'EFmt'
#define kComputeResultCmd         'rslt'
#define kFirstNameFieldID         128
#define kLastNameFieldID          129
#define kEmailFieldID             130
#define kResultTextID             131
```

3. Define the following function prototypes after the #defines but before the main function. These prototypes will allow your main function to refer to other functions that haven't been defined yet.

```
pascal OSStatus MainEventHandler(EventHandlerCallRef handler, EventRef event, void
*userData);
void ComputeResult(WindowRef window);
```

4. Insert the following code into the main function between the calls to DisposeNibReference and ShowWindow:

```
                // We don't need the nib reference anymore.
                DisposeNibReference(nibRef);

                // Install our window event handler
                EventTypeSpec eventSpec = {kEventClassCommand, kEventCommandProcess};
                InstallWindowEventHandler(window,
                                          NewEventHandlerUPP(MainEventHandler),
                                          1,
                                          &eventSpec,
                                          (void*)window,
```

```
                            NULL);

    // The window was created hidden so show it.
    ShowWindow( window );
```

5. Add the following new functions at the end of the `main.c` file, after the `main` function:

```
pascal OSStatus MainEventHandler(EventHandlerCallRef handler, EventRef event, void
*userData)
{
    OSStatus result = eventNotHandledErr;
    HICommand command;

    // get the HICommand from the event
    GetEventParameter(event,
                      kEventParamDirectObject,
                      typeHICommand,
                      NULL,
                      sizeof(HICommand),
                      NULL,
                      &command);

    // if this is a compute event regenerate the result string
    if (command.commandID == kComputeResultCmd) {
        ComputeResult((WindowRef)userData);
        result = noErr;
    }

    return result;
}

void ComputeResult(WindowRef window)
{
    DebugStr("\pComputeResult called");
}
```

6. Save your changes to `main.c`.

7. Build and run Carbon Email Formatter. As you change text fields by clicking with the mouse, Xcode's Run Log provides the following note:

```
ComputeResult called
```

How It Works

Your source code will use the same `ControlID` and command values you entered into your nib file. It's good practice to define symbols for these constants using the `#define` directive, so that you can more easily tell what each value represents. You will need to update this information by hand, because Interface Builder will not create or maintain the information for you.

The default `main` function basically does three things: loads your application's interface from the nib file, initializes the interface, and starts event processing. Loading a menu and window from a nib file is a fairly simple matter, even though it does take several steps. You begin by calling `CreateNibReference`, which will search your application's bundle for a nib with a given name. If a nib file is found, the function creates an IBNibRef data structure representing that nib file and returns that IBNibRef as an output parameter. The SetMenuBarFromNib and CreateWindowFromNib functions both take an IBNibRef and create interface items that match a specific name. For example, the call to CreateWindowFromNib looks in the nib file for a window instance named "MainWindow," actually creates that instance, and returns the window in a WindowRef output parameter. When done creating items from the nib file, you call DisposeNibReference to close the nib file and free any memory it might be using. Note that this doesn't affect the menu or window you built earlier with SetMenuBarFromNib and CreateWindowFromNib.

Initially, Carbon Email Formatter didn't require much in the way of user interface initialization. All it did was open the window built in the CreateWindowFromNib function using ShowWindow. Before displaying the window you used the InstallWindowEventHandler function to tell Carbon that you wanted to be notified when the window receives commands from the event system, which is the first step in handling your own custom Carbon events. Actually, the InstallWindowEventHandler function isn't a function at all; it's actually a precompiler macro that calls into a function called InstallEventHandler. But if InstallWindowEventHandler were a real function, it might look like this:

```
OSStatus InstallWindowEventHandler(WindowRef              inWindow,
                                   EventHandlerUPP        inHandler,
                                   UInt32                 inNumTypes,
                                   const EventTypeSpec *  inList,
                                   void *                 inUserData,
                                   EventHandlerRef *      outRef);
```

The first argument to InstallWindowEventHandler represents the window you are interested in, in your case the window that was created from your nib file. The inHandler argument is the name of the function the Carbon event system will call to handle events for that window. Most Carbon functions that accept function pointers use an intermediate UPP data type, or *Universal Procedure Pointer*, to describe its function pointers. These universal procedure pointers help Carbon keep track of the runtime-specific details of how to use function pointers; for example, Carbon needs to treat function pointers from Mac OS 9 programs differently than it treats function pointers for Mac OS X programs.

The third and fourth arguments to InstallWindowEventHandler describe the events your callback function is interested in handling. The inList argument takes an array of EventTypeSpec structures that specifically identify kinds of events, and the inNumTypes argument indicates the length of that array. Here you simply pass in a pointer to a single EventTypeSpec, so you set the count to 1. The EventTypeSpec itself is a simple C structure composed of eventClass and eventKind fields:

```
struct EventTypeSpec {
  UInt32 eventClass;
  UInt32 eventKind;
};
```

The eventClass field specifies the nature of the event you're interested in, such as keyboard and mouse events. The kEventClassCommand event class generically represents events generated from controls. Legal values for the eventKind field depend entirely on the event class. In the case of kEventClassCommand, the kEventCommandProcess value refers to events sent as a direct result of using a control. So your EventTypeSpec value describes command events sent directly by controls.

The inUserData argument to InstallWindowEventHandler is a pointer value that is simply passed back into your event handler callback function when it is called. Your event handling code is going to need to reference the window that sent the event, so you simply pass the window reference in as this value.

InstallWindowEventHandler can return an EventHandlerRef through its sixth argument, outRef. You can use this EventHandlerRef value to add event types to the handler later on, or remove it entirely. If you want your handler to stay active only for the life of the target window, you can simply supply NULL instead of an existing EventHandlerRef value.

Once your interface is initialized you start event processing by calling Carbon's RunApplicationEventLoop function. From this point on, Carbon handles the details of getting user events from the operating system, handling built-in operations such as quitting, and so on. Carbon will also call your event handler callback to process kEventCommandProcess events sent by the text field controls.

Your event handler callback uses a very specific function prototype:

```
pascal OSStatus MainEventHandler(EventHandlerCallRef handler, EventRef event, void
*userData)
```

The pascal keyword tells the compiler that the callback function should use Pascal calling conventions; a holdover from the old days when the Macintosh Toolbox was written in Pascal. The handler argument is used to forward the event on to the next available handler, somewhat like how Cocoa's NSResponder chain works. This is useful if you want to intercept events normally handled by Carbon; you can capture the event, perform some processing, and then forward the event back to Carbon using the CallNextEventHandler function. The event argument is the event itself, and the userData variable contains the pointer set by InstallWindowEventHandler.

Your MainEventHandler function extracts a HICommand structure from event using GetEventParameter. The GetEventParameter function is intended to be a general way to get information from an event; however, the information available for a given event depends on the event type. For example, event will always refer to kEventCommandProcess events here, so you can ask it for its HICommand structure, which is specific to kEventCommandProcess events. The only piece of the HICommand interesting to the event handler is its commandID field. This commandID should match the code entered in Interface Builders' Command field.

MainEventHandler will call a separate function called ComputeResult to process rslt commands. This function accepts a window argument that it will eventually use to find your application's controls. You passed the window pointer to your MainEventHandler through its userData variable, so you can just feed that value back into ComputeResult. The following code fragment tells the compiler it should treat the userData pointer as if it were a WindowRef; this prevents the compiler from complaining about a type mismatch. This is called *casting* a value to another variable type.

```
(WindowRef)userData
```

The ComputeResult function simply prints a debug message using the DebugStr function. DebugStr takes Pascal-style strings instead of C-style or Objective-C string objects. Pascal strings resemble C-style strings ("string") except they must always begin with \p ("\pstring"). Note that Carbon does provide functions such as c2pstrcpy that allow you to programmatically convert C strings to Pascal strings, although you shouldn't need to do that kind of thing if you are using newer Carbon API.

When you ran Carbon Email Formatter, you may have noticed your debug string didn't print if you switched between text fields using the tab key; it only printed if you switched fields using the mouse. For some reason, Carbon text fields don't send their action commands when you tab out of the text field. One solution to this problem would be to listen for keyboard events and call `ComputeResult` whenever a key is pressed.

Many of the functions here, both those you define and those you use, return `OSStatus` values to report problems within your application. When using Carbon you should pay careful attention to these error codes. Generally, when your program receives an error it should abort its current operation, whatever that may be. For example, when a program is writing to a file, and a write command fails, you should give up trying to write the file. In most cases, you will want to report a meaningful error message back to the user, through an alert panel.

At this point you have written the code that binds your controls' actions to your own source code. Cocoa provided this functionality for free (meaning, without requiring you to write code) through outlets and actions and through Cocoa Bindings. When working with Carbon interfaces you need to manage these details yourself. This example only touched on a few aspects of event handling in a Carbon application. If you need to learn more about handling events in Carbon, read the document entitled "Handling Carbon Events" within your online developer documentation. You can access this document through Xcode's Documentation interface.

In the next Try It Out, you write the code that extracts and replaces the strings in your user interface. This is the final step in making the Carbon Email Formatter example.

Try It Out   Working with Carbon Controls

1. Add the following function prototypes to `main.c`. Remember to add the code at the top of the file, just above the `main` function.

```
CFStringRef GetControlCFString(WindowRef window, int controlNum);
void SetTextViewCFString(WindowRef window, int controlNum, CFStringRef string);
```

2. Change the definition of the `ComputeResult` function to the following:

```
void ComputeResult(WindowRef window)
{
    CFStringRef firstName = GetControlCFString(window, kFirstNameFieldID);
    CFStringRef lastName = GetControlCFString(window, kLastNameFieldID);
    CFStringRef email = GetControlCFString(window, kEmailFieldID);

    if (firstName && lastName && email) {
        CFStringRef result = CFStringCreateWithFormat(kCFAllocatorDefault,
                                        NULL,
                                        CFSTR("%@ %@ <%@>"),
                                        firstName,
                                        lastName,
                                        email);

        if (result) {
            SetTextViewCFString(window, kResultTextID, result);
```

```
            CFRelease(result);
        }
    }
}
```

3. Add the following functions at the end of `main.c`:

```
// GetControlCFString is a helpful function for getting the text data out
// of a control.
CFStringRef GetControlCFString(WindowRef window, int controlNum)
{
    ControlID controlID = { kApplicationSignature, controlNum };
    ControlRef control = NULL;
    OSStatus err = noErr;
    CFStringRef string = NULL;

    // find the control in the specified window
    err = GetControlByID(window, &controlID, &control);
    if (err == noErr) {
        Size actualSize;

        // get a CFStringRef representing the control's contents
        err = GetControlData(control,
                             kControlEntireControl,
                             kControlEditTextCFStringTag,
                             sizeof(string),
                             &string,
                             &actualSize);

        if (err != noErr) {
            string = NULL;
        }
    }

    return string;
}

// SetTextViewCFString is a helpful function for setting a control's text data
// from a CFStringRef.
void SetTextViewCFString(WindowRef window, int controlNum, CFStringRef string)
{
    HIViewID viewID = { kApplicationSignature, controlNum };
    HIViewRef textView;
    OSStatus err = noErr;

    err = HIViewFindByID(HIViewGetRoot(window), viewID, &textView);
    if (err == noErr) {
        // create a temporary buffer to store our unicode characters. you need
        // to do this because the MLTE API (functions that begin with TXN)
        // do not accept CFStrings directly.
        CFIndex length = CFStringGetLength(string);
        UniChar *buffer = (UniChar *)malloc(length * sizeof(UniChar));

        if (buffer) {
// pull the UniCode characters out of the CFString
            CFRange range = {0, length};
```

```
                    CFStringGetCharacters(string, range, buffer);

                    // set the text view control
                    err = TXNSetData(HITextViewGetTXNObject(textView),
                                    kTXNUnicodeTextData,
                                    buffer,
                                    length * sizeof(UniChar),
                                    kTXNStartOffset,
                                    kTXNEndOffset);

                    // destroy the temporary buffer
                    free(buffer);
            }
        }
    }
```

4. Save your changes to main.c.

5. Compile and run Carbon Email Formatter. Note that when you change the text and click between the text fields, the result text view will update with the formatted email address.

How It Works

The new ComputeResult function resembles code found in the Email Formatter applications in Chapter 8: string data is pulled out of the controls, formatted into a new result string, which is recorded in a result text view. The main difference between this function and the earlier Cocoa examples is the use of the CFStringRef data type.

CFString API comes from the CoreFoundation framework, which provides C-level API for low-level system utilities, such as collection classes, file I/O, and XML parsing. Many data types defined by CoreFoundation resemble Objective-C objects vended by the Foundation framework, as shown in the following table. This similarity is intentional, because CoreFoundation was meant to provide Cocoa-like services to Carbon applications.

CoreFoundation Type	Foundation Object
CFArrayRef	NSArray
CFCharacterSetRef	NSCharacterSet
CFDataRef	NSData
CFDateRef	NSDate
CFDictionaryRef	NSDictionary
CFRunLoopTimerRef	NSRunLoopTimer
CFSetRef	NSSet
CFStringRef	NSString
CFTimeZone	NSTimeZone
CFURLRef	NSURL

CoreFoundation's architects took this similarity one step farther by making many CoreFoundation data types completely interchangeable with Foundation objects. In other words, you can pass certain Foundation objects into C functions that expect CoreFoundation data types, and you can send Objective-C messages to CoreFoundation data types as if they were Foundation objects. This symmetry is called *Toll-Free Bridging*, meaning you can use Foundation and CoreFoundation objects to bridge between Carbon and Cocoa without having to convert the data between the different types. You need to cast your object to the receiving type in order to keep the compiler happy; for example, you must cast an NSString object as a CFStringRef before you pass it into a function expecting a CFStringRef.

Not all objects can be bridged between CoreFoundation and Foundation. For example, a CFBundleRef, which manages how CoreFoundation works with file bundles, cannot be exchanged for NSBundle objects, which performs a similar task for Foundation. Only the objects listed in the preceding table can be shared using toll-free bridging.

You added a helper function called GetControlCFString for pulling data out of text fields. GetControlCFString first uses GetControlByID to get a ControlRef describing one of your program's text fields. GetControlByID looks for a control in a window that matches a particular ControlID, and returns a ControlRef representing that control. Your WindowRef value, window, found its way from the main function so you could use it here.

After you retrieved the ControlRef for the control, you used GetControlData to get the value of that control. GetControlData is a polymorphic accessor function that allows you to get data in one of several formats. GetControlData is defined by the following prototype:

```
OSErr GetControlData(ControlRef       inControl,
                     ControlPartCode  inPart,
                     ResType          inTagName,
                     Size             inBufferSize,
                     void *           inBuffer,
                     Size *           outActualSize);
```

GetControlData's first argument, inControl, is the control you want to work with. The inPart and inTagName arguments specify the data you are interested in retrieving. kControlEntireControl means you're interested in the overall value of the control, and kControlEditTextCFStringTag means you want to get text from the control as a CFStringRef. The last three arguments describe the GetControlData function's output. The inBufferSize argument stores the size of the inBuffer pointer passed in by the caller; in this case GetControlCFString is passing the address to a CFStringRef as the inBuffer, so inBufferSize is set to the size of the CFStringRef pointer (not to the size of the string data — remember the CFStringRef is opaque!). GetControlData will return the actual size required of the buffer to return the control data in its outActualSize parameter; although this is useful for programs that need to track raw buffers of information, you aren't really interested in that information here.

The GetControlData function returns an OSErr data type, which is an older precursor to the OSStatus type. You can safely assign OSErr values to OSStatus variables, and otherwise treat them just like OSStatus codes. In this case, if GetControlData fails for some reason, GetControlCFString will return NULL.

SetTextViewCFString works very much like GetControlCFString: first the routine finds the text view control, and then it sets the control's text to that in a CFStringRef. Unfortunately, HITextView objects behave differently from `ControlRef` objects, and you must use entirely different kinds of API to work with them. For example, you can look up an `HIView` object using `HIViewFindByID`:

```
OSStatus HIViewFindByID(HIViewRef    inStartView,
                        HIViewID     inID,
                        HIViewRef *  outControl);
```

`HIViewFindByID` looks for a view identified by an `HIViewID`, which is basically the same as a `ControlID`, and returns it in the `outControl` parameter. Instead of searching within an entire window, like `GetControlByID`, `HIViewFindByID` searches for views within another view. In this case you can simply get a `HIView` that represents the entire window's contents using the `HIViewGetRoot` function and pass that root view into `HIViewFindByID`.

After you have the `HITextView` object, you can set its contents to your `CFStringRef`. Unfortunately, `HITextView` doesn't currently support `CFStringRef` types directly. `HITextView` delegates all its text handling to an older Toolbox system called the *Multilingual Text Engine*, or MLTE. The MLTE API also doesn't consistently support the use of `CFStringRef` types when working with Unicode text; instead it prefers to work with raw `UniChar` arrays.

You can use the `CFStringGetCharacters` function to pull the individual `UniChar` values out of a `CFStringRef`. `CFStringGetCharacters` acts on a range of characters in the string, defined as a `CFRange`:

```
typedef struct {
    CFIndex location;
    CFIndex length;
} CFRange;
```

`CFRange` structs are described as a length of data starting at a specific location. You can refer to an entire string by creating a range that starts at location 0 and runs for the length of the string, as returned by `CFStringGetLength`. Your program dynamically allocates memory for your buffer in order to efficiently support arbitrary lengths of text; it simply uses the `malloc` and `free` system functions for managing this memory.

`SetTextViewCFString` uses the MLTE function `TXNSetData` to update the contents of the text view:

```
OSStatus TXNSetData(TXNObject     iTXNObject,
                    TXNDataType   iDataType,
                    const void *  iDataPtr,
                    ByteCount     iDataSize,
                    TXNOffset     iStartOffset,
                    TXNOffset     iEndOffset);
```

The first argument represents a `TXNObject` that stores text data and other layout information. You can get a `TXNObject` from your `HITextView` using the `HITextViewGetTXNObject` function. The next three rguments describe your data. You set the `iDataType` parameter to `kTXNUnicodeTextData` to tell the system you are working with Unicode text, and you passed the `UniChar` array and its size in as `iDataPtr` and `iDataSize` arguments. The last two arguments, `iStartOffset` and `iEndOffset`, allow you to specify a range of text within the `TXNObject` that will be modified; you can use the `kTXNStartOffset` and `kTXNEndOffset` values to refer to the entire contents of a `TXNObject`.

You now have seen how Carbon marshals data into and out of a few of its control types. Relatively simple operations, such as getting a string from a control, have expanded into a number of complicated function calls. If you need to work directly with Carbon controls, consult the Carbon Control Manager and HIToolbox documentation to learn more about how to use these functions.

Carbon File Manager

The original Mac operating system sought to make working with files as user friendly as possible. That meant favoring visual representations of file system data, such as folder and file icons, over the more traditional command-line access method. In fact, the operating system provided no command-line interface for selecting files of any kind; instead the user selected files and directories using open and save panels.

This philosophy extended into the Mac OS API as well. The Macintosh File Manager API was not built around a command-line interpreter. Instead the File Manager would identify files based on volume, directory, and file identifiers. Volumes were assigned a numeric value when they were discovered by the operating system. On HFS and HFS+ each file system directory had a unique number assigned to it. You could easily find any directory on a volume, no matter where it was, simply by referring to that number.

Over the years, the API evolved to make file references a little easier to work with. The Carbon API currently uses two kinds of structures to identify files: FSSpec and FSRef. While these structures are similar to each other in many ways, there are a few differences to keep in mind. Also, because the Carbon File Manager does not depend on file paths, it can track files on your local HFS disks even if they move. This feature is provided through aliases.

FSSpec and FSRef

System 7 introduced a single data type for referring to individual files or directories, and rolled out new routines that accepted this new data type. That data type was the FSSpec structure:

```
struct FSSpec {
    short       vRefNum;
    long        parID;
    Str63       name;
};
```

The FSSpec had a dramatic impact on other parts of the Toolbox from that period. All new file system features were written using FSSpec data types, such as the Alias files introduced by the System 7 Finder. Other libraries quickly adopted the FSSpec for managing files, such as QuickTime.

In general, the FSSpec served Mac OS quite well as a pathless mechanism for identifying files. But there were a few weaknesses in the data type that became apparent around the time Apple began the transition from traditional Mac OS to Mac OS X. One of the largest problems with the FSSpec type was its lack of Unicode character support for filenames. It was difficult to use FSSpec structures to create files in languages such as Japanese or Chinese without garbling the filename. Since Mac OS and Mac OS X were moving to support multiple localizations with a single operating system version, a replacement for FSSpec was needed.

Carbon introduced a new file type for referring to files to help solve some of these problems: `FSRef`.

```
struct FSRef {
  UInt8        hidden[80];
};
```

The `FSRef` type is opaque, but not in the same way as CoreFoundation objects. You can create `FSRef` objects on your program's stack, and you can dereference the `FSRef` structure. However, the `FSRef` is defined as being simply 80 bytes large; no other information is published regarding the `FSRef` format. That means you have no good way of interpreting the contents of an `FSRef` type yourself. Like other opaque data types, you must go through function calls to interpret and modify `FSRef` structures.

One of the advantages of `FSRef` is better support for Unicode filenames. You can use `FSRef` values to create files with international filenames. Also, the `FSRef` data type plays better with fully qualified file paths and URLs. For example, it's a simple matter to convert an `FSRef` structure to a `CFURLRef` and vice versa.

But the `FSRef` is not a general replacement for `FSSpec`. You can use an `FSSpec` to refer to a file that doesn't exist yet; therefore, you can create a new file using an `FSSpec` function like `FSpCreate`. But `FSRef` types must refer to files and directories that already exist, and file creation works by passing an `FSRef` to a directory along with a new filename. Another disadvantage of relying on `FSRef` is that it still isn't as widely used as `FSSpec` is. This is especially a problem when working with older API that predates Carbon, such as QuickTime. Ultimately, programmers who need to talk to Carbon API on Mac OS X will need to be familiar with using both `FSSpec` and `FSRef` structures for referring to files.

You see a few examples of `FSSpec` and `FSRef` types in action throughout the remainder of this chapter. If you want to dig deeper into the features of these types, consult the Carbon File Manager documentation on your system.

Aliases

The Finder allows you to create aliases of files on your disk. These aliases could stand in for files or folders that reside elsewhere, even on AppleShare file servers, and when you double-click the alias, the original file opens instead. Aliases will also do their best to find the file if the original is moved somewhere else on the same volume. Although aliases appear to be a file system feature, on Mac OS X they really are a feature of the Carbon File Manager.

Applications can take advantage of aliases' ability to locate files for keeping track of documents and document data. For example, Cocoa uses aliases to track entries in document-based applications' Open Recent menus. If you save a file out of TextEdit, rename the file in the Finder, and go to TextEdit's File ⇨ Open Recent menu, the file appears in the list with its new name.

Some documents also refer to other files. For example, an Xcode project refers to various source files. Also, the Slide Master slide show document refers to a number of individual graphic files. Such documents have to deal with the possibility that one of these external files might no longer exist: The user may have moved or renamed the file, or deleted it completely! If a document uses alias data to refer to a file instead of file paths, the application might be able to handle some of these situations automatically.

In the following Try It Out example, you change Slide Master's slide show file format to track image files using aliases. This allows the slide show file to track down images that are moved or renamed on their local HFS volume. Because Cocoa generally prefers to identify files by path, you need to convert the alias data into paths to actually open your image files.

Try It Out   Storing and Resolving Aliases

1. In Xcode, open the Slide Master project from Chapter 8.

2. Add the Carbon framework to your project by choosing Project ⇨ Add To Project. Select /System/Library/Frameworks/Carbon.framework in the Open panel and make sure the Copy Items Into Destination Group's Folder button is not checked.

3. Create new source files of Cocoa Objective-C class type, named Alias.h and Alias.m.

4. Open Alias.h and replace its contents with the following code:

```
#import <Foundation/Foundation.h>
#import <Carbon/Carbon.h>

@interface Alias : NSObject <NSCoding>
{
    AliasHandle mAliasHandle;
}

- (Alias*)initWithPath:(NSString*)path;

- (NSString*)path;

@end
```

5. Open Alias.m and add the following code:

```
#import "Alias.h"

@implementation Alias

- (Alias*)initWithPath:(NSString*)path
{
    self = [super init];

    if (self) {
        FSRef target;
        OSStatus err;

        // convert this path to an FSRef so you can call Carbon File Manager
        // routines.
        err = FSPathMakeRef([path UTF8String], &target, NULL);

        // create a new alias
        if (err == noErr) {
            err = FSNewAlias(NULL, &target, &mAliasHandle);
        }
    }
```

```objc
        return self;
}

- (void)dealloc
{
    if (mAliasHandle) {
        DisposeHandle((Handle)mAliasHandle);
    }

    [super dealloc];
}

- (NSString*)path
{
    NSString *path = nil;
    FSRef target;
    Boolean wasChanged;

    // resolve this alias and return the result into a Carbon FSRef
    OSStatus err = FSResolveAlias(NULL, mAliasHandle, &target, &wasChanged);

    // initialize a UTF8 buffer from the FSRef's path
    if (err == noErr) {
        UInt8 buffer[PATH_MAX];

        err = FSRefMakePath(&target, buffer, PATH_MAX);

        // create a new path string from the UTF8 buffer
        if (err == noErr) {
            path = [NSString stringWithUTF8String:buffer];
        }
    }

    return path;
}

#pragma mark NSCoding Protocol

- (id)initWithCoder:(NSCoder *)decoder
{
    self = [super init];
    if (self) {
        NSData *aliasData;

        // decode our alias data
        if ([decoder allowsKeyedCoding]) {
            aliasData = [decoder decodeObjectForKey:@"AliasHandle"];
        } else {
            aliasData = [decoder decodeObject];
        }

        // convert the alias data into an alias handle
        if (aliasData) {
```

```
                    mAliasHandle = (AliasHandle)NewHandle([aliasData length]);

                    if (mAliasHandle) {
                        [aliasData getBytes:*mAliasHandle];
                    }
            }

            // if an error happened, destroy the object and return nil
            if (!mAliasHandle) {
                [self autorelease];
                self = nil;
            }
        }
    }
    return self;
}

- (void)encodeWithCoder:(NSCoder *)encoder
{
    // create an NSData object of our alias data
    NSData *aliasData;

    aliasData = [NSData dataWithBytes:*mAliasHandle
                             length:GetHandleSize((Handle)mAliasHandle)];

    // encode our alias data
    if ([encoder allowsKeyedCoding]) {
        [encoder encodeObject:aliasData forKey:@"AliasHandle"];
    } else {
        [encoder encodeObject:aliasData];
    }
}

@end
```

6. Open `Slide.h` and replace the existing definition of the `Slide` class with the code that follows. Note that the `Slide` class now uses an `Alias` object to refer to slides instead of an `NSString`.

```
#import <Foundation/Foundation.h>

@class Alias;

@interface Slide : NSObject <NSCoding>
{
    Alias        *mAlias;
    NSImage      *mImage;
}

- (id)initWithPath:(NSString*)filePath;
- (id)initWithAlias:(Alias*)alias;

- (NSString*)filePath;
- (NSImage*)image;

@end
```

7. Switch to Slide.m and replace its contents with the following code:

```objc
#import "Slide.h"

#import "Alias.h"

@implementation Slide

- (id)initWithPath:(NSString*)filePath
{
    Alias *alias = [[[Alias alloc] initWithPath:filePath] autorelease];

    return [self initWithAlias:alias];
}

- (id)initWithAlias:(Alias*)alias
{
    self = [super init];
    if (self) {
        mAlias = [alias retain];
    }
    return self;
}

- (void)dealloc
{
    [mAlias release];
    [mImage release];

    [super dealloc];
}

- (NSString*)filePath
{
    return [mAlias path];
}

- (NSImage*)image
{
    if (!mImage) {
        mImage = [[NSImage alloc] initWithContentsOfFile:[self filePath]];
    }

    return mImage;
}

#pragma mark NSCoding Protocol

- (id)initWithCoder:(NSCoder *)decoder
{
    NSString *path;

    if ([decoder allowsKeyedCoding]) {
        // if you have an alias, use that.
        Alias *alias = [decoder decodeObjectForKey:@"Alias"];
```

```
        if (alias) {
            return [self initWithAlias:alias];
        } else {
            // otherwise, you must be looking at an older version of a slide
            // show document that stores paths. Read the path data.
            NSString *path = [decoder decodeObjectForKey:@"Slides"];
            return [self initWithPath:path];
        }
    } else {
        // Slides only support paths in flat archives.
        path = [decoder decodeObject];
        return [self initWithPath:path];
    }

    // not a valid Slide object.
    [self autorelease];
    return nil;
}

- (void)encodeWithCoder:(NSCoder *)encoder
{
    if ([encoder allowsKeyedCoding]) {
        [encoder encodeObject:mAlias forKey:@"Alias"];
    } else {
        [encoder encodeObject:[self filePath]];
    }
}

@end
```

8. Save your changes to the Alias and Slide files.

9. Build and run the Slide Master project. You should be able to open any existing path-based slide shows created earlier.

10. Create a new slide show document, add some files, save, and close it. In Finder, rename some of the image files. Then reopen the slide show. Slide Master should find all the images, including the files you renamed.

How It Works

The Alias class provides an Objective-C wrapper around an AliasHandle returned by Carbon File Manager's alias handling API. As its name implies, an AliasHandle is a specific kind of Handle. You can create an AliasHandle using the function FSNewAlias, which like most modern Carbon File Manager functions takes FSRef data types as input.

You can use the FSPathMakeRef function to initialize an FSRef variable from a file path:

```
OSStatus FSPathMakeRef(const UInt8 *path,
                       FSRef *ref,
                       Boolean *isDirectory);
```

The `path` argument takes a string like those returned by POSIX file paths. The `ref` argument contains the address of the `FSRef` variable you want to initialize. If `FSPathMakeRef` succeeds, that `FSRef` will refer to the file pointed to by `path`. You can use the `isDirectory` parameter to quickly find out if the path points to a directory or a file; if you don't need that information you can pass `NULL` instead of an address to a `Boolean` variable.

Getting a file path from an `FSRef` is a little more complicated, only because you need to have some memory handy to store the new path. It comes down to one function call, `FSRefMakePath`:

```
OSStatus FSRefMakePath(const FSRef *ref,
                       UInt8 *path,
                       UInt32 maxPathSize);
```

Again the `ref` argument is the address of an `FSRef` value, this time used as input to the function. The resulting path will be copied into a character buffer pointed to by the `path` argument. You will need to make sure this buffer already exists, either as a C character array, or as a piece of memory created through `malloc` or some other allocation function. When initializing path data from an `FSRef` the `Alias` object uses a C character array to hold the path data. The array is defined to be `PATH_MAX` bytes long. This value comes from Darwin headers, and represents the maximum number of bytes allowed in a pathname. The `maxPathSize` argument tells `FSRefMakePath` how much room is available to store in the `path` buffer. If there isn't enough room to store the entire path, `FSRefMakePath` will return an error of `pathTooLongErr` (-2110) and leave `path` unmodified.

The `FSNewAlias` function takes two `FSRef` parameters as input and returns a new `AliasHandle`:

```
OSErr FSNewAlias(const FSRef *fromFile,
                 const FSRef *target,
                 AliasHandle *inAlias);
```

The `fromFile` parameter allows you to create aliases that start in a specific directory. You can use this value to build aliases that function like relative paths. You may set this value to `NULL` if you want to create aliases relative to the volume's root directory. The `target` argument is the `FSRef` you want to build an alias of. If the function succeeds, it will return a newly allocated `AliasHandle` in the `inAlias` value.

Although Carbon supplies a special function for creating `AliasHandle` types, aliases really are just `Handles`. You can safely copy data out of these handles and store them in other ways, and you can dispose of handles using the general `DisposeHandle` function. Recall that a `Handle` data type is really a pointer type that points to another pointer.

The `Alias` class knows how to encode itself using Foundation's `NSCoding` protocol. It does this by storing its `AliasHandle` data in an `NSData` object. You can't just encode the pointer to the `AliasHandle` in the `NSData` object; this could result in an `NSData` object that refers to a handle that hasn't been allocated, leading ultimately to a crash. Instead you simply encode the handle's data. The `GetHandleSize` function returns the size of a handle in bytes. This information, as well as the `Handle` address itself, is enough to create a new `NSData` object. You can make a new `AliasHandle` from an `NSData` object by creating a new handle large enough to hold the `NSData`'s contents, and copying the data into the new `AliasHandle`.

The `Slide` object changed to use `Alias` objects to store an image file's location on disk. `Slide` objects can ask an `Alias` object for its path to actually read the data, so those changes are all fairly simple. The only complication is a version of Slide Master existed that stored full paths to image data instead of aliases. If you want to be able to read those older slide show files you need to continue to support decoding slides from path. This adds a little bit of complexity to Slide's initWithCoder: method. Note that Slide Master now creates only newer alias-based project files. As long as Slide Master can read the old file format, there's no reason to perpetuate it moving forward.

Working with QuickTime

The QuickTime framework is built into Mac OS X as the standard way of playing audio and video media. QuickTime has been around a long time and is packed with a lot of different multimedia features. Because QuickTime was originally designed to run on Systems 6 and 7, most of its API uses Carbon data types and calling conventions. For example, on Mac OS X 10.3 Panther, QuickTime commonly uses FSSpec types for referring to files, and it uses Handle types for passing information into and out of movies and other pieces of media.

QuickTime also heavily depends on QuickDraw, the original Mac OS graphics environment. Although Mac OS X's native 2D graphics library is CoreGraphics, QuickDraw is available on Mac OS X as a transition tool for older Macintosh software, including QuickTime and other applications. QuickDraw was designed to perform very well, even on systems without a lot of memory or systems without a lot of CPU power. On the other hand, QuickDraw does not allow for floating point geometric coordinates or native support for transparency in the same way as CoreGraphics.

The newest release of Mac OS X, 10.4 "Tiger," includes a number of architectural changes to QuickTime. First, a new library called QTKit provides a Cocoa interface for working with QuickTime. This allows Cocoa programmers to work with QuickTime without having to know about Carbon or its programming conventions. Second, Apple is transitioning QuickTime onto CoreGraphics as its 2D imaging model; this means that under the covers QuickTime can stop relying on QuickDraw functions or data structures. This is especially important because Apple also announced that with Mac OS X 1.4, it has stopped actively investing in QuickDraw development. So it seems the time has come for Carbon apps in general to move toward CoreGraphics for drawing. Of course, for applications that must run on Mac OS X 10.3 Panther, or earlier versions of Mac OS X, you still need to use Carbon/QuickDraw when working with QuickTime. And certain QuickTime features, such as writing custom codecs, may be available only through the older C interface, at least for the time being.

You will find a lot of documentation and sample code available for QuickTime, both locally on your computer and on the Internet. These examples will help you navigate through the more than 2,000 functions that make up the QuickTime API. If you aren't satisfied by the QuickTime API documentation, or it's not clear from the documentation how a function should be used, you can find an example that uses that function and study how it works.

In the following example, you add the capability to create QuickTime movies from Slide Master. You perform this task in several steps:

❑   First you add a method to the Slide class that draws the slide's contents into a GWorld.

❑   Then you add three functions that build up a QuickTime movie from a series of GWorld images. Each function is broken out into separate steps, so they are easier to digest.

❑   Finally you write the controller code in SlideShowDocument that ties the whole command together.

Work through the following Try It Out for a more in-depth example of this process.

Try It Out   **Drawing into a GWorld**

1. In Xcode, add the QuickTime framework to your Slide Master project by choosing Project ⇨ Add To Project. Select /System/Library/Frameworks/QuickTime.framework in the Open panel, and make sure the Copy Items Into Destination Group's Folder button is not checked.

2. Open `Slide.h` and import the `Carbon/Carbon.h` header file near the top of the file. The following code shows the file added after the Cocoa header:

```
#import <Cocoa/Cocoa.h>
#import <Carbon/Carbon.h>
```

3. Add the following method to the `@interface` block:

```
- (OSStatus)drawIntoGWorld:(GWorldPtr)world;
```

4. Switch to `Slide.m` and add the following method:

```
- (OSStatus)drawIntoGWorld:(GWorldPtr)world
{
    GWorldPtr oldWorld;
    GDHandle gdh;
    NSString *path;
    FSSpec fsSpec;
    GraphicsImportComponent importer = NULL;
    ImageDescriptionHandle imageDesc = NULL;
    OSStatus err;
    Rect bounds;

    // set this GWorld to be the current QuickDraw port
    GetGWorld(&oldWorld, &gdh);
    SetGWorld(world, NULL);

    // get the current bounds for this world.
    GetPortBounds(world, &bounds);

    // clear the world so you're starting from a clean slate
    EraseRect(&bounds);

    // build a FSSpec for this image
    path = [self filePath];
    if (path) {
        FSRef fsRef;

        err = FSPathMakeRef([path UTF8String], &fsRef, NULL);

        if (err == noErr) {
            err = FSGetCatalogInfo(&fsRef,
                                   kFSCatInfoNone,
                                   NULL,
                                   NULL,
                                   &fsSpec,
                                   NULL);
        }
    } else {
```

```
        err = fnfErr;
    }

    // open the file with a QuickTime GraphicsImporter
    if (err == noErr) {
        err = GetGraphicsImporterForFile(&fsSpec, &importer);
    }

    // get information about the graphic, including its size
    if (err == noErr) {
        err = GraphicsImportGetImageDescription(importer, &imageDesc);
    }

    // center the image within the world
    bounds.left = ((bounds.right - bounds.left) - (*imageDesc)->width) / 2;
    bounds.right = bounds.left + (*imageDesc)->width;
    bounds.top = ((bounds.bottom - bounds.top) - (*imageDesc)->height) / 2;
    bounds.bottom = bounds.top + (*imageDesc)->height;

    GraphicsImportSetBoundsRect(importer, &bounds);

    // draw the image into the new GWorld
    if (err == noErr) {
        err = GraphicsImportDraw(importer);
    }

    // tear down the image description and importer
    if (imageDesc) {
        DisposeHandle((Handle)imageDesc);
    }
    if (importer) {
        CloseComponent(importer);
    }

    // restore the previous QuickDraw port
    SetGWorld(oldWorld, gdh);

    return err;
}
```

5. Save your changes to `Slide.h` and `Slide.m`.

6. Build and Run your project. The `drawIntoGWorld:` method hasn't been hooked up to anything yet, so you can't really test these changes. You add the code that eventually calls this method in the examples that follow. For now, you can make sure the new code compiles, and verify nothing broke during the editing process by running and using Slide Master.

How It Works

All QuickDraw drawing takes place within *ports*. A QuickDraw port is basically a drawing environment capable of rendering QuickDraw commands. Ports are stored using a `GrafPtr` or `CGrafPtr` data type, and are normally associated with specific windows or views. You can draw into a port by activating the port, or *setting* it, and then issuing QuickDraw commands. Recall from earlier that all QuickDraw drawing is relative to the upper-left corner; this is different from Cocoa drawing, which is relative to the lower-left corner.

A GWorld is a special kind of QuickDraw port useful for off-screen drawing. Although GWorlds use a specific data type, GWorldPtr, they are conceptually similar to other port types and can be treated as ports in most situations. You can set the current GWorld using the SetGWorld function call, as in the following pseudocode example:

```
GWorldPtr oldGWorld;
GDHandle oldGDHandle;
GWorldPtr newGWorld;

// initialize newGWorld with some value

GetGWorld(&oldGWorld, &oldGDhandle);
SetGWorld(newGWorld, NULL);

// do your drawing

SetGWorld(oldGWorld, oldGDHandle);
```

When setting a GWorld, it's good practice to save the current GWorld. You should then restore the previous GWorld when you are done drawing. You can use the GetGWorld function for this purpose. Both GetGWorld and SetGWorld take a GDHandle variable as a second argument, which is a Handle to a GDevice structure. When using SetGWorld to set an off-screen GWorld, you are supposed to pass NULL in as the GDHandle parameter.

Although the Slide object already has access to its image in an NSImage object, Mac OS X does not provide an easy, foolproof way to draw an NSImage into a QuickDraw port. Rather than go down that road, drawIntoGWorld: instead re-opens and draws the file using QuickTime's GraphicsImporter API. Aside from the functions for creating and destroying GraphicsImportComponent types, all the functions in this family begin with GraphicsImporter. Some common functions appear in the following table.

Function	Description
GetGrahpicsImporterForFile	Creates a new GraphicsImportComponent instance for working with the specified file. Files are specified as FSSpec structures. QuickTime will do all the work of figuring out what kind of file you have and how to interpret its data.
CloseComponent	Releases resources used by a GraphicsImportComponent, including freeing memory and closing files.
GraphicsImportGetImageDescription	Returns information about the image, such as its size and bit-depth, in an ImageDescriptionHandle.
GraphicsImportSetBounds	Sets a specific rectangle the GraphicsImportComponent should draw into when the time comes. By default, the image will be drawn at 0,0.

Table continued on following page

Function	Description
`GraphicsImportSetGWorld`	Associates a specific GWorld with the `GraphicsImportComponent`. You can use this function to draw into a GWorld without first setting it. Be sure to set the GWorld before calling `GraphicsImportDraw`.
`GraphicsImportDraw`	Draws the image. If the `GraphicsImportComponent` has a GWorld (`GraphicsImportSetGWorld` was called) it will draw into that GWorld. Otherwise, `GraphicsImportDraw` will draw into the current port.

Since `GetGraphicsImporterForFile` requires an `FSSpec` file reference, you must initialize the `FSSpec` from your file path. One way to do this is first convert the file path to an `FSRef` structure, and then use the `FSGetCatalogInfo` function to return the `FSSpec` for that `FSRef`. Remember that because `FSRef` types can refer only to existing files, this approach works only when you're sure the file already exists. Also, `FSGetCatalogInfo` is a useful function for getting a bunch of other useful information out of the Carbon File Manager, such as the file's type and creator, its modification time, and other tidbits.

The `drawIntoGWorld:` method will draw the image into the GWorld at its full scale. If the image is smaller than the GWorld, `drawIntoGWorld:` will use `GraphicsImportSetBounds` to center the image in the GWorld. If the image is too big, the image will still be centered, but the edges will be cropped out of frame.

In the following Try It Out, you add the code that creates a new QuickTime movie.

Try It Out   Creating a New QuickTime Movie

1. In Xcode, create new source files of type Carbon C File, named `QuickTimeMovie.c` and `QuickTimeMovie.h`. If you like, move these files into the Other Sources group within the Slide Master project.

2. Open `QuickTimeMovie.h` and replace its contents with the following:

```
#include <Carbon/Carbon.h>
#include <QuickTime/QuickTime.h>

typedef OSStatus (*SaveImageMovieCallback)(TimeScale timeScale, int imageNumber,
                                           GWorldPtr world, void *userData,
                                           TimeValue *duration);

OSStatus SaveImageMovie(CFURLRef url, Rect frame, TimeScale timeScale,
                        int numberOfImages, SaveImageMovieCallback callback,
                        void *userData);
```

3. Switch to `QuickTimeMovie.c` and replace its contents with the following:

```c
#include "QuickTimeMovie.h"

#pragma mark Function Prototypes

static OSStatus BuildImageVideoTrack(Movie movie, Rect frame,
                                     TimeScale timeScale, int numberOfImages,
                                     SaveImageMovieCallback callback,
                                     void *userData);
static OSStatus BuildImageVideoSamples(Media media, Rect frame,
                                       TimeScale timeScale, int numberOfImages,
                                       SaveImageMovieCallback callback,
                                       void *userData);
static CFIndex GetURLBytes(CFURLRef url, UInt8 *buffer, CFIndex length);

#pragma mark Function Definitions

// SaveImageMovie builds a QuickTime movie and saves it to 'url'. Individual
// frames are provided through a callback function:
//
// SaveImageMovieCallback(TimeScale timeScale, int imageNumber, GWorldPtr world,
// void *userData, TimeValue *duration);
//
// Callers should supply a callback function that does the following:
//
//   1. Draws the specified image into the supplied GWorld. Images are specified
//      by numeric index, beginning with 0 and ending with numberOfImages - 1.
//   2. Return the duration for this image, expressed as a time value in the
//      supplied TimeScale. This allows frames to display at a different rate.

OSStatus SaveImageMovie(CFURLRef url, Rect frame, TimeScale timeScale,
                        int numberOfImages, SaveImageMovieCallback callback,
                        void *userData)
{
    OSStatus err = noErr;
    int urlSize;
    Handle dataRef = NULL;
    OSType dataRefType;
    long createMovieFileFlags = createMovieFileDeleteCurFile | newMovieActive;
    DataHandler dataHandler = NULL;
    Movie movie;

    // create a new dataRef from the URL data. make sure the URL is 0 terminated.
    urlSize = GetURLBytes(url, NULL, 0);
    dataRef = NewHandle(urlSize + 1);
    if (dataRef) {
        GetURLBytes(url, *dataRef, urlSize);
        (*dataRef)[urlSize] = 0;
        dataRefType = URLDataHandlerSubType;
    } else {
        err = memFullErr;
    }
```

```
        // create a new movie file opened for writing at this location
        if (err == noErr) {
            err = CreateMovieStorage (dataRef,
                                      dataRefType,
                                      'TVOD',
                                      smCurrentScript,
                                      createMovieFileFlags,
                                      &dataHandler,
                                      &movie);
        }

        // set the movie timescale
        SetMovieTimeScale(movie, timeScale);

        // create the movie video track
        if (err == noErr) {
            err = BuildImageVideoTrack(movie, frame, timeScale, numberOfImages,
                                       callback, userData);
        }

        // if you succeeded copy the movie data into its storage. otherwise, delete
        // the data handler's file
        if (err == noErr) {
            AddMovieToStorage(movie, dataHandler);
        } else {
            DataHDeleteFile(dataHandler);
        }

        // clean up open memory structures
        if (dataRef) {
            DisposeHandle(dataRef);
        }
        if (dataHandler) {
            CloseMovieStorage(dataHandler);
        }
        if (movie) {
            DisposeMovie(movie);
        }

    return err;
}

static OSStatus BuildImageVideoTrack(Movie movie, Rect frame,
                                     TimeScale timeScale, int numberOfImages,
                                     SaveImageMovieCallback callback,
                                     void *userData)
{
    return noErr;
}

static OSStatus BuildImageVideoSamples(Media media, Rect frame,
                                       TimeScale timeScale, int numberOfImages,
```

```
                                                     SaveImageMovieCallback callback,
                                                     void *userData)
{
    return noErr;
}

// GetURLBytes behaves like CFURLGetBytes except that it returns fully
// qualified URLs (i.e., "file:///Users/Shared/foo.txt") instead of just the
// path section (i.e., "/Users/Shared/foo.txt").
static CFIndex GetURLBytes(CFURLRef url, UInt8 *buffer, CFIndex length)
{
    CFStringRef string = CFURLGetString(url);
    CFIndex lengthUsed = 0;

    if (string) {
        CFRange range = CFRangeMake(0, CFStringGetLength(string));

        // do the conversion. This will just set size if buffer is NULL.
        CFStringGetBytes(string,
                         range,
                         kCFStringEncodingUTF8,
                         0,
                         false,
                         buffer,
                         length,
                         &lengthUsed);
    }

    return lengthUsed;
}
```

4. Save the changes to `QuickTimeMovie.h` and `QuickTimeMovie.c`.

5. Build and Run your project. The `SaveImageMovie` function hasn't yet been hooked up to anything, so you can't really test these changes. But you can make sure the new code compiles, and that nothing else broke during the editing process.

How It Works

The QuickTime API is meant to be extensible and general purpose. The key to this versatility is the careful use of data structures that break multimedia data up into its component pieces. These pieces include *movies*, *tracks*, *samples*, and *codecs*.

The *movie* sits at the top-level of this abstraction. QuickTime movie files are simply containers that hold data. For example, a movie might store video, an audio stream, text information such as subtitles, or all these things at once. QuickTime uses the `Movie` data type for working with movies.

A movie may contain one or more *tracks*, each one containing a particular kind of information. A track's primary job is to reference *media*, which simply put is the data the movie is composed of. Each track has a sense of what kind of media it references. For example, many QuickTime movies, such as trailers for feature films, contain two tracks: a video track and an audio track. QuickTime uses the `Track` data type for working with tracks. Also, QuickTime uses a second data type, `Media`, for gathering up all the media referenced by a track. Each `Track` will have one `Media` associated with it.

QuickTime media is organized into discrete *samples*, or individual units of track data. For example, a video track is normally composed of a series of frames, where each frame is stored as a distinct sample in that video track. Ultimately, samples are just pieces of data, and QuickTime uses `Handle` structures for storing sample data.

The track media is responsible for decoding sample data in a meaningful way, such as rendering an image from JPEG data, or converting compressed audio into a raw waveform that can be played back by your speakers. Tracks rely on *codecs* to perform these conversions. Codecs are specialized pieces of software that are capable of compressing and/or decompressing data in specific formats. Although you can work with QuickTime codecs directly through `ComponentInstance` data types, you more often work with codecs at a higher level, such as the QuickTime `Media` type or the `GraphicsImporter` system.

The process of building a new QuickTime movie in memory involves working with all these pieces, in one way or another. The high-level steps you followed in this example, first creating a movie, then creating a track, then populating the track with media samples, and so on, are fairly standard between QuickTime programs. If you browse through sample QuickTime programs you will see these same steps over and over again with slight variations. In fact, QuickTime itself follows these basic steps when reading a movie file from disk.

There are a lot of individual things to keep track of when building a QuickTime movie. This example broke up this task into separate functions: `SaveImageMovie`, `BuildImageVideoTrack`, `BuildImageVideoSamples`, and the `SaveImageMovieCallback` callback function. Splitting up the program makes the problem a little easier to understand. Also, these functions mimic the division between the movie, track, media, and samples.

The `SaveImageMovie` function creates new `Movie` and an associated file on disk. QuickTime provides a number of functions for creating new QuickTime files, but many of the more common ones, such as `CreateMovieFile`, rely on `FSSpec` types for specifying files. While Slide Master does have some code to convert file paths into `FSSpec` types, it does so through the `FSRef` type, which means Slide Master cannot build an `FSSpec` for a file that doesn't exist yet. Rather than tackle that problem head on, Slide Master instead used a more flexible function for creating movie files, `CreateMovieStorage`:

```
OSErr CreateMovieStorage(Handle        dataRef,
                         OSType        dataRefType,
                         OSType        creator,
                         ScriptCode    scriptTag,
                         long          createMovieFileFlags,
                         DataHandler * outDataHandler,
                         Movie *       newmovie);
```

`CreateMovieStorage`'s first four arguments, `dataRef`, `dataRefType`, `creator`, and `scriptTag`, refer to the new movie file. Together, `dataRef` and `dataRefType` refer to a `DataHandler`, which is another versatile QuickTime abstraction used for describing sources of data that can be read from somewhere. For example, a `DataHandler` might refer to a file on disk, a network stream, or even a buffer of memory. The `dataRef` argument is a `Handle`, the contents of which will depend on `dataRefType`, which is expressed as an `OSType` code. Slide Master uses `URLDataHandlerSubType` data refs, which are `Handles` composed of fully qualified, `NULL` terminated URL strings.

The `creator` argument takes a 4-byte creator code to associate with the new file. `'TVOD'` is the creator code for QuickTime Player. The `createMovieFileFlags` argument describes the script in which the new file should be created. Slide Master uses `smCurrentScript` to refer to the current script.

The createMovieFileFlags argument is a bitmap field that you can use to influence the behavior of CreateMovieStorage. Individual flag values can be combined using the bitwise OR operator: |. SaveImageMovie sets two flags: createMovieFileDeleteCurFile and newMovieActivate. The first flag, createMovieFileDeleteCurFile, tells CreateMovieStorage to delete the target file if it already exists; this allows the users to overwrite a movie if they choose. The second flag, newMovieActivate, tells CreateMovieStorage to activate the new movie structure, which makes it available to other parts of QuickTime.

On success, the CreateMovieStorage function returns two pieces of data: the DataHandler that refers to the new movie file, and a Movie type that refers to the new movie data. You use the Movie value to build the new QuickTime movie in memory, and then write that movie to file using the DataHandler value.

QuickTime uses TimeScale and TimeValue variables to precisely control events in a movie. Every sample in a QuickTime movie is tagged with a unique duration (because each sample could have a different duration, it's best not to think of QuickTime movies has having fixed frame rates). These sample durations are integer TimeValue values relative to a common integer TimeScale encoded in the sample's Media instance. The TimeScale represents the number of time units in a second. For example, a TimeScale of 600 means there are 600 units of time per second. A TimeValue is expressed in terms of its TimeScale. A sample with a duration of 20 time units on a 600 time unit per second track will be displayed for 20 / 600 seconds, or 1/30 of a second. SaveImageMovie uses SetMovieTimeScale to set a TimeScale for the Movie itself.

Once the Movie has been initialized, its contents are synched with the file on disk using a function called AddMovieToStorage. Although you need to call this function when working with movies created from CreateMovieStorage, it's not necessary when using CreateMovieFile. Once the movie has been written to disk, you are done. Don't forget to free your data structures if you don't need them any more.

In the next Try It Out example, you write code that creates a new video track and adds it to your QuickTime movie.

Try It Out   **Creating a New Video Track**

1. In QuickTimeMovie.c, replace the BuildImageVideoTrack with the following:

```
// BuildImageVideoTrack adds a video track and video media handler to the
// specified QuickTime movie. It will delegate adding images to the movie
// to BuildImageVideoSamples below.
static OSStatus BuildImageVideoTrack(Movie movie, Rect frame,
                                     TimeScale timeScale, int numberOfImages,
                                     SaveImageMovieCallback callback,
                                     void *userData)
{
    Track track = NULL;
    Media media = NULL;
    OSStatus err = noErr;

    // create a new track
    track = NewMovieTrack(movie,
                          IntToFixed(frame.right - frame.left),
                          IntToFixed(frame.bottom - frame.top),
```

```
                            kNoVolume);
    if (!track) {
        err = GetMoviesError();
    }

    // create a new media container for handling video content
    if (err == noErr) {
        media = NewTrackMedia(track,
                              VideoMediaType,
                              timeScale,
                              NULL,
                              0);
        if (!media) {
            err = GetMoviesError();
        }
    }

    // begin editing
    if (err == noErr) {
        err = BeginMediaEdits(media);
    }

    // add images to the movie
    if (err == noErr) {
        err = BuildImageVideoSamples(media, frame, timeScale, numberOfImages,
                                     callback, userData);
    }

    // finish editing
    if (err == noErr) {
        err = EndMediaEdits(media);
    }

    // insert the media into the track
    if (err == noErr) {
        err = InsertMediaIntoTrack(track,
                                   0,
                                   0,
                                   GetMediaDuration(media),
                                   fixed1);
    }

    return err;
}
```

2. Save your changes to `QuickTimeMovie.c`.

3. Build and Run your project. Although `BuildImageVideoTrack` will be called by `SaveImageMovie`, the `SaveImageMovie` function hasn't yet been hooked up to anything, so you can't really test these changes. But you can make sure the new code compiles and that nothing else broke during the editing process.

How It Works

Slide Master uses `BuildImageVideoTrack` to add a video track to the new movie. First you must create the track, using `NewMovieTrack`:

```
Track NewMovieTrack(Movie    theMovie,
                    Fixed    width,
                    Fixed    height,
                    short    trackVolume);
```

The `NewMovieTrack` function returns a new `Track` value from a movie, the frame width and height, and a volume setting. For video tracks like this one, you can pass `kNoVolume` in as the volume; for audio tracks, you can pass `kFullVolume` to play the data at your computer's normal volume setting.

The `width` and `height` values are *fixed-precision* floating-point values and are expressed as `Fixed` types. Fixed-precision refers to a way of storing floating-point values using integer data structures. This can provide better performance on CPUs where integer arithmetic is dramatically faster than floating-point arithmetic, and also help avoid binary representation issues found in floating-point types, although both of these advantages come at the cost of precision. Carbon provides a number of functions and macros for dealing with `Fixed` values, most of which are documented in Carbon's Mathematical and Logical Utilities API reference. `BuildImageVideoTrack` uses the `IntToFixed` macro from Carbon's `FixMath.h` header to convert integer values into `Fixed` values; `BuildImageVideoTrack` also uses the `fixed1` macro to get a fixed-precision representation of the number 1.

Once you have a `Track` you can create a `Media` instance, using `NewTrackMedia`:

```
Media NewTrackMedia(Track        theTrack,
                    OSType       mediaType,
                    TimeScale    timeScale,
                    Handle       dataRef,
                    OSType       dataRefType);
```

The `mediaType` identifies `Media` (and thus the `Track`) as referring to a specific kind of data, such as audio or video data. `BuildImageVideoTrack` uses the `VideoMediaType` value provided by QuickTime to tag this as a video track. The `timeScale` argument specifies the time scale for this video track; all the samples in the track will use this time scale. `BuildImageVideoTrack` uses the same `timeScale` as used for the movie time scale in `SaveImageMovie`. You can use the `dataRef` and `dataRefType` arguments to refer to sample data in other files without copying the samples into your own movie. Because Slide Master creates self-contained movie files, `BuildImageVideoTrack` sets these values to `NULL` and 0 respectively.

If either `NewMovieTrack` or `NewTrackMedia` fails, they return `NULL`. You can get a specific error code from QuickTime using the `GetMoviesError` function. In fact, you can use `GetMoviesError` at any time to get the most recent QuickTime error value.

Once the `Media` instance has been created you can start adding samples to the track. You must bracket sample insertion with calls to `BeginMediaEdits` and `EndMediaEdits`. These functions let QuickTime know when you intend to modify track media. Also, after inserting your samples, you must call `InsertMediaIntoTrack` to finish the edit process:

```
OSErr InsertMediaIntoTrack(Track        theTrack,
                           TimeValue    trackStart,
                           TimeValue    mediaTime,
                           TimeValue    mediaDuration,
                           Fixed        mediaRate)
```

The `InsertMediaIntoTrack` function allows you to specify precisely when these samples should start. `BuildImageVideoTrack` sets `trackStart` and `mediaTime` to 0 to store the media at the beginning of the track. `mediaDuration` refers to the total duration of samples being added; you can use QuickTime's `GetMediaDuration` function to just get this total duration from the `Media` instance directly. Finally `mediaRate` refers to a playback multiplier to use with this track. `BuildImageVideoTrack` uses the fixed-precision value `fixed1` to play the movie back at normal (1x) speed.

In this next Try It Out, you insert video samples into the video track you added in the preceding example. Video samples are created by drawing slide images into GWorlds, capitalizing on code you added earlier.

Try It Out   Inserting New Video Samples

1.   In `QuickTimeMovie.c`, replace the `BuildImageVideoSamples` with the following:

```
// BuildImageVideoSamples adds images to the specified media as video samples.
// Again, image data is provided through a callback function.
static OSStatus BuildImageVideoSamples(Media media, Rect frame,
                                       TimeScale timeScale, int numberOfImages,
                                       SaveImageMovieCallback callback,
                                       void *userData)
{
    OSType codecType = kSorenson3CodecType;
    GWorldPtr world = NULL;
    PixMapHandle pixmap;
    long maxSize;
    OSStatus err;
    Handle sample;
    ImageDescriptionHandle imageDesc;
    int i;

    // create a gworld for drawing
    err = NewGWorld(&world, 32, &frame, NULL, NULL, 0);

    // get a pixmap from this gworld and lock it down, so you can talk to the
    // compression manager.
    if (err == noErr) {
        pixmap = GetGWorldPixMap(world);

        LockPixels(pixmap);
    }

    // compute the size required to hold a single frame
    if (err == noErr) {
        err = GetMaxCompressionSize(pixmap,
```

```
                                    &frame,
                                    0,
                                    codecNormalQuality,
                                    codecType,
                                    anyCodec,
                                    &maxSize);
    }

    // reserve space for our sample
    if (err == noErr) {
        sample = NewHandle(maxSize);
        if (!sample) {
            err = GetMoviesError();
        }
    }

    // reserve space image desc handle. QuickTime will adjust the size of the
    // handle as necessary, so it can start trivially small
    if (err == noErr) {
        imageDesc = (ImageDescriptionHandle)NewHandle(1);
        if (!imageDesc) {
            err = GetMoviesError();
        }
    }

    // for each image, grab the gworld from the callback function, and compress
    // it into a video sample.
    for (i = 0; (i < numberOfImages) && (err == noErr); i++) {
        TimeValue duration;

        // ask the client to draw into this gworld and return a proper duration
        // for this time scale.
        err = (callback)(timeScale, i, world, userData, &duration);

        // compress the image. the compressed data will be copied into sample.
        if (err == noErr) {
            err = CompressImage(pixmap,
                                &frame,
                                codecNormalQuality,
                                codecType,
                                imageDesc,
                                *sample);
        }

        // add the sample to the media
        if (err == noErr) {
            err = AddMediaSample(media,
                                 sample,
                                 0,
                                 (*imageDesc)->dataSize,
                                 duration,
                                 (SampleDescriptionHandle)imageDesc,
                                 1,
```

```
                                        0,
                                        NULL);
            }
        }

        // tear down the gworld
        if (world) {
            UnlockPixels(pixmap);
            DisposeGWorld(world);
        }

        // tear down the sample memory
        if (sample) {
            DisposeHandle(sample);
        }
        if (imageDesc) {
            DisposeHandle((Handle)imageDesc);
        }

        return err;
}
```

2. Save your changes to `QuickTimeMovie.c`.

3. Build and Run your project. Although `BuildImageVideoSamples` will be called indirectly by `SaveImageMovie`, the `SaveImageMovie` function hasn't yet been hooked up to anything, so you can't really test these changes. But you can make sure the new code compiles, and that nothing else broke during the editing process.

How It Works

Slide Master uses `BuildImageVideoSamples` to add samples to the new video track. Samples are compressed using an image compression (or video) codec, which cuts down on file sizes and improves playback performance. The process for adding and compressing these samples is simpler than it may appear, involving these five steps:

1. Allocate a `GWorldPtr` to hold uncompressed image data.

2. Allocate `Handle` to hold compressed image data and the sample description.

3. Draw the image into the `GWorldPtr`.

4. Compress the `GWorldPtr`, and capture the result in your `Handle`.

5. Add the sample to the track.

You need to perform these first two steps only once. You will repeat steps 3 through 5 for each image in your movie.

`BuildImageVideoSamples` allocates a `GWorldPtr` using the `NewGWorld` function:

```
OSErr NewGWorld(GWorldPtr *   offscreenGWorld,
                short         PixelDepth,
                const Rect *  boundsRect,
```

```
        CTabHandle      cTable,
        GDHandle        aGDevice,
        GWorldFlags     flags);
```

In order to create a new `GWorldPtr` you need to declare its `PixelDepth` and its `boundRect`. The `PixelDepth` is the number of bits per pixel, and should be 1, 2, 4, 8, 16, or 32. High-quality images should use 32 bits per pixel, since this allows for the most information. The `boundsRect` simply specifies the GWorld's area. The `cTable` argument can point to a specific color table when working with an indexed color depth (2, 4, or 8 bits per pixel), or you can pass NULL to use the default color table. The `aGDevice` parameter allows you to associate a specific `GDHandle` structure with this `GWorldPtr`, but only if you set the `noNewDevice` flag in the `flags` argument; otherwise you can pass NULL here. You can use the `flags` parameter to modify the behavior of `NewGWorld` (such as by setting `noNewDevice`); you can get the default behavior by passing 0.

Creating a `Handle` to store your compressed data is easy; you can just call `NewHandle`. However, you need to first know how much memory you will need to reserve. This value will depend on the codec used to compress your data. You can ask QuickTime to figure out how much memory you will need by calling `GetMaxCompressionSize`:

```
OSErr GetMaxCompressionSize(PixMapHandle          src,
                            const Rect *          srcRect,
                            short                 colorDepth,
                            CodecQ                quality,
                            CodecType             cType,
                            CompressorComponent   codec,
                            long *                size);
```

The `GetMaxCompressionSize` function needs to know about the pixel storage, the area being compressed, and the color depth. You can simply use the same frame passed to `NewGWorld` to set the `srcRect`, and you can ask QuickTime to figure out which color depth to use by setting `colorDepth` to 0. But you must get the pixel storage from the `GWorldPtr`, in the form of a `PixMapHandle`. Once you obtain the `PixMapHandle` via `GetGWorldPixMap` you must lock it down using `LockPixels`. You must remember to unlock the `PixMapHandle` before freeing the `GWorldPtr`.

`GetMaxCompressionSize` also needs to know how you intend to compress the image, including the kind of codec you want, the specific codec you intend to use, and the compression quality. `GetMaxCompressionSize` sets `quality` to `codecNormalQuality` to obtain normal quality images. You can set `cType` to any one of the codecs supplied with QuickTime. For example, `GetMaxCompressionSize` sets `cType` to `kSorenson3CodecType` to get the Sorenson 3 image compression codec. If you aren't interested in maintaining the exact instance of the codec yourself, you can pass the `anyCodec` constant in the `codec` parameter to ask QuickTime to manage this detail for you.

On success, the `GetMaxCompressionSize` function will return the maximum amount of data required to store images compressed with these settings. Because this data will be stored as a sample in a QuickTime movie, `BuildImageVideoSamples` allocates a `Handle` of this size. `BuildImageVideoSamples` also allocates a handle for storing an `ImageDescriptionHandle` structure. Since the image description will be actively resized by QuickTime, you don't need to supply the correct size for this `Handle`.

The `BuildImageVideoSamples` function knows how many images will be added to the movie, but it doesn't yet have the image data for those images. It processes each image one at a time using a `for` loop.

BuildImageVideoSamples draws each image into the GWorldPtr using the SaveImageMovieCallback function stored in the callback variable. This function was (or will be) passed into the SaveImageMovie function by the caller. The callback provides a way for clients of SaveImageMovie to provide image data and the image duration for the requested image, without having to pre-allocate a large number of images up front. Callers also can pass a little bit of state back to themselves through the userData argument. Although you haven't written the code that calls SaveImageMovie yet, it should be clear that this callback will eventually call the Slide class's drawIntoGWorld: method.

You then compress the image data using CompressImage, which resembles the GetMaxCompressionSize call from earlier:

```
OSErr CompressImage(PixMapHandle          src,
                    const Rect *          srcRect,
                    CodecQ                quality,
                    CodecType             cType,
                    ImageDescriptionHandle desc,
                    Ptr                   data);
```

On success, CompressImage initializes your pre-allocated ImageDescriptionHandle passed into desc and writes the compressed data to the pointer passed into data.

This compressed data is then added to the track's Media instance using AddMediaSample:

```
extern OSErr AddMediaSample(Media                  theMedia,
                            Handle                 dataIn,
                            long                   inOffset,
                            unsigned long          size,
                            TimeValue              durationPerSample,
                            SampleDescriptionHandle sampleDescriptionH,
                            long                   numberOfSamples,
                            short                  sampleFlags,
                            TimeValue *            sampleTime);
```

The theMedia argument represents the Media instance created earlier. The dataIn argument is a Handle pointing to your sample data; in this case, the compressed image data. You can use the inOffset argument to adjust QuickTime if your data doesn't appear at the front of your dataIn buffer, but normally you will pass 0. size refers to the amount of data in the sample. You could pass the Handle size you got from GetMaxCompressionSize, but that could result in storing more data than you really need. The ImageDescriptionHandle you got from CompressImage holds the amount of used data in its dataSize field; you should just pass that value into AddMediaSample. The durationPerSample argument is a TimeValue that represents the duration for this sample; BuildImageVideoSamples gets this information from the callback function. Also, BuildImageVideoSamples passes 1 for numberOfSamples, and 0 for sampleFlags to get the default behavior for AddMediaSample. On success, AddMediaSample can return the specific TimeValue where the sample was added; you can pass NULL if you aren't interested in that information.

Once all the samples have been added to the track media, you can clean up the data structures allocated within BuildImageVideoSamples.

In this final Try It Out, you hook up Slide Master's File ⇨ Import menu command. This is the last step in changing Slide Master to write out QuickTime movies. Finally, you will be able to test your hard work!

Try It Out   Hooking Up the Movie Command

1. Open the MainMenu nib file in Interface Builder.

2. Switch to the Classes tab and add a method to FirstResponder called exportMovie:.

3. Open the File menu in the Main Menu editor.

4. Add an item named Export . . . after the Import . . . item. The File menu should resemble Figure 9-6.

Figure 9-6

5. Control-drag from the Export menu item to the FirstResponder icon in the Instances tab, and connect the menu item to the new exportMovie: method.

6. Save your changes to the MainMenu nib file.

7. In Xcode, open SlideShowDocument.h and add the following method to the SlideShowDocument interface:

```
- (void)exportMovie:(id)sender;
```

8. Switch to SlideShowDocument.m and add the following function declaration near the top of the file, before the SlideShowDocument implementation block:

```
static OSStatus DrawSlideInGWorld(TimeScale timeScale, int imageNumber,
                                  GWorldPtr world, void *userData,
                                  TimeValue *duration);
```

9. Add the following code at the end of the SlideShowDocument implementation block:

```
#pragma mark QuickTime

- (NSURL*)selectMovieURL
{
    NSSavePanel *savePanel = [NSSavePanel savePanel];

    [savePanel setAllowedFileTypes:[NSArray arrayWithObject:@"mov"]];
```

```objc
        if ([savePanel runModal] == NSFileHandlingPanelOKButton) {
            return [savePanel URL];
        }

    return nil;
}

- (void)exportMovie:(id)sender
{
    // ask the user for a save location
    NSURL *url = [self selectMovieURL];

    if (url) {
        // make sure QuickTime is initialized
        OSStatus err = EnterMovies();

        if (err == noErr) {
            TimeScale timeScale = 600;
            int i, count = [mSlides count];
            Rect frame = {0};

            // compute the largest frame required for this movie by iterating
            // over all the slides
            for (i = 0; i < count; i++) {
                Slide *slide = [mSlides objectAtIndex:i];
                NSImage *image = [slide image];
                NSSize size = [image size];

                frame.right = MAX(frame.right, (int)size.width);
                frame.bottom = MAX(frame.bottom, (int)size.height);
            }

            // build the QuickTime movie. rather than supply all the sample
            // data up front, which would cause a large spike in memory usage,
            // simply pass in a callback to allow the movie code to get the
            // sample data on demand.
            err = SaveImageMovie((CFURLRef)url,
                                 frame,
                                 timeScale,
                                 count,
                                 DrawSlideInGWorld,
                                 mSlides);

            // open the movie in QuickTime Player
            if (err == noErr) {
                NSWorkspace *workspace = [NSWorkspace sharedWorkspace];

                [workspace openURL:url];
            } else {
                NSString *title = @"Slide Master could not write movie.";
                NSString *msg = @"An unexpected error occurred. (%d)";

                NSRunCriticalAlertPanel(title, msg, @"OK", nil, nil, err);
```

```
            }
        } else {
            NSString *title = @"Slide Master could not initialize QuickTime.";
            NSString *msg = @"An unexpected error occurred. (%d)";

            NSRunCriticalAlertPanel(title, msg, @"OK", nil, nil, err);
        }
    }
}
```

10. Add the following function after the `SlideShowDocument` implementation block:

```
static OSStatus DrawSlideInGWorld(TimeScale timeScale, int imageNumber,
                                  GWorldPtr world, void *userData,
                                  TimeValue *duration)
{
    // get the slide
    NSArray *slides = (NSArray*)userData;
    Slide *slide = [slides objectAtIndex:imageNumber];

    // compute a proper duration for this timescale. for the sake of argument,
    // assume that every frame lasts 2 seconds.
    *duration = timeScale * 2;

    // draw the slide into the GWorld
    return [slide drawIntoGWorld:world];
}
```

11. Save your changes to `SlideShowDocument.h` and `SlideShowDocument.m`.

12. Build and run Slide Master. The Export . . . command should be active for slide show documents. When you choose File ⇨ Export, a save panel appears, allowing you to pick the location for your movie. After the movie is built, it opens in QuickTime Player.

How It Works

The `exportMovie:` method begins by displaying a save panel. The particulars of driving the `NSSavePanel` class are encapsulated into a method called `selectMovieURL:`, which configures the save panel to choose movie files (files with the `.mov` extension), runs the panel, and returns an `NSURL` object representing the user's selection. `selectMovieURL:` will return `nil` if the user cancels the operation. The `NSSavePanel` can return file references either as `NSString`-based file paths, or as `NSURL`-based URLs. In this case, since the `SaveImageMovie` function expects a URL, a URL reference is most convenient.

Once the user has committed to writing a QuickTime movie, `SlideShowDocument` initializes the QuickTime framework by calling `EnterMovies`. Although `EnterMovies` can be called multiple times safely, applications that make use of QuickTime more extensively will want to call `EnterMovies` once, earlier in their launch cycle: for example, in the application delegate's `applicationDidFinishLaunching:` method or in `main` after the menu bar and windows have been loaded.

Then `exportMovie:` prepares to call the `SaveImageMovie` function by computing the movie's frame size. This value will be used by various functions within `QuickTimeMovie.c`. The QuickTime movie's frame should be large enough to hold all the images. `exportMovie:` computes this frame by iterating over each image and saving the largest width and height it sees. It gets a little help from the `MAX` macro built into the C libraries, which simply returns the larger of two expressions.

You will recall the SaveImageMovie function does all the work of writing out a QuickTime movie based on individual images:

```
OSStatus SaveImageMovie(CFURLRef url,
                        Rect frame,
                        TimeScale timeScale,
                        int numberOfImages,
                        SaveImageMovieCallback callback,
                        void *userData);
```

The exportMovie: method passes the NSURL object in as the url argument, taking advantage of Toll-Free Bridging between Foundation and CoreFoundation. The frame argument is set to the Rect computed earlier. Slide Master uses a timeScale of 600 for its movies, which is a fairly arbitrary choice. The number 600 divides evenly in a number of interesting ways, and is often used for movie content meant for display on computers. The numberOfImages argument simply holds count of the mSlides array. exportMovie: passes a function named DrawSlideInGWorld as the callback parameter. This function's job is to provide image data for each slide when SaveImageMovie (or its subfunctions) needs it. In order to do that DrawSlideInGWorld will need access to all the slides, so exportMovie: passes the mSlides array in as the userData parameter.

The actual implementation for DrawSlideInGWorld is fairly simple. It uses its imageNumber parameter and the array passed into userData to find the Slide that needs to be drawn, and then passes its world argument to that Slide's drawIntoGWorld: method. DrawSlideInGWorld also has to return the duration for the image; it computes a duration of 2 seconds using the supplied timeScale.

Once the movie has been written out to disk, exportMovie: asks the NSWorkspace object to open the movie file. NSWorkspace is an AppKit object that's useful for working with the Finder and other user-level system components. In this case, NSWorkspace's openURL: method asks the Finder to open the new movie as if you had double-clicked its icon.

If any of the QuickTime functions fail, exportMovie: will display a short message in an error panel, so you know something went wrong. Cocoa supplies a convenient function, NSRunCriticalAlertPanel, that handles most of the details of working with alerts. Carbon applications can use the somewhat baroque StandardAlert function. Normally applications should be specific with their alert error messages, by telling users exactly what went wrong and suggesting ways they can fix the problem. This is difficult when working with QuickTime because QuickTime's error conditions aren't well documented, and any QuickTime function might return one of thousands of error codes. Slide Master cheats a little and reveals the specific error number to the user, such as in Figure 9-7. This isn't a very friendly thing to do, but sometimes it's better than nothing.

Figure 9-7

Summary

You learned a lot in this chapter, including the following:

❑ How to manage memory using functions supplied by Carbon, CoreFoundation, and Darwin. For the most part, these functions work in the same way: You use one function call to allocate memory, and another to release it. CoreFoundation also supports reference counting, much like Objective-C objects.

❑ How to use Carbon Events to connect Carbon application interfaces up to your custom source code. You register callback functions with Carbon that get called when certain events are generated. User interface elements in your nib file can have specific commands associated with them as well.

❑ Techniques for calling Carbon API from Cocoa applications. For the most part you can simply call Carbon functions from within a Cocoa application. CoreFoundation helps bridge the gap between Carbon and Cocoa by providing data types that can pose as Foundation objects and vice versa.

❑ How to track local files using the Carbon File Manager. Carbon supports aliases, which do their best to resolve files even if they are moved or renamed. These are the same alias files created by the Finder.

❑ How to use the Carbon APIs to write out a simple QuickTime movie. The QuickTime API set can be challenging to work with because of its size. But with a little patience, and an understanding of Carbon programming conventions and the QuickDraw drawing library, you can integrate QuickTime into your applications.

In the next chapter, you learn about various scripting languages available in Mac OS X. Before proceeding, however, try the exercises that follow to test your understanding of the material covered in this chapter. You can find the solutions to these exercises in Appendix A.

Exercises

1. Modify the Carbon Email Formatter application to update its result text view whenever you type in a text field. No nib file changes should be necessary. You will need to register a window event handler for a keyboard event type to receive keyboard events. Once you do that, your event handler will receive these events before the Carbon framework has the chance to interpret them. You must use the `CallNextEventHandler` function to pass the event back to Carbon so text fields will actually update, and then call `ComputeResult` once `CallNextEventHandler` returns.

2. Change Slide Master's `Export` function to write the name of each image into the lower-right corner of the QuickTime movie. Remember you are working with a QuickDraw port at this point (in the form of a `GWorldPtr`) and the `NSString` drawing techniques you learned in Chapter 8 will not directly help you. Instead, use the MLTE function `TXNDrawCFStringTextBox` to draw the filename.

Part III: Script Programming

Overview of Scripting Languages

With its Unix heritage, Mac OS X comes laden with little surprises that are not traditionally of the Mac but now have a home on the platform. Scripting languages are a good example. Before Mac OS X the support for scripting was limited, aside from Apple's own solution — AppleScript. Now you can run any of the scripting languages found commonly on other Unix platforms and Linux directly from your Mac and not have to sacrifice anything. There are even some advantages to using Mac OS X with these languages, such as Cocoa bridging, which allows you to write great looking Cocoa apps in most of the popular scripting languages.

This chapter provides an introduction to scripting in general and an overview of the most important scripting languages on Mac OS X, from the Bash Shell to Python and Perl. Because it would be impossible to cover all scripting languages in one short chapter, a selection of the most important scripting languages has been made. Each of the languages ships with the Mac OS X system, so you can start using them straight out of the box.

In this chapter you learn

- ❑ What a script language is, and how it differs from languages like Java and Objective-C
- ❑ The strengths and weaknesses of the following scripting languages: Bash, AppleScript, Python, Perl, and JavaScript
- ❑ The basic properties of each of the scripting languages, and what each language looks like
- ❑ Where you can learn more about the various scripting languages
- ❑ How to write Dashboard widgets with JavaScript, Cascading Style Sheets (CSS), and HTML

What Is a Script?

In Chapters 6 and 7 you learned about the C and Objective-C programming languages, which form the basis of much of the development taking place on Mac OS X today. These languages are *compiled languages*, which means they have to be converted from source code into object code, which the CPU understands, by a program called a *compiler*. When you write in compiled languages, you have to build your program before you can run it.

A *script* is a program written in an interpreted language. An *interpreted language* is one that does not get compiled before it is executed. Instead, the source code of the program is read directly, one line at a time, by a program called an *interpreter*. An interpreter is similar to a compiler, in the sense that its job is to convert source code into instructions that the computer can execute, but there is an important difference: A compiler performs the entire conversion before the program is run, generating an executable in a form that can be directly understood by the CPU. An interpreter performs the conversion on-the-fly, reading a line of code at a time, interpreting it, and carrying out the corresponding operations before reading the next line.

Another way of looking at it is that a compiled program runs directly on the CPU, whereas a script runs inside an interpreter, which runs on the CPU. This level of indirection means that scripts generally run quite a bit slower than compiled languages, but when this performance penalty is not a concern, they can make your life a lot easier. The flexibility afforded by an interpreter can provide considerable advantages. For example, it is possible for a script to generate and execute new source code while it is running. This is not possible with a compiled program, which must be fully compiled from source code before it is run.

What Is a Scripting Language?

If a script is a program run by an interpreter, it won't come as much of a surprise that a *scripting language* is the programming language that a script is written in. Scripting languages tend be high-level languages, operating closer to the human programmer than the computer CPU. For example, where C allows you to access addresses in memory via pointer variables (see Chapter 6), scripting languages do not generally provide such low-level operations. Instead, they include extensive libraries of functions for dealing with everything from text manipulation, to file handling, and even access to databases. Scripting languages are very powerful, allowing you to get the most done with as little code as possible.

Each scripting language tends to specialize in a particular application domain:

❑ AppleScript is great for scripting applications with a graphical user interface (GUI).

❑ Python and Perl have excellent text-manipulation facilities.

❑ Ruby includes powerful object-oriented (OO) features to aid in structuring large programs.

❑ Bash makes it easy to leverage other commands and programs.

❑ PHP is designed for building websites, with features for accessing databases and producing HTML.

❑ JavaScript is designed to work in web browsers and can be used to create Dashboard widgets on Mac OS X 10.4 "Tiger."

Scripting languages are often referred to as *glue languages*, because they are generally used to glue together other applications and programs. For example, the Bash Shell has a relatively small built-in set of functions; its usefulness stems from an ability to easily execute all of the commands that ship with a

Unix system. Languages like Perl and Python are often used to make different programs work together: The output of one program may be reformatted by the scripting language in such a way that it can be used as the input to another program. AppleScript is typically used to glue together programs with GUIs, perhaps taking an image file from iPhoto, applying some filters to it in Photoshop, and inserting the finished product in a Microsoft Word file.

In the rest of the chapter, you are introduced in more detail to some of these scripting languages and their application domains. You learn how they can make your life a lot easier as a programmer. Even though you won't become proficient in any of the languages by the end of the chapter, you will have a good idea of what each is about, and where you can learn more if your interest is piqued. Two of the languages — Bash and AppleScript — are so important to Mac OS X that they are given special attention in Chapters 11 and 12, respectively.

Bash

Bash is the default shell that ships on Mac OS X. A *shell* is basically an interpreter that offers the user the possibility of direct interaction, in addition to being able to run scripts. If you open the Terminal application, you are presented with a command-line prompt. This prompt is generated by the Bash Shell, and any command you enter is executed by the Bash Shell.

Bash is descended from the original Unix shell: Bourne Shell. The Bourne Shell is a subset of Bash, so you can do everything in Bash that you can do in the Bourne Shell. In fact, on Mac OS X, whenever you request a Bourne Shell, you get Bash.

It cannot be stressed enough how important shell programming, and Bash in particular, is to Mac OS X. Even if you never see a command-line prompt, or run a shell script yourself, you are indirectly making use of Bash every time you start your computer. For example, the configuration process that Mac OS X follows when it is booted is completely controlled by Bash Shell scripts. If you are not convinced, take a look in the /System/Library/StartupItems directory. Go into any one of the subdirectories there (for example, Apache), and use TextEdit to open the file with the same name as the directory (for example, for the Apache directory, open the Apache file). You are now looking at a Bash Shell script.

Why Bash?

Unix shells are not the most glamorous of languages. They tend to be syntactically eccentric, which can throw up some challenges when you are learning to use them. They do have considerable advantages though, which make it worth your while. Shells are particularly adept at running command-line programs, and combining them in ways you would never have thought possible.

Bash provides the usual programming constructions — variables, conditional branching, loops, and functions — but one of its greatest strengths lies in allowing you to easily redirect program input and output. With very few keystrokes, you can retrieve program input data from a file or channel it from the output of another program. The latter is known as a *pipe*, because it is like running the data down a pipe from one program to the next. A good shell scripter can do some amazing things, such as piping the output of one Unix command to the input of a second, and the output of the second command to the input of a third, and so forth.

Shells like Bash are also the primary means of interacting with the Unix core of Mac OS X. If you need to install a new Unix command, move some files around in the heart of the operating system, or edit the Apache Web Server configuration files, you can best do so with Bash. Finder quite rightly puts up barriers to average users entering the places in the operating system traditionally the reserve of Unix users, but Bash invites you to come on in. All you need to do to get an invitation is open the Terminal application in `/Applications/Utilities`, and you are presented with a Bash Shell eagerly awaiting your instructions.

> *Other alternatives to Bash are available on Mac OS X. In fact, originally the default shell was TCSH, but was later changed. Bash is the default shell on the popular Linux operating system, which may have been the reason it was chosen, quite apart from being a very powerful shell. Apple probably wanted to make migrating from Linux to Mac OS X as painless as possible.*

A strength of shells is that they exist on all Unix-based operating systems. They are truly platform agnostic, so if you write a shell script on Mac OS X, it should run fine on a Linux system. The only thing to be aware of is that although the shell itself may not vary much from one system to the next, the commands it is using may. For example, the Linux version of a particular command may use different options to the Mac OS X variant. Mac OS X's Unix command layer is based on a Unix operating system called FreeBSD, so anything that works on FreeBSD should work fine under Mac OS X.

Shell languages tend not to be very advanced, in comparison to other programming languages. Variables are limited to strings, numbers, and arrays. You can't easily create data structures like C's `struct` (see Chapter 6), and object-oriented programming (see Chapter 7), with classes and objects, is a very foreign concept in the world of Bash. Given these restrictions, you shouldn't try to write your next monster-sized application in Bash. Shells are great for small scripts, up to a few hundred lines, but if you need to write a more extensive program, you are better off going for a more powerful scripting language like Python or Perl.

Try It Out   A Bash Example

Chapter 11 is dedicated to Bash scripting, so only a simple example is provided here to give you a feel for what Bash, and other shells, are about. The following script creates a disk image containing a file or directory of the user's choice.

```
#!/bin/sh

# Set variables with input arguments
VOLUME_NAME=$1
DISK_IMAGE_NAME=$1
DMG_SIZE=$2
DIR_PATH=$3

# Functions
CreateImage() {
  echo Creating a volume
  /usr/bin/hdiutil create -quiet "$DISK_IMAGE_NAME.dmg" -fs HFS+ \
      -volname "$VOLUME_NAME" -megabytes $DMG_SIZE
}

AttachVolume() {
  echo Attaching volume
```

```
        local TMPFILE=`mktemp -t "hdiutil_output"`
        /usr/bin/hdiutil attach "$DISK_IMAGE_NAME.dmg" > "$TMPFILE"
        DEV_FILE=`cat "$TMPFILE" | grep 'Apple_partition_scheme' | \
          awk -F' ' '{ print $1 }'`
    }

    DetachVolume() {
      echo Detaching volume
      hdiutil detach -quiet "$1"
    }

    # Main part of script
    CreateImage
    AttachVolume

    cp -r "$DIR_PATH" "/Volumes/$VOLUME_NAME"

    DetachVolume $DEV_FILE
    echo Finished
```

How It Works

The script begins by assigning a number of variables to arguments passed on the command line when the script was started.

```
VOLUME_NAME=$1
DISK_IMAGE_NAME=$1
DMG_SIZE=$2
DIR_PATH=$3
```

The name of the volume, and the name of the disk image itself, which are stored in the variables VOLUME_NAME and DISK_IMAGE_NAME, respectively, are both set to the first argument passed to the script. Arguments are stored in the variables $1, $2, and so forth, in the order passed to the script. The size of the disk image is passed as the second argument and is assigned to the variable DMG_SIZE. The DIR_PATH variable is assigned to the path of the directory or file that will be stored in the disk image.

A number of functions are defined next, beginning with a function that creates a new, empty disk image.

```
CreateImage() {
  echo Creating a volume
  /usr/bin/hdiutil create -quiet "$DISK_IMAGE_NAME.dmg" -fs HFS+ \
      -volname "$VOLUME_NAME" -megabytes $DMG_SIZE
}
```

This function first prints a message using the echo command to indicate that the image is being created. The hdiutil command is then used to create the disk image. It is passed a number of options, including -fs HFS+, which instructs the command to create an HFS+ file system in the disk image. The -megabytes $DMG_SIZE option gives the size of the disk image. The variable DMG_SIZE is used for this purpose.

> **To access the value of a variable in Bash, you need to prepend a $ symbol.**

The name of the disk image is given as $DISK_IMAGE_NAME.dmg. DISK_IMAGE_NAME is a variable, and its value, $DISK_IMAGE_NAME, is a string. In Bash you can combine variable values and literal strings, like .dmg, by simply using them together. The script replaces $DISK_IMAGE_NAME with its string value before invoking the hdiutil command. The hdiutil command gets passed a filename comprising the value of DISK_IMAGE_NAME, and the extension .dmg. hdiutil never sees the DISK_IMAGE_NAME variable itself.

After the image has been created, it needs to be attached as a volume, so that files can be transferred to it. The function AttachVolume achieves this.

```
AttachVolume() {
   echo Attaching volume
   local TMPFILE=`mktemp -t "hdiutil_output"`
   /usr/bin/hdiutil attach "$DISK_IMAGE_NAME.dmg" > "$TMPFILE"
   DEV_FILE=`cat "$TMPFILE" | grep 'Apple_partition_scheme' | \
      awk -F' ' '{ print $1 }'`
}
```

Again, a message is echoed to the script output indicating what is about to take place, purely for the benefit of the user. A local variable, TMPFILE, is declared next; a local variable is not visible outside the function in which it is declared. The TMPFILE variable is assigned to the output of the command on the right-hand side, which is contained between backticks. When a command is contained between backticks, Bash evaluates it, and replaces the whole command with its output. In this case, the command mktemp creates a temporary file, printing the path to the new file as output. This path replaces the contents of the backticks, and TMPFILE is assigned to the path.

The hdiutil command is again invoked, this time to attach the existing disk image, with the name $DISK_IMAGE_NAME.dmg. The output of the hdiutil command is piped to the file at the path stored in the TMPFILE variable. The > is used to redirect the output of a command to a file. The content of the file is replaced by the output of the command; if the file does not exist, a new file is created to contain the data.

The last line of the function defines a new variable called DEV_FILE, which is the device file associated with the attached volume. This file is needed later in the script to detach the volume again. To get the path of the device, the output of the hdiutil command is processed. To understand how this works, you really need to see the output of hdiutil. Here is what it looks like:

```
Initializing...
Attaching...
Finishing...
Finishing...
/dev/disk2              Apple_partition_scheme
/dev/disk2s1            Apple_partition_map
/dev/disk2s2            Apple_HFS                    /Volumes/SomeVolumeName
```

The path of the device that is needed is the first one that appears, /dev/disk2, in the line with Apple_partition_scheme.

To extract this path, a number of different commands are chained together. The command used to get the path is enclosed between backticks and amounts to the following:

```
cat "$TMPFILE" | grep 'Apple_partition_scheme' | awk -F' ' '{ print $1 }'
```

It begins with the cat command, which simply reads the contents of the temporary file and writes it to output. The output of cat is piped to another command: grep. The symbol | is used when you want to pipe the output of one command to another, just as > pipes output to a file. The grep command receives the output of cat as input and extracts all lines that contain the string Apple_partition_scheme. These lines are written to the output of grep, which is piped to the command awk. awk prints the first thing on the line, the /dev/disk2 path. This path is the output of the whole command, and is assigned to the DEV_FILE variable.

The DetachVolume function is considerably simpler, using the hdiutil command to detach the volume stored in the path passed to it as an argument.

```
DetachVolume() {
  echo Detaching volume
  hdiutil detach -quiet "$1"
}
```

Arguments are treated in functions in the same way they are treated for the script as a whole. The first argument is stored in the variable $1 inside the script; the second in $2; and so forth.

The end of the script calls the functions in the appropriate order and copies the file or directory to the volume while it is attached.

```
CreateImage
AttachVolume

cp -r "$DIR_PATH" "/Volumes/$VOLUME_NAME"

DetachVolume $DEV_FILE
echo Finished
```

To pass the argument to the function DetachVolume, it is simply listed after the function name. Function arguments are separated by whitespace. The script ends by printing the string Finished.

This example demonstrates many aspects of Bash Shell programming. You have seen that

❑ Bash includes the usual suspects, like functions and variables.

❑ Shells make it particularly easy to redirect data streams between different commands with pipes.

❑ The power of a shell derives from the Unix commands it invokes. The shell itself is quite primitive in programming terms.

More Information

Chapter 11 covers Bash in detail, so if you are interested in learning to use it, that is the best place to start.

Aside from Chapter 11, the man page for Bash is a good resource for documentation. Open the Terminal utility and enter the command

```
man bash
```

Use the space bar to move down the page, and press q to quit the man program.

Countless sites on the Internet cover Bash in intimate detail. A quick Google search will generate the hits you need to begin exploring Bash. Here are two sites to get you started:

❑ The Ooblick guide to Bourne Shell Programming is an easy-to-read quick introduction to shells (`http://www.ooblick.com/text/sh/`).

❑ The Free Software Foundations, which is responsible for developing Bash in the first place, includes the Bash Reference Manual on its website (`http://www.gnu.org/software/bash/manual/bashref.html`).

AppleScript

Many different scripting solutions are presented in this chapter, but only one can easily be used to script applications with graphical interfaces: AppleScript. AppleScript was created by Apple in the old days of Mac OS, but is now well supported on Mac OS X, and has even been extended to allow fully functional applications to be developed with AppleScript Studio.

Why AppleScript?

AppleScript is not only different than other scripting languages because its main purpose is scripting applications with a graphical interface, but it also looks a lot different because it is targeted not at programmers, but ordinary Mac users. The language reads to a large extent like English. This is a boon for the non-programmer, but some experienced programmers may be put off by the verbosity of the language, and the degree of redundancy; you can often choose between several different constructions to perform a single task in AppleScript.

In the latest versions of Mac OS X, AppleScript can also be used to develop complete applications, with AppleScript Studio (see Chapter 12). AppleScript Studio is included with Apple's development tools and doesn't cost a penny. Using AppleScript Studio, you can add a Cocoa user interface to your scripts, making it easy for non-programmers to develop Mac OS X applications that are indistinguishable from those written natively in Objective-C.

If you want to script your Mac OS X applications, you will want to use AppleScript, but for other tasks it may not be the best choice. To begin with, AppleScript is not a cross-platform solution; it runs only on Mac OS X, so don't expect your AppleScripts to run on your Linux or Windows computer. AppleScript is also not a very good solution for scripting command-line tools, and text processing is better handled with languages like Python and Perl. This doesn't mean AppleScript has no part to play when you are faced with such tasks, because the best solution may involve some combination of AppleScript for handling applications and another scripting language for processing text and data.

Try It Out   **An AppleScript Example**

AppleScript and AppleScript Studio are covered in more detail in Chapter 12, so this section is kept quite brief. To give you an idea of what AppleScript looks like, here is a simple script that creates and sends emails. The emails are personalized with the name of the person they are sent to. The user enters email addresses and names via dialog boxes.

```
set email_text to "Hello <name>. How are you?"

repeat

    (* Get name and address from user *)
    activate
    display dialog "Enter an email address:" & return ¬
        default answer "" as string buttons {"Cancel", "Continue"} default button 2
    copy the result as list to {email_address, button_pressed}

    (* If user wants to proceed, get the name of the person in the email *)
    if the button_pressed is "Continue" then
        display dialog "Enter name:" & return ¬
            default answer "" as string buttons {"Continue"} default button 1
        copy the result as list to {persons_name, button_pressed}

        (* Create personalized email text *)
        set name_offset to offset of "<name>" in email_text
        set end_offset to name_offset + (length of "<name>")
        set text_length to length of email_text
        set email_beginning to get text 1 thru (name_offset - 1) of email_text
        set email_end to get text end_offset thru text_length of email_text
        set personalized_text to email_beginning & persons_name & email_end

        (* Compose and send email *)
        tell application "Mail"
            set new_message to make new outgoing message ¬
                at end of outgoing messages
            tell new_message
                set subject to "Hi!"
                set content to personalized_text as string
                set visible to false
                make new recipient at end of to recipients ¬
                    with properties {name:persons_name, address:email_address}
            end tell
            send new_message
        end tell

    (* If user pressed Cancel button, exit *)
    else
        exit repeat
    end if

end repeat
```

How It Works

This script begins by setting a variable called email_text to a string that contains the content of all the emails to be sent:

```
set email_text to "Hello <name>. How are you?"
```

The string contains a message, with a placeholder used to represent the name of the recipient. There is nothing special about the placeholder; in this case the text <name> has been used, but any unique string is fine. Later in the script, the <name> placeholder is sought in the email text and gets replaced by the actual name of a recipient.

Most of the script is embedded in a loop, which begins with the keyword `repeat`, and ends with `end repeat`. This loop is similar to a `while` loop in C; it continues forever, unless an `exit repeat` statement is encountered.

The first block of code inside the `repeat` prompts the user to enter an email address by displaying a dialog box:

```
(* Get name and address from user *)
activate
display dialog "Enter an email address:" & return ¬
    default answer "" as string buttons {"Cancel", "Continue"} default button 2
copy the result as list to {email_address, button_pressed}
```

A comment appears first, which is ignored by the AppleScript interpreter, followed by the statement `activate`. This tells the script to become the foremost application. After `activate`, the `display dialog` command is used to display a dialog with the text `Enter an email address:`. The `default answer "" as string` ensures that a text field will be included in the dialog for the user to enter the address. The text field is initialized with an empty string. The rest of the `display dialog` command gives a list of the buttons that should appear and indicates which button should be the default.

The following line gets the result of the dialog, which is a list containing the email address entered and the name of the button pressed. A *list* is a built-in type, similar to an array in other languages, which contains an ordered set of entries. The entries are assigned in this case to the variables `email_address` and `button_pressed`.

The next part of the script checks if the user pressed the Continue button, and, if so, proceeds to request that the name of the email recipient be entered:

```
(* If user wants to proceed, get the name of the person in the email *)
if the button_pressed is "Continue" then
    display dialog "Enter name:" & return ¬
        default answer "" as string buttons {"Continue"} default button 1
    copy the result as list to {persons_name, button_pressed}
```

If the user pressed Cancel in the email address dialog, the `else` branch further down is executed, and the command `exit repeat` causes the `repeat` loop, and thereby the script, to terminate.

With the name and email address in hand, the script proceeds to create the text that will become the content of the email. The placeholder <name> must be replaced with the actual name obtained from the script user:

```
(* Create personalized email text *)
set name_offset to offset of "<name>" in email_text
set end_offset to name_offset + (length of "<name>")
set text_length to length of email_text
set email_beginning to get text 1 thru (name_offset - 1) of email_text
```

```
set email_end to get text end_offset thru text_length of email_text
set personalized_text to email_beginning & persons_name & email_end
```

The first non-comment line locates the <name> substring, using the command `offset`, which returns the index of the first character of the placeholder in the `email_text` string. The index of the last character of <name> is then determined by adding the `length` property of the placeholder string to the variable `name_offset`. The following lines split the `email_text` variable into two variables: the first, `email_beginning`, is the text preceding the placeholder and the second, `email_end`, is the text that follows the placeholder. Last, a new variable, `personalized_text`, is created for the email content, which comprises the concatenation of `email_beginning`, `persons_name`, and `email_end`. The `&` operator concatenates (joins) strings together.

With the content prepared, all that is left is to send the email. The application `Mail` is used for this.

```
(* Compose and send email *)
tell application "Mail"
    set new_message to make new outgoing message ¬
        at end of outgoing messages
    tell new_message
        set subject to "Hi!"
        set content to personalized_text as string
        set visible to false
        make new recipient at end of to recipients ¬
            with properties {name:persons_name, address:email_address}
    end tell
    send new_message
end tell
```

A `tell`/`end tell` block allows you to direct a series of commands to a particular variable, in this case the application `Mail`. The first line in the tell block creates a variable called `new_message`, and sets it to a new outgoing message supplied by the Mail application. `make new outgoing message` instructs `Mail` to create a new message, and `at end of outgoing messages` instructs it to append the message to the list of all outgoing messages.

Another `tell` block is then formed to set properties of the `new_message` variable. The properties include the subject and content of the email. The last command in the block creates a new `recipient`, appending it to the list of all `recipients` of the message, and sets the `recipient` properties with the name and email address obtained from the script user.

> Note that setting the properties of the recipient has been achieved using the `with properties` command, rather than the `tell` block used to set properties of the new_message variable. Either approach is legitimate in AppleScript.

After the `new_message` variable has been configured, the email is sent using the `send` command of the `Mail` application. If all goes well, an email should be sent to the email address entered by the user, with the recipient's name replacing the placeholder in the email content.

What you have seen in this example is that AppleScript

❑ Is a verbose English-like language

❑ Makes it easy to carry out commands with applications like `Mail`

435

❏ Allows you to interact with the user via a graphical interface

❏ Is not that adept at string manipulation

❏ Usually includes several ways to achieve any one task

More Information

Chapter 12 covers AppleScript in more detail and deals with building applications with AppleScript Studio. This chapter is a good place to start if you are interested in learning more about AppleScript.

Your hard disk also includes a lot of reference material on AppleScript, including the documentation pages in Xcode and example scripts in the folder `/Applications/AppleScript/Example Scripts`.

Lastly, Apple's website contains some material. The place to begin the search is `http://www.apple.com/applescript`.

Python

Python is an object-oriented (OO) scripting language designed by the Dutchman Guido van Rossum in the early 1990s. It competes to some extent with Perl, which is covered in the next major section of the chapter, but has a very different philosophy than Perl. Python and Perl are both powerful languages, used in a wide variety of situations, from simple text processing to web programming, from GUI development to bioinformatics.

Whereas Perl offers many different ways to perform the same task and can be made very compact — but also unreadable to the non-expert — Python is one of the most elegant and simple languages there is, without sacrificing anything in the way of power.

The best way to convey the Python ethos is to reproduce some parts of *The Zen of Python*, which is a series of statements about Python written by Tim Peters:

❏ Beautiful is better than ugly.

❏ Explicit is better than implicit.

❏ Simple is better than complex.

❏ Readability counts.

❏ There should be one — and preferably only one — obvious way to do it.

You can read the full list at the Python website (`www.python.org/doc/Humor.html#zen`) or by entering the following commands in a terminal window:

```
Macintosh:~/Desktop sample$ python
python
Python 2.3.5 (#1, Mar 20 2005, 20:38:20)
[GCC 3.3 20030304 (Apple Computer, Inc. build 1809)] on darwin
Type "help", "copyright", "credits" or "license" for more information.
>>> import this
```

To summarize The Zen of Python, Python aims to make things as simple as they can be, yet still provides all the power you need.

Why Python?

As I have just touched on, Python provides very powerful programming constructs, such as object-orientation, in a very simple syntax. OO features become particularly important as your programs grow in size and need to be structured. If you are writing a 100-line script, Bash may be fine, but if you want to write a web content management system, Python fits the bill. It competes with compiled languages like C++ and Java in fields not generally associated with scripting, and more than holds its own.

If you have read Chapter 7 on Objective-C, you understand some of the advantages of object-oriented programming (OOP). Python provides all of those advantages in a scripting language. You can order your programs into classes, which contain data and methods, and one class can derive from another, inheriting all of its data and methods.

Like Objective-C, Python is a *dynamically typed* language, which means you do not need to explicitly state the class of the objects in your scripts. However, Python is *strongly typed*, which means that you cannot do something with an object that is not allowed by its class. If you try to do something illegal with an object, an exception will be raised, and your script will exit (unless you catch the exception). You get the best of both worlds when it comes to typing in Python: the ease of programming without explicitly declaring object classes, and the assurance that if you use an object incorrectly, you will find out as soon as your script is run.

Python provides powerful built-in types, such as dynamic arrays and dictionaries, much like those provided by the Cocoa Foundation framework for Objective-C. Python also includes an extensive library, with support for strings, regular expressions, mathematics, interacting with operating systems, running subprocesses, threading, networking, and much more. If it isn't in the Python Library, it is probably available as an extension; anyone can write modules that extend the functionality of Python.

One problem often associated with scripting languages is performance. For many applications, this is not a great concern, but in certain performance-critical cases, it is. Python alleviates this problem to a large extent because modules can be written in C. In fact, Python is even used in scientific applications, which traditionally have high performance demands. This is possible because those (usually small) parts of a program that consume most of the CPU time can be rewritten in C, or reimplemented to make use of existing modules written in C.

Python ships with every copy of Mac OS X and can be found in the framework `/System/Library/ Frameworks/Python.framework`. It also runs on platforms like Windows and Linux, and if you are careful, your scripts can be made to run on any platform without modification.

Mac OS X does ship with one Python package that is not available on any other platform: a set of bindings for the CoreGraphics framework. These bindings allow you to access the Quartz graphics layer in your Python scripts. For example, you could use a Python script to generate PDF files or convert images from JPEG format to PNG. Basically, anything you can do with CoreGraphics, you can do with the Python bindings.

A Mac OS X framework that is not included with the system, PyObjC, allows you to use Python to program with the Cocoa frameworks. You can write fully functional Cocoa programs in Python, which are indistinguishable from those written in Objective-C. In some ways, it is even easier to program Cocoa in Python than it is in Objective-C. For example, Python has automatic memory management, which means you don't have to explicitly release objects; in Objective-C, you do. This, and other differences, can make Python scripts considerably shorter than the equivalent Objective-C program.

If Python has a weakness, it would simply be that it is not as popular as Perl. Many more extensions are available in Perl than in Python, though you could argue that Python has everything you need. This criticism is analogous to one often leveled at the Mac platform: that it does not have as many applications available as on Windows. The usual counterargument is simply that the Mac has at least one good quality representative in each application category. The same could also be said for Python. It has everything you need, and no more.

Try It Out   A Python Example

Two of Python's strengths are its OO features and text handling. The following script demonstrates these aspects by moving through all of the files and directories descended from a given root directory and counting the words in those files that have a particular extension. It not only counts all whitespace-separated words, but also produces a second count with XML tags removed. You could thus use this script to scan your website directories, producing a word count with HTML tags removed.

XML, the eXtensible Markup Language, is a general language for defining how data is structured. It looks like HTML, but is more general; in fact, there is a variant of HTML called XHTML that is defined in XML.

```python
#!/usr/bin/env python

#----------------------------------------
# Counts words after removing HTML/XML tags
#----------------------------------------
import re, string, sys, os

#----------------
# Classes
#----------------
class WordCounter:
    """
    Counts all whitespace separated words in a string.
    """
    def _reduceString(self, str):
        "Removes anything that should not be counted. Here it does nothing."
        return str

    def countWords(self, str):
        "Counts all words in a string"
        str = self._reduceString(str)
        return len( string.split(str) )

class TagRemovingWordCounter (WordCounter):
    """
    Counts all whitespace separated words, after removing XML tags.
    """
    def __init__(self):
        self.tagRegEx = re.compile(r'\<\/?.+?\>')
```

```
        def _reduceString(self, str):
            str = self.tagRegEx.sub( ' ', str ) # substitute space for XML tag
            return str

#----------------
# Functions
#----------------
def CountWords( wordCounter, fileExt, rootDir ):
    """
    Count words with the WordCounter passed in, for a given root directory
    and file extension. All files with the extension passed, that reside
    in the root directory, or any subdirectory, are scanned.
    """
    fileNameRegEx = re.compile( r'.*\.' + fileExt )
    wordCount = 0
    for currentDir, subDirs, files in os.walk(rootDir):
        for fname in files:
            if not fileNameRegEx.match(fname): continue
            filePath = os.path.join(currentDir, fname)
            f = file(filePath)
            fileContentsString = f.read()
            f.close()
            wordCount = wordCount + wordCounter.countWords(fileContentsString)
    return wordCount

def Usage():
    "Return a string with the usage of the script"
    return "Usage: wc.py file_extension root_directory"

#----------------
# Main program
#----------------
def Main():
    """
    The script takes two arguments: a file extension, and a root directory path.
    All files with the extension in the root directory and subdirectories, are
    processed. The number of words in all the processed files are summed and
    printed. The number of words excluding XML-like tags are also printed.
    """
    # Check that two arguments have been passed to the script
    if len( sys.argv ) != 3:
        print Usage()
        sys.exit()

    # Calculate the word count with tags
    wordCounter = WordCounter()
    numWords = CountWords( wordCounter, sys.argv[1], sys.argv[2] )
    print "%-60s %6d" % ("total word count", numWords)

    # Calculate the word count without tags
    wordCounter = TagRemovingWordCounter()
    numWords = CountWords( wordCounter, sys.argv[1], sys.argv[2] )
    print "%-60s %6d" % ("word count without tags", numWords)

if ( __name__ == "__main__" ): Main()
```

How It Works

The script begins with a *shebang*, just like a Bash script:

```
#!/usr/bin/env python
```

A shebang is a line that tells the shell charged with starting a script which program should be used to run it. In this case, the shebang indicates that the script should be run by the `python` interpreter. A full path to the interpreter has not been provided, although that is also possible; instead, the `/usr/bin/env` command has been used, which searches for the `python` program and returns its path for you to the shell. This makes your script more portable because you don't have to keep changing the shebang every time the `python` interpreter is relocated.

A comment follows, describing briefly what the script is for.

```
#----------------------------------------
# Counts words after removing HTML/XML tags
#----------------------------------------
```

Comments in Python are indicated by a # symbol; anything on the line following the # is ignored by the interpreter.

Next, some modules are imported.

```
import re, string, sys, os
```

Python has many different modules in its library, and many more are available from third parties. To use the functions and classes in a module, you first must import it so that the interpreter knows that it must be loaded. In this case, the modules imported are `re`, for regular expressions; `string`, for string handling; `sys`, for aspects related to the environment the script is running in; and `os`, for interacting with the operating system in a platform-independent manner.

The script continues by defining a number of classes, the first of which looks like this:

```
class WordCounter:
    """
    Counts all whitespace separated words in a string.
    """
    def _reduceString(self, str):
        "Removes anything that should not be counted. Here it does nothing."
        return str

    def countWords(self, str):
        "Counts all words in a string"
        str = self._reduceString(str)
        return len( string.split(str) )
```

Classes appear in all OO languages, including Objective-C (see Chapter 7). The name of the class is given after the keyword `class`; in this case, the class is called `WordCounter`.

Just under the class name is an optional comment, which is used only for documentation purposes. In this case, a multiline comment has been used; Python uses " " " to delineate the beginning and end of multiline comments. Documentation comments can be used with any class or function and can be extracted with the program `pydoc` in order to generate HTML documentation. If you run the command

```
pydoc -w ./script_file
```

in the Terminal utility, an HTML file will be generated that you can open in any web browser.

After the comment, the class includes two methods: `_reduceString`, and `countWords`. A *method*, in OO terminology, is a function that belongs to a class. The keyword `def` is used in Python to delineate the beginning of a function or method. It is followed by the name, and a comma-separated list of arguments in parentheses. A colon is used to close off the line.

Unusually for OO languages, the instance to which a method belongs is passed explicitly as the first argument in the argument list. By convention, this argument is called `self`, like the `self` variable in Objective-C classes (see Chapter 7).

To invoke a method, a Java/C++ like syntax is used. This is demonstrated in the `countWords` method:

```
str = self._reduceString(str)
```

The `_reduceString` method is invoked for the `self` object. The variable `str` is passed to the method and then assigned to the value returned by the method.

By now you may have noticed that there are no `end class` or `end def` keywords to indicate where a class or method finishes. How does the Python interpreter know when one method finishes and the next begins? The answer has to do with whitespace. Whitespace, or to be more specific, indentation, is part of the Python language. In most other languages you indent to make code more readable, but the compiler or interpreter ignores the indentation. In Python, indentation is used to delineate the nesting of blocks of code.

Take this simple example:

```
def hello():
    print "hello"
    print "nice day isn't it"
```

This is not the same as the following:

```
def hello():
    print "hello"
print "nice day isn't it"
```

In the second example, the second `print` statement does not belong to the function `hello`, but to the enclosing code block. In C, the first example would be

```
void hello() {
    printf("hello");
    printf("nice day isn't it");
}
```

and the second would be

```
void hello() {
    printf("hello");
}
printf("nice day isn't it");
```

Syntax aside, the _reduceString method of WordCounter takes an argument for the parameter str, and returns it again. This seems pointless, but has a good reason, as will become evident as you read on.

> The prepended underscore in the name _reduceString **has no special meaning to the Python interpreter, but there is a convention among Python programmers that this means a method is** *protected* **— it should be accessed only from inside the defining class and its descendents. The reason this convention has evolved is that the Python language itself does not provide any constructions for controlling access to data or methods. All instance variables and methods of a class can be accessed wherever the class itself is accessible.**

The countWords method accepts a string argument. It first calls _reduceString with the string, before splitting the string into a list of words with the string.split function, and returning the length of the list.

```
return len( string.split(str) )
```

The split function is from the module string, which is prepended to the function name. The split function returns a list of the words that are separated by whitespace in the string passed to the function.

A list is an array-like built-in type for storing objects in order; it is like NSMutableArray from the Cocoa frameworks (see Chapters 7 and 8). You can get the number of elements in a list, or its length, with the len function. This line thus effectively counts the number of words in the string, and returns it.

The second class, TagRemovingWordCounter, is used to count words after XML tags have been removed.

```
class TagRemovingWordCounter (WordCounter):
    """
    Counts all whitespace separated words, after removing XML tags.
    """
    def __init__(self):
        self.tagRegEx = re.compile(r'\<\/?.+?\>')

    def _reduceString(self, str):
        str = self.tagRegEx.sub( ' ', str ) # substitute space for XML tag
        return str
```

It is a subclass of WordCounter; super classes are given in a comma-separated list in parentheses after the class name. After a documentation comment, the method __init__ is defined. __init__ is the initializer method, which is called when a new object is created. There can only be one initializer per class in Python.

In the example, the __init__ method sets an instance variable called tagRegEx. In order to make a new variable in Python, it is not necessary to declare it; you simply use it on the left-hand side of an expression. The type of the variable becomes the type of the object to which it is assigned. Everything in Python is an object, and every variable has the type of the object it is assigned to. If you reassign a variable to a different object, its type will effectively change to the type of the new object.

tagRegEx is assigned to an object representing a regular expression. A *regular expression* is like a formula that can be used to match patterns in strings. You can use them to test if a string matches a particular pattern, or search a string for matching substrings. Regular expressions are not restricted to Python, but are also integral to Perl, and are even used in shell programming, via commands like egrep, sed, and awk. Regular expressions are very powerful, and are covered in Chapter 11, which deals with shell programming.

The function compile, from the module re, is used to create the regular expression object in this case. The regular expression itself, which matches any XML tag, is given between single quotes. The r that precedes the first quote indicates that the string is a *raw string*, which means that the Python interpreter will pass it to the compile function exactly as it is written in the program. If a string is not a raw string, python will substitute characters that have special meaning.

The _reduceString method of TagRemovingWordCounter uses the regular expression object initialized in __init__ to replace all XML tags with whitespace. Because TagRemovingWordCounter is a subclass of WordCounter, this implementation of _reduceString replaces the implementation in WordCounter. When the countWords method is invoked on a TagRemovingWordCounter object, the countWords implementation in WordCounter is executed because it is inherited by the TagRemovingWordCounter class. countWords first calls _reduceString, replacing all tags with whitespace, before using the split function to split the string into words. Effectively, only words outside of tags are counted.

The function CountWords, which follows the classes, traverses the directory structure, visiting each file, and scanning the ones that have the correct file extension.

```
def CountWords( wordCounter, fileExt, rootDir ):
    """
    Count words with the WordCounter passed in, for a given root directory
    and file extension. All files with the extension passed, that reside
    in the root directory, or any subdirectory, are scanned.
    """
    fileNameRegEx = re.compile( r'.*\.' + fileExt )
    wordCount = 0
    for currentDir, subDirs, files in os.walk(rootDir):
        for fname in files:
            if not fileNameRegEx.match(fname): continue
            filePath = os.path.join(currentDir, fname)
            f = file(filePath)
            fileContentsString = f.read()
            f.close()
            wordCount = wordCount + wordCounter.countWords(fileContentsString)
    return wordCount
```

A for loop is used to iterate over all the directories descended from the root directory. The walk function, from the os module, takes a single argument, which is the path to the root directory to be traversed. It returns an iterator object, which can be used in a for loop.

For each directory, the iterator returns three objects: the directory path, a list of subdirectories in the directory, and a list of files in the directory. Python allows you to return as many values from a function as you see fit, unlike most other languages where only one return value is allowed.

A second loop is nested in the first, in order to iterate over the list of files in each directory. A regular expression, fileNameRegEx, is first used in an if statement to test if the filename has the correct file extension. If it doesn't, the continue statement is executed, causing the for loop to begin its next iteration, skipping the code between the continue and the end of the for loop.

If the filename matches the regular expression, indicating that it has the right extension, the name is combined with the directory path using the function os.path.join, to give the path to the file. The built-in file function opens the file and returns an object giving access to its contents. The contents are read with the read method before the file is closed with the close method.

The WordCounter object passed to the function is used to count the words in the string read in, and the variable wordCount, which was initialized to the integer 0 at the beginning of the method, is increased by the word count for the file. When all files have been scanned, wordCount is returned.

The main program in the example script can be found in the Main function. Main is not a special function in Python; you can put your main program in any function you like, or keep it at global scope. Main is responsible in this case for creating WordCounter objects and printing results for the user:

```
# Check that two arguments have been passed to the script
if len( sys.argv ) != 3:
    print Usage()
    sys.exit()

# Calculate the word count with tags
wordCounter = WordCounter()
numWords = CountWords( wordCounter, sys.argv[1], sys.argv[2] )
print "%-60s %6d" % ("total word count", numWords)

# Calculate the word count without tags
wordCounter = TagRemovingWordCounter()
numWords = CountWords( wordCounter, sys.argv[1], sys.argv[2] )
print "%-60s %6d" % ("word count without tags", numWords)
```

It first checks that the script was passed two arguments, namely, the file extension and the path. Arguments are passed via the list variable sys.argv. This contains the name of the script, followed by each argument, so its length should be one more than the expected number of arguments.

The next block of code initializes a WordCounter object. This demonstrates how you actually create instances in Python. You give the class name, followed by the arguments to the __init__ initializer in parentheses, much like a function call. When you create a new object, memory is allocated for the new object, and then the __init__ method is called with the arguments passed.

The CountWords function is passed the wordCounter object, along with the first two arguments of the script. Lists like sys.argv provide access to their elements via indexes. Indexes begin at 0 and are given in square braces after the list variable. The integer returned by CountWords is printed on the next line using the built-in print function.

The last block of code is very similar, but uses a `TagRemovingWordCounter` object. This demonstrates nicely the strength of OO polymorphism (see Chapter 7) and Python dynamicism. Exactly the same function, `CountWords`, works equally well with a `WordCounter` object as a `TagRemovingWordCounter` object. Both classes include the method `countWords` needed by the `CountWords` implementation. Any other class defining a `countWords` method could also be used in the `CountWords` function.

The `Main` function is not called until the last line of the script.

```
if ( __name__ == "__main__" ): Main()
```

This rather strange looking `if` statement is common to many Python scripts. Often you will write Python scripts that could be run as standalone scripts or imported and used in another script. For example, you may want to use the `WordCounter` class in an entirely different setting. You want to import the classes and functions in the example script, but do not want the main program of the word counting script to be executed.

The `if` statement makes this possible, by comparing the built-in __name__ variable with the string "__main__". If the script was run as the main program, __name__ will be equal to __main__; if it was imported by another script, it will not be. `Main` will thus be executed only when the script is the main program.

This has been a lightning fast introduction to Python, and it has barely scratched the surface. Hopefully, you have been able to recognize that Python

- ❏ Has a simple syntax, in which indentation is significant.

- ❏ Includes powerful OO features.

- ❏ Is dynamically and strongly typed. Variables take the type of the objects they are assigned to and can even change type when reassigned.

- ❏ Includes a broad library of modules, with regular expressions, string handling, and file system operations.

More Information

Your first stop for more information about Python is the main Python website (http://www.python.org). This site includes the latest Python releases, documentation, tutorials, articles, and links to other Python websites.

There are a few sites specifically for Python on the Mac. Jack Jansen is responsible for the Python shipped with Mac OS X, and his MacPython website (http://homepages.cwi.nl/~jack/macpython/) includes the latest binaries for the Mac. He also provides add-ons; these include, for example, a package manager than can be used to easily install popular third-party packages not provided by default on Mac OS X.

The pythonmac website (http://www.pythonmac.org) is a portal for Python on the Mac, with links to related sites and a wiki.

You can find examples of Python in the `/Developer/Examples/Python` directory on your hard disk after you install the Xcode developer tools. You can find examples of using the CoreGraphics framework from Python in the folder `/Developer/Examples/Quartz/Python`.

Lastly, if you are interested in using Python with Cocoa, you need look no further than the PyObjC website (`http://pyobjc.sourceforge.net/`). You can find the latest binaries there and documentation for how to get started.

Perl

Perl is a powerful scripting language introduced by Larry Walls in 1987. One of the underlying philosophies of Perl is that there should be many ways to do the same thing, allowing scripters to choose the approach that suits them the best. This can make for some very different styles of programming. It is not uncommon for a regular user of Perl to come across code from another developer and not be able to make heads or tails of it. For that matter, it is not unusual for a Perl hobbyist to come across code that they themselves have written 6 months previous and not be able to make heads or tails of it.

Perl code itself looks something like a cross between C and a Chinese grocery list. The basic syntax is in the C tradition, with code blocks enclosed in curly braces and line endings delineated by semicolons. Perl adds to this basic syntax a wide variety of symbols, each with its own special meaning. These symbols can make Perl code very compact because you can avoid temporary variables, but it takes some time to learn what they all mean. Until you do know what they mean, Perl source code can appear like some form of encryption.

Why Perl?

As Perl matures, it gains more and more functionality, but it began as basically the scripting equivalent of C. It did not have any OO features, but did provide functions, and more powerful data containers like arrays and hashes (dictionaries). String manipulations were central, with regular expressions built into the language directly, rather than accessible via a library.

These days Perl has even more powerful features, like OO, but the philosophy of the language has not changed. Its shining star is still powerful string handling, but it offers much more than that. You can do just about anything in Perl that you can do in other languages, and more. It is popular not only because of its string handling capabilities, but also because it makes interacting with system-level libraries easy, and can be used for CGI programming for the Web.

One of Perl's great strengths is simply its popularity. It was really the first high-level scripting language. The popularity of Perl means that there are many extensions available, in the form of Perl modules. Most of these modules are available on the Comprehensive Perl Archive Network (CPAN) website (`http://www.cpan.org`). CPAN can also be accessed via command-line tools, allowing you to easily download and install Perl modules.

Perl is particularly popular among C programmers, largely because of its familiarity. Perl syntax is based on C, so C programmers have adopted Perl as their scripting language of choice. Perl also holds to other C conventions, like *pass-by-value*. When a variable, such as a string or array, is passed as an argument to a function, a complete copy of the data is made. This is basically the same approach taken by C. Other languages, like Java and Python, use an approach in which data does not get copied when passed to a function. (Perl does provide *references*, which you can use to avoid copying of data.)

As already stated, one of the central premises of Perl is that there should be several ways to achieve a single task. This flexibility gives the scripter a lot of leeway. If you use Perl regularly, you will likely be able to write scripts much more compactly than you can in other languages, which makes it good for writing small helper scripts. For major projects, a more structured style of programming is required in order to produce maintainable code; Perl can also be used for this, but it takes discipline on the part of the scripter not to lapse into the indecipherable code that Perl allows.

On Mac OS X, Perl can be used with the Cocoa frameworks in a number of ways. If you are interested only in using the Cocoa Foundation framework, you can use the `PerlObjCBridge` module, which is included with Mac OS X. If you would like to use the AppKit framework to create Cocoa applications with a GUI, you will need to install the CamelBones framework, which is not included with Mac OS X.

Whether or not Perl has weaknesses depends on who you talk to. Some consider the compact, eclectic syntax a strength; others find it unnecessarily complex and prefer the clean approach of Python. Some consider the "many ways" philosophy of Perl to be empowering, and others just regard it as confusing.

Try It Out   A Perl Example

Because Perl overlaps Python in many application domains, the example provided in this section has the same basic functionality as the Python example given earlier. This will allow you to compare the two languages more directly, to decide what appeals to you the most. The script itself traverses a directory tree, counting the number of words in files with a given extension. The total number of words is counted, along with the number of words with XML-style tags removed.

```perl
#!/usr/bin/env perl
use strict;
use File::Find;

#-----------------
# Global variables
#-----------------
my $numWords;
my $removeTags;
my $fileExtension;

#----------
# Functions
#----------
sub CountWordsInString {
    my $str = $_[0];
    if ( $removeTags ) {
        $str =~ s/\<\/?.+?\>/ /g;
    }
    my @words = split /\s+/, $str;
    $numWords += $#words + 1;
}

# Called by find function
sub CountWordsInFile {
```

```perl
        my $path = $File::Find::name;
        if ( $path =~ /.*\.$fileExtension/ ) {
            open SOURCE_FILE, $path or die ("Could not open file");
            my $contentsString = join '', <SOURCE_FILE>;
            close SOURCE_FILE;
            CountWordsInString $contentsString;
        }
}

sub CountWords {
    my ( $fileExt, $rootDir, $remTags ) = @_;
    $numWords = 0;
    $fileExtension = $fileExt;
    $removeTags = $remTags;
    my @paths = ($rootDir);
    find(\&CountWordsInFile, @paths );
    return $numWords
}

sub Usage {
    return "Usage: wc.pl file_extension root_directory\n";
}


#-------------
# Main program
#-------------
if ( $#ARGV + 1 != 2 ) {
    print Usage();
    exit;
}

# Calculate the word count with tags
my $numWords = CountWords( $ARGV[0], $ARGV[1], 0 );
print "total word count: $numWords\n";

# Calculate the word count without tags
$numWords = CountWords( $ARGV[0], $ARGV[1], 1 );
print "total word count with no tags: $numWords\n";
```

How It Works

The script begins with a shebang, just as the Python script does, but this script uses the `perl` command instead of `python`.

```perl
#!/usr/bin/env perl
use strict;
use File::Find;
```

Two modules are imported: `strict`, and `File::Find`. The Perl use keyword is equivalent to Python's import. The `strict` module causes Perl to report an error if a variable is used before being declared. Using `strict` is optional, but can make debugging scripts easier.

Next, a number of global variables are declared.

```
my $numWords;
my $removeTags;
my $fileExtension;
```

You can declare variables using the my keyword. The type of a variable is indicated in Perl by a prepended symbol, in this case $. $ means that the variable is a scalar. A @ indicates an array, and a % is a hash, which is the same as a dictionary in Python or Objective-C.

A number of functions are defined next. The first counts words in a string passed as argument:

```
sub CountWordsInString {
    my $str = $_[0];
    if ( $removeTags ) {
        $str =~ s/\<\/?.+?\>/ /g;
    }
    my @words = split /\s+/, $str;
    $numWords += $#words + 1;
}
```

You may be wondering where the parameter list is in this function. Perl does not represent parameters in the usual way; instead, arguments are passed via a special variable: @_. @_ is defined in any function and is an array of the arguments passed to the function. In this case, only one argument is expected, so the first element in the array is retrieved using the expression $_[0] and the value stored in the variable $str. The first element in the arguments array is retrieved by supplying the index 0 in square braces, and because the resulting array element has a scalar value, a $ must be prepended, giving $_[0].

An if block checks if XML tags should be removed, as determined from the $removeTags global variable. If tags are to be removed, the following line is executed:

```
$str =~ s/\<\/?.+?\>/ /g;
```

This is an example of a regular expression. The special operator =~ is used to apply the expression on the right-hand side (RHS) to the string variable $str. The RHS is of the general form s/regular_expression/replacement_string/g. This substitutes any substrings matching the regular expression appearing between the first two slashes, with the text between the last two. The regular expression in this case matches an XML tag, and the replacement string is a single space.

The last few lines of the CountWordsInString function split the string into words, and increase the $numWords global variable based on the number of words in the string. The split function is used to split the string into words, which are stored in the array variable @words. The special variable $#words gives the last index in the @words array, so $#words + 1 is the total number of words.

The next function counts the number of words in a particular file by calling the CountWordsInString function:

```
sub CountWordsInFile {
    my $path = $File::Find::name;
    if ( $path =~ /.*\.$fileExtension/ ) {
        open SOURCE_FILE, $path or die ("Could not open file");
        my $contentsString = join '', <SOURCE_FILE>;
        close SOURCE_FILE;
```

```
        CountWordsInString $contentsString;
    }
}
```

This function gets called by the Perl `find` function The `find` function passes the filename via a global variable called `$File::Find::name`. On the first line of the function, `$File::Find::name` is assigned to a local variable called `$path`. The `if` statement then checks to see if `$path` has the file extension stored in the global variable `$fileExtension`. It uses a regular expression to do this, with the `=~` operator. Rather than substituting a string in this case, a match with the regular expression is sought, to determine whether the file path has the correct extension.

If the file has the right extension, it is opened and assigned to the file variable `SOURCE_FILE`. The `or die` part of the expression causes the program to exit after printing the message `"Could not open file"` should the file be unable to be opened. The next line reads the source file, and uses the `join` function to concatenate all the lines into a single string, which is assigned to the `$contentsString` variable. `SOURCE_FILE` is closed, and the `CountWordsInString` function called, with `$contentsString` as argument. Note that parentheses around the argument list are optional in function calls.

The last of the word counting functions initiates the directory tree traversal, using the Perl `find` function.

```
sub CountWords {
    my ( $fileExt, $rootDir, $remTags ) = @_;
    $numWords = 0;
    $fileExtension = $fileExt;
    $removeTags = $remTags;
    my @paths = ($rootDir);
    find(\&CountWordsInFile, @paths );
    return $numWords
}
```

The function begins by initializing the global variables `$numWords`, `$fileExtension`, and `$removeTags`. You have already seen how these variables are used in the earlier word counting functions. `CountWords` then calls `find`, which iterates over the files in the directory trees passed in the second argument. In this case, there is only one directory tree, but it still needs to be passed as an array to `find`. So, the `@paths` variable is created with `$rootDir` as its only entry. An array literal is created by enclosing comma-separated variables and/or literals in parentheses. The function concludes by returning the total word count, `$numWords`.

The main program begins by checking the number of arguments passed to the script, and then performs two word counts: one with tags, and one without:

```
if ( $#ARGV + 1 != 2 ) {
    print Usage();
    exit;
}

# Calculate the word count with tags
my $numWords = CountWords( $ARGV[0], $ARGV[1], 0 );
print "total word count: $numWords\n";

# Calculate the word count without tags
```

```
$numWords = CountWords( $ARGV[0], $ARGV[1], 1 );
print "total word count with no tags: $numWords\n";
```

@ARGV is an array holding the arguments passed to the script. The entries in this array are passed on to the CountWords function. The third argument to CountWords indicates whether or not tags should be removed. A value of 0, which is false, means tags should not be removed; a value of 1, or true, indicates they should be removed.

Perl is a challenging language and not easy to convey in such a short passage. Many subtleties exist, and they have been glossed over here to some extent. Nonetheless, from this example you should have been able to gather that Perl

❑ Has powerful string-handling features and data containers

❑ Provides a library of useful functions, such as find for traversing directory trees

❑ Has syntax similar to C

❑ Uses a whole range of somewhat cryptic symbols to represent special variables

More Information

The Perl Directory is a good place to begin your exploration of Perl (http://www.perl.org). It includes links to many other Perl resources.

CPAN is the best place to look for Perl modules (http://www.cpan.org). It also includes other resources, like documentation, frequently asked questions, and mailing lists.

To write Cocoa applications with Perl, you will need CamelBones, which you can download from the CamelBones website (http://camelbones.sourceforge.net). This site also includes all the documentation and examples you need to get started writing Cocoa applications with Perl.

JavaScript and Dashboard

Netscape originally created JavaScript as a scripting language to make dynamic content for the Web. JavaScript code is usually found embedded in HTML and gets run in a web browser. By giving you access to all the elements of an HTML page via the so-called *document object model* (DOM), JavaScript allows you to take static HTML web content and change it as time passes.

JavaScript looks quite a bit like the Java programming language, but that is where the comparison ends. JavaScript is not Java, nor is it a subset of Java. JavaScript is a simple interpreted language that runs in web browsers, and Java is an extensive compiled language that can be used for a wide variety of different purposes — from developing websites to creating desktop applications.

Java is a compiled language, but it is a compiled language with a difference. The Java compiler converts Java source code into something called byte code, rather than the machine code that runs on the CPU. The byte code is platform independent; when you run a Java application, a program called the Java virtual machine (JVM) reads the byte code and generates machine executable code, which is what is sent to the CPU. In short, the JVM is a bit like an interpreter. As you can see, the distinction between a compiled language and an interpreted language is not that clear when it comes to Java.

Dashboard

Quite aside from its important place in web development, JavaScript has an added attraction for Mac developers. With the coming of Mac OS X 10.4 (Tiger), JavaScript has stepped outside the browser. As you are undoubtedly aware, Dashboard is a new technology that allows you to develop and use *widgets*, which are little utilities that you can display with the press of a key or move of the mouse. What you may not know is that Dashboard is based on web technologies like HTML, CSS, and JavaScript. Put simply, a Dashboard widget is not much more or less than a web page.

If you have experienced Dashboard as a user, you are aware that widgets can come in a variety of forms. Some are like small stand-alone applications, such as a calculator or notepad. Others, like the Weather and Flight Tracker widgets provided by Apple, give you an easy way to access web content. And a third category provides simplified interfaces to existing programs like iTunes.

Dashboard widgets are *bundles*, which are simply folders with a special extension. All applications on Mac OS X are also bundles — folders with the extension .app, which the Finder treats as a single file for most purposes. Widgets also come in bundles, but the extension you give them is .wdgt.

A widget bundle must include a number of different files, including the following:

❏   A main HTML file

❏   A PNG file for the widget bar icon

❏   A PNG file for the default image of the widget, which is displayed during loading

❏   An Info.plist property list file that includes metadata that describes various aspects of the widget, such as its size on the screen

A widget bundle can also include any other files needed for it to function properly, such as images or JavaScript source code.

Dashboard widgets can leverage any technology included with Mac OS X, from AppleScript to OpenGL, but most are built using just three technologies:

❏   **HTML:** Defines the structure of a widget

❏   **Cascading Style Sheets (CSS):** Defines the look of a widget

❏   **JavaScript:** Defines the behavior of a widget

In the next two Try It Outs you learn a little about JavaScript, HTML, and CSS by creating a Dashboard widget. The widget in question, called DashBall, is of the stand-alone utility variety. DashBall, shown in Figure 10-1, is a simple game in which the user hits a tennis ball against the walls of a brick box.

In this first Try It Out, you set up the widget so that it can be displayed but doesn't do anything. In the second Try It Out, you finish the widget, adding ball movement and responding to when the ball gets hit by the user's cursor.

Figure 10-1

Try It Out   Beginning the DashBall Dashboard Widget

1. Create a new folder called DashBall in the Finder. Create a new text file in the folder called
    DashBall.js using any editor (for example, Xcode or TextEdit), and enter the following
    source code:

```javascript
// Wall Coordinates
var wallCoords = {left:40, right:225, bottom:175, top:15};

// Ball Properties
var ball = {
    x:(wallCoords.right + wallCoords.left ) * 0.5,
    y:(wallCoords.top + wallCoords.bottom) * 0.5,
    velocityX:200.0,
    velocityY:200.0 }

if (window.widget)
{
    widget.onshow = onshow;
    widget.onhide = onhide;
}

// Called when widget is loaded
function setup()
{
    setBallPosition();
}

// Called when dashboard is shown
function onshow()
{
}

// Called when dashboard is hidden
function onhide()
{
}

function setBallPosition()
```

```
{
    var ballImage = document.getElementById("ball");
    ballImage.style.top = ball.y;
    ballImage.style.left = ball.x;
}
```

2. Add another text file called `DashBall.css`, and enter the following text:

```css
body {
    margin: 0;
}

image#ball {
    position: absolute;
}
```

3. Add a file called `DashBall.html` to the `DashBall` folder, and enter the following contents:

```html
<html>

<head>

<style type="text/css">
    @import "DashBall.css";
</style>

<script type='text/javascript' src='DashBall.js' charset='utf-8'/>

</head>

<body onload='setup();'>
    <img src='Default.png'>
    <img id='ball' src='TennisBall.png'>
</body>

</html>
```

4. Now add a text file called `Info.plist` to the `DashBall` folder, and insert the following property list code:

```xml
<?xml version="1.0" encoding="UTF-8"?>
<!DOCTYPE plist PUBLIC "-//Apple Computer//DTD PLIST 1.0//EN"
"http://www.apple.com/DTDs/PropertyList-1.0.dtd">
<plist version="1.0">
<dict>
    <key>AllowMultipleInstances</key>
    <true/>
    <key>CFBundleIdentifier</key>
    <string>com.beginningmacosxprogramming.widget.dashball</string>
    <key>CFBundleName</key>
    <string>DashBall</string>
    <key>CFBundleShortVersionString</key>
    <string>1.0</string>
    <key>CFBundleVersion</key>
    <string>1.0</string>
```

```
        <key>DefaultImage</key>
        <string>Default</string>
        <key>MainHTML</key>
        <string>DashBall.html</string>
        <key>Height</key>
        <integer>225</integer>
        <key>Width</key>
        <integer>300</integer>
    </dict>
    </plist>
```

5. Use a drawing or painting program to create the graphics files for DashBall, and save them in the `DashBall` folder. All files should be in PNG format. Use Figure 10-1 as a reference for how the graphics should look. The following table gives details of each of the graphics you need to create.

Filename	Description of Image	Width	Height
Default.png	A rectangular border made of bricks. The space inside the rectangle should be transparent.	300 pixels	225 pixels
Icon.png	A square region of brick wall with rounded corners, and a tennis ball in the center.	82 pixels	82 pixels
TennisBall.png	A tennis ball.	36 pixels	36 pixels

If you do not have the talent or desire to create these images, you can use the ones supplied in the sample code for this chapter, which you can download from www.wrox.com.

6. Use the Finder to change the name of the `DashBall` folder to `DashBall.wdgt`. The icon of the folder should change to indicate that `DashBall.wdgt` is a Dashboard widget.

7. Double-click `DashBall.wdgt` to open it in Dashboard. Drag the widget around on the screen and then close it again.

How It Works

The `Info.plist` file that you supply in a widget's bundle gives Dashboard important information about the widget, such as its size on-screen and the name of the main HTML file. The `Info.plist` file is in Apple's XML property list format, which allows you to include basic types like integers and strings, and to structure data into arrays and dictionaries.

You do not have to edit property lists manually in a text editor if you don't want to. Instead, you can use the Property List Editor application, which is located in the `/Developer/Applications/` `Utilities` *directory, after you install the Xcode developer tools.*

Here is a table describing the entries in the `Info.plist` file of DashBall:

Dictionary Key	Type	Description
AllowMultipleInstances	Boolean	Whether or not a user is allowed to create more than one instance of the widget on the screen. For DashBall this is allowed.
CFBundleIdentifier	String	A unique identifier for the widget. This is used, for example, to store preferences.
CFBundleName	String	The name of the widget in Dashboard.
CFBundleShortVersionString	String	The version number of the widget, as a short string.
CFBundleVersion	String	The full version number of the widget.
DefaultImage	String	The name of the PNG file that is displayed while the widget is loading. The extension should not be included in the name.
MainHTML	String	The name of the main HTML file of the widget. The extension should be included.
Height	Integer	The height of the widget in pixels.
Width	Integer	The width of the widget in pixels.

The only optional key in the table is `AllowMultipleInstances`; the others have to be supplied in every widget you write.

The `Info.plist` file supplies Dashboard with metadata for your widget, but the structure of the widget itself is defined in the main HTML file. For DashBall, this file is called `DashBall.html`, as given in the `Info.plist` file for the key `MainHTML`. If you have any experience with HTML, the `DashBall.html` file should not pose any challenges. It begins by importing the CSS file `DashBall.css`, which is used to define some aspects of the appearance of the widget:

```
<style type="text/css">
    @import "DashBall.css";
</style>
```

The CSS file is very simple in this case:

```
body {
    margin: 0;
}

image#ball {
    position: absolute;
}
```

The first block indicates that the body of the widget's HTML page should have a margin with a width of 0. The second block refers to the image representing the tennis ball. The position property is set to absolute, which means the ball's position can be set to any position on the page.

After importing DashBall.css, the DashBall.html file includes the JavaScript file DashBall.js:

```
<script type='text/javascript' src='DashBall.js' charset='utf-8'/>
```

DashBall.js determines the behavior of the widget, such as how it reacts to events, user generated or otherwise.

The body of the HTML file includes two image files, one of the brick wall box, Default.png, and the other of the tennis ball, TennisBall.png:

```
<body onload='setup();'>
    <img src='Default.png'>
    <img id='ball' src='TennisBall.png'>
</body>
```

The body tag also includes the onload attribute, which is assigned to a piece of JavaScript code that gets executed when the HTML is first loaded. In this case, the JavaScript function setup, which is defined in DashBall.js, is called. The setup function initializes various aspects of the widget.

The JavaScript file DashBall.js begins by defining some variables for the positions of the four walls and the position and velocity of the tennis ball:

```
// Wall Coordinates
var wallCoords = {left:40, right:225, bottom:175, top:15};

// Ball Properties
var ball = {
    x:(wallCoords.right + wallCoords.left ) * 0.5,
    y:(wallCoords.top + wallCoords.bottom) * 0.5,
    velocityX:200.0,
    velocityY:200.0 }
```

You define variables in JavaScript using the var keyword. The wallCoords variable is assigned to an object that has the attributes left, right, bottom, and top. These attributes are initialized to 40, 225, 175, and 15, respectively. Together they define the region that the tennis ball is allowed to explore. The values themselves are taken relative to an origin at the top-left of the page. They were simply determined by trial and error in order to make the ball appear to bounce off the brick walls.

The ball's attributes are its position, given by x and y, and its velocity, given by velocityX and velocityY. The attributes x and y are initialized such that the ball is located in the center of the box defined by wallCoords. The velocity attributes have been chosen arbitrarily; they could just as easily be set to other values to give the ball a different initial speed and/or direction of travel.

An object in JavaScript is basically the same as a dictionary in Cocoa programming (see Chapters 7 and 8), a collection of key-value pairs. In other languages, the terms map, hash table, and associative array are also used to describe such containers.

The next lines of the `DashBall.js` script set the `onshow` and `onhide` attributes of a JavaScript object called `widget`:

```
if (window.widget)
{
    widget.onshow = onshow;
    widget.onhide = onhide;
}
```

`widget` is created by Dashboard and can be used to interact with Dashboard and the rest of the operating system. For example, you can use `widget`'s `system` method to run shell commands and other programs.

The preceding code uses an `if` statement to check whether the `widget` object exists. You need to do this if you want to be able to test your widgets in a web browser such as Safari because the `widget` object exists only when running in Dashboard, not in a browser.

If the `widget` object does exist, two of its attributes, `onshow` and `onhide`, are set to functions defined later in the script:

```
// Called when dashboard is shown
function onshow()
{
}

// Called when dashboard is hidden
function onhide()
{
}
```

In this case, the functions have also been given the names `onshow` and `onhide`, but this is not a requirement. Neither function takes any action at this point; functionality is introduced in the next Try It Out. The function `onshow` is called when Dashboard gets displayed on the screen, and `onhide` is called when Dashboard gets hidden. These attributes of `widget` are quite important because they allow you to halt any expensive calculations that your widget might perform while Dashboard is not in view.

The `setup` function is called when the HTML body is loaded, as you saw in the preceding HTML file. It calls a second function, `setBallPosition`, which positions the ball's image according to the initial coordinates of the ball:

```
// Called when widget is loaded
function setup()
{
    setBallPosition();
}
```

`setBallPosition` moves the ball's image to whatever point in the page corresponds to its x and y coordinates at that point in time:

```
function setBallPosition()
{
    var ballImage = document.getElementById("ball");
```

```
        ballImage.style.top = ball.y;
        ballImage.style.left = ball.x;
    }
```

This function demonstrates how you can retrieve objects representing elements of a web page using JavaScript. The `getElementById` method of the `document` object, which is the root object for the web page, is passed a string identifier for the object sought. The identifier itself is set in the HTML file using the `id` property; in DashBall, the `id` property of the `img` tag corresponding to the ball's image was set to `ball`.

The object returned by `getElementById` corresponds to the `img` element of the ball's image. You can use JavaScript to set attributes of this tag, and thereby affect the relationship of the ball's image to the page. In this case, the `style` attribute of the `img` element is modified. The `style` attribute represents the element's CSS style, and modifying it effectively changes the CSS style of the image. The `setBallPosition` function sets the `left` and `top` attributes of the `img` element's `style` attribute to the x and y attributes of the ball, respectively. This results in the ball's image moving on the page to the coordinates given.

The DashBall widget is not yet complete. You can view it in Dashboard and move it around, but it doesn't do anything. In the following Try It Out, you finish the widget, making the ball move in time and allowing the user to hit it.

Try It Out   Finishing the DashBall Dashboard Widget

1. Use a text editor to open the `DashBall.js` file in the `DashBall.wdgt` bundle. To open the `DashBall.wdgt` bundle in Finder, you need to Control-click on it and select the Show Package Contents item from the contextual menu. Edit the top of the file as highlighted here:

```
// Ball Properties
var ball = {
    x:(wallCoords.right + wallCoords.left ) * 0.5,
    y:(wallCoords.top + wallCoords.bottom) * 0.5,
    velocityX:200.0,
    velocityY:200.0 }

// Physics
var frictionFactor = 0.9;
var elasticityFactor = 0.95;

// Timers
var theTimer = {step:100};
var powTimerId = 0;

// Variables for hitting
var hitting = false;
var hitCoords = new Object();
var ballCoordsAtHit = new Object();
```

2. Edit the `setup`, `onshow`, and `onhide` functions in `DashBall.js` as indicated here:

```
// Called when widget is loaded
function setup()
{
```

```
        setBallPosition();
        theTimer.id = setInterval("updateBall()", theTimer.step);
}

// Called when dashboard is shown
function onshow()
{
    if ( !theTimer.id ) theTimer.id = setInterval("updateBall()", theTimer.step);
}

// Called when dashboard is hidden
function onhide()
{
    clearInterval(theTimer.id);
    theTimer.id = 0;
}
```

3. To finish `DashBall.js`, add the following code to the end of the file and save your changes:

```
function updateBall()
{
    // Apply gravity
    ball.velocityY += 50.0 * ( theTimer.step / 1000.0 );

    // Update position
    ball.x += ball.velocityX * ( theTimer.step / 1000.0 );
    ball.y += ball.velocityY * ( theTimer.step / 1000.0 );

    // Handle bounces. Include a little friction, and inelasticity.
    if ( ball.x > wallCoords.right || ball.x < wallCoords.left )
    {
        ball.velocityX *= -elasticityFactor;
        ball.velocityY *= frictionFactor;
    }
    if ( ball.y < wallCoords.top || ball.y > wallCoords.bottom )
    {
        ball.velocityY *= -elasticityFactor;
        ball.velocityX *= frictionFactor;
    }

    // Make sure ball is in court
    ball.y = Math.max(ball.y, wallCoords.top);
    ball.y = Math.min(ball.y, wallCoords.bottom);
    ball.x = Math.max(ball.x, wallCoords.left);
    ball.x = Math.min(ball.x, wallCoords.right);

    setBallPosition();
}

function startHit() {
    hitting = true;
    hitCoords.x = event.x;
    hitCoords.y = event.y;
    ballCoordsAtHit.x = ball.x;
```

```
        ballCoordsAtHit.y = ball.y;
    }

function finishHit() {
    if ( hitting ) {
        ball.velocityX += 2 * (event.x - hitCoords.x -
            (ball.x - ballCoordsAtHit.x));
        ball.velocityY += 2 * (event.y - hitCoords.y -
            (ball.y - ballCoordsAtHit.y));
    }
    var pow = document.getElementById("pow");
    pow.style.top = ball.y;
    pow.style.left = ball.x;
    pow.style.visibility = 'visible';
    if ( powTimerId ) clearTimeout(powTimerId);
    powTimerId = setTimeout('hidePow();', 2000);
    hitting = false;
}

function hidePow() {
    document.getElementById("pow").style.visibility = 'hidden';
}
```

4. Open the `DashBall.css` file in the `DashBall.wdgt` bundle. Add the following to the end and save the changes:

```
.powtext {
    font: 26px "Lucida Grande";
    font-weight: bold;
    color: white;
    position: absolute;
    visibility: hidden;
}
```

5. Open the `DashBall.html` file in the `DashBall.wdgt` bundle and make the highlighted changes:

```
<body onload='setup();'>
    <img src='Default.png'>
    <span id='pow' class='powtext'>Pow!</span>
    <img id='ball' src='TennisBall.png'
        onmouseover='startHit();'
        onmouseout='finishHit();'>
</body>
```

6. After you have saved all your changes, double-click the bundle file in Finder to open DashBall in Dashboard. The ball should now move. Try hitting the ball with your cursor to see what happens.

7. Install the DashBall widget by moving it either to `/Library/Widgets` or `~/Library/Widgets`. You may need to create the `Widgets` directory first.

8. Open Dashboard and locate the DashBall icon on the widgets bar at the bottom of the screen. Drag out a new instance of the widget and confirm that it works as expected. Hide Dashboard and then show it again. Confirm that the ball begins moving again from the position it had when hidden.

How It Works

Some small changes are made to the elements in the `DashBall.html` file. In particular, a span element is added that includes the text `Pow!`:

```
<span id='pow' class='powtext'>Pow!</span>
```

This text gets displayed for a couple seconds whenever the user successfully hits the ball. The `id` of the element, `pow`, is used to refer to the text in `DashBall.js`. The `class` of the span element, `powtext`, is defined in `DashBall.css`:

```
.powtext {
    font: 26px "Lucida Grande";
    font-weight: bold;
    color: white;
    position: absolute;
    visibility: hidden;
}
```

This CSS code sets a number of attributes of the text, including its font and color. The position of the text on the screen also needs to be changed based on where the ball is hit. So the `position` attribute is set to `absolute`, just as it was for the ball's image. The position of the text can then be given relative to the coordinate system of the page. The last attribute is `visibility`, which determines whether or not the text is visible. Here it is initialized to `hidden`, which means the text is invisible. When the ball is hit, the text is made visible in the JavaScript code.

> The HTML `span` tag allows you to delineate a piece of text in a web page without attaching any special meaning to it. For example, if you use the `<p>` tag, the text automatically takes on all the attributes of a paragraph. By using `<span>`, you can refer to the text in JavaScript and control its look with CSS without assigning it any particular role.

Apart from the new span element, two attributes were also added to the existing img element used to represent the ball's image in the `DashBall.html` file:

```
<img id='ball' src='TennisBall.png'
        onmouseover='startHit();'
        onmouseout='finishHit();'>
```

The `onmouseover` attribute defines a piece of JavaScript that is executed whenever the user moves the cursor into the region covered by the image. The code executed in this case calls the function `startHit`, which is defined in `DashBall.js`. The `onmouseout` attribute is similar, but it is used when the mouse leaves the area covered by the image. When this event occurs, the `finishHit` function is called.

The `startHit` function sets a number of global variables that are declared at the top of `DashBall.js`:

```
function startHit() {
    hitting = true;
    hitCoords.x = event.x;
    hitCoords.y = event.y;
```

```
        ballCoordsAtHit.x = ball.x;
        ballCoordsAtHit.y = ball.y;
    }
```

The `hitting` variable is used to keep track of whether the user is in the process of hitting the ball. It is `true` when the cursor has entered the region of the ball, and `false` at all other times.

The `hitCoords` global variable is used to store the coordinates of the cursor when the ball is hit. It is declared and initialized at the top of `DashBall.js`:

```
    var hitCoords = new Object();
```

The `new` keyword creates a new object, just as in languages like Java and C++. `hitCoords` is initialized to a new object of the class `Object`, which you can simply view as an empty container. To put data in the container, you assign values to attributes as demonstrated in `startHit`; you do not need to declare the attributes before assigning them.

The `event` object in `startHit` contains information about the event that triggered the function call. The attributes `x` and `y` indicate where the event occurred, and these are stored in the `hitCoords` object for later reference. The coordinates of the ball are also stored when it is hit, in the `ballCoordsAtHit` variable.

All the variables set in `startHit` are used in the `finishHit` function to determine the change in the velocity of the ball resulting from the hit:

```
    function finishHit() {
        if ( hitting ) {
            ball.velocityX += 2 * (event.x - hitCoords.x -
                (ball.x - ballCoordsAtHit.x));
            ball.velocityY += 2 * (event.y - hitCoords.y -
                (ball.y - ballCoordsAtHit.y));
        }
        var pow = document.getElementById("pow");
        pow.style.top = ball.y;
        pow.style.left = ball.x;
        pow.style.visibility = 'visible';
        if ( powTimerId ) clearTimeout(powTimerId);
        powTimerId = setTimeout('hidePow();', 2000);
        hitting = false;
    }
```

This function first makes sure that the `hitting` variable is `true`; if it is, it adjusts the `velocityX` and `velocityY` attributes of the `ball` object. The change in velocity is determined by subtracting the coordinates at which the ball was hit, which are stored in `hitCoords`, from the coordinates of the event leading to the `finishHit` call, which are in the `event` object. The movement of the ball is then subtracted, to give the direction of the hit. The change in velocity is set to two times this direction; this scaling was determined simply by trial and error, to give the right "feel" when the ball is hit. You can adjust it to your own liking.

> *The algorithm used to change the velocity of the ball when it is hit is quite primitive. For example, it does not account for the speed of the cursor when the ball is hit. If you like, you can improve the widget by coming up with a more advanced algorithm for hitting the ball.*

The rest of the `finishHit` function displays the `Pow!` text. It first gets an object representing the text using the `getElementById` function; and then it sets the `style` attribute of the element to position the text at the same point as the ball. The `style.visibility` attribute is also set to `visible` so that the text appears on-screen.

Rather than have the `Pow!` text remain on-screen, a timer is used to hide it after two seconds. The `setTimeout` function is used in JavaScript to create a timer that fires only once. The first argument is the JavaScript that is executed when the timer fires. In this case, the `hidePow` function is called, which hides the `Pow!` text again:

```
function hidePow() {
    document.getElementById("pow").style.visibility = 'hidden';
    powTimerId = 0;
}
```

The second argument to `setTimeout` is the time interval before the timer fires, in milliseconds. The return value of the function is an identifier for the timer. It gets stored here in the `powTimerId` variable. The identifier can be passed to the `clearTimeout` function to cancel the timer; an example of this can also be found in `finishHit`, where any previously created timer that has yet to fire is cancelled before a new timer is created with `setTimeout`.

Another timer is used to animate the ball; the timer in question, however, fires repeatedly at regular intervals, rather than just once. The animation timer gets created in the `onshow` function that is called whenever Dashboard appears on-screen; it gets cancelled in `onhide` whenever Dashboard disappears from the screen:

```
 // Called when dashboard is shown
function onshow()
{
    if ( !theTimer.id ) theTimer.id = setInterval("updateBall()", theTimer.step);
}

// Called when dashboard is hidden
function onhide()
{
    clearInterval(theTimer.id);
    theTimer.id = 0;
}
```

As you can see, the `setInterval` function is used to create a repeating timer, rather than `setTimeout`.

> By starting and stopping the animation in this way, the DashBall widget does not take up precious CPU cycles when Dashboard is not on the screen. You will want to take a similar approach to every widget you write.

The animation timer makes repeated calls to the `updateBall` function. This function updates the ball's coordinates and velocity, and finishes off by moving the ball's image on the screen using a call to setBallPosition. The updateBall function is simple enough from a programming point of view, but it's a bit involved in terms of the physics it uses to modify the state of the ball. For example, it adjusts the velocity for gravity and accounts for collisions with the walls, including the effects of friction and inelasticity. The details are left to you to consider; if they are too complicated for your liking, you can either ignore them or change the algorithm to something simpler.

This DashBall example has only scratched the surface of what is possible with Dashboard widgets. For example, no use was made of preferences, for storing data persistently. You could use preferences to allow the user to set the initial velocity of the ball or the strength of gravity acting on the ball, to name but two possibilities.

No direct use of Quartz drawing was made in DashBall either. Dashboard offers an extension to HTML, the canvas tag, and a matching JavaScript class, Canvas, which allow you to use Quartz to draw on your widget. You could, for example, rewrite DashBall such that the space inside the brick box corresponded to a canvas, and the ball was drawn using the methods of the JavaScript Canvas class, which in turn invoke Quartz drawing functions.

Hopefully, the DashBall example has shown you that

❑   JavaScript is an object-oriented language with Java-like syntax.

❑   JavaScript is closely coupled to HTML and CSS via the document object model (DOM).

❑   Dashboard widgets are not much more than dynamic web pages.

❑   Dashboard widgets are generally constructed out of HTML, for structure; CSS, for appearance; and JavaScript, for behavior.

More Information

There are so many web resources for JavaScript that your best option for learning more may be simply to perform a Google search. The Netscape JavaScript Guide is a good starting point (http://wp. netscape.com/eng/mozilla/3.0/handbook/javascript/), and to learn more about the document object model (DOM), which defines the correspondence between JavaScript objects and HTML elements, you should take a look at Mozilla's Gecko DOM Reference (http://www.mozilla.org/docs/ dom/domref/).

The canvas HTML tag and Canvas JavaScript class are described in Apple's Safari documentation, including the Safari JavaScript Programming Topics document and the Safari JavaScript Reference. Both are located in the Xcode Documentation window, in the search group Reference Library ⇨ Apple Applications ⇨ Safari.

To learn more about Dashboard in general, start off with the Dashboard Programming Guide. After you are underway, the Dashboard Reference can come in handy when you want to look up some aspect of the widget class or a key in the Info.plist, for example. Both documents can be found in the Xcode Documentation window in the search group Reference Library ⇨ Apple Applications ⇨ Dashboard. You can find examples of Dashboard widgets in the directory /Developer/Examples/Dashboard after you have installed the Xcode Developer Tools.

Other Scripting Languages

Unfortunately, there isn't enough room in this book to cover all of the scripting languages shipped with Mac OS X. Five of the more important languages have been addressed, but many other good languages have had to be omitted. The following list gives you a very brief overview of some of these remaining scripting languages:

❑ **Ruby:** A relatively new language with similarities to Python. It is an OO language, with very advanced features that are not even found in Python. The RubyCocoa framework allows you to write Cocoa applications in Ruby (`http://www.fobj.com/rubycocoa/doc/`). You can learn more about Ruby at the Ruby website (`http://www.ruby-lang.org`).

❑ **PHP:** A language used mostly to build websites. It can be mixed with HTML to produce web pages that get dynamically built by the web server whenever requested by a client web browser. PHP allows you to easily integrate a database with your website, upload files via a web page, send emails from web forms, and much more. For general information on PHP, there is the PHP website (`http://www.php.net/`), and for an introduction to PHP on Mac OS X, you need look no further than the Apple Developer Connection (`http://developer.apple.com/internet/opensource/php.html`).

❑ **Tcl:** An easy-to-use scripting language tightly integrated with the Tk GUI toolkit. This combination allows you to write cross-platform GUI applications, though you shouldn't expect the polish of a Cocoa application. The Tcl/Tk frameworks provided with Mac OS X do simulate the look of the Mac OS X controls, but it isn't really going to fool anyone—the interface is obviously not Mac native. Tcl is used as the base language of the DarwinPorts project (`http://darwinports.opendarwin.org/`), which aims to make Unix tools easy to install on Darwin/Mac OS X, as well as some other platforms. A good place to begin learning about Tcl/Tk is the Tcl Developer Xchange (`www.tcl.tk/`).

Summary

A script language is a high-level language that is interpreted, rather than being compiled, into object code by a compiler. Mac OS X ships with a many different scripting languages, each with its own application domain, strengths, and weaknesses. This chapter has introduced you to some of the more important of these languages.

In this chapter, you learned that

❑ The Bash Shell can be used interactively, or to run shell scripts. It is a simple language, used extensively in the Mac OS X system, and is particularly good at gluing other commands and programs together.

❑ AppleScript is the only scripting language that gives you access to applications with a GUI on Mac OS X. It has a verbose, English-like syntax and is targeted at non-programmers.

❑ Python is a powerful object-oriented scripting language, with a simple syntax and extensive library. Like Perl, it is very capable when it comes to text manipulation.

❑ Perl is a C-like scripting language that is particularly adept at text manipulation. It generally provides many different ways of achieving a single task. This is either a strength or weakness, depending on your perspective. Perl's syntax is quite compact, but can lead to indecipherable source code if care is not taken.

❑   JavaScript is a Java-like scripting language that can be used to make dynamic web content, but it is of particular interest to Mac developers because it underpins Dashboard.

❑   Dashboard widgets are basically web pages, composed from web technologies such as HTML, CSS, and JavaScript, with a few extensions that allow you to leverage Mac OS X technologies like Quartz.

❑   Other scripting languages on Mac OS X include Ruby, PHP, and Tcl.

In the next chapter, you learn more about the Bash Shell. Before proceeding, however, try the exercises that follow to test your understanding of the material covered in this chapter. You can find the solutions to these exercises in Appendix A.

Exercises

1.   A friend says to you that she is interested in scripting a weekly backup of her user directory. She asks you what you think the best scripting language to use would be. What would you advise, based on what you have learned in this chapter?

2.   Another friend wants to build a complex web content management system. He asks your advice about scripting languages that he could use for the project. What do you suggest?

3.   If you want to extract photos from your iPhoto library, and automatically send them to friends in your Address Book, what would be the best scripting language for the job?

The Bash Shell

At the heart of every Mac OS X system is a Unix core. If you don't look for it, you won't see it, but it's there. Like all Unix-based systems, Mac OS X relies heavily on shell scripts. When you log in to your account at startup — whatever you happen to be doing on Mac OS X — chances are good that a shell script is involved in some way.

If you read Chapter 10, you know that scripts are simple programs that string together Unix commands to perform a task. Scripts are run by a program called a *shell*, which interprets one line of code at a time. On Mac OS X, the default shell is called Bash; Bash is a powerful shell that can be used interactively, or to run scripts.

In this chapter you learn

- ❑ How to configure and use Bash interactively and for running scripts
- ❑ How to use the Terminal application for accessing the command line
- ❑ The most important Unix commands and where to find information about commands
- ❑ Some of the commands only available on Mac OS X
- ❑ Basic shell programming

Getting Started

Before you can start interacting with the operating system via the Terminal application or writing your own shell scripts, some preliminaries need to be taken care of. First, you need to know what a *command-line interface (CLI)* is and the different ways in which it can be used. You need to have an application that can access the CLI and a way to edit scripts and other text files. Finally, you need to configure your Bash Shell before you start using it. This section covers these aspects, preparing you for the next section when you actually begin using the Bash Shell.

The Command-Line Interface

The Mac has always had an excellent graphical user interface (GUI). It's what made the Mac famous to begin with; with Mac OS X, Apple continues to lead the way when it comes to GUI design.

What was never popular under the old Mac OS was the command-line interface. A CLI is a means of interacting with the operating system via textual commands entered on the keyboard rather than by pointing and clicking the mouse. A CLI usually requires the user to enter commands at a simple prompt rather than interacting via controls and menus.

The CLI on the Mac under the old Mac OS was not popular for a number of reasons, but the most important was that earlier versions of the Mac OS did not actually have a CLI. Where Windows users could start up MS-DOS and enter commands to copy files or execute programs, Mac OS users didn't have this option; in all honesty, most didn't want it.

Mac OS X has a rich graphical interface, but it also offers a CLI as a bonus for the power user. The CLI of Mac OS X can be accessed with applications like Terminal and X11 (with `xterm`). The CLI in Mac OS X is actually the Bash Shell, which listens for the commands you enter at the prompt, and takes action accordingly.

> X11 is the GUI used on most other Unix systems, and is equivalent to Aqua on Mac OS X. You can run X11 alongside Aqua by installing the X11 application, which is an optional install with the Mac OS X system. To install it on your Mac, either use a Mac OS X install disk or download the X11 installer package from Apple (`www.apple.com/macosx/features/x11/`).

A CLI is not for everyone. Most will want to stick with what is offered in the GUI; but for others, the CLI offers an extra dimension. It is very powerful, usually offering more options to the user than can be accessed via a GUI. Some things are also much easier to do with the CLI than with a GUI. For example, Mac OS X includes Unix commands that enable you to manipulate files and text in many more ways than are possible using Finder and TextEdit.

Interactive versus Script

You can use the Bash Shell in two different ways: interactively, or for running scripts. When you type commands at a prompt, you are using the shell interactively. One command is performed at a time, as you enter it and press Return. But you can also put a series of commands in a file to form a *script*. You can use the same commands in a script as you enter at the prompt, but the script allows you to perform many commands together and execute that series of commands as many times as you please without having to retype them each time.

Working interactively does not preclude you running scripts. The two can, and usually are, interleaved. You can run any script you like from the shell prompt; usually, a *subprocess* is started to run the script, such as an extra Bash Shell. The shell initiating the script can either wait for the subprocess to exit, or continue on.

The Terminal Application

The easiest way to access Bash on Mac OS X is to use the Terminal application, which you can find in the `/Applications/Utilities` folder. Terminal can be used to open windows, each of which contains a prompt that you can use to enter commands. Each Terminal window is running a different copy of the Bash Shell, so the commands you enter in one window do not influence the Bash Shell in another window.

When you open Terminal for the first time, you may want to change some configurations. One thing you may want to change is the default behavior of windows when the shell it is running exits. When you first use Terminal, windows remain open after a shell exits; you have to close them manually, even though they aren't useful anymore. If you want to change this behavior so that the window closes when the shell exits, choose Terminal ⇨ Window Settings and select Shell from the popup in the Terminal Inspector panel that appears under When the Shell Exits. You can choose either Close the Window or Close Only if Shell Exited Cleanly. When you are finished customizing the window settings, click the Use Settings as Defaults button.

> *The Close Only if Shell Exited Cleanly option refers to the fact that each shell has an exit status when it terminates. The exit status is a simple integer number. If it is zero, the shell exited without any problem; a non-zero value indicates an error occurred. With this option, the window closes only if no errors arise.*

Apart from Terminal, you can also use the X11 application to access the command line. X11 is an optional install with Mac OS X; if you have installed it, it appears in `/Applications/Utilities`. When you start up X11, an `xterm` Terminal appears by default. `xterm` is a Unix command for starting a new terminal window in the X Windows System, which is the windowing system started by the X11 application. You can create a new terminal window in X11 either by choosing Applications ⇨ Terminal or by entering the following at the prompt of an existing terminal:

```
xterm &
```

Editors

Many ways exist to edit text files on Mac OS X, including TextEdit and Xcode. Opening files in these applications from a terminal is quite easy. You can simply issue this command:

```
open filename
```

This opens the file in the Application assigned to the file type. You can choose the Application for any given file type in the Info panel of the file in Finder (select the file and then choose File ⇨ Get Info).

Using external editors with Terminal is certainly possible, but may not be the most convenient solution. You may prefer to remain inside the terminal window to edit files. Unix has a vast assortment of command-line text editing programs, the most widely used of which are vi and emacs. Both are powerful editors, but they have steep learning curves and are beyond the scope of this book.

> *If you talk to Unix users about their preference for emacs or vi, you may well hit a nerve. The competition between these two editors is something akin to a religious war and can prompt very lively discussions.*

Instead of discussing vi or emacs, this chapter introduces a very simple command-line editor that ships with Mac OS X: Nano. Nano is not as advanced as emacs or vi, but it is quite adequate for basic file editing and is intuitive to use. You can edit a file with Nano simply by entering the nano command, followed by the filename:

```
nano filename
```

If the file already exists, it will be opened; if it does not exist, it will be created. Figure 11-1 shows a sample editing session with nano.

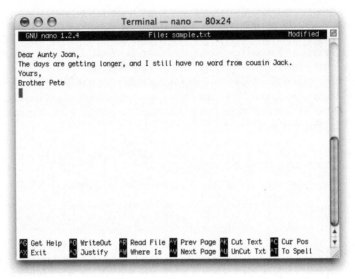

Figure 11-1

Using nano is relatively self-explanatory. You enter text via the keyboard and navigate with the arrow keys. Many commands also can be issued by holding down Control and pressing another key. Some of these commands appear at the bottom of the Nano editing window.

The following table provides a summary of some of Nano's more important commands. More commands are described in Help, which you can access by pressing Control-G.

Command	Description
Control-X	Exits Nano. If you have unsaved changes, Nano prompts you for whether you would like to save them.
Control-K	Cuts the selected text, or a single line if there is no selection. You can't make a selection with the mouse; instead, you set the start position of the selection with Control-^ and move the cursor to the end position with the arrow keys.
Control-U	Pastes the text that was cut with Control-K at the position of the cursor.
Control-^	Sets the starting position of a selection. After issuing this command, use the arrow keys to move the cursor to the end position of the selection.
Control-V	Moves down one full page.
Control-Y	Moves up one full page.
Control-G	Opens the help pages.

Configuring Bash

When a Bash Shell starts up, it can read a number of configuration files. You can customize your Bash Shells by entering commands in one or more of these files. It is common, for instance, to set the PATH *environment variable* in these files. An environment variable is a variable stored by a shell and generally influences the behavior of the shell and any programs that it executes. The PATH variable is a list of paths that are searched for commands and other executable programs.

When you open a Terminal window, you are greeted by an *interactive login shell*. It is *interactive* because you can interact with it in real time, and it is a *login shell* because it was not started by any other shell. When Bash starts a login shell, it executes the commands in the file /etc/profile. Here is the /etc/profile provided with Mac OS X:

```
# System-wide .profile for sh(1)

PATH="/bin:/sbin:/usr/bin:/usr/sbin"
export PATH

if [ "${BASH-no}" != "no" ]; then
        [ -r /etc/bashrc ] && . /etc/bashrc
fi
```

The first line is a comment. On the next two non-blank lines, the PATH variable is set, and the export command is used to export the variable to the shell as an environment variable. PATH is set to a string of colon-separated directory paths, which will be searched in order whenever a command is issued to the shell. The last three lines of the file check whether a file exists at /etc/bashrc; if it does, the commands in the file are executed.

> *In this chapter, the word directory is used interchangeably with folder. These words are testimony to the heritage of Mac OS X, arising out of a marriage between Unix and Mac OS. The word directory is used in the Unix world, and folder was the equivalent term in the original Mac OS. On Mac OS X, either is appropriate.*

The /etc/profile file is read whenever a login shell is started for any user. It should be used for system-wide configuration and not for the configuration options of a particular user. Usually, you do not need to edit /etc/profile at all; you can simply customize the shell from user configuration files.

After /etc/profile, the login shell checks whether a file called .profile exists in the user's home directory. If it does, the commands it includes are executed. You can put into the .profile file any commands you would like to run when a login shell is initiated. You could, for example, add directories to the default PATH variable, like so:

```
PATH=$PATH:~/bin
export PATH
```

This adds the directory bin in your home directory to the existing PATH variable. The value of the PATH variable is retrieved by prepending a $ symbol, as seen on the right side of the first expression. The export command updates the environment variable PATH; without this, the variable would only be changed locally and not outside the .profile file.

Bash allows you to represent a user's home directory by a tilde (~) symbol. So a user's .profile file is located at the path ~/.profile.

Not all shells are login shells. You may start one shell from within another, for example, by simply entering the command bash at the prompt and pressing Return. If you try this, you may not notice any change, but you are actually working inside a new shell. This type of shell is simply called an *interactive shell*; it is not a login shell.

When a new non-login interactive shell starts, the Bash Shell checks for the existence of a file called .bashrc in the user's home directory. If this file exists, it is executed. The .profile file is not executed when a non-login shell starts up. You can use the .bashrc file to customize your shell configuration for non-login shells. Most users don't need to have different configurations for login and non-login shells, so the .bashrc file often simply *sources* the .profile file, like this:

```
source ~/.profile
```

This command simply tells the shell to execute the commands in the file at the path ~/.profile, which means that non-login shells are effectively configured with the same set of commands as login shells.

In the following Try It Out, you use the Terminal application with the Nano editor to create the Bash configuration files ~/.profile and ~/.bashrc and add a few commands to customize your Bash Shell.

Try It Out   Configuring Your Bash Shell

1. Start the Terminal application in /Applications/Utilities.

2. Create the file .profile in your home directory using the Nano editor. To do this, simply issue the following command at the prompt:

```
nano .profile
```

3. Type the following text into the Nano editor. You can use the arrow keys to move around. When you are finished, press Control-X, and answer with a *Y* when prompted whether you would like to save your changes.

```
export PATH=.:$PATH:~/bin
export PS1="\h:\u:\w$ "
alias h history
```

4. Use nano to create the .bashrc file by entering this command:

```
nano .bashrc
```

5. In the Nano editor, add the following line and exit with the key combination Control-X. Be sure you save your changes to .bashrc when prompted.

```
source ~/.profile
```

6. When you are satisfied and want to terminate your Terminal session, enter the following command at the prompt:

```
exit
```

How It Works

This introductory example should help you get familiar with Terminal, Nano, and the Bash configuration files. When you start the Terminal application, a Bash Shell starts, and you receive a prompt. The Bash Shell always has a *current working directory*, and it begins in your home directory. When you create the `.profile` and `.bashrc` files with Nano, they are created in your home directory because that is the current working directory.

The commands added to the `.profile` file are intended to serve as examples and are not by any means compulsory. You can add whatever you like to `.profile`.

The first command extends the PATH variable:

```
export PATH=.:$PATH:~/bin
```

The PATH environment variable is initialized in `/etc/profile` before the `~/.profile` is read. The existing value is not discarded but is extended by the command. The new value of PATH is set to be the old value, as given by `$PATH`, with two directories added: `.` and `~/bin`. The directory represented by the period (`.`) is always the current working directory of the shell, and `~/bin` is the directory `bin` in your home directory. The directory `~/bin` does not have to exist; if it doesn't, Bash simply ignores it when searching for a command. If you create the `~/bin` directory, you could add your own scripts and other *executables* to it, and Bash would find and execute them no matter which directory you happen to be working in.

> *Any file that can be executed by the shell, whether it is a compiled program or script, is often referred to as an executable.*

Many users like to add the current working directory, as given by `.`, to their PATH variable. Adding `.` to the PATH means that the shell will look for executable programs in the current working directory, as well as at other paths. It is quite common to want to execute a program in your current directory, especially if you are writing your own scripts. If you don't include `.` in your path, you need to enter a path in order to run a script in your current working directory, like this:

```
./script_name
```

The order of the paths in the PATH variable is significant. The shell searches the paths in the order they appear, for the first matching executable. When an executable is found, the rest of the paths are ignored. In the example, the shell searches in the current directory (`.`) first, followed by the directories originally in the PATH variable, and lastly in `~/bin`. If you want the executables in a particular directory to have priority, include that directory early in your PATH variable.

The second line of the `.profile` file sets an environment variable:

```
export PS1="\h:\u:\w$ "
```

The PS1 environment variable is used to formulate the prompt string that you see when the Bash Shell is waiting for you to enter a command. You can use any string you like for the prompt, as well as characters with special meanings that are substituted with another string before being displayed. In the example, the hostname (`\h`) is shown, followed by a colon and the user name (`\u`). The current working directory (`\w`) is given last, followed by a `$` symbol and a space. The following table gives some of the more interesting special characters that you can use in your prompt.

Special Character	Description
\d	The date (as in "Wed Nov 20th")
\h	The first section of the hostname
\H	The full hostname
\t	The time in 24-hour format
\T	The time in 12-hour format
\A	The time in 24-hour format, excluding seconds
\w	The path of the current working directory
\W	The last directory in the current working directory path
\!	The number of the command in the history list

The `.profile` file finishes by defining an *alias*. An alias in Bash is an alternative name for a command; when you type the alias, the original command to which it corresponds is executed. In this case, the `history` command, which gives a list of the commands previously given to the shell, is assigned the alias h. Instead of having to type `history` when you want to list the history of commands, with this alias in place you can simply type h.

The `.bashrc` shell, which you will recall is used to configure non-login shells, is designed in this case to simply execute the same set of commands as the `.profile` file:

```
source ~/.profile
```

This is a common approach. Using the `source` command, you can execute the contents of another file in the current shell. Note that this is not the same as running a second script, because when you use `source`, no new shell (subprocess) is started — commands are executed in the existing shell.

The `exit` command allows you to terminate a shell. You can also supply a number to the `exit` command, which is returned to the parent process as the exit code. This is usually used to indicate if an error occurred and what the error was.

Unix Basics

The Unix philosophy, which Mac OS X shares at its lower levels, can be summarized by the old adage that many hands make light work. Unix systems are full of *commands* — small programs that are highly specialized. Each command does one thing, and does it well. Even though the foundations are simple, you can achieve powerful tasks by combining Unix commands. This section covers basic aspects of Unix, some of the most important Unix commands, and how you can combine them to achieve your objectives.

Paths

Much of the time spent interacting with an operating system involves working with files and directories (that is, folders). You have to be able to locate files, view or edit them, move them, remove them, and so forth. But all these actions require that you be able to stipulate to the operating system which file or directory a particular action involves. In Finder, you can select a file and drag it to the Trash if you want to remove it. On the command line, there are no file icons; so you need to give a path to any file or directory you want to use in a command.

Unix paths can take one of two forms: *absolute paths* and *relative paths*. Absolute paths are spelled out in full with respect to the root directory. An absolute path begins with a forward slash, as in the following:

```
cd /Users/terry/Desktop
```

This line uses the `cd` command, which changes the current working directory of the shell. The current directory is set to the `Desktop` folder of user `terry`. The path begins with a forward slash and is thus an absolute path, taken with respect to the root directory of the file system.

Relative paths do not begin with a forward slash and are taken with respect to the current working directory of the shell. If the current working directory in the preceding example is user `terry`'s home directory, the `cd` command could be issued as follows:

```
cd Desktop
```

Because the current working directory is `/Users/terry`, the home directory of user `terry`, entering a relative path of `Desktop` results in the absolute path `/Users/terry/Desktop`.

When working with relative paths, there are a few special symbols that can help you navigate. If you want to refer to the current directory, you can use a single period. The following command, for example, lists the contents of the current working directory of the shell:

```
ls .
```

The period can also be used in paths; the presence of a period effectively leaves the path unchanged. For example, the following command lists the contents of the `Desktop` folder if issued from inside the user's home directory:

```
ls ./Desktop
```

This is completely equivalent to

```
ls Desktop
```

and also to

```
ls ././././Desktop
```

The latter is nonsense, but it demonstrates the impotence of the single period in influencing paths.

Given that the single period has no effect on paths, you may be wondering why you would even need it. Sometimes it is important simply to indicate that something is a path, and a period can achieve that. For example, when issuing commands, the shell searches the paths in your PATH environment variable, but the current working directory is not included unless you have added it yourself. If you have an executable in your current working directory, and you want to run it, you need to give an explicit path, otherwise the shell won't find it. Here is how you can do that:

```
./some_executable
```

Simply issuing the command without the period will result in an error message.

Another special symbol for use in paths is the double period. This moves up to the parent directory of a directory. For example, in order to list the contents of the /Users directory, you could enter the following from your home directory:

```
ls ..
```

Of course, the double period symbol (..) can also be used in paths. Here is how you could list the contents of the /Applications directory from your home directory, using a relative path:

```
ls ../../Applications
```

Wherever the double period occurs in the path, it moves up to the parent directory. Two double periods, as in the preceding example, effectively shift you up two levels of directories: the first one moves you to the /Users directory, and the second one to the root directory /. Once in the root directory, Applications selects the /Applications directory.

Locating and Learning Commands

Unix commands on Mac OS X tend to be stored in a number of standard directories. The most important commands appear in the /bin directory. bin stands for binary; most commands are compiled programs, which means they are in a non-readable binary format rather than a text format.

> *If you look for /bin in Finder, you may be surprised to find it missing. It isn't actually missing, however; it's just hidden. Apple prefers that everyday users not be bothered by low-level details like /bin, and hides them in Finder. You can still navigate to the /bin directory in Finder by choosing Go ⇨ Go to Folder and entering /bin.*

You can list the contents of the /bin command by using the ls command. Here is the output for the command on one particular system:

```
Macintosh:~ sample$ ls /bin
bash          domainname    link      rcp       test
cat           echo          ln        rm        unlink
chmod         ed            ls        rmdir     wait4path
cp            expr          mkdir     sh        zsh
csh           hostname      mv        sleep     zsh-4.2.3
date          kill          pax       stty
dd            ksh           ps        sync
df            launchctl     pwd       tcsh
```

The /bin directory includes the various shells, including bash, as well as fundamental commands for interacting with the file system, such as cp, chmod, mv, and rm. (Details of these commands are provided throughout the "Unix Basics" section.) Even the command used to list the directory contents, ls, resides in /bin.

Mac OS X systems include a second directory intended for binaries typically used by system administrators: /sbin. This directory includes commands for shutting down the system and mounting volumes via a network. The commands in /sbin do not belong to the core of Unix commands, and many are found only on Mac OS X.

Most commands are found in the directory /usr/bin. This directory is intended for less fundamental commands than the ones belonging in /bin. Commands can be added to /usr/bin over time, but the contents of /bin are usually left intact. /usr/bin includes all sorts of commands, from file compression programs to compilers. Any command that is not in /bin, and not intended for system administrative purposes, tends to end up in /usr/bin. The /usr/sbin directory is the analog of /usr/bin for system administrative commands.

You can use the which command to get the path of a command or learn which particular path is used if there are multiple copies of a command. You simply enter which followed by the command name, and it prints out the path that is used if you issue the command in the shell. Here is an example of using which with the emacs command:

```
Macintosh:~ sample$ which emacs
/usr/bin/emacs
```

which works only with commands in the paths defined by your PATH environment variable. If you seek a command outside your path, you will need to use a more general file searching command like find or locate, which are described later in the chapter.

If you want to know how to use a command, or the options that it includes, you can use the man command. Typing in man, followed by a command name, opens documentation in a simple file viewer called less. You can navigate through the documentation by pressing the space bar and quit less by pressing q. Figure 11-2 shows the Terminal window after the command man ls has been issued at the prompt.

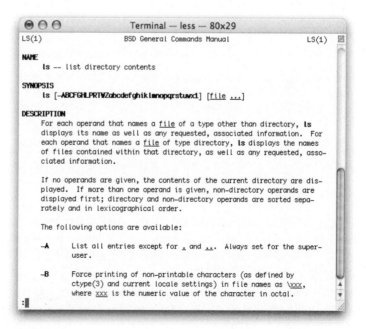

Figure 11-2

Running Commands and Other Executables

By now it should be quite clear that running an executable in a shell is simply a matter of typing its name and supplying any options required. If the command is not in one of the paths in your PATH environment variable, you can run the command by giving an explicit path. You can also use an explicit path if you want to override the search order used by the shell to locate a command. For example, perhaps you have two different versions of a particular command, and you want to specify explicitly which should be run. Using an explicit path to the command achieves this.

When a command or other executable is run, the shell can either wait for it to exit or continue on processing other commands. When the shell blocks and waits, the command is said to be running in the *foreground*; if the shell continues without waiting, the command is running in the *background*. By default, a command runs in the foreground. If you want to run a command in the background, you need to append an & symbol to the end of the line, like this:

```
find . -name "*.txt" &
```

This command searches for text files in the current directory or any of its subdirectories. Because this may take a while, it makes sense to run the command in the background so that you can continue issuing commands while the search proceeds. The & at the end of the line indicates to the shell that it should return from the find command immediately, rather than waiting for it to complete. You get a new prompt, and can continue to issue commands to the shell.

When you run a command or other executable you are actually starting up a new *process*. A process is simply a running program. Commands started from inside a shell are *subprocesses* or *child processes* of the shell and inherit the environment variables of the shell as a result. If the shell exits for some reason while the subprocess is running, the subprocess is terminated by the operating system.

You can pass arguments to a subprocess when it is started simply by including the arguments after the executable name. For example, the following find command is passed three arguments:

```
find / -name "*.doc"
```

The arguments are passed to find as the strings /, -name, and *.doc. The find command interprets the arguments and carries out the request. The shell itself has no understanding of what the arguments represent or which arguments the find command expects to receive; it simply breaks the line into separate strings and passes them to find.

When a command exits, it returns an exit value. This is an integer value, which is usually used to indicate when an error has occurred. A value of 0 means that everything went fine; a non-zero value usually indicates that an error occurred. Often the non-zero value returned is an error code, which can be used to find out exactly what type of error occurred.

To access the error code of a command in Bash, you use the special variable $?. $? is the error code of the last command run by the shell. You can test the value of $? after a command has run to determine if anything went wrong, comparing it to zero, for example. You learn how to perform such tests later in this chapter in the "Shell Programming" section.

If you want to exit a shell, you can use the exit command. With no argument, the exit command sets the exit code to 0. If an error occurs, you will want to set the error code to a non-zero value. To do this, simply supply the error code as an argument to exit, like this:

```
exit 127
```

Here, the exit code has been set to 127.

Bash provides a few other ways to run commands and scripts. The `eval` command can be used to run commands. The commands are executed in the existing shell; no subprocess is initiated. For example, the following lists the contents of the directory `/usr/bin`:

```
eval ls /usr/bin
```

This really becomes useful only when you can evaluate arbitrary strings of commands that are read from file or entered by the user. Strings are covered in greater depth in the "Shell Programming" section.

The `source` command, which you saw earlier, is similar to `eval`, but it executes commands from a file. The commands are again executed in the existing shell, with no subprocess initiated.

With the `exec` command, you can replace the shell with another running script or program. The initiating script is terminated and the newly started executable replaces it, taking its environment, and even *process identity*, the number used to represent the process by the system. If you run the following command

```
exec ls
```

the command `ls` replaces the Bash Shell used to initiate it. When `ls` is finished listing the current working directory, it also exits. Because the shell has terminated, your prompt does not return; depending on your preferences, your Terminal window may close.

If you issue the command

```
exec bash
```

it may seem that nothing has changed, but you have actually started a new Bash Shell, replacing the old one. If you decide you want to use a different shell than `bash` during a Terminal session, you can do it like this:

```
exec tcsh
```

This replaces the existing Bash Shell with a new TCSH Shell.

Redirecting Input and Output

The real strength of shells is their ability to easily combine relatively simple commands to perform complex tasks. To achieve this, it is important to be able to take the data output by one command and use it as input to another command, or to write data to file and read it back in later for further processing. The Bash Shell provides powerful, easy-to-use features for channeling data between commands and files.

Data is channeled from one command to another, or to and from a file, via *pipes*. Pipes are analogous to the plumbing in your bathroom, except that they transmit data instead of water. To pipe data from the output of one command to the input of another, you use the hyphen (|) operator. Here is an example of taking the output of an `ls` command and piping it to a command called `grep`:

```
ls -1 /usr/bin | grep cc
```

Better ways exist to achieve the same effect as this command, but it does demonstrate the workings of a pipe. The command `ls -1 /usr/bin` produces a lot of output, which can be summarized as follows:

```
Macintosh:~ sample$ ls -1 /usr/bin
CFInfoPlistConverter
a2p
acid
aclocal
aclocal-1.6

...

zip
zipcloak
zipgrep
zipinfo
zipnote
zipsplit
zmore
znew
zprint
```

Results differ depending on the commands you have installed in the /usr/bin directory. The output gets piped to the input of the command `grep cc`, which extracts any line containing the text cc. The original output of the `ls` command is reduced to only those commands containing the text cc:

```
Macintosh:~ sample$ ls -1 /usr/bin | grep cc
cc
distcc
distccd
distccschedd
gcc
gcc-3.3
gcc-4.0
perlcc
powerpc-apple-darwin8-gcc-4.0.0
rpcclient
yacc
```

You are not limited to piping data between two commands; you can pipe together as many commands as you like. By way of example, imagine that you were only interested in commands in /usr/bin that contained cc and a digit in their names. Here is one way to list those commands:

```
ls -1 /usr/bin | grep cc | grep -e '[0-9]'
```

The output of this command is

```
Macintosh:~ sample$ ls -1 /usr/bin | grep cc | grep -e '[0-9]'
gcc-3.3
gcc-4.0
powerpc-apple-darwin8-gcc-4.0.0
```

A second pipe has been added, taking the output of the `grep cc` command and piping it into the input of a second `grep`. The second `grep` prints only the lines that contain at least one digit.

You can also pipe data to and from files. To do this, you use the *redirection operators* < and >. The < operator redirects the standard input of a command causing it to be read from a file, like so:

```
grep -i TABLE < index.html
```

Here, the command `grep TABLE`, which prints any line of text containing `TABLE`, is applied to the contents of the file `index.html`. The shell reads `index.html`, channeling the data into the `grep` command, which prints those lines with `TABLE` in them.

Piping the output of a command to file is similar:

```
grep -i TABLE < index.html > table_results.txt
```

This command has been extended, with the output of the `grep` command now being piped to the file `table_results.txt`, rather than being displayed by the shell. After this command has executed, you should be able to open the file `table_results.txt` in an editor such as Nano or TextEdit and find the `grep` output there.

Notice that using > overwrites any existing file. If you want to append the data, rather than replacing the contents of the output file, you can use the >> operator:

```
grep -i TABLE < index.html >> table_results.txt
```

If `table_results.txt` doesn't exist before this command is issued, it is created and the command's output inserted. If the file does exist, the output is appended to the end of the existing data in `table_results.txt`.

Apart from standard output, every command also has a stream of data called *standard error,* which is intended for error messages. You can pipe the standard error to a file using the 2> operator, like this:

```
grep -sdf 2> grep_error.txt
```

The `grep` option given here is invalid, so it prints an error message to the standard error and exits. The file `grep_error.txt` ends up containing the following text:

```
grep: unknown directories method
```

The form of redirection operator used here is not applicable only to the standard error but to any *file descriptor.* The standard error has the file descriptor 2, so the operator 2> pipes the standard error to a file. The standard output has the file descriptor 1, so 1> pipes data to standard output. (The standalone > operator is shorthand for 1>.) Standard input has the file descriptor 0; you can read from standard input with the operator 0<, as well as with the shorthand notation <.

In the next Try It Out, you learn how to redirect data by performing a series of commands interactively in the Bash Shell. The objective is to determine the total amount of RAM available on your Mac by using the command-line tool `system_profiler`.

Try It Out   **Determining Your Memory by Redirecting Data**

1. Open a terminal window in the Terminal application.

2. Enter the command

```
man system_profiler
```

3. Skim the information provided until you think you understand what the `system_profiler` command does. You can use the space bar to move down and press *b* to move back up a page. Press *q* when you are ready to quit the `less` viewer.

4. Back at the Bash prompt, enter the following command:

```
system_profiler SPMemoryDataType
```

The output should look something like this:

```
Macintosh:~ sample$ system_profiler SPMemoryDataType
Memory:

    DIMM0/J21:

        Size: 256 MB
        Type: SDRAM
        Speed: PC133-333

    DIMM1/J22:

        Size: 256 MB
        Type: SDRAM
        Speed: PC133-333

    DIMM2/J23:

        Size: 256 MB
        Type: SDRAM
        Speed: PC133-333

    DIMM3/J24:

        Size: Empty
        Type: Empty
        Speed: Empty
```

5. Now re-enter the command, but pipe the output to a temporary file, like this:

```
system_profiler SPMemoryDataType > sysoutput.tmp
```

6. Open the file `sysoutput.tmp` with Nano to make sure it contains this output:

```
nano sysoutput.tmp
```

7. Exit Nano again by pressing Control-X.

8. Use the `grep` command to read the `sysoutput.tmp` file, and extract the sizes of the RAM modules, like so:

```
grep -e 'Size: [0-9]' < sysoutput.tmp
```

You should see something similar to the following:

```
Macintosh:~ sample$ grep -e 'Size: [0-9]' < sysoutput.tmp
      Size: 256 MB
      Size: 256 MB
      Size: 256 MB
```

9. Repeat the command in step 8, but redirect standard output to a new file:

```
grep -e 'Size: [0-9]' < sysoutput.tmp > grepoutput.tmp
```

10. Enter the following command to extract the numbers in `grepoutput.tmp`:

```
awk '{print $2}' < grepoutput.tmp
```

You should see output that resembles this:

```
Macintosh:~ sample$ awk '{print $2}' < grepoutput.tmp
256
256
256
```

11. Repeat the command in step 10, but pipe the output to a new temporary file:

```
awk '{print $2}' < grepoutput.tmp > awkoutput.tmp
```

12. Process the `awkoutput.tmp` file with the following command:

```
perl -e '$sum=0; while(<>) { $sum+=$_; } print "$sum\n";' < awkoutput.tmp
```

The output displays the total RAM in your computer:

```
Macintosh:~ sample$ perl -e '$sum=0; while(<>) { $sum+=$_; } print "$sum\n";' <
awkoutput.tmp
768
```

Notice that the command is one long line that has been wrapped by the Bash Shell onto the next line. Do not insert a return in the command.

13. Repeat the first few commands of this chain, but instead of generating a temporary file to transfer data, just use a direct pipe from one command to the next, like this:

```
system_profiler SPMemoryDataType | grep -e 'Size: [0-9]'
```

14. Enter the following long command, to duplicate the result of steps 1 through 12 while avoiding temporary files:

```
system_profiler SPMemoryDataType |  grep -e 'Size: [0-9]' | awk '{print $2}' |
perl -e '$sum=0; while(<>) { $sum+=$_; } print "$sum\n";'
```

Again, allow the command to be wrapped by Bash; do not type a return until you have entered the whole command.

15. Remove the temporary files by entering the following three commands at the prompt:

```
rm sysoutput.tmp
rm grepoutput.tmp
rm awkoutput.tmp
```

How It Works

This example is designed to give you lots of practice piping data to and from files and between commands. The commands used throughout the example are covered later in the chapter; for now, concentrate on how data is shifted between the commands, rather than on how the commands themselves actually work.

The `system_profiler` command is used to write information about the memory in your Mac to a temporary file, using the standard output redirection operator >. The data in the temporary file is then read back in to the `grep` command using the standard input redirection operator <. This pattern is followed for the rest of the example, writing data to a file and reading it back in, with each command reducing the data a bit more until the final result is produced.

Rather than introducing temporary files that must be cleaned up later, it is often easier to pipe data directly between commands. This is the approach introduced in the last few steps of the example. Instead of writing the output of each command to a file and reading it back in to the next command, a pipe is used to channel output data from one command to the next. With this approach, the entire sequence of commands can be reduced to a single line, and no temporary files are produced.

At the end of the example, the temporary files are deleted with the command `rm`. `rm` is covered in detail later in the section "Working with Files and Directories."

Navigating the File System

Navigating the file system is somewhat different with Bash than it is with Finder. The shell maintains an environment variable, `PWD`, containing the path to the current working directory. Any relative paths you enter in your commands are interpreted with respect to this path.

Just as you can open different folders in Finder, you can also change the current working directory of a shell. The command `cd` is used for this purpose. To use `cd`, you simply pass the path to a new directory as an argument. The path can be either an absolute path or a relative path. Here is an example of using an absolute path to change to the `/Library/Frameworks` directory:

```
cd /Library/Frameworks
```

To affirm that the current directory did change, you can check the value of the `PWD` environment variable or use the `pwd` command, which prints the path of the current working directory:

```
Macintosh:/Library/Frameworks sample$ echo $PWD
/Library/Frameworks
Macintosh:/Library/Frameworks sample$ pwd
/Library/Frameworks
```

The `echo` command simply prints a string to standard output after values have been substituted for any variables by the shell.

You can also use relative paths with cd, in which case the path is taken relative to the current working directory. So, if the current working directory is your home directory, entering the following command will take you into your Desktop folder:

```
cd Desktop
```

A few special directories in your file system can be reached via shortcuts. Entering cd without any path will take you to your home directory. Your home directory is stored in the environment variable HOME and can also be represented by the tilde (~) symbol. Each of the following commands changes the current working directory to your home directory:

```
cd
cd $HOME
cd ~
```

To change to your Desktop directory, you could use this:

```
cd ~/Desktop
```

You can also access the home directory of another user by appending the user name to the ~. For example, to change to the Desktop folder of the user terry, you could enter this:

```
cd ~terry/Desktop
```

By default you do not have permission to change to the Desktop directory of another user on Mac OS X. To be allowed to do this, the other user would have to change the permissions of the directory to give you access. The "File Permissions" section discusses this in more detail.

Another important directory is the root directory of the file system. This is given by a single forward slash. To change to the root directory, you can issue this command:

```
cd /
```

Navigating a file system is also about knowing what you can navigate to. In Finder, you are automatically presented with a list of available files and folders whenever you open a folder. In Bash, this is not the case; you have to enter a command to list the contents of a directory. The command in question is ls.

If you issue the ls command without any arguments, it lists the contents of the current directory. In the following example, the current working directory is /bin:

```
Macintosh:/bin sample$ ls
bash          domainname    link          rcp           test
cat           echo          ln            rm            unlink
chmod         ed            ls            rmdir         wait4path
cp            expr          mkdir         sh            zsh
csh           hostname      mv            sleep         zsh-4.2.3
date          kill          pax           stty
dd            ksh           ps            sync
df            launchctl     pwd           tcsh
```

If you supply a path to `ls`, absolute or relative, it lists the contents of that directory, no matter what the current working directory happens to be:

```
Macintosh:/bin sample$ cd
Macintosh:~ sample$ ls /var/log/httpd/
access_log       error_log
```

The `cd` command changes the current working directory to the user's home directory. The `ls` command lists the contents of a different directory, namely the `/var/log/httpd` directory used to store log files of the Apache web server.

> *The* `/var/log/httpd/` *directory may be empty if you have never used your Apache web server before, in which case the* `ls` *command given will not print any filenames.*

The `ls` command has a number of useful options. The `-l` option allows you to get detailed information about files and directories, including their size, when they were last modified, and who owns them:

```
Macintosh:~ sample$ ls -l /var/log/httpd
total 936
-rw-r--r--  1 root  wheel  450481  5 Dec 21:35 access_log
-rw-r--r--  1 root  wheel   26433  7 Dec 19:54 error_log
```

In this example, the contents of `/var/log/httpd` have been listed again, but this time by using the `-l` option. The first part of the line indicates the *file mode*, which gives the *permissions* of each file. These determine who is allowed to read, write, or execute a given file. The meanings of the various permissions are discussed later in the chapter.

Other useful information is the file owner, which is `root` for both files in this case; the group of the file, which is `wheel` for both files; the size of the file in bytes, which is 450481 bytes for `access_log` and 26433 for `error_log`; and the date and time they were last modified.

The `-R` option is also quite useful, because it recursively lists subdirectories:

```
Macintosh:~ sample$ ls -R ~tiger/Sites
images            index.html

/Users/tiger/Sites/images:
apache_pb.gif   macosxlogo.gif  web_share.gif
```

This command lists the contents of the `Sites` directory of the user `tiger`, as well as all the subdirectories of `Sites`.

Working with Files and Directories

Knowing how to navigate the file system is one thing, but being able to modify it is just as important. The coming sections cover how you can alter the file system, copying or moving files and directories, creating them, removing them, searching for them, and even compressing and archiving them.

To move a file or directory from one path to another, you use the `mv` (move) command. But this command does more than just move a file or directory from one place to another. It can also be used to change the name of a file or directory or replace one file with another. `mv` simply changes one path, the *source path*, to another path, the *destination path*; if that involves changing the name of the file or directory, that is what happens.

To begin with, consider simply moving a file from one directory to another:

```
mv somefile somedir
```

In this simple example, the file called somefile in the current working directory is moved into the directory called somedir, which is also located in the current working directory. Of course, mv also works with any form of relative or absolute path:

```
mv ~/Desktop/somefile .
```

In this case, mv moves the file somefile in the Desktop folder into the current working directory.

If a file already exists at the destination path, *it is overwritten by the moved file*. You need to be careful not to accidentally delete files you want to keep.

Changing the name of a file is no more involved. You simply ensure that the destination path either doesn't exist or is a file that you want to overwrite. In either case, mv moves the file to the destination path, changing its name appropriately. For example, to change the name of a file called autumn.txt to spring.txt, with both files in the current working directory, you can do this:

```
mv autumn.txt spring.txt
```

After this operation, autumn.txt no longer exists, and the file that used to be called autumn.txt is now called spring.txt.

Other forms of paths are also possible, of course. Here is an example where a file is moved from the user's Desktop folder into the Documents folder and renamed at the same time:

```
mv ~/Desktop/project.doc ~/Documents/lastproject.doc
```

The file originally called project.doc is not only moved to another directory, but its name also gets changed to lastproject.doc. If there is already a file called lastproject.doc in the Documents folder, it will be overwritten and lost.

If you want to avoid accidentally overwriting files when you use mv, you can use the -i option. This will cause mv to prompt you before it overwrites any file. To be really sure you won't accidentally overwrite a file, you can even add an alias to the .profile file, like this:

```
alias mv="mv -i"
```

Now, whenever you enter mv, it will be executed with the -i option included automatically.

Moving directories is similar to moving files, but there are some differences. To change the name of a directory, you simply use a destination path that does not already exist. For example, if there is a directory called projects in the current working directory, and you want to rename it lastyearsprojects, you could do this:

```
mv projects lastyearsprojects
```

Note that if there is already a directory called `lastyearsprojects`, the `projects` directory will not replace it as would happen in the case of files. Instead, the `projects` directory becomes a subdirectory of `lastyearsprojects`. If you want to replace one directory with another, you first have to either move or remove it. (Removing directories is covered shortly.)

Copying files and directories follows similar rules to moving them. The `cp` command is used to copy files from one path to another:

```
cp sourcefile destinationfile
```

Unlike `mv`, the `sourcefile` continues to exist after the `cp` operation; `destinationfile` is a duplicate of `sourcefile`. Just as with `mv`, all manner of paths can be used to stipulate the source and destination files, and if the destination file already exists, it is overwritten.

> The `cp` command had one drawback on Mac OS X prior to version 10.4: it did not copy the resource fork of a file. The *resource fork* is metadata used by the original Mac OS to store information about a file, such as its type. Other operating systems tend to favor the use of file extensions, such as `.txt`, to delineate file type, and Mac OS X now uses a combination of file extension and other metadata.
>
> Mac OS X does still recognize and use resource forks to some extent; so if they exist, it is worth trying to keep them intact. On Mac OS X 10.4 and later, `cp` preserves resource forks; but on earlier versions of the system, resource forks are effectively removed by `cp`. There are, however, a few commands similar to `cp` that you can use to circumvent this problem. One is `ditto`, which can be used to copy files and directories while retaining resource forks. For more information, read the `ditto` man page by typing `man ditto`.

To copy a directory, you have to use the `-r` option with `cp`, like so:

```
cp -r ~/Desktop/sourcedir ~/Documents
```

This copies the directory `sourcedir` in the `Desktop` folder, plus all of its contents, into a new directory called `sourcedir` in the `Documents` folder. If you wanted to rename the copied directory, you could simply do this:

```
cp -r ~/Desktop/sourcedir ~/Documents/destdir
```

Now the copy, while still located in the `Documents` folder, is called `destdir`. If the destination directory already exists, `cp` will not replace it but will make the new copy a subdirectory of the destination directory.

Both `mv` and `cp` can be used with multiple sources, as long as the destination is a directory. For example, the command

```
mv file1 file2 file3 destdir
```

moves the files `file1`, `file2`, and `file3`, which are in the current working directory, to the `destdir` directory, which is also in the current working directory. As always, any form of path can be used for the files and directories in the command.

Removing files is fairly straightforward; you simply use the rm command and give the path to the file:

```
rm somefile
```

This removes the file somefile in the current working directory. You can also remove multiple files, simply by including their paths as arguments to rm, like this:

```
rm ~/Desktop/temp.txt ~/rubbish.doc ~/Documents/project.txt
```

This command removes three different files, which are located in three different directories.

To remove a directory, you either have to supply the -r option to rm or use the rmdir command. Here is an example of each approach:

```
rm -r ~/Desktop/somedir
rmdir ~/Desktop/somedir
```

Making a new directory is achieved using the mkdir command. You give the path to the new directory as an argument:

```
mkdir /Users/tiger/Desktop/newdir
```

This creates a directory called newdir in the Desktop folder of the user tiger.

In the following example, if you tried to issue the command before first creating the newdir directory, an error would result:

```
mkdir /Users/tiger/Desktop/newdir/otherdir
```

mkdir only makes a new subdirectory of an existing directory unless you supply the -p option, in which case it also generates any non-existing intermediate directories. So the preceding command could be made to succeed like so:

```
mkdir -p /Users/tiger/Desktop/newdir/otherdir
```

File Permissions

All of the commands discussed so far will succeed only if you have permission to perform the requested operation. Every file and directory in the file system has a set of permissions; in Finder, you have limited access to these permissions when you select a file, choose File ➪ Get Info, and open the Ownership & Permissions section of the Get Info window. This tells you who owns the file and the operations you are allowed to perform. If you are the owner, you can also change the permissions of the file or folder.

> This section discusses traditional Unix file permissions. Mac OS X 10.4 "Tiger" includes a second means of setting permissions for a file: Access Control Lists (ACL). Access Control Lists are considerably more flexible than traditional Unix permissions, but are also more involved. If you want to learn about ACLs, you can start by reading the man page for the chmod command. This command can be used to interact with ACL attributes.

The Bash Shell gives you even more control over permissions and ownership. You can find out the permissions of a file or directory using the `ls -l` command, as explained earlier. For example, to learn the permissions of the commands in `/bin`, you could enter the following:

```
ls -l /bin
```

The output of this command lists one line for each file. Each line looks something like this:

```
-r-xr-xr-x   1 root   wheel   14380 Mar 21 00:38 cat
```

The owner or user of the file is the third entry on the line, in this case `root`. The permissions of three different types of users are given in the string at the start of the line. The first character in the string indicates the file type, with a hyphen for a file and `d` for a directory. The rest of the string can be broken into three blocks of three characters, giving the permissions of the owner, group, and other users, respectively. Figure 11-3 shows the string in detail.

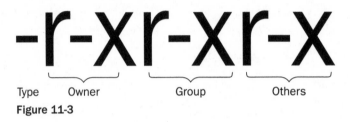

Type   Owner   Group   Others

Figure 11-3

The permissions applying to the owner of the file are in places 2–4, which are `r-x` in this example. The first of these three characters indicates whether the owner has read permission, allowing the contents of the file to be examined or copied, for example. A letter `r` indicates that read permission is granted; a hyphen indicates reading is not allowed.

The second character indicates if the owner is allowed to write to the file, replacing it with another file, or changing its contents. A `w` means writing is allowed; in this example, the owner is not allowed to change the file, so a hyphen appears as the second character.

The last of the three characters pertains to whether the owner can execute the file. If a file is executable, it can be run as a program or script. An `x` here indicates that the file can be executed by the owner, and a hyphen indicates that this is not allowed. This permission is somewhat different for directories because they cannot be executed. For a directory, an `x` indicates that the owner can examine the directory's contents, listing them with the `ls` command, for example.

The remaining six characters in the string are divided between permissions for the file's group, and permissions for all other users. Each file has a group, as well as an owner. The group that a file belongs to is given as the fourth entry on the line printed by `ls -l`; in this example, it is `wheel`. Each user belongs to one or more groups; and if a given user is in the group that a file belongs to, that user has the group permissions.

If a user is not the owner of the file, and also not in the group that the file belongs to, the permissions given by the last set of three characters applies.

If you are the owner of a file, you can change its permissions. The command chmod is used for this purpose. chmod allows you to add or remove permissions for the owner, group, or other users. For example, to make a file executable by the file owner, you could do this:

```
chmod u+x ~/Desktop/somefile
```

The argument u+x indicates that the owner of the file, as indicated by the u, should be granted execute permissions for the file at the path ~/Desktop/somefile. The plus symbol (+) indicates permissions should be granted, whereas a minus symbol or hyphen (-) would indicate permissions should be withdrawn.

Just as you can change the permissions for the file's owner by using a u in the argument string, you can also change permissions for the group by using g and other users by using o. You can even simultaneously update permissions for more than one type of user and/or multiple permission types. Take the following example:

```
chmod ug+rw somefile
```

This command grants read and write permission to the file owner and group users. To remove these permissions again, you can use this command:

```
chmod ug-rw somefile
```

The root user can change a file's owner or group. The chown command is used for this purpose:

```
chown terry somefile.txt
```

This changes the owner of the file given as second argument to user terry. The group of the file is left unchanged.

> root *is known as the superuser and can do anything, regardless of permissions. If you are an administrator on your Mac, you can carry out commands as if you are the superuser using the* sudo *command, which is discussed shortly. You need to be careful when you are carrying out commands as the* root *user because the results of a mistake could be drastic. A mistyped command could easily delete all the files on your file system, so be careful.*

To change the group of a file, the root user can issue a chown command like this:

```
chown :admin somefile.txt
```

The root user can also change the group and owner of a file, or multiple files, simultaneously with chown. Here is such an example:

```
chown terry:admin file1 file2 ~/Desktop/file3
```

The new owner is listed before the colon, and the group after it. The rest of the line contains the paths to the files for which ownership is to be modified.

If you are an administrator of your Mac and need to perform an operation for which you do not have permission, you can use the sudo command. sudo performs an operation as the user root.

By way of example, suppose you want to move a new executable to the /usr/bin folder. /usr/bin is writable only by the root user, so trying to move a file into it causes an error:

```
Macintosh:~ sample$ mv exefile /usr/bin
mv: rename Desktop/temp.py to /usr/bin/temp.py: Permission denied
```

To overcome this restriction, you can use sudo, like so:

```
sudo mv exefile /usr/bin
```

You will be prompted to enter your password; if you enter it, the mv command will succeed. You can use sudo in this way to perform any command for which you don't have permission, including chown.

> The sudo **command expects you to enter your own password when prompted, not that of the superuser** root.

Globbing

If you want to perform a command for several files, it can become tedious typing full names and paths. The Bash Shell allows you to take some shortcuts, using pattern matching within filenames and paths. This is known in the world of shell scripting as *globbing*.

To use globbing, you insert pattern-matching characters into strings to match certain filenames or paths. The pattern-matching characters match zero or more characters in the name or path. Probably the most widely used pattern-matching character is the wildcard *. This special character will match any zero or more characters. For example, used on its own, it matches all files and directories:

```
Macintosh:/bin sample$ cd /bin
Macintosh:/bin sample$ echo *
[ bash cat chmod cp csh date dd df domainname echo ed expr hostname kill ksh
launchctl link ln ls mkdir mv pax ps pwd rcp rm rmdir sh sleep stty sync tcsh test
unlink wait4path zsh zsh-4.2.3
```

This example uses the echo command to print out all the names that * matches, in the directory /bin. Because * matches any number of characters, all the files in /bin are echoed. The Bash Shell replaces the wildcard with the names that it matches before passing the resulting filenames as arguments to the echo command. The echo command itself is not passed the wildcard — the shell interprets any globbing characters before it runs the echo command.

The * character is also useful in combination with non-special characters. For example, suppose you want to list all the text files in your Desktop folder. Here is how you could do it:

```
ls ~/Desktop/*.txt
```

The path ~/Desktop/*.txt matches any file or directory located in the Desktop folder with the extension .txt. The * matches any string, of any length, and .txt only matches names that end in exactly those characters. Together, *.txt matches any name ending in .txt.

The * character is also useful in the middle of a path. Suppose you want to find all .txt files in a subdirectory of the Desktop folder. Here is how you could do that:

```
ls ~/Desktop/*/*.txt
```

Notice that you can use more than one pattern-matching character in each path. The first asterisk matches any directory in the Desktop folder, and the second one, together with .txt, matches any file or directory name ending with the extension txt.

If you only want a wildcard that matches any single character, rather than zero or more like the * character, you can use ?. ? matches one and only one character. The following lists files that have exactly five characters in their names, with blah as the first four:

```
ls blah?
```

A file called blah will not match, but blah0 or blaht will. blah00 will not match, because ? matches exactly one character.

If you want to limit the number of possible characters matched, you can enter the allowed characters in square braces, like this

```
ls blah[01]
```

This would match blah0 or blah1, but not blah2, for example. You can add as many characters between the braces as you like; any of them can match.

You can use various characters to modify the behavior of the pattern-matching braces. If you insert a ^ character directly after the first brace, only characters not included between the braces will match. For example,

```
ls blah[^01]
```

will match blah2, but not blah0 or blah1.

There are also some sets of characters that you can specify within the braces. For example, :alpha: represents alphabetic characters and :upper: represents uppercase characters. So

```
ls blah[:alpha:]
```

will match blaht, but not blah0. For a complete list of character sets, see the Bash man page.

Some of the need for pattern matching is removed by Bash's *autocompletion* feature. If you enter the beginning of a file or directory name at the Bash prompt, you can press the Tab key to see if Bash can complete it for you by considering the possibilities in the given context.

If Bash can find a unique possibility, it inserts it for you, saving you some typing. If it can't, it does nothing. But if you press the Tab key a second time, it shows you all the possible matches. You can then add a few more characters to ensure a unique match and use autocompletion again to finish off.

Autocompletion also works with commands. Try entering system_ and pressing the Tab key. Bash should find the system_profiler command in your path and fill in the rest of the command for you.

In the next Try It Out, you put theory into practice by interacting with your Mac's file system via the Bash Shell. In doing so, you use fundamental commands such as `ls`, `cd`, `mv`, `mkdir`, `chmod`, `chown`, `sudo`, and `rm`.

Try It Out   Interacting with the File System

1. Open the terminal window in the Terminal application.

2. Change to the `/usr/bin` directory and list all commands that contain `gnu`.

```
Macintosh:~ sample$ cd /usr/bin
Macintosh:/usr/bin sample$ ls *gnu*
gnuattach       gnudoit         gnuserv
gnuclient       gnumake         gnutar
```

3. Copy the commands containing `gnu` to your `Desktop` folder and then change to the `Desktop` folder. After typing `Desktop` in the `cd` command, try pressing the Tab key to use Bash's auto-completion feature to finish off the path:

```
Macintosh:/usr/bin sample$ cp *gnu* ~/Desktop/
Macintosh:/usr/bin sample$ cd ~/Desktop
```

4. Make a subdirectory of the `Desktop` folder called `somecommands` and move the commands that you just copied into that subdirectory:

```
Macintosh:~/Desktop sample$ mkdir somecommands
Macintosh:~/Desktop sample$ mv *gnu* somecommands
```

5. Change to the `somecommands` directory and list its contents:

```
Macintosh:~/Desktop sample$ cd somecommands/
/Users/terry/Desktop/somecommands
Macintosh:~/Desktop/somecommands sample$ ls
gnuattach       gnudoit         gnuserv
gnuclient       gnumake         gnutar
```

6. List full details of the `gnutar` command, using `ls -l`:

```
Macintosh:~/Desktop/somecommands sample$ ls -l gnutar
-rwxr-xr-x  1 terry  terry 186024 Apr 29 20:50 gnutar
```

7. Change the permissions of `gnutar`, removing read and execute permissions for all users that are neither the file's owner nor in the file's group:

```
Macintosh:~/Desktop/somecommands sample$ chmod o-rx gnutar
```

8. Change the owner and group of the `gnutar` file to some other user on your system. In the example given here, the new user and group are `tiger`. You should use a user that exists on your system, in place of `tiger`. First try to use `chown` without the `sudo` command. An error should arise. When it does, use the `sudo` command to force the change of ownership. You will be prompted for your password.

```
Macintosh:~/Desktop/somecommands sample$ chown tiger:tiger gnutar
chown: gnutar: Operation not permitted
Macintosh:~/Desktop/somecommands sample$ sudo chown tiger:tiger gnutar
Password: *********
```

9. List full details of the gnutar command again. Notice how the permissions, owner, and group have changed:

```
Macintosh:~/Desktop/somecommands sample$ ls -l gnutar
-rwxr-x---  1 tiger  tiger  186024 Apr 29 20:50 gnutar
```

10. Move down one directory to the Desktop directory and remove the somecommands directory. Answer y when prompted as to whether you would like to override the permissions of the gnutar command:

```
Macintosh:~/Desktop/somecommands sample$ cd ..
Macintosh:~/Desktop sample$ rm -r somecommands
override rwxr-x---  tiger/tiger for somecommands/gnutar? y
```

How It Works

Most of this example involves fairly straightforward changes of directory and copying and moving of files. These are very common actions when working in a shell, and you should learn them well.

In order to list the files containing gnu in the /usr/bin directory, two special globbing characters were used:

```
Macintosh:/usr/bin sample$ ls *gnu*
```

Because the * character matches zero or more characters, *gnu* matches any file or directory name containing gnu, including cases where gnu is at the beginning or end of the name.

After copying the files containing gnu to the Desktop folder, a new directory is created with mkdir, and the commands moved into it with mv. The gnutar command is then singled out for practicing modification of ownership and permissions. First, the rights of other users to read or execute the file are removed, using chmod with the argument o-rx. o refers to users that are neither owner nor in the file's group. The hyphen means that rights are being revoked, and the rx indicates that the rights being revoked are for reading and executing. (Other users did not have write permissions to begin with, so they do not need to be revoked.)

Next, an attempt is made to change the owner and group of the gnutar file. This does not succeed at first because normal users are not allowed to change ownership of a file; only root can change ownership. To overcome this impedance, the sudo command is used to run the chown command.

To finish off the example, the somecommands directory is deleted. Because you do not own the gnutar file, you are prompted if you would like to override the permissions. If you answer in the affirmative, the gnutar file and the rest of the somecommands directory are deleted.

Searching for Files

With the coming of Mac OS X "Tiger," and the Spotlight search technology it contains, you have some pretty powerful tools for finding files and directories available to you on Mac OS X. In addition to the graphical interface, Apple has provided tools for searching with Spotlight from the command line. You can use Spotlight to search for files by name, but it also searches file content and metadata.

Metadata is data about data. It includes information such as a file's name, the date it was created, the type of data it contains, and much more. If you want to know what metadata is associated with a particular file, you can use the `mdls` command to find out:

```
Macintosh:~ sample$ mdls Sites/index.html
Sites/index.html -------------
kMDItemAttributeChangeDate    = 2005-04-21 19:26:03 +0200
kMDItemContentCreationDate    = 2003-10-28 11:05:45 +0100
kMDItemContentModificationDate = 2003-10-28 11:05:45 +0100
kMDItemContentType            = "public.html"
kMDItemContentTypeTree        = ("public.html", "public.text", "public.data",
"public.item", "public.content")
kMDItemDisplayName            = "index.html"
kMDItemFSContentChangeDate    = 2003-10-28 11:05:45 +0100
kMDItemFSCreationDate         = 2003-10-28 11:05:45 +0100
kMDItemFSCreatorCode          = 0
kMDItemFSFinderFlags          = 0
kMDItemFSInvisible            = 0
kMDItemFSLabel                = 0
kMDItemFSName                 = "index.html"
kMDItemFSNodeCount            = 0
kMDItemFSOwnerGroupID         = 501
kMDItemFSOwnerUserID          = 501
kMDItemFSSize                 = 5754
kMDItemFSTypeCode             = 0
kMDItemID                     = 485368
kMDItemKind                   = "HTML document"
kMDItemLastUsedDate           = 2003-10-28 11:05:45 +0100
kMDItemTitle                  = "Mac OS X Personal Web Sharing"
kMDItemUsedDates              = (2003-10-28 11:05:45 +0100)
```

Spotlight command-line tools are located in the `/usr/bin` directory and begin with the letters `md`, which stand for *metadata*. As you can see from the output of the `mdls` command, even a simple HTML file has a lot of metadata associated with it. Each *metadata attribute* is associated with a key; the keys can be seen in the left column of the output of `mdls`, with the data value itself given in the right column.

To search the metadata and content of files, you can use the `mdfind` command. For example, to find all files that include the text `Personal Web Sharing` in the metadata or content, you could issue the following command at the prompt:

```
mdfind "Personal Web Sharing"
```

You can restrict your search to particular metadata attributes by using a simple query string. For example, to search only the metadata attribute `kMDItemFSName` of each file, which contains the filename, you could issue the following command:

```
mdfind "kMDItemFSName == 'Personal Web Sharing'"
```

The string passed to `mdfind` is a query string; in this case the path to any file whose `kMDItemFSName` attribute includes `Personal Web Sharing` will be written out.

Spotlight is an exciting new technology, but it does have one drawback — it works only on Mac OS X 10.4 and later. If you are working on an earlier version of Mac OS X, or a completely different Unix-based operating system, Spotlight will not be available. Luckily, there are some traditional Unix tools that can help you locate files and directories by name.

One of the easiest way to find paths containing a given string is to use the locate command. For example, to find all paths containing the string NSApplication.h, you could issue the following command:

```
Macintosh:~ sample$ locate NSApplication.h
/Developer/ADC Reference
Library/documentation/Cocoa/Reference/ApplicationKit/Java/Classes/NSApplication.htm
l
/Developer/ADC Reference
Library/documentation/Cocoa/Reference/ApplicationKit/ObjC_classic/Classes/NSApplica
tion.html
/System/Library/Frameworks/AppKit.framework/Versions/C/Headers/NSApplication.h
```

As you can see, even a reasonably unique string like this can generate several results. Bear in mind that the string can match anywhere in the path. If it matches a directory name, for example, the whole contents of the directory, and all of its subdirectories, will be printed. Try to be specific about what you are searching for when using locate.

The locate command works with a database of all the files on your file system, which gets updated weekly by Mac OS X. This means that new files are unlikely to be found by the locate command. locate is useful for finding files that do not change often, such as commands, libraries, and header files. It will not be very effective for finding regularly changing files and directories, such as those in your own projects.

> **The** locate **database gets updated once a week on Mac OS X, but only after it has been created. You usually have to create the initial database yourself. To do this, issue the command** sudo /usr/libexec/locate.updatedb **in Terminal.**

A command you can use to search the file system in its current state is find. Of course, find doesn't have the benefit of a database, so it is slower than locate. It has to go through the file system one file/directory at a time, checking the filename, and reporting results. But find has many more options than locate, and is a powerful command to learn.

The most common way of using find is like this:

```
find /System/Library/Frameworks -name NSApplication.h
```

This command searches in the directory /System/Library/Frameworks, and all subdirectories, for any file or directory with the name NSApplication.h.

You can also use globbing characters in the name you pass to find. To search for any file with a name containing darwin in the current working directory or any subdirectory, you could enter this:

```
find . -name "*darwin*"
```

The * characters match zero or more characters in the name, so the path of any file whose name contains darwin, including those that begin or end with darwin, will be printed.

You can also carry out commands on the files you locate with `find`. For this, you use the `-exec` option, which runs a command that you provide, like this:

```
find . -name rubbish -exec rm {} \;
```

This command finds files called `rubbish` in the current working directory or any of its subdirectories. When a file called `rubbish` is found, the command given after `-exec` is performed. The command in this case is `rm`, to remove the file. The path of the located file can be accessed using the special character `{}`, so `rm {}` is the same as typing `rm` followed by the path to the file. Commands following the `-exec` option need to be terminated by a semicolon, but because the semicolon has a special meaning to the Bash Shell, it is escaped with a backslash.

The `find` command is very powerful, with many options. For example, you can list or carry out commands on files that were last modified before a given date. Perhaps you want to remove them after a while. In fact, your Mac OS X system uses the `find` command every day to clean up old files. Take a look in the file `/etc/daily`, which is a Bash script run by Mac OS X every day. You should be able to find a section like this:

```
if [ -d /tmp ]; then
    cd /tmp && {
    find . -fstype local -type f -atime +3 -ctime +3 -exec rm -f -- {} \;
    find -d . -fstype local ! -name . -type d -mtime +1 -exec rmdir -- {} \; \
        >/dev/null 2>&1; }
fi
```

In short, this complicated set of commands uses `find` to remove temporary files and directories located in the `/tmp` directory, after they have not been accessed for a number of days. For more information on the options used in these commands, and `find` in general, read the `find` man page:

```
man find
```

Working with Text

An important part of using a shell is being able to manipulate text, whether the text is the contents of a file or the output of a command that needs to be piped into a second command. Unix systems have a number of powerful tools for working with text, including `grep`, `sed`, and `awk`. This section covers the most important commands for handling text on Mac OS X.

A simple but commonly used command is `echo`. `echo` simply prints out whatever follows it on the line, after the shell has substituted any variable values or special characters. For example, to print a greeting to standard output, you could do this:

```
Macintosh:~ sample$ echo Hello Cupertino !
Hello Cupertino !
```

But you can make your message a bit more flexible by including variables and other special Bash characters:

```
Macintosh:~/Desktop sample$ touch Cupertino
Macintosh:~/Desktop sample$ GREETING=Hello
Macintosh:~/Desktop sample$ echo $GREETING Cuper* !
Hello Cupertino !
```

The `touch` command simply updates the time stamp of the file given as an argument; or, if the file doesn't exist, it creates a new empty file with that name. In this case, an empty file called `Cupertino` is created.

A variable called `GREETING` is then initialized to `Hello`, and the `echo` statement combines the value of the variable, as given by `$GREETING`, with the names of all files and directories in the current directory beginning with `Cuper`. `Cuper*` is interpreted by the shell as a glob and expanded before the string is passed to `echo`. The net result is precisely the same as the first example of using `echo`.

The `cat` command can be used to concatenate (join) a number of files, printing the result to standard output. If used with a single file, it simply writes the contents of the file to standard output. To join two files, creating a third, you could do this:

```
cat file1 file2 > file3
```

After this command, `file3` will first contain the contents of `file1`, followed by the contents of `file2`. `file1` and `file2` themselves will be unaltered. If `file3` exists prior to the operation, it will be overwritten.

`cat` is often used to initiate a chain of operations on the contents of a file rather than using the < redirection operator. For example, you could extract all lines of a file containing the word `Cupertino` by issuing the following command:

```
cat somefile | grep Cupertino
```

The `cat` command writes the contents of `somefile` to standard output. The standard output is piped into a `grep` command, which prints any line containing the text `Cupertino`.

`grep` is a very useful command, which can be used to extract lines of text matching some pattern. In the simplest case, it just searches for a literal match to a string:

```
Macintosh:~/Desktop sample$ grep '<TABLE' index.html
<TABLE WIDTH="85%" BORDER="0" CELLSPACING="15" CELLPADDING="0">
```

The `grep` command searches the file `index.html` for any lines that include `'<TABLE'`, which is an opening tag for a HTML table. Notice the use of single quotes; this is necessary because the < character has a special meaning to the shell (it is the input redirection operator). If you enclose a string in single quotes, the shell will ignore any special meanings, and pass the string unaltered to `grep`.

`grep` can also be used with special pattern-matching strings called *regular expressions*. You can think of regular expressions as being similar to globbing, but do not confuse the two. Although the characters used for pattern matching in globs and regular expressions are often the same, their meanings can be quite different.

Here is a simple example of using a regular expression with `grep`:

```
Macintosh:~/Desktop sample$ grep 'BORDER.*CELLSPACING' index.html
<TABLE WIDTH="85%" BORDER="0" CELLSPACING="15" CELLPADDING="0">
```

The pattern to be matched is `'BORDER.*CELLSPACING'`. This regular expression matches any line that includes the text `BORDER`, followed by zero or more arbitrary characters, and then the text `CELLSPACING`. The period (`.`) character is special in regular expressions. It matches exactly one character, like the `?` in

Bash globbing. The * character has a very different implication in regular expressions; it means that the preceding character can occur zero or more times. In this case, the period is the preceding character, so it can be used to match zero or more arbitrary characters. The complete pattern thus matches any string beginning with CELLSPACING and ending with BORDER, with any characters in between.

Two types of regular expression that you can use with grep are *basic* and *extended*. There is not enough room to cover all the intricacies of regular expressions in this chapter, but they are powerful and well worth learning. To get you started, here is a table of the most important extended regular expression patterns, and what they match. To use extended regular expressions, insert the -E option in front of the regular expression. Basic regular expressions are similar to extended regular expressions, but more restrictive. See the man page of grep for more details.

Pattern	Description	Example	Does Match	Doesn't Match
.	Matches any single character.	char.t	char0t chartt	chart
*	Modifies the meaning of the previous character. A match can occur with zero or more of the previous character in the regular expression.	char*t	chat chart charrt	
+	Similar to *, but requires at least one match. Zero occurrences does not match.	char+t charrrt	chart charrt	chat
{n}	Matches exactly *n* occurrences of the previous character.	char{3}blah	charrrblah	chablah charblah charrblah
[...]	Matches any character given in the square braces.	char[xYz]t	charxt charYt charzt	chart charyt charwt
(...)	Used to group characters together.	char(xyz)*blah	charblah charxyzblah charxyzxyzblah	charxblah charxyblah
|	Allows two different expressions to match.	char(x|yz)+blah	charxblah charyzblah charxxblah charxyzblah charyzxblah charyzyzblah	charblah charzyxblah charyyzzblah

grep is a good command for extracting lines of text, but it can't help you much if you want to modify text. For that you need a more powerful tool, such as sed or awk.

awk is named after its creators — Aho, Weinberger, and Kernighan — and is actually a whole language unto itself. Unfortunately, there isn't the space here to do it justice. It can be used for complex text manipulation, but you can also use it for simple tasks like extracting a word of text based on its position in a line. For example, suppose you wanted to use the wc command to count the number of words in a file. You could do something like this:

```
Macintosh:~/Desktop sample$ wc index.html
    125     799     5754 index.html
```

wc provides the number of lines, words, and characters in the given file. But you are interested only in the number of words; you can extract this number with the following command involving awk:

```
Macintosh:~/Desktop sample$ wc index.html | awk '{ print $2; }'
799
```

In this case, the output of wc has been piped to awk. An awk program is given in between single quotes. awk programs process one line of text at a time, in a repetitive manner. This very simple awk program prints the second whitespace-separated entry on each line that it reads. Because only one line is output by the wc command in this example, awk prints only the string 799, which appears second on the line output by wc.

The number of words in a file can be obtained more easily by simply supplying the -1 option to wc. However, this would not have demonstrated the usefulness of awk, which was the purpose of the preceding example.

The sed command is not a complete programming language like awk, but it is a very powerful editor. A common use for sed is to replace one regular expression with another. For example, the following command replaces any occurrences of the text Apple, with Apple Computer Company:

```
sed -e 's/Apple/Apple Computer Company/g' somefile.txt
```

The resulting text is written to standard output. The first argument to sed, which is enclosed in single quotations, is an editing command; it tells sed what text substitution to make. A substitution command takes the form s/.../.../g, with the regular expression between the first and second forward slashes replaced by the text between the second and third slashes.

Here is a more advanced example, leveraging the possibilities of regular expressions:

```
sed 's/< *[Tt][Aa][Bb][Ll][Ee].*>/<table class="tableclass">/g' index.html
```

This example scans the file index.html for any HTML opening tags for tables. These tags take the basic form <TABLE ...> and can include attributes after the TABLE label. The sed command searches for these tags and replaces them with <table class="tableclass"> when found.

The regular expression used to find the TABLE tags is quite involved. It looks like this:

```
< *[Tt][Aa][Bb][Ll][Ee].*>
```

It begins with the < character, which is followed by a space and a * character. The * indicates that a match can include zero or more of the previous character, namely, the space. A series of five square braces follow, each containing an upper- and lowercase letter. Together, these braces account for the case-insensitivity of HTML, allowing for every legal form of the string table, including TABLE, table,

TaBlE, and taBLE. The regular expression handles the possibility of attributes by including the characters .*, which match zero or more arbitrary characters after the table label. The > terminates the tag.

In the following Try It Out, you use some of the commands you have learned for manipulating text to change the table cell widths in an HTML file.

Try It Out   Editing an HTML File with sed

1. Open a window in the Terminal application.

2. At the prompt, change to your Desktop directory using the cd command:

```
Macintosh:~ sample$ cd ~/Desktop
/Users/tiger/Desktop
```

3. Copy the default index.html file from your Sites folder to the current working directory:

```
Macintosh:~/Desktop sample$ cp ~/Sites/index.html .
```

4. Use cat to pipe the contents of the index.html file into the input of grep, extracting any lines that include tags of the form <TD ...>:

```
Macintosh:~/Desktop sample$ cat index.html | grep -i '<TD.*>'
            <TD COLSPAN=3>
            <TD WIDTH=50%>
            <TD WIDTH=5%></TD>
            <TD WIDTH=45%>
```

5. Using sed, replace all these tags with the tag <TD WIDTH=100>, and put the resulting HTML in a file called new.html:

```
Macintosh:~/Desktop sample$ sed 's/<TD.*>/<TD WIDTH=100>/g' index.html > new.html
```

6. Confirm that the tags have been substituted by using on the file new.html the same grep command as in step 4:

```
Macintosh:~/Desktop sample$ grep -i '<TD.*>' new.html
            <TD WIDTH=100>
            <TD WIDTH=100>
            <TD WIDTH=100>
            <TD WIDTH=100>
```

How It Works

If you haven't modified your Sites directory since installing Mac OS X, it should still include a default index.html file, which is used in this example. If you don't have this file anymore, you can use any HTML file you like as long as it has TD tags.

In step 4, grep is used to extract any line containing an opening table cell tag, which has the label TD. The -i option stands for *case-insensitive*, so grep ignores case, effectively matching tags containing the labels TD, tD, Td, and td.

The sed command replaces the opening table cell tags with the tag <TD WIDTH=100>, using a substitution. Results are redirected with the > shell operator to the file new.html. Notice that in this case, no effort has been made to treat the possibility of tag labels including lowercase letters. This could be achieved by using the pattern `<[Tt][Dd].*>`, but it is not necessary here because the grep command in step 4 already shows that there are no lowercase tags.

The last grep command confirms that the tags have been updated as expected. You can also examine the new.html file for yourself with Nano if you want to be sure everything went as planned.

Process Control

Running short subprocesses in the foreground is fairly straightforward, but if you have something more time-consuming, you will want to run it in the background. You need to be able to monitor the progress of your background process, to find out its status, and whether it has exited. Even if you don't initiate background processes very often yourself, many are run by the root user to handle all sorts of administrative activities.

> Many background processes are *daemons*. Daemons run continuously, and are often started when the system boots up. They typically listen for requests on a network port and act on them when they are received, perhaps starting up other programs.
>
> If you want to see what sort of daemons are running on your system, open the Activity Monitor utility. In an Activity Monitor window, select Administrator Processes from the Show popup button in the toolbar.

The ps command is used to check the status of processes running on your system. If you use it without any arguments, it prints the processes associated with the shell you are using:

```
Macintosh:~ sample$ ps
  PID  TT  STAT      TIME COMMAND
 1112 std  S      0:00.14 -bash
```

Only one process is shown in this case: the Bash Shell itself. Other information given includes the PID, or process identifier; STAT, the status of the process; and TIME, the CPU time consumed. The PID is needed to identify the process in any commands that you issue. The possible status values are given in the following table.

Status Value	Description
D	The process is in disk, and cannot be interrupted.
I	The process is idle. It has been sleeping for longer than 20 seconds.
R	The process is running.
S	The process has just been put to sleep. It has been sleeping for less than 20 seconds.
T	The process is stopped.
Z	The process is a zombie. It is dead.

When you start a process in the background, it appears in the list produced by ps. For example, the following runs the sleep command in the background:

```
Macintosh:~ sample$ sleep 10 &
[1] 1140
Macintosh:~ sample$ ps
  PID  TT  STAT      TIME COMMAND
 1112 std  S      0:00.18 -bash
 1140 std  S      0:00.01 sleep 10
```

The sleep command simply sleeps for the time you give as an argument, in this case 10 seconds. The & has been used to put the command into the background. When you do this, the PID of the subprocess is printed, which is 1140 in this example. When the ps command is issued, the sleep process shows up with the expected PID of 1140.

Without options, ps supplies you only with information about the processes that you own and that were started from the shell. You can get information about other processes that you own using the -x option. The output of ps -x includes any applications that are running, whether you started them yourself or not. For example, apart from the applications you initiated yourself, there are processes for the Finder, Dock, and iCal, which you may not have realized existed.

ps can also be used to get information about other processes running on the system. Many options are available, and you should take a look at the ps man page to decide which ones you would like to include. Using -aux with the command provides enough information for most purposes:

```
Macintosh:~ sample$ ps -aux
USER      PID %CPU %MEM    VSZ    RSS  TT  STAT STARTED     TIME COMMAND
tiger     469 22.9  1.1   92000   7312  ??  S    Sat08PM  3:40.46
/Applications/Utilities/Terminal.app/Contents/Mac
tiger    1108  7.9  9.4  370816  61356  ??  S    5:27AM   7:29.47
/Applications/Microsoft Office 2004/Microsoft Wor
root     1158  3.0  0.1   41932    352 std  R+   6:16AM   0:00.01 ps -aux
tiger     179  3.0  4.8   83264  31700  ??  Ss   Sat06PM 17:17.38
/System/Library/Frameworks/ApplicationServices.fr
tiger    1115  1.0  1.3  103288   8716  ??  S    5:32AM   2:19.98
/Applications/Utilities/Activity Monitor.app/Cont
tiger     527  0.6  4.1  134160  26616  ??  S    7:59AM  18:00.30
/Applications/Internet Explorer.app/Contents/MacO
root     1116  0.3  0.1   27736    576  ??  Ss   5:32AM   1:14.86
/Applications/Utilities/Activity Monitor.app/Cont
root      120  0.0  0.1   27480    348  ??  Ss   Sat06PM  0:03.21 netinfod -s
local
root      122  0.0  0.0   18056    120  ??  Ss   Sat06PM  0:20.49 update
 ...
```

The output has been truncated, but you can see that this set of options gives you information about all processes, and for all users.

One time you will need ps is when something goes wrong and you want to terminate a process. If you can find out the process identifier using ps, you can issue a kill command to stop it. To demonstrate, the sleep command is utilized again:

```
Macintosh:~ sample$ sleep 3600 &
[1] 1180
Macintosh:~ sample$ ps
  PID  TT  STAT     TIME COMMAND
 1112 std  S     0:00.23 -bash
 1180 std  S     0:00.01 sleep 3600
Macintosh:~ sample$ kill -9 1180
Macintosh:~ sample$ ps
  PID  TT  STAT     TIME COMMAND
 1112 std  S     0:00.23 -bash
```

The sleep process is set to sleep for 3600 seconds, or one hour. Instead of waiting for it to exit by itself, the kill command is used with the option -9 and the PID, in order to terminate the process. The last ps command confirms that the sleep process has exited.

> You can use kill to terminate a process in the background, but what about when the process is in the foreground? Simply type Control-C, and the foreground process will be killed.

You can also kill processes by name, rather than process identifier. The killall command is for this purpose.

```
Macintosh:~ sample$ sleep 3600 &
[1] 1183
Macintosh:~ sample$ killall sleep
[1]+  Terminated              sleep 3600
```

killall kills any process belonging to you that matches the name you pass. Processes of other users, including root, are unaffected.

If you do need to kill a process belonging to the root user, or some other user, you can use the sudo command, along with either kill or killall. sudo performs the command as root, and can thus terminate any process. Be careful not to terminate vital processes on your system or you could crash your Mac.

One drawback of ps is that it is static. It prints information about processes running at the time you issue the command, but it never updates. The top command gives similar information to ps, but it continuously updates. Simply issue

```
top
```

and press q when you are ready to exit. top gives all sorts of information, too much to cover here. It is particularly useful though for monitoring the percentage of CPU time that each process is using. Perhaps your system is responding slowly, and you want to know if there is a process hogging the CPU. top can tell you. If you use the -u option, it even orders the processes based on the percentage of CPU time they are using so that you can quickly find the culprit at the head of the list.

Mac OS X Exclusive Commands

If you have experience with other Unix systems, most of the commands discussed in this chapter will be familiar to you. But Mac OS X has a number of commands that are non-standard, and yet very useful.

There are too many to cover in detail, but the following table should give you an idea of what's available. By referencing the man pages, you should be able to figure out how to use each one. If a man page is not available, most commands provide help when you supply the -h option.

Command	Purpose
diskutil	Command-line equivalent of the Disk Utility application. Can be used to check and repair disks and permissions, and erase and partition disks.
ditto	Used primarily for copying files and directories while maintaining file resource forks. It can also be used to create compressed ZIP archives with resource forks intact.
hdiutil	Creates, mounts, and manipulates disk images.
installer	The command-line interface to the Installer application; used to install applications that come in packages.
mount_afp	Mounts an AppleShare file system. This is akin to choosing Go ⇨ Connect to Server in Finder.
open	Opens any document or application, just like you would by double-clicking an icon in Finder.
pmset	Used to control power management. This is of interest to laptop users, because pmset offers more control than is available through the System Preferences application.
system_profiler	Provides the same information found in the System Profiler utility.
SystemStarter	Used to start and stop system services from the command line, such as the Apache web server.

Overview of Other Commands

It is impossible to cover all Unix commands in a single chapter, so a selection of the most important has been presented here. But there are many other commands that you may have use for. The following table gives some of the standard Unix commands that have not been discussed in detail so that you can decide for yourself which are useful. Use the man pages to learn more.

Command	Purpose
crontab	Used to schedule commands to run at regular times. For example, you could schedule a regular cleanup of temporary files, or a backup of your home directory.
curl	Command-line tool for downloading and uploading files. Supports FTP and HTTP protocols.
dig	Tool for interacting with domain name servers (DNS). Can be used to determine the IP address of a host, for example.

Command	Purpose
`ftp`	Used for transferring files to and from servers using the FTP protocol.
`gzip/gunzip`	Compresses/decompresses files with the GZIP format.
`netstat`	Used to get detailed information about the network that the computer is attached to.
`nice/renice`	Used to set or change the priority of a running process so that the kernel allots more or less CPU time to it.
`sftp`	Secure version of `ftp`, based on the SSH protocol. Use it to securely transfer files to or from a server.
`ssh`	Secure shell for remotely accessing a system. It can be used to log in to a remote system, giving access to a command-line interface. It can also be used to run commands on a remote system, and even allows you to encrypt network traffic between two computers using a technique known as *tunneling*. Tunneling can also be used to avoid limitations imposed by a firewall.
`tar`	Creates and extracts archives of files and directories. An archive is a single file that can contain the data of many files and/or directories.
`zip/unzip`	Compresses/decompresses ZIP archives.

Shell Programming

You can do a lot with Unix commands, but if you have to issue the same commands over and over, it can become pretty tedious. Luckily, it's possible to combine a sequence of commands into a script, which can be run as often as you like. This section shows you how to write and run scripts.

Bash also offers a number of rudimentary programming constructions, such as conditional branching and loops, which may be familiar to you from other programming languages. Although these aspects of Bash can be used when working interactively, they are most useful when writing shell scripts. The programming aspects of Bash are also covered in this section.

Scripts

Bash scripts are made up of nothing more or less than the commands you enter at the prompt when working interactively. If you enter these commands in a text file, one per line, in the order they are issued, and you change the permissions of the file so that it can be executed, you have a Bash Shell script.

Take this interactive session:

```
Macintosh:~ sample$ cd ~/Desktop/
/Users/tiger/Desktop
Macintosh:~/Desktop sample$ touch blah
Macintosh:~/Desktop sample$ mkdir blahdir
Macintosh:~/Desktop sample$ mv blah blahdir/
```

If you find yourself repeating these commands often, you might consider inserting them into a script. The script would look like this:

```
#!/bin/bash
cd ~/Desktop/
touch blah
mkdir blahdir
mv blah blahdir
```

The script simply contains the same commands that were entered at the interactive prompt. The only difference is the first line, which is called a *shebang*. A shebang begins with the characters #!, and ends with a path. It tells the shell that is running the script which program to use to interpret it. In this case, another Bash Shell is being used, so the path to the bash command is given. If this were a Perl script, for example, the path to the perl command would be given in the shebang.

When you have added this script to a file, you can run it in two ways. The first is to explicitly use the bash command with the file as an argument:

```
bash scriptfile.sh
```

The bash command is used to run the script in scriptfile.sh. If you take this approach, you do not need to have execute permissions for the file scriptfile.sh. Also, the shebang will be ignored because you are explicitly passing the script as an argument to bash rather than letting the shell decide what to run the script with.

The second and more common way to run a script is to give the script file execute permissions, like this:

```
chmod u+x scriptfile.sh
```

With the script now executable, you can run it like this:

```
./scriptfile.sh
```

You need to include an explicit path to the file, unless you have the current working directory in your PATH environment variable.

When you issue this command, the shell you are using examines the shebang and starts a new Bash Shell that interprets the script.

Variables

You are already acquainted with environment variables in Bash, but not all variables are environment variables. A variable becomes an environment variable when the export command is used. If a variable is not exported, it is visible within the script in which it is defined, but not, for example, in any subprocesses.

Variables are defined by simply assigning them. They do not have to be declared beforehand, as in some other languages. Here is a simple example of defining and using a variable:

```
ADDRESS='1 Shell Street'
echo $ADDRESS
ADDRESS='2 Shell Street'
echo $ADDRESS
```

Running this script results in the following output:

```
1 Shell Street
2 Shell Street
```

The ADDRESS variable is initially assigned to the string '1 Shell Street'. The quotation marks are important; without them, the ADDRESS variable would be assigned only to 1, and the shell would not know how to interpret the rest of the string, resulting in an error. Later in the script, the ADDRESS variable is reassigned to '2 Shell Street'.

To access the value of a variable, you prepend a $ symbol. To summarize, when assigning a value to a variable, you use the variable name without a $, and when you want to substitute the value of a variable, you do use the $. In cases where the shell cannot determine the variable name, you can use curly braces to clarify matters. Take this script, for example:

```
SUBJECT=care
echo $SUBJECTless
```

This results in an error because the shell looks for a variable called SUBJECTless, which doesn't exist. Curly braces are used to fix the problem:

```
SUBJECT=care
echo ${SUBJECT}less
```

The script will now print the text careless.

You will have noticed by now that variable names are usually written in capital letters. This is purely a convention; it is not compulsory. You can use lowercase letters or mix upper- and lowercase; however, if you want your scripts to be easily read by others, consider sticking to the convention.

In each of the preceding examples, the shell substitutes the value of any variables *before* the echo commands are called. This applies to all commands, not only echo. Unless you take certain steps to explicitly prevent variable substitution (discussed in the next section, "Quoting"), the shell substitutes any variables before running the command.

The Bash Shell also provides array type variables. Arrays allow you to include multiple values in a single variable. You access the stored values using an index. Here is an example of defining and using an array:

```
ADDRESS[0]=Hello
ADDRESS[1]=there
ADDRESS[10]=Bob!
echo ${ADDRESS[0]} ${ADDRESS[1]} ${ADDRESS[2]} ${ADDRESS[10]}
```

This script prints this output:

```
Hello there Bob!
```

You index an array using an integer in square braces, with indexes beginning at 0. As you can see, it is not necessary to assign a value for all indexes. In this example, values have been assigned only for indexes 0, 1, and 10. In the echo statement, the value for index 2 is requested. No value has been assigned for index 2, but it does not result in an error; instead, the value is simply an empty string. Only the values of the other three array entries actually appear in the printed output.

When you access the value of an array element, you have to use the curly braces, as shown in the example. If instead you write something like this:

```
echo $ADDRESS[1]
```

the shell first tries to retrieve the value of $ADDRESS. In Bash, this evaluates to the first element in the array, ${ADDRESS[0]}. This value will be substituted and combined with [1], resulting in the output Hello[1], which is not what was intended.

Variables in Bash are global; that is, they are visible throughout the whole script after they have been defined. If you want to limit the visibility of a variable, you can use the local keyword. The following example shows a function that defines two variables, one global and one local:

```
VarFunc() {
  VAR1=value1
  local VAR2=value2
}
VarFunc
echo VAR1 is $VAR1
echo VAR2 is $VAR2
```

Here is the output of this script:

```
VAR1 is value1
VAR2 is
```

Without going into the semantics of functions, which are discussed a little later in this chapter, it should be clear that VAR1 is visible outside the function VarFunc, and VAR2 is not, as witnessed by the fact that an empty string is printed in the second line of the output, rather than the text value2.

You can perform arithmetic with integer variables using the let command. You simply write the expression you want to evaluate on the line after let, like this:

```
Macintosh:~ sample$ ONE=1
Macintosh:~ sample$ let THREE=$ONE+2
Macintosh:~ sample$ echo $THREE
3
```

You cannot perform arithmetic with decimal (floating-point) numbers directly in Bash. If you want to do this, you need to use the command bc or a more powerful language such as Perl or Python (see Chapter 10).

Apart from the variables that you define yourself, the Bash Shell defines a number of useful variables. For example, the process identifier of the shell running the script is given by $$. You can use this when naming files to avoid overwriting output from other runs:

```
echo It\'s a good day, la la la la la la > goodday_output_$$.txt
```

This one-line script writes a string to a file. The filename includes the process identifier (goodday_output_5006.txt) so it is unlikely to overwrite another output file produced by the same script because it will have a different process identifier.

Another set of important shell variables are the *positional parameters*, which correspond to the arguments passed when the script is run. The path of the script is passed in the variable $0, and the arguments are passed in the positional parameters $1, $2, $3, and so forth. The variable $# gives the number of positional parameters. To illustrate, suppose that the following script is inserted in the file argscript.sh:

```
#!/bin/bash
echo The script is called $0
echo There are $# positional parameters
echo First argument is $1
echo Second argument is $2
echo Third argument is $3
```

When this script is run, like this:

```
./argscript.sh arg1 arg2 arg3
```

the following output is produced:

```
The script is called ./argscript.sh
There are 3 positional parameters
First argument is arg1
Second argument is arg2
Third argument is arg3
```

All arguments can also be found in the variable $@. Inserting the following line in the preceding script

```
echo The arguments are $@
```

results in this additional line of output:

```
The arguments are arg1 arg2 arg3
```

Another commonly used shell variable is $?. This gives the exit status of the last command executed in the foreground. Usually, a value of 0 indicates the command succeeded and a non-zero value indicates failure. Here is an example:

```
mkdir tempdir$$
echo Exit code of mkdir was $?
mkdir tempdir$$
echo Exit code of mkdir was $?
```

The second mkdir command causes an error because the directory already exists. The exit code of the successful command is 0, and that of the unsuccessful operation is 1, as you can see from the script output:

```
Exit code of mkdir was 0
mkdir: tempdir5224: File exists
Exit code of mkdir was 1
```

Quoting

Several different types of quotation marks are used in shell programming, and it is important to know the implications of each. For example, double quotations do not have the same meaning as single quotation marks, and the two are often not interchangeable.

Double quotation marks are used to form strings, as you might expect. The shell will perform variable substitution within double quotations, as you can see from the following interactive session:

```
Macintosh:~/Desktop sample$ NAME=David
Macintosh:~/Desktop sample$ TIME="6 o'clock"
Macintosh:~/Desktop sample$ MESSAGE="Meet $NAME at $TIME"
Macintosh:~/Desktop sample$ echo $MESSAGE
Meet David at 6 o'clock
```

The definition of the TIME variable shows that single quotes have no special meaning in a double-quoted string. When defining the MESSAGE variable, the values of the NAME and TIME variables are substituted before the string is assigned to the MESSAGE variable.

If you want to avoid the special meaning of $NAME and $TIME in the shell, you can use single quotation marks:

```
Macintosh:~/Desktop sample$ NAME=David
Macintosh:~/Desktop sample$ TIME="6 o'clock"
Macintosh:~/Desktop sample$ MESSAGE='Meet "$NAME" at $TIME'
Macintosh:~/Desktop sample$ echo $MESSAGE
Meet "$NAME" at $TIME
```

Just as you can use single quotes in a double-quoted string, you can also use double quotes in a single-quoted string. The variable substitutions made in the preceding double-quoted string are not made when single quotes are used.

If you want to use double quotation marks, but force the shell to treat certain characters literally, even when they have a special meaning, you can use the backslash, like so:

```
Macintosh:~/Desktop sample$ NAME=David
Macintosh:~/Desktop sample$ TIME="6 o'clock"
Macintosh:~/Desktop sample$ MESSAGE="Meet \$NAME at $TIME"
Macintosh:~/Desktop sample$ echo $MESSAGE
Meet $NAME at 6 o'clock
```

A backslash preceding a character escapes any special meaning that that character has. It applies not only to variables, as demonstrated here, but to any characters that have special meaning to the shell.

Another type of quotation mark used often in shell programming is the *backtick*. When a command is enclosed in backticks, the command is executed, with the output replacing the command itself. Here is how you could use this approach to rewrite the first example above:

```
Macintosh:~/Desktop sample$ NAME=David
Macintosh:~/Desktop sample$ TIME="6 o'clock"
Macintosh:~/Desktop sample$ MESSAGE="Meet `echo $NAME` at `echo $TIME`"
Macintosh:~/Desktop sample$ echo $MESSAGE
Meet David at 6 o'clock
```

In this case, the echo commands given in the definition of MESSAGE are carried out by the shell and substituted before the string is assigned to MESSAGE. Backticks can be very useful when you want to store the results of a command for further processing. For example, you could list the contents of a directory, storing the resulting string in a variable, as demonstrated by this command:

```
DESKTOP_CONTENTS=`ls ~/Desktop`
```

The `ls` command lists the contents of the user's `Desktop` folder and assigns the resulting output to the `DESKTOP_CONTENTS` variable.

Conditional Branching

Most programming languages provide a mechanism for branching based on a condition or the outcome of a test. This is called *conditional branching*, and Bash also supports it with the `if` command.

The most difficult aspect of learning to use `if` in Bash is constructing conditions. Here is how you could use `if` to test whether an error occurred during the execution of a `mkdir` command:

```
if mkdir hellodir
then
    echo Making hellodir succeeded
else
    echo Making hellodir failed
fi
```

The `if` statement tests if the command given as the condition has an exit value of 0, which indicates success. If so, the commands after the `then` command are executed. If the exit value of the command is non-zero, the commands after the `else` command are executed. The `fi` keyword is used to close the `if` statement.

> *In Bash, the closing keyword of a command is often just the command written backwards. For example, for `if` it is `fi`, and for `case` it is `esac`.*

This `if` command may seem confusing at first because languages such as C and Java behave in the opposite manner: the `if` block is executed when the condition is non-zero or true, and the `else` block is executed when the condition is zero or false. This difference comes about because Bash treats an exit value of zero as success, and all other values as errors.

There is an operator in Bash that allows you to get behavior more similar to what you find in other languages: the `((...))` operator. The preceding example can be rewritten like this:

```
mkdir hellodir
if (( $? ))
then
    echo Making hellodir failed
else
    echo Making hellodir succeeded
fi
```

In this example, the exit value of the `mkdir` command, which is given by the shell variable `$?`, is tested with the `((...))` operator. The `((...))` is an arithmetic evaluation operator, which is actually equivalent to the `let` command. It evaluates the expression, returning 0 if the expression evaluates to a non-zero value, and 1 if the expression is 0.

If rather than performing arithmetic operations, you want to compare string values, you can use the `[[...]]` operator. Here is an example in which the values of three variables are compared using various operators:

```
VAR1="some string"
VAR2="$VAR1"
VAR3="other string"

if [[ $VAR1 == $VAR2 ]]; then
    echo VAR1 and VAR2 are the same
else
    echo VAR1 and VAR2 are different
fi

if [[ $VAR1 != $VAR3 ]]; then
    echo VAR1 and VAR3 are different
else
    echo VAR1 and VAR3 are the same
fi
```

Here is the output of this script:

```
VAR1 and VAR2 are the same
VAR1 and VAR3 are different
```

First, notice that the `then` command, which was previously included on the line following the `if`, is on the same line in this example. This is made possible by the addition of a semicolon behind the `if` command. Separate shell commands can either be written on separate lines or can appear on the same line separated by semicolons. Using the semicolon with an `if` command makes the code a bit more compact.

The assignment of the variables to various strings at the beginning is fairly straightforward, except for `VAR2`. You may be wondering why double quotation marks have been used around the value `$VAR1` on the right-hand side of the assignment. If you don't do this, the shell will expand `$VAR1` as the two words `some` and `string`. The quotation marks used to assign `VAR1` are *not* part of the variable; they are simply there to group the separate words into a single string. If you don't use quotation marks when assigning `VAR2`, it gets assigned to the first word, `some`, and the shell won't know how to treat the extra word `string`. It's a good idea to get into the habit of using double quotes when accessing the value of any string variable, including paths, which often contain spaces.

The conditional expressions themselves are comparisons between strings. The `[[...]]` operator returns 0 if the expression is true, and 1 otherwise. The operators `==` and `!=` can be used in the string comparisons and test for equality and inequality of the strings, respectively. You can also use logical operators, as demonstrated by this example, which extends the preceding script:

```
if [[ $VAR1 == $VAR2 && $VAR2 == $VAR3 ]]; then
    echo VAR1, VAR2, and VAR3 are all equal
elif [[ $VAR1 == $VAR2 && !($VAR2 == $VAR3) ]]; then
    echo VAR1 and VAR2 are equal, but VAR2 and VAR3 are not
elif [[ $VAR1 != $VAR2 && $VAR2 == $VAR3 ]]; then
    echo VAR1 and VAR2 are not equal, but VAR2 and VAR3 are
else
    echo VAR1 and VAR2 are not equal, and neither are VAR2 and VAR3
fi
```

Here is the output for this section of the script:

```
VAR1 and VAR2 are equal, but VAR2 and VAR3 are not
```

This example introduces the elif command, which stands for *else if*. If the condition of an if command is not met, control moves to the first elif. If the condition of the elif is met, such that the expression evaluates to 0, the commands after the next then command are evaluated, and then control jumps down to fi. If the elif condition is not met, control moves to the next elif, and so on. If none of the elif conditions are met, the commands after else are executed.

The conditional expressions in this example make use of many of the available operators. && is the logical AND, which evaluates to true if the expressions on either side of it are true. ||, which is not used here, is logical OR, which is true if either expression is true. Parentheses, such as those used in the first elif expression, can be used to group terms. The unary ! operator is the NOT operator and negates the value of the expression, changing true to false, and vice versa.

The final way of writing test conditions is with the test command, which is equivalent to the [...] operator. test can be used for arithmetic comparisons, but it is most useful for testing file attributes. Here is an example that tests if a particular file exists:

```
if test -e ~/Desktop/tempfile
then
    echo tempfile exists
fi
```

This can also be written as follows:

```
if [ -e ~/Desktop/tempfile ]
then
    echo tempfile exists
fi
```

The test command takes an option used to determine the type of test to be performed for the file given. In this case, the -e indicates that the existence of the file is being tested. If the file exists, the test command evaluates to 0 and the if block is performed, echoing the fact.

You can perform many other tests with the test command by using various options. The following table shows some of the more useful ones.

Option	Test Description
-a or -e	Tests if a file exists. A directory is also considered a file, for this purpose.
-d	Tests if a file exists and is a directory.
-f	Tests if a file exists and is a regular file, not a directory.
-r	Tests if a file exists and is readable.
-w	Tests if a file exists and is writable.
-x	Tests if a file exists and is executable.

Table continued on following page

Option	Test Description
-O	Tests if a file exists and is owned by the user.
-G	Tests if a file exists and is owned by a group of the user.
-nt	Binary operator used to determine if one file is newer than another. The comparison is based on the last modification dates of the two files. The test is true if the file to the left of the operator is newer than the file to the right.
-ot	Similar to -nt, but tests if one file is older than another.

The Bash Shell includes a second conditional branching command that will not be demonstrated here: case. A case command can be used to test an expression for equality with a number of possible values. For more information on the case command, see the bash man page.

Looping

Loops allow you to perform a series of commands repetitively, without having to duplicate them. The while loop continues until the exit status of a command is no longer zero. For example, here is a while loop that has a fixed number of iterations:

```
let i=0
while (( $i < 5 ))
do
    echo $i
    let i=$i+1
done
```

Here is the output of this script:

```
0
1
2
3
4
```

The command given after the while keyword is executed, and its exit value is checked. If it is zero, indicating success, the commands between do and done are executed. This repeats until a non-zero exit value is encountered.

In the example, the command utilizes arithmetic evaluation to determine if the variable i is less than 5. If so, the loop continues; if not, it exits. The commands inside the while block echo the variable and then increment it by one, using the let command.

> *The Bash Shell also includes an* until *loop, which has the same structure as the* while *loop. The difference between the two is that the* until *loop continues as long as the conditional command returns a non-zero exit status and stops when an exit status of zero is encountered.*

while loops are often used to iterate over command-line arguments, using the shift command. Assume the following script is in a file called script.sh:

```
#!/bin/bash

while (( $# ))
do
    echo $1
    shift
done
```

When run with this command:

```
./script.sh 1 2 3 4
```

the output is

```
1
2
3
4
```

In this example, the `while` tests how many input arguments are left, which is given by the shell variable `$#`. When there are none, the `while` loop exits. Each iteration, the command `shift` removes one input parameter — the one in the `$1` variable — and moves all the others to a lower index. `$2` becomes `$1`, `$3` becomes `$2`, and so forth.

The `for` loop is capable of performing the same operations as the example shown at the beginning of this section, with somewhat less code:

```
for (( i=0 ; i<5 ; i++ ))
do
    echo $i
done
```

This is very similar to the `for` loop in the C language, which is described in Chapter 6. Three arithmetic expressions are given inside the arithmetic evaluation parentheses `((...))`. The first is evaluated just once, at the beginning. This is usually used for initializing a counting variable, like `i`. The next is evaluated every iteration, including the first. If it is true, the loop continues; if not true, the loop exits with control transferred immediately to the `done` statement. If the second statement is true, the third statement is evaluated and usually increments the counter variable; the `++` operator increases a variable by one. Each iteration, the commands between `do` and `done` are executed.

Another form of the `for` loop can be used to iterate over a list of words. In the example that follows, it is used to echo a number of names from a string variable:

```
NAMES="Bill Bob Barry Bernice Beatrix"
for name in $NAMES
do
    echo $name
done
```

This is the output:

```
Bill
Bob
Barry
Bernice
Beatrix
```

The `for ... in ...` form of the `for` loop sets the variable given after the `for` keyword to each of the whitespace-separated words in the string given after `in`.

A useful variation on this loop involves leaving out the `in` part of the loop. When you do this, the `for` loop iterates over the input arguments, as demonstrated by this script:

```
#!/bin/bash

for name
do
    echo $name
done
```

Inserting this in a file called `script.sh`, and running the script like this:

```
./script.sh Bill Bob Barry Bernice Beatrix
```

leads to this output:

```
Bill
Bob
Barry
Bernice
Beatrix
```

Functions

If your scripts start to become large, or you find yourself duplicating a lot of code, you may consider using functions. Functions allow you to group commands together, so that they can be executed from anywhere in a script with a *function call*.

You write a function like this:

```
function ChangeToDesktopAndList() {
    cd ~/Desktop
    ls
}
```

This function is called `ChangeToDesktopAndList`. The `function` keyword is optional, but the parentheses following the function name, and the braces, are required. To call this function, you simply enter the function name, like this:

```
ChangeToDesktopAndList
```

The function definition must precede the function call in the script so the shell knows about the function's existence. Wherever you call the `ChangeToDesktopAndList` function, the commands in the function are executed.

Like scripts, functions can also take arguments. And also just like scripts, arguments are accessed in a function using the shell variables $1, $2, $3, and so forth. Here is a more general function than `ChangeToDesktopAndList`:

```
function ChangeToDirAndList() {
    cd "$1"
    ls $2
}


ChangeToDirAndList ~/Desktop -l
```

This function changes to a directory passed as the first argument, and lists the contents, with the options of the `ls` command passed as the second argument. The function call simply lists the arguments separated by whitespace, just as if it were a script. In the example, the `Desktop` folder is the first argument, and the `-l` option is the second.

Note that if your arguments include spaces, you need to use quotation marks to group them. Quotation marks have also been used in the function around the $1 argument, just in case the path passed includes spaces. Here is a function call in which the arguments include spaces:

```
ChangeToDirAndList "$HOME/Desktop/some dir" "-l -a"
```

The only complication is that the environment variable HOME has had to be used in place of the ~ because the shell does not substitute for the ~ in a quoted string.

If you need to explicitly return from a function to the calling code, you can use the `return` command. For example, in this function:

```
function ReturningFunc() {
    ls ~/Desktop
    return
    ls ~
}
```

the last `ls` command is never performed because the function jumps from the `return` command back to the calling code.

In the next Try It Out, you use the various shell programming constructions you have learned to develop a script to find and compress any large files in a given directory and any of its subdirectories.

Try It Out   Writing a Shell Script to Compress Large Files

1. Open a terminal window in the Terminal application.

2. Change to the `Desktop` directory by issuing the following command:

```
cd Desktop
```

3. Create a new file with Nano called `compress.sh`:

```
nano compress.sh
```

4. Enter the following script with Nano in the `compress.sh` file:

```
#!/bin/bash

# Check exit status in $?.
# If non-zero, print it, along with the message in $1.
# If $? is non-zero, exit script if $2 is equal to "YES".
function CheckExitStatus() {
    local EXIT_STATUS=$?
    if (( $EXIT_STATUS )); then
        echo An error occurred, with status $?
        echo Message: $1
        if [[ $2 == "YES" ]]; then
            exit $EXIT_STATUS
        fi
    fi
}

# Function that finds any files larger than 5Mb, and compresses them.
# The directory path $1, and subdirectories, are searched for large files.
function CompressFilesInDirTree() {
    find "$1" -size +5000000c -type f -exec gzip "{}" \;
    CheckExitStatus "Find command failed" YES
}

# Main program. Loop over directories passed via command line arguments.
# Compress any large files in each directory tree.
for dirPath
do
    CompressFilesInDirTree "$dirPath"
done
```

5. Change the permissions of the `compress.sh` file so that it is executable:

```
chmod u+x compress.sh
```

6. Locate a directory tree with a variety of files smaller and larger than 5MB. Copy the whole directory to a temporary directory in the `Desktop` folder:

```
cp -r source_directory ~/Desktop/temp_dir
```

`source_directory` should be the path to the directory you want to copy.

7. Run the `compress.sh` script to compress the large files in `temp_dir`.

```
./compress.sh temp_dir
```

8. Check that the files larger than 5MB that reside in `temp_dir` and its subdirectories have been compressed by the `gzip` command and have the `.gz` extension.

9. Remove the `temp_dir` directory when you are ready.

```
rm -r temp_dir
```

How It Works

The `compress.sh` script begins with a function that checks the exit status of the last command executed and acts based on whether an error occurred:

```
# Check exit status in $?.
# If non-zero, print it, along with the message in $1.
# If $? is non-zero, exit script if $2 is equal to "YES".
function CheckExitStatus() {
    local EXIT_STATUS=$?
    if (( $EXIT_STATUS )); then
        echo An error occurred, with status $?
        echo Message: $1
        if [[ $2 == "YES" ]]; then
            exit $EXIT_STATUS
        fi
    fi
}
```

Before the function definition, there is a comment. A comment can be created by simply using the # symbol; anything after the # on the line is ignored by the shell.

The function name is `CheckExitStatus`, and the first executable line defines a variable called `EXIT_STATUS`, which is visible only inside the function because of the presence of the `local` keyword. `EXIT_STATUS` is assigned to the last exit status, which is given by `$?`. Because `$?` will be reset every time a command is issued, its value is saved in the `EXIT_STATUS` variable.

The `if` block checks if the exit status is non-zero, in which case a couple of messages are echoed. The first argument to the function is a message to the user that is printed if a command failed. The second argument is used in the nested `if` command; if the argument is equal to the string `YES`, the script exits.

The second function does the bulk of the work, searching for files in a particular directory tree and compressing the large ones:

```
# Function that finds any files larger than 5Mb, and compresses them.
# The directory path $1, and subdirectories, are searched for large files.
function CompressFilesInDirTree() {
    find "$1" -size +5000000c -type f -exec gzip "{}" \;
    CheckExitStatus "Find command failed" YES
}
```

The `find` command performs the search. It has a number of options passed to it. The first argument to the function is also used as the first argument to the `find` command. This argument is the root directory of the search. (Note that double quotes have been used to ensure that any spaces in the directory path are not misinterpreted.)

The first option passed to `find` is `-size +5000000c`. This means that `find` should ignore any file smaller than 5000000 bytes, or 5MB. The `-type f` option is included so that `find` searches only for regular files and not directories or other file types. The `-exec` option executes the command given for any file found that matches all criteria. In this case, files are compressed with the `gzip` command.

The CheckExitStatus function is called after the find and passed two strings: one is printed if the command has failed, and the other is a string that indicates whether a failure should cause the script to exit. If YES is passed as the second argument, a failure will cause the script to terminate.

The end of the script, which could be considered the main program, uses a for loop to iterate over any directory paths passed as command-line arguments:

```
# Main program. Loop over directories passed via command line arguments.
# Compress any large files in each directory tree.
for dirPath
do
    CompressFilesInDirTree "$dirPath"
done
```

For each iteration, the CompressFilesInDirTree function is called, passing the directory path as the only argument. The argument is given in quotation marks in case the path includes any spaces, which would cause it to be passed as multiple arguments.

Summary

The Bash Shell plays a vital part in Mac OS X operations, being used at system startup, and for system maintenance. You can use Bash to access a wealth of different Unix commands and combine them to undertake complex operations. These operations would be much more difficult to do with Finder.

In this chapter you learned

- ❑ How to use the Terminal application, and the Nano editor, to use Bash interactively and write shell scripts

- ❑ The most important Bash commands, for performing fundamental operations on files and text

- ❑ About other less fundamental commands, some of which are found only on Mac OS X

- ❑ How you write shell scripts with the programming constructs available in Bash, including conditional branching, looping, and functions

In the next chapter, you learn how to work with AppleScript and AppleScript Studio. AppleScript is quite a different beast to Bash in that it is generally used for scripting applications with a GUI rather than Unix commands. Before proceeding, however, try the exercises that follow to test your understanding of the material covered in this chapter. You can find the solutions to these exercises in Appendix A.

Exercises

1. With the Terminal application, use Bash interactively to create a compressed archive of all the files of a particular type (that is, with a particular extension) located in your home directory or subdirectories.

First locate the files with the `find` command and copy them to a temporary directory. Rather than using the standard `cp` command, which neglects to copy resource forks on versions of Mac OS X prior to 10.4, use the `CpMac` command in the `/Developer/Tools` directory. To learn more about this command, see the `CpMac` man page. Use `ditto` to compress the archive, and `mv` to move it to a backup directory.

Refer to the man pages of the various commands to learn how they are used.

2. Convert the interactive commands you used to complete Exercise 1 into a backup script. You can use the `history` command to see what commands you typed. For more information, see the `history` man page.

Restructure the commands to make the script more readable and robust if necessary, and don't be afraid to introduce shell programming constructs such as conditional branches and functions. Have the script check for errors and send you an email you if one occurs. (*Hint:* See the man page of the `mail` command.)

AppleScript and AppleScript Studio

AppleScript is a scripting language developed by Apple primarily for scripting applications that have a graphical user interface (GUI). It reads like English and is targeted more at the general Mac user than the programming professional. Nonetheless, even the serious programmer has something to gain from AppleScript; without AppleScript, it is virtually impossible to take full advantage of the functionality offered by applications ranging from iPhoto to QuickTime, Mail to Microsoft Word. AppleScript is to GUI applications what the Bash Shell is to Unix commands — the glue that binds them together. (If you don't know what this means, read Chapter 11 on the Bash Shell.)

In recent years, AppleScript has ventured beyond its traditional hunting grounds into application development. By integrating AppleScript with the Cocoa frameworks (see Chapter 8), Apple has made it possible to develop fully fledged Mac OS X applications with AppleScript, using a suite of tools called AppleScript Studio. This makes it possible for non-programmers to easily write applications that look stunning and behave like any other Cocoa application.

This chapter provides an introduction to AppleScript and a brief look at AppleScript Studio. Here are some of the things you learn:

- ❑ The different ways you can use AppleScript scripts, and the tools you can use to create them
- ❑ The basics of the AppleScript language
- ❑ How to script applications like Finder, iPhoto, and QuickTime
- ❑ About the various tools in AppleScript Studio
- ❑ How you can use AppleScript Studio to create applications with the Cocoa frameworks

AppleScript

This section introduces you to the AppleScript language and the many ways it can be utilized. AppleScripts have access to the internals of running applications and can issue commands or request data. By extracting data from one application and feeding it into another, you can create complex workflows with AppleScript. This can end up saving you a lot of repetition in your daily activities, freeing you up for the activities that demand more creativity.

Creating an AppleScript

The tool to use for a basic AppleScript is the purpose-built Script Editor application, which you can find in the `/Applications/AppleScript` folder. Script Editor is a basic editor, but it is designed for AppleScript and has some useful features such as syntax checking and reformatting, which can make scripts easier to read.

Each window of Script Editor (see Figure 12-1) is for a separate script. In the toolbar are buttons for recording a script; stopping the operation in progress; running a script; and compiling, which checks syntax and reformats.

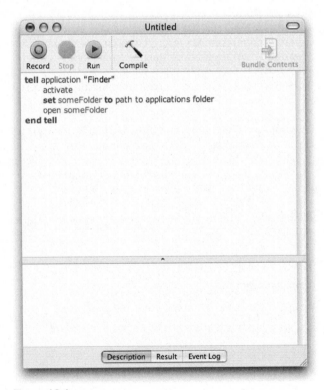

Figure 12-1

The Script Editor also gives you a means to browse the *dictionary* of any application. The dictionary includes the various properties and commands that can be accessed by AppleScript. You can open an application's dictionary by choosing File ⇨ Open Dictionary and then choosing an application.

In this first Try It Out, you write a very simple script with Script Editor, compile, and run it. You also open a dictionary to better understand the script.

Try It Out   Using Script Editor

1. Open the Script Editor application.

2. In the editor window, enter the following script:

```
tell application "Finder"
    activate
    set someFolder to path to applications folder
    open someFolder
end tell
```

3. Click the Compile toolbar button and note the changes in the script.

4. Click the Run toolbar button. A Finder window should appear, displaying the Applications folder.

5. Choose File ⇨ Open Dictionary. In the panel that appears, select Standard Additions in the table and then click the Open button.

6. In the browser view at the top, click File Commands and then select the first of the two Path To commands in the second column. Try to understand the information displayed in the text view at the bottom in relation to the script you entered in step 2.

7. Save the script by choosing File ⇨ Save and typing the name Open Applications Folder. Make sure the File Format popup button is set to Script. Close the script window in Script Editor, and then reopen it by double-clicking the Open Applications Folder script file in Finder.

8. Now save the script again, this time selecting Application from the File Format popup button. Locate the saved file in the Finder, and double-click it. What happens, and how does it vary from what happened in step 7?

How It Works

The script in this example is very simple. It sends several commands to the Finder application. The tell block indicates that commands should go to the application called "Finder". The first command is activate, which tells Finder to become the frontmost application.

The next line sets a variable called someFolder to the path to the Applications folder. Note how similar the last sentence is to the line in the script. AppleScript often really does read like English.

The last command to Finder is open, with the path someFolder passed as an argument. This causes Finder to open a new window with the Applications folder selected.

When you click the Compile button, the AppleScript interpreter checks the syntax of the script for correctness, adds some highlighting and coloring, and sometimes reformats. Reformatting can involve changing indentation, for example, to make the script easier to read. To actually run the script, you need to click the Run button.

The dictionary of Standard Additions documents various standard commands and classes that can be used in your AppleScripts. In this case, the command path to was used to get the path to the Applications directory. The dictionary tells you what arguments can be used with the path to command, and other assorted information.

When you save a script, you can choose various formats. If you choose the Script format, the file opens in Script Editor when you double-click it in Finder. If you want to run the script, you need to use the Run button in Script Editor.

If you save a script as an application, it is given a different extension (.app), which identifies it as an Application to the Mac OS X system. When you double-click the application, it does not open in Script Editor but runs immediately, like any other application. In this example, it opens the Applications folder in Finder, and exits.

> *AppleScript applications can also be referred to as applets.*

Scriptable and Recordable Applications

Not all applications are *scriptable*. A scriptable application is one that can be accessed from an AppleScript. Many applications are not scriptable because the developers did not take the necessary steps to make them so. Making an application scriptable is not difficult, but it also does not happen automatically.

In addition to being scriptable, an application can also be *recordable*. Even fewer applications are recordable than are scriptable. Scripts can be developed for recordable applications simply by opening Script Editor, clicking the Record toolbar button, and carrying out the tasks you want to include in the script. When you are finished, you click the Stop button in the Script Editor toolbar, and you have your AppleScript.

Using this approach is easy because you don't need to write the code yourself; but it has some drawbacks. The first is simply that many applications are not recordable, so you still have to write scripts by hand for those that aren't. The second drawback is that the code produced by Script Editor is very verbose and difficult to follow. It also doesn't include any flow-control constructs like loops or branches; it is simply a list of all the commands you carried out while Record was pressed.

Recording can be useful for simple repetitive tasks and for laying the foundation of a script. You can record a number of actions and then edit the script, introducing more powerful flow-control statements and generally cleaning up the code to form a well-rounded script.

> *There is actually a third category of application: attachable. These applications are even more rare than recordable applications. When an application is attachable, a script can receive notification when certain events occur.*

Apple Events

AppleScripts communicate with one another and with running applications by using *Apple Events*. Apple Events are a means of performing *interapplication communication* and can be used to send messages between scripts and applications running on a single machine or across a network. Each Apple Event can be seen as encapsulating a command sent by one script or application to another script or application, where it is interpreted and usually results in some action being undertaken.

For example, if you have written a line of AppleScript requesting the Finder to open a particular folder, an Apple Event is created to represent this request and sent to the Finder application. Finder attempts to open the folder and sends a reply in the form of a second Apple Event back to your script to indicate whether or not the operation was successful.

Apple Events are represented and transmitted via a *messaging protocol* called the Open Scripting Architecture (OSA), which was devised by Apple in the early '90s. OSA is language agnostic and could be supported by any scripting language. In an ideal world, you could communicate between many different OSA languages, but in practice OSA is only widely used by AppleScript.

> The ideas behind OSA are shared by other more recently developed messaging protocols such as *SOAP* and *XML-RPC*. The latter are built on top of the *eXtensible Markup Language* (*XML*) and are used primarily for *Web Services*. Web Services allow communication between computers via the HTTP protocol, which is used for the Web.
>
> Another form of interapplication messaging on Mac OS X is provided by the Cocoa frameworks. It is called *distributed objects* (*DO*) and allows you to send messages to an object that exists in a different application or even on a different computer, as if it existed locally.

Variables and Data Types

As with most languages, AppleScript uses *variables* to store data. Variables are named vessels for data stored in memory; they can store anything from a simple number, to a string, or even a whole script. AppleScript provides the usual simple data types such as `real` (decimal) and `integer` numbers, and `boolean`, which represents truth values. But there are also more advanced data structures like `string`, which contains text; `list`, which is an ordered collection of data; and `record`, which stores data in key-value pairs. AppleScript even supports object-oriented programming (OOP), which is covered later in the chapter in the "Scripts and Objects" section.

Variable names are case-insensitive in AppleScript and have the usual restrictions: they can contain only alphanumeric characters and the underscore character and cannot begin with a digit. You do not need to declare a variable's type before you use it; to create a variable, you simply assign it a value, like this:

```
set _some_variable to 12.0
```

The `set ... to ...` command is the usual means of setting a variable. In this example, `_some_variable` gets the real number value `12.0`. You can also force a variable to take a particular type by using the `as` keyword:

```
set _some_variable to 12.0 as string
```

In this case, the real number `12.0` is first *coerced* to the string value `"12.0"` before being assigned to `_some_variable`. *Coercion* in AppleScript is similar to what is known as *casting* in other languages, such as C (see Chapter 6). In each case, some data is simply converted from one type to another type.

The limitations placed on variable names can be overridden by enclosing the variable name within | symbols. For example, |5 times as many $'s| is a legal AppleScript variable name.

When you use set, you are actually creating a *shallow copy* of some data, meaning that the variable you assign shares the data with any other variable assigned to the same data. If you want to make a *deep copy*, in which the data is actually duplicated before being assigned to the variable, you use the copy command:

```
copy 12.0 to _some_variable
```

or

```
copy 12.0 as string to _some_variable
```

In most cases, including this example, there is little difference between using set and copy. But with the more advanced data types, it can be important which you choose, as discussed in the following paragraphs.

As already stated, variables don't have a *static type*; they are *dynamically typed*, taking on the type of whatever data they are assigned to. This also means they can change type. Here is an example of a variable first assigned to a real number and then to a string:

```
set x to 5.0 + 5 as number
set x to 5.0 + 5 as string
```

In the first line, x takes the real number value 10.0. In the second line, x is reassigned and has the string value "10.0". You may have thought x would be equal to the string "5.0 + 5", but this is not so. The latter would require the following assignment:

```
set x to "5.0 + 5" as string
```

A string literal is enclosed in double quotation marks.

> Note that the value 5.0 in the preceding examples was coerced to a type called number. Number *is a type that can be used for both* real *and* integer *numbers.*

Another simple data type, boolean, can take the values true and false. You can use the usual comparison operators to create expressions with boolean values. Here are a couple of examples of setting boolean variables:

```
set someBool to true
set anotherBool to 4 < 5
```

In the second example, the variable anotherBool is assigned to the value of the expression 4 < 5, which is true.

String variables are important in any language. In AppleScript, strings are *immutable*, meaning they cannot be changed after they are created. If you need to edit a string, you simply create a new string based on the original one.

AppleScript's string manipulations are relatively primitive when compared to a language like Perl, but you can perform basic operations. You join strings in AppleScript using the concatenation operator &:

```
set address to "18 Hills Hoist Lane, " & "Berryhappy"
```

The variable `address` is assigned the `string` value `"18 Hills Hoist Lane, Berryhappy"`.

If a line in your script gets too long, you can press Option-Return to insert the line continuation character (¬) to continue to the next line. In the preceding example, it would look like this:

```
set address to "18 Hills Hoist Lane, " & ¬
  "Berryhappy"
```

The ¬ is the continuation character. Unlike Objective-C or Java, AppleScript does not have a line termination character. A logical line of code is equivalent to a line in the script, unless a line continuation character is inserted.

AppleScript also includes two important compound data types, which can be used to store collections of data. The first is `list`, which stores ordered collections of data entries, with each entry associated with an index.

> A `list` *is similar to an* `NSMutableArray` *in Cocoa (see Chapter 8); it is a dynamic array that can grow to accommodate new data.*

`List` literals are defined by enclosing comma-separated entries in curly braces, like this:

```
set someList to {1,2,3}
```

The variable `someList` is associated with the `list` containing the integer numbers 1, 2, and 3. It is not necessary for the entries to all be the same type. The following is also legal:

```
set someList to {1,"2",3}
```

Now the second entry is the `string` `"2"`, rather than an `integer`.

To access the entries in a `list`, you can do this:

```
set someEntry to item 2 of someList
```

Here the variable `someEntry` is set to the second entry in the `list`, `someList`. In the previous example, this was the `string` `"2"`. `List` indexes begin at one in AppleScript, not zero as in C and many other languages.

Data types can have various attributes, and AppleScript has a very specific naming scheme for these. An attribute can be either an *element* or a *property*. In the preceding example, `item` is an element of the `list` type. An element is an attribute that can have any number of different values. You use the `item` element of `list` to access the entries in the list. A property is an attribute that has exactly one value. Recognizing the differences between properties and elements is important because you need to use them in quite distinctive ways with AppleScript.

Setting entries of a list after it has been created is also possible:

```
set someList to {"one", "two", "three"}
set item 2 of someList to "2"
```

After the second line has been executed, `someList` will be equal to the `list` `{"one", "2", "three"}`.

To extend a `list` by appending a new value, you can do this:

```
set end of someList to "four"
```

And to insert a value at the beginning you can do this:

```
set beginning of someList to "zero"
```

Finally, the number of entries in a list is accessible via the `length` property:

```
set list_length is length of {1,2,3,4}
```

The variable `list_length` is assigned the value 4, which is the number of elements in the `list` literal. A nice feature of `list`s is that you can use them to assign multiple variables at once, like this:

```
set {x, y, z} to {1, 2, 3}
```

This assigns the entries in the first `list` to those in the second. x is assigned to 1; y to 2; and z to 3.

The second compound data type available in AppleScript is `record`. A `record` stores unordered key-value pairs. In other languages, a `record` is called a *dictionary*, *hash table*, or *map*. A `record` literal in AppleScript is created with curly braces, just like a `list`, but keys are also supplied:

```
set friends_ages to {bob:42, joe:36}
```

The keys are given to the left of each colon, and the values to the right.

To access the values in the `friends_ages` record, you supply a key, like this:

```
set friends_ages to {bob:42, joe:36}
set bobs_age to bob of friends_ages
set joe of friends_ages to 38
```

In the second line, a value is retrieved from the `record` using the keyword `of`. In the third line, an entry in the `record` is modified, changing the value corresponding to the key `joe` to 38 from 36.

Extending a `record` involves the concatenation operator `&`:

```
set friends_ages to friends_ages & {jack:36, jill:37}
```

This actually creates a new `record` by combining the old `friends_ages` record with the literal `record` containing ages for `jack` and `jill`. The newly formed `record` is then assigned to `friends_age`.

Unlike `list`, a `record` doesn't have an element called `items` because the entries in a `record` are unordered. It does have the property `length`, which is the number of entries it contains. In addition, every key used in a `record` is automatically made a property. That is why they work with the `of` keyword, which is usually used to access properties.

It is important to realize that when you assign to a `list` or `record`, you are not actually copying its contents; rather, you are simply creating a reference to the existing data container. A reference is a type similar to a pointer in the C language (see Chapter 6); it basically just stores a memory address. If you actually want to copy the contents, you need to use the `copy` command, rather than `set`:

```
set birthdays to {¬
    terry:date "December 2, 1972", ¬
    ellen:date "May 28, 1968" }

-- Create one reference, and one copy
set ref_to_birthdays to birthdays
copy birthdays to copy_of_birthdays

-- Change terry's birth year to 1974
set terry of birthdays to date "December 2, 1974"

-- Check values
terry of ref_to_birthdays     -- Should give year as 1974
terry of copy_of_birthdays    -- Should give year as 1972
```

This example contains a few new aspects of AppleScript. The first is the date type. As you can see, you can create a date by using an appropriately formatted string, along with the keyword date. The format of the date is quite flexible, but it must be consistent with the settings in the International pane of your System Preferences.

This example also uses comments for the first time. Single-line comments are signified using two hyphens (--); anything following the hyphens on the line is ignored. Multiline comments are delineated by an opening symbol (*, and a closing symbol *).

The main point of this example is to demonstrate that if you use set, you get a reference to the record. If you change the original record, which is birthdays, the set-assigned record also gets updated. On the next to last line, the terry entry in ref_to_birthdays is retrieved; this entry should be the same as in birthdays and show the new year of 1974. The copy will *not* show the new year because it is a completely different record and is not altered by the change to birthdays.

On the last two lines of the script, the terry entries in the two derived records are retrieved. You can use this type of statement to test values in Script Editor. If you open the Result tab in a Script Editor window, you can see the value of the last command run. This can be used to check the values of variables. In this example, you could enter the next to last line if you want to see the value of the terry entry in ref_to_birthdays and enter the very last line for the value of terry in copy_of_birthdays.

AppleScript has many other data types, but none are as important as the ones covered in this section. You will encounter some of the others as you work through the rest of this chapter.

In the following Try It Out, you build up experience with the data types discussed in this section by storing information about a fictional group of friends.

Try It Out   Working with Data

1. Open Script Editor and enter the following in a script window:

```
set joe to { ¬
    full_name:"Joe Blockhead", ¬
    birthday:date "12 February, 1969", ¬
    favorite_colors:{"green", "purple"}, ¬
    favorite_meal:"Spaghetti"}
```

```
set belinda to { ¬
    full_name:"Belinda Blockhead", ¬
    birthday:date "13 February, 1971", ¬
    favorite_colors:{"lilac", "indigo"}, ¬
    favorite_meal:"Beans"}

set peter to { ¬
    full_name:"Peter Whoknows", ¬
    birthday:date "26 June, 1952", ¬
    favorite_colors:{"red", "blue", "pink"}, ¬
    favorite_meal:"Turkey"}
```

2. Click the Compile button to check the script.

3. Add a new line to the end of the script to access the value of Belinda Blockhead's birthday:

```
birthday of belinda
```

4. Run the script by clicking the Run button. Open the Result tab at the bottom of the window and confirm that the birthday shown is correct.

5. Replace the new line added in step 3 with a line to extract the first favorite color of Peter Whoknows:

```
item 1 of favorite_colors of peter
```

6. Rerun the script, again checking the output in the Result tab.

7. Replace the last line of the script again, this time to retrieve the second favorite color of Peter:

```
peter's (item 2 of favorite_colors)
```

8. Rerun the script and check the results.

How It Works

The script defines records for three different individuals. A record can contain any data types; in this case, each record contains a variety: a date, two strings, and a list. It is also perfectly acceptable to embed one record within another.

The rest of the exercise centers on accessing the stored data. Retrieving the birthday of Belinda Blockhead is straightforward, but the favorite colors of Peter Whoknows present more of a problem. How do you access data contained in a compound type that is an entry in another compound type?

You can use one of two approaches. The first involves what is sometimes called an *inside-out reference*. In step 5, you used an inside-out reference:

```
item 1 of favorite_colors of peter
```

The of keyword is used in a chain beginning with the most deeply nested property (the list favorite_colors) and ending with the container at the highest level (the record peter).

The second approach utilizes a *possessive reference*, which is used in C-like languages, including C++ and Java. Step 7 used this approach:

```
peter's (item 2 of favorite_colors)
```

An apostrophe followed by s is used to denote possession. (You were warned that AppleScript is very English-like.) The parentheses are necessary to make clear precisely what is possessed, namely, the second entry of the list favorite_colors.

To compare the AppleScript way with another common form of describing containment relationships, here is how you might write step 7 in Java:

```
peter.favorite_colors.getItem(2)
```

As you can see, the order is exactly opposite to the inside-out approach and is similar to the AppleScript possessive reference form.

In general, the inside-out reference is easier to understand in AppleScript and is the form most commonly used.

Handlers

Handlers are AppleScript subroutines, like functions in the C language (see Chapter 6). A handler includes a block of code that is executed whenever the handler is *called* from somewhere in your script. It has zero or more parameters, which are variables used to pass arguments in, and an optional return value for passing a result back to the *caller*. Unlike C and some other languages, a handler does not need to have been declared or defined before it is used in a script; it can be defined after a call.

Here is a simple handler that adds two numbers together and returns the result. A call is made to the handler to add one and one:

```
on addTwoNums(firstNum, secondNum)
  return firstNum + secondNum
end addTwoNums

addTwoNums(1, 1) -- return value is 2
```

The on keyword precedes the handler's name, followed by a comma-separated list of parameters in parentheses. If there are no parameters, empty parentheses must be used. The handler is terminated by the keyword end, followed by the handler's name. The body can contain any number of statements, and control can be passed back to the caller using the return statement, which may also pass a *return value*.

If you don't enter the name of the handler after the end *statement, Script Editor does it for you.*

The return statement can be used to pass a result back to the caller, but it isn't necessary to include a value or have a return statement at all. If there is no return statement, the value of the last command executed in the handler implicitly becomes the return value. If no value should be returned, a return statement can be used without an argument.

The parameters defined in the preceding example are known as *positional parameters* because they are assigned to the arguments passed to the handler based purely on their position in the parameter list. It is also possible to have *labeled parameters,* in which each parameter is preceded by a preposition, making calls to the handler read more like English. For example, the preceding handler could be rewritten like this:

```
on summing for firstNum against secondNum
  return firstNum + secondNum
end summing

summing for 1 against 1 -- result is 2
```

One advantage of labeled parameters is that the order of the arguments can be varied in the calling code. For example, the following is also a legal call to the `summing` handler, although it doesn't make much sense:

```
summing against 1 for 1
```

A limited number of prepositions are allowed when using labeled parameters, which can sometimes make coming up with appropriate labels a creative challenge. The prepositions available are listed in the following table.

above	below	from	out of
against	beneath	instead of	over
apart from	beside	into	thru
around	between	of	under
aside from	by	on	
at	for	onto	

The `of` preposition is the odd one out; it can be used only for the first label in a handler parameter list. Other than that, there are no restrictions on order.

Labeled parameters are quite restrictive, but luckily AppleScript provides something more flexible: *named parameters*. With named parameters you can call a parameter just about anything you like. Here is an example:

```
on sum given firstNumber:x, secondNumber:y
  return x + y
end sum

sum given firstNumber:5.0, secondNumber:2.0  -- Result is 7.0
```

The keyword `given` must precede the named parameters. The parameters themselves are comma-separated, and each includes a colon, with the parameter name on the left and the variable or value on the right. Like labeled parameters, any order of arguments can be used for named parameters in the calling code.

Named parameters in AppleScript closely resemble the segmented names used in Objective-C (see Chapter 7).

It is also possible to include both labeled parameters and named parameters in one handler. The labeled parameters must come first, and the named parameters last.

```
on append onto firstString given other:secondString
  return firstString & secondString
end appendstring

-- Result of this call is "hello there"
append onto "hello " given other:"there"
```

To understand the mechanics behind argument passing with handlers, it is best to imagine that the parameters in a handler are variables that have been assigned to the arguments passed using the `set` command. If you think like this, you will be able to predict what will happen when you pass a particular type of value.

For example, arguments with simple types such as `real`, `integer`, and `string` are effectively *passed-by-value*. If you change the value of a parameter corresponding to a simple-typed argument, the original argument remains unaffected. If you think about it, this is exactly what would happen if you assigned one variable, say x, to another simple-valued variable, y. If you later change x, y will not be affected. This is what you observe passing simple types to handlers.

The same is not true of compound data types, such as `list`, `record`, `date`, and `script` objects (which you learn about later in the section "Scripts and Objects"). Compound data types are effectively *passed-by-reference*. When you alter the value of a parameter with a compound type, the argument is also changed. This makes sense because if you use `set` to assign a variable x to a compound data value y, and then perform an operation on x, such as appending a new entry to a `list`, y will also be modified.

Here is an example to demonstrate the semantics of argument passing in AppleScript:

```
on changes(numVar, listVar, recordVar)
  set giraffe of recordVar to "A tall animal"
  set end of listVar to 4
  set numVar to 4.0
end changes

set n to 3.0
set l to {1, 2, 3}
set r to {giraffe:"A long animal"}
changes(n, l, r)

n -- value is 3.0
l -- value is {1,2,3,4}
r -- value is {giraffe:"A tall animal"}
```

The argument n is not affected by the reassignment of the parameter `numVar` because it is a simple type. The `list` and `record` variables l and r each reflect the operations performed in the `changes` handler after the call is made.

To finish off this section on handlers, we should point out that not all handlers need to be called from within your scripts. Handlers can also be written to intercept Apple Events sent from outside your code. There is a special `run` handler, for example, that is called to run the main code of a script. If you don't define it explicitly, the statements found in your script at the highest level are executed; but if a `run` handler is found, it is called instead. Here is an example:

```
on run
  say ("hello")
end run

on say (w)
  display dialog w
end say
```

The `run` handler is called when the script is started; it, in turn, calls the `say` handler, which displays a dialog box with the text `hello`. Note that the `run` handler does not need a parameter list because it is special; usually, if you write a handler that has no parameters, you need to include empty parentheses in the definition of the handler.

Control Statements

Control statements relate to the flow of execution of a script and include conditional branching and looping, among other things. AppleScript provides the usual constructions for flow control but adds one or two that you probably won't recognize from any other programming language.

Conditional Branching

AppleScript includes the `if` construct for conditional branching purposes. It tests a `boolean` condition and executes a block of code only if that condition evaluates to `true`. Here is a simple example:

```
if true then
  display dialog "Must have been telling the truth"
end if
```

This is not a particularly interesting example because the condition, which appears after `if`, is always `true`, so the dialog will always be displayed. The `if` statement includes the keyword `then` after the condition, and the block is closed with `end if`. If the condition is `true`, the code between `if` and `end if` is executed; otherwise, it is skipped.

The `if` statement becomes more useful when you actually perform a test:

```
set x to 5.0
set y to 3.0

if x < y then
  display dialog "x was less than y"
else
  display dialog "x was not less than y"
end if
```

The expression `x < y` has been used as the condition in this example. In addition, an `else` block has been included. The code after the `else` is only evaluated if the condition is `false`. In this example, because x is not less than y, the else block will be evaluated, and a dialog displayed with the text x was not less than y.

The if statement can include multiple conditions, using the else if keyword. Here is an example:

```
set x to 5.0
set y to 3.0
set z to 1.0

if (x ≤ y and y ≤ z) or (z ≤ y and y ≤ x) then
  display dialog "y is between x and z"
else if (y ≤ x and x ≤ z) or (z ≤ x and x ≤ y) then
  display dialog "x is between y and z"
else if (x ≤ z and z ≤ y) or (y ≤ z and z ≤ x) then
  display dialog "z is between x and y"
else
  display dialog "An error occurred"
end if
```

Each condition is tested in order, beginning with the condition after if, and proceeding to each else if condition in order. The block of code following the first condition that evaluates true is executed, and all others are skipped. If no condition is true, the else block is executed.

In this example, three different tests compare the three variables x, y, and z. The operator ≤ is generated automatically by Script Editor when you enter <= and compile or run the script. The conditions also include the logical operators and and or, and parentheses are used to group terms. When you run the script, a dialog appears displaying the text y is between x and z.

There is one more form of the if statement: the single-line form. If an if statement has no else block and only a single executable command, it can all be written on a single line, like this:

```
set friends_name to "Bob"
if friends_name is equal to "Bob" then display dialog "Hi Bob!"
```

In addition to demonstrating use of the single-line form of if, this example includes the operator is equal to, which has been used to compare whether two strings are the same.

Looping

AppleScript includes several different constructions for looping. Loops always begin with the keyword repeat and end with the keyword end repeat; however, there are many different variations on the repeat loop. The most basic form loops forever, or until an exit repeat statement is encountered:

```
set x to 0
repeat
  set x to x + 1
  if x = 100 then exit repeat
end repeat

display dialog x as string
```

This example displays a dialog containing the number 100. The code inside the repeat ... end repeat block is executed until x is equal to 100, at which point the exit repeat command causes the loop to terminate.

The loop exit condition in this example can be included in the repeat statement itself using the while or until keywords, like this:

```
set x to 0
repeat while x < 100
  set x to x + 1
end repeat

display dialog x as string
```

or this:

```
set x to 0
repeat until x = 100
  set x to x + 1
end repeat

display dialog x as string
```

In each of these examples, the condition supplied after the while/until keyword is tested *before* each iteration of the loop. The repeat while loop continues as long as the condition is true, and the repeat until continues as long as the condition is false. This explains why the conditions are different in each case. The end result of each example is the same: a dialog is displayed with the number 100.

Often you need to loop over a sequence of regularly spaced integer numbers. There is a repeat loop to handle this too; it is called the repeat with loop. The preceding examples can be rewritten to use this form of repeat:

```
repeat with x from 0 to 100 by 1
end repeat

display dialog x as string
```

As you can see, this is actually the most compact form in this particular instance. The loop variable x is first initialized in the loop to the integer given after from, which is 0. The number given after by is added to x *after* each iteration of the loop, until x is equal to the number after the to keyword, at which point execution jumps to the end repeat and continues from there.

The by keyword is optional in repeat with loops. If you exclude it, the loop variable is incremented by 1 after each iteration. Thus, in this example, it could have been left out. If you need to use numbers other than 1, you need to include by. The numbers supplied must be integers but do not have to be positive. For example, you can have x count backwards to -100 by using an increment of -1 and an end value of -100 after the to keyword.

The repeat with loop is similar to the for loop in the C programming language (see Chapter 6).

The final form of repeat allows you to iterate through the items in a list. For example, the following loop sums items:

```
set sum to 0
repeat with x in {10, 9, 8, 7}
    set sum to sum + x
end repeat

display dialog "The sum is " & sum as string
```

This example displays a dialog with value 34, which is the sum of 10, 9, 8, and 7. The variable after with, x, is repeatedly assigned to values in the list supplied after the in keyword. The list values are assigned in the order in which they appear in the list.

tell

The control statements covered so far are all fairly standard; you could find similar constructions in just about any language. But AppleScript has a few control statements that are peculiar, and nonetheless very important. The most widely used of these is the tell statement, which is used to send commands to applications, among other things.

tell can appear in block form or on a single line. The one-line form looks like this:

```
tell application "Finder" to activate
```

This issues a command to Finder to activate, which means to become the frontmost application. The tell statement consists of the keywords tell and to. A tell statement includes a command, which is activate in this case, and a target to which the command is to be sent, which is Finder. If you run the example script, the Finder application should become active.

Each scriptable application defines a set of commands that can be used in tell statements. To see which commands a particular application defines, you can examine its dictionary by choosing File ⇨ Open Dictionary in Script Editor.

The block form of tell looks like this:

```
tell application "Finder"
    activate
    open desktop
end tell
```

A tell block can contain zero or more commands. In this example, two commands are issued, one to activate and the other to open the Desktop folder. If you run the script, the Finder should become the frontmost application, and a window with the Desktop folder should appear.

tell blocks can also be nested, with each block targeting a different property. For example, imagine that you wanted to get the path to the first photo in your iPhoto library. Here is how you could do it:

```
tell application "iPhoto"
    tell photo library album
        set first_photo to item 1 in photos
        display dialog image path of first_photo as string
    end tell
end tell
```

The outer `tell` block selects the iPhoto application to receive commands. The nested `tell` block targets an object of the class album. This is accessed via a property of the iPhoto application called photo library album.

> *You learn about classes in the "Classes" section later in the chapter. For now, it is enough to know that they can be treated like applications when it comes to issuing commands and accessing properties.*

Inside the nested `tell` block, a variable is set to the first photo in the element photos, which belongs to the `album` class. Because any commands issued in a `tell` block are directed at its target, you do not need to use the `of` keyword to stipulate the album. The next line displays a dialog containing the path to the photo represented by `first_photo`, which is retrieved from the property `image path`.

Two unusual control statements in AppleScript are `ignoring` and `considering`. These are most commonly used to explicitly inform AppleScript to ignore or consider some aspect of text, such as whitespace or punctuation. For example, to compare two strings while ignoring any punctuation, you could do this:

```
ignoring punctuation
    if "Hello, Tom!" = "Hello Tom" then
        display dialog "Strings are equal"
    end if
end ignoring
```

This script displays the dialog indicating that the strings are equal, even though they clearly aren't. The `ignoring` block means that any punctuation in the strings is not considered in the comparison; because all the other characters are the same, the strings are equivalent.

You could rewrite the example to use a considering block, like this:

```
considering punctuation
    if "Hello, Tom!" = "Hello Tom" then
        display dialog "Strings are equal"
    else
        display dialog "Strings are not equal"
    end if
end considering
```

In this case, punctuation is taken into account, and the strings are not equal. If you run the script, a dialog will be displayed to that effect.

Most modern languages provide some form of *exception handling*. Exception handling gives you a mechanism for treating exceptional circumstances and errors. AppleScript includes the `try` block for exception handling. In the following example, an attempt is made to open a file in the `Desktop` folder:

```
set somePath to (path to desktop folder as string) & "temp file"
try
    set fileNum to open for access file somePath with write permission
on error
    close access file somePath
    return
end try
write "Hello Bob!" to fileNum
close access file somePath
```

The `try` block begins with `try`, includes `on error`, and ends with `end try`. The commands given between `try` and `on error` are evaluated, and if an error arises, control is transferred immediately to the `on error` block, and the commands between `on error` and `end try` are executed. These commands are executed only if an error arises; if everything proceeds normally, they are skipped.

This example begins by defining a path. The path to the `Desktop` folder is retrieved first, using the `path to` command from the Standard Additions dictionary. The `path to` command is included in the File Commands group. Paths returned by the `path to` command are colon-delimited. To create a path for a temporary file, the string `"temp file"` is appended to the `Desktop` folder path.

> *Standard Additions are a set of helpful commands and classes included with AppleScript. You can read more about them by choosing File ➪ Open Dictionary in Script Editor and then selecting the Standard Additions item in the table.*

An attempt is then made in the `try` block to open the file with `open for access`. This command is also from Standard Additions, in the File Read/Write group. If an error arises during the attempt to open the temporary file, the `close access` command from Standard Additions is used to close the file, and the script returns. If no error results, execution continues after the `try` block and the text `"Hello Bob!"` is written before the file is closed.

When exceptional circumstances arise, you can *throw* an error, which can optionally include a message string, and/or error number:

```
error "Could not open file." number -52
```

When you do this, control jumps to the `on error` command of the enclosing `try`, even if that `try` block is at a higher level of the script. For example, if an error is thrown from inside a handler, control can jump out of the handler if that is where the enclosing `try` block is located. The `try` block is said to *catch* the error. If there is no enclosing `try` block, the script stops with an error dialog box displayed.

The `try` blocks in the preceding example did not access the message or error number, but you can do that by extending the `on error` command, as in the following example:

```
try
    error "Hi Mum, I failed!" number 2
on error msg number n
    display dialog msg & return & "Error num: " & n as string
end try
```

Parameters in the `on error` block are retrieved just as they are supplied to the `error` command. In this case, the error message is assigned to the `msg` variable, and the error number to the variable n. A dialog is then displayed with this information. The `return` keyword is a global property in this case, *not* the `return` command; it represents the line break character.

There are a couple of other things that you should know about the `on error` block. First, it is optional; if you leave it out, exceptions are caught by the `end try` statement and ignored. Second, you can throw errors from inside the `on error` block. In this way, you can catch an error and throw a different one, perhaps with extra information supplied.

In the following Try It Out, you take the skills you have learned so far, from writing handlers to catching exceptions, and use them to create a stock quote repository. An AppleScript is used to download stock quotes from a Web Service and store them in files.

Try It Out   Downloading and Saving Stock Quotes

1. Open a new script window in Script Editor.

2. Enter the following script in the window:

```
-- Initialize the stock repository, if necessary. It is simply a folder
-- on the Desktop.
on setup_stock_repository()
    set desktop_path to path to desktop folder as string
    tell application "Finder"
        set the repository_folder to desktop_path & "Stock Repository"
        if not (folder repository_folder exists) then
            make new folder at desktop with properties ¬
                {name:"Stock Repository"}
        end if
    end tell
end setup_stock_repository


-- Uses SOAP to download a delayed stock quote
on download_quote(stock_symbol)
    try
        tell application "http://services.xmethods.net:80/soap"
            set quote to call soap {method name:"getQuote", ¬
                method namespace uri:"urn:xmethods-delayed-quotes", ¬
                parameters:{Symbol:stock_symbol}, ¬
                SOAPAction:""}
        end tell
        return quote
    on error
        display dialog "Download failed."
        return ""
    end try
end download_quote


-- Save a price in the repository for the stock symbol given
on save_latest_price given stock:stock_symbol, price:price
    set desktop_path to path to desktop folder as string
    set the repository_folder to desktop_path & "Stock Repository"
    set stock_file_path to repository_folder & ":" & stock_symbol
    try
        set file_number to open for access file stock_file_path ¬
            with write permission
    on error
        close access file stock_file_path
        return
    end try
    set end_of_file to get eof of file_number
    write (price as string) & return to file_number starting at end_of_file + 1
    close access file stock_file_path
end save_latest_price


-- Download and save the price
on archive_stock_price(stock_symbol)
    set price to download_quote(stock_symbol)
    save_latest_price given stock:stock_symbol, price:price
```

```
end archive_stock_price

-- Main script
setup_stock_repository()
archive_stock_price("AAPL")
archive_stock_price("IBM")
archive_stock_price("MSFT")
```

3. Compile the script by clicking the Compile button to make sure it was entered correctly.

4. Run the script by clicking the Run button. You need to be connected to the Internet for the script to work.

5. In Finder, open your Desktop folder and look for a folder called Stock Repository. If you find the folder, open it, and examine the contents of the files contained there. Run the script again, and note how the file contents change.

How It Works

This example brings together many of the aspects of AppleScript that you have learned up to this point in the chapter and a few tricks you haven't seen yet. It defines these handlers:

❑ setup_stock_repository: For setting up a repository to store stock quotes, which is nothing more than a folder containing text files

❑ download_quote: For downloading a stock quote for a given symbol

❑ save_latest_price: For saving a quote for a given symbol to the repository

❑ archive_stock_price: For carrying out the full cycle of downloading and saving a stock quote in the repository

The setup_stock_repository handler creates a folder for the repository, using the Finder:

```
on setup_stock_repository()
    set desktop_path to path to desktop folder as string
    tell application "Finder"
        set the repository_folder to desktop_path & "Stock Repository"
        if not (folder repository_folder exists) then
            make new folder at desktop with properties ¬
                {name:"Stock Repository"}
        end if
    end tell
end setup_stock_repository
```

It uses the Standard Additions command to path in order to retrieve the path to the Desktop folder. In the tell block, it appends the string "Stock Repository" to this path to create the path to the repository folder, and then checks whether the folder already exists. The exists command is defined in the Standard Suite of every application dictionary, including Finder. If the folder does not exist, a new one is created, using another command from the Standard Suite: make.

The download_quote handler uses the SOAP protocol, which is used to access Web Services. With Web Services, you can request a server located somewhere on the Internet to return some data or perform a calculation. In this case, a Web Service is requested to return a time-delayed stock quote for a given symbol:

```
on download_quote(stock_symbol)
    try
        tell application "http://services.xmethods.net:80/soap"
            set quote to call soap {method name:"getQuote", ¬
                method namespace uri:"urn:xmethods-delayed-quotes", ¬
                parameters:{Symbol:stock_symbol}, ¬
                SOAPAction:""}
        end tell
        return quote
    on error
        display dialog "Download failed."
        return ""
    end try
end download_quote
```

The URL of the Web Service is given as the application to the `tell` block. When you do this, AppleScript assumes that the application is a Web Service. Inside the `tell` block, the command `call soap` is issued, which sends a SOAP message to the Web Service. The arguments passed in the SOAP message include the name of the procedure `"getQuote"` and the stock symbol, which is an entry in a `record` containing parameters.

To save a stock quote in the repository, the `save_latest_price` handler uses file writing capabilities provided by the Standard Additions dictionary:

```
on save_latest_price given stock:stock_symbol, price:price
    set desktop_path to path to desktop folder as string
    set the repository_folder to desktop_path & "Stock Repository"
    set stock_file_path to repository_folder & ":" & stock_symbol
    try
        set file_number to open for access file stock_file_path ¬
            with write permission
    on error
        close access file stock_file_path
        return
    end try
    set end_of_file to get eof of file_number
    write (price as string) & return to file_number starting at end_of_file + 1
    close access file stock_file_path
end save_latest_price
```

First, a path to a file is built up. The file is in the repository folder and has the same name as the stock symbol. In the `try` block, the `open for access` command is used to open the file for writing. It returns a file reference number, which is used to refer to the file in other commands.

If opening the file fails, the `try` block catches the error, closes the file, and returns. If the file opens successfully, the `write` command is used to append the price to the end of the file. The `get eof` command gives the number of bytes in the file, which is equivalent to the index of the last character. In order to append, the new data is written to an index one greater than the index given by `get eof`. The handler finishes off by closing access to the file.

The `archive_stock_price` handler does nothing more than call the `download_quote` handler and pass the quote returned to the `save_latest_price` handler:

```
on archive_stock_price(stock_symbol)
    set price to download_quote(stock_symbol)
    save_latest_price given stock:stock_symbol, price:price
end archive_stock_price
```

The main part of the script sets up the repository, and then archives quotes for a few big players in the computer industry:

```
setup_stock_repository()
archive_stock_price("AAPL")
archive_stock_price("IBM")
archive_stock_price("MSFT")
```

This is bit simplistic. A more advanced implementation might prompt you for a stock symbol via a dialog box, or perhaps repeatedly download a particular set of stock quotes at a regular time interval.

Operators

AppleScript includes the usual set of operators found in programming languages, which are used for constructing arithmetic expressions, comparing values, and evaluating logic. The following table describes the operators available and gives simple examples of their use.

Operator	Description	Example	Result
+	Addition operator. Adds two numbers together.	1 + 1	2
–	Subtraction operator. Subtracts the second number from the first.	2 – 1	1
*	Multiplication operator. Multiplies two numbers together.	2 * 2	4
/	Division operator. Divides the first number by the second number.	4.0 / 2	2.0
()	Parentheses. Overrides operator precedence, forcing a different evaluation order.	(1 + 1) * 2	4
=, is, is equal to	Equality comparison operator. true if the left and right numbers are equal.	2 = 2	true
≠, /=, is not, is not equal to	Inequality comparison operator. true if the left and right numbers or not equal.	1 ≠ 2	true

Table continued on following page

Operator	Description	Example	Result
`<`, is less than	Less-than operator. `true` if the left `number` is less than the right one.	2.0 < 5.0	`true`
`>`, is greater than	Greater-than operator. `true` if the left `number` is greater than the right one.	2.0 > 5.0	`false`
≤, `<=`, is less than or equal to	Less than or equal operator. `true` if the left `number` is less than or equal to the right one.	2.0 <= 2.0	`true`
≥, `>=`, is greater than or equal to	Greater than or equal operator. `true` if the left `number` is greater than or equal to the right one.	3.0 ≥ 3.1	`false`
`div`	Integer division operator. Returns the whole number of times that the right `number` goes into the left one. This is similar to the `/` operator, except that the decimal part of the result is effectively discarded. Even though this is the integer division operator, it works with `real` number operands; the result, however, is always an `integer`.	-6.0 div 5	-1
`mod`	Modulus operator. Returns the remainder of a division of the left `number` by the right `number`. This is equivalent to what is left after using the `div` operator. The result is a `real` number if one or both operands are `real`; otherwise it is an `integer`.	-6.0 div 5	-1.0
`^`	Power or exponentiation operator. Raises the first `number` to the second `number`.	2 ^ 3	8
`and`	Logical AND operator. `true` if the left and right `boolean` expressions are both `true`, and `false` otherwise.	1 < 2 and 2 > 1	`true`
`or`	Logical OR operator. `true` if either the left or the right `boolean` expression is `true`. `false` only if both expressions are `false`.	1 > 2 or 1 > 0	`true`
`not`	Logical NOT operator. Has the value `false` if the expression is `true`, and `true` if the expression is `false`.	not 1 > 0	`false`

Equality and Inequality Operators

The equality and inequality operators require more attention than the others. First, those coming from languages such as C may be surprised to find that these operators are not `==` and `!=`. The reason `=` can be used for equality is that it is not used for assignment in AppleScript: the set keyword is used for assignment. In languages such as C, = is the assignment operator, so a different operator is needed for testing equality.

Another aspect of the equality and inequality operators is that they can be used not only to compare numbers but also to compound types such as lists and records. Here is an example of comparisons between some of these data types:

```
{1, 2} = {1, 2}      -- true
{2, 1} = {1, 2}      -- false
{1, 2, 3} = {1, 2}  -- false
{1, 2, 3}    {1, 2} -- true
{Harry:"gray", Bob:"green"} = {Harry:"gray", Bob:"green"}          -- true
{Harry:"gray", Bob:"green"} = {Bob:"green", Harry:"gray"}          -- true
{Harry:"gray", Bob:"green"} is {Tom:"gray", Bob:"green"}           -- false
{Harry:"gray", Bob:"green"} is equal to {Harry:"gray", Bob:"purple"} -- false
```

As you can see, the entries in the list or record must all be equal in order for the data containers to be considered equal. Also, the same number of entries must exist in each container. In the case of a list, the entries must be in the same order; and in the case of a record, both the keys and values must match (the order is not important).

The Concatenation Operator

AppleScript includes a number of other operators, not related to arithmetic or logic. Some you have already seen, such as the concatenation operator &. This is used to join strings and other types, such as records and lists. Here are some examples of using the concatenation operator:

```
"Hello " & "there."            -- "Hello there."
{Bob:"gray"} & {Chris:"orange"} -- {Bob:"gray", Chris:"orange"}
{1,2,3} & {4,5,6}              -- {1,2,3,4,5,6}
```

You can also concatenate types that are not the same. In this case, *implicit coercion* is used to convert the types of the operands such that they can be joined. For example, here are some cases where implicit coercion is needed:

```
1 & 2 & 3                                -- {1,2,3}
{1, 2} & 3                               -- {1,2,3}
{1, 2} & "three"                         -- {1,2,"three"}
"three" & {1, 2}                         -- "three12"
{1, 2} & {Bob:"gray", Chris:"blue"}      -- {1,2,"gray","blue"}
{Bob:"gray", Chris:"blue"} & {1, 2}      -- Error. Can't coerce list to record.
```

Concatenating two or more numbers results in a list. You can append simple types like numbers and strings to the end of a list using the concatenation operator, and you can even add the values of a record to a list using concatenation. You can't add the values of a list to a record because there is no way for AppleScript to assign a key to each value in the list.

The order of operands is important when concatenating. The AppleScript interpreter tries to coerce the operand on the right to a type that can be concatenated to the operand on the left. That is why concatenating a string to a list is different than concatenating a list to a string. In the former case, the string is implicitly coerced to a list and the concatenation operator ends up joining together two lists. In the latter case, the list is coerced to a string by combining its entries, and the concatenation operator ends up combining two strings.

The Contains Operator

AppleScript includes a number of operators that can be used to determine whether or not a string, list, or record contains a given entry or entries. The contains operator is one such operator:

```
"Happy Birthday" contains "Birthday"                      -- true
{1, 2} contains {1}                                        -- true
{1, 2} contains 1                                          -- true
{1, 2} contains 3                                          -- false
{1, 2, 3} contains {1, 2}                                  -- true
{1, 2, 3} contains {1, 3}                                  -- false
{Bob:34, Tom:36, Penny:43} contains {Penny:43, Tom:36}    -- true
{Bob:"gray", Tom:"green"} contains "green"                 -- Error
```

The contains operator works with operands of the same type, such as two lists or two records, but it also works with mixed types if implicit coercion can be used to create compatible types. With strings, contains evaluates to true if the string given on the right is a sub-string of the one on the left.

When used with lists, contains determines whether the list on the right is a sub-list of the one on the left. A sub-list must completely match some contiguous segment of the full list. It is not enough simply to include entries from the full list in the sub-list; the entries must also be in order and contiguous.

This example demonstrates how coercion can be used to check for entries in a list. Whenever contains is used with a number, the number is first coerced to a list, and then the contains operator checks if the newly formed list is a sub-list of the other operand.

The rules for records are similar. contains can compare only two records; because no other type can be coerced to a record, you can use the operator only with explicitly created records. Note that when testing for containment of one record in another, it is sufficient that all key-value pairs are found — the order is not important.

Aside from contains, there are a number of other similar operators. The following table provides descriptions and simple examples of these operators.

Operator	Description	Example	Result
contains	true if the first argument contains the second argument.	{1,2} contains {1}	true
does not contain	true if the first argument does not contain the second one.	{1,2} does not contain {1}	false
is in	true if the second argument contains the first argument.	{1} is in {1,2}	true
is not in	true if the second argument is not contained in the first one.	{1} is not in {1,2}	false
begins with	true if the first argument begins with the first one.	{1,2,3} begins with {1,2}	true
ends with	true if the first argument ends with the second one.	{1,2,3} ends with {2,3}	true

Specifying Elements

As you learned earlier in the chapter, elements are attributes of a data type that can hold any number of different values. One question that this raises is how you specify a particular element. AppleScript gives you lots of different *element specifiers*, each with its own little piece of English grammar — it can all become quite confusing. This section covers these grammatical nuggets and hopefully flattens the learning curve somewhat.

Often you specify an element by name, such as in the following example where an `account` element is requested from the Mail application:

```
tell application "Mail" to get account "tom@completely-fictional.com"
```

The `get` keyword is used, followed by the element and the name as a `string`.

It is also quite common for elements to include an `id`, which is unique. Whereas a name may be able to change, an `id` is immutable and does not change. You can use an `id` to retrieve an element, as in this example:

```
tell application "Address Book"
    set friendsId to get id of person "Erik the Viking"
    set middle name of (get person id friendsId) to "Boris"
end tell
```

This example first stores the `id` of a person from the Address Book application called `"Erik the Viking"`. It then sets the middle name for Erik, using the `id` to access the `person`. The expression in parentheses retrieves the `person` corresponding to Erik. The result is that `"Erik the Viking"` is renamed to `"Erik Boris the Viking"`.

Another common way to access elements is by index. You have already seen this put to use many times with the `list` type. The `item` element gives access to the `list`'s entries:

```
get item 2 of {"one", "two", "three"} -- Result is "two"
```

Or, equivalently, to

```
tell {"one", "two", "three"} to get item 2
```

You can also use negative indexes; these count back from the last element:

```
get item -1 of {"one", "two", "three"} -- Result is "three"
```

Last, you can use a variety of English expressions to refer to specific indexed elements. For example, you can write `get first item`, `get second item`, and so forth. You can also use `get last item` or `get back item` to refer to the last entry in the `list`.

None of these element specifiers are restricted solely to the `item` element of the `list` type — they work with ordered elements of any type.

You may also want to specify a range of indexes of elements. This is quite easily achieved in AppleScript:

```
get items 2 thru 4 of {1,2,3,4,5} -- Result is {2,3,4}
```

Notice that the plural form of the element label has been used, followed by a beginning index, the keyword thru, and an end index. The result is a list containing the requested elements. The word through can be exchanged with thru, and you can optionally designate the beginning index of the list with the keyword beginning and the end by end.

If the elements you want to extract are not stored contiguously, you can use a logical condition to specify them. The where keyword is used for this purpose:

```
tell application "iTunes"
    set play_list to first library playlist of first source
    set track_list to tracks of play_list where artist begins with "Bruce"
    play first item of track_list
end tell
```

If all goes well, this script should play a song by an artist going by the name *Bruce*, assuming there is one in your iTunes library. The logical condition is provided in this line:

```
set track_list to tracks of play_list where artist begins with "Bruce"
```

The where keyword causes each track element in the play_list variable to be tested. Whenever the artist property of the track begins with the text Bruce, the track is added to a list, which is returned after all tracks have been considered.

You can use whose in place of where, and also optionally include the words it or its to make expressions read more naturally. For example, you could write the statement from the preceding example like this

```
set track_list to tracks of play_list where its artist begins with "Bruce"
```

or

```
set track_list to tracks of play_list whose artist begins with "Bruce"
```

You may end up with a grammatical horror story, but AppleScript doesn't care.

So far, you have seen how you can refer to ordered elements in absolute terms by using indexes, but it is also possible to refer to them in terms of their positions relative to other elements. The keywords before/in front of and after/behind can be used to do this. If you run the following script, with a single document containing the text Once upon a time... open in TextEdit, the expressions should evaluate to the values indicated by the comments in the script:

```
tell application "TextEdit"
    tell text of document 1
        get word after word 1         -- "upon"
        get word behind word 1        -- "upon"
        get word in front of word 2   -- "Once"
        get word before word 3        -- "upon"
    end tell
end tell
```

after and behind are equivalent, as are in front of and before.

Sometimes you don't want to refer to a specific element, but to all elements or any element. The every keyword can be used to return a list of all elements, like this:

```
tell application "Finder" to get every folder of home
```

This line returns all the folders in the user's home directory in a list.

The some keyword allows you to randomly select an element:

```
get some item of {1, 2, 3, 4, 5} -- Random results.
```

This line randomly selects an entry in the list each time it is run.

Scripts and Objects

You have seen properties and elements used throughout this chapter, but you haven't yet seen how they are created. A property can be created in a script like this:

```
property greeting:"Good Morning"
display dialog greeting    -- Displays "Good Morning"
set greeting to "Goedemorgen"
display dialog greeting    -- Displays "Goedemorgen"
```

The property is just a global variable like any other, with an initial value assigned to it — in this case the string "Good Morning". Its value can change just like any other variable, as demonstrated on the third and fourth lines.

As you well know by now, you can access properties using the of keyword. To demonstrate this, the following script explicitly creates a *script object*:

```
script Greeter
    property greeting : "Good Morning"
    display dialog greeting
    set greeting to "Goedemorgen"
    display dialog greeting
end script

set greeting of Greeter to "Bonjour"
run Greeter
```

A script object is virtually the same as a top-level script, which is what you create whenever you type something into Script Editor. A script object can have properties, handlers, and other executable statements. The commands in a script object are not executed when they are first read, but when the script is run, using the run command.

As you can see from this example, the properties of a script can be accessed from outside the script itself using the of keyword. In this case, two dialogs appear: one with the text Bonjour, and the other with Goedemorgen. The initial value of the property, "Good Morning", is not displayed because the greeting property gets changed before the script is run.

Perhaps surprisingly, you can't create elements for script objects. Elements are provided only by scriptable applications and built-in AppleScript types.

Script objects allow you to use object-oriented programming (OOP) in AppleScript. Because they can contain data, in the form of properties and other variables, as well as handlers, they have all the ingredients for OOP. (To learn more about OOP, see Chapter 7, which deals with Objective-C.)

The following simple example shows you how you can use script objects for OOP. This example involves script objects representing operating systems, and the first script is called `OperatingSystem`:

```
-- Script object representing general operating systems
script OperatingSystem
    property version : "Unknown"

    on displayDetails()
        display dialog "Version: " & my version
    end displayDetails

    on run
        my displayDetails()
    end run
end script
```

This script object has a single property, `version`, and two handlers, `displayDetails` and run. run was discussed earlier; it is a special handler that all scripts have. When a script is run with the `run` command, this handler gets called. The `run` handler here simply invokes the `displayDetails` handler.

`displayDetails` itself just displays a dialog containing the text `"Version: "`, along with the version number stored in the `version` property. The use of the keyword my is optional in this case; my refers to the enclosing script object and can be used to distinguish a variable or handler belonging to the script from one at a higher level. If there were a global handler called `displayDetails`, for example, using my would make explicit that the version of `displayDetails` in the `OperatingSystem` script should be used.

Things start to get interesting only when you have multiple script objects relating to one another in various ways. Here is the next script object in the example, which is a child of `OperatingSystem`:

```
-- Script object representing the Tiger OS, which is special
script Tiger
 property parent : OperatingSystem
 property version : "10.4"

 on displayDetails()
        display dialog "Tiger Baby!"
        continue displayDetails()
 end displayDetails
end script
```

The `Tiger` script object has its parent property initialized to `OperatingSystem`. You do this in AppleScript to define an *inheritance relationship*. Tiger inherits all the properties and handlers of `OperatingSystem` without having to include them explicitly. So even without adding anything more to the `Tiger` script object, it already has a property called `version` and handlers called `displayDetails` and run. (All script objects have run, of course.)

The rest of the `Tiger` script modifies some of the aspects it inherits. This is called *overriding* in object-oriented (OO) terminology. For example, rather than initializing `version` to `"Unknown"`, it is initialized to `"10.4"`. Without this line of code, `Tiger` would inherit the version `"Unknown"`. The `displayDetails` handler is also overridden; the implementation in `Tiger` displays the message `"Tiger Baby!"`, before calling the `displayDetails` method in `OperatingSystem`. The `continue` keyword is used to stipulate that a handler should be sought in the parent script.

You can pass script objects to handlers just like you can pass other data types to handlers. Script objects, like `lists` and `records`, are passed-by-reference. Their contents are not copied, so any changes made to the object inside the handler still apply after the handler has returned. Here is the next part of the example, which is a handler that displays details of an `OperatingSystem` script object:

```
-- Handler to display an OperatingSystem
on displayOperatingSystem(os)
    os's displayDetails()
end displayOperatingSystem
```

This demonstrates an aspect of OOP known as *polymorphism*. The handler `displayOperatingSystem` simply calls the `displayDetails` handler of the `OperatingSystem` script object passed to it. But the `displayOperatingSystem` handler also works for any script object that has the handler `display Details`, including the child script `Tiger`. Even though the handler only mentions the `Operating System` class, any script object descending from `OperatingSystem` can also be passed to this handler. (For more details on polymorphism, see Chapter 7.)

The last part of the example script uses the script objects and handler defined earlier:

```
-- Create a OperatingSystem object for Panther
copy OperatingSystem to pantherObject
set version of pantherObject to "10.3"
displayOperatingSystem(pantherObject)

-- Create a Tiger object for the Tiger OS, and run it
copy Tiger to tigerObject
run tigerObject
```

To create a new object, you use the `copy` command. You copy the script object to a variable that you then use to represent the object. You can't use the `set` command for this, because `set` does not copy the data contained in the script — it only stores a reference to the script. If you used `set` instead of `copy`, whenever you tried to change the data in one variable all others would also change because they would all refer to the same object.

You can access the properties of a script object in the usual ways, stipulating that the property belongs to the script using the `of` keyword or the possessive form. In this example, an `OperatingSystem` object is created and has its version set to `"10.3"`. It is then passed to the `displayOperatingSystem` handler, which displays a dialog box.

Finally, a `Tiger` object is created, and the `run` command is used to run it. Note that the `Tiger` class does not explicitly define a `run` handler; the `run` handler used is inherited from `OperatingSystem` and calls the `displayDetails` handler. The particular `displayDetails` handler executed is the one in the `Tiger` script, not the one in the `OperatingSystem` script. This is yet another example of polymorphism, in which the handler that ends up being executed depends on the type of the object that is the subject of the call.

Handlers belonging to script objects are called methods in the OO parlance, and calling such a handler is known as messaging because it is like sending a message to the object. (See Chapter 7 for more information.)

Classes

This discussion of different types of objects leads nicely into a discussion of *classes*. A *class* is a type in AppleScript. Earlier in the chapter, the term *data type* was frequently used, but the more correct terminology is *class*. You can use the `class` property of an object to determine its class:

```
script Classy
end script

class of 15             -- integer
class of "82"           -- string
class of {1,2}          -- list
class of Classy         -- script
class of class of Classy -- class
```

Classes are themselves types, as you can see from the last line. They can be compared just like other types; so you can easily test, for example, whether an argument passed to a handler is a `list` or a `record`.

Working with Scripts

You can run AppleScripts from within other AppleScripts, and even from within other programming languages. You use the `run script` command to run a script from within another AppleScript:

```
run script file "DiskName:Users:username:Desktop:somescript.scpt"
```

`run script` is defined in the Scripting Additions dictionary and takes a `file` as an argument. In this case, a `file` object has been created from a path to a script, given in colon-delimited form.

You can also store and load scripts from inside an AppleScript. This is a way to create libraries of commonly used script objects and handlers. Loading is different from running because the `run` handler is not called; the entities in the script are read in but not executed. Here is an example of loading an existing script that was created with Script Editor:

```
set someScript to load script file "DiskName:Users:username:somescript.scpt"
```

The `load script` command is also from the Scripting Additions dictionary.

To use anything from the loaded script, you have to ensure that you indicate the containment relationship explicitly. For example, if this script has a handler called `doSomething`, you could call it in any of the following ways:

```
tell someScript to doSomething()
someScript's doSomething()
doSomething() of someScript
```

You can also store a script using the `store script` command from the Scripting Additions dictionary. This is less common than loading and is not demonstrated here.

You can also run AppleScripts from shells like Bash (see Chapter 11). The `osascript` command, which can be found in the `/usr/bin` directory, allows you to do this. You can run a script or execute a single command. To run a script file, you needn't do more than enter the `osascript` command in a Terminal window, followed by a path to the script file:

```
/usr/bin/osascript script_name.scpt
```

To execute a single command, use the `-e` option:

```
/usr/bin/osascript -e 'tell application "Finder" to activate'
```

To learn more about `osascript`, open the man page in Terminal by entering

```
man osascript
```

You can also run shell scripts from inside AppleScript. To do this, use the `do shell script` command from Standard Additions. Here is an example of using the Unix `grep` command to retrieve all lines in a file containing the word "giraffe":

```
do shell script "grep giraffe ~/Desktop/file_name.txt"
```

To learn more about `grep` and other Unix commands, read Chapter 11.

The next two Try It Outs let you consolidate all the elements of AppleScript you have learned about in this chapter. You write a script that extracts photos randomly from an album in your iPhoto library and combines them into a QuickTime slide show. In the first Try It Out, you develop the simple interface that prompts the user for information used to create the slide show. In the second Try It Out, you add the AppleScript to create the slide show with the information entered.

Try It Out   Creating the User Interface for Slideshow Maker

1. Open Script Editor and in a new document, enter the following script:

```
on run
    try
        set num_photos to prompt_for_number_of_photos_in_show()
        set the_album to prompt_for_album_choice()
    on error msg
        display_error_message(msg)
    end try
end run


on display_error_message(message)
    display dialog message buttons {"OK"} default button 1
end display_error_message


on prompt_for_number_of_photos_in_show()
    set number_of_photos to 0
    repeat while number_of_photos is 0
        try
```

```
              display dialog ¬
                  "How many photos do you want to include in the slideshow?" ¬
                  buttons {"OK"} default answer 10 default button 1
              set dialog_result to result
              set number_of_photos to (text returned of dialog_result) as integer
              if number_of_photos   0 then error "Enter a non-zero positive number"
          on error msg
              display_error_message(msg)
              set number_of_photos to 0
          end try
      end repeat
      return number_of_photos
  end prompt_for_number_of_photos_in_show


  on prompt_for_album_choice()
      tell application "iPhoto" to set album_names to name of albums

      set selected_albums to false
      repeat while selected_albums is false
          choose from list album_names with prompt "Choose an album" ¬
              without multiple selections allowed and empty selection allowed
          set selected_albums to result
          if selected_albums is false then ¬
              display_error_message("Please make a selection")
      end repeat

      set album_name to first item of selected_albums
      tell application "iPhoto" to set the_album to get album album_name
      return the_album
  end prompt_for_album_choice
```

2. Click the Compile button to check that everything has been entered correctly.

3. Click the Run button and respond to the requests provided by the dialog boxes that appear.

4. Rerun the script and try to cause it to crash by entering invalid values for the number of photos to include in the slide show. Note how the script responds to your attempts to confuse it.

How It Works

This version of the Slideshow Maker script begins by prompting the user to enter a value for the number of photos in the slide show, and concludes by asking the user to choose an iPhoto album. The main part of the script comes first and has been included in the run handler. You could just as easily write the contents of the handler at the top level of the script, and nothing would change; if the run handler is not included explicitly, it is generated implicitly.

The run handler maps looks like this:

```
on run
    try
        set num_photos to prompt_for_number_of_photos_in_show()
        set the_album to prompt_for_album_choice()
    on error msg
```

```
            display_error_message(msg)
        end try
    end run
```

Two different handlers are called to request information from the user. The `prompt_for_number_of _photos _in_show` handler requests that the user enter a positive integer representing the number of photos that should be extracted from the iPhoto album and used in the slide show. The `prompt_for _album _choice` shows the user a list of iPhoto albums and asks that a selection be made. The return value of the handler is an object of the `album` class from the iPhoto application.

The commands issued in the `run` handler are all embedded in a `try` block. If any error arises, it is caught at `on error`, and the handler `display_error_message` called to inform the user of the problem. This handler, which appears directly after the `run` handler, does little more than display a dialog box:

```
on display_error_message(message)
    display dialog message buttons {"OK"} default button 1
end display_error_message
```

The `buttons` option for the `display dialog` command from the Standard Additions dictionary allows you to supply a `list` of button titles. In this case, only the OK button is needed. Using the `default button` option, you can give the index of the selected button. By providing a default, you allow the user to dismiss the dialog by simply pressing Return, rather than having to use the mouse to click the button.

The first handler used to interact with the user asks for the number of photos to use in the slide show:

```
on prompt_for_number_of_photos_in_show()
    set number_of_photos to 0
    repeat while number_of_photos is 0
        try
            display dialog ¬
                "How many photos do you want to include in the slideshow?" ¬
                buttons {"OK"} default answer 10 default button 1
            set dialog_result to result
            set number_of_photos to (text returned of dialog_result) as integer
            if number_of_photos    0 then error "Enter a non-zero positive number"
        on error msg
            display_error_message(msg)
            set number_of_photos to 0
        end try
    end repeat
    return number_of_photos
end prompt_for_number_of_photos_in_show
```

The dialog box displayed includes a text field for entering the requested value. The `default answer` option indicates to the `display dialog` command that a field should be included, with the initially displayed value set to `10` in this case. You can include as many text fields as you like in a dialog simply by including multiple `default answer` options.

The value entered by the user is retrieved using the `result` keyword, which always holds the value of the last command executed. `result` has been used in this example to make the code slightly more legible, but it would also be completely acceptable to combine the `display dialog` and `set` commands into a single line, beginning with `set dialog_result to display dialog` . . . .

The result of the `display dialog` command is a `record`. To get the text entered by the user, you access the value corresponding to the `text returned` key. In the example, this is coerced to an `integer` and then compared with 0 to make sure it is a positive number. Any error that occurs is caught by the `try` block, and a `repeat while` loop continues to prompt the user for the number of photos until a valid value is entered. This type of construction, with a loop and error handling code, is a common way of ensuring that your scripts robustly handle user interaction.

The second handler requests that the user choose one of the albums in iPhoto:

```
on prompt_for_album_choice()
    tell application "iPhoto" to set album_names to name of albums

    set selected_albums to false
    repeat while selected_albums is false
        choose from list album_names with prompt "Choose an album" ¬
            without multiple selections allowed and empty selection allowed
        set selected_albums to result
        if selected_albums is false then ¬
            display_error_message("Please make a selection")
    end repeat

    set album_name to first item of selected_albums
    tell application "iPhoto" to set the_album to get album album_name
    return the_album
end prompt_for_album_choice
```

The first line retrieves the names of the albums from iPhoto. The iPhoto application includes an element called `album`; by using the `of` operator to access the name property, with the plural form `albums`, an *implicit loop* is formed. Effectively, the script loops over `albums`, with the `name` retrieved from each one, and added to a `list`. The resulting `list` is what gets assigned to `album_names`. You could achieve the same end result with an explicit `repeat` loop, but the implicit loop is often more elegant.

The `choose from list` command from the Standard Additions dictionary is used to present the albums to the user in a dialog, and accept the user's choice. Two labeled parameters are provided to the command, using the `without` keyword: multiple selections and empty selections are both disallowed. The return value of the `choose from list` command is a `list` of the selected values when a selection was made by the user, and the Boolean value `false` when the Cancel button was clicked. The result is retrieved with the `result` keyword, and stored in the `selected_albums` variable.

Because only one `album` gets used by the script, the `album_name` variable is set to the first `item` of the `selected_albums` list. iPhoto is then told to set the variable `the_album` to the `album` with the name `album_name`; `the_album` is returned from the handler.

In the next Try It Out, you make the Slideshow Maker script fully functional, such that it takes photos from the iPhoto album selected by the user and converts them into a QuickTime slide show.

Try It Out   Finishing Off Slideshow Maker

1.   Open the Slideshow Maker script in Script Editor and modify the `run` handler as follows:

```
on run
    try
```

```
        copy Photo_Archive to photo_arch
        set photo_arch's archive_folder_name to "Test Photo Archive"
        tell photo_arch to setup_archive_folder()
        set num_photos to prompt_for_number_of_photos_in_show()
        set the_album to prompt_for_album_choice()
        add_photos_from_album given Photo_Archive:photo_arch, ¬
            album:the_album, number_of_photos:num_photos
        create_image_sequence_from_folder(photo_arch's archive_folder, 2)
        tell photo_arch to delete_archive()
    on error msg
        display_error_message(msg)
    end try
end run
```

2. Add the following to the end of the Slideshow Maker script:

```
script Photo_Archive
    property original_photo_paths : {}
    property archive_folder_name : "Photo Archive Folder"
    property archive_folder : false

    on setup_archive_folder()
        tell application "Finder"
            set desktop_path to path to desktop folder as string
            set archive_folder_path to desktop_path & archive_folder_name
            if not (folder archive_folder_path exists) then
                set archive_folder to make new folder at desktop ¬
                    with properties {name:archive_folder_name}
            else
                error "Folder called " & archive_folder_name & ¬
                    " already exists on Desktop." number 1
            end if
        end tell
    end setup_archive_folder

    on add_photo_to_archive(the_photo)
        tell application "iPhoto" to set photo_path to image path of the_photo
        if photo_path is not in original_photo_paths then
            set photo_file to POSIX file photo_path as file
            tell application "Finder" to duplicate photo_file to archive_folder
            set end of original_photo_paths to photo_path
            return true
        else
            return false
        end if
    end add_photo_to_archive

    on delete_archive()
        if archive_folder is not false then delete archive_folder
    end delete_archive

end script


on add_photos_from_album given Photo_Archive:the_archive, ¬
    album:the_album, number_of_photos:number_of_photos
```

```
        tell application "iPhoto"
            set num_photos_in_album to count of photos of the_album
            if number_of_photos is greater than num_photos_in_album then
                set number_of_photos to num_photos_in_album
            end if
            set i to 0
            repeat until i is number_of_photos
                the_archive's add_photo_to_archive(some photo of the_album)
                if result is true then set i to i + 1
            end repeat
        end tell
    end add_photos_from_album


on create_image_sequence_from_folder(the_folder, seconds_per_photo)
    tell application "QuickTime Player"
        launch
        activate
        set first_image to first file of the_folder as alias
        open image sequence first_image seconds per frame seconds_per_photo
    end tell
end create_image_sequence_from_folder
```

3. Click the Compile button to check that everything has been entered correctly.

4. Click the Run button and respond to the dialogboxes. You should end up with a QuickTime slide show made up of photos from the album that you selected.

If you don't use iPhoto for digital photos, you can just download a few images from the Internet and import them into your iPhoto library.

How It Works

This script is by the far the most involved you have seen up to this point in the chapter. You may want to read through it several times to better understand how it works. After the user has been prompted for the number of photos in the slide show and an iPhoto album, Finder, iPhoto, and QuickTime Player are used to create and display the slide show. It is a good example of how AppleScript can *glue* Mac OS X applications together to achieve a task in a way not possible in other languages.

The run handler now maps out all the stages required to create the slide show:

```
on run
    try
        copy Photo_Archive to photo_arch
        set photo_arch's archive_folder_name to "Test Photo Archive"
        tell photo_arch to setup_archive_folder()
        set num_photos to prompt_for_number_of_photos_in_show()
        set the_album to prompt_for_album_choice()
        add_photos_from_album given Photo_Archive:photo_arch, ¬
            album:the_album, number_of_photos:num_photos
        create_image_sequence_from_folder(photo_arch's archive_folder, 2)
        tell photo_arch to delete_archive()
    on error msg
        display_error_message(msg)
    end try
end run
```

First, a new instance of a script object called `Photo_Archive` is created using the `copy` command. A `Photo_Archive` simply represents a folder containing photo files. The name of the archive folder is set to `"Test Photo Archive"`, and the handler `setup_archive_folder` is called to create the folder so that photos can be added to it.

The two handlers written in the previous Try It Out are called next, and then the handler `add_photos_ from_album` is used to add the requested number of photos from the iPhoto album to the `Photo_ Archive`. In practice, this involves locating the photos in the file system and copying them to the archive folder using Finder.

With the `Photo_Archive` populated with photos, `create_image_sequence_from_folder` uses QuickTime Player to load them as an image sequence. The `archive_folder` property of `Photo_ Archive` is a folder class from the Finder application; it is retrieved from `photo_arch` and passed to the `create_image_sequence_from_folder` handler. The second argument to the handler is the number of seconds each photo is displayed in the slide show.

The last action taken is to delete the folder controlled by the `Photo_Archive` script object, using the handler `delete_archive`.

The `Photo_Archive` script object begins by defining some properties:

```
script Photo_Archive
    property original_photo_paths : {}
    property archive_folder_name : "Photo Archive Folder"
    property archive_folder : false
```

The `original_photo_paths` property is a `list` used to store the paths of the photos in the archive before they were copied. This is used to avoid copying the same photo more than once into the archive. The `archive_folder_name` was set in the `run` handler and is simply a name for the folder used to store the photos. In this example, the folder is always located in the user's Desktop folder. `archive_folder` is used to store a Finder `folder` class object representing the archive folder. It is initialized to `false` but later set to the `folder` object.

The `setup_archive_folder` was called in the `run` handler to create the folder used to store the copied photos. It does this using the Finder application:

```
on setup_archive_folder()
    tell application "Finder"
        set desktop_path to path to desktop folder as string
        set archive_folder_path to desktop_path & archive_folder_name
        if not (folder archive_folder_path exists) then
            set archive_folder to make new folder at desktop ¬
                with properties {name:archive_folder_name}
        else
            error "Folder called " & archive_folder_name & ¬
                " already exists on Desktop." number 1
        end if
    end tell
end setup_archive_folder
```

It creates a path to the archive folder by concatenating the path to the `Desktop` folder and the name of the archive folder. Using the `exists` command, a check is made to ensure that the folder doesn't already exist. The `exists` command is in the Standard Suite of every application's dictionary.

The remainder of the `Photo_Archive` script object provides handlers for adding photos to the archive and deleting the archive:

```
on add_photo_to_archive(the_photo)
        tell application "iPhoto" to set photo_path to image path of the_photo
        if photo_path is not in original_photo_paths then
            set photo_file to POSIX file photo_path as file
            tell application "Finder" to duplicate photo_file to archive_folder
            set end of original_photo_paths to photo_path
            return true
        else
            return false
        end if
end add_photo_to_archive

on delete_archive()
        if archive_folder is not false then delete archive_folder
end delete_archive

    end script
```

The `add_photo_to_archive` handler has one parameter, which is an object of the class `photo` from the application iPhoto. The first line of `add_photo_to_archive` requests iPhoto to get the path to the `photo`. An `if` block checks if this photo path has already been encountered by using the `is not in` operator with the property `original_photo_paths`. If the photo has previously been added to the archive, `false` is returned, indicating that the photo was not added in the current call.

If the photo has not been added to the archive previously, a `file` object is created to represent it. To do this, a `POSIX file` is created and coerced to a `file`. A `POSIX file` is used when the path is given as a POSIX path, with forward slashes separating directories; this is the type of path used on Unix systems. The `file` class expects a colon-separated path, which was used on versions of Mac OS before Mac OS X. The `image path` property of `the_photo` retrieved from iPhoto is a POSIX path, explaining why a `POSIX file` must be created first.

The next line of `add_photo_to_archive` tells Finder to make a copy of the `photo`'s file in the archive folder. The `duplicate` command, which is used to make the copy, is in the Standard Suite of every application.

The last action taken is to add the `photo`'s path to the `list original_photo_paths` so that it will not be added a second time by a later call. The return value is `true`, indicating the `photo` was added to the archive.

The `delete_archive` handler is very simple. It checks to make sure the `archive_folder` property has been set to something other than the initial value `false`, and if so, uses the `delete` command from the Standard Suite to remove it. The folder is not actually deleted but moved to the Trash. If you want to delete it permanently, you have to empty the Trash.

Once the `Photo_Archive` has been set up and the iPhoto `album` is known, `photos` can be randomly selected from the `album`, and added to the archive; this is the role of the `add_photos_from_album` handler:

```
on add_photos_from_album given Photo_Archive:the_archive, ¬
    album:the_album, number_of_photos:number_of_photos
```

```
        tell application "iPhoto"
            set num_photos_in_album to count of photos of the_album
            if number_of_photos is greater than num_photos_in_album then
                set number_of_photos to num_photos_in_album
            end if
            set i to 0
            repeat until i is number_of_photos
                the_archive's add_photo_to_archive(some photo of the_album)
                if result is true then set i to i + 1
            end repeat
        end tell
    end add_photos_from_album
```

This handler uses a `tell` block to communicate with iPhoto. The first part of the handler compares the `number_of_photos` parameter with the number of photos in the `the_album` parameter. If there are too few `photos` in the `album`, the `number_of_photos` variable is set to the number of `photos` in the `album`.

The last half of the handler includes a loop that adds one randomly selected `photo` at a time from the `album` to the archive. A counter variable, `i`, is used to keep track of how many `photos` have been added to the archive. The result of the `add_photo_to_archive` handler is checked after each call; if it is `true`, indicating the `photo` was successfully added to the archive, the counter is incremented.

The last handler in the script uses QuickTime Player to open the photos in the archive folder as an image sequence:

```
    on create_image_sequence_from_folder(the_folder, seconds_per_photo)
        tell application "QuickTime Player"
            launch
            activate
            set first_image to first file of the_folder as alias
            open image sequence first_image seconds per frame seconds_per_photo
        end tell
    end create_image_sequence_from_folder
```

QuickTime Player is told to `launch`, which causes it to start up without displaying any dialog and then `activate`, which makes it the foremost application. The first `file` in the `folder` parameter is retrieved, coerced to the class `alias`, and assigned to the variable `first_image`.

It is important not to confuse the general `file` class with the `file` class from the `application` Finder. In this case, the class of the first `file` in the `folder` is Finder's `file` class. This can be coerced to the type `alias`, which is very similar to a `file` with a few subtle differences that are not discussed here. The handler concludes with the QuickTime Player command `open image sequence`; the `alias` is passed as an argument, along with the time in seconds to use for each photo.

This example not only utilizes many aspects of AppleScript that you have been exposed to earlier in the chapter, but it also includes more user interaction than previous scripts. In the next section, you learn to go beyond the simple user interfaces you've seen so far and develop complete applications with AppleScript Studio.

AppleScript Studio

Apple has provided a means for you to leverage the power of the Cocoa frameworks from AppleScript: AppleScript Studio. AppleScript Studio is not actually a single program or library; rather, it is a collection of tools that includes applications such as Xcode and Interface Builder. These tools provide the development environment you use for building AppleScript applications.

Of course, development tools are not very useful if AppleScript and Cocoa can't "talk" to one another. So a *bridge* has been built between the two, allowing you to create and manipulate Cocoa objects from AppleScript. The AppleScript–Cocoa bridge forms the centerpiece of AppleScript Studio. It largely succeeds in protecting the AppleScript programmer from the complexities of Cocoa, while still facilitating access to the lion's share of functionality.

In this section, you learn all about the facilities in Xcode and Interface Builder for writing AppleScript applications, as well as how you use the AppleScript–Cocoa bridge. An extensive Try It Out example demonstrates how you write complete applications with AppleScript and take advantage of AppleScript's greatest strength — scripting other applications.

The AppleScript–Cocoa Bridge

The AppleScript–Cocoa bridge allows you to develop complete Cocoa applications in AppleScript, without having to know anything about the Objective-C programming language (see Chapter 7). To achieve this, the bridge effectively mirrors Cocoa objects in AppleScript, and maps AppleScript commands to particular Cocoa methods.

You can issue a command to a particular object in AppleScript, and the command is sent across the bridge to the corresponding Cocoa object where it results in a method being invoked. The Cocoa object behaves exactly the same as if the method invocation had come from an Objective-C program. If the method has a return value, it is sent back over the bridge and converted into an AppleScript object in the process.

The machinery behind the AppleScript–Cocoa bridge is housed in the AppleScriptKit (ASK) framework. This framework is located in the `/System/Library/Frameworks` directory and is included in any AppleScript Studio project you create with Xcode. The framework needs to be initialized by calling a function called `initializeASKFunc`, but the code to do this is inserted automatically by Xcode in the `main.m` file created with any new AppleScript Studio project.

Most of the Cocoa classes available to Objective-C programmers are also available in AppleScript Studio, but they don't have the same names. Cocoa names such as `NSImage` are mapped to more user-friendly AppleScript ones, such as `image`. In addition, fundamental Cocoa types, like `NSArray` and `NSDictionary`, are mapped to built-in AppleScript types such as `list` and `record`. The following table lists the Cocoa classes that correspond to built-in AppleScript types.

Cocoa Type	AppleScript Type
NSString	string
NSArray	list
NSDictionary	record

Cocoa Type	AppleScript Type
NSDate	date
NSPoint	A list of two numbers: x and y.
NSRange	A list of two numbers: beginning and end.
NSRect	A list of four numbers: left, bottom, right, and top.
NSSize	A list of two numbers: width and height.
NSColor	A list of three numbers: red, green, and blue components. Each component ranges from 0 to 65535.

The Cocoa types accessible from AppleScript are defined in the AppleScriptKit dictionary, which is included in each AppleScript application created with Xcode. If you click the AppleScriptKit.sdefsdef file icon in any AppleScript Studio project, Xcode displays the dictionary's contents just as it would appear in Script Editor. Browsing through the dictionary, you find AppleScript classes and commands corresponding to the user interface classes and methods of Cocoa, as well as provisions for functionality such as drag-and-drop and document-based applications.

Not all Cocoa classes and methods are bridged to AppleScript classes and commands, and there will be occasions when you want to define your own Cocoa classes and use them from AppleScript. Luckily, there is a provision for invoking methods of general Cocoa objects and classes from within your scripts: the call method command. In its simplest form, it can be used like this:

```
call method "doSomething"
```

This first looks for a method called doSomething in the delegate of the Cocoa NSApplication object and invokes it if one exists. If there is no doSomething method in the application delegate, the NSApplication class itself is checked for the method. Finally, if neither contains a doSomething method, an error occurs.

For more information on Cocoa classes and methods and design patterns such as delegation, see Chapter 8.

Using call method to call methods in the NSApplication class or in the application delegate is an easy way to execute a piece of Objective-C code. If you don't need to write a whole Objective-C class but would like to execute some code that is easier written in Objective-C than AppleScript, you can simply add a method to the application delegate or a category to the NSApplication class. For example, to include the doSomething method in the NSApplication class, you could define a category like this:

```
// In a header (.h) file
@interface NSApplication (MethodsForAppleScript)
-(void)doSomething;
@end

// In an implementation (.m) file
@implementation NSApplication (MethodsForAppleScript)
-(void)doSomething {
    // Implementation of doSomething goes here
}
@end
```

The category name, `MethodsForAppleScript`, is arbitrary; you can use whatever you like, as long as it is unique for the `NSApplication` class.

> *Categories are an aspect of Objective-C that allows you to add new methods to existing classes. For more information, see Chapter 7.*

The `call method` command can also be used for calling classes and objects other than `NSApplication` and its delegate. To do so, you use either the `of object` or `of class` options, as in the following example:

```
set sheep to call method "alloc" of class "Sheep"
call method "init" of object sheep
call method "makeSheepSound" of sheep
```

The first call is to the Objective-C class method `alloc`. The return value of the `call method` command is an AppleScript object that represents the Objective-C `Sheep` object returned by the `alloc` method. This can be stored in an AppleScript variable and sent messages. Messages sent to the AppleScript object, such as the `init` and `makeSheepSound` messages on the second and third lines, are passed on to the Objective-C `Sheep` object. Note that, as demonstrated by the `makeSheepSound` invocation, you can leave out the keyword `object` when sending a message to an object like `sheep`.

Another variation on the `call method` command allows you to pass parameters to Objective-C methods, like this:

```
call method "writeToFile:atomically:" of sheep ¬
    with parameters {"/tmp/sheep.txt", true}
```

The method arguments are provided to the command in a list, with each entry corresponding to a parameter of the Objective-C method. AppleScript classes, like the `string` and `boolean` types used in the example, are converted to Objective-C types when they are passed across the bridge. The AppleScript string `"/tmp/sheep.txt"` is passed to the `writeToFile:atomically:` method as the `NSString` `@"/tmp/sheep.txt"`, and the `boolean` `true` is passed in as the Objective-C `BOOL` value `YES`.

Using Xcode

An important part of AppleScript Studio is the development environment, and that means Xcode. Xcode includes provisions for managing and editing source code, building, debugging, reading and searching documentation, and browsing the `AppleScriptKit` dictionary. Learning to use these facilities is an important part of learning AppleScript Studio, and with a good basis in Xcode you are 90% of the way there.

> *Xcode is covered in detail in Chapter 3. If you need help with the basics, we recommend turning to Chapter 3 before proceeding further.*

When you create a new project in Xcode by choosing File ⇨ New Project, you can choose two project types that relate directly to AppleScript Studio: AppleScript Application and AppleScript Document-based Application. These titles are self-explanatory. You use AppleScript Application to create a general application with AppleScript Studio, and you use AppleScript Document-based Application to create multiple-document applications. These choices are analogous to those given for pure Cocoa applications.

If you choose AppleScript Application and follow the instructions, you end up with an AppleScript Studio project. This project initially includes a number of files that form the basis of any AppleScript application. These files are summarized in the following table.

File or Bundle	Description
AppKit.framework	The Application Kit framework, which contains the elements of Cocoa used for user interfaces.
Foundation.framework	The Foundation framework, which contains the non-graphical elements of Cocoa.
Cocoa.framework	An umbrella framework that contains both AppKit.framework and Foundation.framework.
AppleScriptKit.framework	The framework that contains the code that bridges AppleScript and Cocoa. Without this, you cannot call Cocoa from AppleScript.
AppleScriptKit.sdef	The AppleScript dictionary for the Cocoa frameworks. Clicking this dictionary reveals the dictionary in Xcode's editor, allowing you to browse the classes and contents made accessible by the AppleScript–Cocoa bridge.
InfoPlist.strings	A property list file found in all Mac OS X applications. It defines aspects of an application, such as its version number.
main.m	The main function, which is written in Objective-C. The main function provided includes code to initialize the AppleScript–Cocoa bridge and pass control to the NSApplication.
MainMenu.nib	The primary Interface Builder file, which contains the main menu and can be used to set up the application's graphical interface.

You also find a file named after the project that has the extension .applescript. You can use this for your script, if you want, or you can remove it and create new AppleScript files. To create a new AppleScript file, you simply choose File ➪ New File and select AppleScript Script File from the AppleScript group.

After you have entered your source code and defined a user interface by editing the MainMenu.nib file in Interface Builder, you will want to build your application. Building an AppleScript application is no different than building any other type of application in Xcode. It simply involves selecting the Build ➪ Build menu item or clicking the Build toolbar button. If all goes well, you should end up with a self-contained application bundle in your build directory that can be run either from inside Xcode, or by double-clicking it in the Finder.

One of the advantages of developing AppleScript with Xcode rather than with Script Editor is that Xcode has an integrated debugger. The debugger works not only with Objective-C and other compiled languages, but also with AppleScript. You can set breakpoints to have program execution stop, step through a script one line at a time, and examine variable values, just as you can when debugging Objective-C or C programs.

For more information on debugging, read Chapter 3, which covers Xcode in detail.

One of the major tasks you are confronted with when learning to use AppleScript Studio is simply learning what classes and commands are available to you via the AppleScriptKit framework. Cocoa is large, and much of it is exposed in AppleScript, making for a relatively steep learning curve. Just as when you are learning to script an existing application, you will probably want to reference the dictionary often to find classes and commands. Simply by clicking the AppleScriptKit.sdef file in Xcode, you can browse the parts of Cocoa exposed by the AppleScriptKit framework.

Xcode also allows you to browse the dictionaries of existing Mac OS X applications, just as Script Editor does. Simply choose File ➪ Open Dictionary, select the application, and the dictionary appears in the active editor.

Apart from the AppleScriptKit dictionary, Xcode also allows you to browse AppleScript and AppleScript Studio documentation. You can open the documentation window by choosing Help ➪ Documentation. To access AppleScript content, open the Reference Library group of the Search Groups list view and click AppleScript. You can find a very useful reference for AppleScript Studio by clicking the API Reference link and then selecting the AppleScript Studio Terminology Reference. This document contains detailed descriptions of all the Cocoa classes and commands exposed in AppleScript via the AppleScriptKit framework, going into greater depth than the dictionary.

Using Interface Builder

Another important piece in the AppleScript Studio puzzle is Interface Builder. Without it, it would be much more difficult for you to create user interfaces for your applications. Interface Builder allows you to lay out the elements of your user interface and label them so that they can be referenced from your AppleScript scripts. You can also indicate which handlers should be called when the user performs an action, such as clicking a button.

For a detailed introduction to Interface Builder, read Chapter 4.

Someone programming in Cocoa or Carbon learns how to connect up outlets and select actions for targets in Interface Builder. However, you don't need to understand these concepts to use AppleScript Studio. Instead, to get each component of the user interface to "talk" to your script code, you configure its AppleScript tab, which is accessible by opening the Inspector window (Tools ➪ Show Inspector). If you choose AppleScript from the popup button at the top, you should see something like what appears in Figure 12-2.

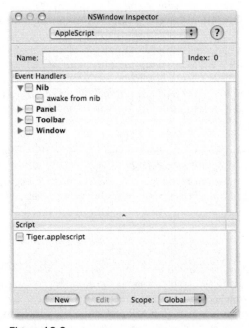

Figure 12-2

At the top of the AppleScript Inspector tab is a text field for entering a name for the interface element. You can use this name to access the element from your scripts. For example, if you selected a window like the one in Figure 12-2 and gave it the name `mainwindow` on the AppleScript tab, you could refer to it in a script like this:

```
set mainWindow to window "mainwindow"
```

You can also refer to interface elements by index, although this is not as robust as naming them because if you later add new elements or remove some, the indexes may change and your script will break. The first window in your application could be referred to like this:

```
set mainWindow to window 1
```

User interface elements are always referenced with respect to their parent container. For a `window`, this is the `application`; but for most other interface elements, it is either a `window` or a super `view`. For example, if you were to add a single `button` to a `window`, naming it `"mainbutton"`, you could refer to it in either of these two ways:

```
set theButton to button 1 of window 1
set theButton to button "mainbutton" of window 1
```

In each case, the containment relationship must be spelled out fully.

Indexing is taken relative to a particular container, whether it's a `window` or `view`. So if a box were introduced to the `window`, and a second `button` added in the box, it would be referenced like this:

```
set buttonInBox to button 1 of box 1 of window 1
```

The second `button` also has the index 1, because its index relates only to `buttons` in the immediate containing view, the `box`. The first `button`'s index relates to any `buttons` contained directly in the `window`.

Returning to the AppleScript Inspector tab (refer again to Figure 12-2), beneath the name field is the Event Handlers list view. This is used to send messages from the user interface to AppleScript scripts when certain events occur. The event handlers are divided up into different groups. If you open any of the groups, you can see a list of the events that can be sent. To indicate that an event should be sent, you check the box next to the handler's name and also check the box of the script that it should be sent to in the Script table view at the bottom of the Inspector tab.

In Figure 12-2, the Nib group is open, and you can see the `awake from nib` handler displayed. This handler is equivalent to the Cocoa method `awakeFromNib`. If you were to check the box next to this handler and then check `Tiger.applescript` in the Script table, the `awake from nib` handler in `Tiger.applescript` would be called after the `window` gets extracted from the Nib file. In `Tiger.applescript`, you would include a handler like the following:

```
on awake from nib theObject
    if theObject is window 1 then
        -- Do something with the window here
    end if
end awake from nib
```

Event handlers are passed a single argument, which is the object that is making the call. In this case, it has been given the parameter name theObject. Sometimes, as is the case here, a handler can be called by multiple objects, and it is necessary to check what object is sending the message by using an if statement. Generally, you either compare the object passed in to an existing object, as in the preceding example, or you check its name property, like this:

```
on awake from nib theObject
    if name of theObject is "mainwindow" then
        -- Do something with the window here
    end if
end awake from nib
```

Many event handlers are available in AppleScript Studio, and the best way to learn them is probably just to use the AppleScript Inspector tab to list them for the interface elements that you are interested in using. Most are self-explanatory; for example, the handler called by a button when it is clicked is called clicked, and whenever a menu item is selected, it calls the choose menu item handler.

There is one more aspect of Interface Builder pertaining directly to AppleScript that you might need to be aware of: the AppleScript palette. If you open the Palettes panel by choosing Tools ⇨ Palettes ⇨ Show Palettes, you should see a script icon in the toolbar. If you click it, the AppleScript palette appears. It includes only one element: ASKDataSource. This can be used to provide a data source for table views that are instantiated in Interface Builder.

If you drag the ASKDataSource icon out into the Instances tab of the main nib window of your Interface Builder document, and connect the dataSource outlet of an NSTableView to it, the table view takes its data from the data source. You populate the ASKDataSource with data in a script; in AppleScript, the ASKDataSource has the class data source. The coming sections demonstrate how to use a data source to populate a table view.

To learn more about connecting user interfaces and AppleScript Studio in general, you can do a lot worse than going through the examples that Apple provides with the developer tools. These are located in the /Developer/Examples/AppleScript Studio directory. They cover everything from using table views to implementing drag-and-drop in your applications.

In the next couple of Try It Out examples, you use AppleScript Studio to develop an application called Piles of Pictures. This application uses AppleScript to retrieve photos from one or more albums in iPhoto and draws them at random positions to form a poster. The drawing is achieved with the aid of Cocoa classes.

The user interface of Piles of Pictures is shown in Figure 12-3. In this first example, you create the user interface in Interface Builder; in the next Try It Out example, you add script code to make the application functional.

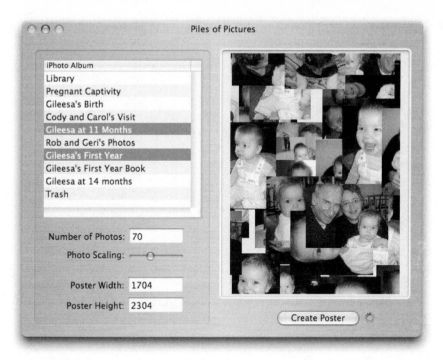

Figure 12-3

Try It Out   Creating the Piles of Pictures User Interface

1. Startup Xcode and choose File ⇨ New Project. When presented with the New Project Assistant, select AppleScript Application from the Application group. Click the Next button. Fill in `Piles of Pictures` for the Project Name and set the directory you would like the project to reside in. Click the Finish button to create the new project.

2. In the Groups & Files pane on the left, open the Resources group and double-click `MainMenu.nib`. The file should open in Interface Builder.

3. Begin laying out the main window, as shown in Figure 12-4. Start by dragging an `NSImageView` from the Cocoa-Controls palette of the Palettes window. Position it on the right as shown. Add an `NSButton` underneath, and open the Inspector window for the button by choosing Tools ⇨ Show Inspector. Enter the title `Create Poster` in the Inspector window. Drag the round `NSProgressIndicator` across and position it next to the button.

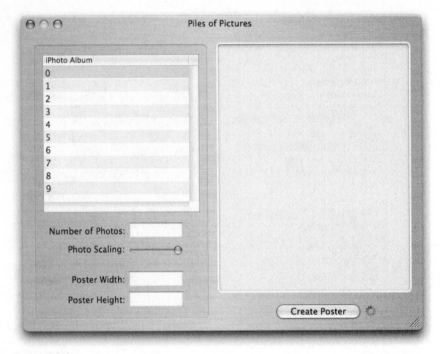

Figure 12-4

4. Drag an NSBox to the left of the window and resize it to fit. Drag an NSTableView, and position it as shown inside the box. Select the NSTableView and enter 1 in the Columns field of the Inspector window. Also make sure the Empty Selection check box is deselected and the Multiple Selection check box is checked. You can also check the Use Alternating Row Background check box if you wish.

5. Select the NSTableColumn by double-clicking the header cell of the NSTableView. Enter iPhoto Album as the Header title.

6. Drag an NSForm from the Cocoa-Text palette into the box. Position it under the NSTableView. Reduce the number of fields in the form to 1 by holding down the Option key while you drag the center-bottom handle upward. Double-click the form cell's label to edit it, and enter Number of Photos. Drag an NSNumberFormatter from the Cocoa-Text palette onto the editable field of the NSFormCell. In the Formatter tab of the Info Window, which should appear automatically, select the format that uses 100 as the Positive example and -100 as the Negative example. Enter 1 in the Minimum field.

7. Repeat step 6 to create the NSForm shown at the bottom of the box in Figure 12-4. This form has two NSFormCells, with the labels Poster Width and Poster Height. Add an NSNumberFormatter to each, selecting the same format as in step 6, but setting the Minimum value to 0 in each case.

8. Add an NSSlider to the box, as shown in Figure 12-4, by dragging it from the Cocoa-Controls palette. In the Inspector window, select Small from the Size popup button and enter 0.0 and 1.0 for the Minimum and Maximum values, respectively. Drag the System Font Text field from the Cocoa-Text palette into the box next to the slider and edit it to read Photo Scaling:.

9. Prepare to adjust the `NSWindow` settings by selecting it in the Instances tab of the `MainMenu.nib` document window. In the Inspector window, check the Has Texture check box. Deselect the Close and Resize check boxes, and enter `Piles of Pictures` for the Window Title.

10. Edit the File menu in the `MainMenu` instance. Double-click the File menu and delete all the menu items it contains except Save. To delete a menu item, select it and press Backspace. Rename the Save menu item to `Save Poster` by double-clicking its title and entering the new name.

11. Instantiate an `ASKDataSource` by dragging it from the Cocoa-AppleScript palette of the Palettes window onto the Instances tab of the `MainMenu.nib` document window.

12. To finish off the user interface, you need to give each element a name and set event handlers. Select each control in turn, and in the AppleScript tab of the Inspector window, configure them according to the following table.

Interface Component	AppleScript Name	Event Handlers
Main image view (`NSImageView`)	`posterimageview`	
Create Poster button (`NSButton`)		Action ⇨ clicked
Progress indicator (`NSProgress Indicator`)	`posterbuildprogress indicator`	
Configuration box (`NSBox`)	`configbox`	
Albums table view (`NSTableView`)	`albumstable`	Nib ⇨ awake from nib
Album name column (`NSTableColumn`)	`albumname`	
Number of photos form (`NSForm`)	`numberofphotosmatrix`	
Photo scaling slider (`NSSlider`)	`scalingslider`	
Poster dimensions form (`NSForm`)	`widthheightmatrix`	
Poster width cell (`NSFormCell`)	`posterwidthcell`	
Poster height cell (`NSFormCell`)	`posterheightcell`	
Main window (`NSWindow`)	`mainwindow`	Nib ⇨ awake from nib Panel ⇨ panel ended
Album data source (`ASKDataSource`)	`datasource`	
Save Poster menu item (`NSMenuItem`)	`saveposter`	Menu ⇨ choose menu item

All event handlers should be connected to the `Piles of Pictures.applescript` script, so ensure that the scripts check box is checked for any interface component that calls an event handler.

13. Save the changes you have made to the `MainMenu.nib` file.

How It Works

Most of this assignment simply involves laying out a user interface with Interface Builder and should not be particularly new to you. If you have read Chapter 4, which covers Interface Builder in detail, you should not find any of this too challenging.

What you probably haven't had to do before is configure the AppleScript tab of each interface component. Most of the components were given a unique name, to make it easier to refer to them in the `Piles of Pictures.applescript` script, which you write in the next section. Some of the controls had event handlers assigned to them, and the main window even had two. When the corresponding events occur, the appropriate event handlers in the `Piles of Pictures.applescript` script are called.

The logic behind the allocation of event handlers is fairly straightforward. When the user clicks the Create Poster button, the `clicked` action event handler is called, and a poster is created with the settings retrieved from the various controls in the configuration box on the left. When the poster is finished, it can be saved. If the user chooses File ⇨ Save Poster, the `choose menu item` handler is invoked to write the image data to file.

The `awake from nib` event handler is used to initially set up the interface. When called by the albums table view, `awake from nib` populates the table with the album names in your iPhoto library. When called by the main window, it sets the initial values of the configuration controls.

The only other event handler is `panel ended` from the `NSWindow`. This event is sent when a save panel sheet that is attached to a window ends. It is used in this case to notify the `Piles of Pictures.applescript` script of the choice made by the user in the save panel sheet that appears when the Save Poster menu item is selected.

In the following Try It Out, you write the `Piles of Pictures.applescript` script to form a working AppleScript application. This script responds to the event handlers sent by the interface components that you set up in this Try It Out and will refer to the interface components using the AppleScript names you provided.

Try It Out   Writing the Piles of Pictures Script

1. Open the Piles of Pictures project in Xcode and click the `Piles of Pictures.applescript` file in the Scripts group of the Groups & Files pane on the left. The script should appear in the main editor. Delete any existing code from the script.

2. Enter the following script into `Piles of Pictures.applescript`:

```
on awake from nib theObject
    if name of theObject is "mainwindow" then
        setControlDefaults()
    else if name of theObject is "albumstable" then
        setupTable()
    end if
end awake from nib

on setControlDefaults()
    tell window "mainwindow"
        tell box "configbox"
            tell matrix "widthheightmatrix"
                set integer value of cell "posterwidthcell" to 1704
                set integer value of cell "posterheightcell" to 2304
            end tell
            set integer value of cell 1 of matrix "numberofphotosmatrix" to 50
        end tell
    end tell
```

```
    end setControlDefaults

on setupTable()
    tell application "iPhoto" to set albumNames to name of albums
    set dataSource to data source 1
    make new data column at end of data columns of dataSource ¬
        with properties {name:"albumname"}
    repeat with albumName in albumNames
        set theRow to make new data row at end of data rows of dataSource
        set contents of data cell "albumname" of theRow to albumName
    end repeat
    set tableView to table view 1 of scroll view 1 of box 1 of window 1
    set data source of tableView to dataSource
end setupTable

on choose menu item theObject
    if name of theObject is "saveposter" then
        display save panel attached to window "mainwindow"
    end if
end choose menu item

on panel ended thePanel with result theResult
    if theResult is 1 then
        set thePath to path name of thePanel as string
        set theImage to image of (image view 1 of window "mainwindow")
        call method "writeImage:toFile:" with parameters {theImage, thePath}
    end if
end panel ended

on clicked theObject
    tell window "mainwindow"
        set posterView to image view "posterimageview"
        tell box "configbox"
            tell matrix "widthheightmatrix"
                set posterWidth to integer value of cell "posterwidthcell"
                set posterHeight to integer value of cell "posterheightcell"
            end tell
            set scaleFactor to float value of slider 1
            set numberOfPhotos to integer value of cell 1 ¬
                of matrix "numberofphotosmatrix"
        end tell
    end tell
    set posterImage to make new image at end of images
    call method "setSize:" of posterImage ¬
        with parameters {{posterWidth, posterHeight}}
    set imagePaths to getPathsToRandomPhotos(getSelectedAlbums(), numberOfPhotos)
    set progressIndicator to progress indicator 1 of window 1
    start progressIndicator
    repeat with imagePath in imagePaths
        set img to load image imagePath
        addImageToPoster(img, posterImage, scaleFactor)
        delete img
    end repeat
    stop progressIndicator
    set image of posterView to posterImage
```

```
    end clicked

on addImageToPoster(img, posterImage, scaleFactor)
    set imageSize to call method "size" of img
    set imageWidth to scaleFactor * (item 1 of imageSize)
    set imageHeight to scaleFactor * (item 2 of imageSize)
    set posterSize to call method "size" of posterImage
    set posterWidth to item 1 of posterSize
    set posterHeight to item 2 of posterSize
    set originX to (random number from -imageWidth to posterWidth)
    set originY to (random number from -imageHeight to posterHeight)
    drawImageOnImage(img, posterImage, ¬
        {originX, originY, originX + imageWidth, originY + imageHeight})
end addImageToPoster

on getSelectedAlbums()
    set selectedRows to selected data rows of table view 1 ¬
        of scroll view 1 of box "configbox" of window 1
    set theAlbums to {}
    repeat with theRow in selectedRows
        set theDataCell to data cell "albumname" of theRow
        set selectedAlbumName to content of theDataCell
        tell application "iPhoto" to get album selectedAlbumName
        set the end of theAlbums to result
    end repeat
    return theAlbums
end getSelectedAlbums

on drawImageOnImage(sourceImage, destImage, destRect)
    call method "lockFocus" of destImage
    set sourceSize to call method "size" of sourceImage
    call method "drawInRect:fromRect:operation:fraction:" of sourceImage ¬
        with parameters {destRect, {0.0, 0.0} & sourceSize, 1, 1.0}
    call method "unlockFocus" of destImage
end drawImageOnImage

on getPathsToRandomPhotos(theAlbums, numberOfPhotos)
    tell application "iPhoto"
        set photoPaths to {}
        repeat numberOfPhotos times
            set end of photoPaths to image path of some photo ¬
                of some item of theAlbums
        end repeat
    end tell
    return photoPaths
end getPathsToRandomPhotos
```

3. Choose File ➪ New File and choose Objective-C Class from the Cocoa group of the New File panel. After clicking Next, enter the name `ApplicationMethods.m` and make sure the Also Create "ApplicationMethods.h" check box is checked before clicking the Finish button.

4. Enter the following code in `ApplicationMethods.h`:

```
#import <Cocoa/Cocoa.h>

@interface NSApplication (ApplicationMethods)
-(void)writeImage:(NSImage *)image toFile:(NSString *)path;
@end
```

5. Enter the following code in `ApplicationMethods.m`:

```
#import "ApplicationMethods.h"

@implementation NSApplication (ApplicationMethods)

-(void)writeImage:(NSImage *)image toFile:(NSString *)path {
    NSData *data = [image TIFFRepresentation];
    [data writeToFile:path atomically:YES];
}

@end
```

6. Build and run the application by clicking the Build and Go toolbar button. If you encounter an error dialog box, double-check the names of each of the interface controls in the AppleScript tab of the Interface Builder Inspector window. It is very easy to supply the wrong label to a control, and an error will result.

7. Assuming that you have an iPhoto Library, select one or more albums in the iPhoto Album table view. Set the number of photos you want to include in the poster and adjust the scaling of the photos. If you want, you can also change the width and height of the poster. Lastly, click Create Poster and wait for the poster to be generated. This can take a minute or two, depending on your settings and computer.

Remember, if you don't use iPhoto for your digital photos, it doesn't mean you can't use it for this example. You can simply open your iPhoto library and import a few images from your hard disk or the Web.

8. Save the poster by choosing File ⇨ Save Poster. Open the saved poster by double-clicking it in Finder.

How It Works

Hopefully the `Pile of Pictures.applescript` script has demonstrated how easy it is to create a useful application with AppleScript Studio, one that is practically indistinguishable from an Objective-C–Cocoa application. With around 100 lines of AppleScript, you can extract photos from iPhoto, draw them on a new image taking full advantage of Cocoa and Quartz, and export the resulting image to a file.

The script begins with the `awake from nib` event handler:

```
on awake from nib theObject
    if name of theObject is "mainwindow" then
        setControlDefaults()
    else if name of theObject is "albumstable" then
        setupTable()
    end if
end awake from nib
```

This handler is called when an interface component is unarchived from a nib file, after any connections with other components have been initialized. Because in Piles of Pictures the awake from nib handler is called for two different objects, the main window and album table view, an if statement is used to recognize which is making a given call. The name property of the caller is used for this purpose. If the caller is the main window, the setControlDefaults handler is called:

```
on setControlDefaults()
    tell window "mainwindow"
        tell box "configbox"
            tell matrix "widthheightmatrix"
                set integer value of cell "posterwidthcell" to 1704
                set integer value of cell "posterheightcell" to 2304
            end tell
            set integer value of cell 1 of matrix "numberofphotosmatrix" to 50
        end tell
    end tell
end setControlDefaults
```

This method sets default values for the controls in the configuration box of the main window. Notice how tell blocks are used to define the containment relationship of the various interface components. Elements are generally identified by name, but sometimes an index is used, as for the numberofphotosmatrix form.

You may be wondering why the NSForms defined in Interface Builder earlier are being ascribed the class matrix in the script. There is no form class in AppleScript that corresponds to NSForm, but NSForm is a subclass of NSMatrix, so you can refer to an NSForm as an NSMatrix. You can thus use the matrix class in AppleScript to refer to NSForms in the user interface. The NSFormCell objects are similarly accessed via the cell class in AppleScript.

Returning briefly to the awake from nib handler, if the caller is the NSTableView, the setupTable handler is called to populate the table view with album names from iPhoto:

```
on setupTable()
    tell application "iPhoto" to set albumNames to name of albums
    set dataSource to data source 1
    make new data column at end of data columns of dataSource ¬
        with properties {name:"albumname"}
    repeat with albumName in albumNames
        set theRow to make new data row at end of data rows of dataSource
        set contents of data cell "albumname" of theRow to albumName
    end repeat
    set tableView to table view 1 of scroll view 1 of box 1 of window 1
    set data source of tableView to dataSource
end setupTable
```

The album names are retrieved from iPhoto in much the same way they were retrieved in scripts earlier in the chapter. The more interesting aspect of this handler is how it makes use of the data source object to populate the table view. The data source is retrieved by index, and assigned to the variable dataSource. A new data column is first added to the data source, with the name albumname. This name is chosen to correspond to the AppleScript name given to the NSTableColumn in Interface Builder.

A repeat loop then iterates over all the album names retrieved from iPhoto. For each album, a new data row is created in the data source. Each data row contains data cells corresponding to the data columns of the data source. The contents of the data cell for column albumname is set to the name of an album each time around the loop.

The last step in setting up the table view is to set its data source property to the newly initialized data source object. The variable tableView is assigned to the table view, and then the data source property is set. Note that in defining the containment relationships, the table view is contained in a scroll view. It is easy to overlook this, because an NSTableView is always contained in an NSScrollView in Interface Builder.

> *Rather than setting the* data source *of the* table view *programmatically, as demonstrated here, you could also use Interface Builder for this. You do so by Control-dragging from the* NSTableView *to the* ASKDataSource, *and connecting the* dataSource *outlet.*

The code to save the poster image to file is distributed over two handlers:

```
on choose menu item theObject
    if name of theObject is "saveposter" then
        display save panel attached to window "mainwindow"
    end if
end choose menu item

on panel ended thePanel with result theResult
    if theResult is 1 then
        set thePath to path name of thePanel as string
        set theImage to image of (image view 1 of window "mainwindow")
        call method "writeImage:toFile:" with parameters {theImage, thePath}
    end if
end panel ended
```

The first event handler is choose menu item, which is called by the Save Poster menu item when it is selected by the user. This method uses the display save panel command to bring up an NSSavePanel for the user to enter a directory and file name. By using the attached to window option, the save panel is made document modal, which means that the panel is displayed as a sheet, and the command exits before the user has finished making a choice.

When the user has entered the relevant information, the second handler, panel ended, is called. The result of the panel, which is the index of the button pressed by the user, is passed to the handler. The OK button corresponds to 1, so an if statement compares the result to 1 to make sure the user didn't click Cancel. If OK was clicked, the file path is retrieved from the path name property of the save panel. The image to be saved is also retrieved from the image view in the main window, and then the call method command is used to call the Objective-C method writeImage:toFile: of the NSApplication class, in order to save the image to a file. The image and path are both passed as arguments.

The writeImage:toFile: method is very simple:

```
@implementation NSApplication (ApplicationMethods)

-(void)writeImage:(NSImage *)image toFile:(NSString *)path {
    NSData *data = [image TIFFRepresentation];
    [data writeToFile:path atomically:YES];
}

@end
```

It is an NSApplication method, in the ApplicationMethods category. The NSImage data is extracted by calling the TIFFRepresentation method, and written to file using NSData's writeToFile:atomically: method. This small piece of Objective-C in an otherwise AppleScript application demonstrates how easy it is to write the parts of your applications in Objective-C, and call them from AppleScript.

When the user clicks the Create Poster button, the clicked handler is called. It initiates the chain of events that retrieves photos and draws the poster. It begins by retrieving the values of the controls in the user interface:

```
on clicked theObject
    tell window "mainwindow"
        set posterView to image view "posterimageview"
        tell box "configbox"
            tell matrix "widthheightmatrix"
                set posterWidth to integer value of cell "posterwidthcell"
                set posterHeight to integer value of cell "posterheightcell"
            end tell
            set scaleFactor to float value of slider 1
            set numberOfPhotos to integer value of cell 1 ¬
                of matrix "numberofphotosmatrix"
        end tell
    end tell
```

The properties integer value and float value are used to access the values of the various controls. If a control contains a string, you would use string value.

The next few lines of clicked create a new image for the poster:

```
set posterImage to make new image at end of images
call method "setSize:" of posterImage ¬
    with parameters {{posterWidth, posterHeight}}
```

The setSize: method is called using the call method command in order to set the size of the image according to the dimensions retrieved from the user interface controls.

The clicked handler concludes by retrieving paths to random photos in the iPhoto albums selected by the user, and drawing each one at a random position on the poster:

```
set imagePaths to getPathsToRandomPhotos(getSelectedAlbums(), numberOfPhotos)
set progressIndicator to progress indicator 1 of window 1
start progressIndicator
repeat with imagePath in imagePaths
    set img to load image imagePath
    addImageToPoster(img, posterImage, scaleFactor)
    delete img
end repeat
stop progressIndicator
set image of posterView to posterImage
end clicked
```

Other handlers are used to carry out various aspects of the procedure. getSelectedAlbums returns a list of the albums selected in the table view. getPathsToRandomPhotos chooses random photos from these `albums` and returns their file paths. `addImageToPoster` draws a photo `image` at a random point on the poster `image` after first scaling it according to the scaling factor entered by the user.

Each `image` is loaded from a file using the `load image` command. After being drawn on the poster `image`, each `image` is deleted using the `delete` command. This is a good way to prevent excessive memory use when you are working with objects, such as `images`, that require a lot of memory.

The `clicked` handler also starts and stops the `progress indicator` to alert the user that the application is busy, and ensures the `image` property of the `image view` is set to the new poster `image` when it is done.

The rest of the script defines the handlers called from `clicked`. `addImageToPoster` prepares to draw a photo on the poster and then calls another handler, `drawImageOnImage`, to do the actual drawing:

```
on addImageToPoster(img, posterImage, scaleFactor)
    set imageSize to call method "size" of img
    set imageWidth to scaleFactor * (item 1 of imageSize)
    set imageHeight to scaleFactor * (item 2 of imageSize)
    set posterSize to call method "size" of posterImage
    set posterWidth to item 1 of posterSize
    set posterHeight to item 2 of posterSize
    set originX to (random number from -imageWidth to posterWidth)
    set originY to (random number from -imageHeight to posterHeight)
    drawImageOnImage(img, posterImage, ¬
        {originX, originY, originX + imageWidth, originY + imageHeight})
end addImageToPoster
```

Most of this code involves randomly selecting a position for the photo on the poster, and calculating `image` dimensions. The `size` method of `NSImage` returns the width and height of the photo `image` in a two-element `list`. These values are scaled by the `scalingFactor` parameter. Random values are chosen for the origin of the photo, which is the left-bottom corner. These values get combined to define the rectangle in which the photo `image` will be drawn in the poster `image` coordinates.

`drawImageOnImage` draws the photo `image` on the poster `image` in the rectangle passed to it. It does this using Cocoa methods:

```
on drawImageOnImage(sourceImage, destImage, destRect)
    call method "lockFocus" of destImage
    set sourceSize to call method "size" of sourceImage
    call method "drawInRect:fromRect:operation:fraction:" of sourceImage ¬
        with parameters {destRect, {0.0, 0.0} & sourceSize, 1, 1.0}
    call method "unlockFocus" of destImage
end drawImageOnImage
```

To draw on an `NSImage` in Cocoa, you first call the `lockFocus` method; after you have finished drawing, you call the `unlockFocus` method. These methods have been invoked here using the `call method` command. The `drawInRect:fromRect:operation:fraction:` method of `NSImage` does the actual drawing. See the `NSImage` documentation for more information about this method.

`getSelectedAlbums` retrieves the names of the albums selected by the user in the `table view` and then requests the `album` objects corresponding to these names from iPhoto:

```
on getSelectedAlbums()
    set selectedRows to selected data rows of table view 1 ¬
```

```
            of scroll view 1 of box "configbox" of window 1
    set theAlbums to {}
    repeat with theRow in selectedRows
        set theDataCell to data cell "albumname" of theRow
        set selectedAlbumName to content of theDataCell
        tell application "iPhoto" to get album selectedAlbumName
        set the end of theAlbums to result
    end repeat
    return theAlbums
end getSelectedAlbums
```

The selected data rows property of the table view class returns the data row objects corresponding to the rows selected by the user. The repeat loop iterates over these data row objects. In each iteration, the content property of the data cell in the data row is retrieved; this is the name of one of the selected albums. The name is used to get the album object from iPhoto, which is added to a list that is eventually returned from the handler.

The last handler in the script is getPathsToRandomPhotos:

```
on getPathsToRandomPhotos(theAlbums, numberOfPhotos)
    tell application "iPhoto"
        set photoPaths to {}
        repeat numberOfPhotos times
            set end of photoPaths to image path of some photo ¬
                of some item of theAlbums
        end repeat
    end tell
    return photoPaths
end getPathsToRandomPhotos
```

This code is very similar to code used earlier in the chapter to randomly access photos in the iPhoto library. It retrieves the number of photos requested at random from the list of album objects passed to it. Notice that there is no attempt made to prevent a photo from being selected more than once, so a poster may contain the same photo two or more times.

Summary

AppleScript is in a category all its own because it is the only scripting language that allows you to directly interact with Mac OS X applications while they are running. For this reason, it fills an important role in Mac OS X programming. Even if your applications are written in languages other than AppleScript, there will often be tasks better left to an AppleScript script. Some knowledge of the language is thus a decided advantage for any Mac OS X developer.

In this chapter you learned

- ❑ How to write AppleScripts with Script Editor, and how to find out about the classes and commands of an application via its dictionary

- ❑ The basics of the AppleScript language, including data types and variables; how to use flow control statements; how to write and call handlers; and how to write and interact with script objects

❑   The differences between properties and elements, and the different ways you can specify a particular element

❑   How to script applications such as iTunes, iPhoto, Finder, and QuickTime

❑   The provisions in Xcode and Interface Builder for writing fully functional Cocoa applications with AppleScript Studio

❑   How you use the AppleScript–Cocoa bridge to work with Cocoa objects in AppleScript scripts

In the next chapter, you learn how to utilize Bash scripts in Cocoa applications written with Objective-C. Before proceeding, however, try the exercises that follow to test your understanding of the material covered in this chapter. You can find the solutions to these exercises in Appendix A.

Exercises

1. Modify the script you completed in the fifth Try It Out example ("Finishing Off Slideshow Maker") so that the user is prompted for the duration of each slide. Make sure you handle invalid user input appropriately.

2. The Piles of Pictures application works fine if the user does not try to do anything unusual, but it doesn't do a good job of taking into account exceptional circumstances. In particular, it doesn't consider the possibility that the user's iPhoto album contains no albums, or that the albums selected by the user are all empty.

    Modify the Piles of Pictures script so that it checks that the user selected at least one album, and that the selected albums are not all empty. If either of these circumstances arises, throw an error, and catch it again in the `clicked` handler. Display an alert panel if an error occurs. (*Hint:* Read about the `alert panel` class in the AppleScriptKit dictionary.)

3. Piles of Pictures allows you to vary the scaling of the photos drawn in the poster, but the same scaling factor applies to all photos. The purpose of this exercise is to allow the user to randomly vary the scaling from one photo to the next, so that the poster ends up with a distribution of different sizes.

    Add a second slider to the Piles of Pictures user interface to allow the user to choose a variation factor from 0.0 to 1.0. Choose a random value for each photo from the range stipulated by the variation factor, and add it to the original scaling factor such that the photos each have a different scaling.

    The variation factor should range over positive and negative values, corresponding to larger and smaller sizes, respectively. You need to ensure that the overall scaling factor of a photo — after applying the variation factor — is between 0.0 and 1.0.

Using Scripts Within Applications

With Mac OS X's large variety of scripting languages, each with its own strengths and application domain, there are often times when you will want to leverage them in your Cocoa applications. The best solution to certain problems may not be Objective-C and Cocoa, but may be a script. At the same time, you don't want to subject your users to the script directly, or the command-line interface — you want the features offered by the scripting language, in a user-friendly Cocoa graphical user interface (GUI). Luckily, Cocoa provides plenty of ways to leverage a script or command-line tool from within a Cocoa program.

In this chapter you learn

❑   The C functions that you can use to run external scripts and programs

❑   Which Cocoa classes can aid you to run external scripts and programs, including NSTask, NSFileManager, NSFileHandle, NSBundle, and NSPipe

❑   How to pass data to and retrieve data from an external program or script, from within a Cocoa application

❑   How to run external programs synchronously and asynchronously from within a Cocoa application

Running Subprocesses with C Functions

Before immediately resorting to Cocoa solutions for running external scripts and programs, you may be wise to remember one thing: Objective-C is a superset of C. Functions are available in the C standard library that may already be powerful enough to serve your purposes, depending on the problem at hand.

If you do not need to perform any complex data transactions with an external program, you may find the C functions simpler to use than the Cocoa classes, which require a number of initialization steps. This section introduces the C functions available to you for starting external scripts and programs, or *processes*, from your Cocoa applications.

> This chapter is mostly concerned with starting *subprocesses* from within a Cocoa program. A *subprocess* is a completely separate program, and does not have access to the same memory address space as the program initiating it.
>
> This contrasts with threads, which are similar, but share the memory space (for example, data structures, variables) of the initiating code.
>
> In short, a thread can use and modify the data stored in your Cocoa application, and a subprocess cannot.

Using the system Function

The `system` function from the C standard library is probably the easiest way to start a subprocess from your Cocoa application. It takes a single null-terminated C string as an argument, and returns an integer error code. The string is simply a shell script, which will be executed by the Bash Shell (see Chapter 11). The return code is simply the exit status of the shell script, which is 0 if no error occurred. Here is an example of using `system` to list the contents of the `/usr/bin` directory, and piping the results to a file:

```
int exitCode =
    system("/bin/ls /usr/bin > ~/Desktop/contents_of_usr_bin.txt");

if ( !exitCode ) {
    NSLog(@"Command succeeded.");
}
else {
    NSLog(@"Command failed with exit code %d.", exitCode);
}
```

The string passed to the system function is not an Objective-C `NSString`, but a plain C `char*` string. It can contain any legal Bash Shell script, so even with this one simple function you can achieve an awful lot.

Just because `system` uses the Bash Shell to run the script passed to it does not mean you can't use other shells, scripting languages, or even fully compiled programs. A Bash Shell is capable of starting its own subprocesses, so you can run whatever you like from within the script passed to system. Here is a simple example of using Perl to perform a calculation from within the shell script:

```
int exitCode = system("/usr/bin/perl -e \"print 4521.9 * 14.5,'\n';\"");
```

In this example, the output of the `perl` command has not been piped to a file, as it was in the previous example. The subprocess shares the standard output stream with the parent process, so the `print` statement writes to the output stream of the parent Cocoa program.

Two double quotation marks had to be escaped with backslashes in the previous command. You will likely need to do this often when preparing scripts in your Cocoa applications, to avoid the special meaning they have for the C compiler.

Given that the shell run by `system` shares the standard output of its parent process, you may be wondering if the standard input is also shared. It is, but it is not trivial to take advantage of this from inside your Cocoa application. It can be useful if you want to create a Cocoa tool that invokes a number of shell scripts to perform some processing of its own standard input data, but in such cases you may be better off avoiding Cocoa altogether, and just using a script. For example, here is a complete Foundation tool that alphabetically sorts the lines of text piped to it in standard input, and prints the results to standard output:

```
#import <Foundation/Foundation.h>

int main() {
    NSAutoreleasePool *pool = [[NSAutoreleasePool alloc] init];

    int exitCode = system("/usr/bin/sort -");
    if ( exitCode ) NSLog(@"Sorting command failed.");

    [pool release];
    return exitCode;
}
```

This program doesn't do anything you can't do with a one-line shell script, but it does demonstrate that subprocesses share their parent process's standard input and standard output streams. The command `/usr/bin/sort` sorts lines in standard input alphabetically, and prints the results. The hyphen (-) in the command indicates that `sort` should take its input from the standard input of the script, which in this case corresponds to the standard input of the Foundation tool.

To compile this program on the command line, copy it into a file called `sorter.m`, and enter the following line into Terminal:

```
/usr/bin/gcc -o sorter sorter.m -framework Foundation
```

To run it, use the following command, where `fileToSort.txt` is any multi-line text file that you want to sort:

```
./sorter < fileToSort.txt
```

Passing data to a subprocess initiated with the `system` function from within a Cocoa program is best achieved by either setting environment variables before calling `system`, or writing data to a file, and reading it back from file in the script.

Passing data via environment variables works because the subprocess inherits the environment of the parent process when it runs, and thus has access to the same environment variables. If you don't have too much data to pass, this is probably the easiest way to transfer data. You can use the C function `setenv` to set the environment, as shown in the following example:

```
#import <Foundation/Foundation.h>

int main() {
    NSAutoreleasePool *pool = [[NSAutoreleasePool alloc] init];

    setenv("FIRST", "40.5", 1);
    setenv("SECOND", "60.7", 1);
```

```
        int exitCode = system("/bin/echo $FIRST + $SECOND | /usr/bin/bc");

        if ( exitCode ) NSLog(@"bc command failed.");

        [pool release];
        return exitCode;
}
```

The `setenv` function takes the name of the variable as first argument, the value of the variable as second argument, and an `int` indicating whether the environment variable should be overwritten if it already exists. A value of 0 for the last parameter indicates the variable should not be overwritten, and a non-zero value indicates that it should be.

In the preceding example, the environment variables FIRST and SECOND are set to 40.5 and 60.7, respectively, with any existing variables that use either name being overwritten. The shell script executed by `system` adds the values in these environment variables using the command `/usr/bin/bc`, which is an arbitrary precision calculator. The program prints 101.2 to output when run.

If you have a lot of data to pass to a subprocess, you are better off writing it to a temporary file, and reading it back into the script. The following example shows you how to use temporary files to pass data back and forth between a Foundation tool and a subprocess, in order to carry out the calculation from the previous example, and print the result from within the Cocoa code:

```
#import <Foundation/Foundation.h>

int main() {
    NSAutoreleasePool *pool = [[NSAutoreleasePool alloc] init];

    // Open temporary file
    NSString *tmpFileName = [[NSProcessInfo processInfo] globallyUniqueString];
    NSString *tmpFilePath =
        [NSTemporaryDirectory() stringByAppendingPathComponent:tmpFileName];

    // Write two numbers to temporary file
    [@"40.5 60.7" writeToFile:tmpFilePath atomically:YES];

    // Set file name in environment
    setenv("FILE_PATH", [tmpFilePath cString], 1);

    // Run the subprocess
    int exitCode =
        system("read FIRST SECOND < \"$FILE_PATH\"\n"
               "/bin/echo $FIRST + $SECOND | /usr/bin/bc > \"$FILE_PATH\"\n");
    if ( exitCode ) NSLog(@"bc command failed.");

    // Read result from file
    NSString *result = [NSString stringWithContentsOfFile:tmpFilePath];
    NSFileHandle *out = [NSFileHandle fileHandleWithStandardOutput];
    [out writeData:[result dataUsingEncoding:NSUTF8StringEncoding]];

    // Delete file
```

```
        [[NSFileManager defaultManager] removeFileAtPath:tmpFilePath handler:nil];

        [pool release];
        return exitCode;
}
```

A temporary file path has been generated by combining the return value of the Cocoa function `NSTemporaryDirectory`, and the `NSProcessInfo` method `globallyUniqueString`. The `NSString` returned by `NSTemporaryDirectory` is a path to a directory that can be used by the process for temporary files. This directory can be removed at some later time by the operating system, so you should use it only for temporary scratch files.

`NSProcessInfo` is a class that contains information about the running process, such as its name and identifier. The method `globallyUniqueString` uses the process information, and details of the host computer, to generate a string that is unique to the process over the whole network that the computer resides on. This is useful for avoiding naming conflicts with other processes.

`NSString` provides a number of functions for manipulating paths; `stringByAppendingPath Component:` is one of these methods. It appends the `NSString` path component passed as the only argument to the messaged path, taking care to include the path separator (`/`) where necessary.

The `NSString` method `writeToFile:atomically:` is used to write two numbers to the temporary file. The second argument is a `BOOL` that indicates whether the method should take the precautionary step of writing the file entirely to a temporary location, before moving it to its final destination. This reduces the risk of the file being only partially written, because the file is guaranteed to be written in full, or not at all. By passing `YES` for this argument, you are making the write operation a bit more robust.

The `setenv` command sets an environment variable with the path to the temporary file, so that the script knows where to read the data. The `cString` method of `NSString` returns a null-terminated `char*` string representing the `NSString`.

The script itself consists of two lines, which are somewhat complicated by the fact that they are embedded in an Objective-C program. For example, new line characters (`\n`) must be given explicitly, and quotation marks have to be escaped with a backslash (`\`). To clarify matters, here is the script as it would be if it were isolated from the program:

```
read FIRST SECOND < "$FILE_PATH"
/bin/echo $FIRST + $SECOND | /usr/bin/bc > "$FILE_PATH"
```

It uses the `read` command to read in the two numbers, and set two variables. `read` reads a line from standard input, which in this case is the temporary file, sets the variable `FIRST` to the first number on the line, and `SECOND` to the second number. `echo` is used to write a summation expression involving these two variables to the standard input of `bc`, which calculates the summation, and writes the result back to the temporary file.

After the `system` function exits, the output of the script is read back into the Cocoa program using the `NSString` method `stringWithContentsOfFile:`, and written to standard output with the class `NSFileHandle`. The temporary file is removed using the default `NSFileManager`, with the method `removeFileAtPath:handler:`.

The preceding example used a temporary file to pass data back and forth between a Cocoa program and a script. Communication was two-way, with the same temporary file being used to pass data in both directions. In more complex scripts, you may have to use multiple files for your communication purposes.

In the next section, you learn about a C function that allows you to avoid using temporary files altogether when communicating with a script.

Using popen to Run Scripts Asynchronously

It is possible to avoid temporary files if you use the C function popen, which stands for "open pipe." This is similar to system, but returns a C FILE type that you can read from or write to. This FILE is connected to the standard input or standard output of the subprocess. Here is how you could perform the calculation from the previous section with popen, instead of temporary files:

```
#import <Foundation/Foundation.h>

int main() {
    NSAutoreleasePool *pool = [[NSAutoreleasePool alloc] init];

    FILE *pipe = popen("read FIRST SECOND; /bin/echo $FIRST + $SECOND | bc", "w");
    fprintf(pipe, "40.5 60.7\n");
    pclose(pipe);

    [pool release];
    return 0;
}
```

The popen function expects the shell script to be passed first, and an operation type second. In this case, "w" is passed, indicating that the file handle returned will be used for writing to the subprocess. The subprocess will receive anything written to the FILE in its standard input stream.

After the pipe is opened, an fprintf call is used to write the data to the standard input of the script, which calculates the result and prints it to standard output. Finally, the pipe is closed with the pclose function.

popen is more difficult to use than system, because it is *asynchronous*, which means it returns before the shell has exited. The system function waits for the script to complete before returning, but popen returns immediately. This is necessary if the preceding script is to work, because the Cocoa program must be able to write to the standard input stream of the subprocess, and it would not be able to do this if popen did not return immediately.

If popen were *synchronous*, like system, the read command in the script would wait for something to appear in the input stream, but the parent process would not be able to execute the fprintf to write anything there. The program would never exit. This situation is called a *deadlock*; a deadlock occurs whenever two or more processes are waiting for each other to do something and are consequently unable to continue.

In the following sections you use the system function to develop a simple file-searching tool called Searcher, based on the Unix command find, with a Cocoa graphical interface. This tool searches for files or directories whose name contains a given string, in a given directory tree. The paths of all files found are displayed in a table, and individual files can be displayed in Finder, or opened directly from the Searcher application.

In the following Try It Out, you develop a Cocoa interface for the Searcher application; in the Try It Out that follows, the file search engine is added, which is nothing more than a shell script containing the `find` command.

Try It Out   Creating a Cocoa Interface for Searcher

1. Create a new Cocoa Application project with Xcode. You can find the Cocoa Application project type in the New Project panel in the group Application. Name the new project `Searcher`.

2. Open the `MainMenu.nib` bundle in Interface Builder by double-clicking it in the Resources group of the Groups & Files panel.

3. Lay out controls in the window as shown in Figure 13-1. You will need to include two editable `NSTextField` instances; two `NSTextField` labels; an `NSTableView`; and three `NSButton` instances.

Figure 13-1

4. Create a new subclass of `NSObject` called `Searcher`, as follows: Click the Classes tab of the `MainMenu.nib` window in Interface Builder. Select `NSObject`, and choose Subclass NSObject from the Classes menu. Name the new class `Searcher`.

5. Instantiate a `Searcher` object by selecting the `Searcher` class in the Classes tab of the `MainMenu.nib` window and choosing Instantiate Searcher from the Classes menu. Double-click the instance to open the Searcher Class Inspector panel and select Attributes from the popup button. In the Outlet tab, add a new outlet called `pathsController`. In the Actions tab, add the three actions `showInFinder:`, `openFile:`, and `search:`.

6. Instantiate an object of the class `NSObjectController` by opening the Cocoa-Controllers panel in the Interface Builder Palettes panel. (The Cocoa-Controllers panel is represented by a cube in the toolbar.) Open the Instances tab of the `MainMenu.nib` window and drag the

NSObjectController icon, which is located in the center of the palette, to the Instances tab. Select the NSObjectController and then click to edit the instance's name, entering SearcherAlias. Open the NSObjectController Inspector panel by selecting Show Inspector from the Tools menu; under Attributes, enter Searcher as the Object Class Name.

7. Control-drag from the SearcherAlias instance to the Searcher instance. When the NSObjectController Inspector panel appears, select the Outlets tab and make sure the content outlet is selected before clicking the Connect button.

8. Now instantiate an NSArrayController in the same manner as the NSObjectController in step 6. Call it PathsController.

9. Bind the PathsController binding contentArray to the SearcherAlias controller, with the Controller Key set to selection and the Model Key Path set to paths. To do this, open the bindings panel of the PathsController: Select it in the Instances tab of the MainMenu.nib window, and select Show Inspector from the Tools menu. Choose Bindings from the popup menu in the NSArrayController Inspector panel. Click the contentArray group, and edit the settings to look like Figure 13-2.

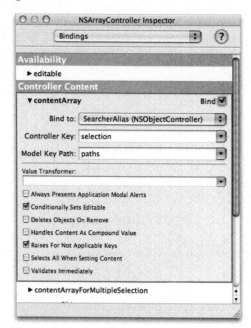

Figure 13-2

10. Set the targets of the Search, Show In Finder, and Open File buttons to the Searcher instance by Control-dragging from each button to the Searcher instance, selecting the appropriate action, and clicking the Connect button. The actions are self explanatory: Search should be connected to search:; Show In Finder to showInFinder:; and Open File to openFile:. Also connect the pathsController outlet of the Searcher instance by Control-dragging from Searcher to the PathsController instance and clicking Connect.

11. Display the NSTableView Inspector panel and set up its attributes as shown in Figure 13-3. If the Inspector window that appears is for the NSScrollView, rather than the NSTableView, you need to double-click the NSTableView to select it. Note that the NSTableView should have only one column. Select that column by double-clicking the column header until the NSTableColumn Inspector panel appears. Select Bindings from the popup menu in the Inspector panel and click the value group. Select PathsController in the Bind to popup button, and arranged Objects as the Controller Key. Leave the Model Key Path unchanged. Click the Bind switch to complete the binding.

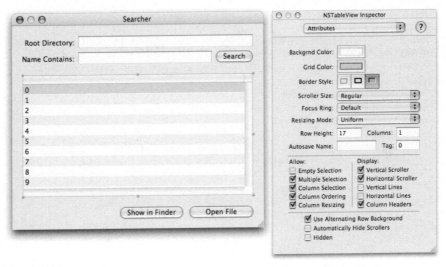

Figure 13-3

12. Bind the value binding of the editable NSTextField to the right of the Root Directory label, according to the following table:

Bind to:	SearcherAlias
Controller Key:	selection
Model Key Path:	rootDirectoryPath
Continuously Updates Value	Checkbox Checked

13. Bind the value binding of the editable NSTextField to the right of the Name Contains label, according to the following table:

Bind to:	SearcherAlias
Controller Key:	selection
Model Key Path:	nameContainsString
Continuously Updates Value	Checkbox Checked

14. Save your changes in Interface Builder, and return to the Searcher project in Xcode. Select the Classes group in Groups & Files, and create a new Objective-C class file called `Searcher.m` by choosing File ⇨ New File. Make sure you elect to create the `Searcher.h` file as well, and in the editor, replace the contents of each file with the following code:

Searcher.h

```
#import <Cocoa/Cocoa.h>

@interface Searcher : NSObject
{
    IBOutlet NSArrayController *pathsController;
    NSArray *paths;
    NSString *rootDirectoryPath;
    NSString *nameContainsString;
}

-(IBAction)openFile:(id)sender;
-(IBAction)showInFinder:(id)sender;
-(IBAction)search:(id)sender;

-(NSArray *)paths;
-(void)setPaths:(NSArray *)paths;

-(NSString *)rootDirectoryPath;
-(void)setRootDirectoryPath:(NSString *)path;

-(NSString *)nameContainsString;
-(void)setNameContainsString:(NSString *)str;

@end
```

Searcher.m

```
#import "Searcher.h"

@implementation Searcher

-(id)init {
    if ( self = [super init] ) {
        [self setPaths:[NSArray arrayWithObject:NSHomeDirectory()]];
        [self setRootDirectoryPath:NSHomeDirectory()];
        [self setNameContainsString:@""];
    }
    return self;
}

-(void)dealloc {
    [paths release];
    [rootDirectoryPath release];
    [nameContainsString release];
    [super dealloc];
}

-(IBAction)openFile:(id)sender {
    NSArray *selectedPaths = [pathsController selectedObjects];
    NSEnumerator *en = [selectedPaths objectEnumerator];
```

```
        id path;
        while ( path = [en nextObject] ) {
            [[NSWorkspace sharedWorkspace] openFile:path];
        }
    }

    -(IBAction)showInFinder:(id)sender {
        NSArray *selectedPaths = [pathsController selectedObjects];
        NSEnumerator *en = [selectedPaths objectEnumerator];
        id path;
        while ( path = [en nextObject] ) {
            [[NSWorkspace sharedWorkspace] selectFile:path
                inFileViewerRootedAtPath:@"/"];
        }
    }

    -(IBAction)search:(id)sender {
    }

    -(NSArray *)paths {
        return paths;
    }

    -(void)setPaths:(NSArray *)newPaths {
        [paths autorelease];
        paths = [newPaths retain];
    }

    -(NSString *)rootDirectoryPath {
        return rootDirectoryPath;
    }

    -(void)setRootDirectoryPath:(NSString *)dirPath {
        [rootDirectoryPath autorelease];
        rootDirectoryPath = [dirPath copy];
    }

    -(NSString *)nameContainsString {
        return nameContainsString;
    }

    -(void)setNameContainsString:(NSString *)str {
        [nameContainsString autorelease];
        nameContainsString = [str copy];
    }

@end
```

15. Build and run the application. The application window should look similar to Figure 13-4, though the user name shown in the paths will be different. Try clicking the Open File and Show In Finder buttons to see what happens.

Figure 13-4

How It Works

This section has dealt primarily with preparing the Cocoa interface of Searcher, and doesn't bear much relation to the main topic of the chapter. But without this interface, Searcher would just be a command-line tool, and there would be no point writing it, because the find command already provides the same functionality.

The main class of the Searcher application is also called Searcher. The Searcher class is actually a controller class that doubles as model. Because Searcher is a simple application, there isn't much point complicating it by creating separate model classes.

Searcher includes the instance variables paths, rootDirectoryPath, and nameContainsString. paths is an NSArray that is used to contain the file paths returned by the search. These paths will be displayed in the NSTableView.

The Searcher class also includes an outlet instance variable: pathsController. This is connected to the PathsController NSArrayController instance, which controls the array of paths returned in a search. This outlet is necessary to retrieve the selected path from the array controller when the Show In Finder and Open File buttons are pressed by the user.

The model data in Searcher is kept in sync with the user interface by the NSObjectController instance SearcherAlias. The content outlet of this controller is set to the Searcher instance. The user interface text fields are bound to keys in SearcherAlias, so that when the directory path or search string is changed by the user, the corresponding model instance variables are updated in the Searcher instance.

The contentArray binding of the NSArrayController is bound to the paths key of SearcherAlias. Whenever a search completes, and the paths NSArray is set in the Searcher instance, PathsController should observe the change via SearcherAlias. The NSTableColumn in the NSTableView, which has its value binding bound to the `arrangedObjects` Controller Key of `PathsController`, will update to reflect the new file paths, and the user will be presented with the search results.

At this point, the `Searcher` application is far from fully operational. The `paths` instance variable of the `Searcher` instance has been populated with a single element, purely for testing purposes. If you click the Show In Finder button, your home directory should be displayed and selected in a Finder window. If you click the Open File button, the contents of your home directory should be displayed in a Finder window. The Search button should not have any effect when clicked.

Each of these buttons has its target set to the `Searcher` instance in `MainMenu.nib`. The Search button is connected to the action `search:`, which is empty. The other two actions make use of the Cocoa class `NSWorkspace` to display or open a file:

```
-(IBAction)openFile:(id)sender {
    NSArray *selectedPaths = [pathsController selectedObjects];
    NSEnumerator *en = [selectedPaths objectEnumerator];
    id path;
    while ( path = [en nextObject] ) {
        [[NSWorkspace sharedWorkspace] openFile:path];
    }
}

-(IBAction)showInFinder:(id)sender {
    NSArray *selectedPaths = [pathsController selectedObjects];
    NSEnumerator *en = [selectedPaths objectEnumerator];
    id path;
    while ( path = [en nextObject] ) {
        [[NSWorkspace sharedWorkspace] selectFile:path
            inFileViewerRootedAtPath:@"/"];
    }
}
```

In each case, the `pathsController` outlet, which is connected to the `PathsController` instance, is queried for the selected objects. An `NSEnumerator` is used in combination with a `while` loop to iterate over all selected paths. The file corresponding to each path is opened and displayed using `NSWorkspace`.

With the user interface of Searcher now complete, in the next Try It Out you add the search engine, which is nothing more or less than the Unix `find` command.

Try It Out   Writing the Search Engine for Searcher

1. Open the Searcher project and select the `Searcher.m` file in the Classes group of the Groups & Files panel. In the editor, modify the `init` method of the class, according to the following highlights:

```
-(id)init {
    if ( self = [super init] ) {
        [self setPaths:[NSArray array]];
        [self setRootDirectoryPath:NSHomeDirectory()];
        [self setNameContainsString:@""];
    }
    return self;
}
```

2. Move down to the `search:` method of the `Searcher` class, and insert the following contents:

```objc
-(IBAction)search:(id)sender {
    // Create a temporary file path for the scripts output
    NSString *tmpFileName = [[NSProcessInfo processInfo] globallyUniqueString];
    NSString *tmpFilePath = [NSTemporaryDirectory()
        stringByAppendingPathComponent:tmpFileName];

    // Set input parameters for the script via the environment variables
    setenv("SEARCH_STRING", [nameContainsString cString], 1);
    setenv("OUTPUT_FILE", [tmpFilePath cString], 1);
    setenv("ROOT_DIR", [rootDirectoryPath cString], 1);

    // Run the find command
    system("find \"$ROOT_DIR\" -name \"*$SEARCH_STRING*\" > \"$OUTPUT_FILE\"");

    // Retrieve output from the output file, and split into separate lines
    NSString *outputString = [NSString stringWithContentsOfFile:tmpFilePath];
    NSArray *newPaths = [outputString componentsSeparatedByString:@"\n"];

    // Set paths array
    [self setPaths:newPaths];

    // Delete the output file
    [[NSFileManager defaultManager] removeFileAtPath:tmpFilePath handler:nil];
}
```

3. Compile and run the program by clicking the Build and Go toolbar item.

4. Try entering the path `/usr` and the search string `darwin`. Click the Search button and wait for the results. You should see something similar to Figure 13-5. Try selecting several of the paths and clicking the Show In Finder button.

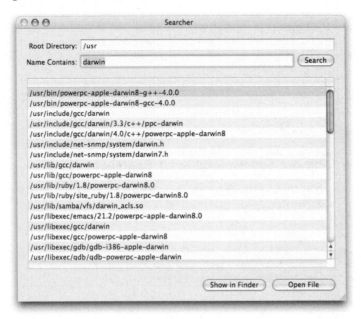

Figure 13-5

5. Enter the full path to your home directory. Enter `txt` as the search string, and click Search. The search could take some time, depending on the size of your home directory, so be prepared to wait. What do you notice about the responsiveness of the application while it is searching? Try selecting some of the search results in the table and clicking the Open File button.

How It Works

The `search:` method is quite similar to some of the examples seen earlier in the chapter. It passes parameters to the `find` command using environment variables, which are set with the `setenv` C function. The `find` command searches at the path passed as the first command-line argument, and all subdirectories, for the string given after the `-name` option. The search string can contain wildcards, and in this case an asterisk has been inserted at the beginning and end of the variable `SEARCH_STRING` so that any name containing the string matches. The output of the `find` command is piped to a temporary file, the path of which is also passed through an environment variable.

You should note that most of the paths in the shell script are enclosed in quotation marks, which have been escaped by backslashes to avoid the special meaning they have in Objective-C. Placing quotation marks around paths in scripts is always a good idea, because if the path passed includes one or more spaces, it is likely to be misinterpreted by the script as multiple separate paths.

When the `find` command completes, control is returned to the Cocoa application, and the `NSString` method `stringWithContentsOfFile:` is used to read the results in from the temporary file. The results are then split into lines using the `componentsSeparatedByString:` method, which returns an `NSArray`.

The `paths` instance variable is set using the `setPaths:` accessor method, and this initiates a chain of updates, due to the bindings defined earlier. The `NSArrayController PathsController` instance observes the change to `paths`, and the `NSTableView` is updated to reflect the new search results.

If you test the application, you will notice it has one serious drawback: The user interface is unresponsive when the `find` command is running. The `system` function is synchronous, so it doesn't return until the script completes. If the script is lengthy, as it can be in this case if you search through a lot of files, the user interface can freeze for some time. This can be very frustrating for the user.

One way to solve this problem is to make the application multithreading. Instead of a single thread of execution, two or more threads work at the same time. Threads are like processes, except they share the same memory address space as other threads in the same program. This means that all threads have access to the same data, which can make programming with multiple threads more complicated.

In this example, one thread could be assigned to updating the user interface, and one to running the script. The user interface would continue to operate via the first thread, even when the `system` function blocks the second thread. Multithreading with Cocoa is not that difficult, so this could be achieved without too much trouble, but it would not solve all problems. For example, suppose you wanted to allow the user to cancel a search. The `system` function provides no provisions for canceling a script once it is started, so the user would have to wait until it is finished, or the script would have to be left running in the background, consuming precious CPU cycles.

A better approach is to use only `system` for running short, simple scripts, and upgrading to the facilities provided in Cocoa for running more complex and lengthier subprocesses. The Cocoa class `NSTask` provides similar functionality to the `system` function, but offers much more control, as you find out by reading the next section.

Running Scripts with Cocoa

Cocoa provides a number of classes that can be used to help run subprocesses and communicate with them. The most important of these classes is NSTask, which allows you to run scripts and other executables, and provides fine control over program arguments, environment variables, and access to standard input and output. NSTask runs subprocesses asynchronously, but provides a method for waiting until the subprocess completes, which is equivalent to running the subprocess synchronously. NSTask also provides methods for suspending, resuming, and terminating a subprocess. In short, NSTask gives you much more control over external scripts than the C system function.

Introducing NSTask

In its simplest form, NSTask can be almost as easy to use as system. Take this example of using a script to list the contents of two directories:

```
#import <Foundation/Foundation.h>

int main() {
    NSAutoreleasePool *pool = [[NSAutoreleasePool alloc] init];

    NSArray *args = [NSArray arrayWithObjects:@"/bin", @"/sbin", nil];
    NSTask *task = [NSTask launchedTaskWithLaunchPath:@"./list.sh" arguments:args];
    [task waitUntilExit];
    int exitStatus = [task terminationStatus];

    [pool release];
    return exitStatus;
}
```

This program creates an NSTask with the convenience constructor launchedTaskWithLaunchPath: arguments:. The launch path of an NSTask is the path to the script or other executable that will be run. The arguments are passed to the script when it is run. They are equivalent to the argv arguments that the main function of a C program is passed when it is started. (Try not to confuse the arguments passed to a program with its environment variables.)

The launchedTaskWithLaunchPath:arguments: method not only initializes the NSTask, it also launches it, meaning that it runs the program or script at the launch path given. It then exits immediately—the launchedTaskWithLaunchPath:arguments: launches the subprocess asynchronously. To avoid having the Cocoa program exit before the subprocess is finished running, a waitUntilExit message is sent to the NSTask, which blocks execution until the subprocess exits. The exit status of the script is retrieved using the NSTask method terminationStatus, and is returned from the Cocoa program.

The missing link in this picture is the script that the NSTask launches. The NSTask is initialized with the launch path ./list.sh. To run the program, the script list.sh must be located in the same directory as the Cocoa executable. Here are the contents of the list.sh file:

```
#!/bin/sh

while (( $# ))
do
  echo
```

```
    echo ===============================================
    echo Contents of Path: $1
    echo ---------------------------
    ls $1
    shift
done
```

You need to make sure that any script you write is given permissions that allow it to be executed. You can do this on the command line by entering chmod u+x script_file. *If you do not make your script file executable, the* NSTask *will not be able to launch it.*

This script loops over its arguments, which were provided by the NSTask, performing an ls command for each path passed. Some echo statements make the output more readable, but it is otherwise a simple script.

$# is a bash variable that contains the current number of arguments, excluding $0. $# is tested in the while loop condition to see if it is 0. The (( )) brackets test the arithmetic value of the $# variable; if it is non-zero, the bracketed expression evaluates to zero, and vice versa. The while loop continues looping as long as the condition is zero, which corresponds to when $# is non-zero.

You may think that this loop will never exit, but $# can change as the script executes. The command shift just before the end of the loop moves all arguments to the left one place. So the contents of $3 are moved to $2, $2 to $1, and so forth. The contents of $1 are discarded, and the number of arguments thus decreased by 1. (The program name, $0, is left unchanged by shift.) The ls statement is always applied to $1, but the contents of $1 change each iteration of the loop, until all arguments have been treated. When there are no more arguments left, the while loop exits.

This simple example demonstrates that NSTask isn't difficult to use, although for very simple scripts, system may be more convenient because the script can be given directly to the function as a string. NSTask expects to be passed a launch path, which implies that a script must exist in a separate file before it can be launched.

Transferring Data with Pipes

NSTask includes methods for accessing the standard input and output streams of a subprocess. Unless you set these explicitly with the setStandardInput: or setStandardOutput: methods, the subprocess launched by NSTask will inherit the standard input and output streams of the parent process—the Cocoa program.

The argument to setStandardInput: and setStandardOutput: should be either an NSFileHandle or an NSPipe. An NSFileHandle is a class typically used for accessing file contents, but can also be used for reading or writing streams such as standard input and output or sockets, which are used in networking. An NSPipe is the Cocoa analog of a Unix pipe: It provides one NSFileHandle for reading and one for writing. Usually one end of a pipe is connected to the output of one process, and the other end to the input of a second process. Data written to the pipe by the first process is channeled to the second process, where it can be read from the pipe.

Earlier in the chapter, the sort command was used to sort the lines of a file into alphabetical order. Here is another example using sort, which sorts data passed to a script via an NSPipe:

```
#import <Foundation/Foundation.h>

int main() {
    NSAutoreleasePool *pool = [[NSAutoreleasePool alloc] init];

    NSString *stringToSort =
        @"melbourne\n"
        @"sydney\n"
        @"perth\n"
        @"adelaide\n"
        @"brisbane\n";

    NSTask *task = [[[NSTask alloc] init] autorelease];
    [task setLaunchPath:@"./sort.sh"];

    NSPipe *inputPipe = [NSPipe pipe];
    NSPipe *outputPipe = [NSPipe pipe];
    [task setStandardInput:inputPipe];
    [task setStandardOutput:outputPipe];

    // Launch task
    [task launch];

    // Write to standard input of script
    NSData *data = [stringToSort dataUsingEncoding:NSUTF8StringEncoding];
    NSFileHandle *inFile = [inputPipe fileHandleForWriting];
    [inFile writeData:data];
    [inFile closeFile];

    // Read output of script
    data = [[outputPipe fileHandleForReading] readDataToEndOfFile];

    // Write the output string
    NSFileHandle *so = [NSFileHandle fileHandleWithStandardOutput];
    [so writeData:data];

    int exitStatus = [task terminationStatus];

    [pool release];
    return exitStatus;
}
```

The script in the ./sort.sh file looks like this:

```
#!/bin/sh
sort -
```

The Cocoa program just shown doesn't use the convenience constructor launchedTaskWithLaunchPath:
arguments: because the standard input and output of the NSTask need to be set before the task is
launched. The launchedTaskWithLaunchPath:arguments: method launches the task immediately, not
giving any opportunity to set the streams.

Instead, the NSTask is simply initialized with init, and accessor methods are used to set the launch path
and standard input and output. Two NSPipes are created using the class method pipe, which returns an

initialized and autoreleased NSPipe object. These two NSPipes are set as the input and output of the NSTask using setStandardInput: and setStandardOutput:, at which point the task is launched with the launch method.

The input data for the script is created by converting the stringToSort NSString variable into an NSData object, using UTF8 encoding. The NSPipe method fileHandleForWriting returns an NSFileHandle object that can be used for writing to a pipe. The input data is written to the file handle returned by this method for the standard input pipe using the NSFileHandle writeData: method. Lastly, the NSFile Handle is closed using the closeFile method. It is important to do this; otherwise the script will wait forever for more input, because it has no other means of determining when the stream has ended.

The output of the script is read from an NSFileHandle provided by the NSPipe that is used for script output. In this example, the data is written directly to the standard output stream of the Cocoa program. The same end result could have been achieved by not setting the standard output of the NSTask at all, because then it would share the standard output of the Cocoa program. However, script output would usually be used inside a program, and setting an NSPipe for script output is the best approach when this is the case.

NSPipe objects can be viewed as temporary files that are used to communicate between two processes in one direction, with one process writing data and the other reading it. You could achieve the same effect by simply writing script input to file with an NSFileHandle, and reading it back in from the script. In fact, this was exactly the approach used earlier in the chapter to pass input to scripts started with the system function. The advantage of using an NSPipe is that you don't have to create and delete a temporary file. You can also read and write to or from an NSPipe in chunks. This is useful if you are processing data in stages, passing one chunk at a time from one process to the other.

In the following Try It Out, you use the Cocoa classes introduced in this chapter to write an application that automatically archives a file or directory at regular time intervals, using a shell script. The idea behind the application is that you can use it to keep a short version history of the files in whatever project you happen to be working on. If you take a wrong turn while working on the project, you can return to one of the archived versions of the project and retrieve some or all of its files. The application is called Crumbs, because it is analogous to dropping breadcrumbs in order to find your way back when you get lost.

Try It Out   Creating a User Interface for Crumbs

1. Create a new Cocoa Application project in Xcode and call it Crumbs.

2. Open the Resources group in the Groups & Files panel and double-click the MainMenu.nib file in order to open it in Interface Builder.

3. Lay out the main window as shown in Figure 13-6. The Frequency popup button should include the items Hourly and Daily, and the Maximum popup should include 5, 10, and 20. Set the Frequency to Hourly; set the Maximum popup to 5.

Figure 13-6

4. In the main window, select the Turn Archiving On button, and display the Inspector panel by selecting Show Inspector from the Tools menu. Enter Turn Archiving Off as Alt. Title and select Toggle in the Behavior popup button.

5. Select the Hourly menu item in the Frequency popup button. In the Inspector panel, set the Tag to 3600. Set the tag of the Daily menu item to 86400. Change the tags of the menu items in the Maximum popup button to match their titles, namely, 5, 10, and 20.

6. In the Classes tab of the `MainMenu.nib` window, select the `NSWindowController` class. Select Subclass `NSWindowController` from the Classes menu and enter `CrumbsController` as the name of the new class. Open the Inspector panel for the class and add two actions: `browseForPathToArchive:` and `toggleArchiving:`. Lastly, create an instance of `CrumbsController` by selecting Instantiate CrumbsController from the Classes menu.

7. Bind the various controls to the Shared User Defaults controller. (The controller appears in the Instances tab of the `MainMenu.nib` window once you create the first binding.) Use the Inspector window shown in Figure 13-7, which is for the Frequency popup button, as a reference. Set the bindings according to the following table.

Control	Binding	Controller Key	Model Key Path
NSTextField for Path	value	values	PathToBeArchived
NSPopUpButton for Frequency	selectedTag	values	ArchivingFrequencyTag
NSPopUpButton for Maximum	selectedTag	values	MaximumArchivedFilesTag
NSButton for Toggling Archiving	value	values	ArchivingState

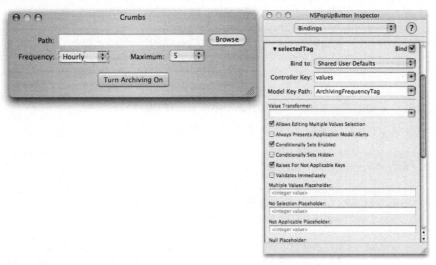

Figure 13-7

8. Control-drag from the Browse button to the CrumbsController instance in the Instances tab of the `MainMenu.nib` window. Select the `browseForPathToArchive:` action and click Connect.

Set the target of the Turn Archiving On button in the same way, connecting it to the `toggleArchiving:` action of the CrumbsController.

9. Connect the window outlet of CrumbsController to the main window by Control-dragging from the CrumbsController instance to the Window instance, and connecting the window outlet in the Inspector window.

10. Create files for the `CrumbsController` class by selecting it in the Classes tab of the `MainMenu.nib` window and selecting Create Files for CrumbsController from the Classes menu. Go to Xcode and move the newly created `CrumbsController.h` and `CrumbsController.m` files to the Classes group in the Groups & Files panel.

11. Open the `CrumbsController.h` and `CrumbsController.m` files in turn in the editor and replace their content with the following code:

CrumbsController.h

```
#import <Cocoa/Cocoa.h>

@interface CrumbsController : NSWindowController {
    NSTimer *timer;
}
- (IBAction)browseForPathToArchive:(id)sender;
- (IBAction)toggleArchiving:(id)sender;

-(void)runArchiveScript;

@end
```

CrumbsController.m

```
#import "CrumbsController.h"

// User default keys
static NSString *PathToBeArchived          = @"PathToBeArchived";
static NSString *ArchivingFrequencyTag     = @"ArchivingFrequencyTag";
static NSString *MaximumArchivedFilesTag   = @"MaximumArchivedFilesTag";
static NSString *ArchivingState            = @"ArchivingState";
static NSString *LastBrowseDirectory       = @"LastBrowseDirectory";


@implementation CrumbsController

+(void)initialize {
    NSUserDefaults *defs = [NSUserDefaults standardUserDefaults];
    NSDictionary *dict = [NSDictionary dictionaryWithObjectsAndKeys:
        [NSNumber numberWithInt:3600],            ArchivingFrequencyTag,
        [NSNumber numberWithInt:5],               MaximumArchivedFilesTag,
        [NSNumber numberWithInt:NSOffState],      ArchivingState,
        NSHomeDirectory(),                        LastBrowseDirectory,
        nil];
    [defs registerDefaults:dict];
}

-(id)init {
    if ( self = [super init] ) {
        timer = nil;
```

```
        }
        return self;
    }

    -(void)dealloc {
        [timer invalidate];
        [super dealloc];
    }

    -(void)awakeFromNib {
        // Toggle archiving, to start timer if necessary
        [self toggleArchiving:self];
    }

    - (IBAction)browseForPathToArchive:(id)sender {
        NSUserDefaults *defs = [NSUserDefaults standardUserDefaults];
        NSOpenPanel *panel = [NSOpenPanel openPanel];
        [panel setCanChooseDirectories:YES];
        [panel setCanChooseFiles:YES];
        [panel setAllowsMultipleSelection:NO];
        [panel beginSheetForDirectory:[defs objectForKey:LastBrowseDirectory]
            file:nil
            modalForWindow:[self window]
            modalDelegate:self
            didEndSelector:@selector(openPanelDidEnd:returnCode:contextInfo:)
            contextInfo:NULL];
    }

    -(void)openPanelDidEnd:(NSOpenPanel *)openPanel returnCode:(int)code
        contextInfo:(void *)contextInfo {
        if ( code == NSOKButton ) {
            NSUserDefaults *defs = [NSUserDefaults standardUserDefaults];
            NSString *path = [[openPanel filenames] objectAtIndex:0];
            [defs setObject:path forKey:LastBrowseDirectory];
            [defs setObject:path forKey:PathToBeArchived];
        }
    }

    - (IBAction)toggleArchiving:(id)sender {
        NSUserDefaults *defs = [NSUserDefaults standardUserDefaults];
        if ( [[defs objectForKey:ArchivingState] intValue] == NSOnState ) {
            // Perform first archive
            [self runArchiveScript];

            // Start timer for future runs
            int seconds = [[defs objectForKey:ArchivingFrequencyTag] intValue];
            timer = [NSTimer scheduledTimerWithTimeInterval:seconds
                target:self
                selector:@selector(runArchiveScript)
                userInfo:nil
                repeats:YES];
        }
        else {
            [timer invalidate];
            timer = nil;
```

```
        }
    }

-(void)runArchiveScript {
    NSLog(@"Running archive script");
}

@end
```

12. Save your changes in Interface Builder and build and run the application in Xcode. Test the Browse button to make sure that the path in the NSTextField updates appropriately when you select a file in the Open panel. Click the Turn Archiving On button a few times and monitor the log messages in the Run Log.

How It Works

As Cocoa applications go, this first version of Crumbs is relatively simple. It uses the shared NSUser Defaults to store data, which is an easy way to have data persistence without having to archive the data to file yourself, or write a multiple document application. Most of the controls are bound to the shared NSUserDefaultsController, which updates the shared NSUserDefaults. The CrumbsController registers default values for each of the keys in its initialize class method, and the rest of the class accesses the stored data via the NSUserDefaults instance returned by standardUserDefaults. The keys used are defined at the top of CrumbsController.m as static NSString variables.

The only complication in Crumbs revolves around NSTimer, which is a class that you may not be familiar with. NSTimer can be used to run a method at some later time, or run it at regular time intervals. When archiving is turned on, the CrumbsController class uses an NSTimer to regularly run the archiving script.

When the toggleArchiving: action is invoked, which occurs whenever the Turn Archiving On button is pressed, an if statement is used to check the user default corresponding to the key ArchivingState. This state corresponds to the state of the Turn Archiving On button: If it has the value NSOnState, indicating that archiving is turned on, a new timer is created with the convenience constructor scheduledTimer WithTimeInterval:target:selector:userInfo:. This NSTimer class method creates a new instance, adds it to the default NSRunLoop, and sets it to fire regularly at the time interval passed.

When the NSTimer fires, it calls the selector passed when it was initialized. In Crumbs, this is the run ArchivingScript method, which at this point only prints a message, but in the next version will run the archiving script. The time interval of the NSTimer is set using the value corresponding to the Archiving FrequencyTag user default, which is bound to the Frequency popup button. By judiciously choosing the tag to correspond to the number of seconds in the interval (for example, Hourly corresponds to a tag of 3600), the tag can be used directly to construct the NSTimer. If you didn't do this, you would need to use an if branch or similar construction to convert from the menu item titles to the time interval in seconds.

When the timer is no longer needed, such as when the toggle button is pressed in the Turn Archiving Off state, it is invalidated by calling the invalidate method. You do not need to release the NSTimer, just as you did not need to retain it earlier. The NSTimer is retained by the NSRunLoop, and when you invalidate it, it stops firing and is automatically released.

With the user interface now complete, the next Try It Out shows you how to introduce the archiving script and finish off the Crumbs application.

1. Open the Crumbs project in Xcode. Open the `CrumbsController.h` file in the editor and make the changes highlighted in the following code:

```
#import <Cocoa/Cocoa.h>

@interface CrumbsController : NSWindowController {
    NSTimer *timer;
    NSTask *task;
}
- (IBAction)browseForPathToArchive:(id)sender;
- (IBAction)toggleArchiving:(id)sender;

-(void)runArchiveScript;
-(void)taskDidTerminate:(NSNotification *)notif;

-(NSTask *)task;
-(void)setTask:(NSTask *)task;
@end
```

2. Open the `CrumbsController.m` file in the Xcode editor. Update the `init` and `dealloc` methods of the class as follows:

```
-(id)init {
    if ( self = [super init] ) {
        // Register for NSTask termination notifications
        [[NSNotificationCenter defaultCenter] addObserver:self
            selector:@selector(taskDidTerminate:)
            name:NSTaskDidTerminateNotification
            object:nil];
        [self setTask:nil];
        timer = nil;
    }
    return self;
}

-(void)dealloc {
    [[NSNotificationCenter defaultCenter] removeObserver:self];
    [task release];
    [timer invalidate];
    [super dealloc];
}
```

3. Add the following accessor method implementations to the `CrumbsController` class:

```
-(NSTask *)task {
    return task;
}

-(void)setTask:(NSTask *)newTask {
    [task autorelease];
    task = [newTask retain];
}
```

4. Modify the implementation of the runArchiveScript and add the method
   taskDidTerminate:, as shown here:

```
-(void)runArchiveScript {
    NSBundle *bundle = [NSBundle bundleForClass:[CrumbsController class]];
    NSString *pathToScript = [bundle pathForResource:@"archive" ofType:@"sh"];
    NSTask *t = [[[NSTask alloc] init] autorelease];
    NSPipe *p = [NSPipe pipe];
    [t setLaunchPath:pathToScript];
    [t setStandardOutput:p];
    [self setTask:t];

    // Set environment variables
    NSUserDefaults *defs = [NSUserDefaults standardUserDefaults];
    NSString *filePath = [defs objectForKey:PathToBeArchived];
    NSString *fileName = [filePath lastPathComponent];
    NSString *maxFiles = [[defs objectForKey:MaximumArchivedFilesTag] stringValue];
    NSDictionary *envDict = [NSDictionary dictionaryWithObjectsAndKeys:
        fileName,    @"BASE_ARCHIVE_NAME",
        filePath,    @"PATH_TO_BE_ARCHIVED",
        maxFiles,    @"MAX_ARCHIVED_FILES",
        nil];
    [t setEnvironment:envDict];

    [t launch];
}
```

```
-(void)taskDidTerminate:(NSNotification *)notif {
    NSTask *t = [notif object];
    int status = [t terminationStatus];
    if ( status != 0 ) {
        NSFileHandle *outFileHandle = [[t standardOutput] fileHandleForReading];
        NSData *stringData = [outFileHandle readDataToEndOfFile];
        NSString *failureReason =
            [[[NSString alloc] initWithData:stringData
                encoding:NSUTF8StringEncoding] autorelease];
        NSAlert *alert = [[[NSAlert alloc] init] autorelease];
        [alert setAlertStyle:NSWarningAlertStyle];
        [alert addButtonWithTitle:@"OK"];
        [alert setMessageText:@"Archiving failed."];
        [alert setInformativeText:failureReason];
        [alert beginSheetModalForWindow:[self window]
            modalDelegate:nil didEndSelector:NULL contextInfo:NULL];
    }
}
```

5. Select the Resources group in the Groups & Files panel and choose File ➪ New File. In the New
   File panel, choose Shell Script and click Next. Enter archive.sh as the name of the file and
   click the Finish button.

6. Add the following content to the new archive.sh file:

```
#!/bin/sh

# Functions for error checking and reporting
StopWithError() {
    echo $1
```

```
        exit 1
}

CheckForError() {
    if [ $? -ne 0 ]; then
        StopWithError "$1"
    fi
}

# Setup the Crumbs archive directory
CRUMBS_ARCHIVE_DIR=~/Documents/Crumbs\ Archives
if [ -e "$CRUMBS_ARCHIVE_DIR" ]; then
    # Path exists already, so check that it is a directory
    if [ ! -d "$CRUMBS_ARCHIVE_DIR" ]; then
        StopWithError "A file occupies the path of the Crumbs archive directory."
    fi
else
    # Path doesn't exist. Create the directory
    mkdir -p "$CRUMBS_ARCHIVE_DIR"
    CheckForError "An error occurred while creating the Crumbs archive directory."
fi

# Check that the path to be archived exists
if [ ! -e "$PATH_TO_BE_ARCHIVED" ]; then
    StopWithError "The file or directory to be archived does not exist."
fi

# Determine path of new archive
DATE_STRING=`date "+%y-%m-%d_%H-%M-%S"`
ARCHIVE_PATH="${CRUMBS_ARCHIVE_DIR}/${BASE_ARCHIVE_NAME}_${DATE_STRING}.zip"

# Create archive
ditto -keepParent --rsrc -c -k "$PATH_TO_BE_ARCHIVED" "$ARCHIVE_PATH"
CheckForError "Could not create archive of $PATH_TO_BE_ARCHIVED at $ARCHIVE_PATH."

# Remove old archives
# First change to the archive directory
cd "$CRUMBS_ARCHIVE_DIR"
CheckForError "Could not change to the Crumb's archive directory."

# Determine how many files need to be removed
numFilesTotal=`ls "$BASE_ARCHIVE_NAME"*.zip | wc -l`
let numToRemove="$numFilesTotal-$MAX_ARCHIVED_FILES"

# Remove files
if [ $numToRemove -gt 0 ]; then
    ls "$BASE_ARCHIVE_NAME"*.zip | head -$numToRemove | \
        sed -e 's/^/"/' -e 's/$/"/' | xargs rm
    CheckForError "Error occurred while removing old archive files."
fi
```

7. Build and run the application. Enter a path to archive and click the Turn Archiving On button. Look in your `Documents` directory to see if a new directory has been created called `Crumbs Archives`. Check that there is a zip file there that contains an archive of the path you entered.

Test the application to see if it archives at regular intervals, and that it discards old archives once the maximum is reached. (You may find it useful to reduce the time interval to test these things. You can also generate new archives by repeatedly clicking the Turn Archiving On button.)

The ditto *command does not work very well with symbolic links, so make sure that when you test Crumbs out, you use a path that does not include any symbolic links.*

How It Works

The most interesting changes in this revision of Crumbs occur in the runArchivingScript method. It begins by using NSBundle to locate the archive.sh script:

```
NSBundle *bundle = [NSBundle bundleForClass:[CrumbsController class]];
NSString *pathToScript = [bundle pathForResource:@"archive" ofType:@"sh"];
```

The method bundleForClass: is called to get the NSBundle, with the CrumbsController class passed as the only argument. The bundle is then queried for the path of a file called archive, with the extension sh, using the pathForResource:ofType: method.

An NSTask is then created with the init initializer, along with an NSPipe for the script's standard output.

```
NSTask *t = [[[NSTask alloc] init] autorelease];
NSPipe *p = [NSPipe pipe];
[t setLaunchPath:pathToScript];
[t setStandardOutput:p];
[self setTask:t];
```

The standard input is not used in Crumbs, but the standard output is utilized to pass error messages back to the Cocoa program when things go wrong. Various aspects of the NSTask are set, including the launch path, which was retrieved from the NSBundle, and the standard output pipe. The NSTask is stored as a CrumbsController instance variable using the setTask: accessor method.

Rather than passing variables to the script via the argument list, environment variables have been used in this Crumbs application:

```
// Set environment variables
NSUserDefaults *defs = [NSUserDefaults standardUserDefaults];
NSString *filePath = [defs objectForKey:PathToBeArchived];
NSString *fileName = [filePath lastPathComponent];
NSString *maxFiles = [[defs objectForKey:MaximumArchivedFilesTag] stringValue];
NSDictionary *envDict = [NSDictionary dictionaryWithObjectsAndKeys:
    fileName,   @"BASE_ARCHIVE_NAME",
    filePath,   @"PATH_TO_BE_ARCHIVED",
    maxFiles,   @"MAX_ARCHIVED_FILES",
    nil];
[t setEnvironment:envDict];
```

The setEnvironment: method allows you to set the environment variables of an NSTask with the keys and values of an NSDictionary. When you use the setEnviroment: method, the NSTask does not inherit any environment variables from the Cocoa program, so you should keep that in mind.

In the preceding code, some of the environment variables are set with values taken from the user defaults, such as the path of the file to be archived. The BASE_ARCHIVE_NAME environment variable is used by the archive.sh script to come up with a name for new archives. Here it is set to the last component of the path, using the NSString method lastPathComponent. The last component of a path is the name of the file or directory being archived.

The runArchiveScript finishes by launching the NSTask, which you will recall runs asynchronously. The runArchiveScript returns before the script has completed, so the user interface should still be responsive if a large file or directory is being archived. The user will be able to update the controls and turn off future archiving, even if the script is still running.

Given that the script is running asynchronously, how does the CrumbsController know when it has exited? If errors arise in the script, the program must know when the script has terminated, so that it can retrieve the error message and display it for the user. The NSTaskDidTerminateNotification notification is used for this purpose. It is posted by the NSTask when the subprocess terminates, for whatever reason. The CrumbsController registers for this notification in the init method, and the method taskDidTerminate: is invoked when the script exits.

The taskDidTerminate: method gets the NSTask instance from the NSNotification, and calls the terminationStatus method to establish if an error occurred:

```
- (void)taskDidTerminate:(NSNotification *)notif {
    NSTask *t = [notif object];
    int status = [t terminationStatus];
    if ( status != 0 ) {
```

If the exit status of the script is non-zero, the error message is read from the script's standard output:

```
NSFileHandle *outFileHandle = [[t standardOutput] fileHandleForReading];
NSData *stringData = [outFileHandle readDataToEndOfFile];
NSString *failureReason =
    [[[NSString alloc] initWithData:stringData
        encoding:NSUTF8StringEncoding] autorelease];
```

An NSAlert is generated from the error message, and displayed as a sheet to the user:

```
NSAlert *alert = [[[NSAlert alloc] init] autorelease];
[alert setAlertStyle:NSWarningAlertStyle];
[alert addButtonWithTitle:@"OK"];
[alert setMessageText:@"Archiving failed."];
[alert setInformativeText:failureReason];
[alert beginSheetModalForWindow:[self window]
    modalDelegate:nil didEndSelector:NULL contextInfo:NULL];
```

When you use NSTask to run a subprocess asynchronously, you often need to set up a method like taskDidTerminate: that is invoked when the NSTaskDidTerminateNotification is posted. Perhaps you need to handle error conditions, or perhaps you only need to notify the user that the subprocess has finished. Whichever it is, this notification can be very useful.

The only thing left to consider is the archive.sh script itself. It begins by defining two functions, which are used for error handling:

```
# Functions for error checking and reporting
StopWithError() {
```

```
        echo $1
        exit 1
}

CheckForError() {
    if [ $? -ne 0 ]; then
        StopWithError "$1"
    fi
}
```

StopWithError writes an error message to standard output, and then exits the program with a status of 1. CheckForError checks the exit status of the last command to be executed, which is stored in the shell variable $?, calling StopWithError if it is not equal to zero. It also takes an error message as an argument, and passes this along to StopWithError if an error has occurred.

The next section of the script sets up a directory to store the Crumbs archives in. The path of this directory is set to Crumbs Archives in the user's Documents directory:

```
# Setup the Crumbs archive directory
CRUMBS_ARCHIVE_DIR=~/Documents/Crumbs\ Archives
if [ -e "$CRUMBS_ARCHIVE_DIR" ]; then
    # Path exists already, so check that it is a directory
    if [ ! -d "$CRUMBS_ARCHIVE_DIR" ]; then
        StopWithError "A file occupies the path of the Crumbs archive directory."
    fi
else
    # Path doesn't exist. Create the directory
    mkdir -p "$CRUMBS_ARCHIVE_DIR"
    CheckForError "An error occurred while creating the Crumbs archive directory."
fi
```

The script tests if a file or directory already exists at the path. If so, it checks to make sure that it is a directory, and not a file. If it is a file, StopWithError is called. If nothing exists at the path, mkdir is used to create a directory there, and CheckForError tests to make sure that the command succeeded.

Next, a test is performed to determine whether the path to be archived exists, and then a path is constructed for the archive file:

```
# Check that the path to be archived exists
if [ ! -e "$PATH_TO_BE_ARCHIVED" ]; then
    StopWithError "The file or directory to be archived does not exist."
fi

# Determine path of new archive
DATE_STRING=`date "+%y-%m-%d_%H-%M-%S"`
ARCHIVE_PATH="${CRUMBS_ARCHIVE_DIR}/${BASE_ARCHIVE_NAME}_${DATE_STRING}.zip"
```

The first half of the archive filename is the name of the file or directory being archived, which is passed to the script in the environment variable BASE_ARCHIVE_NAME. The second half is a string representing the date, which is created on the preceding line with the date command. The format is chosen such that the year precedes the month, which precedes the day, and so forth. With this format, the oldest files appear at the beginning of an alphabetically ordered list, which will become important further on.

The archive itself is created with the `ditto` command, passing the `--rsrc`, `-c`, and `-k` options:

```
# Create archive
ditto --keepParent --rsrc -c -k "$PATH_TO_BE_ARCHIVED" "$ARCHIVE_PATH"
CheckForError "Could not create archive of $PATH_TO_BE_ARCHIVED at $ARCHIVE_PATH."
```

The `ditto` command is useful for copying files and directories, as well as creating compressed archives. The reason it is preferred here to other options, like `gzip` or `tar`, is that `ditto` can preserve file resource forks on versions of Mac OS X prior to 10.4. Resource forks are a type of metadata that originated in the old days of Mac OS. Most archiving commands effectively remove the resource forks on older versions of the operating system. Some programs on Mac OS X still use them, so it is a good idea to preserve them where possible.

The `--rsrc` option indicates that `ditto` should preserve resource forks, and the `-c` option causes it to create an archive, rather than copying the file or directory given. The `-k` option makes `ditto` use the zip format, which is compatible with Windows, and is what Finder generates when you use it to archive a directory or file. The `--keepParent` option tells `ditto` that if it is archiving a directory, it should enter the directory itself in the archive, not just its contents. The last two arguments are the file or directory to be archived, and the path to the new archive.

The `-rsrc` option is not strictly necessary on Mac OS X 10.4 and later because it is the default. On earlier versions of Mac OS X, it is not the default; so including it in the command is a good idea.

The script finishes by removing old archive files. In many ways this is the trickiest part of the whole exercise. The `cd` command is used first to change to the archive directory:

```
# Remove old archives
# First change to the archive directory
cd "$CRUMBS_ARCHIVE_DIR"
CheckForError "Could not change to the Crumb's archive directory."
```

Next, the total number of archive files corresponding to the `BASE_ARCHIVE_NAME` environment variable is established:

```
# Determine how many files need to be removed
numFilesTotal=`ls "$BASE_ARCHIVE_NAME"*.zip | wc -l`
let numToRemove="$numFilesTotal-$MAX_ARCHIVED_FILES"
```

The `ls` command lists the archive files, with the output piped to the `wc` command. `wc` counts the number of lines, words, and characters in standard input; with the `-l` option, only the number of lines is output, which is equivalent to the number of files. The next line uses `let` to subtract the maximum number of archive files from the total number. The maximum number is taken from the `MAX_ARCHIVED_FILES` environment variable, which is set by the `NSTask`.

If the number of files to be removed is greater than zero, a command is issued to remove them:

```
# Remove files
if [ $numToRemove -gt 0 ]; then
    ls "$BASE_ARCHIVE_NAME"*.zip | head -$numToRemove | \
        sed -e 's/^/"/' -e 's/$/"/' | xargs rm
    CheckForError "Error occurred while removing old archive files."
fi
```

The command again lists the files with `ls`, and pipes the output to the `head` command, which writes the first `$numToRemove` file paths to standard output, and ignores the rest. Because `ls` writes the files in alphabetical order, and the naming scheme was chosen so that the oldest files came first, the output of `head` will include the paths of the files that should be deleted.

To avoid filenames with spaces being interpreted as multiple files, each line output by `head` is embedded in quotation marks, using `sed`. The first `-e` option to `sed` causes the start of line character (^) to be replaced with a quotation mark. The second option results in the end of line character ($) also being replaced with a quotation. The quoted paths are passed via `xargs` to `rm`, and the files are deleted.

Summary

This chapter has introduced you to ways of running external programs and scripts from a Cocoa application. You learned the following:

❏ That you can use the C functions `system` and `popen` to run commands and short scripts from inside C and Objective-C programs

❏ That you can communicate with subprocesses started with `system` via environment variables and temporary files, and that subprocesses started in this manner share the standard input and output streams of the parent process

❏ The difference between synchronous and asynchronous functions, and that `system` is a synchronous function and `popen` is asynchronous

❏ That the Cocoa class `NSTask` is more powerful than `system` or `popen`, allowing you to pass arguments to a subprocess, set its environment separately to the parent process, and set its standard input and output streams

❏ That `NSTask` runs asynchronously, and that the notification `NSTaskDidTerminate Notification` is posted whenever a subprocess exits

❏ About the class `NSPipe`, and that you can use it to avoid temporary files when passing data to, and retrieving data from, a subprocess started with `NSTask`

The exercise that follows tests your understanding of the material covered in this chapter. You can find the solution in Appendix A.

Exercise

1. Update the Searcher application so that it makes use of the Cocoa class `NSTask`, instead of the C function `system`. Make sure the Cocoa application's user interface remains responsive if the `find` command must search through many files. (*Hint:* The script should be allowed to run in the background. Do not call a blocking function, such as `waitUntilExit`.)

Exercise Answers

Chapter 1

Exercise 1 solution

The first two apropos commands return far too much information to be useful. The third command, apropos "copy file" returns a reasonable amount of information:

```
Macintosh:~ sample$ apropos "copy file"
CpMac(1)                - copy files preserving metadata and forks
File::Copy(3pm)         - Copy files or filehandles
cp(1)                   - copy files
cpio(1)                 - copy file archives in and out
ditto(8)                - copy files and directories to a destination
directory
```

From that result, you might surmise that CpMac, cp, or ditto would be an appropriate tool for copying files. Of course, the manual entry for each command provides more helpful information.

Exercise 2 solution

The command man -k "copy file" is equivalent to apropos "copy file" and yields the same results as Exercise 1.

Chapter 2

Exercise 1 solution

Use the following steps to collect the sample:

1. Launch /Developer/Applications/Performance Tools/Sampler. The program starts but no windows appear on-screen yet.

2. Choose File ➪ New. A dialog appears allowing you to specify the program you want to sample.

3. Click the Set button next to the Executable text field. This brings up a standard open panel.

4. Select /Applications/Stickies in the Open panel and click the Open button. The Executable text field will be filled with the application's path.

5. Click OK to dismiss the dialog. A Sampler window like the one shown in Figure A-1 appears. Notice the three tabs: Browser, Outline, and Trace. The Browser tab, containing empty Browser and Call Stack views, is selected.

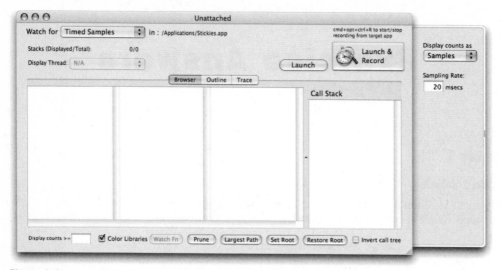

Figure A-1

6. Click the Launch & Record button in the Sampler window's upper-right corner. The Stickies application appears in the Dock, and its windows appear behind the Sampler application.

7. Let Stickies run for a few seconds and click the Stop Recording button. Sampler's Browser and Call Stack views change to display Stickies' call stack information.

The browser area shows a tree containing all the frames recorded by Sampler. The Call Stack table displays the most commonly occurring backtrace that includes the frame selected in the browser. When you first collect sample data, the first frame in the trace is selected and the Call Stack displays the most common backtrace. If you let Stickies run for a few seconds without using it, that backtrace should end with a function called mach_msg_trap, as shown in Figure A-2.

Figure A-2

This means Stickies was just waiting for user input from the window server. Because programs waiting for user input (or sitting in `mach_msg_trap` in general) use no CPU time, this is normally a good thing.

Exercise 2 solution

a. The default output from GetFileInfo lists all file or directories attributes. Note the v in the attributes string represents the invisible attribute. When capitalized, it means the file or directory is invisible.

```
Macintosh:~ sample$ /Developer/Tools/GetFileInfo fileOrFolder
directory: "fileOrFolder"
attributes: aVbstclinmed
created: 08/26/2004 23:47:53
modified: 08/26/2004 23:47:53
Macintosh:~ sample$
```

You can also use the -av flag to test the invisible attribute directly, as shown in the following code. Note that there is no space between the -a and the v. When run with this option, `GetFile Info` prints 1 if the directory is invisible and 0 if it's not.

```
Macintosh:~ sample$ /Developer/Tools/GetFileInfo -av fileOrFolder
1
Macintosh:~ sample$
```

b. According to SetFile's man page, the following command marks a program invisible:

```
/Developer/Tools/SetFile -a V fileOrFolder
```

Unlike with `GetFileInfo`, there is a space between the -a and the V.

This command works as intended on Mac OS X 10.4 "Tiger" systems. However, there is a bug in some versions of Mac OS X 10.3 Panther that causes this command to fail. `SetFile` doesn't properly interpret the string following the -a flag. On those systems, you can work around the problem using -a vV to set the invisible attribute as shown here:

```
/Developer/Tools/SetFile -a vV fileOrFolder
```

And the -a vv argument clears the invisible attribute:

```
/Developer/Tools/SetFile -a vv fileOrFolder
```

   c.   Here is the complete solution:

      1. Launch /Applications/Utilities/Terminal. Note you start out in your home directory.

```
Last login: Sat May 15 23:28:46 on ttyp1
Welcome to Darwin!
Macintosh:~ sample $
```

      2. Create the Secrets directory using the mkdir command.

```
Macintosh:~ sample $ mkdir Secrets
Macintosh:~ sample $
```

      3. Use the SetFile command as shown to mark the program invisible.

```
Macintosh:~ sample $ /Developer/Tools/SetFile -a V Secrets
Macintosh:~ sample $
```

      4. Make sure the invisible bit has been set properly using GetFileInfo.

```
Macintosh:~ sample $ /Developer/Tools/GetFileInfo -av Secrets
1
Macintosh:~ sample $
```

If GetFileInfo returns 1, the file has been marked invisible. However, if GetFileInfo returns 0, you are running a version of Mac OS X with a bad SetFile command. Use the workaround mentioned in part b to set the invisible bit.

```
Macintosh:~ sample $ /Developer/Tools/GetFileInfo -av Secrets
0
Macintosh:~ sample $ /Developer/Tools/SetFile -a vV Secrets
Macintosh:~ sample $ /Developer/Tools/GetFileInfo -av Secrets
1
Macintosh:~ sample $
```

      5. Note the file is still visible from Terminal. That's because Terminal doesn't honor these settings.

```
Macintosh:~ sample$ ls -l
total 0
drwx------    4 sample   sample   136 15 Aug 20:49 Desktop
drwxrwxrwx   12 sample   sample   408 15 Aug 20:49 Documents
drwx------   29 sample   sample   986 15 Jul 01:16 Library
drwx------    3 sample   sample   102 16 May 01:20 Movies
drwx------    6 sample   sample   204  2 Jun 22:50 Music
drwx------    5 sample   sample   170 15 Aug 21:20 Pictures
drwxr-xr-x    7 sample   sample   238  2 Jun 22:50 Public
drwxr-xr-x    2 sample   sample    68 26 Aug 23:47 Secrets
drwxr-xr-x    5 sample   sample   170 16 May 01:20 Sites
Macintosh:~ sample $
```

6. Select Force Quit from the Apple menu. A panel containing a list of applications appears.

7. Select Finder from the list and click the Relaunch button.

8. Look in your home directory for the Secrets folder. It will not appear.

Exercise 3 solution

As you learned earlier in this chapter, you can use man -a intro to list through all the intro man pages. To get a complete list of all the sections, you could simply make note of the sections yourself as they appear in the pages.

You could also use man -k intro to list all the man pages matching the intro keyword, as shown in the following code. Although this does return the section information you're interested in, it returns information for a bunch of other man pages as well.

```
Macintosh:~ sample $ man -k intro
...
glut(3)                     - an introduction to the OpenGL Utility Toolkit
intro(1)                    - introduction to general commands (tools and utilities)
intro(2)                    - introduction to system calls and error numbers
intro(3)                    - introduction to the C libraries
intro(5)                    - introduction to file formats
intro(9)                    - introduction to system kernel interfaces
kerberos(1)                 - introduction to the Kerberos system
math(3)                     - introduction to mathematical library functions
networking(4)               - introduction to networking facilities
...
Macintosh:~ sample $
```

If you want an exact list, you can ask for a list of all the pages named intro using man -a -w intro, shown in the following. Of course -a displays all files with the specified name, and the -w flag tells man to print pages' paths rather than their content. You can then deduce the manual section from the file's directory and file extension.

```
Macintosh:~ sample $ man -a -w intro
/usr/share/man/man1/intro.1
/usr/share/man/man2/intro.2
/usr/share/man/man3/intro.3
/usr/share/man/man5/intro.5
/usr/share/man/man9/intro.9
Macintosh:~ sample $
```

Chapter 3

Exercise 1 solution

Use the proper man page requests that appear in the following table. Note that printf overlaps with a command-line function, so you must specifically request the section for C functions. The section is optional for the other man pages.

Function	Man Page
printf	"3 printf"
scanf	"scanf" or "3 scanf"
pow	"pow" or "3 pow"

Exercise 2 solution

1. Change the instances of int in Calculate.h to double. This includes

```
double calculate(const double a, const double b, const char op);
```

2. Change the instances of int in Calculate.c to double. This includes

```
double calculate(const double a, const double b, const char op)
{
    double result;
```

3. Replace the main function in main.c with the following code:

```
int main (int argc, const char * argv[])
{
    int count;
    double a, b, answer;
    char op;

    // print the prompt
    printf("Enter an expression: ");

    // get the expression
    count = scanf("%lg %c %lg", &a, &op, &b);
    if (count != 3) {
        printf("bad expression\n");
        exit(1);
    }

    // perform the computation
    answer = calculate(a, b, op);

    // print the answer
    printf("%lg %c %lg = %lg\n", a, op, b, answer);

    return 0;
}
```

Exercise 3 solution

1. Add the following include after the other includes in Calculate.c:

```
#include <math.h>
```

2. Add the following case entries to the switch statement. Here is the final switch statement:

```
            case '/':
                result = a / b;
                break;
            case '\\':
                result = (int)a / (int)b;
                break;
            case '%':
                result = (int)a % (int)b;
                break;
            case '^':
                result = pow(a, b);
                break;
```

Your `Calculate.c` file should look like the following:

```
/*
 *  Calculate.c
 *  Calculator
 *
 *  Created by Your Name on Wed Jun 16 2004.
 *  Copyright (c) 2004 __MyCompanyName__. All rights reserved.
 *
 */

#include "Calculate.h"

#include <stdio.h>
#include <stdlib.h>
#include <math.h>

double calculate(const double a, const double b, const char op)
{
    double result;

    switch (op) {
        case '+':
            result = a + b;
            break;
        case '-':
            result = a - b;
            break;
        case '*':
            result = a * b;
            break;
        case '/':
            result = a / b;
            break;
        case '\\':
            result = (int)a / (int)b;
            break;
        case '%':
            result = (int)a % (int)b;
            break;
        case '^':
            result = pow(a, b);
```

```
            break;
        default:
            printf("unknown operator: %c\n", op);
            exit(1);
    }

    return result;
}
```

Chapter 4

Exercise 1 solution

1. Change all the labels so that they are pinned to the upper-left corner. The Autosizing control should look like the one shown in Figure A-3.

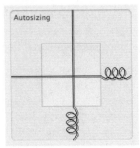

Figure A-3

2. Change all the text fields so that they are pinned to the upper edge of the window, and so that they are flexible in the horizontal direction. The Autosizing control should look like the one shown in Figure A-4.

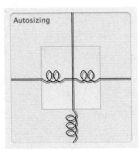

Figure A-4

3. Change the OK and Cancel buttons so that they are pinned to the lower-right corner. The Autosizing control should look like the one shown in Figure A-5.

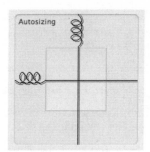

Figure A-5

4. Enable the window's close, minimize, and resize controls by checking these items in the Inspector's Attributes view.

5. Set the window's minimum size to the window's current size by clicking the appropriate Current button in the Inspector's Size view.

Exercise 2 solution

1. Create a new Cocoa ⇨ Application project. Your nib window appears, containing a menu bar and window instances. You won't need the menu bar instance; delete it if you like.

2. Drag the NSTabView object from the Containers palette and drop it in the window.

3. Use the guides to line the tab view against the upper-left corner and resize the tab view to fill the window. Hold down the Option key and move the mouse over the window to verify the tab view's position. Its edges should be 20 pixels from the window's edges, except for the top one, which should be 12 pixels.

4. Double-click the View tab and name it Advanced.

5. Double-click the Tab tab and name it Game.

6. Drag a System Font Text label from the Text palette into the tab view. A selection box should appear within the tab view, as shown in Figure A-6. This indicates you're dragging the control into the tab view itself, not simply into the window.

Figure A-6

7.   Use the guides to position the label a comfortable distance from the upper-left edge of the tab view. Hold down the Option key and move the mouse over the tab view to verify the label's position. The top and left edges should be 20 pixels from the tab view edges.

8.   Change the label to read `Player Name:` and resize the label to fit this new text exactly.

9.   Right-align the text using the Inspector's Attributes view.

10.   Drag a text field from the Text palette into the tab view. Position it directly to the right of the label. Use the Inspector's Size view to make the text field 200 pixels wide.

11.   Duplicate the label and text field, and move the new objects directly below the old ones. They should line up horizontally. Verify the text fields are 8 pixels apart by first selecting one text field and then pointing at the other field while holding down the Option key.

12.   Change the second label to read `Team Name:`.

13.   Click the Advanced tab to select it. The controls in the Game tab will disappear.

14.   Drag a check box from the Controls palette into the tab view. Position it in the upper-left corner of the window: 20 pixels from the left and top edges.

15.   Change the text box to read `Log in automatically`.

16.   Create two more check boxes, `Respawn Immediately` and `Unlimited Ammunition`, and position them immediately below the first check box. All three check boxes should be 20 pixels from the left edge and 8 pixels from each other.

17.   Switch back to the Game tab. Note that the contents of this tab are wider than the contents of the Advanced tab, but the contents of the Advanced tab are taller.

18.   Resize the tab view horizontally to fit the Game tab's contents. There should be 20 pixels between the text fields' right edges and the tab view. You may have trouble finding the tab view's resize controls if you're editing its contents; in this case the tab view will use a special bounding box without resize controls. You can bring the tab view's bounding box back by pressing the Escape key.

19.   Switch to the Advanced tab and resize the tab view vertically until its bottom edge is 20 pixels away from the third check box.

20.   Select all three check boxes, hold the Option key, and move the mouse over the tab control. The check boxes will be 20 pixels away from the top, left, and bottom edges collectively. If you have trouble selecting the check boxes, try clicking one of the boxes and using Command-A to select all.

21.   While holding down the Option key, use the arrow keys to center the check boxes in the tab view. You can nudge 10 pixels at a time by also holding down the Shift key when pressing an arrow key.

22.   Switch back to the Game tab.

23.   Select all the controls, hold the Option key, and center the controls in the tab view.

24.   Resize the window horizontally so there are only 20 pixels between the tab view and the window edge. Leave plenty of space below the tab view for adding buttons.

25.   Drag a push button from the Controls palette and use the guides to position it below and to the right of the tab view. It will be 12 pixels from the lower edge of the tab view and 20 pixels from the window's edge.

26.   Rename this button `OK` and use the Inspector's Attributes view to set Return as its key equivalent.

27. Drag a second push button from the Controls palette and use the guides to position it about 12 pixels away from the OK button.

28. Rename this button `Cancel` and set Escape as its key equivalent.

29. Resize the window vertically so there are only 20 pixels between the OK and Cancel buttons and the window's edge.

30. Test your handiwork by choosing File ⇨ Test Interface.

Chapter 5

Exercise 1 solution

a. TextEdit's `Info.plist` file describes seven different document types:

- ❏ Rich Text Format documents (called `NSRTFPboardType`)
- ❏ Microsoft Word Documents
- ❏ Rich Text Format with Attachments (called `NSRTFDPboardType`)
- ❏ Plain Text Documents (called `NSStringPboardType`)
- ❏ Apple SimpleText Documents
- ❏ HTML Documents
- ❏ Apple Web archives

b. Preview's bundle signature is `prvw`.

c. Terminal's bundle identifier is `com.apple.Terminal`.

d. The exact contents of a `nib` file bundle will depend on what the nib file represents. Files commonly found in nibs include

- ❏ `classes.nib`
- ❏ `info.nib`
- ❏ `keyedobjects.nib`
- ❏ `objects.nib`

Some Interface Builder files might even include images and other resources embedded within the `nib` bundle, but such nibs should be very rare.

e. The current bundle version of the AppKit framework has been `C` throughout the Mac OS X releases to date. Note the version is a single English letter.

f. The current bundle version of the JavaVM framework on your system depends on what you have installed. For example, if you have installed Java 1.4.2, the current version of JavaVM will be `1.4.2`. Unlike AppKit, JavaVM uses traditional version numbers instead of individual English letters.

Exercise 2 solution.

a. defaults domains

b. `defaults -currentHost domains`

c. `defaults read com.apple.Terminal`

Recall that preferences are stored using an application's CFBundleIdentifier. You learned Terminal's bundle identifier in the preceding exercise (1c).

d. `defaults -currentHost read com.apple.HIToolbox`

HIToolbox is a framework, not an application. Even so, it has a CFBundleIdentifier and a preference domain. HIToolbox stores its preferences on a per-machine basis; you should have seen its preference domain go by in exercise 2b.

e. `defaults write MyExamplePref Autosave 1`

Unlike other defaults commands, defaults write command creates a preference file if it doesn't exist.

f. `defaults write MyExamplePref colors -array red orange yellow`

The -array flag tells defaults the following values are actually members of an array. Other flags exist as detailed in the defaults man page.

g. `defaults delete MyExamplePref Autosave`

Chapter 6

Exercise 1 solution

1. Open the Grepper project in Xcode, and make the highlighted changes in the following code to the main.c file:

```
#include <stdio.h>
#include <string.h>

// Global constants
const int MAX_STRING_LENGTH = 256;

// Main function
int main (int argc, const char * argv[]) {

    // Get string to search for, which is the last argument
    const char *searchString = argv[argc-1];

    // Loop over files
    unsigned int fileIndex;
    for ( fileIndex = 1; fileIndex < argc-1; ++fileIndex ) {
        // Get input file path from standard input
        const char *inpPath = argv[fileIndex];

        // Open file
        FILE *inpFile;
```

```
        inpFile = fopen(inpPath, "r");

        // Loop over lines in the input file, until there
        // are none left
        char line[MAX_STRING_LENGTH];
        int lineCount = 0;
        while ( fgets(line, MAX_STRING_LENGTH-1, inpFile) ) {
            ++lineCount;
            if ( strstr(line, searchString) ) {
                printf("In file %s, line %d:\t%s", inpPath, lineCount, line);
            }
        }

        // Close files
        fclose(inpFile);

    } // End loop over files

    return 0;
}
```

2. Select the Grepper executable in the Executables group of the Groups & Files panel on the left of
    the project window. Choose Get Info from the File menu and select the Arguments tab in the Info
    window that appears. Using the + button, add arguments to the Arguments table at the top. Add
    the paths of two or more text files first, and a string to search for as the last argument.

3. Compile and run the program by clicking the Build and Go toolbar item in the main project
    window.

4. Verify from the results that appear in the Run Log window that all the files entered have been
    searched; also note that line numbers now appear for each line printed.

Exercise 2 solution

1. Open the MyAddressBook project in Xcode and select the `AddressBook.h` file in Source group
    of the Groups & Files panel. In the editor, add the following function signature:

```
int RemovePerson( AddressBook *addressBook, char *name );
```

2. Open the `AddressBook.c` file in the editor and add the following function:

```
int RemovePerson( AddressBook *addressBook, char *name ) {
    int n = addressBook->numPersons;

    // Search for person with the name passed
    int i;
    for ( i = 0; i < n; ++i ) {
        Person *person = addressBook->persons[i];
        if ( strcmp( person->name, name ) == 0 ) {
            // Found Person, so delete
            DeallocPerson(person);

            // Reduce number of persons in address book.
            // Also move the last person to the fill the hole formed
            // in the persons array by the removal.
            addressBook->numPersons = n - 1;
```

```
            addressBook->persons[i] = addressBook->persons[n-1];

            return 1; // succeeded
        }
    }

    return 0; // failed
}
```

3. In the `Controller.h` file, add the following function signature:

```
void ProcessDeletePersonRequest(Controller *controller);
```

4. In the `Controller.c` file, add the following function definition:

```
void ProcessDeletePersonRequest(Controller *controller) {
    char name[256];
    printf("You chose to delete an address.\n");
    printf("Please enter the name of the person to delete: ");
    gets(name);

    int personWasRemoved = RemovePerson( controller->addressBook, name );
    if ( personWasRemoved )
        printf("%s was deleted from the address book.\n", name);
    else
        printf("The address of %s could not be found in the address book.\n", name
);
}
```

5. Modify the `ProcessUserChoice` function in `Controller.c` as indicated by the highlights in the following code:

```
int ProcessUserChoice(Controller *controller, char choice) {
    int shouldStop = 0;
    switch (choice) {
        case 'a':
            ProcessNewPersonRequest(controller);
            break;
        case 'f':
            ProcessFindPersonRequest(controller);
            break;
        case 'd':
            ProcessDeletePersonRequest(controller);
            break;
        case 's':
            ProcessSaveRequest(controller);
            break;
        case 'q':
            ProcessSaveRequest(controller);
            shouldStop = 1;
            break;
        default:
            printf("You entered an invalid choice. Try again.\n");
    }
    return shouldStop;
}
```

6. Modify the `PrintUserOptions` function similarly, according to the highlights in this code:

```
void PrintUserOptions(Controller *controller) {
    printf("\nYou can either\n"
            "a) Add an address\n"
            "f) Find an address\n"
            "d) Delete an address, or\n"
            "s) Save your addresses\n"
            "q) Save and Quit\n");
    printf("Please enter your choice (a, f, s, d, or q): ");
}
```

7. Compile and run the program by clicking Build and Go in the toolbar of the main project window. Try adding a number of addresses, and then deleting some. Make sure you can still find addresses that haven't been deleted in the address book afterward.

Something to note about this solution is that there were several places in the existing code that needed to be updated. The changes made were not localized to a small part of the code, but were spread throughout. Having to update many different parts of a program when you need to make changes can introduce bugs and make a program difficult to learn for someone not familiar with it. Object-oriented programming (OOP), which you learn about in Chapter 7, endeavors to localize changes, reducing the impact of changes on existing code.

Chapter 7

Exercise 1 solution

After you have created the Discus project, replace the contents of the `Discus.m` file with the following code:

```
#import <Foundation/Foundation.h>

int main (int argc, const char * argv[]) {
    NSAutoreleasePool * pool = [[NSAutoreleasePool alloc] init];

    // Store data in an array of dictionaries
    NSArray *discs =
        [NSArray arrayWithObjects:
            [NSDictionary dictionaryWithObjectsAndKeys:
                @"CD",                     @"Type",
                [NSNumber numberWithInt:3], @"LengthInMinutes",
                @"Lounge Room",            @"Location",
                @"BB Bonkas",              @"Artist",
                nil],
            [NSDictionary dictionaryWithObjectsAndKeys:
                @"CD",                     @"Type",
                [NSNumber numberWithInt:4], @"LengthInMinutes",
                @"Attic",                  @"Location",
                @"CC Charmers",            @"Artist",
                nil],
            [NSDictionary dictionaryWithObjectsAndKeys:
                @"DVD",                      @"Type",
                [NSNumber numberWithInt:121], @"LengthInMinutes",
```

```
                @"Attic",                    @"Location",
                @"TJ Slickflick",            @"Lead Actor",
                @"LJ Slickflick",            @"Director",
                nil],
            nil];

    // Extract a few entries, and print them in the console
    NSLog(@"The third entry in the library is a %@",
        [[discs objectAtIndex:2] objectForKey:@"Type"]);
    NSLog(@"The director is %@",
        [[discs objectAtIndex:2] objectForKey:@"Director"]);

    // Write the array to file
    NSString *path =
        [NSHomeDirectory() stringByAppendingPathComponent:@"Desktop/discus.plist"];
    [discs writeToFile:path atomically:YES];

    // Read the array back from the file, and write it to the console
    NSArray *newDiscs =
        [[[NSArray alloc] initWithContentsOfFile:path] autorelease];
    NSLog(@"The database contents are:\n%@", newDiscs);

    [pool release];
    return 0;
}
```

The dictionaries and arrays have been populated directly using the methods dictionaryWithObjects
AndKeys: and arrayWithObjects:. Each of these methods takes a comma-delimited list and must be
terminated with nil.

The objectAtIndex: method extracts an entry from an NSArray, and objectForKey: is used to get a
particular value out of an NSDictionary once it has been retrieved from the array. Values are written to
the console with NSLog; the %@ formatting character can be used to format any object, including the
NSStrings and NSNumbers in the example.

The NSString class has a number of methods for working with paths, and stringByAppendingPath
Component: has been used in this example. The NSHomeDirectory function returns the path to the home
directory, and the rest of the path is supplied to the method as the string @"Desktop/discus.plist".

The writeToFile:atomically: method can be used to write Foundation classes such as NSArray,
NSDictionary, and NSString to file in property list format. The property list format is a structured
XML format, as you would see if you opened the file in a text editor. Using this method, along with
initWithContentsOfFile:, makes reading and writing structured data a breeze with Cocoa.

Exercise 2 solution

1. Open the MyAddressBook Objective-C project in Xcode, and select the AddressBook.h file in
    the Source group of the Groups & Files panel. In the editor, add the following method declara-
    tion to the class interface block:

```
-(Person *)removePersonForName:(NSString *)name;
```

2. In the file `AddressBook.m`, add the following method definition to the implementation block of `AddressBook`:

```
-(Person *)removePersonForName:(NSString *)name {
    id person = [[personForNameDict objectForKey:name] retain];
    [personForNameDict removeObjectForKey:name];
    return [person autorelease];
}
```

3. In the `Commands.h` file, add the following interface block:

```
@interface RemovePersonCommand : Command
{
}
@end
```

4. Open the `Commands.m` file in the editor and add the implementation of the `RemovePerson Command` class, as follows:

```
@implementation RemovePersonCommand

+(NSString *)commandIdentifier {
    return @"d";
}

+(NSString *)commandDescription {
    return @"Delete an address";
}

+(NSArray *)requiredInfoIdentifiers {
    return [NSArray arrayWithObject:@"Name of person"];
}

-(NSString *)executeWithInfoDictionary:(NSDictionary *)infoDict {
    NSString *name = [infoDict objectForKey:@"Name of person"];
    Person *p = [[self addressBook] removePersonForName:name];
    return ( p == nil ? @"Address not found" :
        [NSString stringWithFormat:@"Address for %@ was removed from address book",
            name] );
}

@end
```

5. While in the `Commands.m` file, modify the `initialize` method of the `Command` class as high-lighted here:

```
+(void)initialize {
    commandClasses =
        [[NSArray arrayWithObjects:
            [NewPersonCommand class],
            [FindPersonCommand class],
            [RemovePersonCommand class],
            [SaveAddressBookCommand class],
            [QuitCommand class],
            nil] retain];
}
```

6. Compile and run the program by clicking the Build and Go toolbar item. Enter a number of addresses, and then try removing some. Also try to remove someone not in the address book. Test the program to ensure that entries that should remain in the address book are still there after you have removed other addresses.

What should strike you about the changes required in the Objective-C version of MyAddressBook is that they were reasonably isolated from existing code in the sense that very few existing methods needed to be edited. The only existing method that needed changing was the initialize method of the Command class, and the change was very minor. The changes to the program that were made involved mostly extending it with new methods and classes, rather than modifying what already existed. This reduces the risk of introducing bugs when changing a program, and usually makes it easier to understand.

The AddressBook class was modified in much the same way that the AddressBook ADT was modified in the C program of Exercise 2 from Chapter 6. A new method was introduced to remove an entry, in this case by removing it from the NSMutableDictionary personForNameDict instance variable that is used to store instances of Person in the AddressBook. Note that this method is quite a bit simpler than the corresponding C version. That is because the Objective-C version leverages powerful Foundation classes of Cocoa, such as NSMutableDictionary.

Chapter 8

Exercise 1 solution

1. In Xcode, add the following method to SlideShowWindowController.m's PrivateMethods category:

```
- (void)tableDoubleClick:(id)sender;
```

2. Set the table view's double-click action using the following line of code. You need to add this line to SlideShowWindowController's windowDidLoad method.

```
[mTableView setDoubleAction:@selector(tableDoubleClick:)];
```

Normally, double-clicking a row in a table view begins an editing session; this is a common way of changing contents in a table view. If the rows in a table view aren't editable, the table view sends a double-click action along the responder chain. NSTableView doesn't have a double-click action by default, so you must supply one if you are interested in handling double-clicks. The double-click action otherwise behaves just like an NSControl instance's action.

3. Define the following tableDoubleClick: method in SlideShowWindowController's Table View Support section.

```
- (void)tableDoubleClick:(id)sender
{
    int row = [sender clickedRow];

    if (row != -1) {
        Slide *slide = [[self document] slideAtIndex:row];
```

```
        NSString *path = [slide filePath];

        [[NSDocumentController sharedDocumentController]
openDocumentWithContentsOfFile:path display:YES];
    }
}
```

The NSDocumentController singleton class is responsible, among other things, for keeping track of the kinds of documents your application is capable of opening. You can ask the NSDocumentController to open a file at a specific path. If the application is capable of displaying the file at that path in a document, NSDocumentController creates a document for that file, and, if necessary, displays its window on-screen.

4. Save your changes to SlideShowWindowController.m.

5. Build and run Slide Master. When you double-click a row in the table view, the image file opens in its own image document.

Exercise 2 solution

1. SlideImageView must track a file's name in order to display it along with the image data. That's a simple matter of creating accessors for an mFileName instance variable and being careful to retain the objects passed into SlideImageView. SlideShowWindowController will set this information when the table view's selection changes.

In Xcode, add an mFileName instance variable and setFileName: method to SlideImage View.h as shown here:

```
@interface SlideImageView : NSImageView
{
    NSColor    *mBackgroundColor;
    NSString   *mFileName;
}

- (void)setBackgroundColor:(NSColor*)color;
- (void)setFileName:(NSString*)fileName;

@end
```

2. Release the mFileName variable in SlideImageView's dealloc method:

```
- (void)dealloc
{
    [mBackgroundColor release];
    [mFileName release];

    [super dealloc];
}
```

3. Define the setFileName: method with the following code:

```
- (void)setFileName:(NSString*)fileName
{
    if (fileName != mFileName) {
```

```
        [mFileName release];
        mFileName = [fileName retain];
    }

    [self setNeedsDisplay:YES];
}
```

4. Add code in `drawRect:` to draw the filename in the lower-right corner of the screen, as shown in the following:

```
- (void)drawRect:(NSRect)rect
{
    if (mBackgroundColor) {
        [mBackgroundColor set];
        NSRectFill(rect);
    }

    [super drawRect:rect];

    if (mFileName) {
        NSRect bounds = [self bounds];
        NSRect stringRect = NSZeroRect;

        stringRect.size = [mFileName sizeWithAttributes:nil];
        stringRect.origin.x = bounds.size.width - stringRect.size.width;

        [mFileName drawInRect:stringRect withAttributes:nil];
    }
}
```

AppKit provides additional methods on the `NSString` class to draw strings directly into views, and `SlideImageView` uses these methods to draw its filename. First, it calls `sizeWithAttributes:` to measure the visual size of the filename. Once it knows the area required to draw the string, `SlideImageView` builds a rectangle describing exactly where the string should be drawn. `SlideImageView` then draws the string to the screen using `drawInRect:withAttributes:`. `SlideImageView` uses `nil` to use the default drawing attributes for its string.

5. Open `SlideShowWindowController.m` and change `tableViewSelectionDidChange:` to set the image's filename as well as its image:

```
- (void)tableViewSelectionDidChange:(NSNotification *)aNotification
{
    int selection = [mTableView selectedRow];
    NSImage *image = nil;
    NSString *name = nil;

    if (selection != -1) {
        Slide *slide = [[self document] slideAtIndex:selection];

        image = [slide image];
        name = [[slide filePath] lastPathComponent];
```

```
        }

        [mImageView setImage:image];
        [mImageView setFileName:name];
    }
```

6. Save your changes to `SlideImageView.m` and `SlideShowWindowController.m`.

7. Build and run Slide Master. When you view an image in the slide show window, its name appears in the lower-right corner. The name is drawn in black, using a default font value. Note this filename does not appear when you view images in their own document.

Exercise 3 solution

1. In Interface Builder, create a subclass of `NSTableView` called `SlideTableView` in the `SlideShowWindow` nib file's Classes tab.

2. Create new source files for `SlideTableView` and save them to the default location within the Slide Master project.

3. Change your table view's custom class to `SlideTableView`.

4. Save the `SlideTableView` nib file.

5. In Xcode, open `SlideTableView.h` and replace its contents with the following code:

```
#import <Cocoa/Cocoa.h>

@interface SlideTableView : NSTableView
{
}
@end

@interface NSObject (SlideTableViewDelegate)
- (BOOL)tableView:(NSTableView*)tableView keyDown:(NSEvent*)event;
@end
```

6. Switch to `SlideTableView.m` and add the following method to the `SlideTableView` implementation:

```
- (void)keyDown:(NSEvent*)event
{
    id delegate = [self delegate];
    SEL selector = @selector(tableView:keyDown:);
    BOOL handled = NO;

    if (delegate && [delegate respondsToSelector:selector]) {
        handled = [delegate tableView:self keyDown:event];
    }

    if (!handled) {
        [super keyDown:event];
    }
}
```

7.   Open `SlideShowWindowController` and add the following method to the `Table View Support` section:

```
- (BOOL)tableView:(NSTableView*)tableView keyDown:(NSEvent*)event
{
    unichar ch = [[event characters] characterAtIndex:0];
    BOOL result = NO;

    if (ch == 0x7f || ch == NSDeleteFunctionKey) {
        [self keyDown:event];
        result = YES;
    }

    return result;
}
```

8.   Save your changes to the `SlideTableView` and `SlideShowWindowController` files.

9.   Build and run Slide Master. Now when the table view is selected, the Delete key deletes the selected slides. The arrow keys also continue to change the selection.

Chapter 9

Exercise 1 solution

You can solve this problem either by reusing the existing `MainEventHandler` or by creating a new event handler. The solution that follows extends `MainEventHandler`.

1.   In Xcode, replace `main.c`'s call to `InstallWindowEventHandler` with the following code:

```
// Install the window event handler
EventTypeSpec eventSpec[2] = {
    {kEventClassKeyboard, kEventRawKeyDown},
    {kEventClassCommand, kEventCommandProcess},
};
InstallWindowEventHandler(window,
                          NewEventHandlerUPP(MainEventHandler),
                          2,
                          eventSpec,
                          (void*)window,
                          NULL);
```

2.   Replace the entire `MainEventHandler` with the following code:

```
OSStatus MainEventHandler(EventHandlerCallRef handler, EventRef event, void
*userData)
{
    OSStatus result = eventNotHandledErr;

    UInt32 class = GetEventClass(event);

    if (class == kEventClassCommand) {
```

```
        HICommand command;

        // get the HICommand from the event
        GetEventParameter(event,
                          kEventParamDirectObject,
                          typeHICommand,
                          NULL,
                          sizeof(HICommand),
                          NULL,
                          &command);

        // if this is a compute event regenerate the result string
        if (command.commandID == kComputeResultCmd) {
            ComputeResult((WindowRef)userData);
            result = noErr;
        }
    }

    // if this is a keyboard event, forward the event first, and then
    // recompute the events
    else if (class == kEventClassKeyboard) {
        // forward the event
        result = CallNextEventHandler(handler, event);

        // if the event was handled correctly, compute the result
        if (result == noErr) {
            ComputeResult((WindowRef)userData);
        }
    }

    return result;
}
```

3. Save your changes to `main.c`.

4. Build and run Carbon Email Formatter. Now when you type in the text fields, the result text view will update automatically.

Exercise 2 solution

The most direct way to solve this problem is to augment the `Slide` class's `drawIntoGWorld:` method and draw the string while the `GWorldPtr` port is set. In addition, this solution factors the string drawing code into a new private method called `drawFilenameIntoCurrentPort:` to help reduce clutter.

The `TXNDrawCFStringTextBox` function draws a `CFStringRef` into a `textBox` rectangle, and returns the actual area occupied by the string in `textBox`. In order to draw a string in the lower-right corner of the port you will need to know the width of the string in advance; from this information you can compute the string's location. The easiest way to get that information is to call `TXNDrawCFStringTextBox` with the full port bounds rectangle along with an option flag that suppresses drawing. When the function returns, `textBox` will hold the string area, and you can adjust the rectangle to fit in the lower-right corner. This solution adds a small amount to the width returned by `TXNDrawCFStringTextBox` in order to overcome some rounding errors in the function.

Although the `drawIntoGWorld:` method reads the bounds for your `GWorldPtr`, it may modify the value to center the image in the port. Because the unmodified port bounds are also needed to draw the filename, this solution modifies `drawIntoGWorld:` to preserve the port bounds.

1. Open the Slide Master project in Xcode and open `Slide.m`.

2. Add the following method before the `drawIntoGWorld:` method:

```
- (OSStatus)drawFilenameIntoCurrentPort:(Rect)portBounds
{
    OSStatus err = noErr;
    Rect textBox = portBounds;
    TXNTextBoxOptionsData options = {0};

    // get the filename
    NSString *fileName = [[self filePath] lastPathComponent];

    // set the TXN options to not draw the string; this means you can use
    // TXNDrawCFStringTextBox to measure the size of our text.
    options.optionTags = kTXNDontDrawTextMask;

    // measure the text box
    err = TXNDrawCFStringTextBox((CFStringRef)fileName,
                                 &textBox,
                                 NULL,
                                 &options);

    // if all is well, move the textBox to the lower right corner of the
    // port and draw!
    if (err == noErr) {
        // adjust the text width slightly to avoid rounding error
        textBox.right += 5;

        OffsetRect(&textBox,
                   portBounds.right - (textBox.right - textBox.left),
                   portBounds.bottom - (textBox.bottom - textBox.top));

        options.optionTags = 0;

        err = TXNDrawCFStringTextBox((CFStringRef)fileName,
                                     &textBox,
                                     NULL,
                                     &options);
    }

    return err;
}
```

3. Replace the `drawIntoGWorld:` method with the following method:

```
- (OSStatus)drawIntoGWorld:(GWorldPtr)world;
{
    GWorldPtr oldWorld;
    GDHandle gdh;
    NSString *path;
```

```
FSSpec fsSpec;
GraphicsImportComponent importer = NULL;
ImageDescriptionHandle imageDesc = NULL;
OSStatus err;
Rect bounds, portBounds;

// set this GWorld to be the current QuickDraw port
GetGWorld(&oldWorld, &gdh);
SetGWorld(world, NULL);

// get the current bounds for this world.
GetPortBounds(world, &portBounds);
bounds = portBounds;

// clear the world so you're starting from a clean slate
EraseRect(&bounds);

// build a FSSpec for this image
path = [self filePath];
if (path) {
    FSRef fsRef;
    err = FSPathMakeRef([path UTF8String], &fsRef, NULL);

    if (err == noErr) {
        err = FSGetCatalogInfo(&fsRef,
                               kFSCatInfoNone,
                               NULL,
                               NULL,
                               &fsSpec,
                               NULL);
    }
} else {
    err = fnfErr;
}

// open the file with a QuickTime GraphicsImporter
if (err == noErr) {
    err = GetGraphicsImporterForFile(&fsSpec, &importer);
}

// get information about the graphic, including its size
if (err == noErr) {
    err = GraphicsImportGetImageDescription(importer, &imageDesc);
}

// center the image within the world
bounds.left = ((bounds.right - bounds.left) - (*imageDesc)->width) / 2;
bounds.right = bounds.left + (*imageDesc)->width;
bounds.top = ((bounds.bottom - bounds.top) - (*imageDesc)->height) / 2;
bounds.bottom = bounds.top + (*imageDesc)->height;

GraphicsImportSetBoundsRect(importer, &bounds);

// draw the image into the new GWorld
if (err == noErr) {
```

```
        err = GraphicsImportDraw(importer);
    }

    // tear down the image description and importer
    if (imageDesc) {
        DisposeHandle((Handle)imageDesc);
    }
    if (importer) {
        CloseComponent(importer);
    }

    // before you go, draw the filename in the lower right corner.
    if (err == noErr) {
        [self drawFilenameIntoCurrentPort:portBounds];
    }

    // restore the previous QuickDraw port
    SetGWorld(oldWorld, gdh);

    return err;
}
```

4. Save your changes to Slide.m.

5. Build and run Slide Master. Export a slide show document as a QuickTime movie. When the movie appears in QuickTime Player, you will notice the filenames have been added to the lower-right corner of each frame.

Chapter 10

Exercise 1 solution

Backing up files and directories is easily achieved using a standard shell like Bash. Bash can find and copy files using commands like find and ditto. You could use other languages, but Bash is the simplest and most universal solution.

Exercise 2 solution

A web content management system is a complex piece of software, and demands a powerful scripting language. Python or Perl would be most appropriate for this purpose. The object-oriented features of Python would make it particularly attractive for building such an advanced system.

Exercise 3 solution

AppleScript wins this one hands down. It is the only scripting language that allows you to directly access data in applications like iPhoto, Address Book, and Mail.

Chapter 11

Exercise 1 solution

1. Open a terminal window in the Terminal application.

2. Change to the `Desktop` folder using the `cd` command.

```
cd ~/Desktop
```

3. Make a directory to temporarily store copied files in. You should choose a directory name that is appropriate for the type of files you are copying. In this case, the directory name is `TextFiles Backup`.

```
mkdir TextFilesBackup
```

4. Issue the following `find` command to locate files with the extension `txt` that reside in your home directory or a subdirectory thereof. The command copies each file found to the backup directory.

```
find ~ -name *.txt -exec /Developer/Tools/CpMac -r {} ~/Desktop/TextFilesBackup \;
```

The globbing wildcard character `*` matches zero or more characters, so `*.txt` matches any text file. Each file found is copied by the `CpMac` command passed with the `-exec` option. `CpMac` has the advantage of preserving resource forks, whereas `cp` doesn't. The semantics of `CpMac` are very similar to `cp`.

5. Use the following command to compress the backup folder with ZIP compression, while retaining all resource fork information:

```
ditto -c -k --rsrc ~/Desktop/TextFilesBackup ~/Desktop/TextFilesBackup.zip
```

The `-k` option forces `ditto` to use the universal ZIP format, which can be read on most operating systems. The `--rsrc` option means that resource fork data should also be preserved. The name of the directory to be compressed is given first after the options, and the archive file path next.

6. Issue the following three commands to remove the `TextFilesBackup` directory, create a directory for storing backups, and move the ZIP file to it.

```
rm -r ~/Desktop/TextFilesBackup
mkdir ~/Backups
mv ~/Desktop/TextFilesBackup.zip ~/Backups/
```

Exercise 2 solution

1. Open a terminal window in the Terminal application and change to your Desktop directory:

```
cd ~/Desktop
```

2. Using the Pico editor, create a file called `backup.sh` and enter the following script. Then replace the email address `fred@blah.com` with your own email address. Save the file, and exit Pico.

```
#!/bin/bash

# Set email address for error messages
ERROR_EMAIL=fred@blah.com

# Functions
StopWithError() {
    local MSG="An error caused backup script to terminate: $1"
    echo $MSG | mail $ERROR_EMAIL
    exit 1
```

```
}

CheckExitStatus() {
    if (( $? )); then
        StopWithError "$1"
    fi
}

# Configuration variables
FILE_EXT=txt
BACKUP_DIR=~/Backups

# Create backup directory if necessary
if [ -e "$BACKUP_DIR" ]; then
    # Make sure the backup directory is actually a directory
    if [ ! -d "$BACKUP_DIR" ]; then
        StopWithError "The backup path is not a directory"
    fi
else
    # If the backup directory doesn't exist, create it
    mkdir -p "$BACKUP_DIR"
    CheckExitStatus "mkdir failed to create backup directory"
fi

# Variables for temporary files and directories
ARCHIVE_DIR_PATH=`mktemp -d /tmp/backupdir_XXXX`
BACKUP_FILE_NAME=TextFilesBackup_`date +%F_%H-%M`.zip
BACKUP_FILE_PATH="$BACKUP_DIR/$BACKUP_FILE_NAME"

# Locate files with extension given, and copy to archive directory
find ~ -name "*.$FILE_EXT" -type f \
  -exec /Developer/Tools/CpMac "{}" "$ARCHIVE_DIR_PATH" \;
CheckExitStatus "Find command failed"

# Compress the archive directory
ditto -c -k --rsrc "$ARCHIVE_DIR_PATH" "$BACKUP_FILE_PATH"
CheckExitStatus "ditto command failed to compress archive"

# Remove the archive directory
rm -r "$ARCHIVE_DIR_PATH"
CheckExitStatus "Could not remove archive directory"
```

The mktemp command is used to create a temporary directory to copy the files to. The output of this command is the path to the new directory. The -d option indicates that a directory should be created, rather than a regular file. The path of the temporary directory is given last. The XXXX part of the directory name gets replaced by the mktemp command with a unique number.

3. Change the mode of the backup.sh file so that it is executable:

```
chmod u+x backup.sh
```

4. Run the script:

```
./backup.sh
```

5. When the script completes, use Finder to check the contents of the directory ~/Backups for a ZIP archive. Double-click the archive to expand it, and see if it contains text files from your home directory.

6. Try to force an error by removing the backup directory and replacing it with a regular file. See if you receive an email about the error when you rerun the script.

> This script takes no account of multiple files with the same name. If more than one file shares a name, only one of the files will appear in the archive; the others will have been overwritten. You would need to improve the script if you wanted to archive multiple files with the same name.

Chapter 12

Exercise 1 solution

Insert the following handler code into the slide show script:

```
on prompt_for_slide_duration()
    set slide_duration to 0
    repeat while slide_duration is 0
        try
            display dialog ¬
                "How many seconds should each slide in the " & ¬
                "slideshow be displayed?" ¬
                buttons {"OK"} default answer 2 default button 1
            set dialog_result to result
            set slide_duration to (text returned of dialog_result) as real
            if slide_duration    0 then error "Enter a positive number"
        on error msg
            display_error_message(msg)
            set slide_duration to 0
        end try
    end repeat
    return slide_duration
end prompt_for_slide_duration
```

This handler is very similar to others in the script that prompt the user for input. A dialog is displayed requesting the user to enter the number of seconds per slide in the show. The value entered must be a number greater than zero; otherwise an error will arise, and the user will be prompted again.

To complete the exercise, modify the run handler to call the prompt_for_slide_duration handler, and pass the result to the create_image_sequence_from_folder handler.

```
on run
    try
        copy Photo_Archive to photo_arch
        set photo_arch's archive_folder_name to "Test Photo Archive"
        tell photo_arch to setup_archive_folder()
```

```
                set num_photos to prompt_for_number_of_photos_in_show()
                set slide_duration to prompt_for_slide_duration()
                set the_album to prompt_for_album_choice()
                add_photos_from_album given Photo_Archive:photo_arch, ¬
                    album:the_album, number_of_photos:num_photos
                create_image_sequence_from_folder(photo_arch's archive_folder, ¬
                    slide_duration)
                tell photo_arch to delete_archive()
            on error msg
                display_error_message(msg)
            end try
        end run
```

Exercise 2 solution

Begin by adding a `try` block to the `clicked` handler to catch any `errors` that get thrown:

```
on clicked theObject
    tell window "mainwindow"
        set posterView to image view "posterimageview"
        tell box "configbox"
            tell matrix "widthheightmatrix"
                set posterWidth to integer value of cell "posterwidthcell"
                set posterHeight to integer value of cell "posterheightcell"
            end tell
            set scaleFactor to float value of slider 1
            set numberOfPhotos to integer value of cell 1 ¬
                of matrix "numberofphotosmatrix"
        end tell
    end tell
    set posterImage to make new image at end of images
    call method "setSize:" of posterImage ¬
        with parameters {{posterWidth, posterHeight}}
    set progressIndicator to progress indicator 1 of window 1
    start progressIndicator
    try
        set imagePaths to getPathsToRandomPhotos(getSelectedAlbums(),¬
            numberOfPhotos)
        repeat with imagePath in imagePaths
            set img to load image imagePath
            addImageToPoster(img, posterImage, scaleFactor)
            delete img
        end repeat
    on error errorMsg
        display alert "An error occurred while creating the poster." as warning ¬
            default button "OK" message errorMsg ¬
            attached to window "mainwindow"
    end try
    stop progressIndicator
    set image of posterView to posterImage
end clicked
```

The `display alert` command displays an alert panel, in this case a warning. The error message passed via the `error` is displayed in the panel. By supplying the `attached to` option, the alert is given as a sheet on the main window.

650

In the `getSelectedAlbums` handler, add a check to ensure that at least one album has been selected:

```
on getSelectedAlbums()
    set selectedRows to selected data rows of table view 1 ¬
        of scroll view 1 of box "configbox" of window 1
    if (count of selectedRows) is 0 then
        error "There were no albums selected. " & ¬
            "Select one or more albums, and try again."
    end if
    set theAlbums to {}
    repeat with theRow in selectedRows
        set theDataCell to data cell "albumname" of theRow
        set selectedAlbumName to content of theDataCell
        tell application "iPhoto" to get album selectedAlbumName
        set the end of theAlbums to result
    end repeat
    return theAlbums
end getSelectedAlbums
```

If the number of selected rows is zero, an `error` is thrown, which gets caught in the `clicked` handler.

Finally, modify the `getPathsToRandomPhotos` handler so that it checks the number of photos available in the selected albums:

```
on getPathsToRandomPhotos(theAlbums, numberOfPhotos)
    tell application "iPhoto"
        -- Check that there is at least one photo in the albums
        set atLeastOnePhoto to false
        repeat with theAlbum in theAlbums
            if (count of photos in theAlbum)   0 then
                set atLeastOnePhoto to true
                exit repeat
            end if
        end repeat
        if not atLeastOnePhoto then
            error "There were no photos in the selected albums. " & ¬
                "Add some photos to the albums, and try again."
        end if

        -- Choose random paths
        set photoPaths to {}
        repeat numberOfPhotos times
            set end of photoPaths to image path of some photo ¬
                of some item of theAlbums
        end repeat
    end tell
    return photoPaths
end getPathsToRandomPhotos
```

The new code uses a `repeat` loop to iterate over the `albums` passed in. The number of `photos` in each `album` is retrieved using the `count` command, and if it is non-zero, the `atLeastOnePhoto` variable is set to `true` and the loop exits. If after the loop has completed the `atLeastOnePhoto` variable is still `false`, an `error` is thrown.

Exercise 3 solution

In order to update the user interface, follow these steps:

1. Open the `MainMenu.nib` file in Interface Builder by double-clicking its icon in the Groups & Files pane of the Piles of Pictures Xcode project window.

2. Select the Photo Scaling slider and the Photo Scaling text field by holding down the Shift key and clicking each in turn. Duplicate these two views by choosing the Edit ⇨ Duplicate menu item. Double-click the new text field and enter `Scaling Variation:`.

3. Position the new controls to make the interface more aesthetically pleasing. You may need to resize the window and other views to achieve this.

4. Select the new slider and open the AppleScript tab of the Inspector window. Enter `variation slider` in the Name field.

5. Save your changes to `MainMenu.nib` and return to the Xcode project.

Now add the following new handler to the `Piles of Pictures.applescript` script:

```
on varyScalingFactor(scalingFactor, variance)
    set randomVariance to (random number from -variance to variance)
    set scalingFactor to scalingFactor + randomVariance
    if scalingFactor < 0.0 then set scalingFactor to 0.0
    if scalingFactor > 1.0 then set scalingFactor to 1.0
    return scalingFactor
end varyScalingFactor
```

This handler takes the scaling factor and the variation factor. It forms a new scaling factor by adding a random value to the original scaling factor, in the range stipulated by the variation factor. The random number is chosen in the range from `-variance` to `variance`. Negative values result in a smaller scaling factor, and positive ones give a larger scaling factor.

The random number is added to the `scalingFactor` variable. Because this could potentially result in a scaling factor greater than 1 or less than 0, two `if` statements check the value of `scalingFactor`, and adjust it if necessary, such that it ends up in the range 0.0 to 1.0.

To finish off, it is only necessary to call this new handler at the appropriate point in the script. In the `clicked` handler, you need to make this modification:

```
on clicked theObject
    tell window "mainwindow"
        set posterView to image view "posterimageview"
        tell box "configbox"
            tell matrix "widthheightmatrix"
                set posterWidth to integer value of cell "posterwidthcell"
                set posterHeight to integer value of cell "posterheightcell"
            end tell
            set scaleFactor to float value of slider "scalingslider"
            set scaleVariation to float value of slider "variationslider"
            set numberOfPhotos to integer value of cell 1 ¬
                of matrix "numberofphotosmatrix"
        end tell
```

```
        end tell
        set posterImage to make new image at end of images
        call method "setSize:" of posterImage ¬
            with parameters {{posterWidth, posterHeight}}
        set imagePaths to getPathsToRandomPhotos(getSelectedAlbums(), numberOfPhotos)
        set progressIndicator to progress indicator 1 of window 1
        start progressIndicator
        repeat with imagePath in imagePaths
            set img to load image imagePath
            set photoScaleFactor to varyScalingFactor(scaleFactor, scaleVariation)
            addImageToPoster(img, posterImage, photoScaleFactor)
            delete img
        end repeat
        stop progressIndicator
        set image of posterView to posterImage
    end clicked
```

Rather than passing the `scaleFactor` retrieved from the user interface directly to the `addImageTo Poster` handler, it is first adjusted using `varyScalingFactor`, with the result stored in the variable `photoScaleFactor`. This adjusted scaling factor is what is passed to `addImageToPoster`. Because the factor is different for each photo, each photo will be scaled differently in the resulting poster.

Chapter 13

Exercise solution

1. Open the Searcher project in Xcode, and select the `Searcher.h` file in the Groups & Files panel, such that it appears in the editor. Make the highlighted changes in the following code:

```
#import <Cocoa/Cocoa.h>

@interface Searcher : NSObject
{
    IBOutlet NSArrayController *pathsController;
    NSArray *paths;
    NSString *rootDirectoryPath;
    NSString *nameContainsString;
    int searchingState;
    NSTask *task;
}

-(IBAction)openFile:(id)sender;
-(IBAction)showInFinder:(id)sender;
-(IBAction)toggleSearch:(id)sender;

-(NSArray *)paths;
-(void)setPaths:(NSArray *)paths;

-(NSString *)rootDirectoryPath;
-(void)setRootDirectoryPath:(NSString *)path;

-(NSString *)nameContainsString;
```

```
-(void)setNameContainsString:(NSString *)str;

-(NSTask *)task;
-(void)setTask:(NSTask *)task;

-(int)searchingState;
-(void)setSearchingState:(int)newState;

@end
```

2. Open the `Searcher.m` file in the editor and change the `init` and `dealloc` methods as follows:

```
-(id)init {
    if ( self = [super init] ) {
        [self setPaths:[NSArray array]];
        [self setRootDirectoryPath:NSHomeDirectory()];
        [self setNameContainsString:@""];
        [self setSearchingState:NSOffState];
        [self setTask:nil];

        // Register for NSTask termination notifications
        [[NSNotificationCenter defaultCenter] addObserver:self
            selector:@selector(taskDidTerminate:)
            name:NSTaskDidTerminateNotification
            object:nil];
    }
    return self;
}

-(void)dealloc {
    [[NSNotificationCenter defaultCenter] removeObserver:self];
    [paths release];
    [rootDirectoryPath release];
    [nameContainsString release];
    [task release];
    [super dealloc];
}
```

3. Replace the `search:` method in the implementation block of the `Searcher` class with the following two methods:

```
-(IBAction)toggleSearch:(id)sender {
    if ( searchingState == NSOnState ) {
        NSBundle *bundle = [NSBundle bundleForClass:[self class]];
        NSString *pathToScript = [bundle pathForResource:@"search" ofType:@"sh"];
        NSTask *t = [[[NSTask alloc] init] autorelease];
        NSPipe *p = [NSPipe pipe];
        [t setLaunchPath:pathToScript];
        [t setStandardOutput:p];
        [self setTask:t];

        NSDictionary *envDict = [NSDictionary dictionaryWithObjectsAndKeys:
            nameContainsString,    @"SEARCH_STRING",
            rootDirectoryPath,     @"ROOT_DIR",
            nil];
```

```
            [t setEnvironment:envDict];

            [t launch];
        }
        else {
            [self setTask:nil]; // This cancels the task
        }
    }

-(void)taskDidTerminate:(NSNotification *)notif {
    NSTask *t = [notif object];
    if ( t != [self task] ) return; // Make sure we have the latest task
    int status = [t terminationStatus];
    if ( status == 0 ) {
        // Read output, and split it into separate paths.
        NSFileHandle *outFileHandle = [[t standardOutput] fileHandleForReading];
        NSData *stringData = [outFileHandle readDataToEndOfFile];
        NSString *outputString =
            [[[NSString alloc] initWithData:stringData
                encoding:NSUTF8StringEncoding] autorelease];
        NSArray *newPaths = [outputString componentsSeparatedByString:@"\n"];
        [self setPaths:newPaths];
    }
    else {
        // Alert user of error
        NSAlert *alert = [[[NSAlert alloc] init] autorelease];
        [alert setAlertStyle:NSWarningAlertStyle];
        [alert addButtonWithTitle:@"OK"];
        [alert setMessageText:@"The search failed."];
        [alert setInformativeText:
            [NSString stringWithFormat:
                @"The find command used to search failed with error %d.", status]];
        [alert runModal];
    }
    // Reset searching status
    [self setSearchingState:NSOffState];
}
```

4.   Introduce the following accessor methods to the implementation block of `Searcher`:

```
-(NSTask *)task {
    return task;
}

-(void)setTask:(NSTask *)newTask {
    [task interrupt]; // Cancel previous search
    [task autorelease];
    task = [newTask retain];
}

-(int)searchingState {
    return searchingState;
}

-(void)setSearchingState:(int)newState {
    searchingState = newState;
}
```

5. Open the `MainMenu.nib` file by double-clicking its icon in the Resources group of the Groups & Files panel.

6. Change the layout of the main window slightly to match what's shown in Figure A-7. You will need to change the type of the Search button to Round Bevel Button in the Inspector window. Also enter the Alt. Title Stop for the Search button in the Inspector window, and select Toggle in the Behavior popup.

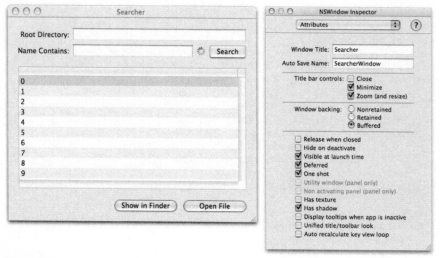

Figure A-7

7. In the Search Button Inspector Window, select Bindings from the popup button at the top, and click the `value` group. Bind the button's value to the `SearcherAlias` controller, with Controller Key set to `selection` and Model Key Path set to `searchingState`.

8. Open the `animate` binding group of the `NSProgressIndicator` in the Inspector panel and enter the same binding information that you entered in step 7 for the Search button.

9. Open the `Searcher` Class Inspector panel by double-clicking the `Searcher` instance in the Instances tab of the `MainMenu.nib` window. Select Attributes in the popup button and change the name of the `search:` action to `toggleSearch:`. You can do this by double-clicking the `search:` action in the Actions tab and entering the new name.

10. Select the Resources group in Groups & Files and then select New File . . . from the File menu. Choose to create a new Shell Script, and give it the name `search.sh`. Open the new file in the editor and insert the following:

```
#!/bin/sh
find "$ROOT_DIR" -name "*$SEARCH_STRING*"
```

11. Save the changes in Interface Builder, and build and run the application. Enter details for a long search and press the Search button. Cancel the search by pressing Stop. Restart the search and wait for it to complete.

The search.sh script is virtually the same as the command passed to system in the previous incantation of the Searcher application. The only difference is that instead of piping output to a temporary file, the output of the find command just goes to the standard output of the script, which is read via the NSPipe back in the taskDidTerminate: method. The temporary file used with the system function is not needed when you use NSTask with NSPipe instances for standard input and/or standard output.

Developer Resources

A number of useful developer resources are available to Mac OS X programmers. These include web sites, mailing lists, and other resources. This chapter provides information about these resources.

Websites

Apple Developer Connection

    http://developer.apple.com/

You can find a wealth of Mac OS X programming information at Apple Developer Connection (ADC), including online documentation, sample code, and software downloads. Most of the ADC content is free or available through a free membership, although some of its services are available only to paid ADC subscribers.

CocoaDev

    http://www.cocoadev.com/

CocoaDev is a *Wiki* website dedicated to Cocoa programming on Mac OS X. Wiki websites encourage public participation by allowing anyone to post and edit content directly on the site. Not only can you browse CocoaDev for answers to your questions, but you can also post your own questions in a discussion area. Later on, you can even post answers to other people's questions.

Cocoa Dev Central

    http://www.cocoadevcentral.com/

Cocoa Dev Central is a Cocoa programming website featuring articles and tutorials. Although less collaborative than the CocoaDev website, the content on Cocoa Dev Central is presented like full-length magazine articles. Also, Cocoa Dev Central links to other Cocoa programming resources on the Internet, so you can find even more information about Cocoa programming.

MacScripter.net

```
http://bbs.macscripter.net/
```

MacScripter.net is a collection of web forums dedicated to AppleScript programming. You can find additional information about writing AppleScripts on Mac OS X there, as well as resources for AppleScript Studio and the Automator tool found in Mac OS X 10.4 "Tiger." MacScripter.net also includes a large section of sample scripts and a section where you can share code with other people.

MacTech

```
http://www.mactech.com/
```

MacTech provides a ton of information aimed at the Mac OS X programmer, including Macintosh news, development articles and tutorials, and sample code. You will find a wide variety of programming content on MacTech, including information for both Carbon and Cocoa programmers.

The Omni Group Developer

```
http://www.omnigroup.com/developer/
```

The Omni Group is a Mac OS X software company best known for the OmniWeb web browser, but it also has a large Cocoa developer website. For example, the website offers information about writing and porting games on Mac OS X. You can even download some of Omni's source code for use in your own projects.

Stepwise

```
http://www.stepwise.com/
```

Stepwise contains a lot of information on Cocoa and WebObjects programming. Although (as of this writing) the site hasn't been updated since 2003 there is still a wealth of introductory Cocoa content available.

Mailing Lists

Apple Mailing Lists

```
http://lists.apple.com/mailman/listinfo/
```

Apple runs mailing lists for a variety of programming topics, including Carbon, Cocoa, AppleScript, and other technologies. Apple engineers frequently contribute to these lists, so they are a good place to get detailed answers to your questions. You can find mailing list archives online at `http://lists.apple.com/archives/`.

Omni Mailing Lists

```
http://www.omnigroup.com/developer/mailinglists/
```

The Omni Group sponsors a few mailing lists for Mac OS X, including development lists for Cocoa and WebObjects, and a mailing list for Mac OS X administration. Archives are also available online.

Other Resources

CocoaDev Chat Rooms

A number of contributors to the CocoaDev website are available in the CocoaDev chat room on the AOL Instant Messenger network. For example, you can connect to CocoaDev from iChat by choosing File ⇨ Go to Chat and entering CocoaDev as the chat name. IRC channels are also available. You can find out more on CocoaDev's website: `http://www.cocoadev.com/index.pl?ChatRoom`.

MacTech Magazine

MacTech Magazine has been providing monthly articles on Macintosh programming for more than 20 years. Current issues feature information about application development in Carbon, Cocoa, and AppleScript. You can also find articles on other technologies such as OpenGL, QuickTime, and various scripting languages. MacTech articles are usually written for a beginning or intermediate programming audience, so there's something there for everyone. You can find out more at MacTech's website: `http://www.mactech.com/`.

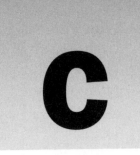

Developer Tools Roadmap

In this chapter, we provide tools that can help you during the development process. Most of these tools are installed by Mac OS X's Developer package, although others are simply part of Mac OS X. These tools include full-featured applications and command-line utilities.

Build Tools

Automator

```
/Applications/Automator.app
```

You can use Automator to automate the way you use many of your Mac OS X applications without forcing you to write Apple Script code. Automator breaks common tasks into individual *actions* that can be linked together into a larger *workflow*. You can then save Automator workflows for later use; they can also be triggered at certain times of day, run when you log in, or run automatically when files are added to a folder. Automator is actually built directly into Mac OS X 10.4 "Tiger." You do not need to install the Developer packages to use it.

Interface Builder

```
/Developer/Applications/Interface Builder.app
```

Interface Builder is a graphic user interface builder for Carbon and Cocoa applications. It is the main tool on Mac OS X capable of reading and writing nib files (.nib). Interface Builder integrates with Xcode to simplify the process of configuring your program's user interface.

Xcode

```
/Developer/Applications/Xcode.app
```

Xcode is Mac OS X's native IDE. It provides a rich user interface for writing, building, and debugging programs, as well as for accessing online developer documentation. Xcode files are arranged into projects, containing one Xcode project file (.xcode), source code, and other resources.

Graphics Tools

Core Image Fun House

`/Developer/Applications/Graphics Tools/Core Image Fun House.app`

Mac OS X 10.4 "Tiger" comes with Core Image, a framework containing tools for manipulating images. Most of Core Image's functionality comes from small plugins called *Image Units*. You can use Core Image Fun House to explore Core Image features and test how various Image Units behave when applied to your images.

OpenGL Driver Monitor

`/Developer/Applications/Graphics Tools/OpenGL Driver Monitor.app`

The OpenGL Driver Monitor allows OpenGL programmers to directly watch activity within the computer's video cards. It helps programmers isolate performance problems within their OpenGL code by showing where the graphics card is spending most of its time. This tool can also display information about the OpenGL capabilities available on your hardware.

OpenGL Profiler

`/Developer/Applications/Graphics Tools/OpenGL Profiler.app`

The OpenGL Profiler is a second tool for monitoring OpenGL performance within a specific application. Like OpenGL Driver Monitor, OpenGL Profiler helps programmers find performance problems by showing how much time specific OpenGL operations take within a particular application.

OpenGL Shader Builder

`/Developer/Applications/Graphics Tools/OpenGL Shader Builder.app`

OpenGL Shader Builder is a specialized IDE for writing, prototyping, and debugging OpenGL vertex and fragment programs. You can export a Shader Builder project as an Xcode project, allowing you to convert your results into a stand-alone application.

Pixie

`/Developer/Applications/Graphics Tools/Pixie.app`

Pixie dramatically magnifies the area around the cursor, allowing you to examine your user interface in minute detail. This is useful for making sure your user interfaces exactly match the specifications described in the Apple Human Interface Guidelines.

Quartz Composer

`/Developer/Applications/Graphics Tools/Quartz Composer.app`

Quartz Composer is a small development environment for writing graphic effects and animations. You program these effects graphically, by selecting various building blocks and wiring them together to create your final composition. These compositions can be integrated into other programs. Mac OS X 10.4 "Tiger" comes with several Screen Saver modules written using Quartz Composer.

Java Tools

Jar Bundler

/Developer/Applications/Java Tools/Jar Bundler.app

Jar Bundler takes a collection of Java class files and other resources and packages them as a stand-alone Mac OS X application. This is useful for distributing pure Java programs to a wide audience of Mac OS X users.

JavaBrowser

/Developer/Applications/Java Tools/JavaBrowser.app

JavaBrowser is a stand-alone class browser for Java objects. You can use JavaBrowser to summarize various Java interfaces available on Mac OS X. These include the standard Java distribution, Apple's Cocoa bindings for Java, and other interfaces.

Performance Tools

Activity Monitor

/Applications/Utilities/Activity Monitor.app

Activity Monitor is a Mac OS X system utility that tracks your computer's activity, such as the currently running processes, CPU load, available memory, and so on. It provides useful graphs for most of this information, including a CPU load meter that you can place in your menu bar or elsewhere on-screen. Activity Monitor can also force-quit troublesome processes, even if they don't appear in the Dock.

BigTop

/Developer/Applications/Performance Tools/CHUD/BigTop.app

BigTop graphs some of your computer's vital statistics, such as CPU load over time. The information is slightly different than that displayed by Activity Monitor. BigTop is part of the CHUD tools installed by Mac OS X's Developer packages.

MallocDebug

/Developer/Applications/Performance Tools/MallocDebug.app

MallocDebug analyzes a program's memory use as it runs. You can use MallocDebug to find places where your program is reserving memory more often than you expect. You can also use MallocDebug to find *memory leaks*, places where memory is allocated but never freed.

MONster

/Developer/Applications/Performance Tools/CHUD/MONster.app

MONster is a low-level hardware sampling tool that can provide very specific information about CPU, operating system, and subsystem performance. Most application programmers want to analyze their software at a higher level, using tools such as OpenGL Profiler, Sampler, and Shark. MONster is part of the CHUD tools installed by Mac OS X's Developer packages.

ObjectAlloc

```
/Developer/Applications/Performance Tools/ObjectAlloc.app
```

ObjectAlloc is similar to MallocDebug, except that it specifically watches for Objective-C object allocations. ObjectAlloc is useful for finding places where your program might be creating and releasing an unusual number of temporary objects, which can have a negative impact on performance.

Quartz Debug

```
/Developer/Applications/Performance Tools/Quartz Debug.app
```

You can use Quartz Debug to analyze the way your program draws its interface. It is useful for finding places where you are wasting time drawing the same area twice or drawing a large area instead of a smaller one. Quartz Debug also provides controls for other CoreGraphics debug options.

Sampler

```
/Developer/Applications/Performance Tools/Sampler.app
```

Sampler shows you how a program's call stack changes over time. It works by stopping your program several times a second and analyzing the stack. You can interpret the sample data using a number of different tools. One advantage to using a tool like Sampler is that it can examine any kind of program, even if the program doesn't have built-in debugging information. Although Sampler can tell you how much time you spent in a given function, it can't tell you how many times that function was called.

Saturn

```
/Developer/Applications/Performance Tools/CHUD/Saturn.app
```

Saturn provides a graphic interface for displaying precise information about how many times a program's functions were called, how long each call took, and so on. You can use Saturn only with special *profiled* versions of your programs. A profiled program contains special debugging code that allows other programs to watch and time every change to your program's call stack. You can use Xcode (or the underlying gcc compiler) to build a profiled version of your program. Saturn is part of the CHUD tools installed by Mac OS X's Developer packages.

Shark

```
/Developer/Applications/Performance Tools/Shark.app
```

Like Sampler, Shark is a statistical sampling tool that examines the state of your CPU as well as the state of your program's call stack while your program is running. After Shark identifies where your program is spending its time, it recommends ways in which you can improve your program's performance. Some of its recommendations are very specific, such as moving variables out of loops if they don't change. Shark is part of the CHUD tools installed by Mac OS X's Developer packages.

Spin Control

    /Developer/Applications/Performance Tools/Spin Control.app

Spin Control can automatically sample applications when they become unresponsive. This can be useful for sampling programs when performance problems are hard to reproduce.

Thread Viewer

    /Developer/Applications/Performance Tools/Thread Viewer.app

Thread Viewer graphs your program's thread usage in real time, allowing you to see if your program is using more threads than you expected. Creating a bunch of unnecessary threads can have a negative impact on your program's performance.

Other Utilities

Bluetooth Explorer

    /Developer/Applications/Utilities/Bluetooth/Bluetooth Explorer.app

Bluetooth Explorer displays the Bluetooth devices connected to your system. You can use it to modify the connection or disconnect the device.

FileMerge

    /Developer/Applications/Utilities/FileMerge.app

FileMerge lists differences between two similar files and allows you to selectively merge the files together. FileMerge also works on entire directories of files.

icns Browser

    /Developer/Applications/Utilities/icns Browser.app

icns Browser is a simple application that lets you see the contents of a Mac OS X icon file (.icns). You cannot modify the contents of the icon file with icns Browser.

Icon Composer

    /Developer/Applications/Utilities/Icon Composer.app

Icon Composer is an editor for creating and editing icon files (.icns). You can drag a separate image into Icon Composer for each icon size in the icon file, or you can just drag a single image into each icon. If necessary, Icon Composer scales the image to fit the icon size.

IORegistryExplorer

    /Developer/Applications/Utilities/IORegistryExplorer.app

IORegistryExplorer lets you browse the devices and services registered with IOKit. It is useful when debugging devices or device drivers.

PackageMaker

```
/Developer/Applications/Utilities/PackageMaker.app
```

PackageMaker builds installation packages (.pkg) for use with Apple's built-in Installer. You point PackageMaker at a content directory, fill in some information about the package, and PackageMaker does the rest.

PacketLogger

```
/Developer/Applications/Utilities/Bluetooth/PacketLogger.app
```

PacketLogger can help you analyze Bluetooth traffic on your computer.

Property List Editor

```
/Developer/Applications/Utilities/Property List Editor.app
```

Property List Editor lets you view and edit property list (.plist) files. Property lists are a standard way to store small collections of hierarchical data on Mac OS X and are often used for application configuration files, simple documents, and preferences.

Repeat After Me

```
/Developer/Applications/Utilities/Speech/Repeat After Me.app
```

Repeat After Me allows you to view and edit waveform files created by Apple's Speech Manager that is built into Mac OS X. You can convert your changes into speech commands that can be fed back into the Speech Manager, allowing you to customize the way your application speaks certain words and phrases. For example, the following text causes the Speech Manager to say "Hi" with a rising tone; you can type the text into TextEdit and speak it by choosing Edit ➪ Speech ➪ Start Speaking:

```
[[inpt TUNE]]
_
h {D 75; P 94.0:0}
1AY {D 235; P 107.6:0 144.6:17 251.2:66 194.2:79}
[[inpt TEXT]]
```

SRLanguageModeler

```
/Developer/Applications/Utilities/Speech/SRLanguageModeler.app
```

You can use SRLanguageModeler to fine-tune your program's speech recognition. If your application responds to a fixed set of commands, you might be able to improve your program's capability to understand those commands using the SRLanguageModeler's tools.

Terminal

`/Applications/Utilities/Terminal.app`

Terminal is a Mac OS X system utility that allows you to access Mac OS X's command-line tools. Each Terminal window houses a command shell such as `/bin/bash`. Terminal responds to familiar text editing techniques such as copy and paste and drag and drop, which can make the command-line interface easier for some people to use.

USB Prober

`/Developer/Applications/Utilities/USB Prober.app`

USB Prober displays information about the attached USB devices, including USB information from the IOKit registry. It is useful for people working on USB devices and device drivers.

Command-Line Tools

DeRez

`/Developer/Tools/DeRez`

DeRez can produce a Rez file (`.r`) from a Carbon Resource Manager file or from a file's resource fork. It's often useful for examining the contents of a resource file or resource fork or for extracting existing resources for use in your own Rez files. Rez files have largely been replaced by nib files for Carbon user interfaces.

diff

`/usr/bin/diff`

`diff` displays differences between two text files. It is more configurable than the FileMerge application, although its results can be harder to interpret.

gcc

`/usr/bin/gcc`

`gcc` is Mac OS X's built-in C/C++/Objective-C compiler. You can use `gcc` to build and link programs from the command line. Xcode uses `gcc` under the covers for compiling source code.

gdb

`/usr/bin/gdb`

`gdb` is Mac OS X's built-in interactive source-level debugger. You can use `gdb` to step into your program's source or object code as the program runs. You can also use `gdb` to display the contents of core files (`.core`) that are saved in `/cores` when programs crash. Xcode uses `gdb` under the covers for its own interactive debugger.

GetFileInfo

/Developer/Tools/GetFileInfo

GetFileInfo prints HFS metadata for specific files. You can use it to read a file's type or creator code, see if the file is invisible, and similar tasks. You can use the related tool SetFile to set this information.

ld

/usr/bin/ld

ld is Mac OS X's built-in object code linker. Normally, you might access ld's functionality through gcc or other programs; but if you have specific linking needs, you can run ld directly. For example, Xcode uses ld to link your program's object files together and produce your project's application, framework, and plug-in binaries.

leaks

/usr/bin/leaks

leaks can analyze a program for memory leaks. It offers a subset of the functionality found in the MallocDebug application.

make

/usr/bin/make

make is a build configuration system common to Unix platforms. make works by reading one or more make files (.make or simply makefile depending on how make is used) that contain a series of rules for working with your project files. On Mac OS X, Xcode largely replaces the need for make; however, most Unix source projects still rely on make files because make is available virtually everywhere.

man

/usr/bin/man

The man command displays information from Mac OS X's built-in Unix manual. It's useful for learning about other command-line programs or for getting programmer documentation for the Darwin System library.

Rez

/Developer/Tools/Rez

Rez produces a Carbon Resource Manager file or a resource fork from a Rez file (.r). Rez files are text files in a specific format used to specify Carbon resources and have largely been replaced by nib files for Carbon user interface configuration.

sample

```
/usr/bin/sample
```

sample analyzes a running process over a period of time and records the process's call stack. You can use sample to get a sense of what a program is doing from the command line. You can simply view the resulting sample file in a text editor or viewer, or you can load the sample file into Sampler to interactively browse through the stack data.

SetFile

```
/Developer/Tools/SetFile
```

SetFile sets a file or directory's HFS metadata, such as its type and creator (for files), invisibility bit, or other data. It is often used in conjunction with GetFileInfo.

top

```
/usr/bin/top
```

top displays various statistics about your computer, such as the amount of memory and CPU time being consumed by running processes. It is a command-line version of the Activity Monitor utility.

Index